D060404ß

Linux®+ Certification Bible

Linux+®
Certification Bible

Trevor Kay

Hungry Minds™

Best-Selling Books • Digital Downloads • e-Books • Answer Networks • e-Newsletters • Branded Web Sites • e-Learning

New York, NY ✦ Cleveland, OH ✦ Indianapolis, IN

Linux® Certification Bible

Published by
Hungry Minds, Inc.
909 Third Avenue
New York, NY 10022
www.hungryminds.com

Library of Congress Catalog Card No.: 2001093590

ISBN: 0-7645-4881-6

Printed in the United States of America

10 9 8 7 6 5 4 3 2 1

1P/RZ/RS/QR/IN

Distributed in the United States by Hungry Minds, Inc.

Distributed by CDG Books Canada Inc. for Canada; by Transworld Publishers Limited in the United Kingdom; by IDG Norge Books for Norway; by IDG Sweden Books for Sweden; by IDG Books Australia Publishing Corporation Pty. Ltd. for Australia and New Zealand; by TransQuest Publishers Pte Ltd. for Singapore, Malaysia, Thailand, Indonesia, and Hong Kong; by Gotop Information Inc. for Taiwan; by ICG Muse, Inc. for Japan; by Intersoft for South Africa; by Eyrolles for France; by International Thomson Publishing for Germany, Austria, and Switzerland; by Distribuidora Cuspide for Argentina; by LR International for Brazil; by Galileo Libros for Chile; by Ediciones ZETA S.C.R. Ltda. for Peru; by WS Computer Publishing Corporation, Inc., for the Philippines; by Contemporanea de Ediciones for Venezuela; by Express Computer Distributors for the Caribbean and West Indies; by Micronesia Media Distributor, Inc. for Micronesia; by Chips Computadoras S.A. de C.V. for Mexico; by Editorial Norma de Panama S.A. for Panama; by American Bookshops for Finland.

For general information on Hungry Minds' products and services, please contact our Customer Care department within the U.S. at 800-762-2974, outside the U.S. at 317-572-3993, or fax 317-572-4002.

For sales inquiries and reseller information, including discounts, premium and bulk quantity sales, and foreign-language translations, please contact our Customer Care department at 800-434-3422, fax 317-572-4002, or write to Hungry Minds, Inc., Attn: Customer Care Department, 10475 Crosspoint Boulevard, Indianapolis, IN 46256.

For information on licensing foreign or domestic rights, please contact our Sub-Rights Customer Care department at 212-884-5000.

For information on using Hungry Minds' products and services in the classroom or for ordering examination copies, please contact our Educational Sales department at 800-434-2086 or fax 317-572-4005.

For press review copies, author interviews, or other publicity information, please contact our Public Relations department at 317-572-3168 or fax 317-572-4168.

For authorization to photocopy items for corporate, personal, or educational use, please contact Copyright Clearance Center, 222 Rosewood Drive, Danvers, MA 01923, or fax 978-750-4470.

is a trademark of
Hungry Minds, Inc.

About the Author

Trevor Kay is a holder of four CompTIA certifications: A+, Network+, Server+, and Linux+. Trevor is also the author of the *Server+ Certification Bible*. Trevor started his IT career working at a local museum as a desktop publisher. From there, he has held many positions, from IT help desk, technical support, and network administrator positions for local companies to having a key roll in the Y2K projects of one of the largest financial institutes in Canada.

Credits

Acquisitions Editor
Katie Feltman

Project Editor
Amanda Munz Peterson

Technical Editor
Joe Byrne

Question Writer
James Russell

Copy Editor
Rebekah Mancilla

Editorial Manager
Ami Frank Sullivan

Senior Vice President, Technical Publishing
Richard Swadley

Vice President and Publisher
Mary Bednarek

Project Coordinator
Jennifer Bingham

Graphics and Production Specialists
Beth Brooks, Laurie Petrone,
Jill Piscitelli, Heather Pope

Quality Control Technician
John Bitter, Valery Bourke, Angel Perez

Permissions Editor
Laura Moss

Media Development Specialist
Travis Silvers

Media Development Coordinator
Marisa Pearman

Proofreading and Indexing
TECHBOOKS Production Services

Cover Image
Anthony Bunyan

This book is dedicated to all my family and friends. Your tremendous support made this book possible.

Preface

Welcome to the *Linux®+ Certification Bible!* This book is designed to help you acquire the knowledge, skills, and abilities you need to pass CompTIA's Linux+ Certification:

* **Exam XK0-001 :** Linux+ Certification

This book is designed to be the only book or course you need to prepare for and pass CompTIA's Linux+ Certification exam, which is one of the newest members of CompTIA's certification family.

This book deals with all of the objectives stated by CompTIA for the Linux+ exam. You learn how to deal with planning a Linux implementation (including installing Linux in a GUI or text-based environment) and configuring the Linux operating system after installation. This book also teaches you how to administrate and maintain your Linux system, troubleshoot common problems, and how to identify, install, and maintain system hardware.

My hope is that you'll find this book the most helpful Linux+ Certification product reference that you've ever read. I also hope that you'll use it not only to prepare for CompTIA's Linux+ Certification exam, but that you'll come back to it again and again as you perform your day-to-day Linux professional tasks.

How This Book Is Organized

This book is organized into seven major parts, followed by a glossary, an index, and one CD. Here's what you'll find in this book:

Part I: Linux Basics

Part I presents the information that you need to understand Linux. This part covers the creator of Linux and a brief history about the development of Linux . The Linux Kernel and the many different types Linux distributions are also discussed.

Part II: Installation

Part II includes the instructions on how to perform a proper installation of Linux. GUI and text-based installations are covered. Identifying all system requirements and validating that they support Linux is also included. The different types of roles and services of Linux system are discussed along with identifying where to obtain software and resources.

Part III: Configuration

Part III is about configuring your Linux system. This part teaches you how to configure X windows with automated utilities and workstations for remote access . This part also covers how to add and configure printers along with information about installing and configuring add-in hardware, reconfiguring the boot loader, and editing basic configuration files.

Part IV: Administration

Part IV covers how to administrate a Linux-based environment. This part shows you how to create and delete users, modify existing users, and create, modify, and delete groups. Next, this part teaches you how to identify and change file permissions, manage and navigate the Linux hierarchy, and mount and manage file systems, devices, common shell commands, and expressions. You also learn how to use network commands to create, extract, and edit file and tape archives by using `tar`. The part ends with the information that you need to manage runlevels; starting, stopping, and restarting services; managing print spool and queues; using vi; and managing and navigating the GUI. It also teaches you how to program basic shell script by using common shell commands.

Part V: Maintaining the Linux System

Part V is about maintaining the Linux system. This part provides you with information on how to monitor and maintain processes, network interfaces, system logs, security, and backup. Areas in this part include creating and managing local storage devices and file systems, understanding functions of the `cron` command, identifying core dumps, and how to run and interpret ifconfig. This part focuses on downloading and installing patches and updates; identifying, executing, and killing processes; monitoring system log files; and how to properly document work performed on a system. This part also teaches you how to perform and verify backups and restores, gives you security best practices, and teaches you how to set daemon and process permissions.

Part VI: Troubleshooting and Maintaining System Hardware

Part VI is about troubleshooting Linux systems. This part provides you with the basic knowledge and skills to identify, inspect, and diagnose problems in the Linux operating system and how to apply remedies by using common commands and utilities. In this part, you learn how to identify and locate the problem by determining whether the problem originates from: hardware, operating system, application software, configuration, or the user. You also learn troubleshooting best practices, editing configuration files based on symptoms using system utilities, using systems boot disk(s) and root disks on workstations and servers to diagnose and rescue file systems. This part also teaches you how to inspect and determine causes of errors from system log files, how to use disk utilities to solve file system problems, and how to recognize common errors. You learn how to take appropriate action on boot errors, how to identify backup and restore errors, how to identify and use trouble-shooting commands, and how to locate troubleshooting resources and updates.

This part also covers the knowledge that you need to maintain your Linux system hardware. This part covers the knowledge and skills you need to install, configure and troubleshoot core and peripheral hardware in a Linux environment. This part includes information on generic hardware issues and Linux specific hardware issues. Topics in this part include: Identifying basic terms, concepts, and functions of system components, including how each component should work during normal operation and during the boot process; removing and replacing hardware and accessories, identifying basic networking concepts; and proper procedures for diagnosing and troubleshooting ATA, SCSI, and peripheral devices. You also find the knowledge on how to properly troubleshoot core system hardware, including processors, RAM, and mainboards.

CD-ROM

The compact disc included with this book contains some excellent resources and programs. You'll find this entire book in Adobe PDF format and a variety of different programs that I hope you will find useful. To find out more about the CD-ROM, please see Appendix A.

How Each Chapter Is Structured

A lot of thought went into the structure and design of this book, particularly the specific elements that will provide you with the best possible learning and exam preparation experience.

Here are the elements you'll find in each chapter:

- ✦ The complete exam objectives that are covered in the chapter
- ✦ A Chapter Pre-Test to test your knowledge before reading the chapter
- ✦ Clear, concise text on each topic
- ✦ Screen shots and graphics that are worth more than a thousand words
- ✦ A Summary

✦ A comprehensive Study Guide that contains:
  • Exam-style Assessment Questions
  • Scenario problems for you to solve,
  • A Lab that you can use to sharpen your skills
  • Answers to Chapter Pre-Test Questions, Assessment Questions, and Scenarios

How to Use This Book

This book can be used either by individuals working independently or by groups in a formal classroom setting.

For best results, I recommend the following plan of attack as you use this book. First, take the Chapter Pre-Test, and then read the chapter and the Key Point Summary. Use this summary to see if you really understand the key concepts. If you don't, go back and reread the section(s) that you're not clear on. Then, do all of the Assessment Questions and Scenarios at the end of the chapter. Remember, the important thing is to master the tasks that are tested by the exams.

The chapters of this book are designed to be studied sequentially. In other words, it's best if you complete Chapter 1 before you proceed to Chapter 2. A few chapters can probably stand alone, but all in all, I recommend a sequential approach.

After you've completed your study of the chapters and reviewed the Assessment Questions in the book, use the test engine on the compact disc included with this book to get some experience answering practice questions. The practice questions will help you assess how much you've learned from your study and will also familiarize you with the type of exam questions you'll face when you take the real exam. After you identify a weak area, you can restudy the corresponding chapters to improve your knowledge and skills in that area.

Although this book is a comprehensive study and exam preparation guide, it does not start at ground zero. I assume that you have the following knowledge and skills at the outset:

✦ Basic terminology and basic skills to use a Linux distribution
✦ Basic mouse skills: being able to left-click, right-click, double-click, use the pointer, and so on.
✦ Basic PC hardware and networking comprehensions

If you meet these prerequisites, you're ready to begin this book.

If you don't have the basic Linux experience or mouse skills, I recommend that you work through a self-study book, such as *Linux For Dummies* (Hungry Minds, Inc.) or the *Linux Bible* (Hungry Minds, Inc.).

Conventions Used in This Book

Every book has its own set of conventions, so I'll explain the icons I've used in this book.

You'll see icons throughout each chapter. Six types of icons are used in this book. Below are the explanations of each icon:

 Caution This icon is used to warn you that something unfortunate could happen if you're not careful. It also points out information that could save you a lot of grief. It's often easier to prevent a tragedy than to fix it afterwards.

Cross-Reference This icon points you to another place in this book for more coverage of a particular topic. It may point you back to a previous chapter where important material has already been covered, or it may point you ahead to let you know that a topic will be covered in more detail later on.

Exam Tip This icon points out important information or advice for those preparing to take the Linux+ Certification exam.

In the Real World Sometimes things work differently in the real world than books — or product documentation — say they do. This icon draws your attention to the author's real-world experiences, which will hopefully help you on the job (if not on the Linux+ certification exam).

Tip This icon is used to draw your attention to a little piece of friendly advice, a helpful fact, a shortcut, or a bit of personal experience that might be of use to you.

 Objective This icon points out exactly where an exam objective is covered in a particular chapter, so you can focus your efforts on the areas where you need the most practice.

Acknowledgments

I would like to thank my brother, Nigel Kay, for his input and contributions to this book and the many hours he spent with me on this project to make this book the best it can be.

Thanks to everyone at Hungry Minds, including Katie Feltman, Acquisitions Editor; Amanda Peterson, Project Editor; Rebekah Mancilla, Copy Editor; Joe Byrne, Technical Editor; and to everyone in the Graphics and Production departments for their hard work and dedication to making this book a reality.

And special thanks to my mother and close friends: Clare Steed, Sharon Kay, Hamish Humphray, Walter Bell, Dell Errington, Anne Greenfield, The Testolin family, Rob (The Sculpture) Heath, Joe Piotrowski, Kevin Benjamin, Russ Francis, Jim Esler, Lisa Mior, Ricki Fudge, Beth Crowe, Elena N. Ranchina, Greg Stephens, Steve Marino, and Ken Dejong for their tremendous support during this project.

Contents at a Glance

Contents

Part I: Linux Basics   1

Part II: Installation   51

Part V: Maintaining the Linux System   381

Chapter 12: Linux Disk and System Management 383

Chapter 13: Process Management 409

Part VI: Troubleshooting and Maintaining System Hardware   479

Chapter 16: Linux Troubleshooting Basics 481

Chapter 17: Troubleshooting the Boot Process 507

Linux Basics

The Linux+ exam covers 14 percent on Linux basics. Understanding how Linux has a wide variety of distributions available; knowing the primary distributions and the packages that are included with each distribution is imperative in order to implement a successful Linux installation for the office or customers.

The chapters in this part focus on defining Linux and exploring its origins. I discuss the GNU GPL; I also discuss specific terms and their meanings, including: Open Source, Closed Source, artistic license, Freeware, and Shareware. This part also goes into detail about the growth of Linux, and I give you a basic understanding of the specific characteristics with which Linux is equipped.

The end of this part will focus on the Linux kernel and how you can determine the status, features, and reliability of the kernel based on its version. Also covered are package and package solutions and the different types of Linux distributions that are available. Knowing and understanding the pros and cons of each distribution will help you to decide what type of distribution is right for you, your company, and your customers.

Basic Linux Concepts

EXAM OBJECTIVES

- ✦ 1.5 Compare and contrast how major Linux licensing schemes work (e.g., GNU/GPL, freeware, shareware, open source, closed source, artistic license)

CHAPTER PRE-TEST

1. What is Linux?

2. What is GNU?

3. What is GPL?

4. What is the difference between Open and Closed Source?

5. What is the difference between Freeware and Shareware?

6. Who created Linux?

7. Why was Linux created?

8. Why is Linux not Unix?

9. What is POSIX and why is it important to Linux?

10. Why is desktop and Enterprise use of Linux growing so rapidly?

✦ Answers to these questions can be found at the end of the chapter. ✦

In this chapter, I introduce you to the basics of Linux and I discuss a brief history of Linux. I also answer several important questions about Linux, including: What are the concepts of GNU, GPL, Open Source, Freeware, Shareware, Closed Source, and Artistic License? How is Linux growing? Why is Linux used on the desktop as well as in the Enterprise? Getting to the bottom of these concepts and ideas will help you to understand Linux and its popularity.

What is Linux?

Linux (pronounced "LIH-nucks") is a 32-bit operating system (OS) that can be used on virtually every computer hardware platform. Originally designed for the Intel x86 platform, it is now available for Intel, Mac, Sparc, Alpha, embedded devices, and many more platforms. Linux is a UNIX-like OS that is very stable, reliable, and flexible. It is used on PCs, professional workstations, servers, routers, and practically every other computing platform. Linux works well in all these environments, and because it is multi-user and multi-tasking, it can perform virtually any job or group of jobs quickly and efficiently. Linux is as powerful as any other operating system, and most importantly, it is free. Linux was created to be a free alternative to UNIX and has become a competitor for all operating systems available today. This fact has enabled Linux to greatly increase its user base, and to be supported and used by the largest corporations and governments in the world. Because of its open nature and technical strengths, Enterprise use of Linux is best illustrated by its large-scale use on the Internet — it powers a majority of Internet applications, including the Apache Web server. Linux has sprung from humble beginnings to become a widely used and respected OS on essentially all computing platforms. Linux is a direct competitor with other high profile operating systems, such as UNIX and Microsoft Windows.

The origin of UNIX

UNIX got its start when a group of researchers from AT&T Bell Laboratories, General Electric, and the Massachusetts Institute of Technology worked together under the Multiplexed Information Computing System, or MULTICS, project in 1968. AT&T Bell Laboratories researchers Ken Thompson and Dennis Ritchie developed UNIX with many of the developments of the MULTICS project. UNIX was intended to be an affordable multi-user and multi-tasking OS, and to help meet those goals, UNIX was rewritten in 1973 using the C programming language. This allowed the UNIX OS to become transportable to other hardware platforms without having to be specifically written for that hardware platform. This ease of transport is still evident today because versions of UNIX are available for practically every computing platform, from PC to Supercomputer. As UNIX grew, Bell Labs licensed it to several users, one of which was the Computer Science department of the University of California Berkeley, creators of the *Berkeley Software Distribution* (BSD). The development of UNIX over the years at Berkeley, with the support of the Defense Advanced Research Projects Agency (DARPA), included the TCP/IP networking protocol suite that now powers the Internet. However, these various distributions of UNIX caused some compatibility problems. To resolve this issue, the Institute of Electrical and Electronics Engineers (IEEE) developed a new American National Standards Institute (ANSI) standard called the *Portable Operating System Interface for Computer Environments* (POSIX). This standard defines how a UNIX-like system needs to operate; this standard also details system calls and interfaces. This ANSI standard resolved most of the compatibility issues and helped UNIX to expand even further. The longer that UNIX was in distribution and with all the advances that were being made, however, one thing became increasingly clear: UNIX was being developed for workstations and minicomputers. This meant that students at major universities were unable to use UNIX applications on their powerful PCs in the late 1980s and early 1990s. And even though Professor Andrew Tannebaum had created Minix, a UNIX-like OS, it didn't have the functionality desired by students like Linus Torvalds.

Who started Linux?

Linus Torvalds started the Linux project while he was a student at the University of Helsinki. He worked to create a UNIX-like operating system equipped with more features than Minix. Torvalds created a Linux kernel that could work with UNIX applications, and in 1991, he released his first kernel for the Intel x86 platform, which was widely distributed over the Internet. A *kernel* is the core of any operating system, and the Linux kernel was built to work like UNIX but doesn't use any of the UNIX code — this is why Linux is not UNIX. The kernel is what allows most software to access the hardware that it is installed on. The key to Linux is its kernel because the kernel allows other programmers to refine it, add to it, and incorporate most of the features and applications of UNIX. Most standard UNIX applications have been ported to Linux, such as windows managers, Internet utilities, program development utilities, and just about every other tool used in computing today. The ability that other programmers have to work on and improve the Linux kernel is a result of the unique way Linus Torvalds distributed the kernel itself, which I discuss in the next section.

GNU and GPL

Objective

1.5 Compare and contrast how major Linux licensing schemes work (e.g., GNU/GPL, freeware, shareware, open source, closed source, artistic license)

The availability of the Linux kernel is different from the UNIX kernel or even the Windows kernel because it is distributed under the GNU (which stands for *GNU's Not UNIX*) General Public License (GPL). This license means that the source code is freely distributed and available to the general public, usually via the Internet. The GNU GPL is used to ensure that everyone has the ability to distribute copies of, use portions of, make changes to, or add packages to the software under this license. The GNU GPL also means that anyone who receives the software — even if they were charged for it — is protected under the GNU General Public License to have the same abilities to make changes and distribute the software. The GNU GPL ensures that no one person or organization can make a change to the kernel without making those changes publicly available. The Free Software Foundation, through fund-raising, supports the GNU project. Information on the GNU project can be found at www.gnu.org, where a description of their goals and the different types of GNU licenses are explained. The GNU GPL is as follows:

Version 2, June 1991
Copyright (C) 1989, 1991 Free Software Foundation, Inc.
59 Temple Place - Suite 330, Boston, MA 02111-1307, USA

Everyone is permitted to copy and distribute verbatim copies of this license document, but changing it is not allowed.

The licenses for most software are designed to take away your freedom to share and change it. By contrast, the GNU General Public License is intended to guarantee your freedom to share and change free software — to make sure that the software is free for all its users. This General Public License applies to most of the Free Software Foundation's software and to any other program whose authors commit to using it. (Some other Free Software Foundation software is covered by the GNU Library General Public License instead.) You can apply it to your programs, too. When we speak of free software, we are referring to freedom, not price. Our General Public Licenses are designed to make sure that you have the freedom to distribute copies of free software (and charge for this service if you want), that you receive source code or can get it if you want it, that you can change the software or use pieces of it in new free programs; and that you know you can do these things. To protect your rights, we need to make restrictions that forbid anyone to deny you these rights or to ask you to surrender the rights. These restrictions translate to certain responsibilities for you if you distribute copies of the software, or if you modify it. For example, if you distribute copies of such a program, whether gratis or for a fee, you must give the recipients all the rights that you have. You must make sure that they, too, receive or can get the source code. And you must show them these terms so they know their rights. We protect your rights with two steps: (1) copyright the software, and (2) offer you this license which gives you legal permission to copy, distribute, and/or modify the software. Also, for each author's protection and ours, we want to make certain that everyone understands that there is no warranty for this free software. If the software is modified by someone else and passed on, we want its recipients to know that what they have is not the original, so that any problems introduced by others will not reflect on the original authors' reputations. Finally, any free program is threatened constantly by software patents. We want to avoid the danger that redistributors of a free program will individually obtain patent licenses — in effect making the program proprietary. To prevent this, we have made it clear that any patent must be licensed for everyone's free use or not licensed at all. The precise terms and conditions for copy, distribution, and modification follow.

TERMS AND CONDITIONS FOR COPYING, DISTRIBUTION AND MODIFICATION

0. This License applies to any program or other work which contains a notice placed by the copyright holder saying it may be distributed under the terms of this General Public License. The "Program", below, refers to any such program or work, and a "work based on the Program" means either the Program or any derivative work under copyright law: that is to say, a work containing the Program or a portion of it, either verbatim or with modifications and/or translated into another language. (Hereinafter, translation is included without limitation in the term "modification".) Each licensee is addressed as "you".

Activities other than copying, distribution and modification are not covered by this License; they are outside its scope. The act of running the Program is not restricted, and the output from the Program is covered only if its contents constitute a work based on the Program (independent of having been made by running the Program). Whether that is true depends on what the Program does.

1. You may copy and distribute verbatim copies of the Program's source code as you receive it, in any medium, provided that you conspicuously and appropriately publish on each copy an appropriate copyright notice and disclaimer of warranty; keep intact all the notices that refer to this License and to the absence of any warranty; and give any other recipients of the Program a copy of this License along with the Program.

You may charge a fee for the physical act of transferring a copy, and you may at your option offer warranty protection in exchange for a fee.

2. You may modify your copy or copies of the Program or any portion of it, thus forming a work based on the Program, and copy and distribute such modifications or work under the terms of Section 1 above, provided that you also meet all of these conditions:

a) You must cause the modified files to carry prominent notices stating that you changed the files and the date of any change.

b) You must cause any work that you distribute or publish, that in whole or in part contains or is derived from the Program or any part thereof, to be licensed as a whole at no charge to all third parties under the terms of this License.

c) If the modified program normally reads commands interactively when run, you must cause it, when started running for such interactive use in the most ordinary way, to print or display an announcement including an appropriate copyright notice and a notice that there is no warranty (or else, saying that you provide a warranty) and that users may redistribute the program under these conditions, and telling the user how to view a copy of this License. (Exception: if the Program itself is interactive but does not normally print such an announcement, your work based on the

Program is not required to print an announcement.) These requirements apply to the modified work as a whole. If identifiable sections of that work are not derived from the Program, and can be reasonably considered independent and separate works in themselves, then this License, and its terms, do not apply to those sections when you distribute them as separate works. But when you distribute the same sections as part of a whole which is a work based on the Program, the distribution of the whole must be on the terms of this License, whose permissions for other licensees extend to the entire whole, and thus to each and every part regardless of who wrote it. Thus, it is not the intent of this section to claim rights or contest your rights to work written entirely by you; rather, the intent is to exercise the right to control the distribution of derivative or collective works based on the Program.

In addition, mere aggregation of another work not based on the Program with the Program (or with a work based on the Program) on a volume of a storage or distribution medium does not bring the other work under the scope of this License.

3. You may copy and distribute the Program (or a work based on it, under Section 2) in object code or executable form under the terms of Sections 1 and 2 above provided that you also do one of the following:

a) Accompany it with the complete corresponding machine-readable source code, which must be distributed under the terms of Sections 1 and 2 above on a medium customarily used for software interchange; or,

b) Accompany it with a written offer, valid for at least three years, to give any third party, for a charge no more than your cost of physically performing source distribution, a complete machine-readable copy of the corresponding source code, to be distributed under the terms of Sections 1 and 2 above on a medium customarily used for software interchange; or,

c) Accompany it with the information you received as to the offer to distribute corresponding source code. (This alternative is allowed only for noncommercial distribution and only if you received the program in object code or executable form with such an offer, in accord with Subsection b above.) The source code for a work means the preferred form of the work for making modifications to it. For an executable work, complete source code means all the source code for all modules it contains, plus any associated interface definition files, plus the scripts used to control compilation and installation of the executable. However, as a special exception, the source code distributed need not include anything that is normally distributed (in either source or binary form) with the major components (compiler, kernel, and so on) of the operating system on which the executable runs, unless that component itself accompanies the executable. If distribution of executable or object code is made by offering access to copy from a designated place, then offering equivalent access to copy the source code from the same place counts as distribution of the source code, even though third parties are not compelled to copy the source along with the object code.

4. You may not copy, modify, sublicense, or distribute the Program except as expressly provided under this License. Any attempt otherwise to copy, modify, sublicense or distribute the Program is void, and will automatically terminate your rights under this License. However, parties who have received copies, or rights, from you under this License will not have their licenses terminated so long as such parties remain in full compliance.

5. You are not required to accept this License, since you have not signed it. However, nothing else grants you permission to modify or distribute the Program or its derivative works. These actions are prohibited by law if you do not accept this License. Therefore, by modifying or distributing the Program (or any work based on the Program), you indicate your acceptance of this License to do so, and all its terms and conditions for copying, distributing or modifying the Program or works based on it.

6. Each time you redistribute the Program (or any work based on the Program), the recipient automatically receives a license from the original licensor to copy, distribute or modify the Program subject to these terms and conditions. You may not impose any further restrictions on the recipients' exercise of the rights granted herein. You are not responsible for enforcing compliance by third parties to this License.

7. If, as a consequence of a court judgment or allegation of patent infringement or for any other reason (not limited to patent issues), conditions are imposed on you (whether by court order, agreement, or otherwise) that contradict the conditions of this License, they do not excuse you from the conditions of this License. If you cannot distribute so as to satisfy simultaneously your obligations under this License and any other pertinent obligations, then as a consequence you may not distribute the Program at all. For example, if a patent license would not permit royalty-free redistribution of the Program by all those who receive copies directly or indirectly through you, then the only way you could satisfy both it and this License would be to refrain entirely from distribution of the Program. If any portion of this section is held invalid or unenforceable under any particular circumstance, the balance of the section is intended to apply and the section as a whole is intended to apply in other circumstances. It is not the purpose of this section to induce you to infringe any patents or other property right claims or to contest validity of any such claims; this section has the sole purpose of protecting the integrity of the free software distribution system, which is implemented by public license practices. Many people have made generous contributions to the wide range of software distributed through that system in reliance on consistent application of that system; it is up to the author/donor to decide if he or she is willing to distribute software through any other system and a licensee cannot impose that choice. This section is intended to make thoroughly clear what is believed to be a consequence of the rest of this License.

8. If the distribution and/or use of the Program is restricted in certain countries either by patents or by copyrighted interfaces, the original copyright holder who places the Program under this License may add an explicit geographical

distribution limitation excluding those countries, so that distribution is permitted only in or among countries not thus excluded. In such case, this License incorporates the limitation as if written in the body of this License.

9. The Free Software Foundation may publish revised and/or new versions of the General Public License from time to time. Such new versions will be similar in spirit to the present version, but may differ in detail to address new problems or concerns. In essence, GNU is an attempt to guarantee certain rights for both users and developers. This sets Linux apart from other most operating systems in the market today is that Linux is Open Source.

Each version is given a distinguishing version number. If the Program specifies a version number of this License which applies to it and "any later version", you have the option of following the terms and conditions either of that version or of any later version published by the Free Software Foundation. If the Program does not specify a version number of this License, you may choose any version ever published by the Free Software Foundation.

10. If you wish to incorporate parts of the Program into other free programs whose distribution conditions are different, write to the author to ask for permission. For software which is copyrighted by the Free Software Foundation, write to the Free Software Foundation; we sometimes make exceptions for this. Our decision will be guided by the two goals of preserving the free status of all derivatives of our free software and of promoting the sharing and reuse of software generally.

NO WARRANTY

11. BECAUSE THE PROGRAM IS LICENSED FREE OF CHARGE, THERE IS NO WARRANTY FOR THE PROGRAM, TO THE EXTENT PERMITTED BY APPLICABLE LAW. EXCEPT WHEN OTHERWISE STATED IN WRITING, THE COPYRIGHT HOLDERS AND/OR OTHER PARTIES PROVIDE THE PROGRAM "AS IS" WITHOUT WARRANTY OF ANY KIND, EITHER EXPRESSED OR IMPLIED, INCLUDING, BUT NOT LIMITED TO, THE IMPLIED WARRANTIES OF MERCHANTABILITY AND FITNESS FOR A PARTICULAR PURPOSE. THE ENTIRE RISK AS TO THE QUALITY AND PERFORMANCE OF THE PROGRAM IS WITH YOU. SHOULD THE PROGRAM PROVE DEFECTIVE, YOU ASSUME THE COST OF ALL NECESSARY SERVICING, REPAIR OR CORRECTION.

12. IN NO EVENT UNLESS REQUIRED BY APPLICABLE LAW OR AGREED TO IN WRITING WILL ANY COPYRIGHT HOLDER, OR ANY OTHER PARTY WHO MAY MODIFY AND/OR REDISTRIBUTE THE PROGRAM AS PERMITTED ABOVE, BE LIABLE TO YOU FOR DAMAGES, INCLUDING ANY GENERAL, SPECIAL, INCIDENTAL OR CONSEQUENTIAL DAMAGES ARISING OUT OF THE USE OR INABILITY TO USE THE PROGRAM (INCLUDING BUT NOT LIMITED TO LOSS OF DATA OR DATA BEING RENDERED INACCURATE OR LOSSES SUSTAINED BY YOU OR THIRD PARTIES OR A FAILURE OF THE PROGRAM TO OPERATE WITH ANY OTHER PROGRAMS), EVEN IF SUCH HOLDER OR OTHER PARTY HAS BEEN ADVISED OF THE POSSIBILITY OF SUCH DAMAGES.

END OF TERMS AND CONDITIONS

Understanding Open Source

Objective
➡

1.5 Compare and contrast how major Linux licensing schemes work (e.g., GNU/GPL, freeware, shareware, open source, closed source, artistic license)

The GNU GPL makes Linux Open Source because it is an acceptable license for Open Source Software. Open Source follows a similar path of the GNU GPL, but it also has many differences. Even though the Open Source Initiative strictly adheres to GNU GPL, it is not a specific license; rather, the Open Source Initiative supports the various types of open source licenses that are available. The idea behind the Open Source Initiative (OSI) is to gather corporate support behind open source. Companies that want to participate in Open Source are allowed to write their own license or use the GNU GPL and submit the license to the OSI for certification. This opens the door for all Open Source software and guarantees not only source code access but also follows the Open Source Definition. Full information on the Open Source Initiative can be found at `www.opensource.org`. The Open Source Definition is as follows:

✦ **Free Distribution** — The license shall not restrict any party from selling or giving away the software as a component of an aggregate software distribution containing programs from several different sources. The license shall not require a royalty or other fee for such sale.

✦ **Source Code** — The program must include source code, and must allow distribution in source code as well as compiled form. Where some form of a product is not distributed with source code, there must be a well-publicized means of obtaining the source code for no more than a reasonable reproduction cost — preferably, downloading via the Internet without charge. The source code must be the preferred form in which a programmer would modify the program. Deliberately obfuscated source code is not allowed. Intermediate forms such as the output of a preprocessor or translator are not allowed.

✦ **Derived Works** — The license must allow modifications and derived works, and must allow them to be distributed under the same terms as the license of the original software.

✦ **Integrity of The Author's Source Code** — The license may restrict source-code from being distributed in modified form only if the license allows the distribution of "patch files" with the source code for the purpose of modifying the program at build time. The license must explicitly permit distribution of software built from modified source code. The license may require derived works to carry a different name or version number from the original software.

✦ **No Discrimination Against Persons or Groups** — The license must not discriminate against any person or group of persons.

✦ **No Discrimination Against Fields of Endeavor** — The license must not restrict anyone from making use of the program in a specific field of endeavor. For example, it may not restrict the program from being used in a business, or from being used for genetic research.

✦ **Distribution of License** — The rights attached to the program must apply to all to whom the program is redistributed without the need for execution of an additional license by those parties.

✦ **License Must Not Be Specific to a Product** — The rights attached to the program must not depend on the program's being part of a particular software distribution. If the program is extracted from that distribution and used or distributed within the terms of the program's license, all parties to whom the program is redistributed should have the same rights as those that are granted in conjunction with the original software distribution.

✦ **License Must Not Contaminate Other Software** — The license must not place restrictions on other software that is distributed along with the licensed software. For example, the license must not insist that all other programs distributed on the same medium must be open-source software.

Understanding Closed Source

In Closed Source software, such as Microsoft products, the creators are the only ones who can access and modify the software source code. Of course, this also means that they are the only ones who are authorized to refine, add to, and fix bugs in the software. This is the most restrictive of the software licensing methods.

Selecting Closed Source as the licensing method often draws the wrath of GNU GPL and Open Source supporters. The Open Source and GNU GPL supporters see Closed Source as a restriction that should be lifted to allow anyone to fix, improve, or change the software for the benefit of the software and its community of users. Companies that select Closed Source as the licensing method for the software that they release are often trying to protect "intellectual property," and therefore see little benefit to opening the software to others. This is a major philosophical difference between Closed Source and Open Source software licenses.

Understanding Artistic License

Artistic License takes a different philosophical approach. It is different from Open Source or GNU GPL because Artistic License is a more restrictive license. Artistic License requires that any modifications to a software package remain in some control of the Copyright Holder. This defeats the reason for Open Source and GNU GPL because if the Copyright Holder does not like the direction (even if it improves the software) the Copyright Holder can stop the changes. Perl is a good example of Artistic License and of the issues that this license can cause.

Is Freeware really free?

Freeware is software that the creator or copyright holder gives away for no charge. This may seem to indicate that the software is not protected by a license. This impression, however, is not accurate because Freeware, even if it is free of charge, is often covered by one of the many licensing methods. Sometimes companies or individuals will release software as Freeware but control the software under a Closed Source license. This may seem strange, but consider the freeware as a service to introduce users to a company or individual's software. The company or individual may use the same core programming to create all of the software that they offer, so they may not want to release the code under an Open Source license. Thus, Freeware has no charge, but it isn't always *free*.

Is Shareware never free?

Shareware is software that a creator has decided to give away with a string attached. The attached string is that if you want to continue using the software, you must send a payment to the creator. Some creators use the honor system, but most shareware is designed to turn itself off after a certain amount of time. Considering this situation, you may wonder if shareware has to be Closed Source. The answer is no, because it can be licensed under any of the licensing methods; however, it does seem to make more sense to make shareware Closed Source in order to limit the distribution.

A comparison and contrast of licensing methods

Naturally, you should make comparisons when determining which licensing method to select. Keep the following points in mind when choosing a licensing method:

The **GNU GPL** is restricted to the exact terms of the published GNU GPL and can't be changed. This is more restrictive than some software authors desire.

The **Open Source Licensing** method has the GNU GPL as a subset, but it also allows software authors the capability to write their own license, as long as that license follows the Open Source Initiative standards.

Closed Source Licensing is used for any software in which the copyright holder doesn't want to share the source code of a software package in any way. This is the usual method of licensing by commercial companies and prevents others from using the code to customize the software for redistribution.

Note   This doesn't mean that Closed Source software is never customized and redistributed. Recently, two of the most popular computer games have had their *cores* (or engines) licensed to other companies for customization and redistribution as several new games. This is an excellent way for one company to make more money off of a software program while the purchasing company saves development cost.

Artistic Licenses are generally used by software authors who want to give others limited access to the code of a software program. In fact, this is often the case when software authors want to prevent software from being altered too dramatically from the original code.

Freeware and Shareware are variations on these various licensing methods. Freeware may or may not be GNU GPL or Open Source, but the creator doesn't charge for the software. Usually Freeware and Shareware are not descriptive of the Open or Closed Source nature of the program. By using the GNU GPL or Open Source Initiative license, the developers of Linux and its associated programs have allowed the use, change, and redistribution of these programs under the GNU GPL or Open Source method to create excellent growth in the OS world.

The Growth of Linux

The growth of Linux is subject to some debate, but the best indicators of the power of Linux are the following:

✦ Major companies that support it, such as Intel, IBM, Dell, and Google

✦ Governmental use as the only operating system in offices or throughout an entire country

✦ The increase of non-technical users who use Linux as their operating system

The major companies support Linux as an alternative to other operating systems on the market because there is a great demand for the reliability and security of Linux that the other operating systems often can't provide. These corporations determined that there was a need to support, install, sell, or use Linux in the day-to-day workings of the company. For example, Dell and IBM may sell, install, and support Linux as an operating system on their PCs through server lines of equipment — simply because users ask for it. In addition, Google uses Linux to power its search engine because Linux has proven itself to be stable and *clusters* (lots of servers working as one) well.

Another area representing the growth of Linux is the increase of Linux within governmental offices. Several countries have determined that Linux should be *the* operating system of choice, and in some cases, the *only* operating system that is used in government offices or throughout the country. These governments have determined that Linux fits their needs better than other operating systems for economical, political, and technical reasons.

Furthermore, many non-technical users are now using Linux as their operating system of choice. Whether they saw a TV show, read an article, or saw an experienced user utilize Linux in a helpful way, non-technical users are trying Linux out or switching to it as an alternative to other operating systems — and then staying with Linux after it proves itself to be stable, reliable, and easy to use. Last year, according to the market research firm International Data Corporation (IDC), Linux operating system growth outpaced all other client and server operating systems.

Linux on a Personal Computer

At one time, the use of Linux on the PC was only for the technical professional or hobbyist. This is changing rapidly because the impression that Linux is always stable but difficult for the end user is being replaced by the idea that Linux is easy to install, set up, and use. Almost every distribution of Linux has an easy-to-use graphical interface that even the novice user can follow. Linux distributions are also using some excellent hardware probing tools for easier installation on any PC. Most creators of Linux distributions understand that the user may want to dual-boot with Microsoft Windows or Mac OS, so they make this an easy option to perform. The addition of Windows-like Desktop managers and GUI environments has eased the transition for traditional Mac OS and Microsoft Windows users into the Linux environment. All of these updated features are making Linux a viable choice for the home or business PC user. However, Linux still has some disadvantages because some tasks continue to be difficult to perform. For example, the novice user is still afraid of using the UNIX command line, and many other tasks involve a more in-depth knowledge of the Linux environment that a novice user may not have. Behind the GUI interface, however, is the power, stability, and reliability that UNIX and Linux bring to the PC — regardless of the platform. A familiar interface, overlaying a powerful operating system, lets everyone use Linux and benefit from it.

Graphical installation

The fact that the common user has the ability to operate a Linux PC the same way as a competing OS is a tribute to the speed at which Linux has developed. This growth has powered several changes in Linux, the first of which is the installation interface. Most distributions have left the command line behind, opting for an easy-to-understand graphical installation. (Don't worry; the command line is still there for those who want to use it.) These graphical installation programs provide mouse support, a basic windows system, and easy push button control panels that allow users to walk through the installation process fairly easily. Using this method, any user who can install or upgrade Microsoft Windows or Mac OS can install or upgrade Linux. This is the first key development that is allowing Linux to grow.

Hardware detection

The second development that is contributing to the growth of Linux is its hardware detection and support. All major distributions of Linux for the PC have excellent hardware detection. Through the use of advanced hardware detection and some support for plug-and-play devices, Linux can detect and load the correct device drivers for various types of hardware. This enables the user to ignore the previous task of manually configuring the PC for the hardware that it contains. The ability to detect most new hardware and automatically load proper drivers has eased the difficulty of Linux installation on most PCs.

Graphical user interface

Because most users transitioning from the Microsoft Windows or the Mac operating system are used to a graphical environment, Linux had to have a similar interface to remain competitive. Both the K Desktop Environment (KDE) and GNU Network Object Model Environment (GNOME) are very competent GUI environments. They include most (if not all) of the features that the Microsoft Windows or Mac OS graphical interfaces offer, and they add several excellent utilities, such as word processors, database programs, spreadsheets, accounting programs, and many more. Several commercial programs, such as WordPerfect, are also available for Linux. The maturing process of the Linux graphical interface is not complete, but they are extremely comparable to the other GUIs on competitive operating systems.

Linux limitations on the PC

There are some prominent issues that must be resolved before more users will have the desire to switch to Linux. Most commercial application software is written for Microsoft or Mac OS, and even though some are ported to Linux, a large number of popular software applications are still not available. Some hardware is also not supported to the fullest capability possible. Linux relies on vendors to make their drivers or hardware open to developers. Some manufacturers don't release information for their hardware. This lack of information can cause the user some difficulty in configuring the hardware — especially if no drivers are available for the device. It can take a long time for a developer to write a Linux driver for recently released hardware devices. These issues are decreasing in number as new releases of the Linux kernel make improvements on support for 3D graphics, USB, IEEE1394, and virtually any other new hardware technology.

Linux succeeds on the PC

Because Linux is now providing support for almost every piece of hardware, has an easy installation interface, and gives users an excellent GUI to work with, Linux has become the fastest growing operating system today. Perhaps Linux will soon be seen as the best operating system for the PC — and it is completely possible that Linux will displace other operating systems as the primary OS for every PC platform.

Linux on workstations

Because Linux will work with virtually any hardware device, it can also be ported easily to work on virtually every hardware platform. This ability has allowed Linux to be installed on the professional workstation. This ability to run on any workstation platform may provide users with the following:

✦ New life for older workstations with slower hardware

✦ A common operating system environment across different platforms

✦ Software portability to all hardware platforms

These benefits can enable general users and users in companies and governments to work on the same operating system across various hardware from PCs to workstations.

Because Linux was created with UNIX compliance in mind, it inherits the portability of UNIX. Portability means that it can be adapted to practically any hardware, so you will see it on everything from embedded chips to multi-processor servers. The porting to various workstation platforms allows Linux to replace vendor-specific operating systems and provide a current, common, and POSIX-compliant operating system, which can be used to provide a common operating system environment to all hardware devices. Linux can thus save a user, company, or government the expense of replacing or upgrading the vendor-specific operating system on the old workstations.

Linux on servers

Because UNIX is an excellent server operating system, Linux inherits the UNIX capability of providing efficient and stable server services. The stability of Linux makes it a natural selection to provide services to many users. Because Linux supports all the major services that are on the market today and can easily scale upwards to support additional services and applications, it fulfills all the needs that a server must provide. Linux runs on virtually every platform, so it is able to replace less capable and unreliable operating systems. Linux does have some limitations, but as stated previously, Linux is rapidly resolving these deficiencies as the kernel is improved and evolved.

Stability

Servers require stability. Linux is a very stable operating system — often running for years without a reboot — so it can easily provide a reliable server to any user, company, or government. The reliability of Linux can be traced to the kernel, and because the GNU GPL allows anyone to fix problems with the kernel, it is continually evolving its stability through constant improvements. The kernel, the core system, and other services can run as modules, thus adding to the stability of Linux. Additionally, if a module were to crash, it can be stopped and restarted separately from the operating system; this is a good way to update drivers and other services that are running on the server. By providing a very stable environment, Linux is very well suited to be a server.

Services

Linux provides the base operating system for a server environment, but its popularity has come from the wide variety of applications and services that have been developed for it by Linux programmers. These services are usually released under Open Source or GNU GPL methods and are improved and modified to work as stable and efficient as possible.

A large majority of Internet Web servers are powered by using Linux and the Apache Web server. This combination is an excellent choice as it has proven to be stable, secure, and reliable for many years. To increase interoperability between operating systems, programmers have created a program called Samba that allows Linux to communicate with Microsoft Windows environments. These are only a few of the services available on a Linux server but it does demonstrate that Linux can compete in any environment and provide the services needed for a diverse user base.

Linux fails?

Like any operating system, Linux has some limitations and issues. For example, it is not the best operating system in every environment; other operating systems seem to handle new technologies quicker than Linux, due to the fact that Linux can only support emerging technologies as drivers are written for them. For users in the non-corporate world, this means they are programming these drivers for Linux in their spare time. With some manufacturers and companies not releasing their hardware specifications in time, it can take a very long time for a newer technology to be supported under Linux.

Summary

In this chapter, I explore what Linux is, why it was created, how it was created, and what standards it uses. I also list the licensing of Linux and compare it to the other methods of licensing software. Finally, I illustrate the growth of Linux in various environments. For the exam, keep these key points in mind:

✦ Know the differences between the types of licensing

✦ Be able to describe the differences between Linux, Unix and other operating systems

✦ Know the strengths of the Linux platform, and why its usage is growing so fast

✦　　✦　　✦

STUDY GUIDE

The Study Guide section provides you with the opportunity to test your knowledge about Linux. The Assessment Questions will help you to understand the basics of Linux, and the Scenarios provide practice with real situations. If you get any questions incorrect, use the answers to determine the part of the chapter that you should review before continuing.

Assessment Questions

1. What operating system inspired Linux?

    A. Minix

    B. POSIX

    C. UNIX

    D. GNU

2. Who created the first Linux kernel?

    A. Andrew Tannebaum

    B. Linus Torvalds

    C. Ken Thompson

    D. Dennis Ritchie

3. Linux was originally created to run on what platform?

    A. Sparc

    B. PowerPC

    C. Intel x86

    D. Alpha

4. AT&T Bell Laboratories, General Electric, and the Massachusetts Institute of Technology worked together under what project?

    A. MULTICS

    B. GNU

    C. Open Source

    D. BSD

5. The Linux kernel is distributed under which licensing method?

   A. Artistic

   B. GNU GPL

   C. Closed Source

   D. Freeware

6. What does GNU mean?

   A. It is free

   B. It is not UNIX

   C. It is Open Source

   D. It is Linux

7. What does GPL mean?

   A. General Public License

   B. Generic Public License

   C. GNU Public License

   D. Good Public License

8. What may be seen as a drawback of the GNU GPL?

   A. It is too restrictive

   B. It is free to use

   C. It costs too much

   D. It is ambiguous

9. The Open Source Initiative differs from the GNU GPL by?

   A. Allowing changes to the GNU GPL

   B. Accepting any licenses

   C. Accepting certain licenses

   D. Remaining Open Source

10. Open Source and GNU GPL both seek to?

   A. Guarantee the ability to change, add to, and redistribute software

   B. Guarantee that the software is always free

   C. Provide copyright licensing to prevent distribution

   D. Provide all software for no charge

11. Closed source software is meant to?

    A. Never be updated

    B. Always be purchased

    C. Prevent others from access to the software code

    D. Prevent others from writing code for the software

12. Freeware is not always Open Source because?

    A. It is Open Source because it is free

    B. It doesn't always allow redistribution

    C. It is always Closed Source

    D. It is under the GNU GPL

13. What is an advantage that Linux offers by remaining POSIX-compliant?

    A. UNIX compliance

    B. Minix Standard

    C. MULTICS compliance

    D. GNU standard

14. Which of the following uses an Artistic license?

    A. GNU

    B. UNIX

    C. Linux

    D. Perl

15. What does POSIX stand for?

    A. Portable Operating System Interface for Computer Environments

    B. Portable Operating System Interface for UNIX

    C. Portable Operating System Interface for LINUX

    D. Portable Operating System Interface for Experience

16. Is all Shareware protected by a Closed Source License?

    A. No, Shareware can be Open Source or Closed Source; it just requires a fee for its use.

    B. No, Shareware is Open Source but requests a fee for its use.

    C. Yes, Shareware is Closed Source and requires a fee for its continued use.

    D. Yes, Shareware is Closed Source unless you pay the fee.

17. Which of the following may it be an advantage of Linux on a PC?

    A. Easy to install

    B. Easy to configure

    C. Easy to use

    D. Works with any software

18. Which of the following is a popular Linux Web service?

    A. Internet Information Server

    B. Apache

    C. Samba

    D. Windows

19. Why is Linux a good server operating system?

    A. It is very stable.

    B. It is the best operating system at every task.

    C. It allows proprietary changes for redistribution.

    D. It isn't a good server operating system.

20. Why is Linux growing so rapidly?

    A. It can only be used on one machine for each GNU GPL.

    B. It can't be redistributed without Linus Torvalds's permission.

    C. It is easily ported to any hardware and then easily installed.

    D. It may be hard to work with, but it is very stable.

Scenarios

The following three scenarios will test your knowledge of some ways in which Linux can resolve issues.

1. You have just upgraded your old PC to the fastest PC on the market. You want to resell it but you also don't want to violate any licensing for the OS. What can you do to avoid violating a software license?

2. Your company just replaced some old workstations because they can't run the newest proprietary software. You want to use the old workstations to create an Internet Café in the company break room. The old software doesn't include an Internet browser. How can you resolve this issue?

3. Your company is short of funds but needs a reliable file server set up. You have managed to get a server but not an operating system license. Which OS can you use to set up the server?

Answers to Chapter Questions

Chapter Pre-Test

1. Linux is a UNIX-like operating system.

2. GNU stands for *GNU's not UNIX* and is attempting to create a UNIX-like OS.

3. GPL stands for *General Public License,* which was established with GNU to guarantee that it would remain free.

4. Open Source allows anyone to make changes and redistribute software, whereas Closed Source restricts those rights to the copyright holder.

5. Freeware is software that carries no fees, but Shareware requests or requires a fee.

6. Linus Torvalds started the Linux project while a student at the University of Helsinki.

7. To provide an UNIX-like OS.

8. Linux doesn't use a UNIX kernel and is Open Source.

9. The POSIX standard allows POSIX software to run on any POSIX OS.

10. Linux is an Open Source UNIX-like OS that provides the stability and functionality for both the individual desktop, and Enterprise server environments.

Assessment Questions

1. C. UNIX inspired the Linux OS because Linus Torvalds wanted to use UNIX tools but didn't want to buy a UNIX license. Minix is a UNIX-like tool created by Professor Andrew Tannebaum, GNU is an ongoing project to create a UNIX-like OS, and POSIX is an IEEE standard for UNIX. For review, see the "Who started Linux?" section.

2. B. Linus Torvalds created the first Linux kernel and released it to the general public in 1991. Ken Thompson and Dennis Ritchie helped to create UNIX, and Andrew Tannebaum created Minix. For review, see the "Who started Linux?" section.

3. C. Linux was originally created to run on the Intel x86 platform. Sparc and Alpha are not PC platforms and although the PowerPC is a PC platform, it isn't the PC that Linus Torvalds used. For review, see the "Who started Linux?" section.

4. A. AT&T Bell Laboratories, General Electric, and the Massachusetts Institute of Technology worked together on the MULTICS project to create a Multiplexed Computing System. BSD was and is a licensee of UNIX code, Open Source is an initiative for free software, and the GNU project is attempting to create a UNIX-like OS. For review, see "The origin of UNIX" section.

5. B. The Linux kernel is distributed under the GNU GPL and guarantees that users will remain free to change, add to, and redistribute Linux. The artistic licensing method is more restrictive, Closed Source restricts code access, and Freeware is not a license at all. For review, see the "GNU and GPL" section.

6. B. GNU's Not UNIX, or the GNU project, is attempting to create a UNIX-like OS. It is free and Open Source and it is not Linux (although Linux is often called *GNU/Linux* for GNU applications running on the Linux kernel). For review, see the "GNU and GPL" section.

7. A. GPL stands for *General Public License* and it was created to protect the intent of the GNU project. For review, see the "GNU and GPL" section.

8. A. The possible drawback of the GNU GPL is that it is more restrictive than some companies may prefer when distributing Open Source Software, because the source code can't be combined with code that is not under the GPL.. For review, see the "Understanding Open Source" section.

9. C. Open Source differs from the GNU GPL by accepting certain licenses that follow the standards of Open Source. No changes can be made to the GNU GPL, and this is why it is sometimes considered to be restrictive. Open Source accepts only those licenses that follow the OSI standard. GNU GPL is a subset of the Open Source standard, but is only one of many acceptable licenses for Open Source. For review, see the "Understanding Open Source" section.

10. A. Open Source and GNU GPL both seek to guarantee the ability to freely change, add to, and redistribute software. The GNU GPL and Open Source licensing methods don't forbid charging for distribution of software, they simply require that the software remain changeable and redistributed. This license is used to prevent restrictions on distribution and to prevent anyone from charging fees for software. For review, see the "GNU and GPL" and "Understanding Open Source" sections.

11. C. Closed Source software is meant to prevent users from accessing the source code, changing it, and then redistributing it. Closed Source doesn't prevent others from writing updates or additions to the software, it only seeks to prevent others from accessing the source code for the software. For review, see the "Understanding Closed Source" section.

12. B. Freeware is not always Open Source because it doesn't always allow redistribution. Freeware is not indicative of the licensing method, it just means that the copyright holder gives it away. It also doesn't mean that you may change or improve the software and then redistribute it. For review, see the "Is Freeware really free?" section.

13. A. POSIX is used to provide UNIX compliance. Minix is not a standard; the MULTICS project helped form the basics for UNIX; and the GNU standard is essentially a project to create a new UNIX-like kernel. For review, see the "The origin of UNIX" section and the "GNU and GPL" section.

14. D. Perl uses the Artistic license. UNIX usually uses the Closed Source method; however, this is changing because GNU uses the GPL method — as does Linux. For review, see the "Understanding Artistic License" section.

15. A. POSIX stands for *Portable Operating System Interface for Computer Environments.* It is the standard for ensuring compatibility between UNIX versions. For review, see the "The origin of UNIX" section.

16. A. Shareware is not Open Source or Closed Source, but does require a fee for its use. Usually, it is Closed Source, but this is not always the case. For review, see the "Shareware is never free?" section.

17. D. One disadvantage of Linux is that not as much commercial software has been written for it as for Microsoft or Mac OS. For review, see the "Linux limitations on the PC" section.

18. B. The Apache Web server is the most popular Web server in use on the Internet. Internet Information Server is the Microsoft Web server, while Samba is software that allows Linux access to Microsoft network services. For review, see the "Services" section.

19. A. Linux is a good server operating system because it is very stable. Although Linux is an excellent OS, it isn't the best for every situation and it isn't proprietary. For review, see the "Linux on servers" section.

20. C. Linux is growing so rapidly because it is easily ported to any hardware and then easily installed. It can also be easily installed on as many machines as necessary, and it isn't limited to one machine for each GNU GPL. It can be changed and redistributed without permission from anyone. For review, see the "The Growth of Linux" section.

Scenarios

1. Linux can be downloaded and installed on the old PC without violating any software licensing because it is covered under the GNU GPL.

2. Install Linux on the workstations and configure any of the many Web browsers available to provide the Internet services.

3. Linux is released under an Open Source licensing method — the GNU GPL — and can be installed on any server to provide the necessary file server.

Linux Kernel and Distributions

EXAM OBJECTIVES

✦ 1.7 Identify strengths and weaknesses of different distributions
   and their packaging solutions (e.g., tar ball vs. RPM/DEB)

✦ 1.9 Identify how the Linux kernel version numbering works

✦ 1.10 Identify where to obtain software and resources

CHAPTER PRE-TEST

1. What are the ways that the Linux kernel is released?

2. Who determines the release of the Linux kernel?

3. What does the version number of the Linux kernel signify?

4. Where are the best Linux resources?

5. What are Linux packages?

6. What are Linux applications?

7. What is a Linux distribution?

8. What are the major standard Linux distributions based on?

9. For what platforms are Linux distributions released?

10. What are the major reasons to purchase and use a Linux distribution?

◆ Answers to these questions can be found at the end of the chapter. ◆

In this chapter, you will learn more about the Linux kernel, including information on how you can use kernel versions to determine the status, features, and reliability of the kernel. This chapter also includes a listing of Linux resources, and I discuss an easy way to use these resources. In fact, I show you how to use Linux resources in order to learn how to install, modify, and use packages and applications. Packages and applications are usually distributed as a vendor distribution, so I will discuss these distributions and also list some of the most popular ones. After this chapter, you should have a better understanding of these important Linux concepts, and you should be able to identify the kernel version, Linux resources, packages, applications, and distributions — and how they are used to create a software package that you may want to use.

Linux Kernel

The *kernel* is the core of the operating system and provides the ability for software to access the hardware systems. Because the Linux kernel is used to access hardware, the kernel is often updated. These updates to the kernel are used to provide or improve support for newer technologies, such as SCSI controllers, Ultra ATA, USB, IEEE-1394, video cards, and other devices that are not properly supported by the previous kernel. The Linux kernel uses modules to add support for new devices and improve support for existing devices.

The use of modules prevents the entire Linux kernel from requiring constant replacement because the administrator can simply update the module to improve or provide support for the desired device. Modules, however, have limits, and you may have many reasons to update and recompile the entire kernel — to achieve, for example, better stability, performance, and improved support for all hardware. Keeping track of kernel changes can be a challenge, but by using a simple numbering system, Linux users can identify their current kernel version.

Kernel versions

Objective

1.9 Identify how the Linux kernel version numbering works

The kernel versions are used to determine the status, feature set, and reliability of the kernel. This kernel version numbering system ensures the availability and easy identification of each kernel. This system is summarized in the following list (Table 2-1 lists major kernel versions, including basic information about each version):

- ✦ **Major number:** This is the leftmost number, and it reflects a major change in the kernel.

- ✦ **Minor number:** This is the middle number and reflects the stability of a particular kernel. Even numbers indicate a stable release, and odd numbers indicate a developmental release.

✦ **Revision number:** This is the last number and indicates the version of the overall release. For example, 2.4.4 is the fourth subversion of the 2.4.0 kernel.

Exam Tip   Linux kernel version numbering is used often and is an important subject. You don't have to memorize every detail about each Linux kernel, but you should understand the revision numbers and the purpose of updating the kernel.

Table 2-1 Linux Kernel Versions				
Kernel	**Date**	**Size**	**Status**	**Subversions**
0.01	17 September 1991	63,263	Stable	2
0.10	3 December 1991	90,032	Stable	2
0.95	8 March 1992	116,059	Developmental	4
Pre-0.96	22 April 1992	131,606	Pre-Release	0
0.96a	22 May 1992	174,003	Stable	4
0.96b	22 June 1992	181,231	Stable	2
0.96c	5 July 1992	191,894	Stable	2
0.97	1 August 1992	233,862	Developmental	7
0.98	29 September 1992	320,917	Stable	6
0.99	13 December 1992	426,483	Developmental	79
Pre-1.0	6 March 1994	1,009,290	Pre-Release	0
1.0	13 March 1994	1,016,601	Stable	9
1.1.0	6 April 1994	1,013,691	Developmental	95
1.2.0	7 March 1995	1,850,182	Stable	13
1.3.0	12 June 1995	2,052,167	Developmental	100
2.0-pre1	12 May 1996	4,570,261	Pre-Release	13
2.0	9 June 1996	4,718,270	Stable	39
2.10	30 September 1996	4,897,927	Developmental	132
2.2.0-pre1	28 December 1998	10,455,343	Pre-Release	8
2.2.0	26 January 1999	10,592,549	Stable	19
2.3.0	11 May 1999	11,208,792	Developmental	51
2.3.99-pre1	15 March 2000	16,027,466	Pre-Release	8
2.4.0-test1	25 May 2000	16,989,873	Pre-Release	11
2.4.0-Pre-release	31 December 2000	19,341,926	Pre-Release	0
2.4.0	4 January 2001	19,788,626	Stable	4 and counting

Kernel availability

Objective

1.10 Identify where to obtain software and resources

The availability of the kernel is clearly protected by the GNU GPL licensing method, and this protection allows users to download the Linux kernel in all of its various forms from the Internet. You can download the kernel from several locations, but all kernel releases are kept at `www.kernel.org` and include a brief or detailed description of the release. Customized kernels are available from the creators of various Linux distributions, but Linus Torvalds, who created the Linux kernel, has customarily released the most updated version of the kernel.

Linux Distributions

Objective

1.7 Identify strengths and weaknesses of different distributions and their packaging solutions (e.g., tar ball vs. RPM/DEB)

1.10 Identify where to obtain software and resources

Because of the Open Source nature of the Linux kernel, which allows anyone to modify or enhance the base kernel with other software, Linux is available in a wide variety of distributions.

A Linux *distribution* is a collection of software packages, utilities, and tools, and is based on the version of a Linux kernel. Distributions are often created with a specific purpose in mind, such as an embedded Web server or a special network server for an ISP. Most are general-purpose distributions, meaning that they come with a wide variety of software packages, tools, and applications that can be installed by the end user, resulting in ultimate flexibility.

Each distribution comes with its own characteristics and special tools, created by the distribution company to increase the value of their version of Linux. Most of these distributions can be obtained for free (in keeping with the GPL license) but many companies also sell commercial distributions. Most Linux vendors center their business on a service support model for their distribution.

The following sections list the most popular types of Linux distributions available.

Beehive

The goal of Beehive Linux is to provide a fast, simple, and secure i686 optimized Linux distribution. The distribution is small—approximately 250MB—and installs at about 120MB. Therefore, this distribution has the benefit of being able to quickly configure a new system without having to install the added modules for older hardware that must be removed from the kernel in order to achieve optimal performance. This timesaving benefit is intended for the experienced user. Because Beehive Linux doesn't include support for any hardware other than i686 CPUs, the kernel installs already optimized for the speed of this processor. The lack of support for other features on older machines, such as built-in menus and GUIs, allows the experienced user to get a Linux workstation or server up quickly and provides the optimized performance and security that this distribution is attempting. The primary drawback of Beehive Linux is the limited support for new Linux users. Because Beehive Linux is intended for the experienced user, there is no easy-to-follow installation or Windows-like environment. Beehive Linux is available at www.beehive.nu/.

BlueCat

BlueCat Linux is a Linux distribution that is enhanced to meet the requirements of embedded device developers. BlueCat includes enhancements for LynuxWorks' cross-development and embedding tools, and is royalty-free. LynuxWorks is a founding member of the real-time operating systems (RTOS) industry, creating its first product in the late 1980s for the NASA-funded space station program. With the introduction of its Linux strategy, it is now a leader in the embedded Linux market. Here are more details about BlueCat Linux:

✦ Allows the development of embedded devices without the cost of using a non-open source tool.

✦ Matches the requirements of embedded small devices to large-scale multi-CPU systems.

✦ Supports the ARM (7 with MMU, 7 with SOC, 9), Intel x86, MIPS R3000 and R4000, Motorola PowerPC, PowerQUICC, StrongARM and Super-H architectures with an embedded target of Intel IA-32, Motorola PowerPC, PowerQUICC II, or compatible processors.

This distribution is an example of the niche market for Linux and is available at www.lynuxworks.com/.

Caldera OpenLinux

OpenLinux was designed by Caldera for corporate commercial use. The OpenLinux distribution includes all the GNU software packages, as well as many other well-known software and system packages. It is POSIX (Portable Operating System Interface for Computer Environments) compliant (as is Linux, but not all distributions of Linux), so it adheres to the ANSI (American National Standards Institute) standard for UNIX. Although OpenLinux is distributed free of charge, Caldera provides support for an additional fee. Caldera's support ranges from the eDesktop package to the eServer package. The eDesktop was designed for basic workstation installations and the eServer includes software packages, such as DHCP, DNS, FTP, and mail for the server environment. Caldera is also a major UNIX system provider with SCO OpenServer UNIX — the world's best selling UNIX server operating system — and UnixWare 7, which Caldera uses to provide unified UNIX with Linux solutions. Caldera provides excellent support for the registered user but limited support for the non-registered user. OpenLinux is available at www.caldera.com/.

Debian

Debian was created by a group of volunteer programmers. It is an entirely noncommercial project but does provide support for commercial products in the distribution. Corel and Sun currently maintain software associations with Debian. Although Debian uses the Linux kernel, it is known as *Debian GNU/Linux* because it distributes GNU software with its distribution (as do all Linux distributions). The Debian distribution is fairly easy to install and configure but is usually preferred by more experienced Linux users because Debian is entirely noncommercial and support is limited; as a result, some new Linux users will avoid it altogether. The Debian distributions can provide support for Alpha, ARM, Intel, Macintosh 68k, PowerPC, and Sparc Platforms, and is available at www.debian.org/.

Corel

Corel Linux was designed specifically for the desktop computer. Corel is a Debian-based distribution with a four-step graphical installer that requires very little user interaction — thus making it one of the easiest distributions to install for the novice. This distribution features a customized KDE drag-and-drop environment, including an easy-to-use browser style file manager. Corel Linux is very easy to install on non-customized hardware and provides very good support on the average desktop. The Corel Linux distribution also provides easy support for a dual boot PC. Because Corel Linux is a very customized distribution designed for easy installation and use, it has pushed away some traditional Linux users. The ability to provide this ease of installation does not allow much user interaction or intervention, and therefore prevents some users from installing Corel Linux on customized hardware. The customized desktop has also caused some advanced users to dislike the Corel Linux distribution. Corel specializes in the novice Linux user and co-existence with another operating system for the novice Linux user and is available at http://linux.corel.com/.

DragonLinux

DragonLinux was created to run on top of versions of Microsoft Windows or any version of DOS. This is a complete Linux operating system that specializes in the beginning user, who will enjoy the quick install and the software's ability to co-exist with the existing desktop environment, which may also be beneficial to the experienced user. DragonLinux does not require you to repartition your hard drive. The main advantage provided by DragonLinux is that most Linux distributions can co-exist with Microsoft products — but the products do require their own separate partition. The benefits of DragonLinux, however, are also its disadvantages. Because it installs on top of Windows or DOS, it uses the file structure of the host operating system. Therefore, users don't benefit from enhanced Linux file systems, such as the Reiser file system, or the added stability of a UNIX-like system. DragonLinux is available at `www.dragonlinux.net/`.

Elfstone

Elfstone Linux was not designed to dual-boot or share disk partitions with other operating systems. Elfstone is perhaps the most Unix-like of all commercial distributions, and therefore provides excellent support for engineers, network administrators, and programmers. Elfstone Linux provides an interface that is a Motif/Athena hybrid to provide a fast and intuitive interface. Because it isn't designed as a dual-boot system, Elfstone Linux is a drawback for anyone who is not dedicated to running only Linux. The Elfstone Linux distribution is available at `www.elflinux.com/linux.html`.

Gentoo

Gentoo Linux considers itself to be a meta-distribution or Linux technology engine. It supports advanced features including dependencies, "fake" installs, package management, unmerging, virtual packages, and more. The tools let you install only the packages that you need to run your system. For example, if you don't select GNOME, then none of the modules will include GNOME support. But if you do select GNOME support, then all the modules will be installed. This helps to control the installation of useless packages and therefore prevents the bloat that other systems experience. Although the Gentoo system is very advanced, it is slow to develop and has yet to be adopted by other distributions, and is therefore less attractive to users. The Gentoo distribution is available at `www.gentoo.org/`.

Hard Hat Linux

Hard Hat Linux is the leading Linux distribution for embedded applications. It is designed to provide the scalability, dependability, and performance that is required by embedded systems. Hard Hat supports the x86, PowerPC, StrongARM, MIPS, SH, and SPARC platforms. Hard Hat Linux is best known for being selected as IBM's, PowerPC-based set-top box controller chips Linux port. Therefore, Hard Hat Linux is not intended for the common user, but rather for those creating, modifying, and supporting the embedded systems. More information on Hard Hat Linux can be found at `www.mvista.com/`.

KRUD

Kevin Fenzi is the co-author of *The Linux Security HOWTO* and creator of Kevin's Red Hat Über Distribution (KRUD). KRUD is based on Red Hat 7.0, which includes the most up-to-date security and application errata. This distribution was created to make it easy for users to keep up on all the latest errata and package updates every month, and to make a Linux system more secure after the initial install. KRUD uses several specialized tools to determine the necessary updates, and then updates all packages on a system, including the dependencies. Because the KRUD distribution is based on Red Hat Linux, it has all the features of Red Hat Linux, plus the added benefit of the latest security and application errata from Kevin Fenzi. This distribution is available as a monthly subscription and is beneficial to users who want to keep their systems very up-to-date. The drawback of KRUD may be the fact that users must rely on someone else to provide security for their systems. This can be a false sense of security, because every system has a different level of risk that should be assessed on an individual basis. Furthermore, even though you may have the latest package updates, you are not ensured the proper configuration of the package for your individual machine. KRUD has various purchasing options and is available yearly for $65 from `www.tummy.com/krud/`.

LinuxPPC

LinuxPPC is a distribution dedicated to the PowerPC platform. LinuxPPC supports the Gnome desktop, and provides support for USB. This distribution also provides the PowerPC chip the ability to run Linux and introduce Mac users to Linux. Although it is dedicated to supporting the PowerPC platform, this distribution is not the only one that supports PowerPC, and more recognized distributions are supporting this platform. Because of this support by other Linux vendors, LinuxPPC is often less desirable to the end user. The LinuxPPC distribution also lacks some of the better support of its commercial competitors. LinuxPPC is available at `http://linuxppc.org/`.

Mandrake

Mandrake is a distribution that is based on the Red Hat distribution. Many users believe that Mandrake Linux is actually just Red Hat with some enhancements, but it has evolved well beyond that. Mandrake includes several enhancements to the Linux configuration, such as DrakX, a graphical installer, and Mandrake Control Center, which is used to easily perform most system tasks. These tools make it much easier to configure hardware and software for Linux. This is an important innovation because it helps Linux to move to the non-technical user's desktop. Mandrake also includes an extensive collection of windows managers and the latest KDE, Gnome, and kernel. Mandrake Linux strives to be easy to configure out of the box and to make more difficult tasks, such as 3-D acceleration, easier on the user. These enhancements to the Mandrake Linux distributions have influenced many other Linux distributions to be more user-friendly. The Mandrake Linux Internet site at `www.linux-mandrake.com` provides excellent support with online documentation, user groups, and e-mail support. The disadvantages of Mandrake Linux are that it is limited to the x86 platform and support is not as good as some other commercial distributions.

Phat Linux

Phat Linux is a distribution that has been specially made to run on a Windows computer without the need of partitioning a hard drive to support a separate Linux partition. It includes a very easy, Windows-based installation program, and can be installed on computers running Windows 95 and 98. Phat Linux comes bundled with most of the typical Linux applications and services such as X windows, Gnome, KDE, Apache web server, FTP server, and other popular utilities. The disadvantages of Phat Linux, is that it has to be run from DOS mode on the Windows computer. Phat Linux is geared towards new Linux users who would like to try out Linux, without having to rearrange their hard drive to accommodate it.

Red Hat

Red Hat is one of the most popular Linux distributions currently available. Red Hat is the creator of the RPM (Red Hat Package Manager) system that is now available for use in most distributions of Linux. Red Hat supports the latest kernels and adds a number to the kernel version number to indicate the patch that has been applied; for example, the number 2.2.18-10 indicates that the Red Hat patch 10 has been applied to the kernel.

Note   Red Hat has formed alliances with many companies, including IBM, Sun Microsystems, Oracle, in order to create and maintain software support.

Red Hat has an ever-expanding distributions base that includes support for Alpha, ARM, Intel, m68k, SGI, and Sparc hardware platforms. All of these distributions are available from several FTP sites and from Red Hat's own FTP server. The Red Hat distribution also supports an extensive online set of documentation, including FAQs, a Getting Started Guide, HOW-TO, Installation Guide, Red Hat's Hardware Compatibility List, and Tips for Linux, which are all freely available under the GNU GPL.

Red Hat's business model is to sell superior support. Although Linux is free and the Red Hat distribution is also free, many users purchase support packages from Red Hat. The support ranges from installation and configuration to Enterprise support for e-commerce and database operations. Red Hat has also created a widely accepted (yet difficult) certification of The Red Hat Certified Engineer. All of these features have led Red Hat to become one of the most popular distributions. Red Hat is available at `www.redhat.com/`.

Slackware

Slackware, which was created by Patrick Volkerding, is considered to be an expert distribution of Linux. Since its first release in April of 1993, Slackware has strived to remain as UNIX-compliant as possible. Therefore, it is sometimes considered to be more difficult to use than other Linux distributions. Slackware supports the Alpha, Intel, and Sparc platforms and includes most of the same desktops and software packages as other Linux distributions. Because it is UNIX-compliant, Slackware is an excellent distribution for a user who prefers a standard Unix environment. Slackware is much more user-friendly than its reputation would seem to indicate, but many users remain hesitant to try it. Slackware is available from www. slackware.com/.

StormLinux

StormLinux, by Stormix, has created enhancements and applications for Linux by using the Debian GNU/Linux distribution. One of these enhancements is the Storm Administration System (SAS), which allows you to easily manage tasks, such as network set-up and managing user profiles. The Storm Package Manager allows you to easily manage files by installing, updating, and deleting them in order to provide a clean, updated, and secure system. StormLinux provides many more customized tools to improve upon the Debian distribution. StormLinux is also not as current as other Linux distributions, but is available as StormLinux Open Edition for download from www.stormix.com/.

SuSE

SuSE is distributed by a German company and is very popular in Europe. It is one of the fastest growing distributions worldwide and has been ported to most languages. SuSE's unique expertise in Linux and its global development team are dedicated to Open Source software and have contributed to the recognition of SuSE as one of the best and most complete Linux distributions. SuSE has made substantial contributions to major Linux projects, including kernel development, XFree86, ALSA (Advanced Linux Sound Architecture), and USB support for Linux, among others. It uses the Yast or Yast2 installer, which provides an easy installation process. The SuSE professional distribution comes with many CDs that include software packages, such as Star Office, WordPerfect, and Koffice, and many commercial products. The SuSE Personal supplies everything that home and small business users would expect in a desktop system. SuSE also supports a wide range of server-specific distributions, including Database Server with DB2, Groupware Server with Lotus Domino R5, and eMail Server II. SuSE provides excellent support via an extensive online set of documentation, which includes FAQs, support documents, and a Hardware Compatibility List. SuSE Linux does not, however, provide the level of free support that is provided by some of its direct competitors. SuSE supports Alpha, IBM's eServer iSeries (the successor to AS/400), IBM S/390, Intel, PowerPC, and Sparc, and is available from www.suse.com/.

TurboLinux

TurboLinux is distributed by Pacific Hitech and supports only the Intel platform. TurboLinux is well known for its own packages, such as TurboPkg (for application updating), the TurboDesk X-windows environment, and Cluster Web Server. Like most distributions of Linux, it does support the RPM system. TurboLinux is the clustering technology leader in Linux and is the market leader in Asia. TurboLinux supports the x86 platform, and although it currently supports the Alpha platform, this support will end soon. TurboLinux provides free online documentation for users to browse through, FAQs, and package updates. The support from TurboLinux is not as easy to access as the support from other commercial providers, and the variety of supported platforms is limited. TurboLinux is available at `www.turbolinux.com/`.

Yellow Dog Linux

Yellow Dog Linux is for PowerPC computers and may co-exist with Mac OS in a dual-boot environment. It is a graphical environment that runs on older Apple hardware and is stable and fast. Yellow Dog is based on Red Hat 7.0, but includes a simplified booting structure and a custom-built (by Terra Soft Solutions) graphical installer, which also has the more advanced Black Lab Linux. Yellow Dog Linux is dedicated to the PowerPC platform and provides online FAQs, general questions, hardware compatibility, installation guide, yaboot or BootX (provides dual-boot), and *yup* (which stands for Yellow Dog update program), which are all easy to use. Because Yellow Dog supports only the PowerPC platform, it only has limited appeal to other general Linux users. It is available at `www.yellowdoglinux.com/`.

Mini and Specialty Distributions

Linux also comes in mini, micro, and specialty distributions. These are used to perform very specific functions and several are listed in the following section.

Astaro

Astaro distributes Astaro Security Linux, which offers extensive protection for local networks against hackers, viruses, and other risks associated with connecting to the Internet. The Astaro Security Linux provides firewalling capabilities, NAT (network address translation), masquerading, proxies with content-filter, user authentication and SMTP with virus protection, VPN (virtual private networking), traffic accounting, and easy administration. The Astaro distributions are available via download at `www.astaro.com`.

KYZO

KYZO's unique LinuxROM distribution runs entirely from a bootable Flash ROM, which gives you the server system security, reliability, and ease of use that isn't available from hard drive-based operating systems. The KYZO LinuxROM distributions use a special compact flash card and circuit board with an IDE connector to turn any PC into a file, print and CD servers, Internet and VPN gateway, and Web cache services. It eliminates the use of the hard drive to improve reliability. KYZO provides demonstration versions for download at `www.kyzo.com/`.

FlightLinux

FlightLinux is a concept that uses a real-time variation of the Open Source Linux Operating System for onboard spacecraft use. The Open Source Linux concept with a modified, real-time, embeddable kernel better addresses the unique problems of spacecraft onboard computers. FlightLinux is the subject of a NASA Advanced Information System Technology (AIST) research effort. More information is available at `http://flightlinux.gsfc.nasa.gov/`.

LEM

LEM is an embedded version of Linux that can fit on less than an 8 Meg Disk Partition (Base install + Graphical User Interface). LEM is supported by Mandrake Linux, is based on Mandrake 6.1, and is easily scalable. The base version includes all the basic shell commands. You can also add Xfree SVGA windows system, and TCP/IP is built-in. This is not the smallest embedded version of Linux, but LEM may be used when an X windows server is needed. The LEM distribution is available at `http://linux-embedded.com/`.

NetMAX

NetMAX Linux is a good example of how companies can use Open Source distributions to create a niche for themselves. NetMAX is based on Red Hat, and provides services that range from file servers to ISP (Internet Service Provider) hosting. The customized version of Red Hat allows NetMAX to sell the distribution at a premium and creates an easy-to-use software package that non-technical users can implement. Although Netmax provides an excellent niche solution for ISPs, all of these types of services are available from other distributions without the complex licensing that NetMAX uses. NetMAX is available at `www.netmax.com/`.

Packages and Packaging Solutions

Objective   1.7 Identify strengths and weaknesses of different distributions and their packaging solutions (e.g., tar ball vs. RPM/DEB)

Almost every distribution listed in the preceding sections originally began as a customized version of the Red Hat or Debian distribution. Several outstanding distributions were not originally created from one of these distributions, but most distributions include many of the same GNU packages. A *package* is a set of binary code that creates a program, which can be as simple as PING or as complex as an Office suite application. These binary code sets are packaged together to allow a user to download one file that contains an entire program, instead of all the individual files that comprise the program. These packages are usually compressed and sometimes use a package manager. The most common package types are Tarball, RPM, and DEB. Each of these package types provides the package in a single file.

Red Hat Package Manager

One of the most popular tools for the installation of applications and programs is the Red Hat Package Manager (RPM), which was originally created for the Red Hat distribution. RPM is an open utility available to everyone and is distributed under the GNU GPL. RPM provides features that make it easier for users to maintain a Linux system by enabling the RPM to control installing, uninstalling, and upgrading software packages. The advantages of RPM are outlined in the following list:

✦ RPM manages upgrading to allow the intelligent, fully automated, in-place upgrades of your system including notification of needed software dependencies.

✦ RPM supports powerful queries that search through individual files to indicate which package a file belongs to; these queries also search through entire system databases for the installed packages.

✦ RPM can perform system verification. For example, when a user deletes files, the RPM can verify that no files required for a package have been deleted. If a file required by a package has been deleted, RPM will identify which file (or files) is missing and the package can be reinstalled.

✦ RPM supports the Pristine Sources concept, which can provide the original source software with any patches that were used.

A complete set of instructions is also included to provide details to users of the RPM package. Packages with Red Hat Package Manager use the extension of .rpm. For more information on the RPM, see www.redhat.com.

Debian Package Management System

Much like the Red Hat Package Manager, the Debian Package Management System is used to create easier installation of packages from binary code containing executables, configuration files, MAN/info pages, copyright information, and other documentation. These packages are distributed in a Debian-specific archive format that uses the .deb extension.

Debian's packaging tools can be used to manage and change packages (or parts of a package), or break down packages into a more manageable size for transportation. These tools also aid in the creation of package archives and simplify the installation of remote packages from an FTP server. The Debian package follows the format

```
<name >_<Version Number>-<Debian Revision Number>.deb
```

to provide information before accessing the package. The Debian Package Management System provides many of the same features of RPM.

Tarball

Archiving by using Tar places several files or the contents of a directory or directories into one file, which is commonly called a *Tarball*. Using Tarballs is a good way to create backups and archives. Usually, tar files end with the .tar extension, which is often compressed by using GZIP or ZIP to create a compressed archive of the files or directory. Unlike RPM or the Debian Package Management System, a Tarball doesn't check for dependencies, it doesn't require documentation, and it doesn't place the files where they belong in the Linux file structure. Tarball usage is almost required when working with Linux, but package managers are improving rapidly and someday the Tarball may be a thing of the past.

Linux Resources

Objective   1.10 Identify where to obtain software and resources

One of the best sources of information on how to use Linux commands is the MAN pages. The term *MAN pages* is a short form for *manual* pages, and they are like an on-line manual for your system. The MAN pages are an excellent resource when using any UNIX or Linux system. To access a MAN page, type man **<program name>** at the command prompt to display the written instructions for a program. Some programs don't include MAN pages, but most do.

Tip   MAN pages are very useful and should be the first stop when you need information about a program and its various options and proper syntax.

When the MAN pages don't provide enough information, the Linux HOWTO pages can provide the guidance needed to complete a task. Linux HOWTO pages are listed at many Linux Web sites. The HOWTOs are an excellent resource and often give you every bit of information that you may need to complete a given task. HOWTOs are especially useful if you are not exactly sure which program you need to provide a specific service or to complete a task. If you do know what you want to do, then you can always use the mini-HOWTOs as a refresher on how to perform a task or provide a service. You can find both HOWTOs and mini-HOWTOs at `www. linuxdoc.org`, which also provides MAN pages, FAQs, and guides, which are excellent resources. The most important resources for Linux are on the Internet and free of charge; however, very complicated issues often require more than the above resources can provide. When these free resources are not enough, don't hesitate to use the resources of the distribution that you are using.

Summary

This chapter explores more detailed information on the Linux kernel. The Linux kernel versions are listed and illustrated and the numbering methods are explained. The availability of the Linux kernel via the Web or through one of the many available distributions is demonstrated. The definition of a package and the methods that you can use to create a package are discussed. Finally, some of the many resources available for Linux uses are described.

✦   ✦   ✦

STUDY GUIDE

The Study Guide section provides you with the opportunity to test your knowledge about the objectives covered on the exam. The Assessment Questions provide understanding of the basics of Linux, and the Scenarios provide practice with real situations. If you get any questions incorrect, use the answers to determine the part of the chapter that you should review before continuing.

Assessment Questions

1. What allows new hardware to be supported by the Linux kernel without reinstalling the entire kernel?

   A. Modules

   B. Plug-in

   C. Tarball

   D. Patch

2. What is the first section of the Linux kernel version used to provide?

   A. Major number

   B. Minor number

   C. Revision number

   D. Patch level

3. What does the major number in the Linux kernel version mean?

   A. Large changes in the kernel

   B. Stability of the kernel

   C. Every change to the kernel

   D. Which Red Hat Linux system is applied

4. What does an odd minor number indicate?

   A. Stable kernel

   B. Developmental kernel

   C. Pre-Release kernel

   D. Beta kernel

5. What does an even minor number indicate?

    A. Stable kernel

    B. Developmental kernel

    C. Pre-Release kernel

    D. Beta kernel

6. Where can you find a previous version of the kernel?

    A. www.linux.org

    B. www.linuxc.com

    C. www.kernel.com

    D. www.kernel.org

7. Where can you find the most up-to-date information on Red Hat Linux?

    A. www.redhat.org

    B. ftp.redhat.org

    C. www.redhat.linux.com

    D. www.redhat.com

8. Which of the following supports only the PowerPC platform?

    A. Bluecat

    B. Yellow Dog

    C. Red Hat

    D. DragonLinux

9. Kevin Fenzi was the co-author of which Linux HOWTO?

    A. Linux security

    B. Tar

    C. Linux kernel

    D. Hurd

10. KYZO Linux runs from which media?

    A. Hard drive

    B. Diskette Drive

    C. CD-ROM

    D. Flash memory

11. Which of the following is being used in IBM's PowerPC-based set-top box?

    A. Hard Hat

    B. Elfstone

    C. BlueCat

    D. LEM

12. Which of the following Linux distributions specializes in clustering capabilities?

    A. Corel

    B. LinuxPPC

    C. DragonLinux

    D. TurboLinux

13. The Linux creation for NASA is?

    A. KRUD

    B. Astaro

    C. KYZO

    D. FlightLinux

14. A set of files that install to create a program are called what?

    A. Distribution

    B. Package

    C. Tarball

    D. Source code

15. Red Hat Package Manager is covered under which license?

    A. GNU GPL

    B. Closed Source

    C. Freeware

    D. Artistic License

16. RPM provide all but which of the following?

    A. Pristine sources

    B. Package dependencies

    C. System verification

    D. Upgrading install packages

17. Red Hat Package Manager uses which of the following extensions?

   A. .tar.gz

   B. .rpm

   C. .deb

   D. .tar

18. The Linux mini-HOWTOs would most likely be found at?

   A. www.linux.org

   B. www.linuxdoc.org

   C. www.kernel.org

   D. www.minihowto.org

19. Where is the first place to look for information when you are trying to figure out which options can be used with the PING command?

   A. HOWTO

   B. Mini-HOWTO

   C. Man pages

   D. FAQs

20. Which of the following is not a compressed file?

   A. .tar

   B. .rpm

   C. .deb

   D. .tgz

Scenarios

The following scenarios test your knowledge of some Linux Resources.

1. If you are unsure of how — or even what — program to use to complete a task, where should you go to find free assistance?

2. You have just installed the newest kernel 2.5.0, but it doesn't seem to work on your system properly, and is not very stable. What is most likely the cause?

3. You need to quickly install a software package for a user. Why would an RPM package be a better choice than a Tarball package?

Lab Exercises

Lab 2-1 Examining kernel information

1. Using an Internet accessible PC and Web browser, look up the latest version of the Linux kernel at `www.kernel.org` and record it.

2. Note if the kernel is stable or developmental.

3. Find documentation on updating a kernel to the new version.

4. Find detailed and quick-start directions for performing the upgrade.

5. Verify that the upgrade is compatible on the PC that you are using.

Answers to Chapter Questions

Chapter Pre-Test

1. The Linux kernel is released via the Internet, as it has been since its inception.

2. Linus Torvalds releases the newest kernel versions.

3. It shows the major features, stability, and revisions.

4. You can find many Linux resources, the best of which are `www.linux.org`, `www.kernel.org`, and `www.linuxdoc.org`.

5. A Package is a set of binary code that creates a program.

6. These are programs that run on the Linux kernel

7. A distribution is a Linux kernel distributed with customized programs

8. The major Linux distributions are based on Red Hat or Debian Linux.

9. Linux has been released for virtually every computer platform.

10. Buying a Linux distribution often entitles you to support from the vendor.

Assessment Questions

1. A. Modules allow new hardware to be supported by the Linux kernel, Plug-ins are for Web browsers, Tarball is a package creation, and a patch fixes an existing issue. For review, see the "Linux Kernel" section.

2. A. The first section of the Linux kernel version provides the major number, the second section provides the minor number, the third section provides the revision, and the fourth section provides the patch on Red Hat systems. For review, see the "Kernel versions" section.

3. A. The major number in the Linux kernel version is used to indicate a major change in the kernel. The minor number indicates the stability, revision numbers indicate every change, and Answer D is the applied patch in a Red Hat system. For review, see the "Kernel versions" section.

4. B. An odd minor number indicates a developmental kernel, an even number indicates a stable kernel, a pre-release can have either number, and Linux doesn't use Beta kernels. For review, see the "Kernel versions" section.

5. A. An even minor number indicates a stable kernel, an odd number indicates a developmental kernel, a pre-release can have either number, and Linux doesn't use Beta kernels. For review, see the "Kernel versions" section.

6. D. Previous versions of the kernel are stored at `www.kernel.org`; `www.linux.org` supports information about Linux but directs you to `www.kernel.org`; `www.linux.com` doesn't support previous Linux kernel archives; and finally, `www.kernel.com` is a commercial site. For review, see the "Linux Kernel" section.

7. D. The most up-to-date information on Red Hat Linux is at `www.redhat.com`, `www.linux.org` and `www.kernel.org` are not devoted to Red Hat, and `www.redhat.linux.com` is not supported by Red Hat Linux. For more information, see the "Red Hat" section.

8. B. Only Yellow Dog uses the PowerPC platform; Bluecat is for embedded systems; Red Hat supports virtually all platforms; and DragonLinux was created to run on top of Microsoft products. For more information, see the "Linux Distributions" and "Yellow Dog Linux" sections.

9. A. Kevin Fenzi was the co-author of Linux Security HOWTO; he didn't write the HOWTO for tar, the kernel, or the Hurd. For more information, see the "KRUD" section.

10. D. KYZO Linux runs from compact flash memory; it doesn't run from hard drives or CD-ROM. For more information, see the "KYZO" section.

11. A. Hard Hat Linux is being used in IBM's PowerPC-based set-top box. Elfstone is a server Linux distribution; Bluecat is for embedded devices but not for this particular device; and LEM was not selected for the IBM box. For more information, see the "Hard Hat Linux" section.

12. D. TurboLinux is a clustering leader; Corel and DragonLinux don't cluster; and LinuxPPC is for the PowerPC and is not a clustering leader. For more information, see the "TurboLinux" section.

13. D. The Linux creation for NASA is FlightLinux. Astaro is a router replacement; KYZO is an embedded solution for PCs; and KRUD is a customized version of Red Hat. For more information, see the "FlightLinux" section.

14. B. Files that create a program are called a *package*. A *distribution* is a group of packages; Tarball is a single file made from many files; and source code creates a program. For more information, see the "Packages and Packaging Solutions" section.

15. A. Red Hat Package Manager is covered under the GNU GPL. It isn't Freeware, nor is it covered under an Artistic License or Closed Source license. For more information, see the "Red Hat Package Manager" section.

16. B. RPM provides all but package dependencies; it informs the installer of missing dependences, but doesn't install or reinstall them. RPM provides for upgrading, verification, and pristine sources. For more information, see the "Red Hat Package Manager" section.

17. B. Red Hat Package Manager uses the .rpm extension; Debian uses .deb; Tarball uses .tar; and a GZIP Tarball uses .tar.gz. For more information, see the "Red Hat Package Manager" section.

18. B. You can most likely find the Linux mini-HOWTOs at `www.linuxdoc.org`; the others support Linux in other ways or don't exist. For more information, see the "Linux Resources" section.

19. C. The first place to look for information when you are trying to use the PING command is the MAN pages; the others may work, but when in doubt, use the MAN pages. For more information, see the "Linux Resources" section.

20. A. Tar is an archive—not a compression; tar is usually compressed with GZIP; RPM and Debian are compressed files. For more information, see the "Tarball" section.

Scenarios

1. The best place to start is `www.linuxdoc.org` because this site supports guides, HOWTO, mini-HOWTOs, and FAQs. A secondary place to look is `www.redhat.com`. For more information, see the "Linux Resources" section.

2. Kernel 2.5.0 is a developmental kernel and may not be configured to support your hardware, or be very stable. For review, see the "Linux Kernel" section.

3. RPM is designed to install a program completely, whereas Tarball just opens up and dumps the files wherever you open it. For more information, see the "Red Hat Package Manager" section.

Installation

After you have decided on the type of Linux distribution that you want and what role this system will play, you must plan the implementation. Identifying all system hardware and verifying that it is supported by Linux is essential for a successful implementation. The chapters in this part walk you through pre-implementation planning and the installation process in either in a GUI (graphical user interface) or a text-based environment. Installing Linux will be a customary routine on the job and a prevalent topic on the CompTIA Linux+ exam. In fact, 12 percent of the exam is focused solely on the installation of Linux. This part teaches you everything that you need to know for the CompTIA Linux+ exam, but also what you need to know in the real world when installing Linux.

Pre-Installation Planning

EXAM OBJECTIVES

- ◆ 1.2 Identify all system hardware required and validate that it is supported by Linux (e.g., CPUs, RAM, graphics cards, storage devices, network interface cards, modem)

- ◆ 1.3 Determine what software and services should be installed (e.g., client applications for workstation, server services for desired task), check requirements and validate that it is supported by Linux

- ◆ 1.6 Identify the function of different Linux services (e.g., Apache, Squid, SAMBA, Sendmail, ipchains, BIND)

- ◆ 1.8 Describe the functions, features, and benefits of a Linux solutions as compared with other operating systems (e.g., Linux players, distributions, available software)

- ◆ 1.10 Identify where to obtain software and resources

- ◆ 1.11 Determine customer resources for a solution (e.g., staffing, budget, training)

CHAPTER PRE-TEST

1. Where can Linux be used in the Enterprise?

2. Can Linux be used as a Windows file server?

3. Can Linux be used to prevent outside access?

4. Is e-mail supported by Linux?

5. Can Linux provide the services required of a Web server?

6. Can Linux co-exist with an Apple Macintosh?

7. Does Linux provide the type of services that are offered by other operating systems?

8. Can Linux replace every other operating system?

9. Is Linux limited by hardware compatibility?

10. Where can a customer find information about a Linux service?

✦ Answers to these questions can be found at the end of the chapter. ✦

In this chapter, you will learn about the roles that Linux can fulfill in an enterprise environment. I will discuss many of the services that Linux can provide, and these services will show you that Linux is comparable to all other operating systems currently in use. The compatibility of Linux with most of today's hardware will demonstrate the flexibility that it provides. This flexibility enables Linux to provide services, such as file storage, e-mail connectivity, and Internet services, and to interoperate with other file systems. In addition we'll look at various Linux packages and distributions that provide enterprise services and identify where these options can be obtained. Finally, we'll round out the chapter with a discussion on the needs of the customer and how the customer can provide the resources to use Linux effectively in the enterprise environment.

Linux In the Real World

Objective

1.3 Determine what software and services should be installed (e.g., client applications for workstation, server services for desired task), check requirements and validate that it is supported by Linux

1.6 Identify the function of different Linux services (e.g., Apache, Squid, SAMBA, Sendmail, ipchains, BIND)

The great benefit of Linux is that it can be used from the desktop to the server in the enterprise environment. How is this possible? Unlike other operating systems, Linux supports virtually every service that users may need. For example, an administrator can install Linux on a PC and use it to perform word-processing tasks, surf the Web, dial up with a modem, DSL, or cable — or connect via a network interface card (NIC), share files, and even play games. Playing games may not be the goal in an enterprise environment, but Linux is capable of supporting Web servers, files servers, database servers, and many more server-based applications. Linux can provide these services through the packages that are included with a distribution or through a download of these software packages to a Linux PC or server. Because Linux works on most platforms, it has a wide range of uses in the enterprise environment.

Setting up a desktop user is now as easy with Linux as it is with most other operating systems. The end user can now use a PC to perform daily tasks with Linux. Included with most Linux distributions are fully functional word processors, e-mail programs, spreadsheets, database programs, graphic views and manipulators, Web browsers, file transfer, printing support, presentation software, and virtually every other type of program supported by rival desktop operating systems. The availability of these features allows the enterprise user to create documents, chart profits or production, read and send e-mail, transfer files, create and view Web pages, and many other tasks that they need to perform. All of these abilities make Linux a capable operating system for the desktop enterprise environment.

Word Processing

A PC with a Microsoft operating system may use Microsoft Word or Corel WordPerfect for word-processing tasks, whereas a Linux-based system can use Corel WordPerfect, Kword, AbiWord, StarOffice Writer — or one of many other Linux-based word processors. Using Linux instead of a Microsoft or Apple operating system can present problems with word processing because Microsoft doesn't have a version of MS Word for Linux. This can cause some issues with compatibility of file formats, but because all these word processors can save in a format compatible with other word processors, compatibility isn't as difficult an issue as it may once have been. The ability to use a compatible word processor allows Linux to be easily integrated into an enterprise word processing solution.

Spreadsheets and databases

Although word processing may be one of the most needed tools in an enterprise environment, spreadsheets and databases may have equal or even greater importance in some workplaces. With Linux, users can create high quality spreadsheets and databases files with programs such as Corel Quattro, StarOffice Base, KSpread, or one of many other available programs. These programs are highly useable and capable of creating a spreadsheet or database in any office environment. With these applications, Linux is able to provide the required compatibility with programs that are used in other operating systems. Programs such as Corel Quattro, StarOffice Base, and KSpread can easily create a spreadsheet or database that is compatible in format with other commercial applications. Such compatibility is vital because interoperations with other versions of databases and spreadsheets make Linux a viable selection in the enterprise environment.

Web browsing

Although word processing, spreadsheets, and databases are very important in today's enterprise environment, Web browsing may have as much significance in performing and staying informed in the business world. Linux can be used to support Web browsing with several programs, such as Netscape, Opera, and Konqueror. Netscape, Opera, and Konqueror support most Web sites, and users find the browser interfaces easy to use. Therefore, Linux enables users to browse the Internet as easily as they can with any other operating system — but some problems can occur. One of the problems that can arise when using Linux to browse the Web is non-compatibility with some Web sites that use certain proprietary code. The reality of the current Web marketplace is that Microsoft products have become widely used in many areas. Because Web designers have no formal standard that must be adhered to when building a Web page, it is possible, and increasingly common, for designers to leverage browser-specific features built into Microsoft's Internet Explorer. Because Microsoft does not support a Linux version of Internet Explorer, some Web pages may not display as intended on the popular Linux browser applications. If the browser doesn't understand the information being sent from the Web page, it may fail to display the page or cause part or all of a page to be corrupted. As the popularity of Linux — and Linux Web browsers in particular — increases, it will hopefully encourage Web developers to write code that adheres to industry standards, rather than create proprietary solutions that only work on certain browsers.

E-mail

Because Netscape also supports the standards for Internet mail, its mail component — which uses POP3 and SMTP — can be used to read and send e-mail. Many other e-mail clients are available, such as Kmail and StarOffice Mail. Although these mail programs may easily work for most users, some features are not supported by these mail programs. Groupware programs, such as Microsoft's Exchange, provide non-standard applications for scheduling and other group-orientated tasks. Users and organizations that require these types of "all-in-one" messaging systems may find that Linux is not the right choice for them. However, Linux's ability to support standardized e-mail makes the task of setting up, configuring, and maintaining a pure, standards-based e-mail server easier for the users and support personnel. These types of e-mail programs are well documented and often have guided setup programs, which create a reliable and comfortable environment for the user and the enterprise.

File transfer

The ability to download files is also included in Linux via TCP/IP standards, such as FTP (File Transport Protocol) and TFTP (Trivial File Transport Protocol). These are standards supported in the TCP/IP stack that is included with Linux. At the command prompt, you can use the FTP command just as you would in any operating system that includes the TCP/IP networking protocol. Many users, however, don't enjoy performing file transfers at the command line because somewhat cryptic commands may confuse the novice user. Several utilities, such as gFTP, KFTP or Igloo FTP Pro, provide graphical user interfaces (GUI) that work in a Windows environment and provide easy-to-use file transfer clients. These tools are very similar to the tools that are available in virtually every other operating system — thus making Linux just as useful and reliable.

More, more, and more applications

Linux provides virtually any application that a user in the enterprise environment needs. For example, do you need a chat or pop-up client to make interoffice communications easier? Try kiam, kicq, kpopup, kTuxPop, or kYahoo, which all provide connectivity to instant messaging applications, such as AOL Instant Messenger (AIM), Yahoo instant messaging, and even Winpopup compatibility. Integrated office suites, such as KOffice and StarOffice, provide a complete package of Office-compatible programs, including Kivio, which is a Visio-style flowcharting application. Linux also includes PIM (Personal Information Manager) and Palm organizer support software, and programs that allow users to manipulate graphics, such as GIMP, Krayon, and the vector drawing application, Killustrator. You can also send a fax by using Linux with programs such as sendfax, kphonecenter, and SendfaKs. Scheduling tools are also available in software packages, such as StarOffice Schedule. Presentation applications include Corel Presentations, Kpresenter, and StarOffice Impress, among others.

Virtually *any* software program is available for Linux; however, some applications have issues of non-compatibility due to the Closed Source nature of commercial applications. Microsoft has yet to port any of their very popular software versions to the Linux operating system. Many Microsoft formats are not supported on the Web or in e-mail programs. This is one reason that an enterprise may not fully deploy Linux as a desktop service. Regardless of how well Linux is suited for the desktop, however, you have many compelling reasons for deploying Linux on the server side, and possibly replacing UNIX, Microsoft, and Novell desktops in the enterprise server environment.

The Server and DNS

The Linux operating system is typically used as a server in the enterprise because it is a very stable and complete operating system. Because Linux has been developed to be a UNIX-like operating system, it can perform almost any job that a UNIX server can perform. And because Microsoft Windows and Novell Netware Servers are now providing most of the same services that are provided by UNIX servers, you can use Linux to perform these duties in place of the Microsoft or Novell operating system-based servers. Also, because Linux is very stable, it has proven to be very reliable and has therefore been accepted into the server rooms, farms, and clusters of major companies for operating mission-critical services. Linux is especially suited for Internet applications and services such as DNS, e-mail, firewall, FTP, proxy, Web file and print, and many other popular Internet services. These servers are able to provide the services that you need in the enterprise environment in a reliable, inexpensive, and well-supported way.

When you install a Linux server, Domain Name System (DNS) is one of the many popular Internet options available. DNS is a distributed Internet directory service. DNS resolves system names to IP addresses. This is an important service because it allows users to connect to machines by their name rather than an obscure IP address, which can be easily forgotten.

DNS directory service consists of DNS data, DNS servers, and Internet protocols for retrieving data from the servers. Resource records for each host are made available by the DNS directory, using special text files organized into *zones*. Zones are kept on authoritative servers that are distributed all over the Internet, which answer queries according to the DNS network protocols. Most servers are authoritative for some zones and perform a caching function for all other DNS information. Most DNS servers, however, are authoritative for just a few zones, but larger servers are authoritative for tens of thousands of zones. By breaking the DNS into smaller zones and then those zones into domains, the load on any one machine is lightened. This also improves the reliability of the Internet by not requiring one server or group of servers to have all the information. Because this is a hierarchical configuration, the enterprise organization can establish a DNS server to control access to the organizational network. This can be done on a Linux server by enabling a specific piece of software. Small businesses can use this software to allow users to connect to the Internet, or large organizations can use it to establish domains and eventually a DNS zone server of their own. Creating, using, and providing a DNS server allows the enterprise to control access to specific servers. To see this service in action:

1. Select your favorite Web site.

2. Open a console prompt.

3. Type the command **ping www.linux.org**

4. Press enter.

Your display will look something like this:

```
Pinging www.linux.org [198.182.196.56] with 32 bytes of data:

Reply from 198.182.196.56: bytes=32 time=80ms TTL=232
Reply from 198.182.196.56: bytes=32 time=80ms TTL=232
Reply from 198.182.196.56: bytes=32 time=71ms TTL=232
Reply from 198.182.196.56: bytes=32 time=70ms TTL=232

Ping statistics for 198.182.196.56:
    Packets: Sent = 4, Received = 4, Lost = 0 (0% loss),
Approximate round trip times in milli-seconds:
    Minimum = 70ms, Maximum =  80ms, Average =  75ms
```

This display shows that DNS resolved the name www.linux.org to the IP address 198.182.196.56.

A Linux Web server

Whereas DNS resolves a name to an IP address allowing users to connect to Web pages, a Web server provides the actual Web page. Linux is used throughout the Internet to provide this service. The most popular software that Linux uses to provide Web pages is the Apache Web server. Apache exists to provide commercial-grade software capable of providing HyperText Transfer Protocol, or HTTP, which is a standard for creating documents to be viewed over the Internet. Apache is the leading Internet Web server with over a 60 percent market share, according to the Netcraft survey (www.netcraft.com/survey). Apache Web Server powers Web sites over other commercial software at a rate of more than 3 to 1, and will continue to do so because it is a robust, stable, and free alternative to other software. This may be the best example of Linux because the Apache Web server is not only capable but is preferred in the enterprise environment.

Linux e-mail server

E-mail is one of the most important services utilized by the end user. It is the most commonly used communications medium for users to communicate internally and externally. Using e-mail within an organization requires the support of an e-mail server. The most common mail server program is the Sendmail package. Sendmail supports all the services necessary to provide a comprehensive e-mail server. Sendmail supports connectivity to a mail user agent (MUA), mail transfer agents (MTAs), several transfer protocols, and delivery agents. Other programs also perform this function, such as Postfix.

✦ **MUA** is an application that is run directly by the user and provides the ability to compose and send outgoing messages as well as to display, file, and print messages. Examples of MUAs are Netscape Composer, Kmail, StarOffice Mail, elm, mailx, mh, and zmail.

✦ **MTAs** are used to transfer messages between e-mail servers. MUAs send messages to the transfer agent, which then transfers the message to another MTA; this MTA then either passes the message to a known MUA or to another MTA. This process continues until the MTA knows the destination MUA and delivers the message.

✦ **Transfer agents** are responsible for properly routing messages to their destination. The language spoken between transfer agents is known as a *transfer protocol*. The most common transfer protocol is SMTP (Simple Mail Transfer Protocol), but there are many more, including the well known UUCP (Unix-to-Unix copy) and X.400.

✦ **Delivery agents** are used to place a message in a user's mailbox. When the message arrives at its destination, the final transfer agent gives the message to the appropriate delivery agent, which adds the message to the user's mailbox. In Linux, the most common delivery agent is the procmail service.

Linux also supports commercial products, such as the Lotus Domino server, to provide e-mail services. The ability of Linux to perform these tasks — specifically the Sendmail application — allows it to be used as a full function e-mail server.

File servers

Linux is an excellent platform for providing access to file systems that may be local or remote. File servers are a necessity in the enterprise environment so that users may safely store their data in a central location. These file server services may be needed for other Linux, UNIX, Microsoft, and Apple clients or servers.

The ability of Linux to be used as a network file server is comparable to UNIX. UNIX uses the Network File System (NFS), which is a distributed file system, to mount a remote file system or directory and to treat those files or directories as if they were local. Linux uses the NFS software package, which includes commands and daemons for NFS, Network Information Service (NIS), and other services.

| Note | NIS was originally created by Sun Microsystems and was originally called *Sun's Yellow Pages*—this terminology is sometimes still used. |

Support for NFS normally requires that each system be configured to access each resource or device with a configuration file. The inclusion of NIS in Linux allows the server to maintain the configuration files for the entire network. This makes administration of network resources and devices easier, because only the NIS files must be updated instead of every client. It's natural to expect Linux to provide services for other Linux or UNIX clients, but what about Microsoft clients?

Microsoft created the Server Message Block (SMB) protocol to provide the ability to share files and resources. SMB was created for use in the small local area network (LAN) environment and proved to be unsuitable for larger networks. As a result, Microsoft created the Common Internet File System (CIFS), which is based on SMB and Network Basic Input Output System (NetBIOS) of previous Microsoft networking. For Linux to provide support for Microsoft clients requires a service to run on each client or a Linux service that understands Microsoft protocols. Enter Samba, a software program created by Andrew Tridgell, which allows Linux clients to communicate with Microsoft resources using the SMB protocol. Samba is Open Source, and is available from `www.samba.org`. The last piece of the puzzle may require Linux to support Macintosh operating system clients.

Macintosh computers use AppleTalk to provide access to remote file systems and printers. Linux can provide network file services to Mac OS clients with the Netatalk implementation of AppleTalk. This allows Apple clients the ability to access files, directories, and printers on a Linux server. To provide the Netatalk service, Linux is required to have kernel level support for the AppleTalk Datagram Delivery Protocol (DDP). Most Linux distributions include this support. Apple's latest MAC OS, called OS X is based on BSD UNIX, so NFS support may be provided or added to the new Mac OS. The support for Mac, Microsoft, UNIX, and Linux clients allows Linux file servers to exist and excel in the enterprise environment.

Proxy, news, and search servers

Linux provides for proxy, news, and search services with several different software packages. Linux provides a proxy-caching server that caches Web information, which increases the client's access speed, and also reduces bandwidth costs to a company. The most popular proxy-caching server for Linux is called *Squid*. Squid is a high-performance proxy-caching server that supports FTP, gopher, and HTTP data objects. It is used to *cache* (store information) that was previously accessed by clients. When a user makes a request for a Web page, Squid checks to see if it has a copy of the requested information in its cache. If Squid has this information, it checks to see if the information is current, updates it if necessary, and then forwards this information to the client. This saves the client time if the information was previously accessed and saves the company money and resources because Squid removes the need to access the requested information from the Internet. Squid also allows the creation of access control lists (ACL), thus enabling the filtering and tracking of Web traffic that the clients are requesting. Therefore, Squid provides an excellent proxy server with comprehensive Web-filtering tools.

News servers are supported in Linux by InterNetNews package (INN) and Leafnode. Leafnode is a USENET software package designed for small sites with few readers and only a slow link to the Net, and is therefore not really beneficial in the enterprise environment. INN, however, is a full Usenet system that includes a NNTP (Network News Transport Protocol) server and a newsreading server. INN was originally written by Rich Salz, but has since been taken over by the Internet Software Consortium (ISC). InterNetnews is used to exchange messages between networks of news servers.

✦ News articles are placed into newsgroups.

✦ Each individual news server locally stores all articles that it has received for a given newsgroup.

✦ The newsgroups are organized in hierarchical fashion ensuring that all messages are distributed to local servers, making access to stored articles extremely fast.

Searching for documents in a newsgroup or on the World Wide Web can be a challenge to the user. Due to the vast amount of information available, it can be a daunting task to search individual web sites and newsgroups for a particular piece of information. Luckily, you have Dig (or the ht://Dig system), which is a complete World Wide Web (WWW) indexing and searching system for a domain or intranet. Dig is intended to provide a searching and indexing system for local websites and Intranet information. Although it is competent for its intended area of use, it is not meant to replace large-scale Internet search engines, such as Google, Yahoo, Lycos, Infoseek, or AltaVista. Dig supports both simple and complex searches. It supports Boolean search methods, with arbitrarily complex Boolean expressions and *fuzzy search methods* to search both HTML and text documents. Fuzzy search methods use exact, soundex, metaphone, common word endings, synonyms, and configurable algorithms to search the documents. Dig can be configured to search subsections of the databases for any number of keywords, and to then send the output to a customized HTML template. You can use Dig to index a server or parts of a server that are protected by a username and password.

FTP servers

The FTP (File Transfer Protocol) is a protocol that allows computers to send and receive files over the Internet. A counterpart to FTP is TFTP, or *Trivial File Transfer Protocol*. TFTP is the connection-less protocol that is often used for streaming files, such as audio or video, where missing one piece of information is less important than continuing the stream of information. Due to the design of the protocol, different machines using different operating systems and different hardware can exchange files in a safe manner. FTP provides for guaranteed delivery of data from an FTP server to the FTP client. Most versions of Linux come with some form of FTP server package. After the server is configured, users can connect to it with any FTP client.

Firewalls

A *firewall* protects the resources of a private network from unauthorized access from an outside network. A typical firewall is often created on a *router*, or a specially designated computer, which acts as a gateway to separate the outside network from the internal network. This creates a secure path so that only authorized incoming requests are allowed into the private network. An inexpensive Linux machine with a connection to the outside network and with another connection to the internal network can be used as a firewall. Linux provides many resources to create a firewall, including ipchains, Netfilter (which uses iptables and NAT or Network Address Translation), and IP Masquerade. Firewalls are very important servers that must be constantly updated and tested. The ability of any firewall solution is only as good as the person administering it. If you have the world's best firewall but don't keep it up-to-date, vulnerabilities may be discovered that can compromise the firewall.

ipchains

ipchains work by using a set of rules to filter traffic. The rules are initially organized into three groups (called *chains*):

✦ The *input chain* is used to control which packet comes into the box.

✦ The *forward chain* intercepts packets that come from one network and are destined for another network but are routed through the firewall.

✦ The *output chain* examines packets that are leaving the firewall.

The chain that is used to decide the fate of the packet depends on where the packet was intercepted. Several basic targets and functions are used with ipchains, including:

+ ACCEPT, which allows the packet to pass through

+ DENY, which denies access by the packet

+ REJECT, which denies access and notifies the sender

+ MASQ, which masquerades the packet

+ REDIRECT, which sends the packet to a local socket or process on the firewall

+ RETURN, which sends the packet to the end of the chain and lets the default target process the packet

Netfilter

Netfilter uses a true package-filtering tool to filter incoming packets. To perform this task, Netfilter uses iptables. These tables are established with rules based on particular network protocols. Therefore, different tables with rules can be created to select packets according to different criteria. After the packet is selected and passed to the table, the table handles the dropping or accepting of the packet. This greatly reduces the overhead of packet filtering because only the table that handles the packet actually determines the status of the packet — and not an entire set of rules, as in ipchains.

NAT

NAT (Network Address Translation) is the translation of an IP address that is used within one network to a different IP address known within another network. One network is designated as the *inside* network and the other is designated as the *outside* network. Typically, NAT is used to map a user's local network address to an outside IP addresses, and resolves the IP address on incoming packets back into its local IP address. This helps to ensure security because each outgoing or incoming request must go through a translation process that also offers the opportunity to qualify or authenticate the request or match it to a previous request. NAT also conserves on the number of IP addresses that are needed and lets a single public IP address communicate with external networks. Every packet coming from the internal network will be seen from the outside world as coming from that particular IP address. Most of today's inexpensive routers use NAT to provide services such as sharing dedicated digital connections. IP Masquerade is really a form of NAT that is used with ipchains.

Stateful packet inspection

Stateful Packet Filtering Firewalls operate around the connections between network firewalls. In filtering packets by the information that is contained within the packet header, firewalls allow or deny access to the network. Stateful filtering firewalls analyze individual data packets as they pass through. In addition to the packet header, Stateful inspection also assesses the packet's payload and looks at the application protocol. It can then make access decisions based on the source, destination, and service that is requested by the packet. With this level of information, the firewall is able to make a more informed policy decision than can be made by traditional firewalls. Although Stateful inspection offers the highest level of security, none of the current Linux-based firewalls currently support this method.

Determining Linux Roles and Services

Now that I've shown you how Linux can support servers with DNS, e-mail, file, firewall, FTP, proxy, Web, and many other server services and clients with word processors, e-mail programs, spreadsheets, database, graphic views and manipulators, Web browsers, file transfer, printing support, presentation, and virtually every other type of program, it's time to determine the roles and services that a system may require. You can use Linux for all the roles that I have discussed, and in fact, Linux is often used for all of these and many more.

Comparing Linux with other operating systems

Objective

1.8 Describe the functions, features, and benefits of a Linux solutions as compared with other operating systems (e.g., Linux players, distributions, available software)

Because Linux can support all of the services that other operating systems can, how do they compare? Because Linux is a true 32-bit OS with real multiuser and multiprocessing capabilities, it compares very well to other operating systems. The proof is in the real world uses of Linux.

Use on the Web

The search engine Google is a prime example of the ability of Linux to compete with other operating systems. Google is one of the premier search engines on the Internet and it runs on a Linux cluster. Over 60 percent of Web servers run Apache Web Server, which is completely supported under Linux and provides all of the efficiency and reliability of a high-end UNIX server. Linux has proven its capability to provide all the services that are needed in a server or desktop environment.

Installation

Installation of Linux is comparable to UNIX, Mac, and Microsoft operating systems. All of these operating systems provide a friendly user interface that allows the installation of the operating system with very little user input. The fact that Microsoft includes an extremely large number of device drivers with the initial installation package makes it attractive to non-technical users and gives it a slight advantage in this area. For the more technical user, Linux can also be installed from the command line, enabling a variety of advanced installation options.

Stability

After it is configured, the reliability of the operating system is clearly an issue to be considered. Because Linux is UNIX-like, it has gained many of the benefits of UNIX. For example, UNIX has always been considered one of the most reliable and stable operating systems available, but Linux is clearly in the same class of service as UNIX. The Microsoft operating systems are usually considered to be less stable; however, they have made great strides with recent releases of their enterprise software and hope to be rid of that reputation. It is clear, however, that UNIX and Linux are considered to be the best choices for services regarding stability.

New technology

Although Linux has improved greatly in many areas over the years, it still trails in the ability to support new technology as well as UNIX or Microsoft. Because Linux relies on private and public developers and volunteers to create device drivers for new and often expensive hardware, it is obvious why Linux can't support as many new devices as these other commercial operating systems. For example, in the case of support for Fibre Channel drive arrays, Linux clearly supports the technology but has also been shown to trail both UNIX and Microsoft Server 2000 in data throughput under load. This will change as Fiber Channel matures, but at this time, Linux clearly has some issues to resolve. Although Linux has some ground to gain on correcting the issues of new technology support, it excels in the support of older hardware. While other operating systems often abandon the support of older hardware, Linux continues to provide useful applications for old systems.

Cost

Finally, and perhaps most importantly, the cost of all these operating systems is an issue that can't be overlooked. Linux is freely licensed and can be installed in as many desktops or servers that you desire. Microsoft has traditionally used a single purchase license and client licensing method, but they are moving to a new licensing method that requires renewal of a software license on a regular basis. UNIX, which was once considered to be the most costly to purchase, is now being led by Sun Microsystems, which is currently distributing their Solaris binary code for no charge with media available for a drastically reduced price. Linux is clearly the winner here. Even fully supported distributions that are available for purchase are usually much less expensive than the competition. However, the initial cost of Linux does not mean that the long-term costs are lower than other operating systems. A belief persists that Linux costs more in the long run because it requires a more knowledgeable support staff, and that when users encounter problems, it often takes longer to resolve. Indeed, the ability to support any operating system requires a knowledgeable staff, and all operating systems have issues that can be difficult to resolve, but the long-term cost of any operating system is very comparable and no operating system is clearly less or more expensive than the others. Although Linux has not separated itself as a clear leader in every situation, it has shown that it should be considered and performs well versus its competition.

Hardware compatibility

Objective ➤ 1.2 Identify all system hardware required and validate that it is supported by Linux (e.g., CPUs, RAM, graphics cards, storage devices, network interface cards, modem)

The hardware compatibility of Linux has always been one of its big advantages. Although Linux doesn't support the newest technologies on a level comparable to other operating systems, it does provide excellent support for most other hardware. Linux also supports perhaps the largest list of hardware platforms. Because it was built to be UNIX-like, Linux also benefits from the easy portability to other platforms, and has been shown to run on virtually every platform available. This is an enormous benefit for Linux because it has become the standard for installations on embedded devices, and this fact alone may help Linux to gather more support on other platforms as it matures and receives more coverage. The ability of Linux to work on many platforms and on most of the hardware in the marketplace can make determining compatibility of a specific piece of equipment difficult. Thankfully, most Linux distributions support a Hardware Compatibility List (HCL) on their Web sites.

Exam Tip Understand the Hardware Compatibility List (HCL) because it is an important concept and will be covered on the exam.

The HCL shows all the hardware that the vendors tested with their distribution of Linux. By providing the HCL, a system and all of its components can be verified as compatible with Linux *before* the operating system is installed. This way, a user knows if the CPU, RAM, graphics cards, storage devices, network interface cards, modem, and virtually any other hardware component will be supported.

Linux software packages and package distribution types

Objective ➤ 1.10 Identify where to obtain software and resources

Not all software services and applications are included in every distribution. If the software package is not available in the distribution, it is usually available for download from the Internet. The software packages that have been discussed in this chapter are typical services that are necessary for a desktop or server system. The following is a list of many of the sites that can provide most of these software packages:

✦ http://www.abiword.org/

✦ http://www.apache.org/

✦ http://www3.corel.com

✦ http://www.htdig.org/

✦ http://www.isc.org/products/INN/

✦ http://koffice.kde.org/

✦ http://www.konqueror.org/

✦ http://www.leafnode.org/

✦ http://www.linux.org

✦ http://www.linuxdoc.org

✦ http://www.lotus.com/home.nsf/welcome/domino

✦ http://netfilter.filewatcher.org

✦ http://www.netscape.com/

✦ http://www.opera.com/

✦ http://www.proftpd.net/

✦ http://www.sendmail.org/

✦ http://www.squid-cache.org/

✦ http://www.sun.com/software/star/staroffice/

✦ http://www.trolltech.com/

Although these Web sites have excellent support for the software packages, sometimes you may have a need for more information. This information is available in the MAN pages and documentation that are included with most software packages.

Determining customer resources

Objective   1.11 Determine customer resources for a solution (e.g., staffing, budget, training)

After you have determined a need for a desktop or server system, you also need to determine the ability of the customer to provide the resources necessary to install and support these systems. The hardware is just the beginning. If a desktop installation has been selected, then you must have a PC on which to install the operating system. After Linux is installed, you may need to purchase some specific software to integrate the PC into the existing network. You will also need ongoing maintenance to keep the distribution up-to-date and you will need to repair any hardware failures in the PC. For a server installation, not only is there a requirement verifying hardware compatibility and all the desktop installation requirements, there is also the requirement for expansion and scalability of the server to be able to support an increased userbase in the future. Because servers often expand beyond the initial hardware, the expansion of the server should be verified before the installation begins. The customer's ability to upgrade the server should also be taken into account. Finally, you face the ongoing cost for staff to support the systems. Budgets must be allocated not only for staff but also for equipment maintenance, replacement, and continued training to properly keep the systems up-to-date and running.

Summary

In this chapter, I discussed the ability of Linux to be used in the enterprise environment. I demonstrated the ability of Linux to perform everyday tasks required of a desktop and of a server in the enterprise environment, along with the software needed to provide these services. I also alerted you to the fact that these software packages may need to be downloaded or installed after the installation of the base operating system. I also pointed out that the hardware should be verified with the help of the HCL, which is provided by the Linux vendors. Linux was also compared to other operating systems with respect to cost, services provided, and budget and staffing support requirements.

✦　　✦　　✦

STUDY GUIDE

The Study Guide section provides you with the opportunity to test your knowledge about the Linux+ exam objectives that are covered in this chapter. The Assessment Questions provide practice for the real exam, and the Scenarios provide practice with real situations. If you get any questions wrong, use the answers to determine the part of the chapter that you should review before continuing.

Assessment Questions

1. Which of the following is a popular word processor that is available for both Microsoft and Linux operating systems?

   A. Corel WordPerfect

   B. Microsoft Word

   C. Opera

   D. Domino

2. Which of the following is not a spreadsheet program for Linux?

   A. Corel Quattro

   B. StarOffice Base

   C. Kspread

   D. Excel

3. What is the name of the KDE-based Web browser?

   A. Netscape

   B. Opera

   C. Konqueror

   D. Internet Explorer

4. Which of the following is not available for Linux?

   A. AOL instant messenger

   B. Yahoo messenger

   C. ICQ

   D. MSN instant messenger

5. What service does DNS provide?

    A. Automatic addressing

    B. Name to IP mapping

    C. WINS resolutions

    D. UUCP transfer

6. What is the most common protocol used for an e-mail server?

    A. SMTP

    B. SNMP

    C. Sendmail

    D. X.400

7. What software package provides Microsoft SMB support for Linux?

    A. NetBIOS

    B. Samba

    C. NFS

    D. DDP

8. The Squid application provides which service for a Linux system?

    A. E-mail

    B. News

    C. Proxy

    D. Firewall

9. Which of the following is the protocol used for news and newsgroups?

    A. Leafnode

    B. INN

    C. Squid

    D. NNTP

10. Which of the following is an example of an application that provides searching capabilities on an intranet or domain?

    A. Dig

    B. Gopher

    C. SSL

    D. NNTP

11. Which of the following applications is an example of an FTP server?

   A. Apache

   B. Squid

   C. TFTP

   D. wu-ftpd

12. Which of the following applications is an example of a kernel embedded, rules-based firewall?

   A. ipchains

   B. Netfilter

   C. NAT

   D. Stateful Packet Inspection

13. What does NAT stands for?

   A. Network Advertised Translation

   B. Network Address Translation

   C. Network Address Transport

   D. Network Acceptable Translation

14. Which is Linux least likely to provide excellent support for?

   A. An external Ultra Wide SCSI HDD

   B. An Ultra ATA HDD

   C. A Fibre Channel HDD

   D. An Iomega ZIP drive

15. Which of the following is used to verify that the NIC works with Linux?

   A. HCL

   B. SUNW

   C. MAN pages

   D. www.linux.org

16. Which of the following Web sites are helpful in configuring a Web server?

   A. www.apache.org/

   B. www.isc.org/products/INN/

   C. www.squid-cache.org/

   D. www.trolltech.com/

17. Which of the following Web sites can be used to gather information about creating a firewall?

    A. `www.htdig.org/`

    B. `www.leafnode.org/`

    C. `http://netfilter.filewatcher.org`

    D. `www.squid-cache.org/`

18. Which of the following can be used with NFS to provide remote file access for UNIX systems?

    A. NIS

    B. NAT

    C. NNTP

    D. SMB

19. Which of the following is the task that the Sendmail server provides?

    A. MTA

    B. MUA

    C. MDA

    D. DDP

20. Which of the following is a connection-less protocol for file transfer?

    A. SMTP

    B. FTP

    C. TFTP

    D. UUCP

Scenarios

1. A company wants to create a Web server on their intranet. Which Linux package can be used to supply this service?

2. An accounting office has DSL (Digital Subscriber Line) Internet access that they want to secure and share among several users. Which service that Linux offers should they use?

Answers to Chapter Questions

Chapter Pre-Test

1. Linux can be used in the enterprise at every level, from the desktop, to the server.

2. Samba provides connectivity with windows-based PCs or servers by using the SMB protocol.

3. Linux can be used to install a firewall that can limit or prevent unauthorized access.

4. Linux supports e-mail through use of standards-based software such as Sendmail, which is based on the Simple Mail Transport Protocol (SMTP).

5. Linux supports the most popular Web server in use today, which is the Apache web server.

6. Linux can provide file and print services for the Mac OS with support for the Appletalk protocol.

7. Linux can provide every major service that is offered by other operating systems, which makes it an attractive alternative.

8. Linux is very competitive with rival operating systems in terms of cost, reliability, and efficiency, and is a viable choice in most situations.

9. Because drivers for hardware devices are created as they come out by mostly volunteer developers, sometimes Linux does not support very new technologies.

10. Linux offers many places to gather information about the services that it can run, including — but not limited to — the sites that maintain the service software, `Linux.org` and `Linuxdocs.org`, and the MAN pages for the service.

Assessment Questions

1. A. WordPerfect is a popular word processor that is available for both Microsoft and Linux operating systems. Microsoft Word has not been ported to Linux; Opera is a Web browser; and Domino is an e-mail server. See the sections "Word Processing" and "Spreadsheets and Databases" for more information.

2. D. Excel is a Microsoft Product that has not been ported to Linux. The others have all been created or ported to Linux. See the section "File servers" for more information.

3. C. The KDE-based Web browser is Konqueror. Netscape and Opera are excellent Web browsers, but they are not part of KDE; neither is Internet Explorer. See the section " Web browsing" for more information.

4. D. MSN Instant Messenger is not available for Linux; the others are all available in some form for Linux. See the section "More, more, and more applications" for more information.

5. B. DNS provides name to IP mapping; DHCP supplies automatic addressing; WINS is a Microsoft service; UUCP is an old file transfer protocol. See the section "The Server and DNS" for more information.

6. A. SMTP is the most common protocol for an e-mail server. Sendmail is a software package that supports SMTP. SNMP is simple network management protocol, and X.400 is not the primary e-mail service in use today. See the section "Linux e-mail server" for more information.

7. B. The Samba software package provides for Microsoft SMB support in Linux so that Linux machines can connect to Microsoft network resources. NetBIOS is a Microsoft protocol; NFS is used to support UNIX; and DDP is used to support the MAC OS. See the section "File servers" for more information.

8. C. Squid provides the Proxy service, which caches and filters web traffic. E-mail is supported by sendmail; news is supplied by INN; and firewalls are created with ipchains and Netfilter. See the section "Proxy, news, and search servers" for more information.

9. D. NNTP protocol is used for news services. LeafNode and INN are examples of news servers, and Squid is a proxy server. See the section "Proxy, news, and search servers" for more information.

10. A. Dig is the common name of the service that provides searches on an intranet or domain. The others are all services not related to searching on an intranet or domain. See the section "Proxy, news, and search servers" for more information.

11. D. wu-ftpd is an example of a common FTP server application. Apache is a web server, Squid is a proxy server, and TFTP is actually a protocol used for connectionless FTP transfers. See the section "FTP servers" for more information.

12. A. ipchains is an example of the Linux firewall software that is built-in to the kernel. Netfilter is a separate firewall application, NAT is merely a Network Address Translation table, and stateful packet inspection is an advanced firewall filtering technique. See the section "Firewalls" for more information.

13. B. NAT stands for *Network Address Translation*. See the section "Firewalls" for more information.

14. C. Linux is least likely to provide excellent support for Fibre Channel because this is the newest hardware. See the section "Hardware compatibility" and "Comparing Linux with other operating systems" for more information.

15. A. HCL is where you should look first to learn if Linux supports a particular hardware device. SUNW is the stock ticker for Sun Microsystems; the MAN pages may have some hardware information, but they are usually used for software configuration and information; and finally, `Linux.org` does not support an extensive hardware list. See the section "Hardware compatibility" for more information.

16. A. The site `www.apache.org` is helpful for configuring the Apache Web server. The others do not support Web servers. See the section "A Linux Web server" for more information.

17. C. The following Web site can be used to gather information about creating a firewall: `http://netfilter.filewatcher.org`. The other Web sites don't support firewall software; Squid is for proxy services, Leafnote is a news server; and Dig is a search server. See the section "Firewalls" for more information.

18. A. NIS is used with NFS to provide remote file access for UNIX systems. NAT is used to allow many IPs to use a single IP to access the Internet; NNTP is a news server protocol; and SMB allows the remote access of a windows system to Linux and Linux to windows. See the section "File servers" for more information.

19. A. MTA is the task that a Sendmail server provides, which is transferring mail from one network or host to another. MUA is a mail user agent; MDA is a mail delivery agent; and DDP is Datagram Delivery Protocol. See the section "Linux e-mail server" for more information.

20. C. TFTP is an example of a connection-less protocol for file transfer. The others are connection-oriented. See the section "FTP servers" for more information.

Scenarios

1. To create a Web server, you should install the Apache Web server. To provide better services for local users, add a Squid proxy server to cache Web pages to decrease the amount of traffic going to the Internet.

2. To protect the internal network from unauthorized users from an outside network, a firewall server should be installed. In order to share the Internet connection, the NAT service should be set up to allow all machines to connect to the Internet using one IP address.

Installing Linux

EXAM OBJECTIVES

+ 1.1 Identify purpose of Linux machine based on predetermined customer requirements (e.g., appliance, desktop system, database, mail server)

+ 1.3 Determine what software and services should be installed (e.g., client applications for workstation, server services for desired task), check requirements and validate that it is supported by Linux

+ 1.4 Determine how storage space will be allocated to file systems. (e.g., partition schemes)

+ 1.7 Identify strengths and weaknesses of different distributions and their packaging solutions (e.g, tar ball vs. RPM/DEB)

+ 1.8 Describe the functions, features, and benefits of a Linux solutions as compared with other operating systems (e.g., Linux players, distributions, available software)

+ 1.9 Identify how the Linux kernel version numbering works

+ 2.1 Determine appropriate method of installation based on the environment (e.g., boot disk, CD-ROM, Network (HTTP, FTP, NFS, SMB))

+ 2.2 Describe the different types of Linux installation interaction and determine which to use for a given situation (e.g., GUI, text, network)

+ 2.3 Select appropriate parameters for Linux installation (e.g., language, time zones, keyboard, mouse)

+ 2.4 Select packages based on the machine's "role" (e.g., Workstation, Server, Custom)

Continued

EXAM OBJECTIVES (CONTINUED)

✦ 2.5 Select appropriate options for partitions based on pre-installation choices (e.g., FDISK, third party partitioning software)

✦ 2.6 Partition according to your pre-installation plan using fdisk (e.g., /boot, / , /usr, /var/home, SWAP)

✦ 2.7 Configure file systems (e.g., (ext2) or (ext3) or REISER)

✦ 2.8 Select appropriate networking configuration and protocols (e.g., modems, Ethernet, Token-Ring)

✦ 2.9 Select appropriate security settings (e.g., Shadow password, root password, umask value, password limitations and password rules)

✦ 2.10 Create users and passwords during installation

✦ 2.11 Install and configure Xfree86 server

✦ 2.12 Select Video card support (e.g., chipset, memory, support resolution(s))

✦ 2.13 Select appropriate monitor manufacturer and settings (e.g., custom, vertical, horizontal, refresh)

✦ 2.14 Select the appropriate window managers or desktop environment (e.g., KDE, GNOME)

✦ 2.16 Install boot loader (e.g., LILO, MBR vs. first sector of boot partition)

CHAPTER PRE-TEST

1. What different methods are available for installing Linux?

2. What tools are available for hard drive partitioning?

3. What are the supported partition types in Linux?

4. What are the benefits of a journaling file system, and which ones support this feature in Linux?

5. What is the default networking protocol in Linux?

6. How can you make your Linux system more secure during installation time?

7. Can additional user accounts be created during the installation of Linux?

8. What are the benefits and the disadvantages of an X-Windows system and windows manager?

9. What is the purpose of a boot loader?

10. How is an additional software package installed during the initial installation of Linux?

✦ Answers to these questions can be found at the end of the chapter. ✦

This chapter is about installing Linux. First, I will show you how to install Linux based on the customer's needs and requirements. Then, I will show you how to use different file systems to fulfill those installation needs. I will also discuss how to select the required services in order to meet the requirements of the users needs.

I will walk you through a Linux installation step-by-step, showing you the appropriate method of installation, the different types of installation interaction, how to select appropriate parameters (such as language, time zones, keyboard, and mouse), the different packages based on the Workstation, how to choose between a Server or a Custom installation, partitioning based on pre-installation choices and the tools to accomplish partitioning. Other installation tasks include configuring the network, security, and passwords, Xfree86 with video cards, monitors and the desktop windows managers. Then, finalizing the installation and reasons for recompiling and adding packages to the installation will be illustrated.

Final Preparations for Installation

Objective

1.1 Identify purpose of Linux machine based on predetermined customer requirements (e.g., appliance, desktop system, database, mail server)

1.3 Determine what software and services should be installed (e.g., client applications for workstation, server services for desired task), check requirements and validate that it is supported by Linux.

1.8 Describe the functions, features, and benefits of a Linux solutions as compared with other operating systems (e.g., Linux players, distributions, available software)

You have a few tasks to complete before you can begin the actual installation. One of the most important tasks is to verify the type of installation that you wish to use. Is the user absolutely sure that she wants to have just a workstation or server? This is an important decision and should be verified beforehand. For example, the user may think that she wants only a desktop system, but perhaps she also wants to share documents on the intranet or Internet? If so, a Web server installation may be more appropriate.

Verification

If you verify the services that the user wants from his or her machine prior to installation, you may save yourself the task of reconfiguring at a later date. Most installation types can be verified by using a checklist, similar to the one that is used during the installation of Linux. The checklist can be a very complicated table or as simple as the list shown in Table 4-1.

Table 4-1
Linux installation checklist

Workstation System	Selected Installation Type or Service
Word Processor	
Spreadsheet	
Database	
Graphics	
E-Mail client	
Web browser	
Programming languages	
Application development tools	
Networking	
Commercial Applications	

Server System	Selected Installation Type or Service
Web server	
File Server	
Database Server	
Mail Server	
Application Server	
Terminal Server	
E-commerce Server	
Proxy Server	
DNS Server	
DHCP Server	
News Server	
Search Server	
FTP Server	
Firewall	
Commercial server application	

You should consider this table to be only a partial list of possible options. Each installer should customize the verification list to make the installation process easier. Having this checklist should help installers to determine if a user needs a workstation or server type installation. Generally, however, users don't always know which service they want to use. Therefore, the installer should employ some probing questions to ascertain whether the user wants to share any files or services with others. The following is a list of sample questions that installers can ask their users:

✦ Do you want to have others use your files, system, or documents over an intranet or the Internet?

✦ Which result do you desire the most — sharing of network resources, prevention of outside access to the network, or controlling access?

✦ Do you need to run any high-end applications or services such as Web and FTP?

Using these questions will allow the installer to determine whether the user needs only a workstation, server, or appliance. Here is a breakdown of each type of installation:

✦ **Workstation installation:** Generally does not provide services to anyone but the user of the machine.

✦ **Server installation:** Provides services to users anywhere on the intranet or Internet.

✦ **Appliance system:** Used only to provide special network services, such as routing, proxy, or firewall services; are often minimum hardware configurations that are customized to provide the given service.

✦ **Thin server:** A special distribution customized to provide only one service; are easy to configure and are often customized to provide the best service for one particular task.

Package selection

No matter which type of server installation you choose, you still need to configure it with the required software packages that are needed for your specific applications. Every installer's goal is to make installations easier, a list should be created of software packages that allows for the installation of the client's desired service. A good example of this is shown in Table 4-2:

Table 4-2
Detailed installation list

Type of System or Service	Distribution or Package	Notes
Server Installation	___Red Hat ___Mandrake ___ SuSE ___TurboLinux ___Caldera ___ Debian ___ Slackware ___ Krud	There are many more distributions than this and some are considered better at certain tasks
Web Server	___Apache ___Tux Web Server* ____Other	System to provide a Web page?
File Server	___Samba ___NFS ___Netatalk ___Other	Share files on the intranet?
Database Server	___MySQL ___PostgreSQL ___Oracle ___Other	Database of employees?
Mail Server	___Sendmail ___Domino** ___other	Provide e-mail to and from the Internet?

* Tux Web Server is a fast Web server included with Red Hat Linux

**Domino is an e-mail server from Lotus

The installer can customize this installation list to the current environment that he or she is working in. Using a list ensures that the installation meets the needs of the client, and also allows the client to learn of other possible uses of Linux. Because some clients may be using another operating system to provide a service, such as a Windows file server, they may not know that Linux can also provide that service. Informing your clients of this fact can be an excellent way to move them from other operating systems to Linux.

Final hardware verification

Even though you have already checked the system against the Hardware Compatibility List (HCL), it is best to actually verify some information — such as the hardware details — before proceeding with the installation of Linux, because some details may need to be clarified. For example, some hardware makers may use several different chipsets to create a piece of hardware; therefore, it is wise to verify that the video card is version x, y, or z of a chipset. This is also true of hard drives; the size may be the same but they may have different structures. Suppose that one 30GB hard drive has 16,383 cylinders, 16 heads, and 63 sectors with 60,030,432 LBA (logical block addressing) to have a total capacity of 30,760MB; another 30GB hard drive has the same 16,383 cylinders, 16 heads, and 63 sectors, but with 60,032,448 LBA for a capacity of 30,736MB. These two drives also work at different speeds: The first has runs at 7200 RPM, and the second drive runs at 5400 RPM. This difference may seem inconsequential, but when you are setting up a server environment, it may cause problems down the road. Therefore, a checklist similar to the one that you made for software packages may be helpful when finalizing the preparations just prior to installing Linux. This list may look like the one shown in Table 4-3.

Table 4-3 Detailed hardware list		
System Component	**System Contains (examples)**	**Reason Needed**
CPU	Intel Pentium II	Kernel customization
System Memory	256 MB SDRAM	Swap file allocation
System Board	Intel BX based	Special features of the board
Video Card	3Dfx Voodoo 5500	Configuration of X-windowing
Monitor	Generic monitor capable of 1600x1200 at 85Hz	Configuration of X-windowing
SCSI controllers	Adaptec 2940	System installation from or to SCSI Media
Network Interface Card (NIC)	3COM 905B	Configure Networking
Sound cards	Creative Labs SB Live	Sound Configuration
Hard Disk Drive (HDD)	Seagate ST39204LW	Available space for partitioning
CD-ROM, CD-RW, DVD	Yamaha CRW2100SZ	System installation from media and system usage after installation
Specialty Cards	Xpeed's X400 ADSL PCI Adapter	Advanced features

For each customized installation of Linux, you may need to know many more items, but these are the basics.

Pre-installation partitioning planning

Objective   1.4 Determine how storage space will be allocated to file systems. (e.g., partition schemes)

The last item on your pre-installation agenda is to plan the partition table of the Linux installation. Again, the use of a list will help you to direct and verify the required file systems needed for the installation. Although it is possible to set up a system with just a root partition and a swap file, you will usually benefit from creating more than just the minimal requirements. Table 4-4 is an example of the form that you can use for this process.

Table 4-4
Linux partitions

Partition	Partition Types	Reason for Partition
/	ReiserFS, ext2 or supported	Root file system
/bin	ReiserFS, ext2 or supported	Executables
/boot	ReiserFS, ext2 or supported	Files required to boot system
/dev	ReiserFS, ext2 or supported	Represent the devices attached
/etc	ReiserFS, ext2 or supported	System configuration files
/home	ReiserFS, ext2 or supported	User files
/lib	ReiserFS, ext2 or supported	Binaries to support executables
/opt	ReiserFS, ext2 or supported	Optional Software
/proc	ReiserFS, ext2 or supported	Special files for extracting or sending information to the kernel
/sbin	ReiserFS, ext2 or supported	Executables for the root user
Swap	Linux swap partition type	Disk swapping space
/tmp	ReiserFS, ext2 or supported	Temporary files
/usr	ReiserFS, ext2 or supported	System files
/usr/local	ReiserFS, ext2 or supported	Software locally installed but protected from system upgrades
/var	ReiserFS, ext2 or supported	System log files, spools, or lock files
/<Customized directory>	ReiserFS, ext2 or supported	For special files or applications

Table 4-4 is a general list of the most common partitions that are created when Linux is installed. Here are a few general rules for partitioning:

✦ The swap partition should be at least equal to the size of memory installed on the system.

✦ Some installers prefer to install a swap partition twice the size of memory, but this is not required.

✦ The / or root partition is the only partition that is absolutely required to boot the system.

Exam Tip The uses of the various partitions is a very advanced subject. For the exam, remember which types of files are stored in which partitions, and you may be able to find the particular file fairly easily or avoid a wrong answer on the test.

The other partitions, such as /usr and /bin, are used to organize the system files and to create default mount points that are pre-configured when the system is installed. The Linux installation program will create most of the other default partitions. Custom partitions, however, are not created by the Linux installation program; these are usually used to store user data, and specialized applications. The more organized a system is, the easier it is to manage, move, update, and fix damaged files. By planning the software, hardware, and partitions, the installation of the Linux system will progress smoothly and in an organized manner.

Installing Linux

Objective 2.1 Determine appropriate method of installation based on the environment (e.g., boot disk, CD-ROM, Network (HTTP, FTP, NFS, SMB))

2.11 Install and configure Xfree86 server

2.12 Select Video card support (e.g., chipset, memory, support resolution(s))

2.13 Select appropriate monitor manufacturer and settings (e.g., custom, vertical, horizontal, refresh)

2.14 Select the appropriate window managers or desktop environment (e.g., KDE, GNOME)

At this point, all of the planning is complete and it is time to start the installation.

Tip The installation of Linux by a network server is an excellent way to install Linux on a large number of systems that will be similarly configured.

This ability is important because it can be installed on a system that has no diskette drive or CD-ROM for a corporate environment — or other similar mass production need.

The way that you decide to install Linux may have been part of the planning, because you have several methods to choose from. First, Linux supports bootable diskettes that hold a small portion of the Linux kernel and allow the further installation of Linux. Some Linux distributions actually use only diskettes to create the Linux system — but those distributions are not commonly used today. Second, Linux also includes support for bootable CD-ROMs or DVDs, which are now more common for user and enterprise installation methods. Finally, you also have the ability to install the Linux system from an NFS or other network server. This option is usually only chosen for the enterprise environment, or by the user with a very good broadband connection.

The CD-ROM installation method is the most common method that users employ to install Linux. Because Linux can be installed in as little as 15 minutes, this method imposes no time constraints on its user. The CD-based installation is usually interactive and requires that the person performing the installation make selections for the type of installation, packages to be included, and configurations of the installation. The following steps will illustrate the CD-ROM method of installation of Linux. A bootable CD can start the CD-ROM installation of Linux. After Linux has begun installing, the choices begin.

Text or GUI installation

Objective

2.2 Describe the different types of Linux installation interaction and determine which to use for a given situation (e.g., GUI, text, network)

The type of interface is the first selection in the installation process that the installer must make. Most modern Linux installations will launch to a GUI (graphical user interface) based installation by default. GUI is usually the easiest installation to follow and use; some do almost everything for you (much like a Microsoft installation), but others walk you through each step of the installation. GUI installations require some minimal hardware. GUI installations are capable of detecting most hardware, and usually have excellent tools for setting up the system; however, if the system doesn't have enough memory, processor power, or video capability, the GUI installation is not appropriate and the text-based installation should be chosen instead.

The text installation uses a very basic command line interface, or *shell*, which allows the installer to easily install Linux on older and slower machines (even machines that lack a video card) by using a terminal. Other reasons that you may have for using the text installation instead of GUI include:

✦ Text installations use minimal graphics. Therefore, it is usually faster to move from screen to screen.

✦ Text installations can create a batch file to answer your questions for mass installations.

In the Real World

Mass installation and upgrades are a fact of life in the real world of big corporations and governments. Failures usually occur when the installer did not correctly identify the hardware, did not properly configure the network, or was given the wrong source files for the installation or upgrade. Therefore, always make sure to verify the hardware, network configuration, and source files, and perform a test installation at each site.

Performing mass installations used to be challenging, but programs like Kickstart from Red Hat are eliminating the difficulties. With Kickstart, an installer can set up a server to automatically respond to client requests for software downloads, which can be customized. So no matter which type of installation you need, Linux can supply it. All you have to do is select the installation method, as shown in Figure 4-1.

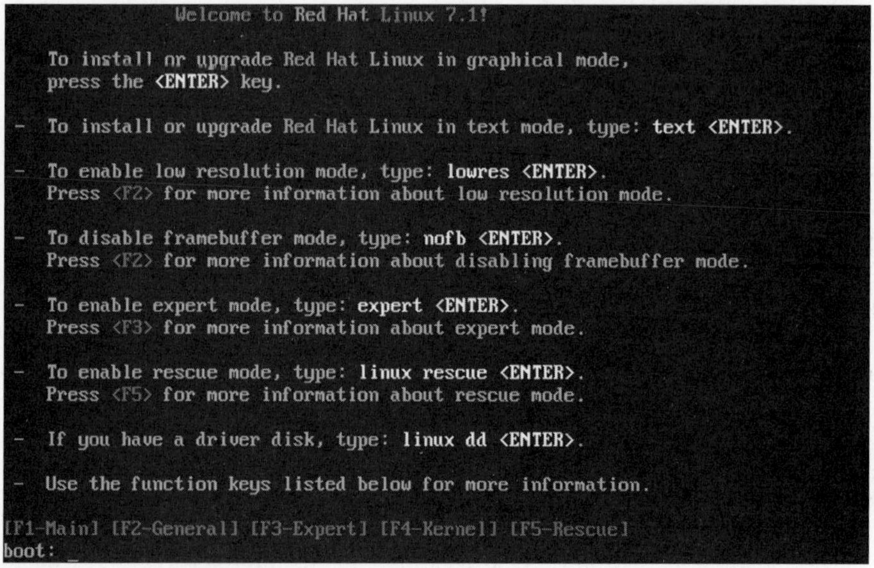

```
                Welcome to Red Hat Linux 7.1!

     To install or upgrade Red Hat Linux in graphical mode,
     press the <ENTER> key.

  -  To install or upgrade Red Hat Linux in text mode, type: text <ENTER>.

  -  To enable low resolution mode, type: lowres <ENTER>.
     Press <F2> for more information about low resolution mode.

  -  To disable framebuffer mode, type: nofb <ENTER>.
     Press <F2> for more information about disabling framebuffer mode.

  -  To enable expert mode, type: expert <ENTER>.
     Press <F3> for more information about expert mode.

  -  To enable rescue mode, type: linux rescue <ENTER>.
     Press <F5> for more information about rescue mode.

  -  If you have a driver disk, type: linux dd <ENTER>.

  -  Use the function keys listed below for more information.

[F1-Main] [F2-General] [F3-Expert] [F4-Kernel] [F5-Rescue]
boot: _
```

Figure 4-1: The Red Hat Linux welcome screen

After you have selected the method of installation, Linux will begin to detect hardware. Even though Linux hardware probing is fairly accurate, I recommend that you observe the detection of hardware before the installation program moves to the GUI, shell, or command line interface for the installation of Linux. Figure 4-2 shows the hardware detection screen.

This screen shows the detection of hardware in the machine, including the lines:

```
PIIX: IDE controller on PCI bus 00 dev 38
```

This is the PCI controller for the IDE interface based on the primary chipset in the machine. If the installation doesn't detect the controller needed for hard drive access, however, the installation won't be able to continue. Although this doesn't happen very often, it is worth your while to watch the major and minor hardware detection at this stage. After basic hardware has been detected, the installation moves to the next phase—basic interface setup.

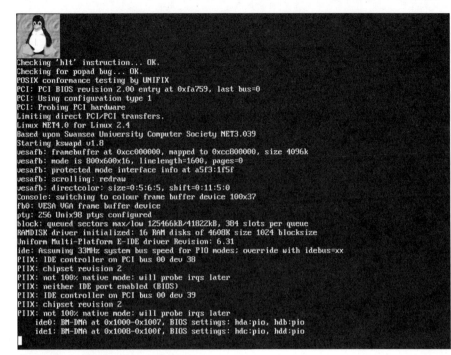

```
Checking 'hlt' instruction... OK.
Checking for popad bug... OK.
POSIX conformance testing by UNIFIX
PCI: PCI BIOS revision 2.00 entry at 0xfa759, last bus=0
PCI: Using configuration type 1
PCI: Probing PCI hardware
Limiting direct PCI/PCI transfers.
Linux NET4.0 for Linux 2.4
Based upon Swansea University Computer Society NET3.039
Starting kswapd v1.8
vesafb: framebuffer at 0xcc000000, mapped to 0xcc800000, size 4096k
vesafb: mode is 800x600x16, linelength=1600, pages=0
vesafb: protected mode interface info at a5f3:1f5f
vesafb: scrolling: redraw
vesafb: directcolor: size=0:5:6:5, shift=0:11:5:0
Console: switching to colour frame buffer device 100x37
fb0: VESA VGA frame buffer device
pty: 256 Unix98 ptys configured
block: queued sectors max/low 125466kB/41822kB, 384 slots per queue
RAMDISK driver initialized: 16 RAM disks of 4608K size 1024 blocksize
Uniform Multi-Platform E-IDE driver Revision: 6.31
ide: Assuming 33MHz system bus speed for PIO modes; override with idebus=xx
PIIX: IDE controller on PCI bus 00 dev 38
PIIX: chipset revision 2
PIIX: not 100% native mode: will probe irqs later
PIIX: neither IDE port enabled (BIOS)
PIIX: IDE controller on PCI bus 00 dev 39
PIIX: chipset revision 2
PIIX: not 100% native mode: will probe irqs later
    ide0: BM-DMA at 0x1000-0x1007, BIOS settings: hda:pio, hdb:pio
    ide1: BM-DMA at 0x1008-0x100f, BIOS settings: hdc:pio, hdd:pio
```

Figure 4-2: The hardware detection screen

Basic setup of Linux

Objective ▶

2.3 Select appropriate parameters for Linux installation (e.g., language, time zones, keyboard, mouse)

At this point, you need to provide some general information to the Linux installation before it can proceed. The following sections outline this information.

Language

First, the installer must select the language that the installation will proceed in. This choice sets the language for the rest of the installation. If the wrong language is selected, the installer may find that he or she won't be able to read the options correctly to move forward or backward in the installation process. Therefore, you should use care in selecting the language, as shown in Figure 4-3.

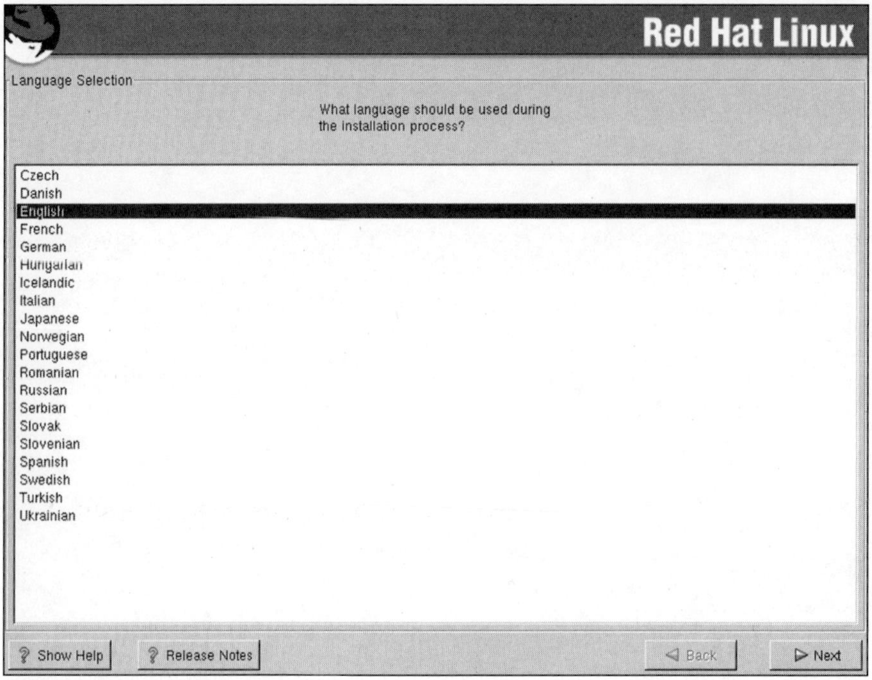

Figure 4-3: The Red Hat language selection screen

Licensing agreement

You must accept a licensing agreement before continuing to install the Linux operating system and any additional packages included with the distribution. Read this statement completely because it may contain licensing that doesn't meet the needs of the installation. If you do find an issue with the licensing agreement, don't install the software — find a distribution without the hindering license or with the knowledge that the license needs to be followed.

Keyboard and mouse

After the installer has agreed to the license, the system usually presents some other simple configuration questions, which usually involve the following:

- ✦ The selection of a mouse

- ✦ The selection of a keyboard model

- ✦ The type of installation

- ✦ The level of security of the installation

- ✦ The layout that is being used

- ✦ The selection of special features, such as Internet buttons

After these configuration questions have been answered and the features correctly selected, the installer can move on to selecting the mouse attached to the unit. Hopefully, the mouse has already been working at a minimum level. However, you select the actual type of mouse from a list that gives you the option of allowing a two-button mouse to emulate a three-button mouse. Notice the help window in Figure 4-4 that provides some basic help in selecting the correct mouse.

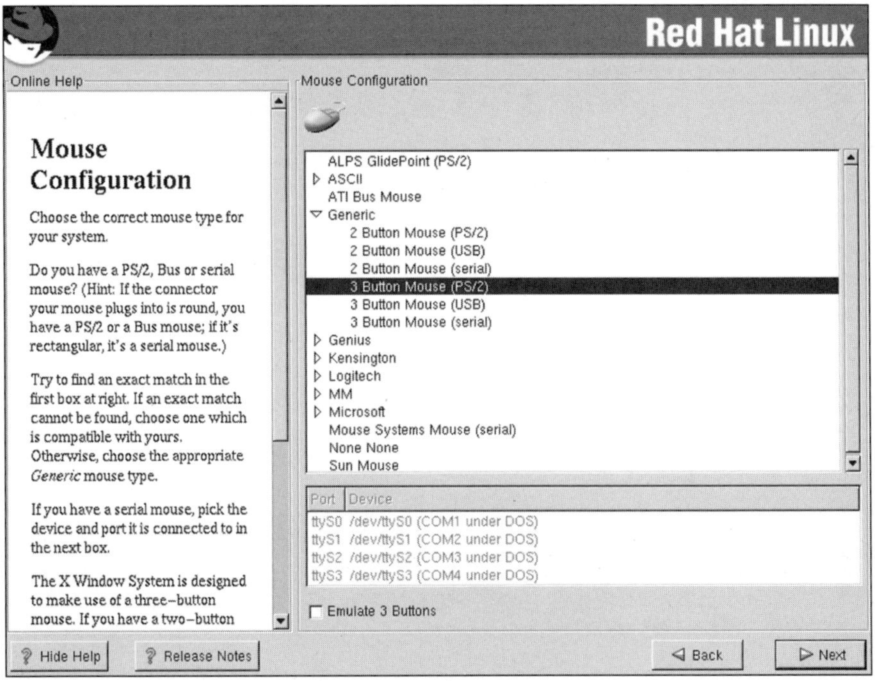

Figure 4-4: The Red Hat mouse configuration screen

Unlike other operating systems, Linux uses the capabilities of a three-button mouse to provide various features:

✦ The left button is the standard button for selecting items in a windows environment

✦ The right button is used to bring up a secondary menu in the active window

✦ The third button is used for special features of an application or window

This usually completes the basic configuration, and the installer can continue with the installation of Linux.

Selecting the machine type

 2.4 Select packages based on the machine's "role" (e.g., Workstation, Server, Custom)

After these basic configurations have been completed, most distributions will ask for the type of installation that the installer desires. Most installers use the format shown in Figure 4-5.

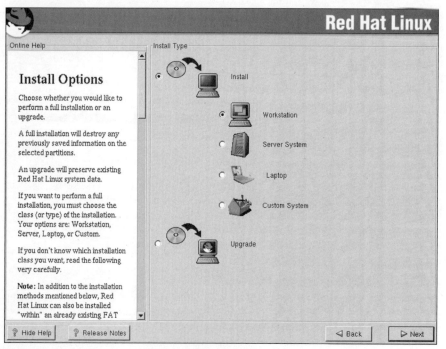

Figure 4-5: The Red Hat installation type screen

The options you can choose are a Workstation, Server System, Laptop, Custom System or Upgrade. The following sections break these down:

Workstations

Workstation configurations are generally the best choice for end users who do not need all the server applications installed. The Workstation installation includes the standard software packages that are needed to perform daily tasks. This includes software to perform Web browsing, to create documents and spreadsheets, and to retrieve e-mail. Some Workstation class packages allow the installation of commercial software to be included with the installation of Linux. Selecting a Workstation installation does not, however, limit the system to this role, but it does use a configuration that is meant for workstations.

Caution   Installation classes, such as workstation, are predetermined configurations in some Linux distributions and may limit or provide no options during the installation.

The pre-configuration usually includes not only the default software packages, but also some workstation-specific features, such as the hard drive partitioning and the security level the system starts at. Because additional packages can be added to the workstation, users can change the role of the system to provide services that are normally provided by a server.

Server Systems

By selecting Server at this point in the installation process, the installer is selecting basic features and configuration of a server. This includes the partitioning of the hard drive (including packages for providing services that a server can supply) and customized priorities for running applications. The selection of a Server configuration does not limit the system to this role, but does configure it to perform the tasks that a server is called upon to perform.

Laptops

Although Linux excels at performing on a server, Linux has had difficulty performing on a laptop. This is changing for many reasons, one of which is the standardization of laptop hardware, which has enabled Linux to provide better support for laptops. As a result, Linux has created a custom installation that provides for the needs of laptop hardware, including special hardware support, advanced power management, and a minimized volume of software to be installed.

Custom Systems

Customized Systems range from the most minimized system to the most complete installation of Linux. This option allows the installer to configure virtually every feature of the Linux installation. More advanced users may desire this installation method to achieve the most customized installation possible. This option also requires the most knowledge of how to configure Linux.

Upgrades

The final installation option is the ability to upgrade the existing installation of the Linux operating system. This is usually best used on the same distribution of Linux, because structural differences may exist between different distributions, which can cause unreliable upgrading.

Whether you choose a Workstation, Server, Laptop, Custom, or Upgrade installation the subsequent screens for disk partitioning will vary depending on your selection, so select the appropriate options as required.

Partitioning the hard disk drive

1.4 Determine how storage space will be allocated to file systems. (e.g., partition schemes)

2.5 Select appropriate options for partitions based on pre-installation choices (e.g., FDISK, third party partitioning software)

2.6 Partition according to your pre-installation plan using fdisk (e.g., /boot, / , /usr, /var/home, SWAP)

2.7 Configure file systems (e.g., (ext2) or (ext3) or REISER)

The next step in your installation is to partition the hard drive. This is performed automatically for Workstation, Server, and Laptop installation classes. The automatic configuration standards that can be set up by selecting a Workstation, Laptop, or Server class, however, usually won't work if the hard drive has an existing partition. At this point in the installation, or if a custom installation has been selected, a manual configuration of the partition must be performed. Disk Druid and fdisk are the usual partition utilities that are offered at this point, but others may be presented depending on your distribution. Disk Druid is the recommended tool for most users and is an easy-to-use and capable partitioning tool. Disk Druid is illustrated in Figure 4-6.

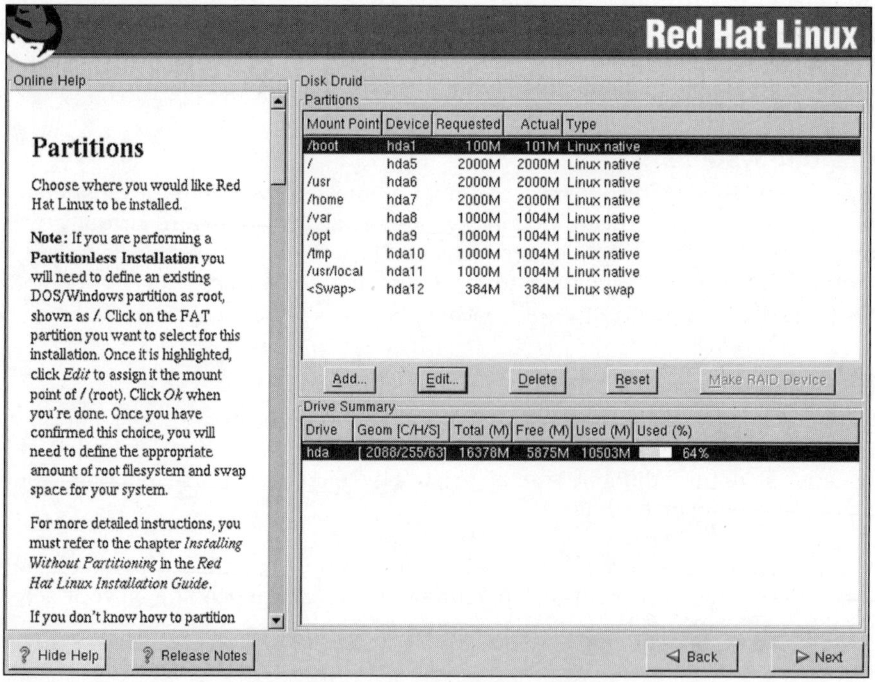

Figure 4-6: Hard Drive Partitioning with Disk Druid screen

The other major tool that is used for partitioning is `fdisk`. `fdisk` offers fast and easy-to-manage tools for partitioning. The most common partition file system types are ext2 or Linux native, Linux swap, and the newer Reiser File System or ReiserFS. Linux, however, also supports the following partitions: DOS FAT 16, Win98 FAT32, Linux RAID, Linux Logical Volume Manager, BSD/386, NetBSD, Solaris Boot Partition, UNIX System V, and virtually every other partition type available.

Exam Tip   For the exam, it's important to know the major Linux partition file systems, which include ext2, ext3, Linux swap, and ReiserFS. You should also understand the interaction that Linux has with the other major file systems in Microsoft and UNIX worlds.

These partition file system options are important for dual boot systems or on systems that are used to test potential operating systems. The Reiser File System may be the preferred partition type to use for a Linux-only system. Because the ReiserFS is a journaling file system, it allows for faster recovery from unexpected problems, such as power outage. It also uses a method to write to the hard drive that is faster and more secure. You can better understand the benefit of the ReiserFS if you know a little about how the ext2 file system writes information to a hard drive.

The ext2 partition first caches the data, and then writes it to the hard drive. If a power outage occurs while the system is operating, the file system can become corrupted because some of the data in the cache may not have been written to the drive. The next time Linux boots, it should detect this corruption, and run the fsck utility to correct any damage that was done.

The ReiserFS method adds additional safety by performing file writes in a more intelligent fashion. The ReiserFS system uses the following method:

1. Cache the data in RAM

2. Perform a preparatory command to write the data to the hard drive

3. Write the data to the hard drive

4. Verify the write to the hard drive

5. Clear the cache

If a power failure occurs, the journaling system is able to detect partially written data and can "back out" the data upon power restoration. By using this method, the Reiser file system prevents most of the data corruption that can occur, and therefore does not usually run fsck when an unexpected power loss is experienced. Therefore, because of the journaling capabilities, the ReiserFS is usually considered to be better than ext2. Another benefit of the ReiserFS is that it uses fast balanced trees. Balanced trees provide more robust performance and a sophisticated algorithmic file system. This method allows even small 100 byte files to be written into one block, while other file systems place each file into their own block. This speeds the handling of small files and saves space. Another space-saving feature of the ReiserFS is that it doesn't use fixed space for the allocation for *inodes* — which are data structures that hold information about files in a Unix file system — thus saving approximately six percent of the overall disk space.

Each file contains an inode, and files are uniquely identified in the file system by their inode numbers. Each inode contains the following information:

✦ device where the inode resides

✦ locking information

✦ mode and type of file

✦ number of links to the file

✦ owner's user and group IDs

✦ number of bytes in the file

✦ access and modification times

✦ time that the inode was last modified

✦ addresses of the file's blocks on disk

Yet another advanced feature of the ReiserFS is that it uses plug-in based, object-oriented, balanced tree algorithms. This allows the plug-in based objects to improve performance of the ReiserFS as newer algorithms are created to resolve issues found in the current objects. Therefore, monthly updates can improve performance of an already good file system. This is now the recommended file system and should be used on most modern installations of Linux — unless a specific reason dictates otherwise. The ext3 file system — once thought to be the next journaling system for Linux but is still in development — may never be used because the ReiserFS has found a home on most systems.

After you have selected the file system, you must create the individual file structure. Workstations generally employ a basic structure that includes a / (slash) partition, a /home partition, and a swap partition (a variant of this is to also include a /usr partition). The most basic structure is a / and swap partition. The size of these partitions should be determined by the size of the hard drive, but given the low price of hard drives, installers can use a size structure similar to the information presented in Table 4-5.

Table 4-5 Simple workstation partition		
Partition	**Size**	**Notes**
/	500 MB	Usually this is enough space
/usr	2900 MB	Often has many subdirectories
/home	12000 MB	Lots of space for users
Swap	256 MB	Determined by the amount of system memory

This table shows a simple structure that could be used. Each individual system needs to be sized according to the needs of the server, which often include the preceding structures and an additional partition of /var. This structure changes the sizes of the partitions to a partition scheme similar to the one demonstrated in Table 4-6.

Table 4-6 Simple server partition		
Partition	**Size**	**Notes**
/	256MB	Usually this is enough space
/usr	2900MB	Often has many subdirectories
/home	6900MB	Lots of space for users
/var	5500MB	Need for large system logs
Swap	384MB	Determined by the amount of system memory, the recommended minimum is equal to the RAM in the system

After you have determined and entered the partitioning using either Disk Druid or `fdisk`, the partitions need to be activated. To do this, the partition table must be written to the hard drive. Until this point, all of the information that has been entered exists only in memory. After you have committed the partition to the hard drive, the existing data on a hard drive will be lost, and the new partitions will be placed on the drive. Also up to this point, a reboot of the system will return the system to its previous state. After the partition is written, a new operating system must be installed. When this decision has been made, the screen shown in Figure 4-7 — or one like it — will be presented.

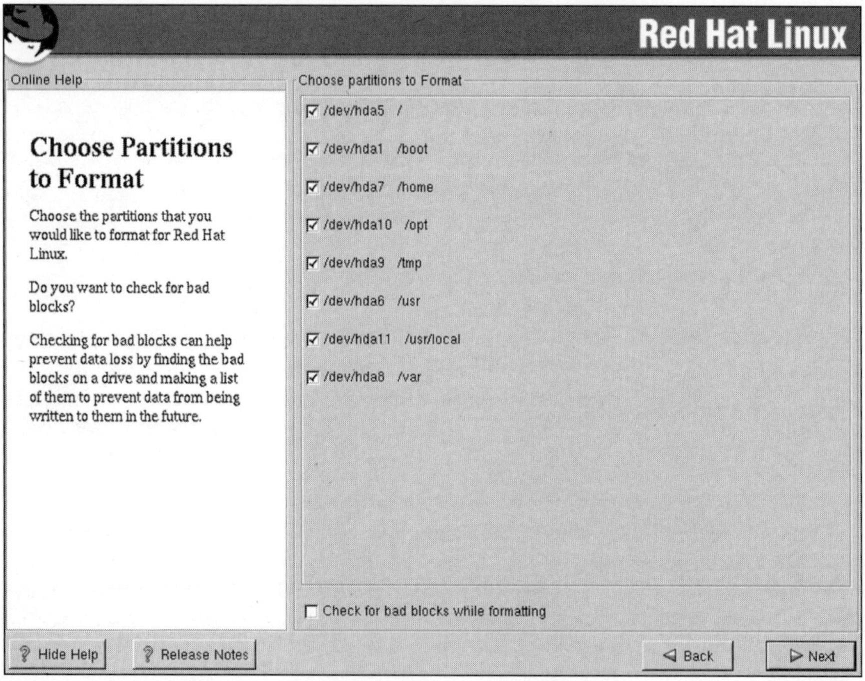

Figure 4-7: The Red Hat "choose partitions to format" screen

On this screen, you can select the partitions to be written, plus you are given the option to test the hard drive for bad blocks while the formatting is being done. I recommend taking this action on all but the most trusted hard drives because even brand new drives may have been damaged in shipping or installation. This is the final opportunity to abandon the installation without changing the existing system. To continue from this point will complete the partitioning of the system and its preparation for the installation of Linux.

Installing a boot manager

Objective   2.16 Install boot loader (e.g., LILO, MBR vs. first sector of boot partition)

The next selection in the Red Hat Linux installation is to choose the type of boot loader and its location. A *boot loader* is used to boot the operating system into the intended operating system, which is achieved by loading a bootstrap onto the hard drive. This bootstrap then tells the computer system where to find the next part of the operating system to be loaded. Sometimes the bootstrap will reference a menu that allows the computer system to choose from several operating systems. LILO is the default boot loader on most Linux systems; however, GRUB is also an option. GRUB is a multi-system boot loader created by the GNU project. There are also commercial products that can provide this bootstrap and can be used as the boot loader or boot manager for a Linux system. LILO, or Linux Loader, is used to boot the system into Linux and also provides many tools for troubleshooting a system that does not boot properly. LILO can be used to boot backup copies or different versions of the operating system's kernel, and it can, as previously stated, allow for a dual boot of the Linux operating system and another operating system. Using LILO to perform the duties of a boot loader is fairly straightforward, but be aware of a couple of notable points:

✦ The location of the bootstrap can be placed in the Master Boot Record (MBR) or the first sector of the boot partition. The Master Boot Record is generally used, but on some systems that are running multiple operating systems, this may not be the best selection because LILO may not work properly with the other operating system.

✦ Because Microsoft Windows NT and 2000 uses NTFS as the file system, LILO won't be able to boot the Microsoft system. This is not true of Microsoft Windows NT installations that use FAT 16 partitions or Microsoft Windows 2000 installations that use Win98 FAT 32 partitions. In situations were LILO is not loaded in the Master Boot Record, the first boot block of the drive containing Linux is usually used.

Caution   When planning to Dual-Boot Linux with any other product, back up the data on the existing operating system before proceeding with the second operating system installation.

Figure 4-8 illustrates the screen that Red Hat uses to determine were LILO is loaded (if it is loaded at all). The installation of LILO can be bypassed if another boot loader is used, such as GRUB or a commercial product.

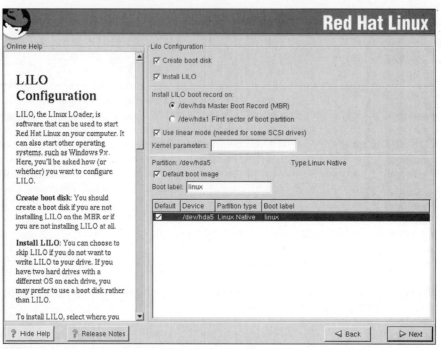

Figure 4-8: The Red Hat LILO configuration screen

Creating the Boot Diskette

The next noticeable feature included with the Red Hat installation and in most distributions is the option to make a bootable diskette that can be used to recover a non-bootable system, or to boot the system if LILO is not installed in the Master Boot Record (MBR). Finally, the installer must select the default system to be booted. On a system that may have both Microsoft Windows 98 and Linux, LILO can be set to boot either system by default with the option to boot the other one. This is a useful tool for those who want to run Linux but have a desire or need to use Microsoft or other operating systems. After LILO, GRUB, or another boot manager has been determined and loaded, the system will be able to boot Linux or any other operating system.

Networking

Objective 2.8 Select appropriate networking configuration and protocols (e.g., modems, Ethernet, Token-Ring)

At this point, the operating system is now bootable, so the next step in the Red Hat installation is to set up networking. Networking is what Linux was created to do; because Linux is a UNIX-like operating system, it has inherited the powerful TCP/IP features of UNIX and uses them by default. Although this isn't the next step in every Linux distribution, the choices are all very similar to the Red Hat installation menus. Networking is detected during the initialization of the system and is therefore presented from the installer at this stage. The network card that is detected is given an interface name. In this case, the name is *eth0*, as shown in Figure 4-9, but it can also be given interface names that map to other protocols such as token ring, FDDI, or PPP (or PPPoE used with some xDSL cards) if using a modem or other device. Although this can be accomplished with a modem, not all Linux distributions configure modem networking during installation.

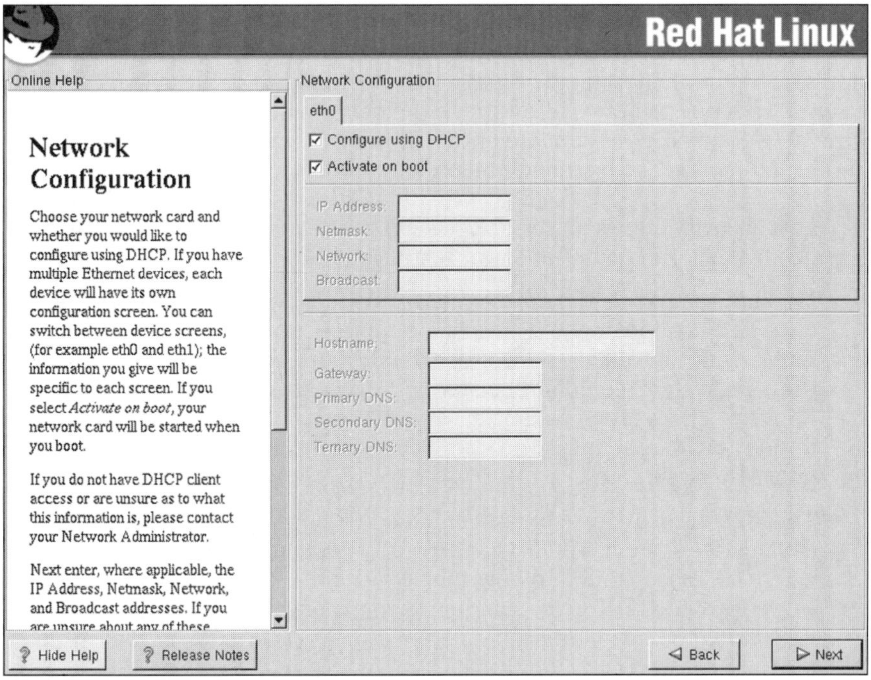

Figure 4-9: The Red Hat network configuration screen

To configure the Ethernet card, the installer must have information about the availability of Dynamic Host Configuration Protocol, (DHCP), which allows the system to lease an IP address for a limited amount of time. The lease is renewed if the client requests an update before the lease expires and if the server approves the renewal. Therefore, if a DHCP server is available, this is usually the easiest and best option for configuring an Ethernet NIC, or network interface card. If a DHCP server is not available, then a static address must be used; otherwise, networking will not start. Usually, if static addresses are used, a network administrator controls which addresses are used and on what equipment. A request for an IP address from the network administrator will generally result in an IP address for the system. That IP address will have the format of 4 octets of information. This can be in binary, hex, or decimal form, but is usually in decimal and is seen when you ping an address. For this example, I use 192.168.0.50, which is part of a class C address and uses a subnet mask of 255.255.255.0 by default.

The subnet mask is used to break up groups of computers so that they can work more effectively on the network. After the IP and subnet mask have been input, the system will complete the network and broadcast sections. The installer will then need to input the Hostname of the system that will ID the system, the Gateway (usually a router) that will usually provide access to the Internet or intranet, and up to three DNS (domain name system) that will be used to resolve machine names to IP addresses. After all these networking items are configured, the system should be ready to work on the network. Although the networking is configured, the security of the networking is not complete until a firewall setting has been selected. This firewall setting is set to low, medium, or high; here is a breakdown of each setting:

✦ **Low security** allows all services access to the machine and is usually only used in a closed environment or testing situations.

✦ **Medium security** is the default and opens most of the known ports for operation. This is important, because if a required service is blocked, then the system may not be able to network correctly. For example, if DNS were blocked, then the system would not be able to resolve the Fully Qualified Domain Name, or FQDN (such as the server `www.linux.org`), and therefore, would not be able to reach the Web site. The medium setting is the default because it opens these services.

✦ The **high security** level blocks all but a few services, such as DNS, and really isolates the system. This level of security is most appropriate on a server where access is limited to only the services that the system provides. If a server provides FTP services, then perhaps only these services that provide FTP should be open. This will prevent attacks on another service from affecting the FTP server.

Firewall services are now set up during installation and usually use a screen, as shown in Figure 4-10, to enable the configuration of the firewall.

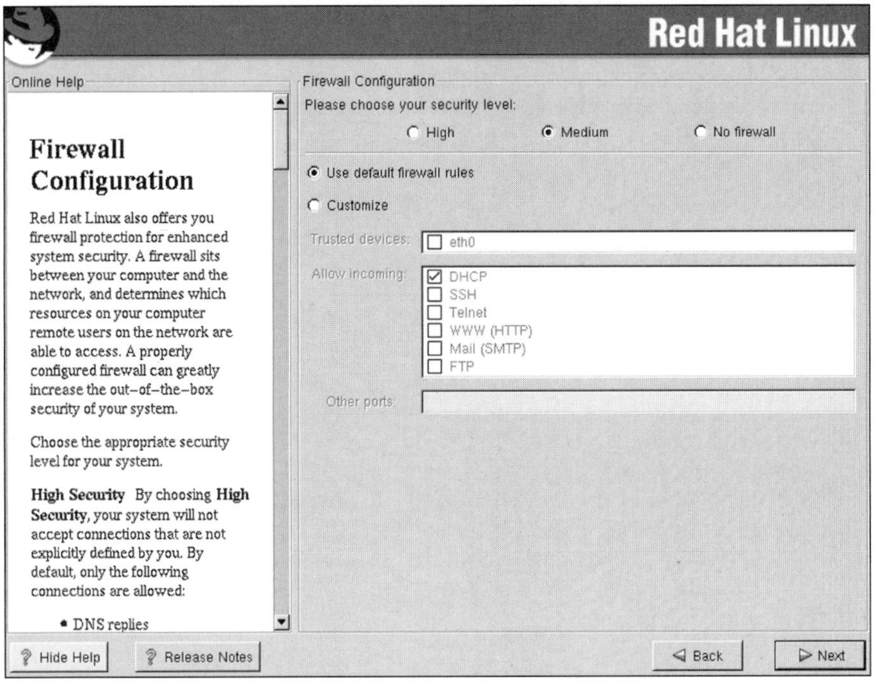

Figure 4-10: The Red Hat firewall configuration screen

After the appropriate boxes have been checked, the networking portion of the installation is complete and additional information can be entered.

Additional installation information

Objective

2.3 Select appropriate parameters for Linux installation (e.g., language, time zones, keyboard, mouse)

At this point in the installation, the system asks for additional languages to be supported. This is a simple screen that allows an installer to select languages to be supported on the system above and beyond the native language that is selected very early in the installation. After this is completed, the system will ask for the installer to select the time zone of the system. This includes a world map, with a red "X" marking the city selected as the physical location of the system. This map is interactive, so if the city to be designated as the location of the system is illuminated by a yellow dot, the installer should simply point and click and the yellow dot will become a red "X" to denote its selection. If the system is going to be set to a UTC, or Universal Coordinated Time, then this option may also be selected at this point. After these additional settings are completed, the system moves to user accounts.

Accounts and passwords

2.9 Select appropriate security settings (e.g., Shadow password, root password, umask value, password limitations and password rules)

2.10 Create users and passwords during installation

To enable users to logon to the system, user accounts and passwords must be created during or after installation. The first password and account that should be created is that of the *root* user. This is the most powerful account on the system and should only be used when other forms of accounts can't perform the specific task. The root account is the equivalent of Supervisor or Administrator accounts in other network operating systems. Because the root account is the most powerful account on the system, it is especially important to use good password rules when creating it. Because the account name is already known, a weak password will make the system even easier to break into. Therefore, I highly recommend that you create a very secure password for the root account. Creating secure passwords is an art form. The rules about what to do and what not to do are highly detailed. In fact, entire books have been written on the subject of security, so if you are a system administrator and you want to create the absolute best passwords, use the tools at your disposal. To create a fairly safe password, you need to follow just a few of the most important rules, including:

✦ Use letters, numbers, and special characters

✦ Include at least eight total characters

✦ Don't use words that can be found in the dictionary

✦ Don't use dates of significance, such as a birthday or anniversary

✦ Use the string in an unrepeated way

An example of a good password is *g0-2b8k!*—this meets the minimal length and does not have any pattern. Although it may seem hard to remember, it is the only way to create a password that is more secure than *abc-123*, which has been used on many systems before. User accounts should also employ these password rules, but most users will want to use passwords that are easier to remember. They can do so by substituting numbers for letters. In this way, a user can create the password *!pa55-w0rd,* which is much more secure than *!pass-word*. This may not be the best way to create passwords, but it does create memorable and harder-to-break passwords.

In the Real World Sometimes the use of password rules ends up defeating the purpose of the passwords in the first place. Be very sure to use password rules that the users can live with. If a rule is too difficult, or if the users have passwords that are difficult to remember, chances are likely that they will write them down. This causes the password to be extremely unsecured. A better method of password security is to create difficult-to-break passwords that are easy for the users to remember. For situations that require more security, you may need to seek hardware solutions to provide the level of security that you want to achieve.

Figure 4-11 illustrates the root password and the user creation screen that Red Hat Linux uses during installation; other versions of Linux use a similar GUI screen. This utility creates the root password and perhaps a few user accounts — in order to prevent running as root all the time — and uses the asterisk to hide the passwords from prying eyes. After the passwords have been created, the next screen displays the manner in which they are stored, as shown in Figure 4-12.

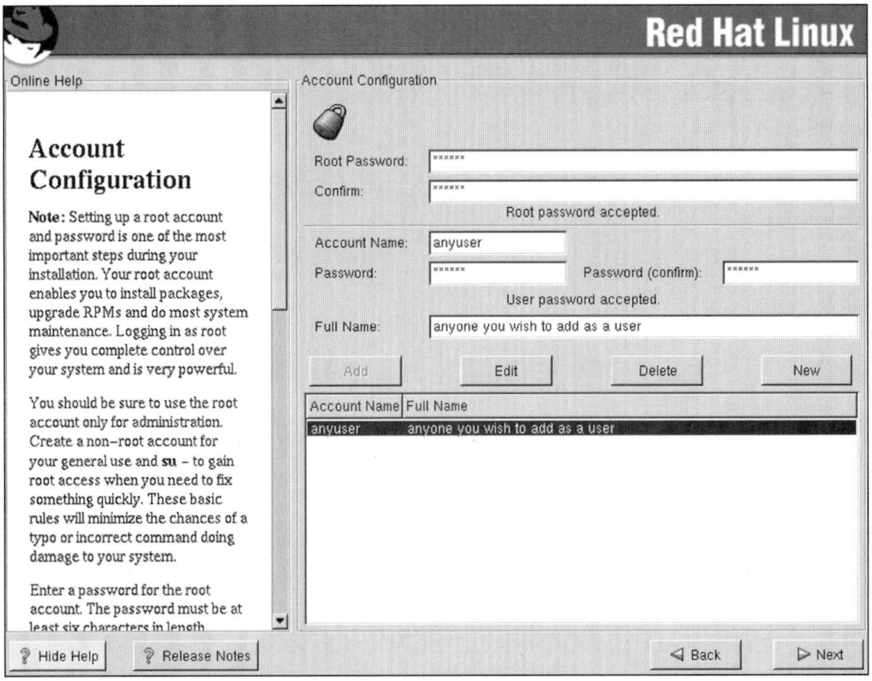

Figure 4-11: The Red Hat account configuration screen

Figure 4-12 demonstrates that the Enable MD5 Passwords is checked in the screen, thus showing that MD5 encryption is to be used. MD5-based encryption is used to create a 128-bit "fingerprint" of the input. It is more secure than older versions and is recommended unless you have a specific need for backward compatibility with an older encryption method. More details are available in the Request for Comments: 1321 on MD5, available at www.faqs.org/rfcs/rfc1321.html.

The next item to configure is to enable or disable shadow passwords, which is activated by default, and is used to provide another layer of protection to the created passwords. Shadow passwords or Shadow Utilities provide more protection for the system's authentication files by moving the encrypted passwords (normally found in /etc/passwd) to /etc/shadow, which is readable only by root. This file includes information about password aging, and prompts for passwords to be changed when they are too old. This feature is activated by default and should remain on for the added features and security that it provides for the system.

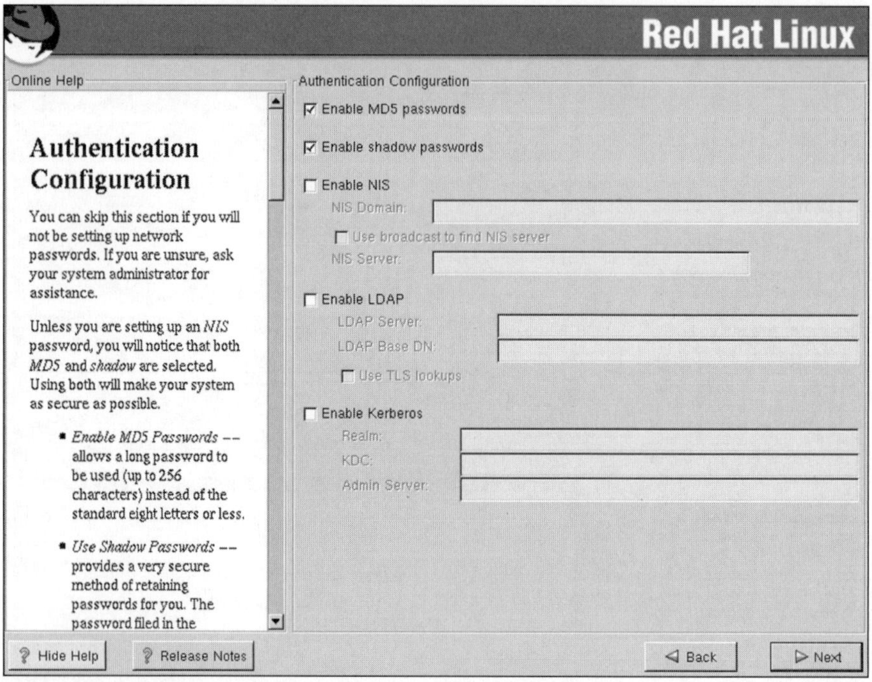

Figure 4-12: The Red Hat authentication configuration screen

Network Information Service (NIS) is used to log onto a UNIX- or Linux-created domain. NIS is used for support of the NFS and controls access to network shares. This does not improve system security, but can be used to improve network security.

Lightweight Directory Access Protocol (LDAP) is a protocol for accessing online directory services and provides directory services in intranet or extranet systems. It can be used to control access to resources on the network in a way similar to NIS, or even DNS.

Kerberos is an authentication method that uses strong encryption. It is used as a network authentication protocol and uses secret-key cryptography to provide the strong encryption. It is used in the client/server environment to provide clients a secure login on the server end, and to also ensure the security of the server. This allows the client to prove its identity to a server (and vice versa) across an insecure network connection. It is available for free from MIT (Massachusetts Institute of Technology) or in many commercial products. If your network is vulnerable to security risk, you may benefit from installing a Kerberos server and authenticating user and server interaction. The security of a system is only as good as the users and the passwords that they are allowed to use. Creating password rules and using the available security methods will greatly enhance the system's security.

Additional packages to install

After you have secured the system with user accounts and passwords, the installation program gives you the option to install or remove software packages. Here you can include services that are normally found on a server or vise versa, and add or remove packages as needed. In the Red Hat Linux installation program, the added services are listed in an easy-to-use method, as illustrated in Figure 4-13.

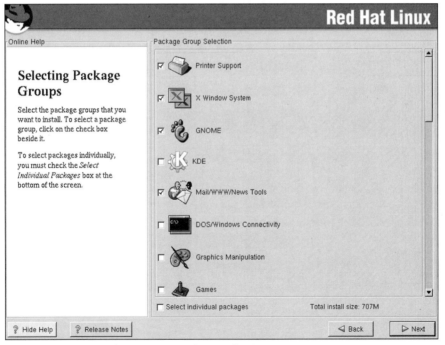

Figure 4-13: The Red Hat group package selection 1 screen

Figure 4-13 shows many of the services that can be used on a workstation system. By checking one of these boxes, the installation will include services for printing, the X Windows System, KDE and GNOME windows managers, mail, the Web, news readers, DOS and Windows connectivity to provide access to a Microsoft server, graphics manipulators, and games. The application package checklist, which is shown in Figure 4-14, is capable of installing a multimedia system, providing laptop support, and creating a network-capable workstation (use an NIC to connect), a dial-up capable workstation (use a modem to connect), and basic servers. These server packages are customized for the distribution that is being installed, including a news server capable of hosting a newsgroup, and NFS, Samba, and IPX Netware connectivity servers that provide file sharing with UNIX, Microsoft Windows, and Netware.

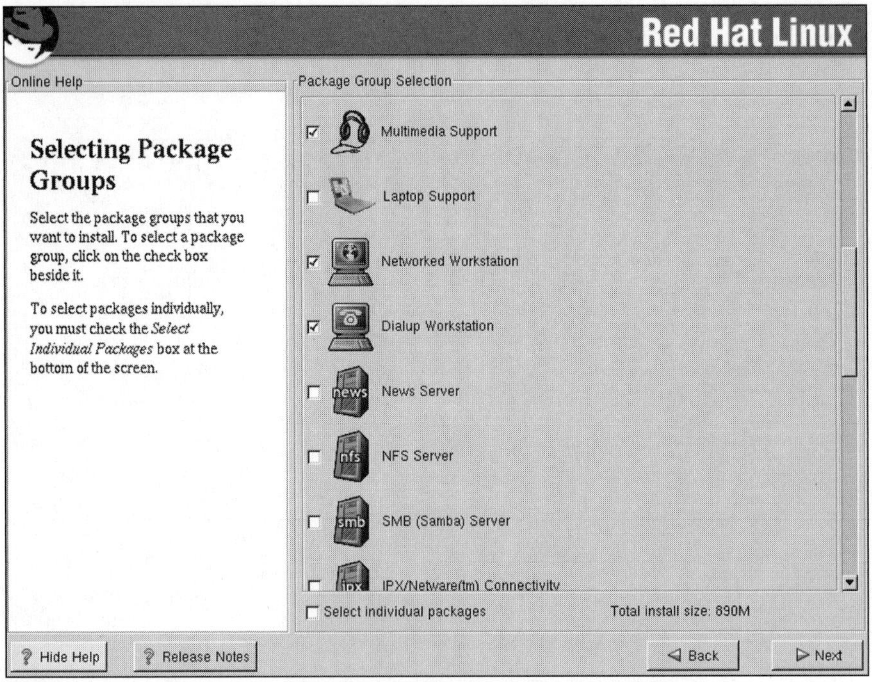

Figure 4-14: The Red Hat group package selection 2 screen

You can also install services for FTP file transfer, SQL databases systems, Web services, and DNS, as shown in Figure 4-15. All these services are normally used on a server (such as a Web server); however, they can also be used on a desktop system to provide simple Web pages. The selection of network management tools include the Simple Network Management Protocol (SNMP), which is used to manage network devices, such as hubs, switches, routers, servers and workstations. You can also install authoring and publishing tools with a simple check of a box.

Figure 4-15: The Red Hat group package selection 3 screen

Finally, the installation program provides the option of selecting the following:

   ✦ **Emacs,** which is a powerful self-documenting, customizable, and real-time display editor.

   ✦ **Development packages,** which are used to create programs and services with tools like C++.

   ✦ **Kernel development,** which is a means to distribute the tools to allow anyone to customize, tweak, and create new kernels for the Linux operating system.

You also have the ability to select all of the available packages for installation on the system. Figure 4-16 shows the final selections for the packages screen.

Figure 4-16: The Red Hat group package selection 4 screen

At this point, you have reached your last chance to remove packages or to install additional ones before the files are written to the hard drive. You can also take advantage of a check box at the bottom of the screen, which will allow the installation of individual packages. By checking this box and proceeding, the installer is able to use the screen shown in Figure 4-17 to make even more detailed package selections.

After you have selected all of the optional packages and any dependencies, the installation selection process is almost complete.

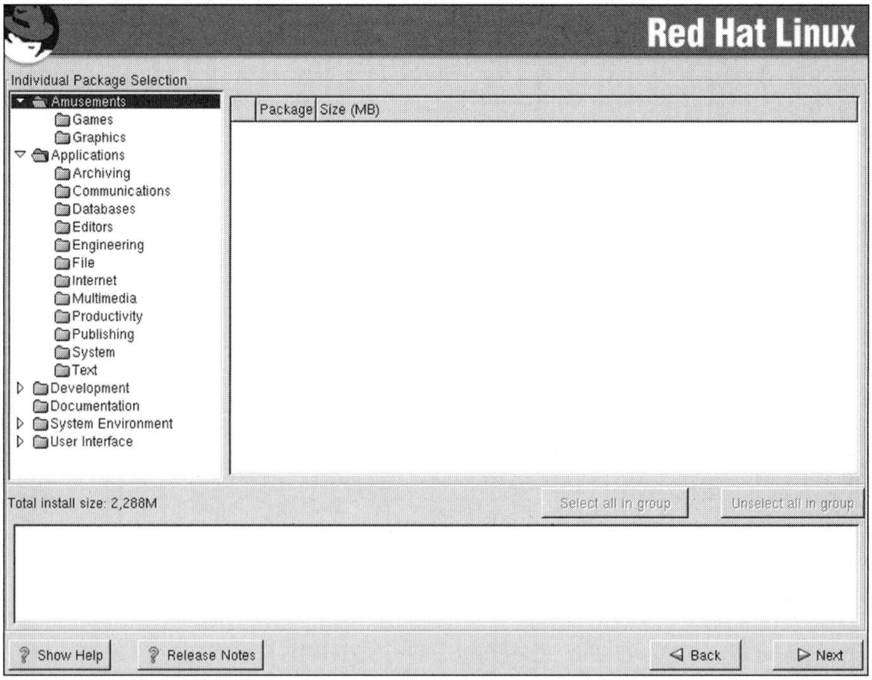

Figure 4-17: The Red Hat individual package selection screen

GUI installation

Objective

2.11 Install and configure Xfree86 server

2.12 Select Video card support (e.g., chipset, memory, support resolution(s))

2.13 Select appropriate monitor manufacturer and settings (e.g., custom, vertical, horizontal, refresh)

2.14 Select the appropriate window managers or desktop environment (e.g., KDE, GNOME)

The installation of the GUI, or graphical user interface, is the next part of the installation process. Often, you configure a GUI interface in Linux by using XFree86, which is a freely redistributable Open Source implementation of the X Window System that runs on UNIX, Linux, versions of BSD, Mac OS X (Darwin), Solaris for the x86 platform, and OS/2. XFree86 is the base software that provides the support between the hardware and graphical user interface. The KDE, GNOME, Enlightenment, Blackbox, AfterStep, twm and fvwm windows managers all run XFree86 as the interface to provide hardware support. The ability of Xfree86 to provide hardware support is constantly being updated by the XFree86 Project, Inc., located at www.xfree86.org, and currently provides support for not only the x86 platform, (hence the X in Xfree86), but also for Alpha, PowerPC, Sparc, and in-the-works MIPS CPUs. As Xfree86 has evolved, it has provided better and better support for more variations of hardware, and also provides high-end 3-D support. Although most windows managers, such as enlightenment, use the Xfree86 X-Windows System, it is KDE and GNOME that are the most used windows managers on today's Linux systems.

Obtaining video card information

When configuring a system to use Xfree86, you are often required to have detailed information about the video card and monitor. Although Xfree86 does an excellent job of detecting video cards, sometimes it will identify the class of the video card — S3 968, for example — but not the exact chipset, such as S3 968 with TI3026 chipset. Therefore, when installing the Xfree86 system, you should know the manufacturer and the model of the video card, the video card chipset, and the amount of memory that the video card contains. As Xfree86 evolves, this is becoming less of a requirement.

Monitors suffer many of the same detection errors, which is partly due to the fact that monitors are created by so many different manufacturers. Xfree86 allows you to manually input the information to get the best performance out of your monitor. You need the following information in order to correctly configure the monitor:

✦ The horizontal and vertical refresh rate in Hz

✦ The maximum color depth (only on old monitors)

✦ The maximum screen resolution

With this information in hand, it is time to configure the system. Figure 4-18 shows the menu in the Red Hat setup, and Figure 4-19 shows the Xfree86 menu.

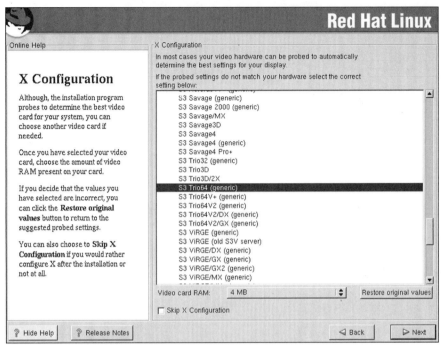

Figure 4-18: The Red Hat X configuration screen

Configuring the X windows system

To configure the X Windows system, you need to use the Xfree86 configuration utility. The screens in Figures 4-18 and 4-19 demonstrate the ability of Xfree86 to interface with other programs in order to provide hardware support for any windowing program or windows manager. Red Hat has placed a single menu that accesses the Xfree86 submenu for the Video Card menu shown in Figure 4-20.

The next Red Hat installation screen, shown in Figure 4-21, shows the manufacturers of the monitor. This is an extensive list, as Red Hat contains support for virtually every monitor that may be on a system. This corresponds to the Xfree86 menu for monitor selection.

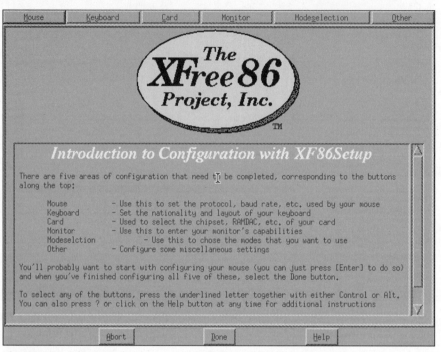

Figure 4-19: The introduction to configuration with XFree86 screen

The screen in Figure 4-21 enables you to select the depth of color and screen resolution. *Color depth* allows the system to display images as close to the true colors that a video card can provide. Selections usually include 16-bit, 24-bit, and 32-bit color. These are implementations of binary math that provide 4 bits for 16 colors, 8 bits for 256 colors, 16 bits for colors, 24 bits for 1,6777,216 colors, and 32 bits for 4,294,967,296 colors. By allowing the selection of color depth, the installation enables the user to select between color quality and screen resolution.

Screen resolution is the number of pixels used to fill the screen. By setting the screen resolution to 640 × 480, for example, means that the video card will use 640 pixels wide by 480 pixels high to fill the monitor. Therefore, if you select the setting of 1024 × 768, then the screen can contain more data but will be smaller in size than the screen resolution setting of 640 × 480. This is because the video card is now using 1024 — almost twice the number 640 — pixels wide and 768 pixels high to fill the screen. Selecting a higher screen resolution usually results in reduced color depth capabilities because the amount of memory on the video card provides the ability to select different color depths and screen resolutions. On this system, the screen resolution is set to 1024 × 768 and the color depth is at 16 bits or High Color, as shown in Figure 4-22.

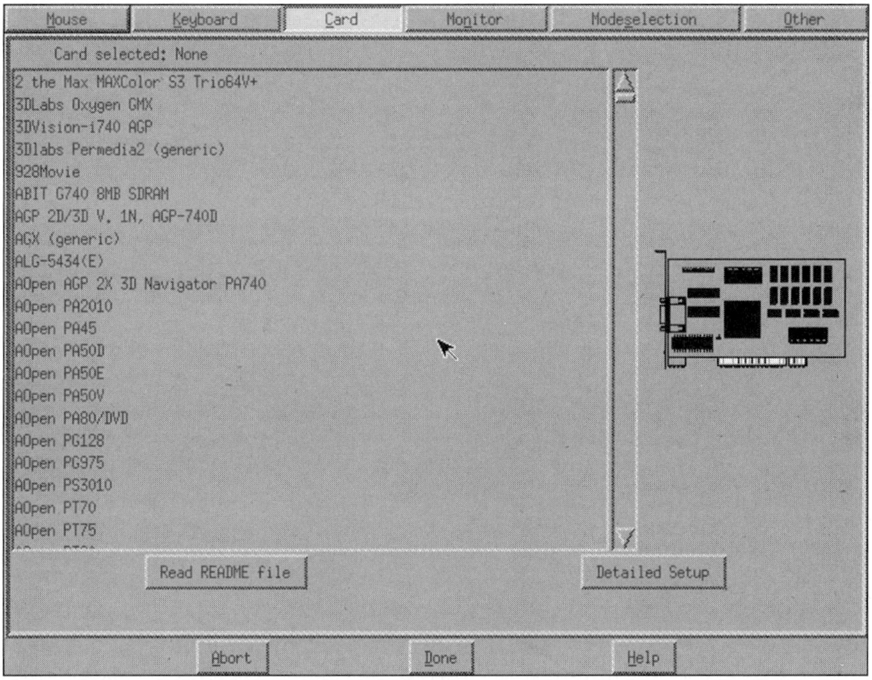

Figure 4-20: The Xfree86 video card selection screen

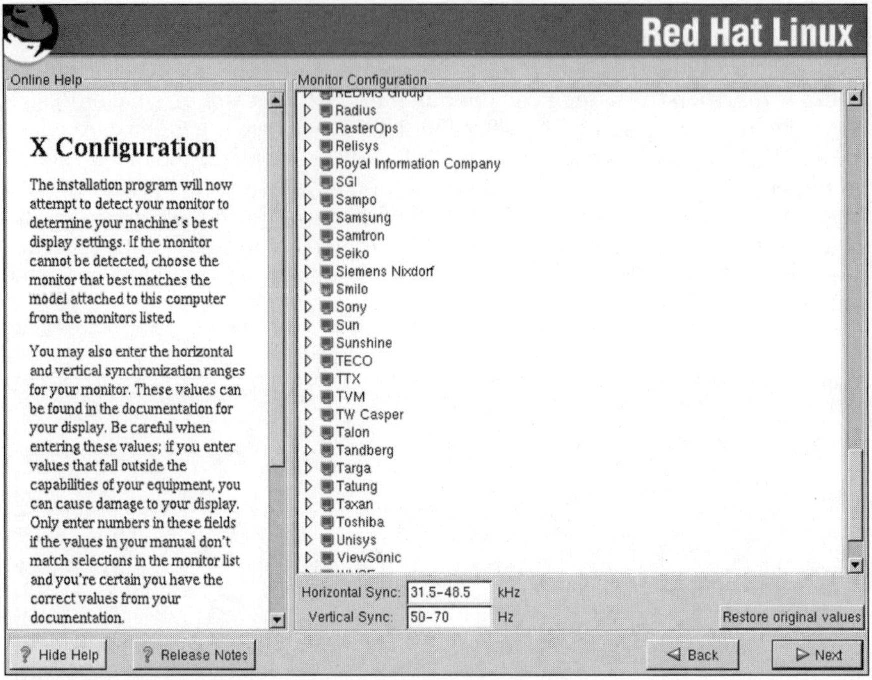

Figure 4-21: The Red Hat monitor configuration screen

Because the video card has only 4MB of memory, the color is limited to 16 bits at 1024 × 768, but if you select 800 × 600, you can use 24-bit color, as shown in Figure 4-23.

The XFree86 menus are a little different because this task is broken down into two steps:

1. **Select the resolution capabilities of the monitor.** Notice in Figure 4-24 that the installer doesn't choose by brand name or by monitor type, but strictly based on the resolution capabilities of the monitor. Continue to the monitor menu and select the resolution capabilities of the attached monitor.

2. **Select the color depth and screen resolution on which the X Windows System will be run.** You make this selection at the Modeselection screen. The selection settings on the screen will be limited by the abilities of the video card and the monitor. The screen resolutions are located in the center of the screen, and the color depth is located along the lower left part of the screen. Figure 4-25 shows the screen as it appears in the XFree86 setup program.

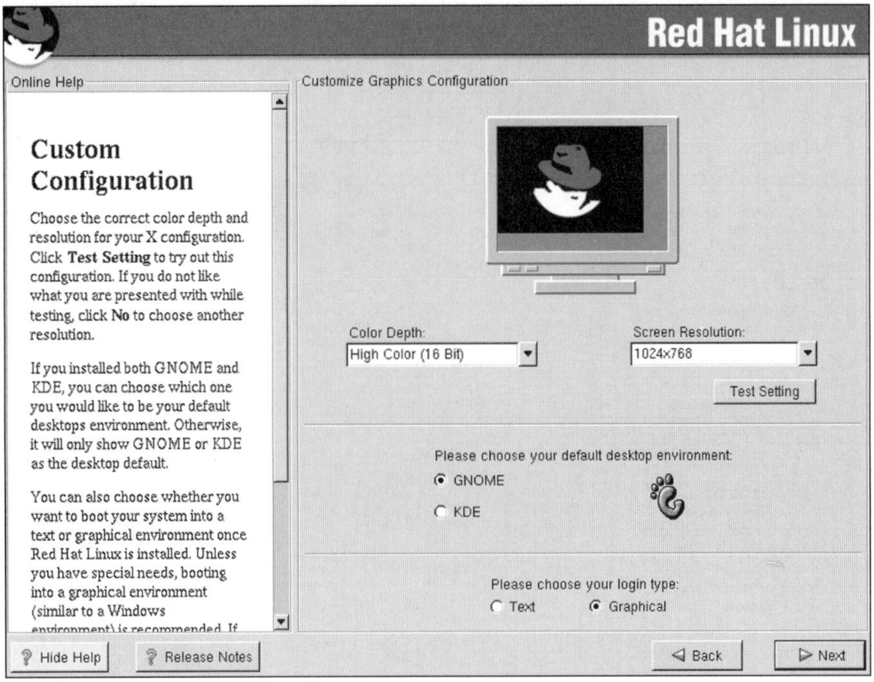

Figure 4-22: The Red Hat customized graphics configuration screen

Tip Notice also that the mouse doesn't move when the installer attempts to select the monitor. If this method of installing the X Windows System is selected, the mouse must be manually configured. On a modern system, the installer manually configures the mouse by tabbing to the mouse menu, pressing enter to select it, selecting the type of mouse attached to the system, and then selecting apply. This will instantly bring the mouse on-line and make it available for the rest of the installation.

Selecting the windows manager or desktop environment

After you have selected the color depth and screen resolution, you must now choose the windows manager, or desktop environment. The Red Hat distribution includes the GNU Network Object Model Environment — or GNOME — which is the default desktop environment for Red Hat, and K Desktop Environment — or KDE — as the choices for windows managers. Here is a brief comparison of the two:

✦ GNOME is more like the X Windows System, and KDE more resembles MAC OS or Microsoft Windows.

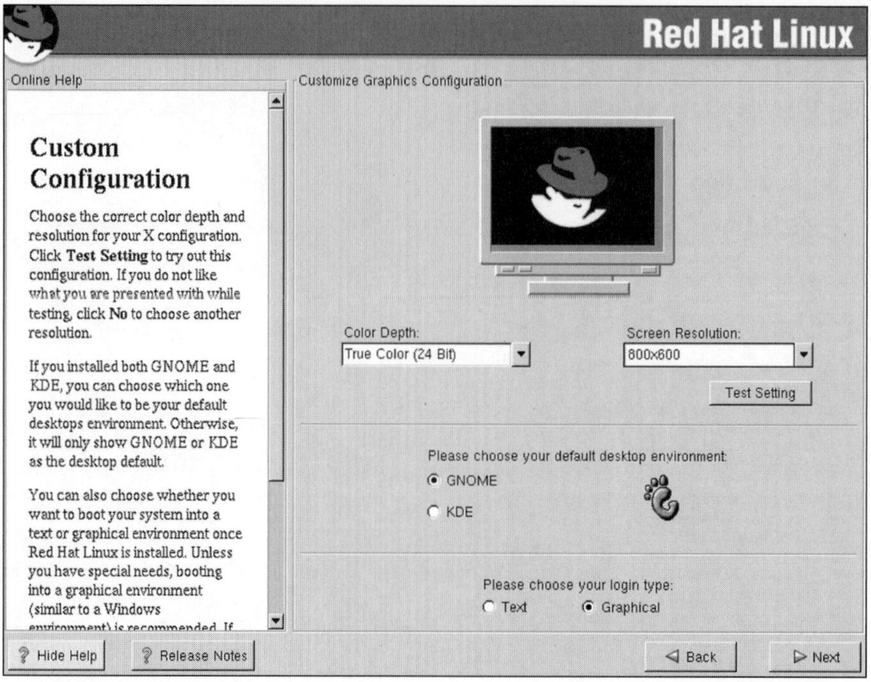

Figure 4-23: The Red Hat customized graphics configuration at 800 × 600 screen.

✦ The KDE environment provides the stability of UNIX, and therefore Linux, with a contemporary desktop environment similar to Mac OS or Microsoft Windows 95/98/NT/2000. GNOME is part of the GNU project and was created as a completely free desktop for the user, as well as a powerful application framework for the software developer.

When choosing your installation packages, the installer was able to select both the GNOME and KDE packages. If the installer selected both, then this selection just sets the active windows. The last choice of this set of screens is to either boot to a command line login or graphical login by starting the selected windows manager and then logging in through the desktop environment. After finalizing these settings, the system will test the selected color depth, screen resolution, and desktop environment with a screen similar to the one shown in Figure 4-26.

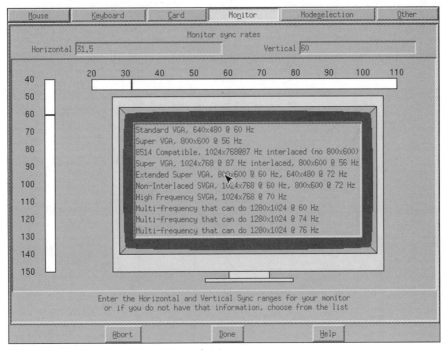

Figure 4-24: The Xfree86 monitor selection screen

Confirming the test is the last step before rebooting the system. This is the end of the installation of Red Hat Linux. Although other distributions don't follow this pattern step-by-step, they do use similar choices. After the system is rebooted, it is ready for use or further configuration.

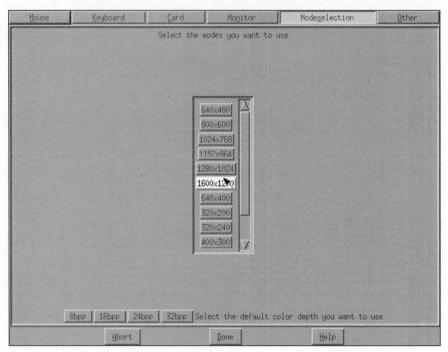

Figure 4-25: The Xfree86 mode selection screen

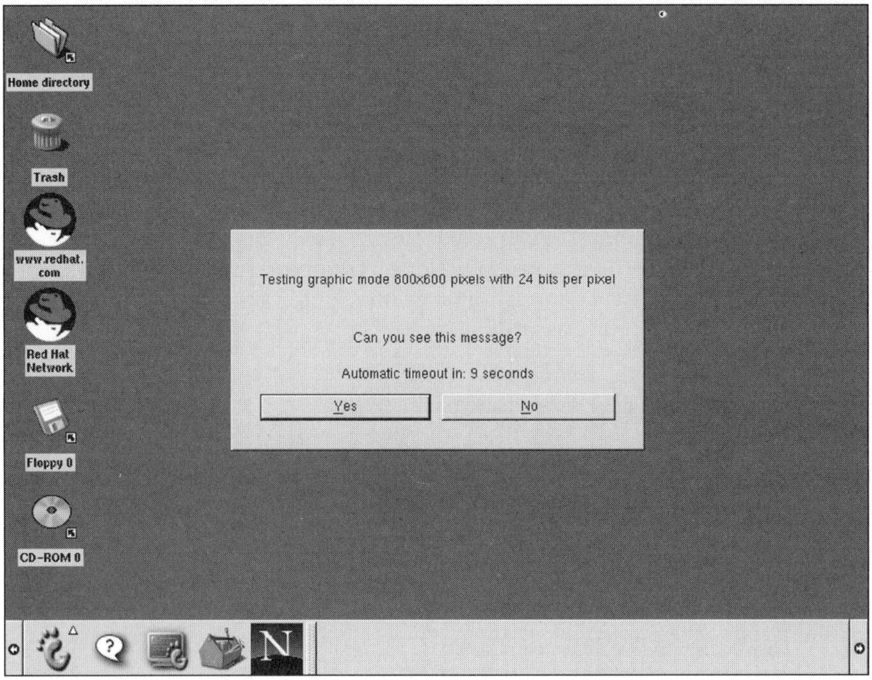

Figure 4-26: The Red Hat testing graphics mode at 800X600

Summary

This chapter details the installation of Linux. I show you the final preparations to make before actually installing Linux, along with several tables to help initialize the installation. I also walk you through the actual step-by-step installation of Linux, demonstrating the importance of knowing what hardware, services, and packages to install.

✦　　✦　　✦

STUDY GUIDE

The Study Guide section provides you with the opportunity to test your knowledge about the Linux+ exam objectives that are covered in this chapter. The Assessment Questions provide practice for the real exam, and the Scenarios provide practice with real situations. If you get any questions wrong, use the answers to determine the part of the chapter that you should review before continuing.

Assessment Questions

1. When installing Linux, what should you do before beginning the installation?

   A. Install the boot manager

   B. Obtain a detailed hardware list

   C. Partition the hard drive

   D. Configure the GUI interface

2. What information is stored in the /etc partition?

   A. Executable files

   B. Binaries to support executables

   C. System files

   D. System configuration files

3. Which of the following packages is used to provide file sharing?

   A. Samba

   B. Squid

   C. KRUD

   D. Apache

4. Which of the following is usually included on a server installation of Linux?

   A. Web browser

   B. Programming languages

   C. Database Server

   D. Application development tools

5. Which of the following methods is not used to install Red Hat Linux on many computers in an enterprise environment?

   A. Kickstart

   B. CD-ROM

   C. Floppy

   D. Internet

6. What is the default user interface for the installation for most Linux distributions?

   A. Text

   B. GUI

   C. NFS

   D. Terminal

7. Which of the following installation classes is normally used on a Laptop computer?

   A. Workstation

   B. Custom

   C. Server

   D. Laptop

8. What is almost always the first choice when installing Linux?

   A. Keyboard

   B. Mouse

   C. Language

   D. Time zone

9. Which Linux installation class provides the most complete or minimal installation?

   A. Server

   B. Custom

   C. Laptop

   D. Workstation

10. Which of the following is a journaling file system?

    A. ext2

    B. FAT16

    C. Linux extended

    D. Reiser

11. The fdisk MAN page recommends which tool to use for partitioning a hard drive?

    A. cfdisk

    B. fdisk

    C. Disk Druid

    D. partition

12. What feature makes the ReiserFS updateable?

    A. plug-in based objects

    B. balanced trees

    C. Inodes

    D. caching

13. What is the minimum recommended swap partition size on a system with 512 MB of RAM?

    A. 256 MB

    B. 1024 MB

    C. 512 MB

    D. 768 MB

14. On a system that already has Microsoft Windows NT 4.0 with an NTFS partition, where would you install LILO to allow for a dual bootable system?

    A. Master Boot Region

    B. Last sector of the boot partition

    C. First sector of the NTFS partition

    D. First sector of the boot partition

15. What does DHCP provide for a Linux system?

    A. Name resolution

    B. IP addressing

    C. FTP services

    D. Host name configuration

16. What must be assigned on the account configuration screen?

    A. Root password

    B. Account name

    C. User ID

    D. User name

17. What is the purpose of the MD5 option on passwords?

    A. compression

    B. Encrypted network logon

    C. Encryption

    D. Move passwords to a secure partition

18. What is Kerberos used for?

    A. Encrypt passwords

    B. Move passwords to a secure partition

    C. Secure directory services

    D. Encrypted network logon

19. What provides hardware support for desktops in Linux?

    A. KDE

    B. XFree86

    C. GNOME

    D. Enlightenment

20. Which of the following is the GNU windows manager?

    A. GNOME

    B. KDE

    C. Enlightenment

    D. X Windows System

Scenarios

1. The ABC Toy Company wants to set up a file server on the intranet so the toy designers can share the plans for the newest Walking and Talking Penguin doll. The development division has put the entire budget into this toy, but the toy development manager has an unknown server that can be used for this project. What should the system installer do to prepare for installation?

2. The Widget Corporation has decided that all 50,000 computers in the company should have Linux installed due to licensing issues with the current OS provider. All the systems in the company are identical — thanks to excellent planning by the IT department. This project needs to happen as fast as possible, but at all costs must be completed by the end of the month. The IT staff, however, does not have the manpower to perform installations at each machine independently. What are some of the solutions that a Linux distribution can provide to fulfill this need?

Lab Exercises

Lab 4-1 Linux Installation

The objective for this hands-on lab is to gain experience in installing Linux on a PC. You should be able to use any distribution of Linux for this installation exercise.

1. On an unused PC, or on a PC with no OS, prepare to install Linux. Carefully document the types of hardware present in the system. Verify that the Linux distribution of your choice will support the PC and all the hardware. Use a checklist to verify this information.

2. Plan the installation of Linux, including the role that it will be used for. Decide which additional packages to install, and the method of installation. Check the hardware support information needed, and consider the partitioning of the hard drive, including the use of a boot loader. Use a checklist to verify each step.

3. Perform the installation of Linux. Be sure to use the checklist from Step 2 to verify that all the steps of this installation are followed.

4. Install one additional package that is not included on the checklist and document the installation of the package.

5. After the installation is complete, reboot the system and be sure that it boots Linux.

Answers to Chapter Questions

Chapter Pre-test

1. You can perform the installation of Linux in many ways: From floppy disks, (not the most common method), from CD-ROM media (one of the most popular methods), or over a network connection. This provides connectivity to virtually any file server that can provide the installation files. You can also use automated installation methods, such as Kickstart, which allow the installation of Linux to proceed without user intervention.

2. The primary tools for partitioning a disk with or for Linux are fdisk, cfdisk, Disk Druid, or a similar product and commercial partitioning programs, such as Partition Magic.

3. Linux supports virtually every available partition; check with the individual Linux distribution that is being installed for the file systems that it supports. The most common Linux file systems are ReiserFS, ext2, and Linux swap.

4. Because a journaling file system keeps track of the entire process of writing a file to the disk, it is able to recover from unforeseen problems, such as power outages, much easier and with more reliability.

5. TCP/IP is the default networking protocol for all UNIX and UNIX-like operating systems.

6. By installing the minimum of services needed, you will not open up your system to various security holes that may be present in certain services. For example, installing the FTP or HTTP service even through you are not using it can make your system vulnerable to attacks on these services.

7. Most Linux installations offer the ability to add additional users; this is recommended because performing all tasks as the root user can be undesirable. It is usually preferred to login as a standard user then change into the root user for root user privileges.

8. The X Windows System and windows managers provide a GUI interface that many users find more comfortable. The use of a GUI uses processing power and therefore slows the system down. It may be recommended to use an X Windows System for a workstation and only command line on the database server.

9. A boot loader allows you to choose which operating system to launch when a system is started. An example of a Linux boot loader is LILO.

10. Additional software is installed in most Linux distributions with a menu-driven selection method.

Answers to Assessment Questions

1. B. The creation of a detailed hardware list may prove to be important for several sections of the installation. The boot manager, partition, and GUI are all performed during the installation. For review, see the "Final hardware verification" section.

2. D. The partition /etc contains the system configuration files for the Linux system. Executable files are contained in /bin, binaries to support executables are contained in /lib, and system files are contained in /usr. For review, see the "Pre-installation partitioning planning" section.

3. A. Samba is used to provide file sharing for Microsoft Windows systems. Squid is used to provide proxy services; and KRUD is a Linux distribution. For review, see the "Package selection" section.

4. C. Database Server is the only service that usually requires a server installation. The other services are usually installed on a workstation. For review, see the "Verification" section.

5. A. Red Hat Linux features Kickstart for mass installations. The others can be used but don't provide the best performance. For review, see the "Text or GUI installation" section.

6. B. Most Linux distributions now use a GUI interface for installation. Text installations are usually used for systems with limitations; terminal installations are used for systems without a video card; and NFS is an installation media access method. For review, see the "Text or GUI installation" section.

7. D. Usually a laptop installation is selected for a laptop. Although you can use a custom installation, it isn't the most likely choice; workstation and server installations won't provide for the special needs of a laptop. For review, see the "Selecting the machine type" section.

8. C. The first choice is almost always the language to use. The others are later in the installation. For review, see the "Basic setup of Linux" section.

9. B. The custom installation is the most configurable installation. The other installation classes have a default set of files that doesn't provide for a minimum or maximum installation. For review, see the "Selecting the machine type" section.

10. D. The Reiser is the only journaling file system. The others are not journaling file systems. For review, see the "Partitioning the hard disk drive" section.

11. A. The MAN page for `fdisk` recommends the use of `cfdisk`. The others are not recommended in the MAN pages. For review, see the "Partitioning the hard disk drive" section.

12. A. The ability of the ReiserFS to be updated with plug-ins is a major benefit of this journaling file system. Inodes are used to hold data structure information about files; balanced trees are used to provide fast journaling; and finally, caching is used in the journaling system. For review, see the "Partitioning the hard disk drive" section.

13. C. The minimum recommended swap size is equal to the amount of memory in the system. The other does not meet this standard. For review, see the "Partitioning the hard disk drive" section.

14. D. The first sector of the boot partition is used in this situation because LILO is not compatible with NTFS. Selecting the Master Boot Region would render Microsoft Windows unbootable; the others are not valid selections. For review, see the "Partitioning the hard disk drive" section.

15. B DHCP stands for *dynamic host configuration protocol*, and is used to provide IP addressing, including the subnet mask, default gateway, and DNS server addresses. For review, see the "Networking" section.

16. A. The only requirement is for a root password, the others are available but not required. For review, see the "Accounts and passwords" section.

17. C. MD5 is an encryption method that uses a 128-bit fingerprint for identification. Compression is used with Gzip; passwords are moved with Shadow utilities to /etc/shadow; and network logon is not a use of MD5. For review, see the "Accounts and passwords" section.

18. D. Kerberos is used for secure network logon. For review, see the "Accounts and passwords" section.

19. B. Xfree86 provides the support between the hardware and graphical user interface. All the others are windows managers. For review, see the "GUI installation" section.

20. A. GNOME is the GNU windows manager. For review, see the "Selecting the windows manager or desktop environment" section.

Scenarios

1. The installer should inventory the system to make sure that it is capable of supporting the duties of a file server. It should be checked for appropriate processing capabilities, storage, memory, and networking. The server and all the hardware in it should be verified as compatible with the Linux distribution selected. The installation should be planned, including the class installation, partitioning of the hard drive, and all networking settings. Any other packages or preferences should also be determined. All this information should be documented.

2. Linux has many tools that can be used to create an automatic installation of Linux; this includes Red Hat's Kickstart, NFS installations, and many more preconfigured installation methods.

Advanced Installation

- ✦ 2.1 Determine appropriate method of installation based on the environment (e.g., boot disk, CD-ROM, Network (HTTP, FTP, NFS, SMB))

- ✦ 2.2 Describe the different types of Linux installation interaction and determine which to use for a given situation (e.g., GUI, text, network)

- ✦ 2.5 Select appropriate options for partitions based on pre-installation choices (e.g., FDISK, third party partitioning software)

- ✦ 2.6 Partition according to your pre-installation plan using fdisk (e.g., /boot, / , /usr, /var/home, SWAP)

- ✦ 2.7 Configure file systems (e.g., (ext2) or (ext3) or REISER)

- ✦ 2.8 Select appropriate networking configuration and protocols (e.g., modems, Ethernet, Token-Ring)

- ✦ 2.15 Explain when and why the kernel will need to be recompiled

- ✦ 2.16 Install boot loader (e.g., LILO, MBR vs. first sector of boot partition

- ✦ 2.17 Install and uninstall applications after installing the operating system (e.g., RPM, tar, gzip)

- ✦ 2.18 Read the Logfiles created during installation to verify the success of the installation

- ✦ 2.19 Validate that an installed application is performing correctly in both a test and a production environment

CHAPTER PRE-TEST

1. What are the types of text-based installations?

2. What tool is included with most distributions of Linux to partition a hard drive?

3. Do all distributions support the Reiser File System (ReiserFS)?

4. Why is a text installation preferred over a GUI installation?

5. What systems can be dual-booted with Linux?

6. What are the major differences between the GUI and a text- or shell-based installation?

7. Can the Linux kernel be updated after installation?

8. What are the reasons for updating the Linux kernel?

9. Where can a user verify the installation of services?

10. What should be done to test and document the installation of Linux?

✦ Answers to these questions can be found at the end of the chapter. ✦

The ability to install the Linux operating system in various environments is a valuable skill. This chapter illustrates the text-based — perhaps more appropriately termed *shell-based* — installation of Linux. In many installation situations, the installation and configuration of graphical X-windows is not needed, and the operating system can be installed in a simple text mode. This may also be necessary in the event that your video card is not supported in the X-windows environment. After I have demonstrated how to perform a GUI and text-based installation, you will be able to perform virtually any required installation.

The installations that you will be called on to perform may include connecting to a network server to install Linux. You can connect to network servers of all types in order to install Linux. You can use this ability to install Linux over an LAN, intranet, or the Internet to roll out many workstations at once or to supply a remote user with the same interface that the local users have.

After the installation of Linux is complete, it's time to focus on the use of the tools that come with Linux or that may be added to the installation. Both the installation of Linux and its tools should be tested in the lab and user environment to verify that they are installed correctly. Log files can also be used to verify the accuracy of the installation of Linux and some of its applications.

Finally, documentation of all the settings that are used to install Linux should be filed for future reference. These files should consist of valuable data that may include items such as any preparatory documentation, installation information, any errors or difficulties that were encountered, and packages that were installed or added. This is not only helpful for future reference but sets a pattern for other work, such as upgrades or repairs, to also be documented. These installation techniques provide a skill set that will be very well respected.

Alternative to the GUI Installation

Objective

2.2 Describe the different types of Linux installation interaction and determine which to use for a given situation (e.g., GUI, text, network)

The GUI installation is the preferred method for most distributions of Linux. This preference is driven by the popularity of the GUI installation among other operating systems. Although GUI installations can be much simpler to use, they are not always the best method, however. A Linux system that is intended to be a firewall or router needs all the system resources that can be provided, so it may be beneficial to install a minimal video card or no video card at all. And even though this may free up some system resources, it does prevent the installation of Linux in a GUI environment. This is a benefit of installing Linux in text mode — it uses fewer system resources to provide the interface.

In the Real World

A Linux distribution will usually indicate the minimum recommended system requirements for the GUI installation, and you can use this to determine if the system requires a text-based installation.

If the system does not have enough processor power or memory, the GUI interface will provide a message (usually early in the GUI installation) stating that the system is low on resources and suggesting that perhaps a text-based installation is a better option. By selecting a text-based installation, you will experience many differences from the GUI installation. The major differences are usually the customized menus and specialized tools that don't work in a command-line or shell environment.

Command Line installation

Objective

2.5 Select appropriate options for partitions based on pre-installation choices (e.g., FDISK, third party partitioning software)

2.6 Partition according to your pre-installation plan using fdisk (e.g., /boot, / , /usr, /var/home, SWAP)

2.7 Configure file systems (e.g., (ext2) or (ext3) or REISER)

By selecting a text-based installation, you are given one of two alternatives. The command line is one of these alternatives. The bootable diskette or CD-ROM may initiate a minimal kernel to allow the use of a command line interface, as shown in Figure 5-1.

```
Welcome to the Slackware Linux bootable installation CD! (version 7.0.0)

######  IMPORTANT!  READ THE INFORMATION BELOW CAREFULLY.  ######

- You will need one or more partitions of type 'Linux native' prepared.  It is
  also recommended that you create a swap partition (type 'Linux swap') prior
  to installation.  For more information, run 'setup' and read the help file.

- If you're having problems that you think might be related to low memory (this
  is possible on machines with 8 or less megabytes of system memory), you can
  try activating a swap partition before you run setup.  After making a swap
  partition (type 82) with cfdisk or fdisk, activate it like this:
     mkswap /dev/<partition> ; swapon /dev/<partition>

- Once you have prepared the disk partitions for Linux, type 'setup' to begin
  the installation process.

- If you do not have a color monitor, type:   TERM=vt100
  before you start 'setup'.

You may now login as 'root'.

slackware login:
```

Figure 5-1: The command line interface

This command line interface usually requires the login of root with no password. After this is completed, the steps required to prepare the system are very similar to the GUI interface; the order, however, may be different. The instructions given in the command line interface are to partition the hard drive and possibly activate a swap partition. To perform these tasks, you should use cfdisk or fdisk for disk partitioning. The command mkswap /dev/<partition>, and then swapon /dev/<partition> can be used to create the swap partition. To proceed, type cfdisk at the command prompt and use cfdisk to partition the hard disk drive. The interface of cfdisk is shown in Figure 5-2.

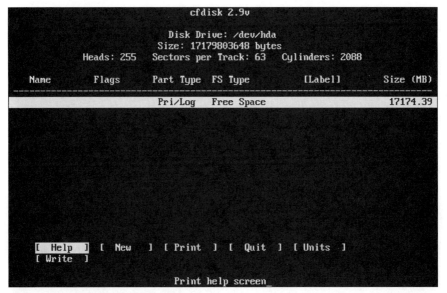

Figure 5-2: The partitioning tool cfdisk

This interface provides tools for HELP, NEW (partition creation), PRINT (the partition table), QUIT (the program), UNITS (unit of hard drive space in MB or sectors), and WRITE (commit partitions to disk), which will allow the creation of the partition(s) needed for the installation of Linux. Select NEW from the menu to create the first partition; this allows the input of the size of the partition. The menu then displays, as shown in Figure 5-3.

Select TYPE to select the partition type from the menus shown in Figures 5-4 and 5-5.

These are the menus of the possible partitions that can be supported by cfdisk. Notice that the ReiserFS is not supported here — remember that not all Linux distributions support the ReiserFS yet. The creation of partitions continues until all of the requirements of the pre-installation partition plan have been fulfilled. Be sure to create at least one bootable partition — otherwise, the system may be installed but unable to boot. The partitions are then committed to the hard drive with the write command. Be sure to verify that these partitions are correct because after they have been committed to the hard drive, it will be changed and any data will be lost, as shown in Figure 5-6.

```
01 FAT12                    40 Venix 80286           86 NTFS volume set
02 XENIX root               41 PPC PReP Boot          87 NTFS volume set
03 XENIX usr                42 SFS                    93 Amoeba
01 FAT16 <32M               4D QNX4.x                 94 Amoeba BBT
05 Extended                 4E QNX4.x 2nd part        A0 IBM Thinkpad hiberna
06 FAT16                    4F QNX4.x 3rd part        A5 BSD/386
07 HPFS/NTFS                50 OnTrack DM             A6 OpenBSD
08 AIX                      51 OnTrack DM6 Aux1       A7 NeXTSTEP
09 AIX bootable             52 CP/M                   B7 BSDI fs
0A OS/2 Boot Manager        53 OnTrack DM6 Aux3       B8 BSDI swap
0B Win95 FAT32              54 OnTrackDM6             C1 DRDOS/sec (FAT-12)
0C Win95 FAT32 (LBA)        55 EZ-Drive               C4 DRDOS/sec (FAT-16 <
0E Win95 FAT16 (LBA)        56 Golden Bow             C6 DRDOS/sec (FAT-16)
0F Win95 Ext'd (LBA)        5C Priam Edisk            C7 Syrinx
10 OPUS                     61 SpeedStor              DB CP/M / CTOS / ...
11 Hidden FAT12             63 GNU HURD or SysV       E1 DOS access
12 Compaq diagnostics       64 Novell Netware 286     E3 DOS R/O
14 Hidden FAT16 <32M        65 Novell Netware 386     E4 SpeedStor
16 Hidden FAT16             70 DiskSecure Multi-Boo   EB BeOS fs




                    Press a key to continue_
```

Figure 5-3: The partition submenu of `cfdisk`

```
17 Hidden HPFS/NTFS         75 PC/IX                 F1 SpeedStor
18 AST Windows swapfile     80 Old Minix             F4 SpeedStor
1B Hidden Win95 FAT32       81 Minix / old Linux      F2 DOS secondary
1C Hidden Win95 FAT32 (     82 Linux swap            FD Linux raid autodetec
1E Hidden Win95 FAT16 (     83 Linux native          FE LANstep
24 NEC DOS                  84 OS/2 hidden C: drive   FF BBT
3C PartitionMagic recov     85 Linux extended









    Enter filesystem type: 82
```

Figure 5-4: Choosing the partition type in `cfdisk`

```
                            cfdisk 2.9v

                      Disk Drive: /dev/hda
                      Size: 17179803648 bytes
            Heads: 255   Sectors per Track: 63   Cylinders: 2088

     Name          Flags      Part Type  FS Type      [Label]        Size (MB)
    ------------------------------------------------------------------------
     hda1          Boot       Primary    Linux                          501.75
     hda2                     Primary    Linux swap                     254.99
     hda3                     Primary    Linux                         8003.20
                              Pri/Log    Free Space                    8414.47




         [Bootable]  [ Delete ]  [  Help  ]  [Maximize]  [ Print  ]
         [  Quit  ]  [  Type   ]  [ Units  ]  [ Write  ]

              Change the filesystem type (DOS, Linux, OS/2 and so on)
```

Figure 5-5: The partition submenu of cfdisk

```
                            cfdisk 2.9v

                      Disk Drive: /dev/hda
                      Size: 17179803648 bytes
            Heads: 255   Sectors per Track: 63   Cylinders: 2088

     Name          Flags      Part Type  FS Type      [Label]        Size (MB)
    ------------------------------------------------------------------------
     hda1          Boot       Primary    Linux                          501.75
     hda2                     Primary    Linux swap                     254.99
     hda3                     Primary    Linux                         8003.20
     hda4                     Primary    Linux                         8414.47




     Are you sure you want write the partition table to disk? (yes or no): yes

                      Writing partition table to disk...
```

Figure 5-6: The partitions are committed to the hard drive.

This completes the partitioning of the hard drive and has readied the system for installation of Linux.

Install the Linux system

2.1 Determine appropriate method of installation based on the environment (e.g., boot disk, CD-ROM, Network (HTTP, FTP, NFS, SMB))

2.6 Partition according to your pre-installation plan using fdisk (e.g., /boot, / , /usr, /var/home, SWAP)

2.7 Configure file systems (e.g., (ext2) or (ext3) or REISER)

After the hard drive has been partitioned, the main setup program is started. This initiates a shell program — the second type of text-based installation — which will be used to continue the installation of the Linux kernel and any additional packages. The menu is a text-based installation, but it is using a shell program to display the information in a more organized manner, as shown in Figure 5-7.

```
┌─────────── Slackware Linux Setup (version 7.0.0) ───────────┐
│ Welcome to Slackware Linux Setup.                            │
│ Select an option below using the UP/DOWN keys and SPACE or ENTER. │
│ Alternate keys may also be used: '+', '-', and TAB.         │
│  ┌──────────────────────────────────────────────────────┐  │
│  │ HELP       Read the Slackware Setup HELP file         │  │
│  │ KEYMAP     Remap your keyboard if you're not using a US one │
│  │ ADDSWAP    Set up your swap partition(s)              │  │
│  │ TARGET     Set up your target partitions             │  │
│  │ SOURCE     Select source media                        │  │
│  │ SELECT     Select catagories of software to install  │  │
│  │ INSTALL    Install selected software                  │  │
│  │ CONFIGURE  Reconfigure your Linux system              │  │
│  │ EXIT       Exit Slackware Linux Setup                │  │
│  └──────────────────────────────────────────────────────┘  │
│                                                             │
│           <  OK  >          <Cancel>                        │
└─────────────────────────────────────────────────────────────┘
```

Figure 5-7: The Slackware Linux Setup Shell

This shell has many options — the first of which supplies the Help files for the installation. You can use these help files to answer any unresolved questions before continuing the installation. The next option allows for the customization of the keyboard, depending on the country and language you wish to set it for.

More disk configurations

The addswap command will activate the swap partition for the rest of the installation. You can also use mkswap /dev/<partition> and then swapon /dev/<partition> at the command prompt before entering setup to activate the swap partition; this is the method that I recommend. After the swap partition has been activated, you can configure the partitions that were created with the cfdisk command. Use the TARGET menu command to set up the target partitions, which create the file system necessary for this installation. The menu then displays a list of the partitions that you previously created — not including the swap partition — and allows you to select a partition. Selecting a partition prompts a menu, as illustrated in Figure 5-8, which shows that the first partition selected is the /, or root partition.

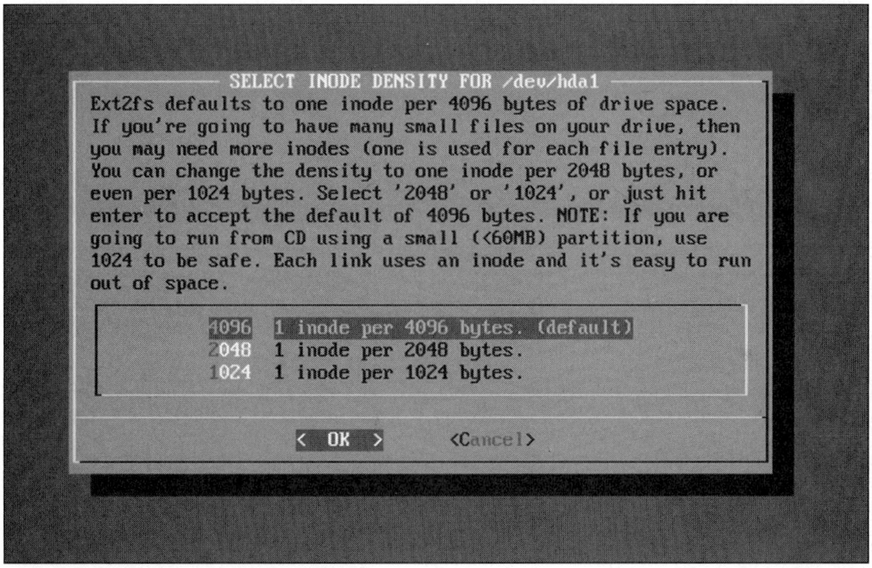

Figure 5-8: Selecting Inode Density

This installation section allows you to select the size of disk Inodes, which is a data structure that holds information about files in a Unix file system. The menu provides a useful help function to let you know why certain selections would be made. Basically, the smaller the files you want to install on the system, the smaller the Inode should be. For example, suppose that you have a database server of names and addresses. These files are very small, so if you select the smaller Inode size of 1024, while wasting a small amount, you save 3072 bytes per file saved. After you have selected the Inode, the partition is formatted and the partition selection menu returns, showing that the partition is now in use. Continue selecting partitions and creating the file systems according to your pre-installation plan.

Select the source and packages

At this point, the partitioning is complete, and your next step is to select the installation media. You have plenty of options to choose from, as shown if Figure 5-9.

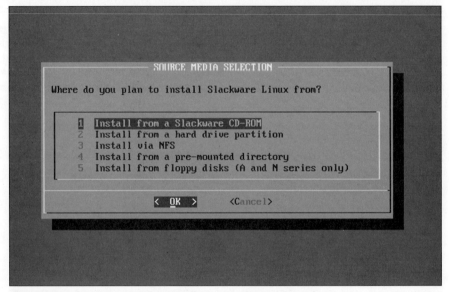

Figure 5-9: The Source of the Installation Media is selected

The installation media can consist of a CD-ROM, HDD, NFS, a pre-mounted directory, or even a floppy (although this is not the fastest method).

In the Real World Using a NFS, or any other network installation of Linux, poses a security risk. Although most network installations proceed safely, the system is susceptible to attack during installation because most security measures of the system are not in place. For example, the system may be altered or reconfigured before it is complete. To prevent possible problems, isolate any installation from the network.

Select the CD-ROM method of installation, and the package selection screen appears. Here, you can make selections of large groups of packages, including the most common packages that come with Linux. Select the options that fulfill the needs of the machine and meet the pre-installation plan. The large groups of packages don't always contain the specific packages that you want. The next screen allows you to select among the other packages in one of several ways, as shown in Figure 5-10.

Cross-Reference See the network installation section for more on NFS installations.

```
┌──────────────── SELECT PROMPTING MODE ────────────────┐
  Now you must select the type of prompts you'd like to see during
  the installation process. If you have the drive space, the 'full'
  option is quick, easy, and by far the most foolproof choice. The
  'newbie' mode provides the most information but is much more
  time-consuming (presenting the packages one by one) than the
  menu-based choices. Otherwise, you can pick packages from menus
  using 'expert' or 'menu' mode. Which type of prompting would you
  like to use?

     ┌──────────────────────────────────────────────────┐
       full     Install everything (up to 996 MB of software)
       newbie   Use verbose prompting (and follow tagfiles)
       menu     Choose groups of packages from interactive menus
       expert   Choose individual packages from interactive menus
       custom   Use custom tagfiles in the package directories
       tagpath  Use tagfiles in the subdirectories of a custom path
       help     Read the prompt mode help file
     └──────────────────────────────────────────────────┘

            <  OK  >          <Cancel>
```

Figure 5-10: Selecting Optional Packages

You actually have the ability to select every package in the distributions, but this option is seldom used in working environments because it uses a lot of space and does not provide the security that is desired in most environments. Needlessly installing services and applications can open up your system to network activity that may compromise your system, such as FTP or HTTP. The menu grouping selects the packages in a pre-bundled way, as deemed best by the distribution. The expert mode is intended only for advanced installers who can select not only the packages, but also the dependencies for the packages selected. For example, one package often requires another package to be installed in order for it to function correctly. In most expert modes, the system requires that the installer ensure that all dependent services and files are installed in order to install the package and enable it to function properly. Finally, you also have the ability to call a file that has a pre-determined configuration. You can use this ability, for example, to retrieve a configuration of the desired packages from a diskette or other media. In fact, this is an excellent way to install the same packages on several workstations in a large environment, such as a government or corporate office. A Help menu item can provide some assistance in using the package selection menu. After you select any of these options, the installation of the individual packages will proceed. Some choices require interaction from the installer, while others simply start installing all the files to the hard drive.

Finalize the installation

Objective   2.16 Install boot loader (e.g., LILO, MBR vs. first sector of boot partition.)

After the installation has completed, the system asks to be configured. If the system isn't configured, it may not boot; this is not true of all distributions, but most distributions will compile the kernel so that it is actively able to boot the system. Then the shell script proceeds by creating a bootable diskette, which is advisable because you can use this diskette to boot the system in case of emergencies, such as boot failures, system crashes, and even to repair a damaged system. After the boot diskette has been created, the system then configures a modem or other device to be used for remote login or dial-in or dial-out. This is a potentially complicated task, because you must know the port that the modem or other device is using, such as COM1 or COM2. Finally, you may be presented with some other customization choices, such as font selection, but the next major menu is the installation of LILO, or LInux LOader, which prompts you to install the bootstrap.

Exam Tip The character sequence of "LILO" informs you of the success or failure of the boot process. The first "L" indicates that the primary boot loader has been started. "I" appears as soon as the secondary boot loader has been loaded. The second "L" appears when the secondary boot loader signals that it has been loaded. If any problems have occurred, a two-digit hex error code appears, which is documented in LILO's manual. If no problems occur, the "O" displays along with the boot prompt.

The next configuration is for the LILO text console, which displays the messages that were created during the boot process. Your next selection is to choose the location for the LILO installation. Select this location according to your pre-installation plan. After LILO is installed, your next step is to manually configure the network, which usually requires the predetermined network configuration, including a static IP address or the use of DHCP (Dynamic Host Configuration Protocol).

Cross-Reference See Chapter 4 for more information about configuring networking.

After networking has been completed, you are prompted to complete the configuration of the mouse, the time zone, and the X Window System. After you have completed these tasks, the system is ready to be rebooted.

Network installations of Linux

Objective 2.2 Describe the different types of Linux installation interaction and determine which to use for a given situation (e.g., GUI, text, network)

2.8 Select appropriate networking configuration and protocols (e.g., modems, Ethernet, Token-Ring)

If you have a closed network environment, a LAN with no outside connection, or a LAN with an extremely secure firewall, you may want to choose to allow the network to install Linux for you. If you do choose the installation of Linux by NFS (Network File System) or another network method, you are required to use a supported network interface card (NIC). Therefore, when starting an installation via NFS or other network method, remember to perform the following tasks:

✦ **Verify that the network card is supported.**

✦ **Select the driver that supports your network card.** In most cases, you are offered the opportunity to supply additional parameters to assist the Linux kernel in communicating with your card.

✦ **Configure the networking protocol to access the server.** In most cases, the networking protocol is TCP/IP and NFS. For a TCP/IP installation via NFS, the required parameters will most likely be those listed in Table 5-1.

Table 5-1
Configuration for Network Installation

Configuration Needed	Configuration Data (examples)	Reason for Information
IP Address	192.168.0.100	IP address for stations to access the network
Netmask *	255.255.255.0	Used to determine the size of the network
Network Address	192.168.0.0	Used to determine the network address
Broadcast Address	192.168.0.255	Where broadcasts are made
NFS Server Name	Linux_nfs	What server to request files from
File Directory	/mnt/cdrom	Where the server keeps the files necessary for installation
Domain Name	Fully Qualified Domain Name (FQDN)	The name of the network in use
Host Name	Linux_workstation	The rest of the FQDN for the workstation
Gateway	192.168.0.1	Not used, unless the server is not on the local network
Name Server	192.168.0.250	Where to convert the NFS Server Name to IP address

* Often called *sub-netmask*

Most often, information from this table is all that you will need. After this has been put into the Linux installation program, it connects to the NFS server (or another server being used) and begins the installation of the files. This installation method is often started with a diskette and can therefore be run on several machines at once. After the network configuration is complete, differences are essentially indistinguishable between a network installation and a CD-ROM-based installation. The network installation does have a few drawbacks — consisting mostly of security issues and NIC driver availability — but is an excellent way to install Linux on many machines simultaneously at one or many locations.

Review of a Linux Installation

I have covered the steps for both GUI and text-based Linux installations. You must complete some general tasks during both of these installations, the first of which is to prepare for the installation. This preparation includes the following tasks: Make a list, and determine which resources you need, which packages you need to supply the software, and which system configuration that you want to use during installation.

Cross-Reference   See Chapter 4 for more information on preparing to install Linux.

After the preparation is complete, the installation can begin — but first, you must complete a series of general tasks.

Installation media

First, you must select the source of the installation files, which include CD-ROM, local hard drive, diskette, or Network Server — and is determined for each individual installation. The CD-ROM version is used for most Linux distributions because the Linux system does not have to be connected to the network, which provides an added layer of security. Network installations require an NIC that is supported by Linux, a network connection, and server resources to supply the installation files.

Initial selections

Second, you select the customization of the language, keyboard, and mouse — decisions that affect the rest of the installation.

Installation type or class

Third, select the type of installation class. In some environments, a workstation, server, or laptop installation will work, but usually the custom installation class is the best option because it will allow only the required services to be installed. This choice creates not only a customized system, but also a system that is often more secure than any of the other installation classes.

Disk partitioning and formatting

Fourth, configure the hard drive for use by Linux. This is a complicated step because even though many tools are available to aid you in this task, you will only truly benefit from pre-planning and experience. The common tool used in this step is fdisk, which is included in almost every major distribution. Other tools include

Disk Druid, and third party tools, such as Partition Magic, which can be used to create the partitions required for Linux. After you have selected one of these tools, you have basically two more selections to make — the file systems to use and the partitions to create. The most popular file system may be ext2, but the ReiserFS is gaining ground due to its journaling capabilities because of this reason, this is the file system that I recommend. The creation of partitions (or slices for UNIX/BSD users) is truly according to the preferences of the installer because only one partition is required. Although configuring a disk is a challenging task, the tools are getting much better and can sometimes perform most tasks automatically.

Installing LILO

Fifth, the installation of a boot loader is usually necessary for most systems. LILO is a standard boot loader for Linux (although you may encounter security issues); GRUB is the GNU project counterpart. Boot loaders not only boot the system, but they also allow the system to possibly boot other operating systems. LILO can also be installed to only a diskette and thus render a system non-bootable unless the diskette is present. This possibility can provide local security for the system because without the diskette — which can be locked in a safe or stored off-site — the system won't boot.

Network configuration

Sixth, configure Linux networking. During installation, the system is usually configured for some basic networking, which can include modem use or access, terminal connections, LAN or WAN connections, and many others. Broadband connections and devices are also becoming basic networking options.

User accounts

Seventh, create user accounts with passwords that conform to good password practices. That is, create a password with a minimum of eight characters and also use a mixture of alpha, numeric, and special characters. This rule holds especially true for the root user account because this is the most privileged account on the system.

Authentication methods

Eighth, create authentication methods that protect the passwords; good security practice suggests enabling both MD5 and shadow passwords. MD5 enables encrypted passwords to be used, and shadow passwords prevent all users from reading the encrypted passwords (in other words, the shadow password file is only readable by the root user).

Package selection and installation

Finally, select only those packages that are required for the machine to provide the desired service. By limiting the number of installed packages, the number of potential security vulnerabilities will also be limited. Therefore, when installing a workstation, don't install everything because doing so opens the systems to the security risk of a Web server — even if the workstation is not using the software to provide Web pages.

A Dual-Boot Installation of Linux

Linux can accomplish most tasks quite easily, but some software programs will only run on a different operating system. In these situations, you may want to create a system that will be able to use two operating systems. This is called a *dual-boot system,* which Linux supports very well. You will probably encounter some issues when creating a dual-boot system, but planning can resolve these issues. The most important rule to follow when creating a dual-boot system is to use a method that doesn't destroy the data already existing on the HDD. The best way to accomplish this is to create an installation path. Some systems work extremely well with Linux, but others are not so Linux-friendly. The ability to establish a dual-boot system is a growing need and a skill that any installer should consider learning.

Linux with Microsoft Windows

Linux can be installed with most Microsoft products fairly easily, which is due to the ability of Linux to use the FAT16 and FAT32 partition types.

Caution   Linux does not support FAT32 before the 2.0.34 kernel release. If you are using an older version of Linux, verify that the kernel is at least at this level if you want FAT32 support. This level of support allows operating systems to share files.

These types of partitions are used for Microsoft Windows 9x, ME, DOS, and Windows 3.1, and allow LILO to be installed with options to boot both Linux and these Microsoft products. The task of creating a dual-boot system on a PC with Microsoft Windows 9X already installed is fairly straightforward:

1. Begin installing Linux on a Microsoft Windows 9X system.

2. When prompted, place LILO in the MBR or in the Linux root partition's boot sector.

3. If LILO is installed in the MBR, it will read the existing operating system partition(s) and create a DOS or Windows menu item.

4. If it is installed on the root partition of Linux, the root partition of Linux must be set as the active partition to boot from.

Tip Before attempting to create any dual-boot system (or before installing or using another operating system, partitioning software, or boot manager), be sure to back up all data on the existing operating system. If the configuration fails or is done improperly, the existing operating system may be rendered useless and all data may be lost.

The LILO menu item allows the previously installed version of Microsoft Windows to be selected when booting the system. Sometimes, however, this fails to work, so the root user in Linux — the file /etc/lilo.conf — must be edited. The file looks something like this:

```
boot=/dev/hda
map=/boot/map
install=/boot/boot.b
prompt
timeout=50
message=/boot/message
linear
default=linux

image=/boot/vmlinuz-2.4.2-2
     label=linux
     read-only
     root=/dev/hda7
```

You will need to add lines to the file to enable the ability to boot a separate Windows partition. Before adding these in, you will need to ascertain which hard drive and partition contains Windows. Table 5-2 outlines the way that Linux identifies the various hard drive types.

Table 5-2 Linux HDD Identification	
Disk Locations	**Linux Disk Identification**
Primary IDE controller-drive 0 or Master	/dev/hda or hda
Primary IDE controller-drive 1 or Slave	/dev/hdb or hdb
Secondary IDE controller-drive 0 or Master	/dev/hdc or hdc
Secondary IDE controller-drive 1 or Slave	/dev/hdd or hdd
SCSI Controller-SCSI ID 0	/dev/sda or sda
SCSI Controller-SCSI ID 1	/dev/sdb or sdb
SCSI Controller-SCSI ID 2	/dev/sdc or sdc

This hard drive identification table is an excellent place to start when you are attempting to determine hard drive naming in Linux. This table is only a basic one, however, because it only takes into account single IDE or SCSI controllers. The partitions contained on the disk are numbered 1-X, where X is the total number of partitions. Therefore, in the preceding example of the /etc/lilo.conf, the hard drive is /dev/hda or the master Primary IDE controller. Microsoft Windows 9X is installed on the first partition of this drive, or hda1. To add Microsoft Windows to the LILO menu, simply add the following lines:

```
other=/dev/hda1
label=windows
```

You can boot Microsoft Windows from LILO by typing **windows** at the LILO boot prompt. This method also works if Microsoft Windows 9X has been added to a Linux PC. You may have to reinstall LILO to be able to boot the system, but this is a situation that you are prepared for if you created the bootable diskette during the installation of Linux. From this diskette, you are capable of restoring LILO if it was damaged during the installation of Microsoft Windows.

Linux with Microsoft Windows NT and 2000

Dual booting with Windows NT and 2000 is more complicated. If you use a FAT16 or FAT32 partition for the Microsoft Windows NT or 2000 operating system, then the method used for Microsoft Windows 9X should work. If, however, NTFS is the file system that you use, the NT boot loader is not compatible with LILO in the MBR. This means that LILO must not be installed in the MBR or the Microsoft operating system won't boot. To get around this situation, install LILO in the root partition of Linux and on a diskette. Complete the installation of Linux and reboot the system with the diskette that you used to boot Linux. After you are in Linux, use the following commands to copy a binary image of the boot sector to a blank diskette:

```
mount -t msdos /dev/fd0 /mnt/floppy

dd if=/dev/hda5 bs=512 count=1 of=/mnt/floppy/linux.bin
```

Then, remove the floppy and reboot the system into Microsoft Windows NT or 2000. You will need to edit the file boot.ini at this point. Open boot.ini in a plain text editor, such as notepad, and add the following line:

```
c:\linux.bin="Linux"
```

Save the file boot.ini and exit the text editor. Then, copy the file linux.bin from the floppy to the HDD in the root directory of the Microsoft Windows HDD. This allows the startup menu of Microsoft Windows NT or 2000 to display the Linux line and gives it the linux.bin file, which contains directions detailing where to boot this operating system. This should allow Linux to dual-boot with Microsoft Windows NT or 2000.

Linux and Solaris

You can easily dual-boot Linux with Solaris. To create a dual-boot between Linux and Solaris:

1. Install Linux on the system. Create partition 8 for Linux root, and partition 7 for Linux swap, leaving partition 1 for SunOS root and partition 2 for SunOS swap.

2. Install SILO (Sparc Improved Boot Loader), which is the LILO equivalent in the Sun platform world, in the Linux root partition.

3. Allow SILO to create an entry in nvalias to allow the system to boot.

4. Boot the system to verify that the Linux installation was successful.

5. Halt the system and proceed to install Solaris. When the Solaris installer asks if data should be preserved, do so to save the Linux partitions.

6. Continue to install Solaris in partition 0 (the first partition that was created).

7. Answer "yes" when the installation program inquires about making the new root partition the default boot in NVRAM. Then continue the installation as usual. After the installation is complete, the system prompts you to be rebooted into Solaris. Do this to verify the installation of the Solaris operating system, and then halt the system.

8. Enter the "show-disks" to list the disk paths that are needed to dual-boot the system. You also need the path formats for the disk, which you can obtain with the "devalias" command. With this information, enter the following to allow the system to dual-boot on an IDE system with one disk:

```
nvalias linux <disk_path_from_above>@0,0:h
nvalias solaris <disk_path_from_above>@0,0:a
```

(to boot Solaris by default)

```
setenv boot-device disk:a
```

(to boot Linux by default)

```
setenv boot-device disk:h
```

This configuration allows Linux to dual-boot with the Solaris operating system.

Linux and other operating systems

Linux can be configured in many ways to dual-boot with other operating systems. The one major responsibility to keep in mind is to always back up the data on the existing operating system to protect it — just in case anything goes wrong. Dual-booting a system with Linux and other operating systems allows you to run multiple operating system on one computer. This is helpful if you have certain applications or tools that only can run in one particular operating system.

Installing Additional Software with gzip and tar

2.17 Install and uninstall applications after installing the operating system (e.g., RPM, tar, gzip)

Many software packages can't be installed with the Linux distribution because most commercial software won't allow it. Many programs are a collection of binaries and libraries, compressed with the gzip utility, and brought together as one file with the tar utility.

The *gzip (GNU zip) utility* is the GNU compression utility that was designed to replace the original, Unix compress utility. The gzip utility is used to compress files in order to save space and speed transfer of large files. The first step is to unzip the file, which you can do with gunzip, which unzips Gzip files, by using the format gunzip <file name>.gz. When finished, you will be left with a file with the extension .tar.

A *tar file* is a single archive of multiple files; it can be created on a disk or tape. It supports spanning of media, which can save the data across multiple media such as floppy diskettes, and supports incremental and differential backups to allow great flexibility in use. Therefore, you can use tar on previously created archives to extract files, to store additional files, or to update or list the files that were already stored.

To extract files from the tar archive, use the tar utility to extract the individual files. The tar command takes the form of tar -xvf <file name>.tar. .tar. When the file extraction is complete, you will be able to compile and run the binaries to install the program.

Installing Additional Software with RPM

2.17 Install and uninstall applications after installing the operating system (e.g., RPM, tar, gzip)

2.19 Validate that an installed application is performing correctly in both a test and a production environment

RPM stands for Red Hat Package Manager, and is an open packaging system available to everyone. RPM is used to retrieve source code, and packages it into source and binary form. The binaries can then be installed and tracked, and the source is easy to rebuild. RPM maintains a searchable database of all the installed packages and is used to track all the files of the packages and can provide information about the installed packages. The RPM database is used to give the RPM command the ability to install, upgrade, and remove software packages. RPM uses switches to perform specific tasks. Table 5-3 lists most of the switches used by RPM.

Table 5-3
Red Hat Package Manager Installation Commands

Switches used with the `rpm` command	Switch performs this task
-i or --install	Used to install from RPM
--dbpath <path>	Uses <path> to find RPM database
--excludedocs	Do not install documentation
--force	Ignore package and file conflicts
--ftpport <port>	Use <port> as the FTP port
--ftpproxy <host>	Use <host> as the FTP proxy
-h	Print hash marks during installation
--ignorearch	Do not verify package architecture
--ignoreos	Do not verify package operating system
--includedocs	Install documentation
--nodeps	Do not check on dependencies
--noscripts	Do not execute pre- and post-install scripts
--percent	Prints percentages during installation
--prefix <path>	Relocate the package to another <path> if possible
--rcfile <rcfile>	Set alternate rpmrc file to <rcfile>
--replacefiles	Replace files owned by another package
--replacepkgs	Replace a package with a new copy
--root <path>	Set alternate root to <path>
--test	Performs installation test only
-v	Display additional information
-vv	Display debugging information

The most basic installation command for RPM is `rpm -i filename-1.2-2.i386.rpm`. The most common command that is used to install an RPM, however, is `rpm -ivh filename-1.2-2.i386.rpm`, which displays additional information, and displays hash marks to illustrate that the RPM is still working, which is helpful for large RPMs that take a longer time to install. You can use the other options, but in general, this is a basic RPM installation command.

Exam Tip   You need to know the format and switches that are used with the RPM command.

Removing software with RPM

RPM has the ability to remove software packages from the system. Use the switches in Table 5-4 to accomplish this task.

<table>
<tr><th colspan="2">Table 5-4
Red Hat Package Manager Erase Commands</th></tr>
<tr><th>Switches used with
the `rpm` **command**</th><th>Switch performs this task</th></tr>
<tr><td>-e</td><td>Erase or remove one or more packages</td></tr>
<tr><td>--dbpath <path></td><td>Use <path> to find the RPM database</td></tr>
<tr><td>--nodeps</td><td>Do not check on dependencies</td></tr>
<tr><td>--noscripts</td><td>Do not execute pre- and post-install scripts</td></tr>
<tr><td>--rcfile <rcfile></td><td>Set alternate rpmrc file to <rcfile></td></tr>
<tr><td>--root <path></td><td>Set alternate root to <path></td></tr>
<tr><td>--test</td><td>Performs installation test only</td></tr>
<tr><td>-v</td><td>Display additional information</td></tr>
<tr><td>-vv</td><td>Display debugging information</td></tr>
</table>

The `rpm -e filename-1.2-2.i386.rpm` command erases or removes the package. You can use an optional command to give more information, such as `rpm -evv filename-1.2-2.i386.rpm`, which gives detailed information about the removal of the package.

Caution Use the erase switch with great care because RPM may remove packages that are required for the system to function. The system can be rendered useless if the wrong package is removed from the system.

Upgrading software with RPM

RPM can also be used to upgrade a package, which is no small task. To accomplish this, RPM tracks the installation and removal of previous packages in order to correctly install an upgrade to an existing RPM package. Table 5-5 lists the switches that you use to upgrade an RPM package.

Table 5-5 Red Hat Package Manager Upgrade Commands	
Switches used with the rpm **command**	**Switch performs this task**
-U or --upgrade	Used to upgrade an RPM
--dbpath <path>	Use <path> to find RPM database
--excludedocs	Do not install documentation
--force	Ignore package and file conflicts
--ftpport <port>	Use <port> as the FTP port
--ftpproxy <host>	Use <host> as the FTP proxy
-h	Print hash marks during installation
--ignorearch	Do not verify package architecture
--ignoreos	Do not verify package operating system
--includedocs	Install documentation
--nodeps	Do not check on dependencies
--noscripts	Do not execute pre- and post-install scripts
--oldpackage	Permit the upgrading to an older package
--percent	Prints percentages during installation
--prefix <path>	Relocate the package to another <path> if possible
--rcfile <rcfile>	Set alternate rpmrc file to <rcfile>
--replacefiles	Replace files owned by another package
--replacepkgs	Replace a package with a new copy
--root <path>	Set alternate root to <path>
--test	Performs installation test only
-v	Display additional information
-vv	Display debugging information

Upgrading packages can be accomplished by using the command `rpm -U file-name-1.4-4.i386.rpm`. A more common way to upgrade is to use the command `rpm -Uvh filename-1.4-4.i386.rpm`, which displays additional information and provides hash marks during installation. Notice that anything similar to the `rpm -ivh filename-1.2-2.i386.rpm`, is also correct. The only difference is the use of the -U upgrade switch to perform an upgrade versus an installation with the -i switch. The -U is really a combination of the -i and -e switches, and because of this, you can use it to install packages even when you have no upgrade to perform. The upgrade does not erase any files that are normally removed during an upgrade; therefore, it still installs the package by using the installation feature of upgrading. This is why many people who have used RPM for years may not use the -i switch to install packages; instead, they use the -U switch to perform installations and upgrades.

Query the RPM software

The query command in RPM allows you to query what has been installed, upgraded, and erased. This is a powerful tool, which you can use to query files for an individual package or to learn all the packages that are installed on the system. Table 5-6 shows the switches that are used with RPM and the query command.

Table 5-6
Red Hat Package Manager Query Commands

Switches used with the rpm command	Switch performs this task
-q or --query	Query the installed package(s)
-a	Query all installed packages
-c	Display a list of configuration files
-d	Display a list of documentation files
--dbpath \<path>	Use \<path> to find RPM database
--dump	Display all verifiable information about each file
-f \<file>	Query package owning \<file>
-g \<group>	Query packages belonging to \<group>
-i	Display summary package information
-l	Display a list of the files in a package
\<null>	Display full package label
-p \<file> (or "-")	Query a package \<file> (URLs are okay here)
--provides	Display the capabilities the package provides
--qf or --queryformat	Display the queried data in a custom format
-R or --requires	Display the capabilities requirement of the package
--rcfile \<rcfile>	Set alternate rpmrc file to \<rcfile>
-s	Displays the state of each file in the package
--scripts	Show the scripts associated with a package

Switches used with the rpm command	Switch performs this task
--root \<path\>	Set alternate root to \<path\>
-v	Display additional information
-vv	Display debugging information
--whatprovides \<x\>	Query packages providing capability \<x\>
--whatrequires \<x\>	Query packages requiring capability \<x\>

The ability to query the installed files is a very useful tool because you can learn which version of the C libraries is installed on a system. The following is an example:

```
[root@localhost /root]# rpm -q tar
tar-1.13.19-4
[root@localhost /root]#
```

You can also use the query command to see all the RPM packages on the system; the following is an example:

```
[root@localhost /root]# rpm -qa |more
indexhtml-7.1-2
specspo-7.1-1
pciutils-devel-2.1.8-19
cdda2wav-1.9-6
db3-3.1.17-7
gdbm-1.8.0-5
libjpeg-6b-15
mailx-8.1.1-20
esound-0.2.22-1
mpg123-0.59r-10
at-3.1.8-16
less-358-16
netpbm-9.9-5
playmidi-2.4-12
aspell-0.32.6-2
rmt-0.4b21-3
setserial-2.17-2
ntsysv-1.2.22-1
tar-1.13.19-4
mount-2.10r-5
crontabs-1.9-2
wget-1.6-2
cyrus-sasl-1.5.24-17
--More--
```

In the preceding example, notice the use of the pipe (I) and more commands; if these options are not used, the list of RPM packages scrolls by very quickly. Finally, the query command is so useful because it has this format: The query is first, then the files to be queried, and finally the information to be queried for.

Verify the RPM software

Objective

2.19 Validate that an installed application is performing correctly in both a test and a production environment

You can also use RPM to verify that the software on the system is in working order. Use this verify command to make sure that the packages are still configured properly, to verify that no changes have been made to the system, or to verify that an accidental remove of files did not damage the system. Table 5-7 lists the switches that are used with the verify command.

<table>
<tr><td colspan="2">Table 5-7
Red Hat Package Manager Verify Commands</td></tr>
<tr><td>*Switches used with
the* rpm *command*</td><td>*Switch performs this task*</td></tr>
<tr><td>-V or --verify</td><td>Verify the installed package(s)</td></tr>
<tr><td>-a</td><td>Verify all installed packages against the RPM database</td></tr>
<tr><td>--dbpath <path></td><td>Use <path> to find RPM database</td></tr>
<tr><td>-f <file></td><td>Verify package owning <file></td></tr>
<tr><td>-g <group></td><td>Verify the packages belonging to <group></td></tr>
<tr><td>--nodeps</td><td>Do not check dependencies during verification</td></tr>
<tr><td>--nofiles</td><td>Do not verify file attributes</td></tr>
<tr><td>--noscripts</td><td>Do not execute verification scripts</td></tr>
<tr><td>-p <file> (or "-")</td><td>Verify against a specific package <file></td></tr>
<tr><td>--rcfile <rcfile></td><td>Set alternate rpmrc file to <rcfile></td></tr>
<tr><td>--root <path></td><td>Set alternate root to <path></td></tr>
<tr><td>-v</td><td>Display additional information</td></tr>
<tr><td>-vv</td><td>Display debugging information</td></tr>
</table>

The verify command is very important in the installation of Linux because it enables the installer to verify that all packages are installed correctly. You can use the following command to verify all RPM packages installed on the system during installation or when adding packages.

```
[root@localhost /root]# rpm -Va |more
.M......    /var/spool/at/.SEQ
S.5....T c /usr/share/a2ps/afm/fonts.map
S.5....T   /boot/kernel.h-2.4.2
.......T   /lib/modules/2.4.2-2/modules.dep
.......T   /lib/modules/2.4.2-2/modules.generic_string
.......T   /lib/modules/2.4.2-2/modules.isapnpmap
.......T   /lib/modules/2.4.2-2/modules.parportmap
.......T   /lib/modules/2.4.2-2/modules.pcimap
.......T   /lib/modules/2.4.2-2/modules.usbmap
missing    /etc/identd.key
S.5....T c /etc/X11/fs/config
missing    /usr/share/ssl/certs/stunnel.pem
```

Do not be surprised that some files won't be verified, because RPM is very strict about passing the verification.

Verify the package files

The files contained in a package may be just as important as the verification of the package. To verify the individual files, answer the following questions:

✦ Is the organization listed?

✦ Have unauthorized changes been made to it?

✦ Can it be trusted not to compromise the system?

You can resolve these questions with the file verification command. Table 5-8 shows the switches for this command.

Table 5-8
Red Hat File Verify Commands

Switches used with the rpm command	Switch performs this task
-K or --checksig	Verify one or more package files
--nopgp	Do not verify any PGP signatures
--rcfile <rcfile>	Set alternate rpmrc file to <rcfile>
-v	Display additional information
-vv	Display debugging information

The command to verify a file may look something like this:

```
[root@localhost /root]# rpm -K rpm-2.3-1.i386.rpm
rpm-2.3-1.i386.rpm: size pgp md5 OK
```

A failed verification may look like this:

```
[root@localhost /root]# rpm -Kv rpm-2.3-1.i386.rpm
rpm-2.3-1.i386.rpm:
Header+Archive size OK: 278686 bytes
Good signature from user "Red Hat Software, Inc.
<redhat@redhat.com>".
Signature made 1996/12/24 18:37 GMT using 1024-bit key, key ID
CBA29BF9

WARNING: Because this public key is not certified with a
trusted signature, it is not known with high confidence that
this public key actually belongs to: "Red Hat Software, Inc.
<redhat@redhat.com>". MD5 sum OK:
8873682c5e036a307dee87d990e75349
```

You can use this type of verification to prevent the installation of corrupt or tampered files on a production system.

The tools that are included in the RPM are impressive, with their ability to detect dependencies, and install support files on the fly. The fact that Red Hat opened up RPM for every Linux distribution is equally impressive, because RPM has become a Linux standard for installing, removing, upgrading, querying, and verifying the packages installed on a Linux system.

Upgrading the Kernel

Objective ➡   2.15 Explain when and why the kernel will need to be recompiled

Immediately after installation, you may encounter situations in which you are required to upgrade the system. Although the Linux kernel has seen many advances, it may not fulfill the needs of your system. For this reason, the kernel (which is available at www.kernel.org/) is updated often. You may have several reasons to update the kernel on your system, including the following:

✦ **Stability:** Although a released stable kernel is usually of high quality, many issues can still arise. This is why additional kernel releases are often more stable than the previous release.

✦ **Hardware support:** You probably need to upgrade to a version 2.0 kernel or higher in order to achieve support for many of the new hardware devices that are available today. For example, the 2.4 kernel has vastly improved support for Fibre Channel devices. This is not the only reason to upgrade a kernel, but it is perhaps the most driving force behind kernel development. The ability to use Linux with USB, IEEE-1394, Fibre Channel, and many other new technologies drives developers to create a new kernel to provide better support for these pieces of hardware.

✦ **Hardware platforms:** The newest processors often benefit from having the kernel optimized for their use. By providing an updated kernel, the system will be able to use the CPU more efficiently.

✦ **Package support:** Some software packages don't run well—or don't even run at all—on older kernel versions, and these packages are often required to use the Linux system.

Regardless of the reasons for upgrading the kernel, installers should be competent at performing this task.

Upgrading a Linux Kernel

To carry out a Linux kernel upgrade, perform the following:

1. Make sure that you have a working emergency boot disk available—just in case a mistake is made while upgrading the kernel. If a boot disk was not created during the installation, use the `mkbootdisk` command to make one. The standard command is similar to `mkbootdisk --device /dev/fd0 2.4.x`, where 2.4.x is the full version of the current kernel.

2. Test the boot disk to make sure that it will boot the system. This will protect the system in case the upgrade fails by giving the option to restore the old kernel.

3. Clear out any configuration files from previous builds of the kernel. You can do this with the `make mrproper` command, which will clean up the source tree.

After you have completed these steps, you can choose from several methods to perform the upgrade, which are listed here.

✦ **make config:** An interactive text program. Components are presented and you answer with Y (yes), N (no), or M (module).

✦ **make menuconfig:** A graphical, menu-driven program. Components are presented in a menu of categories; you select the desired components in the same manner that you used in the Red Hat Linux installation program. Toggle the tag corresponding to the item that you want included by answering Y (yes), N (no), or M (module).

✦ **make xconfig:** An X Window System program. Components are listed in different levels of menus, which you select by using a mouse. Again, answer with Y (yes), N (no), or M (module).

✦ **make oldconfig:** This is a non-interactive script that sets up your Makefile to be the default settings. If you're using the Red Hat patched kernel, it sets up the configuration for the kernel that is shipped for your box. This is useful when setting up your kernel to known working defaults and then turning off features that you don't want.

Tip   If you are using a pre-configured installation file, which is used to configure identical systems, you may omit the `mrproper` and `make config` commands and use the `make dep` and `make clean` commands to prepare the system for the new kernel.

After you have completed one of these methods, your next step is to edit the Makefile, found at `/usr/src/linux/Makefile`, and change the line EXTRAVERSION = to a new name for the newly created kernel configuration file. This allows you to have the old working kernel and the new kernel on your system at the same time. Use the `make bzImage` to build the kernel and add any modules with the `make modules` command. Then install the modules — even if none were built — with the `make modules_install` command. Rename the original kernel in /boot and copy the new kernel to /boot. Now edit `/etc/lilo.conf` to include the newly created kernel and run `/sbin/lilo`. The following is an example of what you can do to the lilo.conf file.

```
image=/boot/vmlinuz-2.2.16-12
    label=linux
    initrd=/boot/initrd-2.2.16-12.img
    read-only
    root=/dev/hda8

other=/dev/hda1
    label=dos

image=/boot/vmlinuz-2.2.16-12
    label=linux
    initrd=/boot/initrd-2.2.16-12.img
    read-only
    root=/dev/hda8

image=/boot/vmlinuz-2.2.18-12.upgrade
    label=test
    initrd=/boot/initrd-2.2.18-12upgrade.img
    read-only
    root=/dev/hda8

other=/dev/hda1
    label=dos
```

This allows the system to boot off the previous kernel and the new kernel at the same time. Another way that you can perform the upgrade to a new kernel is to use the RPM utility, which allows the updating of the kernel with the powerful tools included in RPM. Although many installers don't like to perform kernel updates with RPM, it should be included in your repertory of skills.

System Log Files

Objective 2.18 Read the Logfiles created during installation to verify the success of the installation

During the installation of Linux and additional software packages, system logs are created. These logs are created on the system to allow for verification of installation and for troubleshooting if the installation goes poorly. Table 5-9 shows the major system configuration and log files and includes a brief description of each one.

Table 5-9
System Configuration and Log Files

File	Description
/etc/sysconfig	Directory on Red Hat Linux that holds system configuration files
/etc/rc.d	Directory that holds system startup and shutdown files
/etc/rc.d/rc.sysinit	Initialization file for the system
/etc/rc.config	Configuration file for SuSE Linux system
/etc/rc.d/rc.local	Initialization file for custom commands
/etc/rc.d/rc.modules	Loads kernel modules on startup of the system
/etc/rc.d/init.d	Directory that holds many of the daemons, servers and scripts for the System V init startup control standard
/sbin/init.d	Directory that holds many of the daemons, servers, and scripts for a SuSE system
/etc/rc.d/rc(1-8).d	Directories for the different runlevels; these directories hold links to scripts in the /etc/rc.d/init.d directory (on SuSE these are located in /sbin/init.d/rc(1-8).d)
/etc/rc.d/init.d/halt	Operations performed each time the system is shut down. Some distributions use the name rc.halt
/etc/rc.d/init.d/lpd	Start up and shut down the lpd printing daemon

(Continued)

Table 5-9 *(continued)*

File	Description
/etc/rc.d/init.d/inet	Operations to start and stop the inetd Internet services daemon
/etc/rc.d/init.d/network	Operations to start and stop the network connections
/etc/rc.d/init.d/httpd	Operations to start and stop the httpd Web server daemon
/etc/X11	X Windows configuration files
/etc/lilo.conf	LILO configuration file
/etc/fstab	Listing of the Linux file systems and automatically mount file systems
/etc/hosts	Hosts configuration file
/mnt	Holds removable media file systems mount points
/etc/inittab	The default state and terminal connections
/etc/passwd	Contains user password and login information
/etc/shadow	Contains user-encrypted passwords
/etc/group	Contains a list of groups and the configuration for each group
/etc/syslog.conf	Contains the names and locations of system log files
/proc/	Contains hardware configurations of the system
/var/log/boot.log(.x)	Show the completion of daemons and other system functions, (.x) shows there are several corresponding to system boots
/var/log/cron (.x)	Show the weekly and daily cron jobs completed, (.x) shows there are several corresponding to system boots
/var/log/dmesg	Contains hardware detected on boot up
/var/log/maillog (.x)	Mail logs for system information, (.x) shows there are several corresponding to system boots
/var/log/secure (.x)	RSA key generation log, (.x) shows there are several corresponding to system boots
/var/log/spooler (.x)	Spooler generation log, (.x) shows there are several corresponding to system boots
/var/log/fax	Directory of fax log files
/var/log/httpd	Directory of httpd Web daemon log files
/var/log/news	Directory of news daemon log files
/var/log/samba	Directory of samba log files
/var/log/squid	Directory of squid log files
/var/log/uucp	Directory of uucp log files

This table provides a list of just some of the locations of important system files that you can use to configure and verify how the system is functioning. Knowing the location of the files and what they are used for will aid you in quickly troubleshooting a system when problems arise.

The Final Test of the Installation

 2.19 Validate that an installed application is performing correctly in both a test and a production environment

At this point, you have installed the system and additional software, and you have checked that the system and its logs are functioning. You need to complete the final testing of the system, which usually means that the system is ready to be deployed into a production environment. You should have documented everything that you have done to the system. Your documentation should include the checklists that you used to install the system, all the hardware that you included, the partitioning scheme that you used, and the networking configurations, packages, and other system configurations, and any other packages that you installed before deployment. This documentation should provide a system history that will make it easy for others to follow what has been done and how to resolve issues that may arise. After you have completed this documentation, it's time to give the end user access to the system. This is the final stage of testing, because the end user will be able to try and perform their daily functions which tests proper system functionality. If no issues arise during final testing, the system is fully functional. This completes the installation of Linux and the deployment into the production environment.

Summary

This chapter explains many of the basics of Linux system installation. This task involves several major areas:

- ✦ Preparation for Installation
    - Verify that the hardware is supported
    - Plan the partitioning of the HDD
    - Plan the configuration of the network
    - Plan the system class
    - Plan for the installation of additional packages

✦ Installation of Linux

- Media selection
- Initial selections
- Installation type
- Disk partitions and formatting
- LILO or GRUB installation
- Network configuration
- Root and user account information
- Authentication configuration
- Package selection and installation

✦ Post Installation

- Installing additional packages
- Verification of installed packages
- System log's location and usage
- Recompiling the kernel
- Documentation and deployment

✦   ✦   ✦

STUDY GUIDE

The Study Guide section provides you with the opportunity to test your knowledge about the Linux+ exam objectives that are covered in this chapter. The Assessment Questions provide practice for the real exam, and the Scenarios provide practice with real situations. If you get any questions wrong, use the answers to determine the part of the chapter that you should review before continuing.

Assessment Questions

1. What is the main alternative to a GUI installation?

 A. Text

 B. Command line

 C. Shell

 D. Graphical

2. What is the recommended partitioning tool included with every distribution of Linux today?

 A. Disk Druid

 B. Format

 C. fdisk and cfdisk

 D. Partition Magic

3. Which of the following file system types supports journaling?

 A. ext2

 B. FAT32

 C. Reiser

 D. FAT16

4. What is the purpose of the `swapon` command when installing Linux in command line interface mode?

 A. Create a swap partition

 B. Create and activate a swap partition

 C. Create a swap area in RAM

 D. Activate a created swap partition

5. When would an Inode of 1024 be used instead of the default 4096?

    A. A few very large files are expected on the system

    B. A few very small files are expected on the system

    C. Many large files are expected on the system

    D. Many small files are expected on the system

6. What condition is indicated if only the LI appears when attempting to boot a Linux system with LILO?

    A. Primary boot loader has been started

    B. Secondary boot loader has been loaded

    C. Tertiary boot loader has been loaded

    D. Secondary boot loader signals it has been loaded

7. Which of the following is required with a network installation of Linux?

    A. FQDN

    B. Gateway

    C. NIC

    D. CD-ROM

8. When creating a Dual-Boot system, where is the recommended place to install LILO?

    A. MBR

    B. Extended partition

    C. The first partition of the HDD

    D. Linux root partition's boot sector

9. Where should LILO *not* be installed when Linux is being added to a system that is already using Microsoft Windows 2000 with NTFS?

    A. MBR

    B. Extended partition

    C. The first partition of the second HDD

    D. Linux root partition's boot sector

10. What is `gzip`?

    A. An installation program

    B. A compression utility

    C. An archive utility

    D. A file system

11. What is `tar`?

    A. An installation program

    B. A compression utility

    C. An archive utility

    D. A file system

12. Which is the standard command used to uncompress `gzip` files?

    A. `uzip`

    B. `unzip`

    C. `GNUzip`

    D. `gunzip`

13. What is the RPM switch for only installing packages?

    A. -i

    B. -U

    C. -I

    D. -e

14. What is the command used to install an RPM package named `filename1.2-2.i386.rpm`?

    A. `rpm -i filename-1.2-2.i386.rpm`

    B. `rpm -ivh filename-1.2-2.i386.rpm`

    C. `rpm -evh filename-1.2-2.i386.rpm`

    D. `rpm -U filename-1.2-2.i386.rpm`

15. What is the command used to remove an RPM package named `filename1.2-2.i386.rpm`?

    A. `rpm -i filename-1.2-2.i386.rpm`

    B. `rpm -ivh filename-1.2-2.i386.rpm`

    C. `rpm -evh filename-1.2-2.i386.rpm`

    D. `rpm -Uvh filename-1.2-2.i386.rpm`

16. The following command can be used to install an RPM package: `rpm -Uvh filename-1.2-2.i386.rpm`. What functions does this perform?

    A. Upgrades with additional information and hash marks.

    B. Installs with additional information and hash marks.

    C. Does not upgrade if an older package is not already installed. If the older package exists, then upgrades with additional information and hash marks.

    D. Installs the package with additional information and hash marks, then removes old packages.

17. Which command is used to see which RPM version of tar was installed on the system?

    A. `rpm -q tar`

    B. `rpm -V tar`

    C. `rpm -K tar`

    D. `rpm -Q tar`

18. Where are the automatically mounted file systems listed?

    A. `/etc/lilo.conf`

    B. `/etc/fstab`

    C. `/etc/inittab`

    D. `/etc/syslog.conf`

19. Where would the processor type be determined?

    A. `/etc/fstab`

    B. `/etc/rc.d`

    C. `/proc/cpuinfo`

    D. `/etc/sysconfig`

20. Where are most of the boot-up log files kept?

    A. `/etc/log/`

    B. `/var/log/`

    C. `/sbin/log/`

    D. `/root/log/`

Scenarios

1. The Linux system is installed and the user wants to install a new program. The system supports the RPM method of installation. What should you do before installing, during install, and after installation of the RPM package?

2. A user wants to use Linux to perform a specific task. He is required to use Microsoft Windows to support his e-mail program. What are the steps necessary to install Linux to dual-boot on this system?

Lab Exercises

Lab 5-1 Linux Software Installation

The objective for this hands-on lab is to gain experience in installing additional software on a Linux PC. You should be able to use any distribution of Linux for this installation exercise.

1. Download an RPM software package to install on the Linux system.

2. Query for an existing version of the RPM software on the system.

3. Verify the files that are associated with the RPM software (if it exists on the system).

4. Install or upgrade the RPM package in the test mode only.

5. Install or upgrade the RPM package on the system.

6. Verify the installation of the RPM software.

7. Test the software to verify that it works.

8. Remove the RPM software from the system.

9. Verify that the RPM software has been removed.

Answers to Chapter Questions

Chapter Pre-test

1. There are two types of text-based installations: command line and shell.

2. The basic disk partitioning tool included with most distributions of Linux is fdisk.

3. Not all distributions support the ReiserFS.

4. A test installation is preferred over a GUI for speed and resource issues.

5. Virtually any operating system can be dual-booted with Linux.

6. The major differences between a GUI and text installation are the customized menus and specialized tools of the GUI that don't work in text mode.

7. The kernel can be (and often is) updated and even upgraded after installation of Linux.

8. The major reasons to upgrade a Linux kernel are to provide hardware support, stability, and package requirements.

9. You have many ways to verify the installation of a service. RPM packages can be verified; log files can be checked for services, such as Web servers; and you can test the service at the machine, or another machine for network services.

10. All the pre-installation planning, installation selections, and configurations — and all the post installation configurations and added packages — should be documented. These should be kept in a standard place for all systems, which may be attached to the system, in a file cabinet, or on a file server.

Assessment Questions

1. A. The alternative to a GUI installation is a text installation. Command line and shell are types of text installation and graphical is a GUI installation. For review, see the "Alternative to the GUI Installation" section.

2. C. `fdisk` and `cfdisk` are the most popular disk partitioning tools for Linux, and are available with most distributions. Disk Druid is a Red Hat specific partitioning tool, while Partition Magic is a third party tool. For review, see the "Command Line installation" section.

3. C. Reiser is a Journaling File System; the others are not. For review, see the "Command Line installation" section.

4. D. The `swapon` command can be used to activate a created swap partition; it does not create a swap partition. For review, see the "More disk configurations" section.

5. D. When many small files are expected on the system, it's best to use an Inode of 1024. This saves space on so many small files and is the only time you need to add the overhead of the smaller Inodes to the system. For review, see the "More disk configurations" section.

6. B. The secondary boot loader has been loaded when LI appears. "L" signifies that the primary boot loader has been started and "LIL" signals that the secondary boot loader has been loaded. For review, see the "Finalize the installation" section.

7. C. In this list, only an NIC is required; the others may be needed for installation, but not for a network installation on a LAN. For review, see the "Network installations of Linux" section.

8. D. When creating a dual-boot system, the safest place to install LILO is the Linux root partition's boot sector. On some systems, the other choices can render the system inoperable. LILO can't be placed on the extended partition, but it can be placed in an extended partition. For review, see the "A Dual-Boot Installation of Linux" section.

9. A. The loader, boot.ini, with Windows 2000 is not compatible with LILO, and the reference to the Windows 2000 partition will be removed. LILO can be installed in the MBR if preferred, but it will have to be specially configured to boot the Windows 2000 partition. For review, see the "Linux with Microsoft Windows NT and 2000" section.

10. B. `gzip` is a compression utility created by the GNU project. It is not a file system, installation program, or archive utility. For review, see the "Installing Additional Software with gzip and tar" section.

11. C. `tar` is an archive utility that is used to create tape backups. It is not a file system, installation program, or compression utility. For review, see the "Installing Additional Software with gzip and tar" section.

12. D. The standard command used to uncompress `gzip` files is `gunzip`. For review, see the "Installing Additional Software with gzip and tar" section.

13. A. The command line switch for installing an RPM is -i. For review, see the "Installing Additional Software with RPM" section.

14. B. The most common command used to install an RPM package is `rpm -ivh filename-1.2-2.i386.rpm`. The -i and -U will work, but aren't normally used because the vh switches provide more feedback. The -evh switch will remove the package. For review, see the "Installing Additional Software with RPM" section.

15. C. The most common command used to remove an RPM package is `rpm -evh filename-1.2-2.i386.rpm`. The others commands are used to install RPM packages. For review, see the "Removing Software with RPM" section.

16. B. The command `rpm -Uvh filename-1.2-2.i386.rpm` performs the installation of the package with additional information and hash marks, and then removes old packages. For review, see the "Upgrading software with RPM" section.

17. A. The `rpm -q tar` is used to see which RPM version of tar was installed on the system. The other answers either won't work or won't return the desired results. For review, see the "Query the RPM software" section.

18. B. The automatically mounted file systems are listed in the file `/etc/fstab`. The other files contain different data. For review, see the "System Log Files" section.

19. C. The processor type is determined in the `/proc/cpuinfo file`. The other files contain different data. For review, see the "System Log Files" section.

20. B. Most of the boot-up log files are kept in `/var/log/`. The other locations contain different data or don't exist. For review, see the "System Log Files" section.

Scenarios

1. The RPM tools should be used to query or verify the installed packages to confirm the installation of any previous packages; the signature of the new package should also be checked. The RPM should be installed or upgraded by first using the test mode to verify that it works, and then it should be installed. Then query the RPM system and verify the installation of the RPM package.

2. The steps to creating a dual-boot system are as follows:

a. You should always begin with backing up all the data on the system before starting.

b. Perform the same checklist that you used to install Linux on any system.

c. Execute the installation and verify that LILO is installed.

d. Finalize the dual-boot configuration and test-boot each operating system.

e. Document all processes completed.

Configuration

Configuring is a constant task when maintaining a Linux workstation or server. The chapters in this part detail how to configure your Linux system for better performance and functionality. In a corporate environment, you will have to get your Linux systems on the network, and you will have to configure printers and peripherals, along with the user interface. On top of these duties, you will also have to swap space, edit basic configuration files, and document all of your work. CompTIA focuses 15 percent of the exam on configuration. Thus, the chapters in this part focus on every exam objective related to configuration so you will be able to fully understand how to configure your Linux system and be able to apply this knowledge when taking the exam.

Configuring X-Windows

- ◆ 3.1 Reconfigure the Xwindow system with automated utilities (e.g., Xconfigurator, XF86Setup)
- ◆ 3.14 Document the installation of the operating system, including configuration

CHAPTER PRE-TEST

1. What is the X Window System?

2. Where are the software and resources for the X Window System?

3. What applications are used to configure the X Window System?

4. What are the benefits of a manual configuration versus a GUI configuration of the X Window System?

5. What files are used to support or document the X Window System?

6. What are the major components of the X Window System?

7. What are the available Desktop Environments?

8. What are the benefits of a Desktop Environment?

9. Can the X Window System be used on remote systems?

10. What are the benefits of using the X Window System in the enterprise?

✦ Answers to these questions can be found at the end of the chapter. ✦

The X Window System is a complex graphical system that can be used for GUI applications in the desktop or enterprise environment. The ability to configure the X Window System for desktop or enterprise use is a valuable skill and requires the use of many tools. To use these tools, you must have knowledge of the X Window System and the concepts behind it. The X Window System utilizes several layers of software to provide these graphical services. These services provide the base X Window System, and ease configuration by breaking it down into more manageable pieces.

What is the X Window System?

The X Window System is used to provide a GUI interface for most Linux and UNIX systems. The X Window System was created in 1984 by the Massachusetts Institute of Technology's Laboratory for Computer Science in cooperation with the Digital Equipment Corporation as part of Project Athena. The origins of the X Window System are based in the work of the Xerox Corporation's Palo Alto Research Center (PARC) and in the W windowing package, which was created by Paul Asente. In 1987, MIT released the X Window System as X11; it is very similar to the versions of X11 in use today. MIT developed the X Window System, but it was turned over to the X Consortium for further development. More information on the history of X Windows is available at `www.x.org`.

`www.x.org` is the worldwide consortium empowered with the stewardship and collaborative development of the X Window System technology and standards. `www.x.org` provides official X Window System updates to the general public — free of charge. This organization also controls the evolution of the X11R6 specifications and provides for revisions and updates to the package. The main X Window System that is used with Linux is XFree86, which is produced by the XFree86 Project, located at `www.xfree86.org`. XFree86 is a freely re-distributable Open Source implementation of the X Window System that runs on Linux, UNIX, BSD versions, Mac OS X (also known as Darwin), Solaris (x86 series) operating systems, and OS/2. These organizations provide the X Window System for most Linux systems.

The X Window System

For the X Window System to maintain portability and be able to work across different hardware and software platforms, it was created using four components — the X Server, X Client, X Protocol, and X Window manager — that interact to provide the GUI interface.

The X Server

The *X Server* is the software that provides the direct hardware support for the entire X Window System. The most common version of X Servers used in Linux is XFree86. These XF86 servers are provided by two methods:

✦ Pre-4.0 versions of XFree86 contain individual servers for over 15 types of hardware; the major units of this hardware are Mach64, S3, and SVGA video card chipsets.

✦ Version 4 of XFree86 contains modules that provide service for a single XF86 server.

These improvements enable more standard support across all types of hardware. With this X Server support, Linux has the ability to support most hardware for the entire X Window System.

The X Client

An *X Client* is the software that requests services from the X Server. The X Server then returns information to the X Client to be displayed on the video output system. By using a client/server system, the X Window System gains an advantage in that the client has the ability to be local or remote.

When discussing an X Window System client environment, you need to be familiar with several terms, which are shown in Table 6-1.

Table 6-1	
X Client Terms	
Terminology	*Reference For*
Screen	The entire desktop displayed
Root Window	The background of the screen
Window Manager	The main interface between the X Window System and the user
Pointer	The cursor that is used to represent the position of the mouse or other pointing device
Window	Any frame displayed by an application
Terminal Emulator	A window providing an emulated terminal

X Client and Server communications

The X Protocol provides the communications between the client and the server. This protocol was developed to provide a network-capable, transparent graphical user interface for the UNIX operating system. This GUI was designed to be much different than the one used in Microsoft Windows.

The X Protocol distributes the processing of applications by specifying a client-server relationship at the application level. Therefore, by using a layered approach, the X Window System has separated the application part from the hardware part, which accomplishes the following:

✦ Allows the hardware system to be separated from the software

✦ Allows a single workstation to run an X Client for many physically separate machines or for one remote machine that has excess computing power (to be used to supply the X Server for many X Clients)

✦ Allows remote system management in a GUI environment or a true client-server environment and distributed processing

Creating the client layer as device-independent and the server layer as device-dependent accomplishes this distributed processing. X Protocol further provides a common windowing system by specifying an asynchronous network protocol for communication between an X client and an X server. The following are some advantages that the X Window System gains from this approach:

✦ Local and remote computing are actually the same to the user and developer

✦ The X server can easily support a variety of languages and operating systems

✦ X clients can easily support a variety of languages and operating systems

✦ Applications don't suffer a performance penalty when used locally or remotely

X Window Manager

The final part of the X Window System is the manager that the user interfaces with. Many Window Managers are available, including AfterStep, Enlightenment, fvwm, and Window Maker. The X Window Manager provides the user with a common GUI environment, which allows the use of common desktops across not only Linux systems, but also any system that can use the X Window System.

Tip   The most common desktop systems that are used today are GNOME and KDE. These should not be confused with the role of Window Managers, because they provide the full desktop environment, while the Windows managers affect the look and feel of the X Windows system.

GNOME

The GNOME project, available at www.gnome.org, is part of the GNU project and was created to provide an entirely free desktop environment for free systems, as shown in Figure 6-1. Moreover, GNOME provides a user-friendly suite of applications and an easy-to-use desktop.

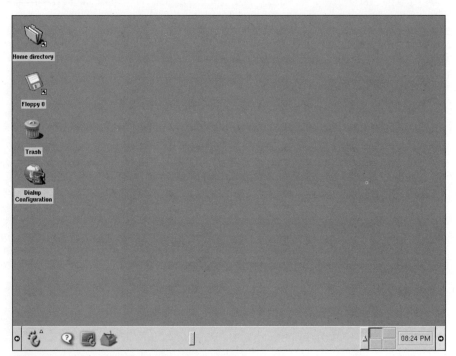

Figure 6-1: The GNOME Desktop Environment

GNOME currently uses a Window Manager to provide the interface — the most common interfaces that are used are Enlightenment and Window Maker. GNOME provides several user friendly features, such as a file and display manager, that familiar environment for users used to the Microsoft Windows system, and an excellent desktop environment with many tools.

To increase the user friendly design of their desktop, the GNOME project created the GNOME Usability Project. The goal of the GNOME Usability Project is to facilitate the use of GNOME, making it as enjoyable and intuitive as possible. This goal has directed GNOME toward a standard user interface with established guidelines for GNOME developers to aid them in making applications.

GNOME is easy to use, but it is also cutting-edge technology. GNOME offers a very modern desktop, which was created by using the GTK+ Tool Kit, XML, and CORBA. CORBA, which stands for *Common Object Request Broker Architecture*, provides open, vendor-independent architecture that applications can use over networks. CORBA uses the standard protocol IIOP to provide this common network transport, which also allows any program using the protocol to interoperate with any other CORBA-based program — regardless of the computer, operating system, programming language, or network.

GTK+ is a multi-platform toolkit for creating graphical user interfaces. GTK+ is part of the GNU Project and uses the GNU GPL to ensure that all developers — even those developing proprietary software — can use it. GTK+ has a C-based, object-oriented architecture and uses the following libraries:

✦ **GLib** — provides many useful data types, macros, type conversions, string utilities, and a lexical scanner

✦ **GDK** — is a wrapper for low-level windowing functions

✦ **GTK** — is an advanced widget set

These libraries allow GTK+ to provide maximum flexibility and an excellent, standardized interface for graphical user interfaces. Through the use of these tools, GNOME utilizes the latest in cutting edge programming technology, and with other included GNOME tools and applications, such as GNOME Office, provides the user with a stable, standard, and useful graphical user interface. The Gnome Office suite consists of many useful productivity tools for the common end user. The software available in Gnome Office is summarized in Table 6-2.

Table 6-2 GNOME Office Suite	
Application	**Task Provided**
AbiWord	A multi-platform word processor
Gnumeric	A spreadsheet application
Achtung	A GNOME presentation program
GNOME-DB	A database connectivity
GIMP	An extremely powerful and versatile graphics and image-editing program
Sketch and Sodipodi	Vector drawing packages
Eye Of GNOME	An image viewer
Balsa	A flexible and powerful e-mail client
Evolution	An integrated calendaring, e-mail application and personal information manager
Dia	A structured diagrams program similar to Visio

Continued

Table 6-2 (continued)	
Application	**Task Provided**
Guppi	A plotting and graphing program
MrProject and Toutdoux	Project management tools
GnuCash	A personal finance manager
Gfax	Used to send and receive faxes
Galeon	A fast and standards-compliant Web browser

These applications round out the ability of GNOME to provide a complete desktop for end users. Because GNOME is part of the GNU project, it is covered by the GNU GPL, which ensures that all users and developers have access to GNOME. This makes GNOME an excellent, powerful, flexible, and free desktop environment.

KDE

The K Desktop Environment (KDE), which is available at www.kde.org, is another major desktop environment for Linux, UNIX, and UNIX-like operating systems, as shown in Figure 6-2.

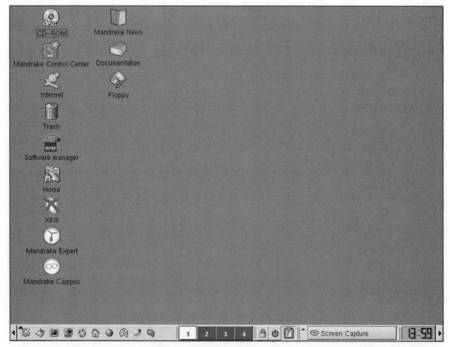

Figure 6-2: The K Desktop Environment

Unlike GNOME, the KDE includes a very sophisticated window manager (KWin), but it can utilize other Window Managers if configured to do so. KDE is a powerful, Open Source, graphical desktop environment that provides ease of use, contemporary functionality, and outstanding graphical design. KDE also provides a high quality developmental framework that allows for quick and easy creation of applications. KDE uses the Qt C++ cross-platform toolkit, which is also released (since version 2.2) under the GNU GPL to provide the framework. Qt is a product of a Norwegian company — Troll Tech — and is available from the Troll Tech FTP server at `ftp://ftp.troll.no/`. The KDE desktop provides a familiar environment for users who have previously used Microsoft Windows. KDE is very portable and can run on Linux, Solaris, FreeBSD, IRIX, HP-UX, and other versions of UNIX.

The K Desktop Environment expands on this excellent foundation with a wide variety of applications. Table 6-3 shows a list of included KDE applications.

Table 6-3
K Desktop Environment Applications

Suite	Application	Task Provided
KOffice	KWord	A FrameMaker-like word processor application
KOffice	KSpread	A spreadsheet application
KOffice	KPresenter	A presentation application
KOffice	Kivio	A flowcharting program
KOffice	Krayon, also known as Kimageshop	A painting and image editing application
KOffice	KPlato	A project management application
KOffice	KChart	A chart-drawing application
KOffice	KFormula	A formula editor
KOffice	Kuger	A business report tool
Konqueror	Konqueror	A file manager
Konqueror	Konqueror	The canvas for all the latest KDE technology, from KIO slaves to component embedding via the KParts object interface
Konqueror	Konqueror	An Open Source Web browser with HTML4.0 compliance, supporting Java applets, JavaScript, CSS1 and (partially) CSS2, as well as Netscape plugins
Konqueror	Konqueror	A universal viewing application

Also available are audio, games, and many more applications for KDE. These applications enable KDE to provide an excellent, powerful, flexible, and free desktop environment.

Usually, you select a window manager or desktop environment during the installation of Linux, but the desktop or window manager that you desire may not be up-to-date or included with the Linux distribution. To resolve this, most desktops and window managers are available for download from the Web sites shown in Table 6-4.

Table 6-4
Window Manager and Desktop Environment Software Resources

Window Manager and Desktop Environment	Software resources
AfterStep	`www.afterstep.org`
Blackbox Window Manager	`http://blackbox.alug.org`
Enlightenment	`www.enlightenment.org/pages/main.html`
FVWM F Virtual Window Manager	`www.fvwm.org`
Fvwm95 Virtual Window Manager 95	`ftp://mitac11.uia.ac.be/pub`
GNOME desktop environment	`www.gnome.org`
IceWM Ice Window Manager	`http://icewm.sourceforge.net` **and** `www.icewm.org`
K Desktop Environment	`www.kde.org`
MWM Motif Window Manager	`www.opengroup.org/openmotif`
OLVWM OpenLook Virtual Window Manager	`www.phys.columbia.edu/~flame/olvwm.html`
Sawfish extensible window manager	`http://sawmill.sourceforge.net`
SCWM Scheme Constraints Window Manager	`http://scwm.sourceforge.net`
Window Maker	`www.windowmaker.org`
XFce desktop environment	`www.xfce.org`
Others	`www.xwinman.org`

Configuring X Window Systems

Objective 3.1 Reconfigure Xwindow with automated utilities (e.g., Xconfigurator, XF86Setup)

You are often required to configure or reconfigure the X Window System, after the installation of Linux. This may be because you didn't have the proper drivers or the correct configuration when you first installed Linux. To complete this configuration, you will often use several tools and files, including X, `xinit`, `.xinitrc`, XF86Setup, and xf86config. The X file is a symbolic link, or *symlink*, to the X Server that is being used for the system — usually located at /usr/X11R6/bin/ directory. The `xinit` program is used to start the X Window System. After it starts, the X Window System uses the file `.xinitrc`, which contains the configuration information. If there is no `.xinitrc` file, then `xinit` uses the following default configuration:

```
xterm -geometry +1+1 -n login -display :0
```

This file can be manually edited to configure the X Window System; however, the XF86Setup and xf86config tools can also be used to configure the system with menu-driven programs. XF86Setup is a GUI program that starts a default X Window System, which allows the configuration of the X Window System.

Cross-Reference For more information about configuration of the X Window System during installation, see the section "Configuring the X Windows System" in Chapter 4.

Sometimes, however, the default system won't work; in such a case, the `xf86config` program can be used to configure the X Window System at the command line. To use `xf86config` to configure the X Window System, the user must be logged in as the root user. Then the user can type **xf86config** at the command prompt to launch the program. The text shown in Figure 6-3 displays the initial configuration screen of **xf86config**.

This screen provides information about the program `xf86config`, such as the location of the file. The screen also informs you that the program creates a basic configuration, and that should know as much as possible about your video card to aid in the configuration. After reading this information, press Enter to continue to the next screen, as shown in Figure 6-4.

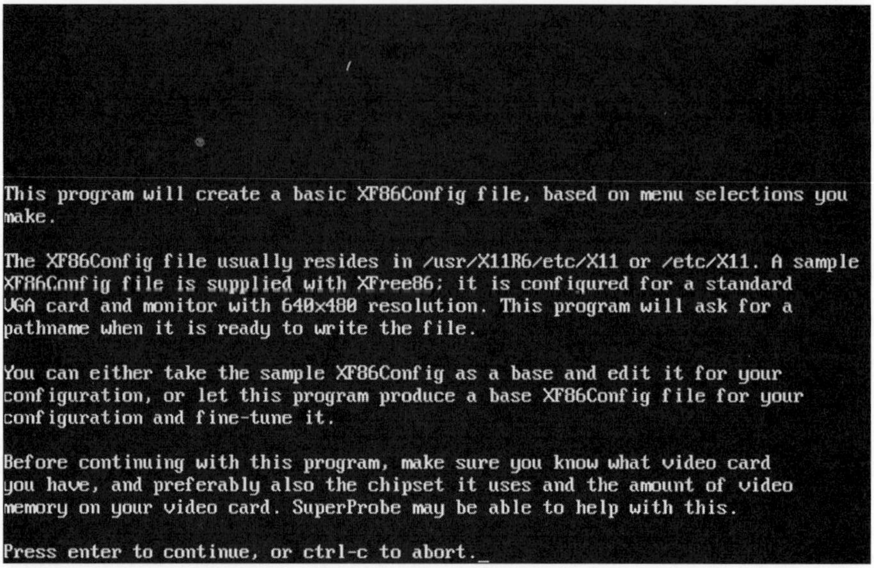

Figure 6-3: The Initial xf86config Screen

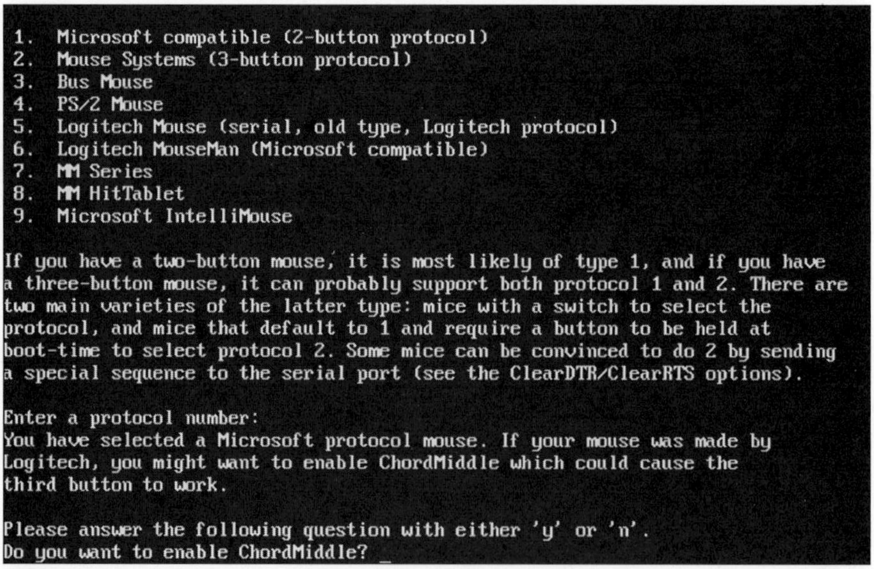

Figure 6-4: The xf86config Mouse Configuration Screen

Figure 6-4 shows the mouse type selected and includes the selection of several mouse types. The following is a list of selections that you will make at this point:

1. **Select the mouse type that most represents the mouse attached to your system.** If you need help in this area, I recommend using the MAN pages. In the case of x86config, however, the MAN page is not very helpful — so some trial-and-error testing of the mouse configuration may be required.

2. **Select CordMiddle if you have a third button on a Logitech mouse with Microsoft compatibility.** After you have selected the mouse type in Step 1, the program prompts for the use of CordMiddle, which enables the use of a third button on some mouse devices.

3. **Enable Emulate3Buttons if CordMiddle does not work with your mouse.** This selection is prompted on all mouse types.

4. **Give the full device name for the attached mouse.** This is the physical location of the mouse on the system and is most likely functional with the default selection of /dev/mouse. If possible, use this for ease of identification.

Caution

If the selection of /dev/mouse does not work, then you probably need to do some investigation of the mouse interface. A Serial port mouse may be mapped to /dev/ttys0 and a PS2 mouse may be on /dev/psaux. You have many options to help you install your particular type of mouse. For example, /dev/tsmo will work for a PS2 mouse, so your best option is to probe for the mouse information when configuring a mouse. Information about the detected devices can be found in the dmesg file and in /proc. Using the information found in these locations should eliminate or narrow the choices for the full device name for the attached mouse.

5. **Configure the monitor.** The screen shown in Figure 6-5 provides important information required for the configuration of the monitor in xf86config, including the vertical refresh rate and the horizontal sync rate. (You should have included these rates when gathering information prior to installation.) With this documented information, you can select the monitor's horizontal sync capabilities at display resolutions. Select a predefined range or manually select the range from the list shown in Figure 6-6. However, don't select a monitor setting that is outside the capabilities of the monitor in use.

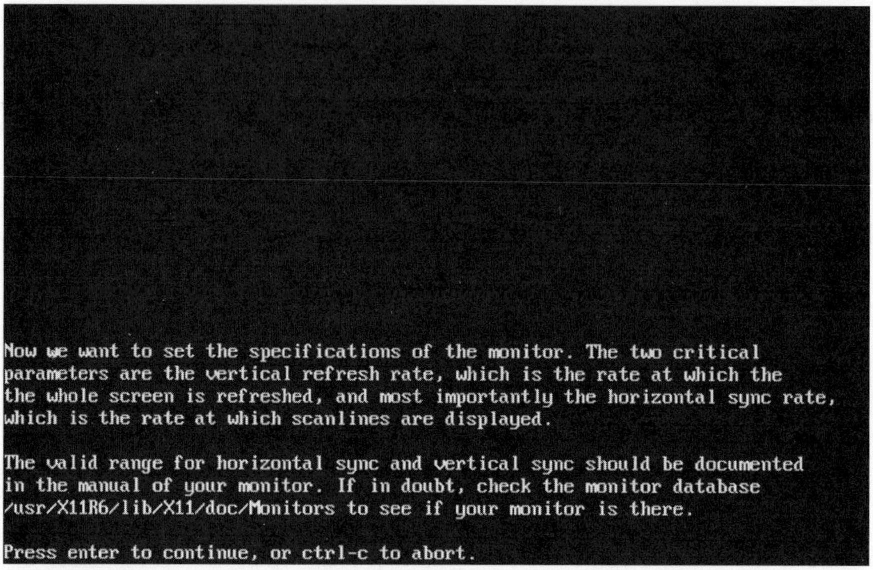

Now we want to set the specifications of the monitor. The two critical
parameters are the vertical refresh rate, which is the rate at which the
the whole screen is refreshed, and most importantly the horizontal sync rate,
which is the rate at which scanlines are displayed.

The valid range for horizontal sync and vertical sync should be documented
in the manual of your monitor. If in doubt, check the monitor database
/usr/X11R6/lib/X11/doc/Monitors to see if your monitor is there.

Press enter to continue, or ctrl-c to abort.

Figure 6-5: The xf86config Monitor Warning Screen

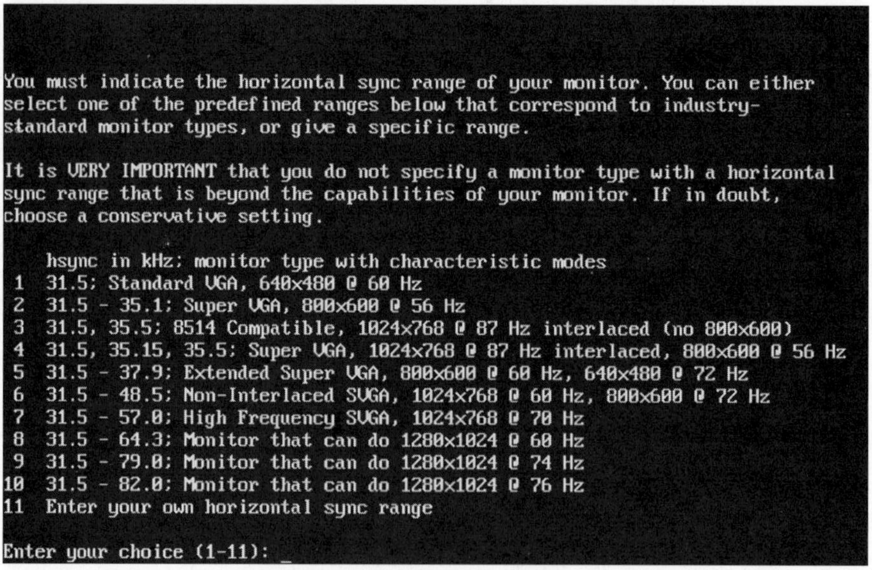

You must indicate the horizontal sync range of your monitor. You can either
select one of the predefined ranges below that correspond to industry-
standard monitor types, or give a specific range.

It is VERY IMPORTANT that you do not specify a monitor type with a horizontal
sync range that is beyond the capabilities of your monitor. If in doubt,
choose a conservative setting.

     hsync in kHz; monitor type with characteristic modes
 1   31.5; Standard VGA, 640x480 @ 60 Hz
 2   31.5 - 35.1; Super VGA, 800x600 @ 56 Hz
 3   31.5, 35.5; 8514 Compatible, 1024x768 @ 87 Hz interlaced (no 800x600)
 4   31.5, 35.15, 35.5; Super VGA, 1024x768 @ 87 Hz interlaced, 800x600 @ 56 Hz
 5   31.5 - 37.9; Extended Super VGA, 800x600 @ 60 Hz, 640x480 @ 72 Hz
 6   31.5 - 48.5; Non-Interlaced SVGA, 1024x768 @ 60 Hz, 800x600 @ 72 Hz
 7   31.5 - 57.0; High Frequency SVGA, 1024x768 @ 70 Hz
 8   31.5 - 64.3; Monitor that can do 1280x1024 @ 60 Hz
 9   31.5 - 79.0; Monitor that can do 1280x1024 @ 74 Hz
10   31.5 - 82.0; Monitor that can do 1280x1024 @ 76 Hz
11   Enter your own horizontal sync range

Enter your choice (1-11): _

Figure 6-6: The xf86config Monitor Configuration Screen

6. Select the video card capabilities. At this stage of configuration, a screen warns that you need the information that you've gathered about the video card. Select the chipset, then choose the general type of card, as shown in Figure 6-7. Then, select the RAMDAC and ClockChip setting used with the video card. This can vary from card to card—even in the same model—so use care when verifying this information.

Cross-Reference For more information about hardware identification, see Chapter 5.

After you have selected these settings, the program asks you to save the configuration file, which is the final step of the basic configuration of the X Window System. You can use the xf86config, XF86Setup, and many more configuration utilities to not only configure the X Window System, but to also reconfigure it. Remember this method for performing configurations or reconfigurations: Back up the working configuration and document every selected setting to allow reconfiguration if the system is damaged and to prevent poor configurations from being repeated.

```
0   2 the Max MAXColor S3 Trio64V+           S3 Trio64V+
1   2-the-Max MAXColor 6000                  ET6000
2   3DLabs Oxygen GMX                        PERMEDIA 2
3   3DVision-i740 AGP                        Intel 740
4   3Dlabs Permedia2 (generic)               PERMEDIA 2
5   928Movie                                 S3 928
6   ABIT G740 8MB SDRAM                      Intel 740
7   AGP 2D/3D V. 1N, AGP-740D                Intel 740
8   AGX (generic)                            AGX-014/15/16
9   ALG-5434(E)                              CL-GD5434
10  AOpen AGP 2X 3D Navigator PA740          Intel 740
11  AOpen PA2010                             Voodoo Banshee
12  AOpen PA45                               SiS6326
13  AOpen PA50D                              SiS6326
14  AOpen PA50E                              SiS6326
15  AOpen PA50V                              SiS6326
16  AOpen PA80/DVD                           SiS6326
17  AOpen PG128                              S3 Trio3D

Enter a number to choose the corresponding card definition.
Press enter for the next page, q to continue configuration.
```

Figure 6-7: The `xf86config` Video Card Configuration Screen

Custom X Window System Programs

The configuration tools XF86Setup and xf86config are not the most user-friendly tools. Most distributions include configuration programs that allow you to reconfigure the X Window System, Window Manager, and desktop environment. User-friendly applications—such as the Mandrake Control Center, shown in Figure 6-8—allow you to easily select all settings in one screen.

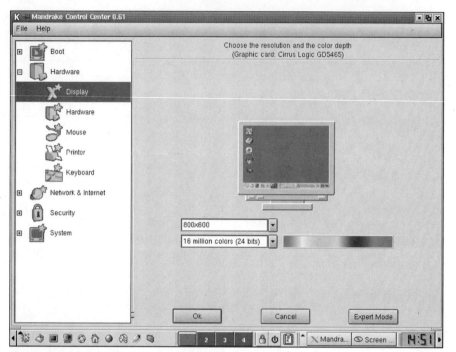

Figure 6-8: The Mandrake Control Center

These applications often allow you to configure the monitor and video card at the same time. Red Hat Linux uses Xconfigurator, which you can use as the initial configuration utility or to reconfigure an X Window System. SuSE uses the SaX and SaX2 (for XFree86 4.0) utilities to configure the X Window System. These are just a few of the custom programs that are available in distributions for configuring the X Window System. These various graphical configuration utilities, however, are customized for each distribution and often contain support files for hardware that are not included in the XFree86 package.

Exam Tip   Custom programs are not available in all distributions of Linux; therefore, you should focus on the generic tools XF86Setup and xf86config. It is important for the exam that you gain experience with these two tools. All tools, however, use the same format, so don't ignore the custom tools — especially Xconfigurator, which is included with Red Hat.

Manual Configuration of the X Window System

You can also manually manipulate the X Window System with the use of the configuration file. The initialization file for the X Window System is often the xf86config file, which is often located at /etc/X11/XF86Config. Every setting is available at this location for configuration by manually editing the text. This requires skill — and often trial-and-error — to see what setting works best. However, there are several different options for configuring the file, which are separated into different sections. These sections are shown in Table 6-5.

Table 6-5	
The xf86config file	
File Section	*This area effects*
Files	Location of support files including font and red, green, blue, or rgbfile
ServerFlags	Used to troubleshoot and disable features
Keyboard	Keyboard protocol used
Pointer	Mouse device, type, and features
Monitor	Monitor information
Device	Video card information
Screen	Combined monitor and device information

The xf86config file is a long file that must be edited in several locations in order to function correctly. This is why the GUI, Command Line, and Shell tools have evolved to the point that manual configuration is seldom — if ever — used to configure an X Window System. However, manually editing or using the XF86Config program can be an exceptionally efficient way for the experienced administrator to configure the X Window System.

Documentation

Objective

3.14 Document the installation of the operating system, including configuration

Whether you choose a GUI, Command Line, or Shell Tool to configure the X Window System, the selected settings should be clearly documented, as should the hardware used. The following information should be included in this documentation:

✦ Monitor make and model

✦ Vertical refresh rate of the monitor

✦ Horizontal sync rate of the monitor

✦ Resolution capabilities of the monitor

✦ Color depth capabilities of the monitor

✦ Video card make and model

✦ Video card Chipset

✦ Video card RAMDAC

✦ Video card available memory

✦ Video card ClockChip

✦ XF86 version

✦ XF86 setup program used

✦ Resolutions selected

✦ Color depth selected

✦ Mouse type selected

✦ Video card selected

✦ Monitor selected

These are most of the settings that should be documented; of course, any other configurations made during the configuration of the X Window System should also be documented.

Exam Tip   Know the information that is required for video card and monitor selection during the installation and configuration of the X Window System.

Summary

This chapter explains many of the basics of the X Window System. This task can be broken down into three areas:

✦ Preparation

• Monitor hardware information

• Video card hardware information

• Planned display settings and window manager

✦ Configuration

• Select GUI, text, or custom X Window System configuration program

• Select mouse type

• Select monitor type

• Select video card type

- Configure the settings
- Test the settings

✦ Documentation

- Monitor make and model
- Vertical refresh rate of the monitor
- Horizontal sync rate of the monitor
- Resolution capabilities of the monitor
- Color depth capabilities of the monitor

✦   ✦   ✦

STUDY GUIDE

The Study Guide section provides you with the opportunity to test your knowledge about the Linux+ exam objectives that are covered in this chapter. The Assessment Questions provide practice for the real exam, and the Scenarios provide practice with real situations. If you get any questions wrong, use the answers to determine the part of the chapter that you should review before continuing.

Assessment Questions

1. Which organization controls the official releases and updates of the X Window System?

    A. www.x.org

    B. www.xfree86.org

    C. www.linux.org

    D. www.mit.edu

2. Which part of the X Window System controls the hardware?

    A. X Client

    B. X Server

    C. X Protocol

    D. Window manager

3. Which part of the X Window System controls the internal communications?

    A. X Client

    B. X Server

    C. X Protocol

    D. Window manager

4. Which part of the X Window System provides the user interface?

    A. X Client

    B. X Server

    C. X Protocol

    D. Window manager

5. Which part of the X Window System controls software application requests?

    A. X Client

    B. X Server

    C. X Protocol

    D. Window manager

6. What are the major advantages/disadvantages of the X Window System for network usage? (Choose all that apply.)

    A. Local and remote computing are actually the same to the user and developer

    B. Applications don't suffer a performance penalty when used locally or remotely

    C. Local and remote computing are actually controlled differently for the user and the developer

    D. Applications do suffer a performance penalty when used locally or remotely

7. Which of the following use the Common Object Request Broker Architecture?

    A. KDE

    B. GNOME

    C. Enlightenment

    D. Sawfish

8. Which window manager does KDE use by default?

    A. Enlightenment

    B. Sawfish

    C. KWin

    D. Blackbox

9. Which of the following is a command line-based setup program for the X Window System?

    A. `XF86Setup`

    B. `XF86Config`

    C. `SetupXF86`

    D. `Xconfigurator`

10. Where is the .xinitrc usually stored on a Linux system?

    A. /etc/X11R6/bin/

    B. /var/X11R6/bin/

    C. /lib/X11R6/bin/

    D. /usr/X11R6/bin/

11. What is the default physical location of the mouse when using XF86Config?

    A. /dev/mouse

    B. /dev/psaux

    C. /dev/ttys0

    D. /dev/tsmo

12. Which of the following customized X Window System configuration programs are included with distributions of Linux? (Choose all that apply.)

    A. Xconfigurator

    B. XF86Setup

    C. Sax2

    D. XDrake

13. Which file can be manually edited to adjust the X Window System configuration?

    A. /usr/X11R6/bin/.xinitrc

    B. /etc/X11/XF86Config

    C. /etc/X11/.xinitrc

    D. /usr/X11R6/bin/XF86Config

14. What is "X" a symbolic link to?

    A. X Client

    B. X Server

    C. xinitrc

    D. XF86Config

15. Which of the makes use the QT programming toolkit?

    A. GNOME

    B. KDE

    C. Enlightenment

    D. Blackbox

16. What program, included with GNOME, provides a word processing application?

    A. KWord

    B. AbiWord

    C. Word

    D. WordPerfect

17. What program, included with KDE, provides graphic manipulation?

    A. Photoshop

    B. GIMP

    C. Krayon

    D. Konqueror

18. Which of the following is part of the GNU project?

    A. KDE

    B. GNOME

    C. XFce

    D. Sawfish

19. Which of the following should be documented when installing a monitor with the X Window System? (Choose all that apply.)

    A. Horizontal sync

    B. ClockChip

    C. RAMDAC

    D. Vertical refresh rate

20. Which of the following should be documented when installing a video card with the X Window System? (Choose all that apply.)

    A. Horizontal sync

    B. ClockChip

    C. RAMDAC

    D. Vertical refresh rate

Scenarios

1. The X Window System has been corrupted on 50 identical systems. What are three utilities that can be used to reconfigure the damaged systems, deploy the repair, and backup the information that will be required to make future failures easier to correct.

2. The installation of the X Window System has been completed successfully on the company workstations. The manager wants to know what information should be documented. What information should be documented for the X Windows installation?

Lab Exercises

Lab 6-1 Linux

The objective for this hands-on lab is to gain experience in configuring and reconfiguring the X Window System. Any distribution of Linux may be used for this exercise.

1. Back up the configuration files for the current X Window System.

2. Start the XF86Config program and configure the X Window System. Be sure to note each step used and compare with the configuration used during the initial installation.

3. Verify that the installation works correctly.

4. Repeat as often as needed to become efficient at configuring the X Window System with XF86Config.

Lab 6-2 Linux

The objective for this hands-on lab is to gain experience in configuring and reconfiguring the X Window System. Any distribution of Linux may be used for this exercise.

1. Back up the configuration files for the current X Window System.

2. Start the XF86Setup program and configure the X Window System. Be sure to note each step used and compare with the configuration used during the initial installation.

3. Verify that the installation works correctly.

4. Repeat as often as needed to become efficient at configuring the X Window System with XF86Setup.

Lab 6-3 Linux

The objective for this hands-on lab is to gain experience in configuring and reconfiguring the X Window System. Any distribution of Linux may be used for this exercise.

1. Back up the configuration files for the current X Window System.

2. Start the custom X Window System configuration program that is included with the Linux distribution of your choice and configure the X Window System. Be sure to note each step used and compare with the configuration used during the initial installation.

3. Verify that the installation works correctly.

4. Repeat as often as needed to become efficient at configuring the X Window System with the custom X Window System configuration program.

Answers to Chapter Questions

Chapter Pre-test

1. The X Window System provides the GUI capabilities in Linux. It provides the X Server for support of the hardware, X Client for support of the software, the X Protocol for local and remote connections between the X Server and Client, and finally, a Window Manager.

2. The software and resources for the X Window System are at `www.X.org` and several other Web sites.

3. The X Window System is configured with XF86Config, XF86Setup, and several custom programs that are included with Linux distributions.

4. Configuring the X Window System manually with a text editor or XF86Config can be a fast and easy way for a very experienced administrator to configure the X Window System.

5. The files used for the X Window configuration are X, xinit, .xinitrc, and xf86config.

6. The major parts of the X Window System are the X Client, X Server, X Protocol, and Window Manager.

7. The most dominant desktops used in Linux are KDE and GNOME.

8. Desktop environments often include several useful applications and provide a full-featured desktop for the user.

9. The X Window System can be used for remote systems; this is actually a major feature of the system because it works equally well on remote and local systems.

10. The ability to use the X Window System to manage remote systems is an enormous advantage for administrators. This allows the administrator to install, test, and troubleshoot user issues remotely while not changing the environment.

Assessment Questions

1. A. The X Consortium at www.x.org controls the official release and updating of the X Window System. MIT turned over control of the X Window System to the X Consortium; www.linux.org maintains information about Linux; and www.xfree86.org creates a distribution of the X Windows System for the x86 platform. For review, see the "What is the X Window System?" section.

2. B. The X Server controls the hardware; the X Client controls the software; the X Protocol controls communication; and the window manager provides the user interface. For review, see the "The X Window System" section.

3. C. The X Protocol controls communication; the X Client controls the software; the X Server controls the hardware; and the window manager provides the user interface. For review, see the "The X Window System" section.

4. D. The window manager provides the user interface; the X Client controls the software; the X Server controls the hardware; and the X Protocol controls communication. For review, see the "The X Window System" section.

5. A. The X Client controls the software; the window manager provides the user interface; the X Server controls the hardware; and the X Protocol controls communication. For review, see the "The X Window System" section.

6. A and B. The advantages of local and remote computing are actually the same to the user and developer; applications don't suffer a performance penalty when used locally or remotely. The others are not disadvantages of remote network use of the X Window System; the major disadvantage is a performance impact from using many X Window Systems on a network. For review, see the "X Client and Server communications" section.

7. B. GNOME uses CORBA (or Common Object Request Broker Architecture) to provide open, vendor-independent architecture that applications can use over networks. The others don't use CORBA. For review, see the "GNOME" section.

8. C. KDE uses the KWin window manager by default. GNOME does not include a specific window manager by default, but is usually installed over Enlightenment, Window Maker, or Sawfish. Enlightenment and Sawfish are window managers. For review, see the "KDE" section.

9. B. The `XF86Config` program is the command line setup program for the X Window System. The others are GUI or Shell programs for the X Window System configuration. For review, see the "Configuring X Window Systems" section.

10. D. The usual location of the file is `/usr/X11R6/bin`. For review, see the "Configuring X Window Systems" section.

11. A. The default location for the mouse device is `/dev/`mouse. For review, see the "Configuring X Window Systems" section.

12. A, C, and D are all custom-created programs for configuring the X Window System on particular Linux distributions. XF86Setup is not distribution-specific; it is included with the XF86 system. For review, see the "Custom X Window System Programs" section.

13. B. The default location of the configuration file for the X Window System is `/etc/X11/XF86Config`. For review, see the "Manual Configuration of the X Window System" section.

14. B. X is a symbolic link or *symlink* to the X Server. The others are not linked to X. For review, see the "Configuring X Window Systems" section.

15. B. KDE uses QT; the others don't. For review, see the "KDE" section.

16. B. AbiWord is the program included with GNOME for word processing. The others may be available, but they are not the defaults. For review, see the "GNOME" section.

17. C. Krayon is included with KDE to provide graphic manipulation. The others may be available but are not the defaults. For review, see the "KDE" section.

18. B. GNOME is part of the GNU project; the others are not. For review, see the "GNOME" section.

19. A and D. Both horizontal sync and vertical refresh rate are information used with monitors. ClockChip and RAMDAC are used with video cards. For review, see the "Configuring X Window Systems" section.

20. B and C. ClockChip and RAMDAC are used with video cards. Both horizontal sync and vertical refresh rate are information used with monitors. For review, see the "Configuring X Window Systems" section.

Scenarios

1. You can configure the X Window System in several ways. First, you can use the custom configuration program that is included with the distribution. Second, you can use the XF86Setup or XF86Config programs included with the X Window System for the x86 system. The third, and probably simplest way, is that you can modify the file manually, and copy the corrected configuration to the other systems. You can also deploy the repaired system by manually configuring each system, but copying the corrected configuration file from the first system to the other identical systems is much more efficient. This way, only one configuration file needs to be backed up, as they are all identical. For review, see the "Manual Configuration of the X Window System" and "Configuring X Window Systems" sections.

2. The following information should be given to the manager:

   • Monitor make and model

   • Vertical refresh rate of the monitor

   • Horizontal sync rate of the monitor

   • Resolution capabilities of the monitor

   • Color depth capabilities of the monitor

   • Video card make and model

   • Video card Chipset

   • Video card RAMDAC

   • Video card available memory

   • Video card ClockChip

   • XF86 version

   • XF86 setup program used

   • Resolutions selected

   • Color depth selected

   • Mouse type selected

   • Video card selected

   • Monitor selected

   For review, see the "Documentation" section.

Configuring Networking

EXAM OBJECTIVES

+ 3.2 Configure the client's workstation for remote access (e.g., ppp, ISDN)

+ 3.4 Configure basic network services and settings (e.g., netconfig, linuxconf; settings for TCP/IP, DNS, DHCP)

+ 3.5 Configure basic server services (e.g., X, SMB, NIS, NFS)

+ 3.6 Configure basic Internet services (e.g., HTTP, POP, SMTP, SNMP, FTP)

+ 3.13 Load, remove, and edit list modules (e.g., insmod, rmmod, lsmod, modprobe)

+ 3.14 Document the installation of the operating system, including configuration

+ 3.15 Configure access rights (e.g., rlogin NIS, FTP, TFTP, SSH, Telnet)

+ 7.8 Identify basic networking concepts, including how a network works

CHAPTER PRE-TEST

1. What is the TCP/IP protocol?

2. What are DNS, WINS, NIS, and DHCP?

3. What are SMB and NFS?

4. What is the purpose of the PPP protocol?

5. What are HTTP, POP, SMTP, and SNMP?

6. What is FTP and TFTP?

7. What are Telnet, rlogin, and SSH?

8. What is a gateway and what is a netmask?

9. What is the standard protocol of the Internet?

10. What are the standard Internet e-mail client protocols?

✦ Answers to these questions can be found at the end of the chapter. ✦

The ability to network is the primary function of Linux. Installing networking may include basic configuration of network services, access rights, client services, Internet services, and remote access. If you know the features of most of the available services, you should be able to prevent major security risks and perform a basic configuration of these services. In fact, you should know that you could make a career out of performing each of these tasks individually. The goal of this chapter is to make you familiar with most of the available services and to show you their basic configurations.

Basic Network Services

Objective

3.4 Configure basic network services and settings (e.g., netconfig, linuxconf; settings for TCP/IP, DNS, DHCP)

7.8 Identify basic networking concepts, including how a network works

A number of services are available to the Linux system to provide networking. In general, these services can be used in any environment and can be divided into two types — clients and servers — and can be used in any environment. Clients use their services to connect to servers and servers use their services to provide information to clients. This relationship is true of every networking system in use, including so-called "peer-to-peer" systems in which both systems act as a client and a server. The major networking protocol for Linux is the Transmission Control Protocol and Internet Protocol (TCP/IP) protocol. TCP/IP provides all network services used in the Linux environment. TCP/IP is the primary protocol of the Internet, so interfacing your local Linux network services to the Internet is very straightforward. You must configure these services at the most basic level. You can use these services after you get them running, but keep the following warning in mind: Although client-side services are usually safe, these services have proven to be insecure in some situations. Therefore, always consult network security information or another source before activating one of these services in any environment. In general, you are required to configure the basic network services — even if it is just to connect to the Internet — so you may benefit from some background information before beginning configuration.

TCP/IP Protocol Suite

The TCP/IP suite is used everyday by anyone who accesses the Internetor or uses a local LAN. The strength of TCP/IP comes from its development: It was designed to be robust and includes two sets of systems — connection-oriented (TCP) and connectionless (UDP) protocols — that allow the remote connection to clients or servers. Table 7-1 lists many of the most popular protocols and services that they provide.

Table 7-1
The TCP/IP Protocol Suite

System	Port (default)	Service provided
FTP	20-21	File Transfer Protocol allows the transfer of files from one system to another with Transmission Control Protocol (TCP) to ensure delivery and directory visibility.
SSH	22	Secure Shell, sometimes known as *Secure Socket Shell*, provides secure access to a remote computer.
Telnet	23	Telnet protocol allows communication with remote systems, usually to access and use the remote system.
SMTP	25	Simple Mail Transfer Protocol used in sending and receiving e-mail. Because it is limited in its ability to queue messages, it is normally used for server-to-server mail transfer.
DNS	53	Domain Name System is used to translate a user-friendly name, such as www.linux.org, to the related IP address, 198.182.196.56 for www.linux.org.
DHCP and BOOTPS	67	Dynamic Host Configuration Protocol is a communications protocol that automates the assignment of Internet Protocol (IP) addresses in a network. Bootstrap Protocol is a protocol that automatically configures a network user and boots or initiates an operating system. BOOTPS is the server-side protocol.
BOOTPC	68	Bootstrap Protocol is a protocol that automatically configures a network user and boots or initiates an operating system. BOOTP is the client-side protocol.
TFTP	69	Trivial File Transfer Protocol is used much like FTP; TFTP, however, uses the User Datagram Protocol (UDP) and does not ensure delivery or provide directory visibility.
Gopher	70	Gopher provides a way to bring text files from all over the world to a viewer on your computer. It has been replaced by the HTTP protocol.

System	Port (default)	Service provided
Finger	79	Finger is a program that tells you the name associated with an e-mail address.
HTTP	80	The Hypertext Transfer Protocol is the set of rules for exchanging files (text, graphic images, sound, video, and other multimedia files) on the World Wide Web.
POP (3)	110	Post Office Protocol 3 is the most recent version of a standard protocol for receiving e-mail downloaded to clients from servers. POP (3) is an alternative to IMAP.
RPC	111	SUN Remote Procedure Call is a protocol that one program can use to request a service from another host on the network without having to understand network details.
RPC	135	Microsoft RPC.
SMB/CIFS	139	SMB/CIFS/CIFS server.
IMAP	143 and 220	Internet Message Access Protocol is a standard protocol for accessing e-mail from your mail server; it is not downloaded until instructed to do so.
SNMP	161	Simple Network Management Protocol governs network management and the monitoring of network devices.
rlogin	221	Remote login is a command that allows an authorized user to log in to other machines (host) on a network and to interact as if the user were physically at the host computer. It has been replaced by SSH and is less known than telnet.
SSL/TSL	443	The Secure Sockets Layer protocol is used for the secure transmission of data on the Internet. TLS is the successor to the Secure Sockets Layer (SSL). It uses the same port but provides more security and is backwards-compatible with SSL; most browsers now use TSL.
SMB/CIFS	445	The Server Message Block Protocol provides a method for client applications in a computer to read and write to files on — and to request services from — server programs in a computer network. It is used to connect to the Microsoft Windows Platform.

Exam Tip   Don't try to memorize these ports; instead, focus on configuring the services and learn what protocol provides what service, such as HTTP for Web pages.

Connection protocols needed

Because the TCP/IP protocol suite is limited to network routing and transportation of information, you may need other protocols to network other systems.

Point-to-Point Protocol

The simplest and most widely used modem-based protocol is the Point-to-Point Protocol (PPP). PPP communicates between two computers by using a serial interface; for example, a personal computer is connected by an analog phone line to a server. Many users access the Internet from home by dialing a modem that connects to a modem pool, which then establishes a point-to-point connection by using PPP. This protocol can also be used for server-to-server connections and router-to-router connections. PPP provides a static connection between two pieces of equipment. It can also be used in many broadband, xDSL or cable, Internet connections with Ethernet.

Ethernet

Ethernet is the most widely used Local Area Network (LAN) access method. It is used to connect most workstations, servers, and routers at hubs that create the LAN.

Ethernet uses the IEEE 802.3 standard to provide connectivity to a network. Ethernet and PPP are the most commonly used access methods, but they aren't the only ones used.

Serial Line Internet Protocol

SLIP, or Serial Line Internet Protocol, is an alternative to PPP. SLIP is not used very widely because it doesn't provide for error detection and it doesn't support synchronous connections.

WAN protocols

Linux can directly support almost any connection, including xDSL, cable, leased lines, and more. To support these connections, Linux employs PPPoE, Frame Relay, and other high-speed interface connection methods. These are not basic configurations of the Linux system, but you should be aware of them.

Other network protocols

Other network protocols include Yellow Pages or NIS (Network Information System) and NFS (Network File System), which use the SUN Remote Procedure Call (part of TCP/IP) to provide networking services. NIS is used to provide access to all systems on a network while only requiring one authentication. NFS is used to provide for file viewing and storage on a remote system.

Configuring Basic Network Services

Objective

3.4 Configure basic network services and settings (e.g., netconfig, linuxconf; settings for TCP/IP, DNS, DHCP)

3.15 Configure access rights (e.g., rlogin NIS, FTP, TFTP, SSH, Telnet)

Basic network services are often configured during the installation of a Linux distribution. Sometimes these services are not completed or need to be changed after installation. To do so, you can choose from several tools to configure basic network services in the Linux operating system. The most common tools are `netconfig` and `linuxconf`. Because `linuxconf` and `netconfig` are often very similar in usage, they are illustrated together in this chapter. Some distributions use the `netconfig` as part of the `linuxconf` suite. Other distributions customize the `netconfig` and `linuxconf` programs for their own configuration. You must have root access to use either program; after you have acquired root access, follow these steps:

1. Log in as the root user.

2. Type the command **linuxconf.**

3. Press Enter to be greeted by the program, as shown in Figure 7-1.

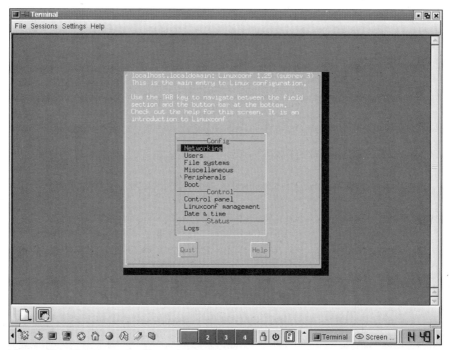

Figure 7-1: The Linux Configuration Screen

Figure 7-1 shows that the `linuxconf` program can be used to configure networking, users, file systems, miscellaneous, peripherals, boot, control panel, `linuxconf` management, date and time, and finally, logs.

4. Select Networking to display the screen shown in Figure 7-2. (Also notice that Figure 7-3 from `netconfig` is identical.)

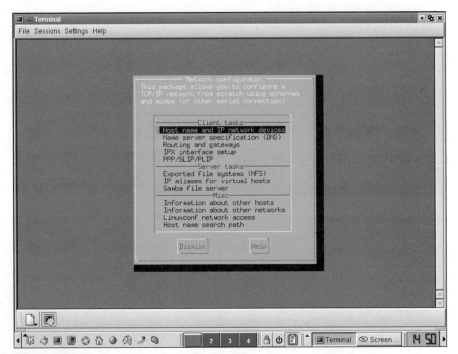

Figure 7-2: The Linux Network Configurator from `linuxconf`

These two screens are identical, but this is not always the case. Figure 7-4 shows the `netconfig` screen from Red Hat 7.1.

The Red Hat program contains less functionality than the preceding `netconfig` program; it only allows some basic configurations, as shown in Figure 7-5.

Because the `netconfig` program has been customized by most distributions, it can be either a very complete configuration program or a very basic one. You should remember that all the settings in the `linuxconf` program can also be used in the `netconfig` program. In light of this fact, I won't discuss any more information related to `netconfig`, because you can use the information in `linuxconf` for all versions of the `netconfig` program.

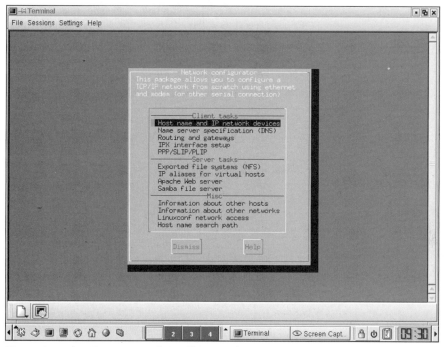

Figure 7-3: The Linux Network Configurator from `netconfig`

Figure 7-4: The Red Hat `netconfig` Program

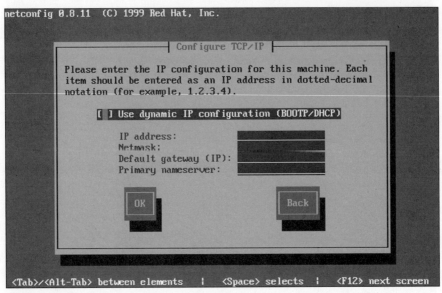

Figure 7-5: The Red Hat Configure TCP/IP Screen

Exam Tip   Be sure to practice with several versions of the `linuxconf` and `netconfig` programs.

Host name

By selecting the Host name and IP network devices, you can configure networking, including the tasks of setting the host name (this is the Fully Qualified Domain Name, or FQDN) and configuring any NIC(s), as shown in Figure 7-6.

You should enter the host name of your computer and your domain name here. Although most users don't need a host name and domain, a server that is intended for users to access from the Internet or an intranet should have this information. This information will be used at a DNS (Domain Name System) server to allow the translation of the domain name to the IP address for the system. (For more information on DNS, see the DNS section later in the chapter.)

You can also set up alias names for your host here.

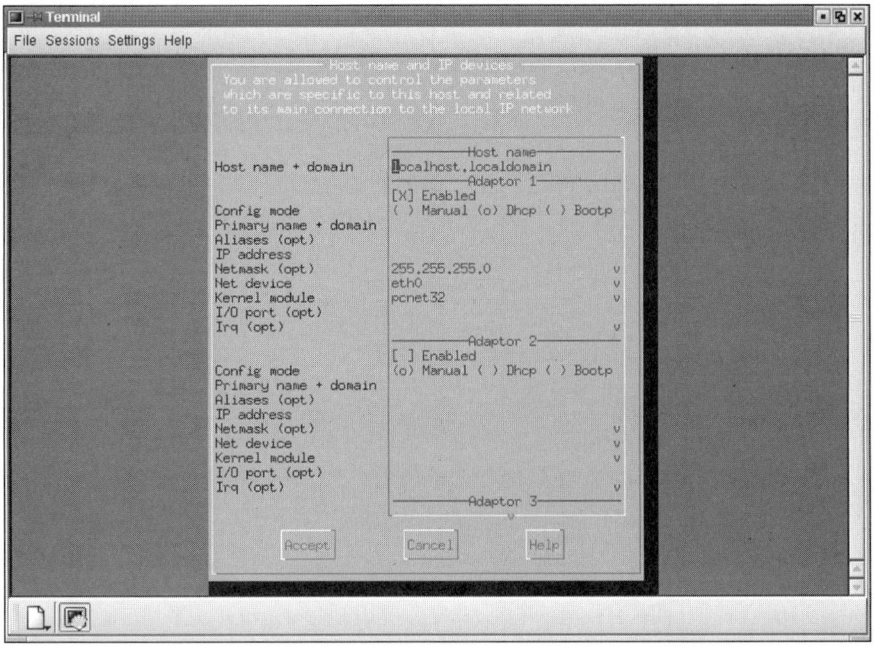

Figure 7-6: The Host Name and IP Configuration Screen

IP addressing

The network configuration program allows you to configure all network cards in the system; this is important if you plan to use the system to connect two LAN segments or to filter or route traffic. TCP/IP requires all stations participating in the LAN or WAN to have an IP address. IP addresses are logical numbers, such as street addresses or phone numbers, which are broken into four groups or *octets*. These four groups of numbers are usually separated by periods (for example, 192.168.0.101). Octets are really representations of the binary numbers. In fact, the binary numbers are just zeros and ones that create all the numbers used in an IP address. An IP address is a 32-bit number — thus, 4 sets of 8 binary numbers — that must be unique to one and only one piece of equipment attached to the network. Using binary math, or by just multiplying $2 \times 2 \times 2 \times 2 \times 2 \times 2 \times 2 \times 2 = 256$, you arrive at 256 total available numbers (starting with 0 and ending with 255). Therefore, the range of the numbering system available for IP addresses is 0 to 255.

IP addresses originate from the Internet Assigned Numbers Authority (IANA). (see www.iana.org/ for more information). These addresses are assigned to Internet Service Providers (ISP), who then distribute them to customers. Since duplication of IP addresses on a network is a serious problem, the network administrator should be consulted before randomly assigning IP addresses to servers and other IP devices. A system usually contains only one NIC or adapter, but you may experience some situations in which you use several NICs, such as routing and other specialized servers. Thus, the only NIC is usually listed as adaptor 1. You can verify this; in Figure 7-6, for example, notice that in the listing next to Net device, adapter 1 has a net device but adapter 2 does not. Manual IP addressing is selected if the administrator can provide a static address. The address should then be entered into the IP address field. If the network is using dynamic IP addressing, as in this example, the administrator is managing a DHCP (Dynamic Host Configuration Protocol) server which is providing IP addresses, so the DHCP option should be selected. You can also select bootp, which is an older type of dynamic addressing system.

DHCP

The Dynamic Host Configuration Protocol (DHCP) is used to automate the task of assigning IP addresses to network devices. Client computers (and other IP devices) can be configured to request an IP address, and other necessary IP settings, from a DHCP server upon entering the network. DHCP servers are configured with a range, or pool, of IP addresses to manage. A Linux system can also be set up to be a DHCP server.

Using the DHCP protocol, client devices send out a broadcast asking for a local DHCP server. Although this is always a local network broadcast, routers can be configured to forward DHCP requests to other network segments. When a DHCP server receives a request, and it has unassigned addresses, it offers one from its address pool to the client. The client then accepts the address and any other information the DHCP server is configured to provide. Most of the time this additional information will be the address of the default gateway and DNS servers. The DHCP server will also set a Time To Live (TTL) value for this lease. The client PC must renew the IP address before the TTL expires or it will need to obtain new IP information from a DHCP server in order to remain on the network. Lease renewals are requested when half of the TTL time has past up to the time that the TTL has expired.

Netmask

An IP address actually contains two pieces of information. The first part of the address identifies a specific network and the second part identifies a specific host, or device, on that network. The only way to determine what part of the IP address is the network portion and which is the host portion is to use a netmask. The netmask is added to the IP address in a binary mathematical process, which creates a new 32-bit number. The point at which this result differs from the added value of the netmask identifies the network side of the IP address. By manipulating the netmask value, an ISP or private network administrator can create numerous "sub" networks from a single IP address class. This specifically allows ISPs to better utilize the shrinking number of available public IP addresses. Advanced discussions of IP addressing and subnetting is beyond the scope of this book—although you will find many books dedicated to just this subject.

Hardware resources

The next items to configure in the networking menu are the network card device, kernel module, I/O (input/output) port, and IRQ (interrupt request). I/O and IRQ are optional because they already indicate the resources of the hardware network device being used.

| Objective |

3.13 Load, remove, and edit list modules (e.g., insmod, rmmod, lsmod, modprobe)

Many network cards are loaded by Linux as a kernel module, meaning that it runs right out of the kernel itself. The following commands are useful in manipulating network card modules:

✦ insmod — Inserts a module into the kernel. For example, if you need to load a 3Com network driver into the kernel for your system, you would use the command, insmod 3c90x

✦ rmmod — This command removes a module from the kernel

✦ lsmod — This lists the modules that are currently loaded into the kernel

✦ modprobe — An advanced command that allows you to automatically load modules using a prepared list stored in a file

DNS

The Domain Name System (DNS) translates a user-friendly domain name, such as www.linux.org, into an IP address. By setting DNS servers in your network client, you are telling the client which DNS server to go to when looking up address names. There is a primary and secondary server, because if the first server is not working when you look up an address, the client will go to the secondary to try the operation.

DNS configuration is illustrated in Figure 7-7.

Routing and gateways

This network configuration section allows you to set your default gateway and routing tables. Typically, for most end user systems, you will only need to set your default gateway, which should be your primary router on your network. More advanced server configurations may need static routes set to different networks. Figure 7-8 shows the information that you are presented when you select routing and gateways.

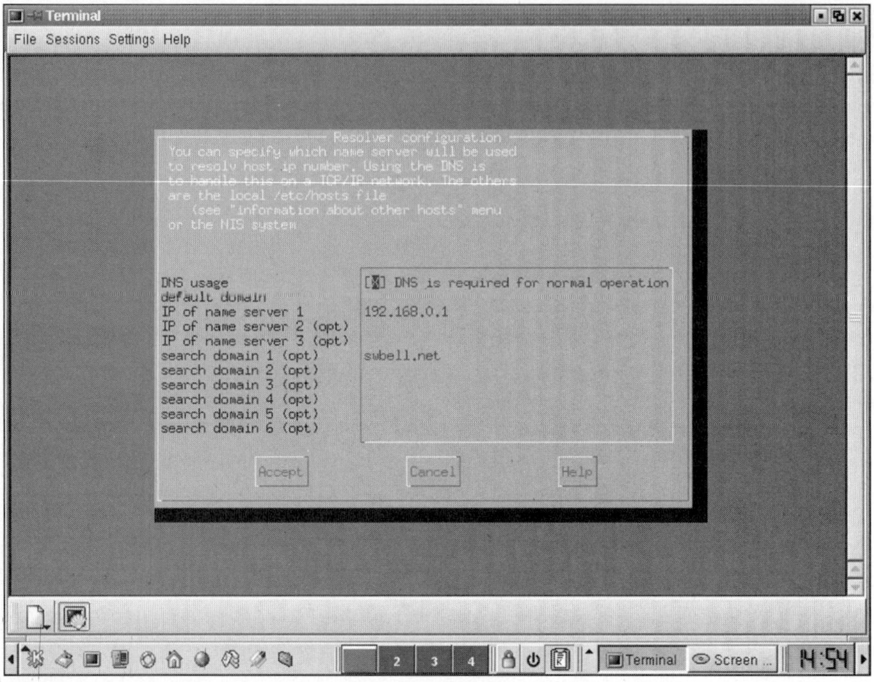

Figure 7-7: The Resolver Configuration (DNS) Screen

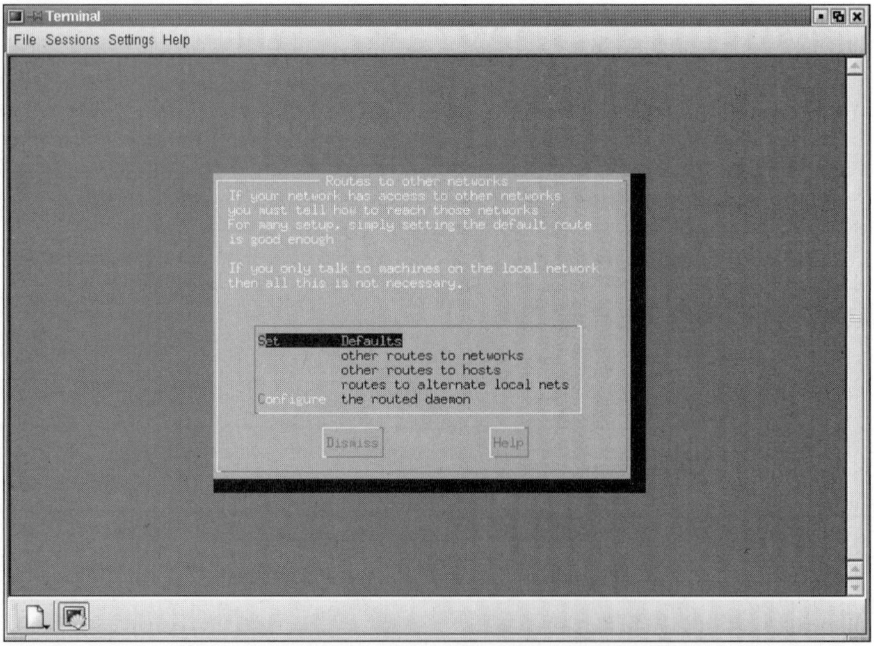

Figure 7-8: The Routing and Gateway Configuration Screen

PPP, SLIP and PLIP connections

The final client configuration task is the configuration on PPP, SLIP and PLIP connections. These are external connections to the system that can be used to create remote connections. You can use any one of these methods to connect a home system to an ISP for Internet access or to gain remote access to a corporate system for administrative purposes. These access methods all provide different features, but PPP is the most commonly used.

Objective ▶ 3.2 Configure the client's workstation for remote access (e.g., ppp, ISDN)

The Point-to-Point Protocol, or PPP, is used to create a connection over a serial device — usually an analog or ISDN modem for client systems, and a high-speed connection for WAN connections. For the purpose of this book, we will only discuss the use of PPP over serial modems (including standard analog and ISDN); however, you should be aware that PPP can also be used in high-speed digital connections as well. If you select PPP/SLIP/PLIP from the menu in Figure 7-3, a menu displays, which enables you to configure the logical device. Choose from the following selections:

✦ Dismiss and return to the previous screen

✦ Ask for help

✦ Add a device configuration

By selecting this last option, you can move forward, and a menu appears, as shown in Figure 7-9.

Some facts to keep in mind:

✦ PPP is used for most modem connections.

✦ SLIP also provides for modem connections, but to a very limited extent. PPP has mostly replaced SLIP except in very basic environments.

✦ PLIP is used to create local connections with the parallel port; this is useful for connecting systems that are closely located and to provide a faster interface than the serial port.

If you select PPP from the PPP, SLIP, and PLIP menu, the PPP configuration screen displays, as shown in Figure 7-10.

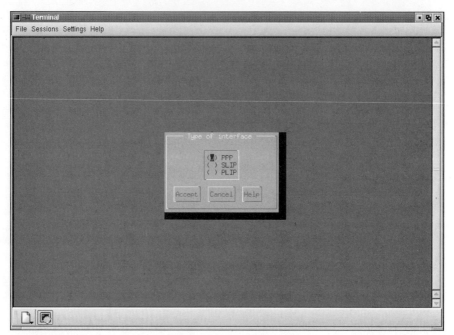

Figure 7-9: Select the type of interface to be configured.

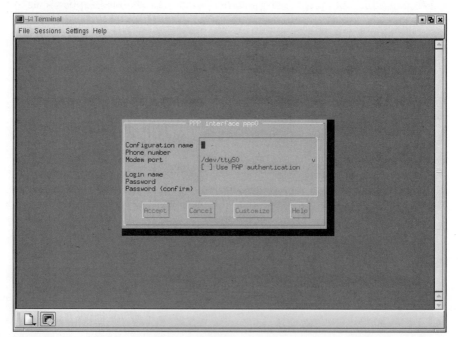

Figure 7-10: Configure the PPP connection

To configure the PPP connection, simply insert the following:

✦ The name of the configuration, such as Dial-ISP

✦ The telephone number to be dialed

✦ The modem port to be used (usually /dev/ttyS0 for com1 or serial A and /dev/ttyS1 for com2 or serial B)

✦ The authentication method (check the ISP instructions; they may indicate that PAP authentication is to be used)

✦ The login name (usually the user name created when the account is established)

✦ The password with confirmation

This is usually enough information to configure a PPP connection with linuxconf or netconfig. However, you may be able to set more advanced features using the customize option. Select the customize option to display the menu shown in Figure 7-11.

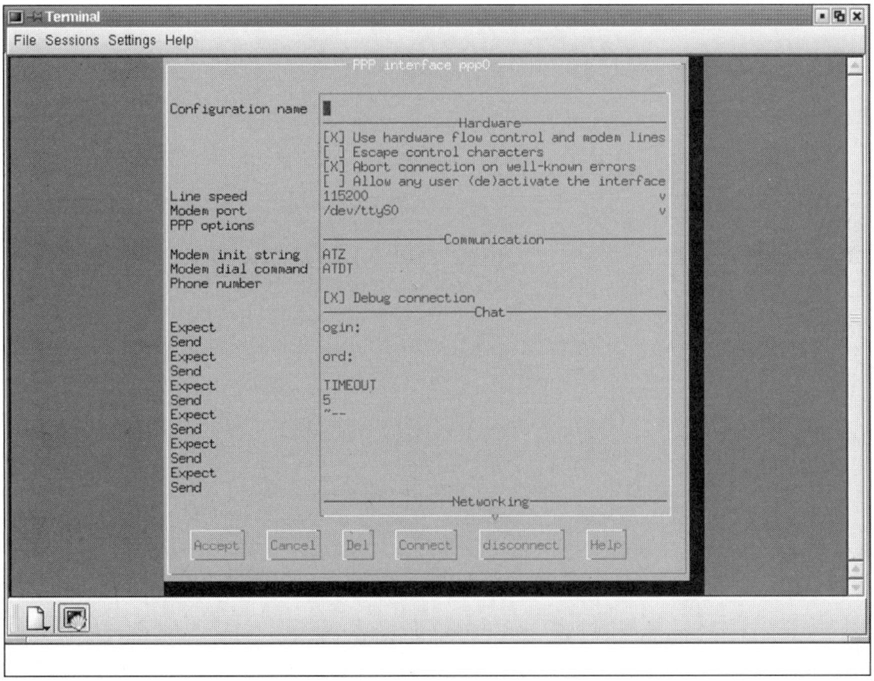

Figure 7-11: Customizing the PPP connection

From this menu, you can configure the modem in more detail, including the following:

✦ You can turn off many normal standards, such as hardware flow control, which is useful when connecting two machines directly with the serial port.

✦ You can enable escape control characters that are normally automatically negotiated during connection creation.

✦ You can choose to attempt to stay connected if known errors occur. This option is usually left "on," so that you can troubleshoot the connection.

✦ You can choose to allow any user to connect or disconnect the configured connection. You may consider this option if you don't want users to know the root user password in order to establish the newly created connection.

✦ You can select the line speed. For troubleshooting connections that don't connect completely or disconnect often, this is very useful. By choosing a lower connect speed, you can see if the system will react better with less errors than at a higher speed.

Server Tasks with `linuxconf`

The `linuxconf` program can configure some basic server functions for the Linux system.

NFS

You can use the `linuxconf` program to configure the NFS (Network File System) clients, thus allowing other UNIX and UNIX-like systems to share resources. The menu, which is shown in Figure 7-12, allows you to configure shared resources, comments, client names, and privileges.

Sun Microsystems developed NFS, which has been designated as a file server standard. NFS uses the SUN Remote Procedure Call, which is a protocol that one program can use to request a service from a program (located on another computer in a network) without requiring an understanding of the network details. It normally uses the NIS for naming resolution. NFS is portable to other UNIX-like systems, such as Linux, and even Microsoft clients with the use of the Sun Solstice Network Client.

In the Real World   Sun Microsystems has extended NFS to WebNFS, which extends the use of NFS to the Internet. WebNFS offers several advantages over HTTP and FTP: It doesn't require the opening and closing of connections for each requested file, and large file downloads are supported and can be downloaded in sections to ease recovery. Netscape, Oracle, IBM, Apple, and Novell have announced support for WebNFS. Sun hopes that the World Wide Web Consortium will adopt it as a standard for the Internet.

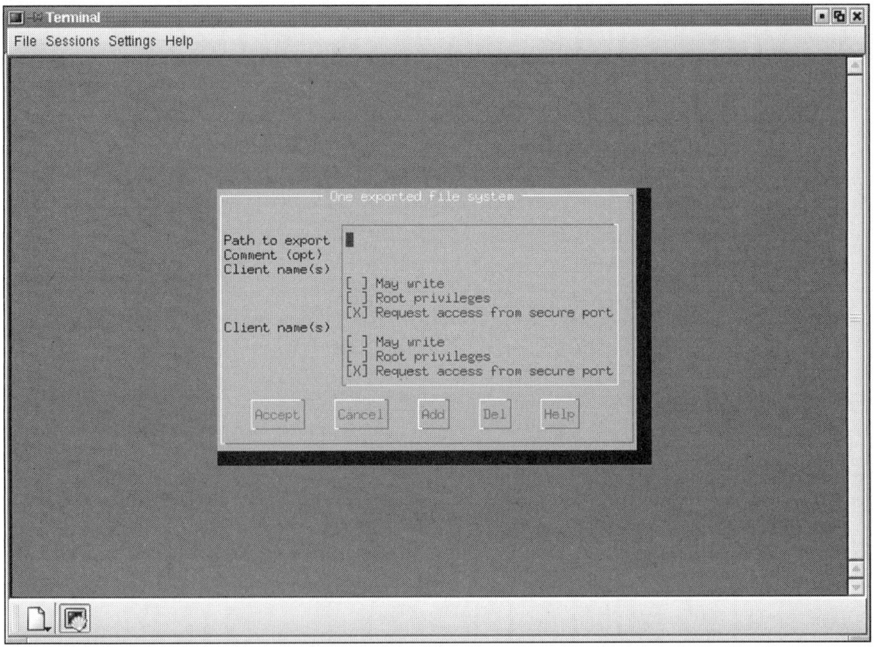

Figure 7-12: Configuring a NFS Share

IP aliases for virtual hosts

IP aliases allow the system to create virtual servers, and are used to create virtual systems on one interface. Figure 7-13 demonstrates this by showing the screen that follows the initial selection of the interface that will have virtual hosts.

Exam Tip   Most Linux users with only six months of experience probably haven't used Virtual Hosts; however, you should be aware of their existence and the basics of how to create them.

To create a range of virtual hosts, follow these steps:

1. At the virtual host configuration screen, enter a range of IP addresses. For example, use a range of 192.168.0.200-250 for a system on a 192.168.0.0 network.

2. In the "Configure domain name server" menu, select the "IP allocation space" entry, enter the range, and type in "Virtual domains" as a short description.

3. Go into the DNS and add a host for the domain with a FQDN. Then hit **ctrl-X** to prompt Linuxconf to compute the first unused IP address in the IP aliases range. Use this IP address.

4. Use the httpd configuration and add a section for the new FQDN. Repeat this as often as necessary for additional virtual hosts.

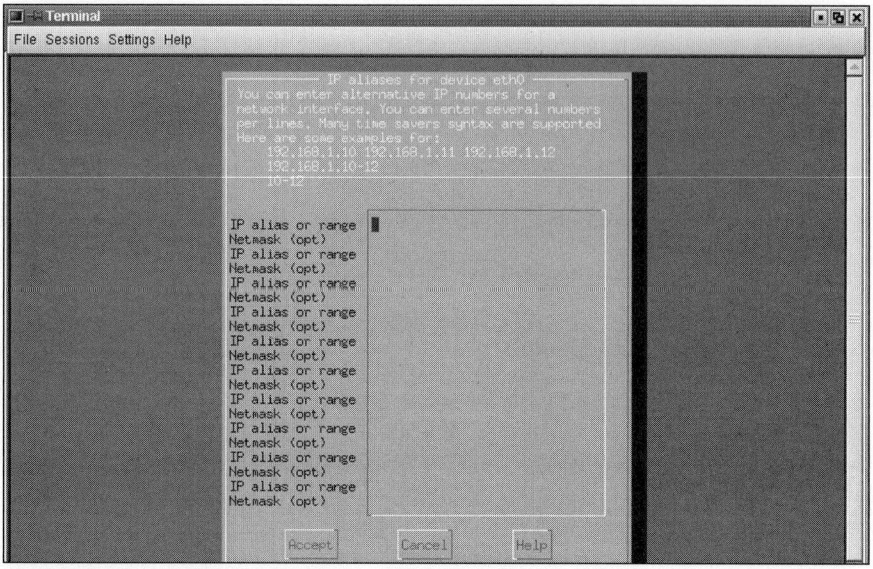

Figure 7-13: Creating Virtual Hosts for an Ethernet Connection

Virtual hosts work very well for service providers to enable many personal Web sites or commercial sites on one physical server.

Apache Web Server

The Apache Web server is currently the most popular Web server. Apache exists to provide commercial-grade software that is capable of providing for the Hypertext Transfer Protocol (HTTP). HTTP is a standard for creating documents to be viewed over the Internet. The standardization of HTTP was started within the IETF (Internet Engineering Task Force) in late 1994 and has evolved into the standard method of displaying Web pages. The linuxconf program can perform a basic configuration on the Apache server. To do this,

1. Choose Networking ➪ Server Tasks ➪ Apache Web Server.

2. When you select the Apache Web server, a menu appears that allows configuration of the Web server.

3. Select the defaults option to allow the input of information for the default configuration.

Basic section

This section includes the entry of the Web administrator or Web master's e-mail address. The domain IP address allows several virtual domains to share a single IP address, which should also be entered in this configuration. The server name is used if DNS or the host's file name resolution is not working correctly, or if the server has a name different than the FQDN. The document root is the file system location of the files used for the Web service. Figure 7-14 shows that the location is the default of /var/www/html.

The next option to configure is for script aliases, which provide the location of script files, such as CGI (Common Gateway Interface), to be run with the Web site. Next you must configure a user ID and group ID, which are used to control access to the Web server. Usually this ID is a created account, called "Apache" for example, that has only read capabilities and perhaps writes to a temporary directory for executables. Don't allow too much access to users accessing the system because they can make unwanted changes to the system.

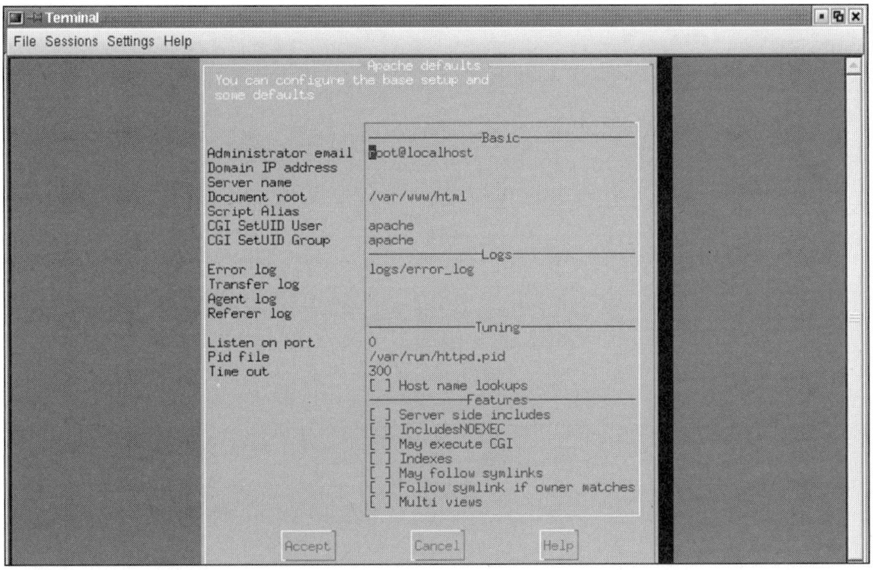

Figure 7-14: Default Configuration of the Apache Web Server

Logs section

The next section in the Apache configuration is for log files.

✦ **Error logs:** Review this log on a Web server because it can indicate problems with the Web server and be used to correct the errors. A common location for this file is /var/log/httpd/error_log. Look for this log on a system using the Apache server.

✦ **Transfer logs:** Are used to track all traffic or access to the Web server and are filed in the Common Log File format. This file may grow quite large for very busy Web servers, so spend some time planning your file locations.

✦ **Agent logs:** Tracks Web page access.

✦ **Referrer logs:** If access to the server was generated by a link from another page, the access is logged here.

Tuning section

The tuning section allows the custom configuration of some of the performance settings of the Apache server. The following list details the configuration options:

✦ **Private Web sites:** When a user requests a Web page by typing `www.linux.org`, the browser assumes that — unless otherwise instructed — it will use the default port for HTTP, which is 80, which is used for all public web sites. If you wish to hide your private web sites on a different access port, you can set it to something like 8080. This way, clients will have to specify the web page on that port to get a connection.

✦ **PID (process identifier) file location:** This is seldom changed because it holds the PID of the main process.

✦ **Timeout:** This is used to disconnect clients who connect to the Web server but don't make a request of the system.

✦ **Host name lookup:** This allows the system to log not only the IP address of the connecting client but also the name of the client. Unfortunately, this option has two major drawbacks:

  • It creates much more network traffic when looking up every client host name.

  • The Web page won't be displayed until the task is completed, therefore slowing the display of the Web page to the client.

This is an excellent tool for very small Web sites to track users. The action that this tool accomplishes, however, can be completed in more efficient ways — especially for large Web sites.

Features

The Features section controls the ability to activate advanced items such as scripting. The features include the following:

✦ **Server side includes option.** Can be used with the extension shtml. The server-side include command simply expands to the contents of a given file and allows bits of HTML or text to be shared between pages for ease of updating.

✦ **NOEXEC option.** Activates the Server side includes option, but uses SSI tags to disable CGI scripts.

✦ **Indexes option.** Allows a list of available files in the Web directory to be displayed if the default index.html file is not present. If this option is turned off, then Error 404, "file not found," is returned as an error message.

✦ **May follow symlinks option.** Must be turned on if symbolic linked folders or files are to be followed when accessed on an Apache server.

✦ **Follow symlinks if owner matches option.** Continues the May follow symlinks option with the added verification that the owner of the file is accessing the symbolically linked file or directory and that all others are denied access.

✦ **Multi views option.** Allows for the client and server to negotiate the language and format of the data to be returned. This allows the server to have language and data files added to support several languages.

After you have chosen the features, the basic configuration of an Apache server has been completed. The creation and maintenance of a Web server is a tasking job and usually requires a Web master. However, the ability to create a basic Web server can be valuable to both small and large companies.

Samba File Server

Microsoft created the Server Message Block (SMB/CIFS) protocol to provide the ability to share files and resources. Samba is a software program that offers a version of SMB/CIFS that allows Linux clients to able to connect to Microsoft network resources such as file shares and printers. The `linuxconf` program can complete the basic configuration of Samba by selecting Samba file server from the networking section of the program. During Samba configuration, the default menu appears, offering the following options: Default setup for user's home, default setup for printers, netlogon setup, and disk shares. The Samba configuration menu is shown in Figure 7-15.

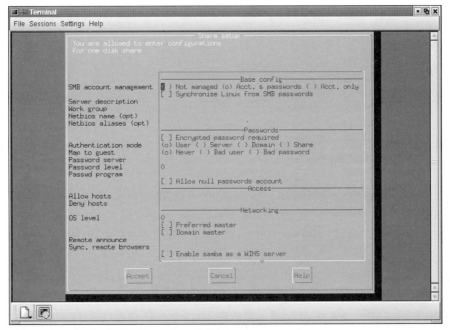

Figure 7-15: Default Configuration of Samba

Basic configuration

The basic configuration section includes the SMB/CIFS account management. This area allows the selection of options including managed and unmanaged, accounts and passwords, account only option, and the ability to synchronize Linux from SMB/CIFS passwords. The following list summarizes these items:

✦ "Not managed" means that each new user of the created Samba shares must be added manually by using the `SMB/CIFS passwd -a` command to add each and every account.

✦ The account and password option allows linuxconf access to both password databases (/etc/passwd and Samba's file at `/etc/SMB/CIFS passwd`) to allow all users to access the Samba shares.

✦ The account only option is used to create and delete accounts in the SMB/CIFS password database.

✦ The next option allows the update of passwords from Microsoft Windows users to the `/etc/SMB/CIFS passwd` password database.

✦ The last option in the basic configuration section allows Samba to alias another server for SMB/CIFS purpose. This allows two SMB/CIFS names to direct clients to the same system, which is very useful when replacing two file servers with one.

Passwords

Passwords control access to the system. The following is a list of options that can be set for passwords:

✦ **Encrypted passwords:** This option sets the type of encryption level. This information may be needed as there are a number of different ways that Microsoft Windows can encrypt the data.

✦ **Authentication mode:** Allows you to select the source of authentication. You can choose from the user, server, domain, or a network share.

✦ **Map to guest mode:** provides tracking of failed user and password access to the Samba server.

✦ **Access:** You can allow accounts with null or no password to use the system. This setting reduces security, but also allows virtually everyone access to a system.

Access

The access section is used to provide or deny access to specific clients. The following is an example:

```
allow host = 192.168.0.*.*  EXCEPT 192.168.0.200
allow host = 10.0.0.0/255.255.0.0
allow host = mybox, hisbox, herbox
```

The first entry allows all users on the 192.168.0 network to access the server except IP 192.168.0.200. The second entry allows all users on the 10.0.x.x network to access the server. The third entry allows only hostnames of mybox, hisbox, and herbox to access the server. This can be quite useful because you can grant access to certain sections of a site while denying access to others — even if they are on the same LAN segment (this is also expandable to the WAN network).

The deny feature works the same except it prevents users from accessing the system. Using the above entries to deny access would look like this:

```
deny host = 192.168.0.*.*  EXCEPT 192.168.0.200
deny host = 10.0.0.0/255.255.0.0
deny host = mybox, hisbox, herbox
```

Networking

The networking section allows the Linux server to perform network services that are normally provided by Microsoft NT or 2000 Servers. The services are controlled by the OS level selected and allow the Samba server to take precedent over another server for duties in the Microsoft environment. The option to be the preferred master can be enabled to allow the Linux system to be selected as the browse master in the Microsoft workgroup.

Caution   This option should be used with care in the Microsoft environment because new Microsoft operating systems often force elections and create a large amount of broadcast traffic in an attempt to become the preferred master.

By selecting the WINS server option, you enable Samba to act as a WINS (Windows Internet Naming Service) server for name resolution of IP addresses to NetBIOS names.

Auto accounts

Auto account creation is controlled by using the Add user script and Delete user script. These are advanced scripts that create and delete accounts based on connections being created with the Samba server. When authentication is confirmed or denied, the account is either added or deleted as required.

Features

Several features are available with the Samba server package, which are described in the following list:

✦ **Guest account** is used to establish which account will be used by clients accessing files or services labeled as Public Access. The user will have all rights of the account used as the Guest account.

✦ **Dead time** is used to terminate connections that remain inactive for the specified amount of time in seconds. This prevents improperly connected or disconnected connections from staying active and using resources.

✦ **Debug level** sets the value of the debug parameter in the SMB.conf file. This can be used to make the system more flexible in the configuration of the system.

✦ **Default service** allows a default service to be specified in cases where the requested service can't be found.

✦ **Show all available printers** allows all configured printers to be browsed by Microsoft Windows clients.

✦ **WinPopup command** allows a program to be configured to respond on the Linux system to WinPopup information set to the system.

Home directories

Although similar to the default setup, this home directory option also provides specialized configuration for home directory shares. This section is illustrated in Figure 7-16.

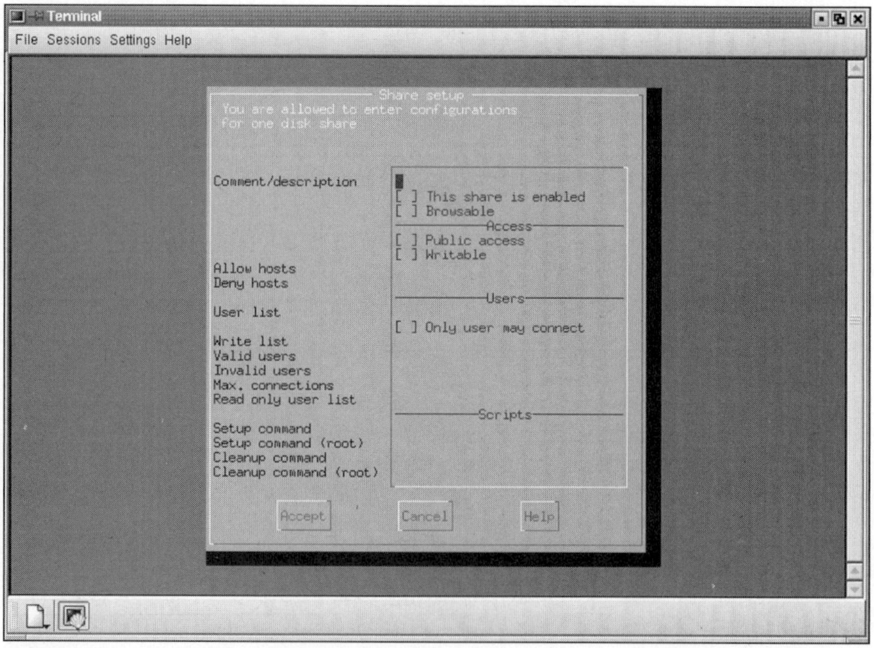

Figure 7-16: Default setup for the user's home

Comment and description

The comment/description field provides a comment or description about a share when a client views it. Set the share as active to automatically include it in browsing lists. Set the share as browseable to include it in net view and browse lists.

Access

The access section establishes the type of access allowed for the share. If you select public access, then no password is needed to connect to the share and the rights of the guest account will be used during access. The writable option determines if clients can create or modify files in the share.

Users

This section allows users to access a share. To enable access, you need to create a list of user names in a comma-delimited list. You won't achieve good security this way, but you can allow systems that don't provide a username to connect to the share. Use the Write list to allow read and write access for a list of users to the shared resource. The Valid Users option provides a list of users that should be allowed to log in to the service. The Invalid users option prevents a specific user from accessing the system. All of these user lists take on the following format (the @ denotes a Linux user group):

```
list: root john fred @linux
```

The Max connections option is used to limit the maximum number of connections to the system at one time. If this number is zero, then an unlimited number of connections are possible. The read only list is a list of users who have read-only privileges on the system.

Scripts

This section provides for scripts to be run when connections or disconnections to the system are made. You can use the Setup command to send the user a message every time he or she logs in. This can be a "message of the day" with a script like the one provided in the help file:

```
csh -c 'echo \"welcome to %S!\" | \ /usr/local/samba/bin/s -M %m -I %I' &
```

If the user connects often, however, this message may become somewhat repetitive. The setup command (root) can also be handy because it provides the same service as the setup command but with root capabilities. Therefore, you can use it to mount file systems before a connection is completed. You can also use this command to mount a CD-ROM before finalizing a connection. Use the cleanup command to create a task to be completed when a client disconnects. Again, the root option gives you the ability to perform the task as the root user. The following is an example of a cleanup command (root):

```
/sbin/umount  /mnt/cdrom
```

This is only an example of what can be done. You can create scripts to provide daily messages or mount file systems at the creation of a connection or reverse the process for disconnections.

Defaults setup for printers

The menu for the configuration of default printers is shown in Figure 7-17.

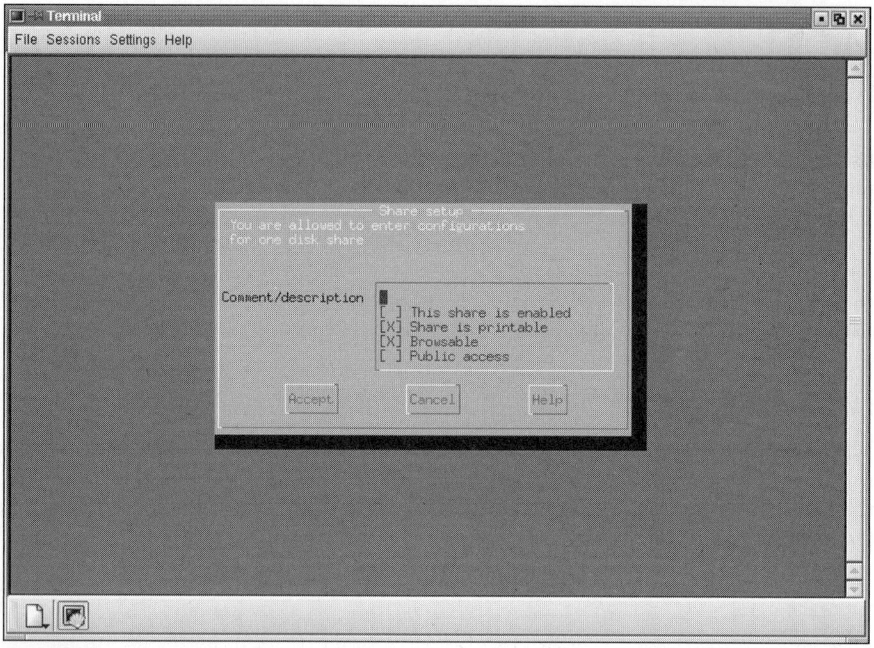

Figure 7-17: Default setup for printers

This is the most basic configuration receives no help from the `linuxconf` program. The first option is to enable the share, which will make it accessible to clients. The second option sets the share to be a printer. Set the share as browsable for shares to be included in net view and the browse list. Finally, public access allows anyone to use the share (even without a password) by using the guest account.

Netlogon setup

The Netlogon setup menu, shown if Figure 7-18, allows the configuration of logon connections.

This menu allows you to enter the title of the share, which can be used to identify it. The default status of this share is to have the enable option on, allowing connections to the share. The final item in the first section is to select the file system to be exported. This file system may be something as simple as a general share of all documents that are used by every network user.

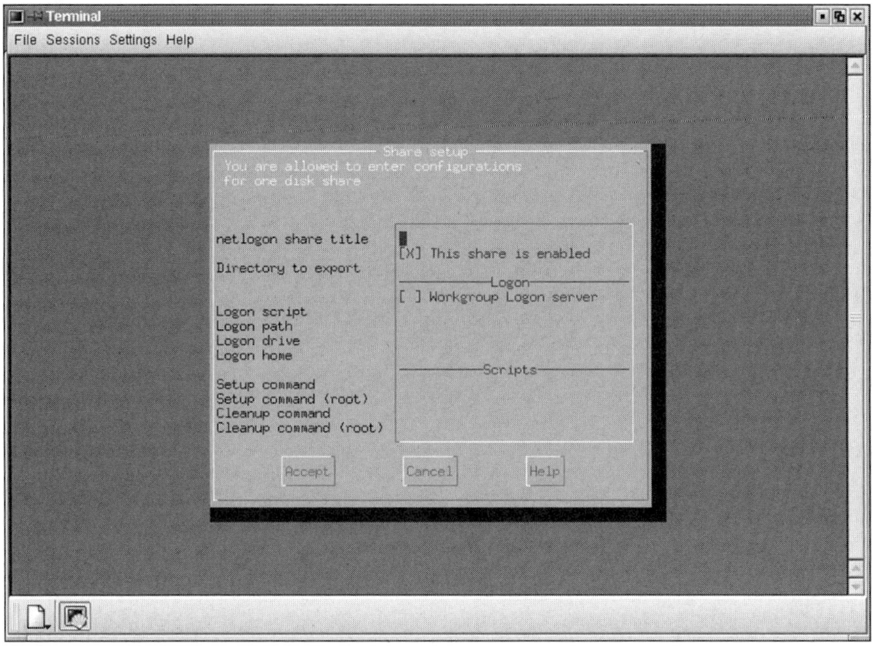

Figure 7-18: The Netlogon Setup Menu

Logon

This section is used to create customized logon setup for users. The logon server is activated to allow an entire group of users to receive a set of drives. This includes the script that is used for the clients, the path to the logon, the logon drive, and the logon home. The network administrator normally provides these items.

Disk shares

Disk shares are created with the final menu item. When you select this, another menu appears, showing current shares and provides the ability to add new shares. Select Add from the menu to display the menu shown if Figure 7-19.

You need to give the share a name. This name will be used to connect from a remote computer to this share and is usually user friendly. Any comments about the share are then added for additional help.

Base information

Set the share as browsable to include the share in network views and browse lists. The Inherit Setting from Share option will copy settings from a template to allow a quick setup. The Directory to Export option provides the path of the resource to be shared, for example: /home/guest.

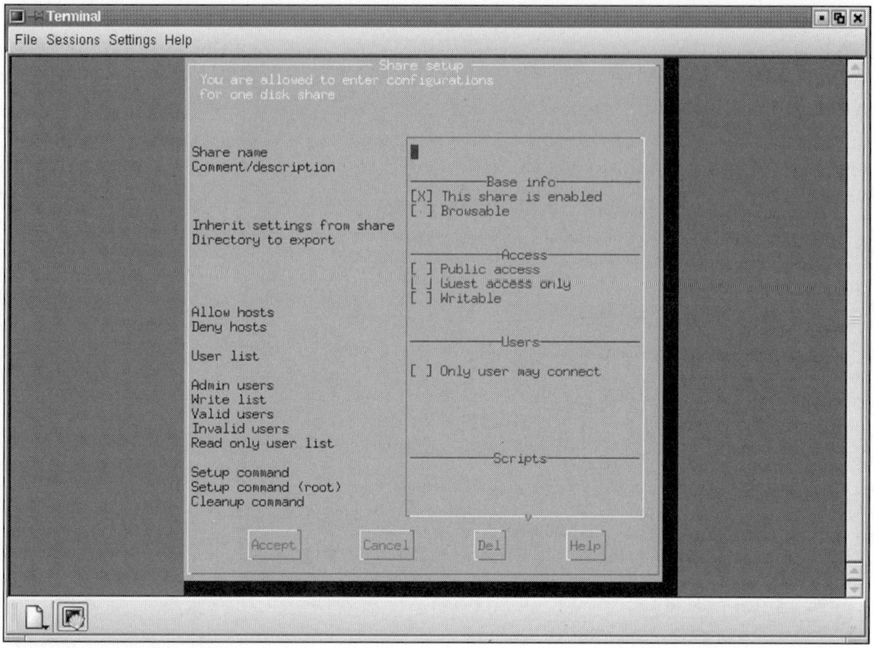

Figure 7-19: Creating disk shares

Access

In the access section, you can establish the type of access allowed for the share. If you select public access, then no password is needed to connect to the share and the rights of the guest account will be used during access. If you select the guest option, then only guest access to the share is permitted (this will have no effect if public access is not also activated). The writable option determines if clients can create or modify files in the share.

Users

This section lists the users who have administrative privileges to the share. This doesn't apply for admin users who already have access.

Scripts

Magic scripts are used to specify the name of a file that — if opened — will be executed by the server when the file is closed. This allows UNIX scripts to be run on behalf of the client at the Samba server. Output from this file will be sent to the destination in the magic output option, which is listed in features. The script is deleted upon completion.

Features

The Force user option forces all connections that are made to the service to be made with this user name. This still requires the user to connect with a valid user name and password, but after they connect, they will be seen by the system as the forced user. Force group name does the same thing with a group account. The Don't Descend feature is used to show directories that are not empty as empty. Take the /proc directory for example; if you don't want users to nose around this directory, you can list it as Don't Descend and it will appear empty to clients. The Guest account option provides the default account used for public access areas. The Max connections option is used to limit the maximum number of connections to the system at one time. If this number is zero then an unlimited number of connections are possible.

At this point, you have completed a basic configuration of Samba and you have acquired a basic knowledge of the SMB/CIFS system. Although network administrators usually configure and maintain Samba servers, the ability to work with Samba is a valuable skill.

Configuring Client Services

 3.5 Configure basic client services (e.g., X client, SMB/CIFS, NIS, NFS)

3.15 Configure access rights (e.g., rlogin NIS, FTP, TFTP, SSH, Telnet)

When configuring a client, you need to configure the services that the client may use. This includes the X client, SMB/CIFS, NIS, and NFS. These services are selected during installation, but you may need to perform some of the configurations after installation.

> **Cross-Reference**
>
> The X client was configured in Chapters 4, 5, and 6. For more information, use the X Configuration sections in those chapters.

SMB/CIFS

The SMB/CIFS client is part of the Samba suite and can be selected during installation. This package can also be added to a system by using one of the methods discussed in Chapter 5. The `SMB/CIFS client` can access an SMB/CIFS/CIFS server. It offers an interface similar to that of the `ftp` program. The `SMB/CIFS client` command launches the client Table 7-2 lists the switches needed for connection. The switches are listed in order of use from closest to the command to furthest from the command; the table also includes a description of the switch for the SMB/CIFS client software.

Table 7-2
SMB/CIFS Client Switches

Switch	Description	Example
servicename	The service that you want to use on the server in the format of a NetBIOS name.	//server/service
password	The password required to access the specified service on the specified server.	users password
-b	This option changes the transmit/send buffer size when getting or putting a file from/to the server. The default is 65520 bytes.	-b 1500
-d	The higher this value, the more detail will be logged to the log files about the activities of the client, ranging from 0-10 and A.	-d 1
-D	Change to initial directory before starting.	-D /tmp
-U	Sets the SMB/CIFS username or username, often includes [%pass] to include the password.	-U user[%password]
-W	Overrides the default workgroup specified in the workgroup parameter of the SMB/CIFS.conf file for this connection.	-W usergroup
-M	This option sends messages to another computer by using the "WinPopup" protocol.	cat message.txt | SMB/CIFS client -M user
-A	This option allows you to specify a file from which to read the username and password used in the connection.	-A filename
-N	Suppresses the normal prompt for password.	-N
-l	Specifies a base file name into which operational data from the running client will be logged.	-l logfilename
-L	Lists services available on a server.	-L host
-I	IP address is the address of the server to connect to. Often used with –L.	-I 10.0.0.250

Switch	Description	Example
-E	Causes the client to write messages to the standard error stream (stderr) rather than to the standard output stream.	-E
-c	A command string separated by semicolons to be executed instead of prompting from stdin. -N is implied by -c.	-c command string such as -c 'print -'
-i	This specifies a NetBIOS scope that SMB/CIFS client will use to communicate when generating NetBIOS names.	-i scope
-O	TCP socket options to set on the client socket. The SMB/CIFS.conf MAN page lists the valid options.	-O socket options
-p	This number is the TCP port number that will be used when making connections to the server instead of the standard TCP port.	-p port
-R	Name resolution order with the options of "lmhosts," "host," "wins," and "bcast".	-R lmhosts
-s	Provides the location of the SMB/CIFS.conf file.	-s SMB/CIFS .conf
-T	The SMB/CIFS client may be used to create tar compatible backups of all the files on an SMB/CIFS /CIFS share.	//server/share "" -N -Tc backup.tar *

Exam Tip   Know the switches but also the format for all commands used in Linux.

These switches from Table 7-3 are used to create the connection. After the connection is complete, the user is presented with a new prompt that looks like this:

```
SMB/CIFS :\>
```

This prompt indicates that the client is ready and waiting to carry out a user command. The user commands are shown in Table 7-3.

Table 7-3
SMB/CIFS Client Commands

Command	Description	Example
?	Used to provide information about a command.	? [command]
!	The ! command will execute a shell locally and run the specified shell command.	! [shell command]
cd	Used to change directories, or if no directory is requested, it will list the current directory.	cd [directory name]
del	The client will request that the server attempt to delete all files matching "mask" in the current directory.	del <mask>
dir	A list of the files matching "mask" in the current directory will be retrieved and displayed.	dir <mask>
exit	Exit the program SMB/CIFS client; this will terminate all connections.	exit
get	Get a remote file <name> and copy it to the local file [name]. This is a binary transfer.	get <remote file name> [local file name]
help	Used to provide information about a command.	help [command]
lcd	The current working directory on the local machine will be changed to the directory specified.	lcd [directory name]
lowercase	When lowercasing is toggled ON, local filenames are converted to lowercase when using the get and mget commands.	lowercase
ls	A list of the files matching "mask" in the current directory will be retrieved and displayed.	ls <mask>
mask	This command allows the user to set up a mask, which will be used during recursive operation of the mget and mput commands.	mask <mask>
md	Used to create a new directory with a specified name.	md <directory name>

Command	Description	Example
mget	Copy all files matching mask from the server to the machine running the client.	mget <mask>
mkdir	Used to create a new directory with a specified name.	mkdir <directory name>
mput	Copy all files matching mask from the machine running the client to the server.	mput <mask>
print	Print the specified file from the client through a printable service on the server.	print <file name>
printmode	Set the print mode to suit either binary data or text.	printmode <graphics or text>
prompt	Toggle prompting for filenames during operation of the mget and mput commands.	prompt
put	Copy the file called "local file name" from the client to the server with optional "remote file name."	put <local file name> [remote file name]
queue	Displays the print queue, showing the job ID, name, size, and current status.	queue
quit	Exit the program SMB/CIFS client; this will terminate all connections.	quit
rd	Remove the specified directory.	rd <directory name>
recurse	Toggle directory recursion for the commands mget and mput.	recurse
rm	Remove all files in the current directory with the match the <mask>.	rm <mask>
rmdir	Remove the specified directory.	rmdir <directory name>
tar	Perform the tar operation.	tar <c|x>[IXbgNa]
blocksize	Must be followed by a valid (greater than zero) blocksize. Causes tar file to be written out in blocksize*TBLOCK (usually 512 byte) blocks.	blocksize <blocksize>
tarmode	Changes tar's behavior with regard to archive bits.	tarmode <full|inc|reset|noreset>
setmode	A version of the DOS attrib command to set file permissions.	setmode <filename> <perm=[+|\-]rsha>

NIS client configuration

The NIS is configured for the client in order to allow them to participate in an NIS network. To participate as an NIS client, you need the ypbind, ypwhich, ypcat, yppoll, ypmatch programs. The most important program is ypbind, so it must be running at all times; it is a daemon process and needs to be started from the system's startup file, such as /etc/init.d/nis, /sbin/init.d/ypclient, /etc/rc.d/init.d/ypbind, and /etc/rc.local. Hopefully, you planned for these packages during the installation of the Linux distribution and they are already installed and configured to start when the system boots. If this is not the case, and if the files are needed for installation, they are available at www.kernel.org (tarball) and www.redhat.com (for RPM versions).

Cross-Reference   See Chapter 5 for more information on software installation.

The location of the ypbind daemon is typically the /usr/sbin directory. The other binaries (ypwhich, ypcat, yppasswd, yppoll, ypmatch) are normally located in /usr/bin. Most current ypbind versions have a configuration file called /etc/yp.conf. For host lookups, you must add "nis" to the lookup order line in your /etc/host.conf file, or you can configure it with linuxconf, as shown in Figure 7-20.

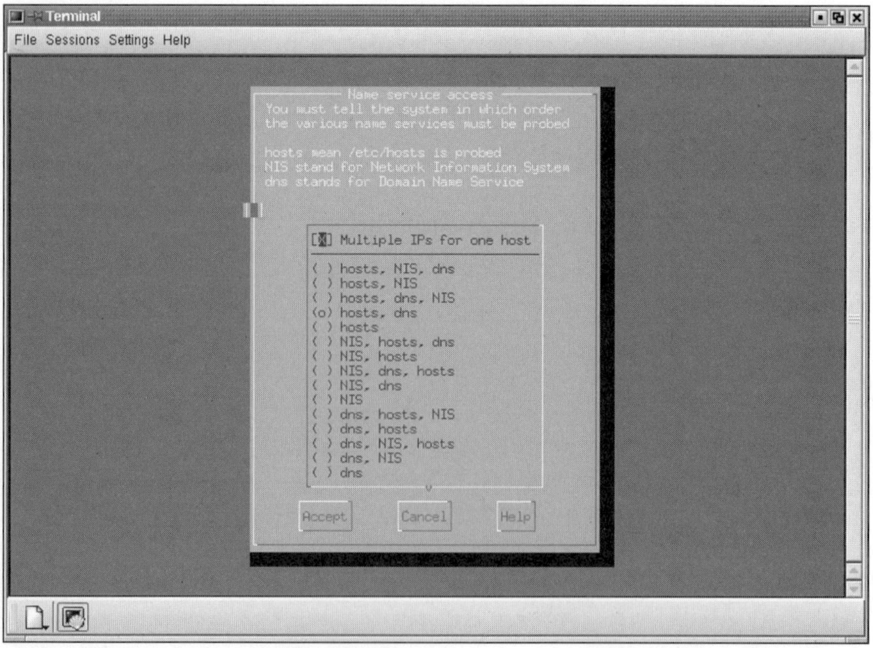

Figure 7-20: Configuring NIS with linuxconf

✦ POP3 TCP/IP port used; the default is 110 and is usually used but can be changed

✦ SMTP server name (used for outgoing mail)

✦ SMTP TCP/IP port used, the default is 25 and is usually used but can be changed

✦ Authentication method used

Using these settings with any mail client software should allow the configuration of mail accounts. Another feature also included with many mail clients is the ability to access News servers. These can be configured inside the mail client and require the following additional information.

✦ Server name

✦ NNTP TCP/IP port used, the default settings are 119 for standard connections and 563 for SSL connections (usually used but can be changed)

✦ User name and password preferences

This enables the configuration of POP3, SMTP, and NNTP for clients in most environments.

FTP

The standard for distributing files on the Internet is the File Transfer Protocol (FTP). It is the simplest way to exchange files between computers on the Internet. With a simple command line interface, a user can use FTP to perform updates, deletes, renames, moves, and copies of files at a server. Web browsers make FTP requests to download files that are selected from a Web page. To use FTP, a user can use the switches and commands shown in Table 7-4.

Table 7-4
FTP Client Switches and Commands

Switch/Command	Description
-d	Enable debugging.
-g	Disable filename "globbing."
-i	Turn off interactive prompting during multiple file transfers.
-n	Do not attempt "auto-login" upon initial connection.
-t	Enable packet tracing (not used).

Continued

Table 7-4 (continued)

Switch/Command	Description
-v	Show all responses from the remote server, as well as report on data transfer statistics. This is turned on by default if ftp is running interactively with its input coming from the user's terminal.
! [command]	Run command as a shell command on the local machine. If no command is given, invoke an interactive shell.
$ macro-name [args]	Execute the macro-name that was defined with the macdef command.
account [passwd]	Supply a supplemental password required by a remote system for access to resources once a login has been successfully completed.
append	Append a local file to a file on the remote machine.
ascii	Use ASCII, the default.
bell	Sound a bell after each file transfer command is completed.
binary	Use binary.
bye	Terminate the FTP session with the remote server and exit ftp.
case	Toggle remote computer file name case mapping during mget commands.
cd remote-directory	Change the working directory on the remote machine to remote-directory.
cdup	Change the remote machine's working directory to the parent of the current remote machine's working directory.
close	Terminate the FTP session with the remote server, and return to the command interpreter.
cr	Toggle RETURN stripping during "network ASCII" type file retrieval.
delete remote-file	Delete the file remote-file on the remote machine.
debug [debug-value]	Toggle debugging mode. If an optional debug-value is specified it is used to set the debugging level.
dir [remote-directory] [local-file]	Print a listing of the directory contents in the directory, remote-directory, and, optionally, placing the output in local-file. If no directory is specified, the current working directory on the remote machine is used. If no local file is specified, output is sent to the terminal.
disconnect	Terminate the FTP session with the remote server, and return to the command interpreter.

Switch/Command	Description
form [format-name]	Set the carriage control format subtype.
get	Retrieve the remote-file and store it on the local machine.
glob	Toggle filename expansion, or "globbing," for mdelete, mget, and mput. If globbing is turned off, filenames are taken literally.
hash	Toggle hash-sign (#) printing for each data block transferred.
help [command]	Print an informative message about the meaning of thecommand.
lcd [directory]	Change the working directory on the local machine.
ls [remote-directory] [local-file]	Print an abbreviated listing of the contents of a directory on the remote machine.
macdef macro-name	Define a macro.
mdelete [remote-files]	Delete the remote-files on the remote machine.
mdir remote-files local-file	Like dir, except multiple remote files may be specified.
mget remote-files	Expand the remote-files on the remote machine and do a get for each file name thus produced.
mkdir directory-name	Make a directory on the remote machine.
mls remote-files local-file	Like ls, except multiple remote files may be specified.
mode [mode-name]	Set the "transfer mode" to mode-name.
mput local-files	Expand wild cards in the list of local files given as arguments and do a put for each file in the resulting list.
nmap [inpattern outpattern]	Set or unset the filename mapping mechanism.
ntrans [inchars [outchars]]	Set or unset the filename character translation mechanism.
open host [port]	Establish a connection to the specified host FTP server with optional port selection.
prompt	Toggle interactive prompting.
proxy ftp-command	Execute an FTP command on a secondary control connection.
put local-file remote-file	Upload a local file to the remote machine.
pwd	Print working directory.
quit	Terminate the FTP session with the remote server and exit ftp.

Continued

Table 7-4 *(continued)*

Switch/Command	Description
quote arg1 arg2 ...	Send the arguments specified, verbatim, to the remote FTP server. A single FTP reply code is expected in return.
recv remote-file [local-file]	Retrieve the remote-file and store it on the local machine.
remotehelp [command-name]	Request help from the remote FTP server.
rename from to	Rename the file retreived from the remote machine.
reset	Clear reply queue.
rmdir directory-name	Delete a directory on the remote machine.
runique	Toggle storing of files on the local system with unique filenames.
send local-file [remote-file]	A synonym for put.
sendport	Toggle the use of PORT commands.
status	Show the current status of ftp.
struct [struct-name]	Set the "file structure" to struct-name.
sunique	Toggle storing of files on remote machine under unique file names.
tenex	Set the "representation type" to that needed to talk to TENEX machines.
trace	Toggle packet tracing (not used).
type [type-name]	Set the "representation type" to type-name.
user user-name [password][account]	Identify yourself to the remote FTP server.
verbose	Toggle verbose mode.
? [command]	Print an informative message about the meaning of command.

The FTP command is not much use without the FTP server service running on the remote system. To provide this feature, the FTP program requires the ftpd daemon. Luckily, the ftpd daemon is started by the inetd by default. The inetd daemon listens for connections on port 20, in the /etc/inetd.conf and initiates the appropriate daemon when an FTP connection is requested.

TFTP

The commands that are used to transfer files between hosts using the Trivial File Transfer Protocol (TFTP) are `tftp` and `utftp`. This is the UDP or "best effort delivery" for downloading files. It does not provide all the tools of FTP but does provide the following switches and commands:

- ✦ ascii
- ✦ binary
- ✦ connect
- ✦ get
- ✦ mode
- ✦ put
- ✦ quit
- ✦ -w or -p Writes
- ✦ -r or -g or -o Reads

A `tftp` command may look like this:

```
tftp server1
```

SNMP

The Simple Network Management Protocol (SNMP) is used to perform network management and the monitoring of network devices and their functions. Each device or client system running SNMP contains an information database which contains specific hardware, software and diagnostic information that can be relayed to an inquiring host. The specific service that runs SNMP on your Linux system is `snmpd`.

 Exam Tip The full topic of SNMP is out of the scope of this book, but for the exam, know the purpose of the protocol.

Remote Access

Objective 3.15 Configure access rights (e.g., rlogin NIS, FTP, TFTP, SSH, Telnet)

One of the primary uses of Linux is to provide remote access to devices and other systems. A variety of utilities provide remote access; the most common utilities are `rlogin`, `telnet`, and SSH. These utilities allow a system to connect to a remote system and perform tasks as if they were actually physically located at the remote system. These programs must be active on both the local and remote system. This requires a daemon to be running for the server host side. This daemon may be started manually for one-time access or at boot-up to provide remote access on a continual basis. You should realize that by providing remote access to a system, increases the security risk for that system for unauthorized access. To reduce the risk of unsecured remote access, I recommend that you use the most secure access methods as often as possible.

Rlogin

Remote login (rlogin) is a utility that allows an authorized user to log in to other Linux or UNIX machines on a network and perform tasks as if the user were physically located at the remote (often called the *host*) computer. The rlogin program uses the terminal type description from the local system and uses it on the remote system. The rlogin program uses rhost authorization method to provide security. The rhost authorization uses the combination of the hosts.equiv and .rhosts files to authenticate users. These files are used to list hosts and users, which are allowed by the local system (the system being accessed) to make a connection via rlogin and SSH. These files use the format of hostname [username]. The hostname uses the FQDN or address, +@netgroup, or the + wildcard, which allow all hosts for this field. The username may use the user name on the remote system, the +@netgroup, or the + wildcard, which allows all users for this field or have no entry at all. To create a connection to a system with rlogin, use the command switches in Table 7-5.

Table 7-5
rlogin Client Switches

Switch	Description	Example
-D	This enables socket debugging on the TCP sockets used for communication.	-D
-E	Used to stop any character from being recognized as an escape character.	-E
-e	Used to specify the character to be used as the escape character.	-e character
-l	Used to specify an alternate user name for the remote login.	-l username
-t	Used to change from the default terminal type, ansi, and use the only other available terminal type, dumb.	-t dumb or ansi
-8	The -8 option allows an eight-bit input data path at all times.	-8
-K	This turns off all Kerberos authentication if available.	-K
-L	Used to allow the rlogin session to be run in litout mode, see tty4 for more information.	-L

Switch	Description	Example
-k	This requests `rlogin` to obtain tickets for the remote host-in-realm realm instead of the remote host's realm as determined by krb_realmofhost	-k
-x	The -x option turns on DES encryption for all data passed via the `rlogin` session.	-x

The `rlogin` command is not much use without the server side service running on the remote system. To provide this feature, the `rlogin` program requires the `rlogind`. The `rlogind` daemon is the server for `rlogin` and provides the authentication for connections. The server checks the remote system's source TCP/IP port and if it isn't in the range 512-1023, the server aborts the connection. Then the server checks the remote system source address and hostname. After this is completed, authentication takes place. The `rlogind` daemon is usually located at `/usr/sbin/rlogind` and is normally started with the inetd. Luckily, the `rlogind` daemon is started by the inetd by default. The inetd daemon listens for connections on certain Internet sockets in the /etc/inetd.conf and initiates the appropriate daemon.

The `rlogin` command and rlogind daemon are used to provide remote access to a system, however it has some issues with security, as some earlier versions allowed root access by mistake. Also, `rlogin` can only be used to connect UNIX, UNIX-like, and Microsoft systems.

Telnet

`Telnet` is used to communicate with another host by using the `Telnet` protocol. `Telnet` provides a standard method for terminal devices and terminal-oriented processes to interface. `Telnet` is commonly used by terminal emulation to connect to remote systems, which allows the connection to routers, switches, hubs, and printers. However, `telnet` can also be used for terminal-to-terminal communication.

To telnet to a host, server1 for example, simply enter the command:

```
telnet server1
```

You will then connect and should display a login prompt for you to authenticate with the system.

`Telnet` requires the `telnetd` daemon to connect to remote systems. The `telnetd` daemon is started by default by inetd, but telnetd must be enabled in the /etc/inetd.conf file. The inetd daemon listens for `telnet` information on port 23. When detected, it then activates the `telnetd` daemon and passes this traffic on.

`Telnet` can be used to provide remote access to many systems but not as secure as `telnet` sends passwords as clear text.

OpenSSH

The OpenSSH suite includes the secure shell (SSH) program, which replaces `rlogin` and `telnet`. The suite also has secure copy (SCP), which replaces `rcp`, and `sftp`, and `ftp`. Also included is `sshd`, which is the server side of the package, and the other basic utilities, such as `ssh-add`, `ssh-agent`, `ssh-keygen`, and `sftp-server`. OpenSSH supports SSH protocol versions 1.3, 1.5, and 2.0. OpenSSH is available at `www.openssh.com` and is a free version of SSH. The following distributions currently support OpenSSH:

✦ OpenBSD

✦ Debian Linux

✦ FreeBSD

✦ Suse Linux

✦ Redhat Linux

✦ Mandrake Linux

✦ BSDi BSD/OS

✦ NetBSD

✦ Computone

✦ Conectiva Linux

✦ Slackware Linux

✦ Stallion

✦ Cygwin

✦ e-smith server and gateway

✦ Engarde Linux

SSH obtains configuration data from the following sources (in this order):

✦ Command line options

✦ Users configuration file ($HOME/.ssh/config)

✦ System-wide configuration file (/etc/ssh_config)

For each parameter, the first obtained value is used. The SSH client provides for connectivity to remote systems and uses the commands shown in Table 7-6.

Table 7-6
SSH SWITCHES

Switches	Description
-a	Disables forwarding of the authentication agent connection.
-A	Enables forwarding of the authentication agent connection.
-b bind_address	Specifies the interface to transmit from machines with multiple interfaces or alias address.
-c blowfish|3des	Selects the cipher to use for encrypting the session. 3des is used by default. It is believed to be secure and is presumably more secure than the des cipher.
-c cipher_spec	For protocol version 2 a comma-separated list of ciphers can be specified in order of preference.
-e ch|^ch|none	Sets the escape character for sessions with a pty.
-f	Requests ssh to go to background just before command execution. This is useful if ssh is going to ask for passwords or pass-phrases, but the user wants it in the background.
-g	Allows remote hosts to connect to local forwarded ports.
-i identity_file	Selects the file from which the identity (private key) for RSA or DSA authentication is read. Default is $HOME/.ssh/identity in the user's home directory.
-k	Disables forwarding of Kerberos tickets and AFS tokens.
-l login_name	Specifies the user to log in as on the remote machine.
-m mac_spec	For protocol version 2 a comma-separated list of MAC (message authentication code) algorithms can be specified in order of preference.
-n	This must be used when ssh is run in the background. A common trick is to use this to run X11 programs on a remote machine.
-N	Do not execute a remote command.
-o option	Can be used to give options in the format used in the config file. This is useful for specifying options for which there is no separate command-line flag.
-p port	Port to connect to on the remote host.
-P	Use a non-privileged port for outgoing connections. This can be used if your firewall does not permit connections from privileged ports.

Continued

Table 7-6 *(continued)*

Switches	Description
-q	Quiet mode. Causes all warning and diagnostic messages to be suppressed. Only fatal errors are displayed.
-s	May be used to request invocation of a subsystem on the remote system.
-t	Force pseudo-tty allocation. This can be used to execute arbitrary screen-based programs on a remote machine, which can be very useful when implementing menu services.
-T	Disable pseudo-tty allocation.
-v	Verbose mode. Causes ssh to print debugging messages about its progress.
-x	Disables X11 forwarding.
-X	Enables X11 forwarding.
-C	Requests compression of all data (including stdin, stdout, stderr, and data for forwarded X11 and TCP/IP connections).
-t	Multiple -t options force tty allocation, even if ssh has no local tty.
-L port:host:hostport	Specifies that the given port on the local host is to be forwarded to the given host and port on the remote side.
-R port:host:hostport	Specifies that the given port on the remote host is to be forwarded to the given host and port on the local side.
-1	Forces ssh to try protocol version 1 only.
-2	Forces ssh to try protocol version 2 only.
-4	Forces ssh to use IPv4 addresses only.
-6	Forces ssh to use IPv6 addresses only.

A standard SSH command may appear: `ssh [-l login_name] [hostname | user@hostname] [command]`

SSH requires the sshd daemon to connect to remote systems. It is normally started at boot from /etc/rc and uses a couple of protocol versions that provide varying security.

✦ **SSH protocol version 1:** Each host has a host-specific RSA key (normally 1024 bits) used to identify the host. Additionally, when the daemon starts, it generates a server RSA key (normally 768 bits). This key is normally regenerated every hour if it has been used, and is never stored on disk.

✦ **SSH protocol version 2:** Each host has a host-specific DSA key used to identify the host. However, when the daemon starts, it does not generate a server key. Forward security is provided through a Diffie-Hellman key agreement. This key agreement results in a shared session key.

When a user successfully logs in, sshd does the following:

✦ If the login is from a tty, prints last login time and /etc/motd (unless prevented in the configuration file or by $HOME/.hushlogin.

✦ If the login is on a tty, records login time.

✦ Checks /etc/nologin and prints contents and quits (unless root).

✦ Changes to run with normal user privileges.

✦ Sets up basic environment.

✦ Reads $HOME/.ssh/environment.

✦ Changes to user's home directory.

✦ Use in order $HOME/.ssh/rc, /etc/sshrc exists, otherwise runs xauth.

✦ Runs user's shell or command.

This sets up a secure and user-friendly environment to perform remote system access using an SSH client. Open SSH is currently the best method of remote access.

Documentation

Objective

3.14 Document the installation of the operating system, including configuration

The configuration of networking services on a Linux system should include the documentation of all settings. This is important for record keeping, rebuilding services, and to provide records of what has been done. The system settings selected should be clearly documented and include every configuration for any of the services used in networking the system.

Summary

This chapter explains many of the basics of configuring a Linux system. This task is comprised of three major areas:

✦ The use of linuxconf and netconfig

- linuxconf
- netconfig
- TCP/IP
- Hostname
- DHCP
- DNS
- Gateways
- PPP, SLIP
- NFS
- NIS
- Apache
- SMB/CIFS

✦ Configuration of Internet Services

- Web access
- E-Mail
- FTP
- TFTP
- SNMP

✦ Configuration of Remote Access

- rlogin
- TELNET
- OpenSSH Protocol Suite

✦　　✦　　✦

STUDY GUIDE

The Study Guide section provides you with the opportunity to test your knowledge about the Linux+ exam objectives that are covered in this chapter. The Assessment Questions provide practice for the real exam, and the Scenarios provide practice with real situations. If you get any questions wrong, use the answers to determine the part of the chapter that you should review before continuing.

Assessment Questions

1. TCP is a _____ oriented protocol? (Fill in the Blank)

   A. Connection

   B. Connection-less

   C. Transmission

   D. Transfer

2. PPP is most often used to create?

   A. Ethernet point-to-point connections

   B. Serial point-to-point connections

   C. Parallel point-to-point connections

   D. LAN connections

3. NIS and NFS use what TCP/IP system to provide their service?

   A. DNS

   B. DHCP

   C. RPC

   D. Yellow Pages

4. Which program can be used to configure not only basic network services but also several network server services?

   A. config

   B. linuxconfig

   C. netconf

   D. linuxconf

5. A host name is most often used to provide which name?

    A. IPX

    B. FQDN

    C. POP3

    D. DHCP

6. IP addresses are?

    A. 24-bit numbers

    B. 48-bit numbers

    C. 32-bit numbers

    D. 8-bit numbers

7. IP addresses are originally assigned by?

    A. ISP

    B. DHCP

    C. DNS

    D. IANA

8. DHCP is used to provide what automatically for clients?

    A. IP addressing

    B. Domain name

    C. Internet name

    D. IPX addressing

9. When attempting to connect to `www.linux.org` the return host unknown is returned. Which service is most likely not functioning properly?

    A. DHCP

    B. NIS

    C. DNS

    D. WINS

10. What other networking information is usually provided in conjunction with an IP address?

    A. Subnet mask

    B. DNS

    C. Samba

    D. PPP

11. PPP is preferred to SLIP for which reasons (choose all that apply)?

    A. Secure password authentication

    B. Static IP addressing

    C. Dynamic IP addressing

    D. Asynchronous communications

12. NFS normally uses which naming service to provide file sharing?

    A. DNS

    B. NIS

    C DHCP

    D. WINS

13. What is the most common Linux Web server in use today?

    A. IIS

    B. Tux

    C. FastTrack

    D. Apache

14. Samba is used to provide support for which protocol?

    A. Network File System

    B. Internetwork Packet Exchange

    C. Dynamic Host Configuration Protocol

    D. Server Message Block

15. What is the most common location of the SMB/CIFS client software installation?

    A. `/usr/samba/bin/`

    B. `/etc/samba/bin/`

    C. `/lib/samba/bin/`

    D. `/bin/samba/`

16. What command provides the entire NIS password database?

    A. `usr/sbin/ypbind`

    B. `ypcat passwd.byname`

    C. `cat passwd ypbind`

    D. `cat ypbind`

17. What programs are used to download files from a remote server (choose all that apply)?

    A. TFTP

    B. TELNET

    C. FTP

    D. SNMP

18. What command is used to load a module into the kernel?

    A. `lsmod`

    B. `modprobe`

    C. `rmmod`

    D. `insmod`

19. What programs can provide remote access to systems (choose all that apply)?

    A. `rlogin`

    B. `Telnet`

    C. SNMP

    D. SSH

20. What is the most secure method of remote access?

    A. `rlogin`

    B. `Telnet`

    C. SNMP

    D. SSH

Scenarios

1. The sales manager wants to ensure the security of the server. One of her worries is about the services on the system that are installed automatically. What is the danger with having unneeded services running on your system?

2. The CFO wants to use Linux to replace an aging Microsoft Windows NT server. What services can Linux use to provide all the services in a Microsoft Windows NT environment?

Lab Exercises

Lab 7-1 Configuring Networking

The objective for this hands-on lab is to gain experience in configuring Linux networking. You should be able to use any distribution of Linux for this installation exercise.

1. Login as the root user

2. Start the `linuxconf` or `netconfig` program

3. Use the program to configure network services

4. Save the settings

5. Test the configuration using `ifconfig -a` and accessing a network

Answers to Chapter Questions

Chapter Pre-test

1. Transmission Control Protocol and Internet Protocol (TCP/IP) suite is the default protocol of the Internet, and all Linux systems.

2. Domain Name System is the naming system of the Internet; Windows Internet Naming Service is the Microsoft naming service; Network Information System is used in UNIX and is often called Yellow Pages; and Dynamic Host Configuration Protocol is used to assign IP addressing and can be used with all of the other services.

3. SMB/CIFS (System Message Block) and NFS (Network File System) are both protocols that allow network access of file systems.

4. Point-to-Point Protocol is a connection method used to create serial connections.

5. HyperText Transfer Protocol, Post Office Protocol, Simple Mail Transfer Protocol and Simple Network Management Protocol are used with TCP/IP to provide network services.

6. File Transfer Protocol and Trivial File Transfer Protocol are used to transfer files.

7. Telnet, rlogin, and SSH are the most common methods of remote access.

8. Gateways are usually routes to other networks and netmask defines the network scope.

9. TCP/IP is the standard protocol of the Internet.

10. POP3 and IMAP are the standard Internet e-mail client protocols. SMTP is usually a server side protocol.

Assessment Questions

1. A. TCP is a connection-oriented protocol. For review, see the "TCP/IP Protocol Suite" section.

2. B. PPP is most often used to create serial point-to-point connections. For review, see the "Point-to-Point Protocol" section.

3. C. NIS and NFS use the RCP TCP/IP protocol. NIS is a similar service to DNS, DHCP is not used to provide NIS or NFS, and NIS is also known as Yellow Pages. For review, see the "Other network protocols" section.

4. D. The programs used for network configuration are `linuxconf` and `netconfig`. The others are not standard programs for network configuration. For review, see the "Configuring Basic Network Services" section.

5. B. The host name is most often used to provide the Fully Qualified Domain Name. The others are not naming systems. For review, see the "Host name" section.

6. C. IP addresses are 32-bit numbers. The others are not correct. For review, see the "IP addressing" section.

7. D. IP addresses are controlled by IANA; however, most clients receive IP addresses from ISPs. DHCP and DNS use IP addressing but are not assigning authorities. For review, see the "IP addressing" section.

8. A. The DHCP service is used to automatically assign IP addresses to clients. It does not provide the other services. For review, see the "DHCP" section.

9. C. When attempting to connect to a Web site, the major service used is DNS. DHCP is for IP addressing and NIS and WINS are normally used for LAN or Intranet naming. For review, see the "DNS" section.

10. A. A subnet mask identifies the class subnetting for that particular IP address. For review, see the "IP addressing" section.

11. A and D. PPP is preferred because it provides secure password authentication, error detection, and both synchronous and asynchronous communications. For review, see the "Point-to-Point Protocol" and "Serial Line Internet Protocol" sections.

12. B. NFS uses the NIS system. The others are not normally used for NFS sharing. For review, see the "NFS" section.

13. D. The Apache Web server is the most common Web server in use today. For review, see the "Apache Web Server" section.

14. D. Samba is used to support the Microsoft SMB/CIFS systems. Samba is not used to support NFS, IPX or DHCP. For review, see the "Samba File Server" section.

15. A. The most common location of the Samba client files is /usr/local/ samba/bin/ or /usr/samba/bin/ directory. For review, see the "SMB/CIFS" section.

16. B. The command used to display the NIS password database is ypcat passwd.byname. The others do not provide the information. For review, see the "NIS client configuration" section.

17. A and C. FTP and TFTP are used to download files from a remote server. Telnet is used for remote access and SNMP is used for management. For review, see the "FTP" and "TFTP" sections.

18. D. The insmod command is used to load a module into the kernel. For review, see the "Hardware resources" section.

19. A, B, and D. To provide remote access Linux uses rlogin, Telnet, and SSH. For review, see the "Remote Access" Section.

20. D. SSH provides the best security of all the programs listed. For review, see the "OpenSSH" section.

Scenarios

1. The sales manager is wise to be worried about what services are started automatically. By default, the inetd daemon starts the ftpd, rlogind, rexecd, rshd, talkd, telnetd, and uucpd daemons, which can create many security holes. Editing inetd.conf can be done to stop these services from automatically being started.

2. Linux can replace most of the services that a Microsoft Windows NT server can provide with the Samba service.

User Environment Settings

◆ ◆ ◆ ◆

EXAM OBJECTIVES

◆ 3.3 Set environment variables (e.g., PATH, DISPLAY, TERM)

◆ 3.7 Identify when swap space needs to be increased

◆ 3.8 Add and configure printers

◆ 3.9 Install and configure add-in hardware (e.g., monitors, modems, network interfaces, scanners)

◆ 3.10 Reconfigure boot loader (e.g., LILO)

◆ 3.11 Identify the purpose and characteristics of configuration files (e.g., BASH, inittab, fstab, /etc/*)

◆ 3.12 Edit basic configuration files (e.g., BASH files, inittab, fstab)

◆ 3.14 Document the installation of the operating system, including configuration

CHAPTER PRE-TEST

1. What is the purpose of PATH?

2. What is the purpose of TERM?

3. Can the swap file be reconfigured?

4. Where is the `inittab` file located?

5. Where is the `fstab` file located?

6. What is a basic editor?

7. Can users have different shells on the same system?

8. What is BASH?

9. What should be done before editing any system configuration file?

10. What is the main reason to use a shell?

✦ Answers to these questions can be found at the end of the chapter. ✦

The user environment is constantly changing, and as a result, systems require the addition of new hardware, the expansion of current hardware, and software changes. The system maintainer may be required to perform several configurations when adding any piece of hardware. This job may include the reconfiguration of swap space, printers, configuration files, hardware profiles, and other environmental variables. The system maintainer may also need to reconfigure LILO and the kernel modules — or even upgrade the kernel. After these tasks have been completed, several of the critical system files may also need to be reconfigured. In this chapter, you will learn how to handle the addition of hardware or software by reconfiguring the user environments.

Adding Hardware

Objective 3.9 Install and configure add-in hardware (e.g., monitors, modems, network interfaces, scanners)

When maintaining or deploying systems, new hardware is often required to support the users' needs. This new hardware may consist of additional memory, video cards, network cards or modems, I/O controllers, printers, and many others. These devices must be configured for the Linux system in order to use them correctly, which often requires the physical installation or connection of the device.

When installing or connecting any device to a system, you must follow the installation instructions for the device. These instructions usually include antistatic guidelines and directions for proper grounding and environmental conditions; you should make sure that you have followed these instructions before attempting any hardware change. If you don't follow the instructions, you may not see any immediate, adverse effects; the damage, however, has been done and the system will show the effects of the damage in time.

For example, monitors are often installed and connected while the system is still powered on. This can be a big mistake because voltage will damage the system if you experience an accidental misconnection of the cables. The same warning goes for printers and most other external devices. Hot plug devices, such as USB, are an exception to this rule because they don't require the system to be powered down for installation. High-end servers usually offer hot plug and swap devices, including hard drives and even PCI cards, that require special consideration. These systems, however, are beyond the basic configuration of a Linux system. Maintaining a Linux system often requires the installation and configuration of new devices, but Linux provides the tools to perform these configurations.

Memory

3.7 Identify when swap space needs to be increased

3.12 Edit basic configuration files (e.g., BASH files, inittab, fstab)

The addition of memory to a system is often required to meet the demanding needs of new applications. In most cases, Linux handles the addition of memory quite well; however, you do need to make several considerations. Memory is often added to increase the memory available to programs, which can render the swap file inadequate for the amount of installed memory. The recommended size of the swap file is twice the available RAM. To reconfigure the Linux swap partition created during installation or to create a swap partition after installation, you should edit the /etc/fstab file accordingly, or use the many disk partitioning tools available to you such as fdisk. If you want to adjust the size of a swap partition, you must disable the current swap partition, which you can do by editing the fstab file (this controls the file systems that are used on boot). The following is an example of the fstab file:

```
/dev/hda1 / reiserfs defaults 1 1
none /dev/pts devpts mode=0620 0 0
/dev/hdb5    /home  reiserfs     exec,dev,suid,rw,usrquota 1 2
/mnt/cdrom /mnt/cdrom supermount fs=iso9660,dev=/dev/cdrom 0 0
/mnt/floppy /mnt/floppy supermount fs=vfat,dev=/dev/fd0 0 0
none /proc proc defaults 0 0
/dev/hda6 /usr reiserfs defaults 1 2
/dev/hda7 /var reiserfs defaults 1 2
/dev/hda5 swap swap defaults 0 0
```

To disable the swap file, simply remark the entry:

```
#/dev/hda5 swap swap defaults 0 0
```

VI

You can use any editor to edit the file, but you may want to consider vi, which is a very good, basic text editor. You will find that vi is very simple to use, and even though vi has many commands, you can perform most simple editing using the commands shown in Table 8-1.

Table 8-1
VI Commands

Switch	Task performed	Notes
a	Enter insert mode. The characters typed in will be inserted after the current cursor position	
i	Enter insert mode. The characters typed in will be inserted before the current cursor position	
r	Replace one character under the cursor	
u	Undo the last change to the file	
x	Delete character under the cursor	
<esc>	Used to exit editing mode	This key is in the upper left corner on the keyboard
:	Used to prepare to exit and save	Used after <esc>
w	Writes the file when used after :	Used after <esc>
q	Quits vi when used after :	Used after <esc>
!	Forces command ignoring other factors	Used to overwrite files or quit without saving

1. Open the file in the vi editor to begin editing the fstab file. Use the command vi /etc/fstab or by moving to the directory where fstab is contained (usually /etc and using the command vi fstab).

2. After you have opened the file, edit the file by using the arrow keys to move down the file to the line containing the swap file information.

3. Comment out the relevant line configuring the swap using the i command and adding a semicolon (;) to the beginning of the line.

4. The changes must be saved, so use the <esc> keystroke to exit editing mode. Then, : to move to prepare to save and w to write or save the file.

5. After you have saved the file, you can exit the file by using : and q.

This action disables the mounting of the swap partition at boot and allows the configuration of a larger swap partition. To boot the system without the swap partition enabled, simply reboot the system after editing the fstab file. Be aware, though, that system performance may decrease drastically upon a reboot. At this point, you can create a new swap partition by using any of the hard disk (HD) partitioning tools discussed in Chapters 4 and 5; `cfdisk` is usually the preferred tool. The typical `cfdisk` screen looks like this.

```
                  çfdisk 2.10s

                 Disk Drive: /dev/hda
                 Size: 2111864832 bytes
        Heads: 128  Sectors per Track: 63  Cylinders: 511

     Name    Flags   Part Type FS Type    [Label]    Size (MB)
     ------------------------------------------------------------
     hda1    Boot    Primary  Linux                   260.12
     hda5            Logical  Linux swap              417.01
     hda6            Logical  Linux                   957.88
     hda7            Logical  Linux                   474.81




     [Bootable] [ Delete ] [ Help ] [Maximize] [ Print ]
     [ Quit ] [ Type ] [ Units ] [ Write ]

          Toggle bootable flag of the current partition
```

Swap

In the cfdisk output, the swap partition is listed even though it has been disabled; you can verify this by using the mount command to view mounted systems after rebooting the system. Use the `cfdisk` program to delete the current swap partition and to create a new swap partition. Your system may not have extra free space, however, so you must back up, resize, and then restore another file system in order to create a larger swap partition. After you have created the larger swap partition, you must activate it with `mkswap /dev/<partition>`. Therefore, in the preceding example, <partition> would be hda5, and then `swapon /dev/<partition>`. Then, you can mount the swap by entering the line into `fstab`, `/dev/hda5 swap swap defaults 0 0`, or — if the partition is the same as before — by removing the comment from the line and rebooting the system.

In the Real World The creation of a new swap partition is most often made on a second hard drive to improve system performance.

After you have successfully created swap space, the system will have improved performance and better reliability.

Adding a hard drive

After you have installed the drive, add a hard drive to mirror the creation of the swap partition. To physically install a hard drive, you must plan several items, including:

✦ Determine the type of hard drive that you need — usually IDE (Integrated Drive Electronics) or SCSI (Small Computer System Interface)

✦ Determine the current settings of devices in use. For IDE, this includes the channel (primary or secondary) and device on channel (master or slave). For SCSI, the ID's used are 0-15 for wide SCSI or 0-7 for narrow devices.

✦ Select an unused ID for the new hard drive

✦ Plan the file system for the new hard drive

✦ Install the new hard drive

✦ Partition and format the file system for the new hard drive

✦ Mount the newly created file system

By using this general guide for installing a hard drive, the configuration can proceed simply and easily. The use of IDE or SCSI can be seen with formatting disk tools that identify disks as hda or sda; "h" represents IDE, and "s" represents SCSI disks.

The selection of the settings for the drive, however, is a bit more complicated. You must first select a free device ID while avoiding any current devices attached to the system. Normally, IDE devices are simpler because they have only two devices attached to one cable. You have three options for addressing IDE devices: Master, slave, and cable select. When adding devices to an IDE cable, the existing device is most often a master device. You can only determine this, however, by actually verifying the ID in use.

In the Real World Don't be fooled by the system detection of the hard drive during system initialization. When a hard drive is installed as the only device, it is often automatically detected as the master device. However, if you attach a second device, a jumper must be installed to assign the drive as master or slave. If you don't do this, the first drive or both of the drives will not be detected by the system.

To verify the device ID's, you need to physically look at the device's jumpers, which are similar to the one shown in Figure 8-1.

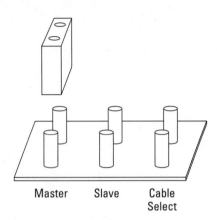

Master   Slave   Cable
Select

Figure 8-1: A Device Jumper

Most drives have a jumper map label attached to make the task of determining the
ID a little easier. Figure 8-1 shows only three jumpers, but often more options are
available to allow the disk to be configured for older systems that may not support
the features of the drive. Master devices are usually bootable on the primary IDE
channel. Some systems can boot from other devices, but for the sake of consis-
tency, the master drive on the primary IDE controller is the boot device for IDE systems. However, it is best to verify the device mapping, such as hda or hdb, to
ensure that the hardware ID matches the system identification.

Cross-
Reference

See Chapter 5 for more information about verifying hard drive ID and Linux
identification.

After you have determined the system and the current device's ID, you can add the
new hard drive. For this example, assume that the current drive is the master on
the primary IDE controller and that the new drive is the slave on the primary IDE
controller. Using correct ESD (electro-static discharge) protection methods —
usually, you use a grounding strap — place the jumper over the correct set of pins
to assign the drive to slave status. Insert the drive into the system and attach to the
cable.

In the
Real World

Verify that the cable is not "cable select" by inspecting the cable for breaks. A break
usually consists of a small hole in the cable, and is used to automatically assign
addresses to devices. If the system is using "cable select," both devices should set
to use cable select.

After you have configured the IDE device, what should you do about SCSI? SCSI
devices, like IDE, also are configured with separate device ID's. SCSI is most often
used in servers, but can also be used on workstations. Basic wide SCSI configuration uses up to 16 IDs to identify SCSI devices; one of these devices is used for the
SCSI controller. Most newer SCSI devices can be configured by setting the ID number on a special numbered switch. Some SCSI devices use jumpers to set the ID of
the device, and they use a binary system to identify the number. The 4 jumpers

are representatives of the place markers 0, 2, 4, 8 (and are labeled as such) in the binary math scheme; reading from left to right the numbers are as follows: 8, 4, 2, 0. Table 8-2 demonstrates how this works.

	Table 8-2 SCSI ID's		
Binary Number	**SCSI ID**	**Jumpers used**	**Linux ID**
0000	0	: : : :	sda
0001	1	: : : |	sdb
0010	2	: : | :	sdc
0011	3	: : | |	sdd
0100	4	: | : :	sde
0101	5	: | : |	sdf
0110	6	: | | :	sdg
0111	7	: | | |	sdh
1000	8	| : : :	sdi
1001	9	| : : |	sdj
1010	10	| : | :	sdk
1011	11	| : | |	sdl
1100	12	| | : :	sdm
1101	13	| | : |	sdn
1110	14	| | | :	sdo
1111	15	| | | |	sdp

Narrow SCSI devices use only three jumpers, so only the information shown up to "7" in the table applies. Using this information to verify the SCSI IDs is often a fairly simple task; however, not all SCSI drives use an easy-to-set jumper pattern. Always verify IDE and SCSI jumpers with the drive manufacturer. Select an unused ID and add the SCSI drive to the system in the same manner as you would add an IDE device. (Note one exception to this: SCSI devices can have many more IDE devices on one controller.) After you have installed the hard drive into the system, it must be configured in order for Linux to use it. You can configure the hard drive by using a disk-partitioning tool, such as cfdisk.

Cross-Reference   See Chapter 5 for more information about using cfdisk.

Unlike the original Linux installation, in which filesystems are created automatically, you need to make a filesystem on your new hard drives manually. On some systems you can use a setup utility, but most often you will use manual configuration. The mkfs command is used to build a Linux file system on a device — usually a hard drive partition. The use of mkfs is performed with the switches shown in Table 8-3.

Table 8-3 Switches used with mkfs	
Switch	**Description**
-V	Produce verbose output, including all file system-specific commands that are executed.
-t fstype	Specifies the type of file system to be built. If it is not specified, the default file system type (currently ext2) is used.
fs-options	File system-specific options to be passed to the real file system builder. Although not guaranteed, most file system builders support the following options.
fs -c	Check the device for bad blocks before building the file system.
fs -l filename	Read the bad blocks list from filename.
fs -v	Produce verbose output.

The standard command used to create a file system looks similar to this:

```
mkfs [-V] [-t fstype] [fs-options] filesys [blocks]
```

When this command completes, the mkfs program returns an exit code with 0 on success and 1 on failure. After this program is used, the file system is created and must be mounted, which you do by using the mount command, and can be auto-mounted by using the fstab file. This allows the new hard drive to be used and completes the installation of the hard drive.

Video and monitor

 3.10 Reconfigure boot loader (e.g., LILO)

When video cards and monitors are installed on the Linux system you usually are only required to reconfigure the X Window System by using Linux video configuration tools such as XF86config. However, you may experience situations in which you desire more complex configurations, including an update of the XF86 program or the Desktop Environment. You may want to perform these configurations in order to provide the best support of the newly installed video card.

Cross-Reference   See Chapter 5 for more information about installing and upgrading software.

You can install any necessary modules by using the following information, according to the Linux HOW TO. You need to decide what to compile into the kernel such as which modules to include. You will make the actual choices during the compilation, during the second stage of the following sequence of instructions:

```
cd /usr/src/linux
make menuconfig
make dep clean modules modules_install zImage
```

After you have completed these commands, you need to map out the module dependencies, which you can do by using the following command:

```
depmod -a
```

At this point, you need to add the newly created kernel to the boot menu of LILO, by adding the following lines to the `lilo.conf` file, which is normally located at `/etc/lilo.conf`:

```
image=/usr/src/linux/arch/i386/boot/zImage
 label=new
 alias=n
 read-only
 vga=ask
 optional
```

A complex `lilo.conf` may look something like this:

```
boot=/dev/hda
map=/boot/map
install=/boot/boot.b
vga=normal
default=linux
keytable=/boot/us.klt
lba32
prompt
timeout=50
message=/boot/message
menu-scheme=wb:bw:wb:bw
image=/boot/vmlinuz
     label=linux
     root=/dev/hda1
     initrd=/boot/initrd.img
     append=" quiet"
     vga=788
     read-only
```

```
image=/boot/vmlinuz
    label=linux-nonfb
    root=/dev/hda1
    initrd=/boot/initrd.img
    read-only
image=/boot/vmlinuz
    label=failsafe
    root=/dev/hda1
    initrd=/boot/initrd.img
    append=" failsafe"
    read-only
other=/dev/hdb1
    label=windows
    table=/dev/hdb
    map-drive=0x80
        to=0x81
    map-drive=0x81
        to=0x80
other=/dev/fd0
    label=floppy
    unsafe
```

Use care when editing this file or you risk losing access to one of your other operating systems that are defined in LILO. Next, using a text editor, create a new file called /etc/rc.d/init.d/modules.init, which is the most common name used in most Linux distributions, that will be used to configure modules into the kernel. Enter the following text in the new file:

```
# Modules initialisation.
#
# Start up the module auto-loading daemon.
/sbin/kerneld

# Mount all currently unmounted auto-mounted partitions.
/sbin/mount -a
```

Then, the following commands are used to enable the newly created file:

```
cd /etc/rc.d
chmod 755 init.d/*
cd rc3.d
ln -s ../init.d/modules.init 05modules.init
```

You can now reboot the system and use the new kernel with the new modules. Some distributions require a different configuration, so be sure to verify the location of the files and the commands to use for your specific distribution. The preceding commands should work with most Red Hat and Debian-based distributions. You can use this method with other devices, such as Ethernet cards and modems. After you have installed any of these devices, you must configure them by using the tool for the device; netconfig or linuxconf work well for network devices.

Printers

Objective 3.8 Add and configure printers

The task of configuring printers for the modern Linux system can entail a large number of steps by the administrator. Linux can support serial, parallel, USB (Universal Serial Bus), and network printers. However, Linux makes the installation of these printers easy with the linuxconf program. To use the linuxconf program, follow these steps:

1. From the main menu of linuxconf, select the Peripherals option and then select the Printer option.

2. If the lpd (line printer spooler) daemon, which provides the ability to print, is not installed or configured correctly, you are presented with the option to configure it.

3. Use the options shown in Figure 8-2 to allow the configuration of a printer.

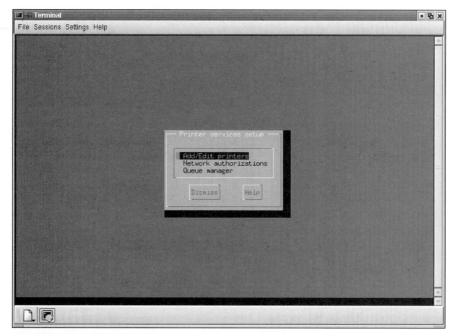

Figure 8-2: Configure a printer

4. Select Add/Edit printers to name the printer. When you select the add option, you are presented with the menu shown in Figure 8-3.

Figure 8-3: Add a printer

5. From this menu, you can also choose to configure a local printer, a remote printer, an SMB/Windows printer, and a Netware Printer (NCP). Enter the name of the printer and select the method of connection to the printer. Then make any additional configurations to allow the newly attached printer to be used on the system.

Configuration files

3.11 Identify the purpose and characteristics of configuration files (e.g., BASH, inittab, fstab, /etc/*)

Several files, which are listed in Table 8-4, control the configuration of many devices.

Table 8-4
System Configuration Files

File	Description
/etc/sysconfig	Directory on Red Hat Linux that holds system configuration files
/etc/rc.d/rc.sysinit	Initialization file for the system
/etc/rc.config	Configuration file for SuSE Linux system
/etc/rc.d/rc.local	Initialization file for custom commands
/etc/rc.d/rc.modules	Loads kernel modules on startup of the system
/etc/rc.d/init.d	Directory that holds many of the daemons, servers, and scripts for the System V init startup control standard
/sbin/init.d	Directory that holds many of the daemons, servers, and scripts for a SuSE system
/etc/rc.d/init.d/lpd	Start up and shut down the lpd printing daemon
/etc/rc.d/init.d/inet	Operations to start and stop the inetd internet services daemon
/etc/rc.d/init.d/network	Operations to start and stop the network connections
/etc/X11	X Windows configuration files
/etc/lilo.conf	LILO configuration file
/etc/fstab	List of Linux file systems to mount automatically at startup
/etc/inittab	The default state and terminal connections

Cross-Reference See Chapter 5 for more information on system files.

Editing these system files with the vi editor allows for the manual configuration of the Linux system and enables new devices and other environmental variables.

Setting environment variables

Objective ➡   3.3 Set environment variables (e.g, PATH, DISPLAY, TERM)

Setting up environmental variables, such as the display, terminal, initialization level, system paths, and many other settings are configuration parameters that affect all of your Linux sessions. One of the major files used to control a Linux system is the inittab file, usually found at /etc/inittab, and this file usually contains information similar to the following:

```
# inittab    This file describes how the INIT process should set up
#        the system in a certain run-level.
#
# Author:    Miquel van Smoorenburg, <miquels@drinkel.nl.mugnet.org>
#        Modified for RHS Linux by Marc Ewing and Donnie Barnes
#

# Default runlevel. The runlevels used by RHS are:
#   0 - halt (Do NOT set initdefault to this)
#   1 - Single user mode
#   2 - Multiuser, without NFS (The same as 3, if you do not have
#     networking)
#   3 - Full multiuser mode
#   4 - unused
#   5 - X11
#   6 - reboot (Do NOT set initdefault to this)
#
id:5:initdefault:

# System initialization.
si::sysinit:/etc/rc.d/rc.sysinit

l0:0:wait:/etc/rc.d/rc 0
l1:1:wait:/etc/rc.d/rc 1
l2:2:wait:/etc/rc.d/rc 2
l3:3:wait:/etc/rc.d/rc 3
l4:4:wait:/etc/rc.d/rc 4
l5:5:wait:/etc/rc.d/rc 5
l6:6:wait:/etc/rc.d/rc 6

# Things to run in every runlevel.
ud::once:/sbin/update

# Trap CTRL-ALT-DELETE
ca::ctrlaltdel:/sbin/shutdown -t3 -r now

# When our UPS tells us power has failed, assume we have a few minutes
# of power left. Schedule a shutdown for 2 minutes from now.
# This does, of course, assume you have powerd installed and your
# UPS connected and working correctly.
pf::powerfail:/sbin/shutdown -f -h +2 "Power Failure; System Shutting Down"
```

```
# If power was restored before the shutdown kicked in, cancel it.
pr:12345:powerokwait:/sbin/shutdown -c "Power Restored; Shutdown Cancelled"


# Run gettys in standard runlevels
1:2345:respawn:/sbin/mingetty tty1
2:2345:respawn:/sbin/mingetty tty2
# Run gettys in standard runlevels
1:2345:respawn:/sbin/mingetty tty1
2:2345:respawn:/sbin/mingetty tty2
3:2345:respawn:/sbin/mingetty tty3
4:2345:respawn:/sbin/mingetty tty4
5:2345:respawn:/sbin/mingetty tty5
6:2345:respawn:/sbin/mingetty tty6

# Run xdm in runlevel 5
# xdm is now a separate service
x:5:respawn:/etc/X11/prefdm -nodaemon
```

The previous file shows how the INIT process sets up the system for a certain run-level. The INIT process is used to start specific services for specific run levels and general services for every run level. In the preceding example, the default run level is indicated in the line `si::sysinit:/etc/rc.d/rc.sysinit`, several items run in standard run levels, and the X Window System runs in run level 5. Editing the configuration file for the INIT process can be useful to start services for a specific run level or all run levels. One of the major jobs of the `inittab` file is to set up the environment variable TERM, which should normally contain the name of the type of terminal, console, or display-device type to be used.

Exam Tip The `/etc/inittab` file will control the TERM environment, so be familiar with the location and format of the file.

This information is critical to any program that is screen-oriented, including editors, mailers, and remote access programs. A default TERM value is set on a per-line basis and nearly always provides all the services needed for a workstation console. However, you can edit the terminal parameters to use a different configuration depending on the needs of a user. Use the `inittab` file to set up user-specific TERM environment specifications when the default settings are not acceptable.

BASH

Objective 3.11 Identify the purpose and characteristics of configuration files (e.g., BASH, inittab, fstab, /etc/*)

3.12 Edit basic configuration files (e.g., BASH files, inittab, fstab)

The Bourne Again SHell (BASH), is the *shell*, or command language interpreter, for the GNU operating system and is standard for most Linux systems. BASH has many features that allow it to perform well in the Linux environment, including command and filename completion, command line editing, history commands and events, detailed shell operational control, and aliasing. BASH is widely used because of these abilities. To verify the use of BASH on a system, use the env command to list information shown below:

```
bash-2.04$ env
PWD=/home/bill
TMPDIR=/tmp/
LC_MESSAGES=en_US
REMOTEHOST=192.168.0.6
HOSTNAME=dhcppc1
NLSPATH=/usr/share/locale/%l/%N
LESSKEY=/etc/.less
LESSOPEN=|/usr/bin/lesspipe.sh %s
LANGUAGE=en_US:en
PS1=\s-\v\$
LESS=-MM
USER=bill
LS_COLORS=no=00:fi=00:di=01;34:ln=01;36:pi=40;33:so=01;35:bd=40;33;01:cd=40;33;0
1:or=01;05;37;41:mi=01;05;37;41:ex=01;32:*.cmd=01;32:*.exe=01;32:*.com=01;32:*.b
tm=01;32:*.bat=01;32:*.tar=01;31:*.tgz=01;31:*.tbz2=01;31:*.arc=01;31:*.arj=01;3
1:*.taz=01;31:*.lzh=01;31:*.lha=01;31:*.zip=01;31:*.z=01;31:*.Z=01;31:*.gz=01;31
:*.bz2=01;31:*.bz=01;31:*.tz=01;31:*.rpm=01;31:*.jpg=01;35:*.jpeg=01;35:*.gif=01
;35:*.bmp=01;35:*.xbm=01;35:*.xpm=01;35:*.png=01;35:*.tif=01;35:*.tiff=01;35:
LC_TIME=en_US
MACHTYPE=i586-mandrake-linux-gnu
MAIL=/var/spool/mail/bill
INPUTRC=/etc/inputrc
LANG=en
LC_NUMERIC=en_US
TMP=/tmp/
LOGNAME=bill
SHLVL=1
LC_CTYPE=en_US
SHELL=/bin/bash
HOSTTYPE=i586
OSTYPE=linux-gnu
HISTSIZE=1000
TERM=ansi
HOME=/home/bill
PATH=/usr/local/bin:/bin:/usr/bin:/usr/X11R6/bin:/usr/games
SECURE_LEVEL=3
LC_MONETARY=en_US
RPM_INSTALL_LANG=en_US:en
LC_COLLATE=en_US
_=/usr/bin/env
```

Notice the line

```
SHELL=/bin/bash
```

Documentation

Objective 3.14 Document the installation of the operating system, including configuration

I can't stress enough the importance of documenting the configuration of any system. You can store this documentation on diskette, tape, CD-ROM, network drive, or even paper. Use this documentation to recreate damaged systems and to provide a path for others to follow. Always include a set of formalized documentation of the systems that are supported — even if it is only a home system — because it will make system recovery that much easier.

Summary

This chapter explains many of the basics of Linux system configuration. The areas of this task include:

◆ Hardware upgrades and additions

- Hardware installation
- Swap File Configuration
- Mounting with `fstab`
- Booting with `lilo.conf`
- Document all changes

◆ Editing system files

- Editing with `vi`
- Backing up files before editing
- Document all changes

◆ User environments

- Using `inittab` to set environments
- TERM controls terminal, console, or display-device type to be used
- BASH (the Bourne Again SHell)

STUDY GUIDE

The Study Guide section provides you with the opportunity to test your knowledge about the Linux+ exam objectives that are covered in this chapter. The Assessment Questions provide practice for the real exam, and the Scenarios provide practice with real situations. If you get any questions wrong, use the answers to determine the part of the chapter that you should review before continuing.

Assessment Questions

1. With respect to a Linux system's RAM, how large should the swap file be?

   A. The same size as RAM

   B. Twice the size of RAM

   C. Ten times the amount of RAM

   D. Half the amount of RAM

2. Which command would you use to create a backup of the `fstab` to the file `fsold`?

   A. `copy fstab fsold`

   B. `cp fstab fsold`

   C. `mv fstab fsold`

   D. `cp fsold fstab`

3. What VI command is used to exit the edit mode?

   A. q

   B. w

   C. <esc>

   D. !

4. What key combination will exit VI and not save the changes made?

   A. : !

   B. : u!

   C. : w!

   D. : q!

5. Which command is used to activate a swap partition?

    A. `/dev/hda5 swap swap`

    B. `mkswap /dev/<partition>`

    C. `swapon /dev/<partition>`

    D. `mkswapon /dev/<partition>`

6. What are the options for IDE hard drive addressing?

    A. Master and Slave

    B. ID 0-15

    C. Master, Slave, and Cable Select

    D. ID 0-7

7. The /dev/sdc disk drive has failed on a Linux system. Which SCSI ID does this drive represent?

    A. 1

    B. 2

    C. 3

    D. 4

8. How many SCSI IDs are available on a narrow SCSI controller?

    A. 7

    B. 8

    C. 15

    D. 16

9. How many SCSI IDs are available on a wide SCSI controller?

    A. 7

    B. 8

    C. 15

    D. 16

10. What command would you use to create a file system on a new hard drive?

    A. `mkfs`

    B. `cfdisk`

    C. `linuxconf`

    D. `format`

11. What daemon is used to service printing requests?

    A. local printer daemon

    B. line printer spooler daemon

    C. line printer service

    D. logical printer spooler daemon

12. The `fstab` file is used to perform which function?

    A. Initialization file for custom commands

    B. Start up and shut down the `lpd` printing daemon

    C. The default state and terminal connections

    D. Automatically mount file systems

13. The `inittab` file is used to perform which function?

    A. Initialization file for custom commands

    B. Start up and shut down the `lpd` printing daemon

    C. The default state and terminal connections

    D. Automatically mount file systems

14. What command can you use to verify the current active shell?

    A. `shell`

    B. `BASH`

    C. `proc`

    D. `env`

15. Which of the following indicates that the shell is BASH?

    A. `SHELL=/bin/bash`

    B. `SHELL=/bin/bashshell`

    C. `SHELL=/bin/BASH`

    D. `SHELL=/etc/bash`

16. Where is the file `bashrc` located?

    A. `/etc/profile`

    B. `/etc`

    C. `/home`

    D. `/home/username`

17. Where is the file . `bashrc` located?

   A. `/etc/profile`

   B. `/etc`

   C. `/home`

   D. `/home/username`

18. What function does the . `bash_profile` file perform?

   A. Login initialization file

   B. Shell configuration file

   C. Shell login file

   D. Logout functions

19. What function does the . `bash_logout` file perform?

   A. Login initialization file

   B. Shell configuration file

   C. Shell login file

   D. Logout functions

20. What is the function of the . `bashrc` file?

   A. Login initialization file

   B. Shell configuration file

   C. Shell login file

   D. Logout functions

Scenarios

1. The system administrator has noticed that several users have requested to use a shell other than the default BASH shell. How can the administrator allow this while still allowing other users of the system to use BASH?

2. The Linux system used to save all the MP3 files created from a personal collection have filled up the Linux system's hard drives. A new hard drive has to be installed. What steps should be taken to perform this upgrade?

Lab Exercises

Lab 8-1 Using the VI editor

The objective for this hands-on lab is to gain experience in using the VI editor. You should be able to use any distribution of Linux for this installation exercise.

1. Log into a Linux system with only user rights.

2. Use VI to create a simple text file.

3. Practice using the common commands within VI.

4. When you're comfortable with the VI editor, open a system file for editing. Be sure to back up the file first.

5. Save the file after editing.

6. Restore the previous file.

7. Repeat as needed until you're comfortable with the VI editor.

Lab 8-2 Adding a hard drive

The objective for this hands-on lab is to gain experience installing a hard drive, partitioning it, creating a file system, mounting it, and editing a system file to use the newly created file system. You should be able to use any distribution of Linux for this installation exercise.

1. Install a hard drive.

2. Partition the hard drive.

3. Create a file system on the drive.

4. Mount the file system.

5. Edit the system file to auto mount the newly created drive on boot.

Answers to Chapter Questions

Chapter Pre-test

1. PATH is used to set the directories searched for any command entered.

2. TERM environment variable is used to set name of the terminal, console, or display-device type to be used.

3. The swap file should be configured to support the system memory and user applications.

4. The `inittab` file is normally stored in the /etc directory.

5. The `fstab` file is normally stored in the /etc directory.

6. A basic editor included with Linux is VI.

7. Multiple shells can be used on the same system and even by the same user.

8. BASH (Bourne Again SHell) is the shell, or command language interpreter, for the GNU operating system and is standard for most Linux systems.

9. Before editing any system files, you should back them up to a safe location first, so that you can recover the original if you make an error.

10. The main use of a shell is to provide services, including command and file-name completion, command line editing, history commands and events, detailed shell operational control, and aliasing.

Assessment Questions

1. B. Typically, the size of the swap file should be twice the size of installed RAM. For review, see the "Adding Hardware" section.

2. B. The command `cp fstab fsold` backs up the fstab file. The others won't work to back up the file. For review, see the "Memory" section.

3. C. The <esc> key is used to exit edit mode in VI. The others are used to perform different VI functions. For review, see the "VI" section.

4. D. The command string that will exit VI without saving the changes is: q!. The : w! overwrites the file and the others are not used. For review, see the "VI" section.

5. B. The `mkswap /dev/<partition>` command is used to activate the swap partition. The other commands don't activate the swap partition. For review, see the "Swap" section.

6. C. The options for IDE drive addressing are Master, Slave, and Cable Select — not only Master and Slave. The numbering system 0-7 and 0-15 are used in SCSI addressing. For review, see the "Adding a hard drive" section.

7. B. The SCSI ID that matches sdc is 2. SCSI ID 1=sdb, 3=sdd, and 4=sde. For review, see the "Adding a hard drive" section.

8. B. There are 8 SCSI IDs on a narrow SCSI bus. For review, see the "Adding a hard drive" section.

9. D. There are 16 SCSI IDs on a wide SCSI bus. For review, see the "Adding a hard drive" section.

10. A. The `mkfs` command is used to create file systems. The `cfdisk` command creates partitions, `linuxconf` is used to configure the Linux system, and format is not a standard Linux command. For review, see the "Adding a hard drive" section.

11. B. The daemon that processes print requests is the line printer spooler daemon. For review, see the "Printers" section.

12. D. The fstab file is used to automatically mount file systems. The others are not functions of fstab. For review, see the "Adding a hard drive" section.

13. C. The /etc/inittab file is used to perform the default state and terminal connections for a Linux system. The inittab file does not perform the other functions. For review, see the "Configuration files" section.

14. D. The env command will display the current active shell. The others are not used to verify the active shell. For review, see the "BASH" section.

15. A. The line SHELL=/bin/bash indicates that the BASH shell is the default shell. For review, see the "BASH" section.

16. B. The bashrc file is usually located in the /etc directory. It is not normally in the other directories. For review, see the "BASH" section.

17. D. The . bashrc file is usually located in the /home/username directory. It is not normally in the other directories. For review, see the "BASH" section.

18. A. The function of the . bash_profile file is to provide login initialization commands. For review, see the "BASH" section.

19. D. The function of the . bash_logout is to provide logout functions. For review, see the "BASH" section.

20. B. The function of the . bashrc file is to provide shell configuration commands. For review, see the "BASH" section.

Scenarios

1. The use of multiple shells is supported and can be configured by placing the appropriate files in the user's home directory and creating the proper configuration files. For review, see the "BASH" section.

2. You should install the hard drive, partition the disk, create a file system on the partition, mount the partition, and add any additional configurations.

Administration

Administrating a Linux network environment will be a common task. You will have to add new users and delete former users. You will also have to issue passwords and set the proper permissions for each user or group. The chapters in this part detail the common tasks that an administrator must know how to perform in order to keep the network (and the users on it) running smoothly. Every day, you will have to use common shell commands; create, extract, and edit files; manage run levels; and even start, stop, and restart services. On the Linux+ exam, 18 percent is focused on administration but understanding the basic functions of the common administration commands and being able to navigate the Linux hierarchy will get you one step closer to being a Linux professional and passing the Linux+ exam.

General Linux Administration

EXAM OBJECTIVES

+ 4.1 Create and delete users

+ 4.2 Modify existing users (e.g., password, groups, personal information)

+ 4.3 Create, modify and delete groups

+ 4.4 Identify and change file permissions, modes and types by using chmod, chown and chgrp

+ 4.5 Manage and navigate the Linux hierarchy (e.g., /etc, /usr, /bin, /var)

+ 4.6 Manage and navigate the standard Linux file system (e.g., mv, mkdir, ls, rm)

+ 4.8 Mount and manage filesystems and devices (e.g., /mnt, /dev, du, df, mount, umount)

CHAPTER PRE-TEST

1. Creating a user normally requires what information?

2. Creating a group of users normally requires what information?

3. What commands or programs are most often used to create users?

4. What commands or programs are most often used to create groups?

5. What are the common directories in Linux?

6. What commands are used to manage and navigate files and directories?

7. What commands are used to mount and manage file systems?

8. What commands are used to identify and manage file permissions?

9. Which of the commands that are used to manage users, groups, directories, file systems, and permissions, do not require the use of root privileges?

10. What commands can be used to manage users and files without the need for root access?

✦ Answers to these questions can be found at the end of the chapter. ✦

Every Linux system requires basic system administration, which includes the creation and management of users and groups of users. In order to allow your users and groups to access data, you must set up permissions to the required files and directories on the system. The administrator must manage these permissions in order to prevent unauthorized access to the file systems, and accidental damage to core system files.

Basic User and Group Administration

Basic user and group administration on a Linux system is an important skill. Among the expectations of this skill is the ability to add and remove users and groups of users. The current users and groups of users must be modified throughout the life of a Linux system.

What are users and groups?

A *user account* is an individual account that is created for the purpose of granting access based on an individual login. This login is used to determine access levels to the Linux system, including file access, directory access, program access, and access for any other user task. User accounts prevent each user that logs in from having administrative rights. Restricting administrative rights is an important security measure and prevents mischievous activity by allowing only the appropriate system rights for each user.

The administrator must also assign appropriate rights for groups of users. A *group* is a logical grouping of users who have the same needs, and group accounts are used to simplify administration of file and directory permissions. This is accomplished by creating a group account, assigning permissions rights to this account, and then adding the appropriate individual users to the group. An example of this might be a payroll department for a company. By creating a Payroll group, you can assign the users who are responsible for payroll activities to a group with access permissions to payroll files. Furthermore, it's probably not a good idea to allow others access to the payroll system. Because the payroll system is most likely comprised of many systems, you can cut down on the overhead of assigning permissions by using groups instead of enabling access to each system for each individual user.

Creating users

4.1 Create and delete users

Some users can be created during the installation of the Linux operating system; however, you will need to add more users as the system is used. You can add more users by employing the adduser command. To use the adduser command, you must have administrative rights. With the adduser command, you can choose from several different options to assign to created users — these options are shown in Table 9-1.

Table 9-1
Options for adduser

Option	Description
-c comment	The new user's password file comment field.
-d <home directory>	The new user will be created using <home directory> as the value for the user's login directory.
-e YYYY-MM-DD	The date the user account will be disabled in the format year-month-date (2001-12-31)
-f #	Sets the number of days after a password expires until the account is permanently disabled. -1 disables the feature and 0 disables the user account when the password expires.
-g	The group name or number of the user's initial login group.
-G	A list of groups of which the user is also a member.
-m	The user's home directory will be created if it does not already exist. The -k option copies the files contained in skeleton_dir to the home directory; if this option is not used, then the files in /etc/skel will be used.
-M	The user's home directory will not be created even if the default is to create the home directory.
-n	A group having the same name, because the user will not be created. This is distribution-specific.
-r	Used to create a system account and requires the -m option to create a home directory.
-p <password>	The encrypted password as returned by the password generator.
-s <shell>	Assigns the <shell> as the user's login shell.
-u <uid>	The numerical value of the user's ID must be unique, unless the -o option is used. The default is to the next available number greater than 99.
No Options	The useradd command displays the current default values.
--help	Provides program help.

With these switches and options, you can use the `adduser` command to create new users. The following files are used to support the addition of users:

✦ `/etc/passwd`: Contains user account information

✦ `/etc/shadow`: Contains secure user account information

✦ `/etc/group`: Contains group information

✦ `/etc/default/useradd`: Contains the default information for adding users

✦ `/etc/login.defs`: Contains the system-wide default login settings

The most common command used to add a user is `adduser` <username>. In enterprise environments, however, the command often includes the -p to assign an initial password and -g to assign a group. The `adduser` command is an important tool in the administration of users.

Change user information

Objective

4.2 Modify existing users (e.g., password, groups, personal information)

You can change user information by using several tools. The tools that are most often used are `chfn`, `chsh`, and `usermod`. Linux administrators use these commands to provide basic user management in the Linux environment.

The `usermod` command

The `usermod` command is the command most often used to administer user accounts. This command uses the -c, -d, -e, -f, -g, -p, -s, and -u options that were shown previously in Table 9-1 and the following options shown in Table 9-2.

Table 9-2	
Options for usermod	
Option	**Description**
-l <login name>	Changes only the user's account name to <login name>. This does not change the home directory of the user.
-L	Locks the user's password, effectively disabling the password.
-U	Unlocks the user's password, reverses the -L option.
--help	Provides program help.

The usermod command provides access to not only the settings available when creating an account, but also to the settings for changing an account name and locking and unlocking an account. These settings make the usermod command an excellent tool for basic administration of the user account.

The chfn **command**

Another tool that is often used to provide basic user account administration is chfn. The chfn command is used to change the finger information provided by the /etc/passwd file. This file provides four fields that are displayed when the finger command is used to identify a user.

Cross-Reference   Use the finger command to gather information based on a user name. The command can accept user names and return real information about that user.

The Linux finger command displays four pieces of information: full name, location, work phone, and home phone. This information can be useful to identify users by using the finger command. The command employs options to assign this information, as shown in Table 9-3.

Table 9-3 Options for chfn	
Option	**Description**
-f <full name>	Assigns the full name of the user.
-o <office>	Allows the assignment of the location or office room.
-p <phone number>	Assigns the office phone number.
-h <phone number>	Assigns the home phone number.
-v	Prints version information.
-u	Prints usage message.
--help	Provides program help.

The chfn command allows administrators to provide basic real world information about a user to the finger command.

The chsh command

Use the change shell command, or chsh, to change a user's default shell only. This allows only the shell to be changed and uses the options shown in Table 9-4.

Table 9-4
Options for chfn

Option	Description
-s <shell>	Specifies the login shell.
-l	Lists the available shells in /etc/shells.
-v	Prints version information.
-u	Prints usage message.
--help	Provides program help.

Deleting users

Objective   4.1 Create and delete users

Use the userdel command to remove users who no longer require access to a system. The userdel command doesn't have many options. The format of this command is userdel <login>, where <login> is the user's account name. The only option for the userdel command is -r, which, when implemented, removes the user's files in the home directory and the user's mail spool. Files are often not removed in order to allow restoration of a user and access to the user's files if necessary.

Creating groups

Objective   4.3 Create, modify and delete groups

You can create groups by using the groupadd command. The creation of a group uses the options shown in Table 9-5.

	Table 9-5 **Options for** groupadd	
Option	**Description**
-g <gid>	The <gid> is a numerical value assigned to the group. 0-499 are normally used for system accounts; therefore, 500 and above are used for newly created groups.
-r	Instructs the groupadd command to add a system account.
-f	Prevents groupadd from exiting with an error when a group already exists on the system.
-o	Allows non-unique <gid> to be used with the -g option.
--help	Provides program help.

The syntax for the groupadd command is: groupadd <groupname>. This command writes to the following files:

✦ /etc/group: Contains group account information

✦ /etc/gshadow: Contains secure group account information

The groupmod **command**

4.3 Create, modify and delete groups

Use the groupmod command to adjust previously created groups. The groupmod command has only a few options. The -g <gid> is used to change the group identification number and must be unique unless the -o option is used. When this command is used, all files that are associated with the old group ID must be manually modified to reflect the new group ID. The -n option is used to change the name of a group and uses this format: -n <new group name>. Use this option, for example, to change the name of an existing group to a more representative name, or in the enterprise world, to a new organizational name. This command writes to the following files:

✦ /etc/group: Contains group account information

✦ /etc/gshadow: Contains secure group account information

The groupdel **command**

Objective

4.3 Create, modify and delete groups

Use the `groupdel` command to remove a group of users. This command is used with the group name in order to remove a group from the Linux system. This command can only be used if the group exists, and you must manually check all files to verify that no files are assigned with the deleted group name as the file group ID. Finally, the primary group may not be removed until all users are removed from the group. This command writes to the following files:

✦ `/etc/group`: Contains group account information

✦ `/etc/gshadow`: Contains secure group account information

Getting Around Linux

You must be able to navigate and manage the Linux hierarchy, set file and directory permissions, and mount and un-mount file systems and devices. The following sections detail the Linux directory hierarchy and where important files can be found, and also the common commands used to traverse these directories.

Navigating Linux

Objective

4.5 Manage and navigate the Linux hierarchy (e.g., /etc, /usr, /bin, /var)

The Linux system uses a hierarchical file system structure, meaning that the system has a primary directory (/ or root) and sub-directories that are used to manage the files. When a user logs in, the system places the user in a default directory, which is usually the user's home directory. Each directory can be referred to by using an exact path name. Because the Linux system is a hierarchy, any user (including root) can verify the directory that they are currently using.

To see what your current directory is, use the command `pwd` or *print working directory*. This command displays the current working directory. Therefore, when a user logs in, the most common reply to the `pwd` command is `/home/<username>`, where <username> is the logged-in user. After the current directory is known, the user can move to the desired directory. To move from directory to directory, use the `cd` (change directory) command.

The `cd` command is mainly used to move from directory to directory by using the syntax, `cd </directory>`. Use the `cd` command to change the current working directory to one directory level up. For example, use the `cd` command in the `/home/user` directory to change the current working directory to /home. To move back to the user directory, use the `cd /user` command or just `cd` user. Note that the command without the forward slash "/" will only work for directories located under the current one. Another navigation method is to use the `cd` command with the full directory path of the desired directory, for example, `cd /home/user/files/documents`.

See Chapter 4 for more information on common Linux directories and their normal contents.

Common file and directory commands

Objective ▶ 4.6 Manage and navigate the standard Linux file system (e.g., mv, mkdir, ls, rm)

After choosing the working directory, the user must know how to use common file and directory commands. These commands can be used to list, copy, move, delete, and create files and directories on the Linux system.

The ls command

To list files on a Linux system, use the ls command. The ls command employs the options shown in Table 9-6.

Table 9-6
Options for ls

Option	Description
-a	List all entries including all those normally not displayed.
-A	List all entries including all those normally not displayed except the working and parent directories.
-b	Forces the printing of non-printable characters in the octal \ddd notation.
-B	Ignore backup or do not list files ending with the ~.
-c	Uses the time of last modification of the i-node for sorting or printing.
-C	Multi-column output that is the default output method. This method sorts down the columns.
--color[=WHEN]	Used to supply color to file types, where [=WHEN] is auto, always, or never.
-d	List only the name of a directory not the contents — useful with the -l option to return directory status.
-D	Used to generate output designed for Emacs' dired mode.
-f	Force each argument to be interpreted as a directory and list the name found in each slot. This option turns off -l, -t, -s, and -r options and turns on -a option.

Option	*Description*
-F	Used to identify the contents of a directory, returning (/) for directories, (>) for doors, (*) for executable files, (|) for FIFO's, (@) for symbolic links and (=) for AF_UNIX address family sockets.
-g	List in long format, giving mode, ACL indication, number of links, group, size in bytes, and time of last modification for each file, often ignored in newer version.
-G	Don't display group information.
-h	Print sizes in human readable format.
-H	Supplies the block sizes for each entry but uses powers of 1000 not 1024
-i	Prints the i-node number for each file.
-l	Use a long listing format.
-L	List the file or directory the link references rather than the symbolic links.
-m	List the files across the page separated by commas.
-n	List in long format, giving mode, ACL indication, number of links, owner's UID, group's GID, size in bytes, and time of last modification for each file.
-N	Used to print raw entry names.
-o	List in long format, giving mode, ACL indication, number of links, owner, size in bytes, and time of last modification for each file.
-p	Places a (/) after each listing of a directory, some implementations include the -F features.
-q	Force printing of non-printable characters in file names as a question mark (?).
-Q	Used to enclose entry names in double quotes.
--quoting-style=WORD	Use quoting style WORD for entry names: literal, locale, shell, shell-always, c, escape.
-r	Reverses the order of sort to supply reverse alphabetic or date list.
-R	Recursively list subdirectories encountered.
-s	Supplies the block sizes for each entry.
-S	Sort by file size.
-t	Sorts by time stamp instead of name.
-T --tabsize=COLS	Assume tab stops at each COLS instead of 8.

Continued

Table 9-6 *(continued)*

Option	Description
-u	Used with the -t option to sort by last time accessed instead of the default last modified.
-U	Don't sort, just display entries in directory order.
-v	Sorts by version.
-w --width=COLS	Assume screen width supplied instead of current value.
-x	Multi-column output with entries sorted across the page.
-X	Sort alphabetically by entry extension.
-1	Print one entry per line of output.
--help	Provide help with the program.
--version	Provides version information about the program.

Use the ls command to view the files and directories of a Linux system. For example:

```
$ ls /boot
System.map@          chain.b          map
System.map-2.4.3-20mdk config@           message
boot-graphic.b      config-2.4.3-20mdk  message-graphic
boot-menu.b         grub/           os2_d.b
boot-text.b         initrd-2.4.3-20mdk.img us.klt
boot.0300           initrd.img@       vmlinuz@
boot.b@             kernel.h        vmlinuz-2.4.3-20mdk
```

The cp command

Use the cp command to copy files and directories in the following format: cp [options] <source> <destination>. Use this command to copy a file or directory from the source to the destination. The cp command employs the options shown in Table 9-7.

Table 9-7
Options of cp

Option	Description
-a	Preserve links and file attributes if possible and copy directories recursively.
-b	Make a backup of each existing destination file.
-d	Preserve links.

Option	Description
-f	Automatically remove existing destinations.
-i	Prompt before overwriting the destination.
-l	Link files instead of copying.
-p	Preserve file attributes if possible.
-P	Append source path to DIRECTORY.
-r	Copy recursively and treat non-directories as files.
-R	Directories are copied recursively.
-s	Create symbolic links instead of copying.
-S --suffix=SUFFIX	Override the default backup suffix.
-u	Copy only files when the source file is newer than the destination, or the destination does not exist.
-v	Verbose mode that explains what is being done.
-x	Stay on this file system.
--help	Provides help with the program.
--version	Provides version information about the program.

The cp command can be used like this:

```
[user@dhcppc1 user]$ cp /home/user/myfile /tmp/
[user@dhcppc1 user]$ ls /tmp
kde-root/   ksocket-root/   mcop-user2/ mcop-user/
kde-user/   ksocket-user/   mcop-root/  myfile
```

Anyone who uses a file system needs the ability to copy files from one location to another. Linux provides the cp command to perform this task.

The mv command

You can move files on the Linux system by using the mv command. This command takes on the following format: mv [options] <source> <destination>. The mv command is a very capable tool for moving files in the Linux environment. The available options for the mv command are shown in Table 9-8.

	Table 9-8 **Options of** mv	
Option	**Description**	
-b	Make a backup of each existing file before removal.	
-f	Automatically remove existing destinations.	
-i	Prompt before overwriting the destination.	
-S --suffix=SUFFIX	Override the default backup suffix.	
-u	Move only older or brand new non-directories.	
-v	Verbose mode that explains what is being done.	
-V --version-control=WORD	Override the normal version control.	
--help	Provide help with the program.	
--version	Provide version information about the program.	

The mv command can be used as follows:

```
[user@dhcppc1 user]$ mv /tmp/myfile /home/user/
[user@dhcppc1 user]$ ls /home/user
Desktop/ myfile nsmail/ tmp/
```

The rm **command**

Use the rm command to delete files on a Linux system. This command uses the following format: rm [option] <file>. Use this command with the options shown in Table 9-9.

	Table 9-9 **Options of** rm	
Option	**Description**	
-d	Unlink directory, even if non-empty.	
-f	Ignore nonexistent files.	
-i	Prompt before any removal.	
-r -R --recursive	Remove the contents of directories recursively.	
-v	Verbose mode that explains what is being done.	
--help	Provide help with the program.	
--version	Provide version information about the program.	

The rm command is used as follows:

```
[user@dhcppc1 user]$ rm /home/user/myfile
rm: remove `myfile'? y
[user@dhcppc1 user]$ ls /home/user
Desktop/ nsmail/ tmp/
```

The touch **command**

To create a file that does not exist on a Linux system, use the touch command. This command uses the following format: touch [options] <file>. This command employs the options shown in Table 9-10.

	Table 9-10
	Options of touch

Option	Description
-a	Change only the access time.
-c	Do not create any files.
-d --date=STRING	Parse STRING and use that instead of the current time when marking the file.
-f	A BSD option ignored in Linux but allowed.
-m	Change only the modification time.
-r	Use the files time instead of the current time.
-t [[CC]YY]MMDDhhmm[ss]	*STAMP [[CC]YY]MMDDhhmm[ss] used instead of current time.
--help	Provide help with the program.
--version	Provide version information about the program.

If the touch command is used on a file that does not exist, and the -c option is not specified, the file will be created. You can also use this command to modify dates on files to reflect a different time than the data and time that is already assigned. Use this command to ensure that a file is backed up on a specific archive, or to show that the file is used before you purge old files. Finally, use the touch command to create a file where one did not previously exist, as shown by the following:

```
[user@dhcppc1 user]$ ls /home/user
Desktop/ nsmail/ tmp/
[user@dhcppc1 user]$ touch /home/user/myfile2
[user@dhcppc1 user]$ ls /home/user
Desktop/ myfile2 nsmail/ tmp/
```

The mkdir **Command**

You can create a directory on a Linux system by using the mkdir command. This command is commonly used in the following format: mkdir [options] <directory name>. This command employs the options shown in Table 9-11.

<table>
<tr><td colspan="2" align="center">Table 9-11
Options of mkdir</td></tr>
<tr><td>*Option*</td><td>*Description*</td></tr>
<tr><td>-m, --mode=MODE</td><td>Set permission mode (as in chmod), not rwxrwxrwx - umask.</td></tr>
<tr><td>-p, --parents</td><td>Make parent directories as needed.</td></tr>
<tr><td>--verbose</td><td>Print a message for each created directory.</td></tr>
<tr><td>--help</td><td>Provide help with the program.</td></tr>
<tr><td>--version</td><td>Provides version information about the program.</td></tr>
</table>

The mkdir command looks like this:

```
[user@dhcppc1 user]$ ls /home/user
Desktop/ myfile2 nsmail/ tmp/
[user@dhcppc1 user]$ mkdir --verbose /home/user/mydir
mkdir: created directory `mydir'
[user@dhcppc1 user]$ ls /home/user
Desktop/ mydir/ myfile2 nsmail/ tmp/
```

The rmdir **Command**

Use the rmdir command to remove a directory on a Linux system. This command is commonly used in the following format: rmdir [options] <directory name>.

Exam Tip   Notice that most commands use the same format—[command] [options] [argument]. This convention is helpful for remembering the proper syntax for any command.

This command uses the options shown in Table 9-12.

Table 9-12
Options of `rmdir`

Option	Description
--ignore-fail-on-non-empty	Ignore failures that are the result of a non-empty directory.
-p, --parents	Remove the directory, and then attempt to remove each part of the path name.
--verbose	Print a message for each removed directory.
--help	Provide help with the program.
--version	Provide version information about the program.

The `rmdir` command looks like this:

```
[user@dhcppc1 user]$ ls /home/user
Desktop/ mydir/ myfile2 nsmail/ tmp/
[user@dhcppc1 user]$ rmdir --verbose /home/user/mydir
rmdir: removing directory, /home/user/mydir
[user@dhcppc1 user]$ ls /home/user
Desktop/ myfile2 nsmail/ tmp/
```

Setting File and Directory Permissions

4.4 Identify and change file permissions, modes and types by using chmod, chown and chgrp

Administrators not only have to navigate files and directories, they must also control access to these files and directories. To do this, the administrator must use several commands to restrict file and directory use. For example, log in as a standard user and then attempt to `cd` into the /root or another user directory. Attempting this action returns the following information:

```
[user@dhcppc1 user]$ cd /root
bash: cd: /root: Permission denied
[user@dhcppc1 user]$
```

This information shows that the /root directory has permissions that deny most users from having access, as shown in the following:

```
drwx------  9 root   root    888 Aug 4 22:05 root/
```

This information shows that the root directory is not available to anyone but the root user. To change the permissions to a file or directory, use several tools, such as chmod, chown and chgrp, to control access.

The chmod **command**

The chmod command enables you to change file access permissions in Linux. This command uses the following format: chmod [OPTION]... {MODE | --reference=FILE} FILE, and can use OCTAL-MODE instead of MODE, with the symbolic mode format shown as [ugoa...][[+-=][rwxXstugo...]...][,...]. The following characters, shown with the meaning of their letters and symbols, select the new permissions for the file or directory:

Owner types

✦ u = The user who owns it

✦ g = Other users in the file's group

✦ o = Other users not in the file's group

✦ a = All users

Permission actions

✦ + = Selected permissions are added to the existing permissions of each file

✦ - = Selected permissions are removed from the existing permissions of each file

✦ = = Selected permissions are assigned as the only permissions of each file

Permission types

✦ r = Read

✦ w = Write

✦ x = Execute for files or access for directories

✦ X = Execute only if the file is a directory or already has execute permission for some user

✦ s = Sets user or group ID on execution

✦ t = Saves program text on swap device

✦ u = The permissions that the user who owns the file currently has for the file

✦ g = The permissions that other users in the file's group have for the file

✦ o = The permissions that other users, not in the file's group, have for the file

✦ a = All users

The octal uses 4 bits (0-7) represented as 4, 2, and 1 (adds to 7), with the first digit used to set the user ID (4), group ID (2), or save the text image attributes (1). The second digit is used to select permissions for the user who owns the file, the third digit is used to select permissions for other users in the file's group, and the fourth digit is used to select the permissions for other users not in the file's group; all use 4 for read, 2 for write, and 1 for execute. The chmod command also uses the options shown in Table 9-13.

Table 9-13 **Options of** chmod	
Option	*Description*
-c --changes	Similar to verbose but only reports when a change is made.
-f -- silent --quiet	Suppresses most error messages.
-R --recursive	Changes files and directories recursively.
--reference=RFILE	Uses RFILE's mode instead of MODE values.
--verbose	This option prints a message for each file processed.
--help	Provides help with the program.
--version	Provides version information about the program.

The basic use of the chmod command looks similar to the following:

```
[user@dhcppc1 user]$ chmod --verbose 4420 myfile
mode of myfile changed to 4420 (r-S-w----)
[user@dhcppc1 user]$
```

This command can be used to change the permissions on directories, as well as files, and should be used with care because it may cause access issues if used improperly.

The chown **command**

Use the chown command to change the user and/or group ownership of each listed \ file, which you can do by taking the first non-option argument in the standard format of the chmod command—chown [OPTION]... OWNER[.[GROUP]] FILE. If the first option is only a user name, or UID, then that user is made the owner of all files listed. If the user name is followed by a colon or period and a group name with no spaces, then the group ownership is also changed. If no group is included, but the colon (:) or period (.) is included, then the user's login group is assigned group ownership. This command can also omit the user name and include only the period or colon and group to change the group ownership of the files listed; this is the same function as chgrp. The options available to the chown command are shown in Table 9-14.

Table 9-14
Options of chown

Option	Description
-c --changes	Similar to verbose but only report when a change is made.
-f -- silent --quiet	Suppresses most error messages.
-h	This option affects symbolic links instead of the referenced file.
-R --recursive	Change files and directories recursively.
--reference=RFILE	Uses RFILE's mode instead of MODE values.
--verbose	This option will print a message for each file processed.
--help	Provide help with the program.
--version	Provide version information about the program.

The chown command often looks like the following (for the file 'newfile', created by user, in the directory /tmp):

```
[root@dhcppc1 /home]# chown --verbose user2 /tmp/newfile
owner of /tmp/newfile changed to user2
```

The chgrp **command**

The change group command uses the following format: chgrp [options] GROUP FILE. This command works very similarly to the chown command, but is used to only change group ownership of a file. The chgrp command uses the same options as the chown command. The chgrp command allows group ownership of a file to be changed independent of the permissions on the file or ownership of the file.

Mounting and Managing File Systems

Objective

4.5 Manage and navigate the Linux hierarchy (e.g., /etc, /usr, /bin, /var)

4.8 Mount and manage filesystems and devices (e.g., /mnt, /dev, du, df, mount, umount)

The Linux system administrator must daily mount and manage the file systems. This task also includes the mounting and un-mounting of devices. The administrator must determine the available resources in order to manage the file systems properly. The administrator can perform these tasks by using the tools provided by the Linux operating system.

Mount

The mount command is a powerful tool used to mount directories and devices on a Linux system. The simplest application of the mount command is to use it with no options or arguments. If the command is used on its own, it will return information similar to the following:

```
[user@dhcppc1 user]$ mount
/dev/hda1 on / type reiserfs (rw)
none on /proc type proc (rw)
none on /dev/pts type devpts (rw,mode=0620)
/mnt/cdrom on /mnt/cdrom type supermount (rw,fs=iso9660,dev=/dev/cdrom)
/mnt/floppy on /mnt/floppy type supermount (rw,fs=vfat,dev=/dev/fd0)
/dev/hda6 on /usr type reiserfs (rw)
/dev/hda7 on /var type reiserfs (rw)
/proc/bus/usb on /proc/bus/usb type usbdevfs (rw,devmode=0664,devgid=43)
```

This example shows the currently mounted devices and directories. Notice that the first device, hda1, is the primary IDE controller-master device, which contains the / or root directory. Mounts for the CD-ROM drive, FDD, /usr directory, /var directory, and USB on /proc/bus/usb are also available to the system. The mount command shows all the mounted devices on the system, and the hardware path for file systems, such as /var on partition /dev/hda7. This partition is commonly used to determine currently mounted devices and directories. The options available for the mount command are listed in Table 9-15.

Table 9-15
Options for `mount`

Option	Description
-a	Mount all filesystems mentioned in fstab of a given type.
-F	Fork off a new incarnation of mount for each device. This will perform the mounts on different devices or different NFS servers in parallel and is used in conjunction with the -a option.
-f	This ``fakes'' mounting the file system by performing the mount without making the actual system call.
-h	Provides the help file information.
-L label	Mount a partition that has the specified label.
-n	Mount without writing information in /etc/mtab.
-r	Mount the file system as read-only.
-s	Allows incorrect or sloppy mount options rather than failing.
-t vfstype	Used to indicate file system type. More on this option in the -t option section.
-u uuid	Mount the partition that has the specified uuid and requires the file /proc/partitions, available since Linux 2.1.116.
-V	Display mount version.
-v	Use verbose mode.
-w	Mount the file system read/write. This is the default.
-o argument	Options are specified with a -o flag followed by a comma separated string of options. More on this option in the -o option section.

These options are used to `mount` a device. The following is a common command, which is used to `mount` the diskette drive on a Linux system.

```
[root@dhcppc1 user]# mount -v /mnt/floppy
/mnt/floppy on /mnt/floppy type supermount (rw,fs=vfat,dev=/dev/fd0)
```

Notice that the file system type is listed and can be assigned by the -t option.

The -t option

The -t option is used to indicate the file system type to be mounted. This allows you to mount other types of file system formats, such as msdos and vfat for Microsoft Windows. For most types, the `mount` program issues a simple `mount` system call; no detailed knowledge of the filesystem type is required because the `mount` command will probe the file system. If the probe fails, then the file /etc/filesystems is checked and those file types are attempted.

The -o option

The -o option has many available arguments that allow it to provide the mount command more flexibility, as shown in Table 9-16.

| | Table 9-16 |
| | **Arguments for the -o Option** |

Argument	Description
async	All I/O to the file system should be done asynchronously.
atime	Update inode access time for each access. This is the default.
auto	Can be mounted with the -a option.
defaults	Use default options: rw, suid, dev, exec, auto, nouser, and async.
dev	Interpret character or block special devices on the file system.
exec	Permit the execution of binaries.
noatime	Do not update inode access times on this file system.
noauto	Can only be mounted explicitly.
nodev	Do not interpret character or block special devices on the file system.
noexec	Do not allow execution of any binaries on the mounted file system.
nosuid	Do not allow set-user-identifier or set-group-identifier bits to take effect.
nouser	Forbid a non-root user to mount the file system. This is the default.
remount	Attempt to remount an already-mounted file system.
ro	Mount the file system read-only.
rw	Mount the file system read-write.
suid	Allow set-user-identifier or set-group-identifier bits to take effect.
sync	All I/O to the file system should be done synchronously.
user	Allow an ordinary user to mount the file system.

Umount

The opposite of mounting a drive is to unmount it, so that it cannot be accessed. Use the umount command to unmount a file system. If a floppy diskette drive is mounted, unmount the diskette before removing it. To perform this task, use the following umount command :

```
[root@dhcppc1 user]# umount -v /mnt/floppy
/mnt/floppy umounted
```

The umount command uses the normal structure of umount [options] argument. The arguments are devices, directories, or -t [file system type]. The options available for the umount command are shown in Table 9-17.

Table 9-17
Options for umount

Option	Description
-a	Un-mount all file systems mentioned in /etc/mtab.
-h	Provides the help file information.
-n	Un-mount without writing information in /etc/mtab.
-r	In case umount fails attempt to mount the file system as read-only.
-t vfstype	Used to indicate file system type. More on this option in the -t option section.
-V	Display umount version.
-v	Use verbose mode.

Mounted file systems

One of the main reasons for adding a new mounted file system is that the current file systems don't provide the required resources for the users. Before adding a new file system via the mount command, however, you should view the systems that are currently being used. Linux has several ways to view this information — the most common are the du and df commands.

The du command

The du command is used to summarize disk usage of each file and recursively for directories. This command provides an extensive list of all the files and their usage of storage space. You may use the du command to determine the space used on a diskette as shown in the following:

```
[root@dhcppc1 floppy]# ls
picture.bmp*
[root@dhcppc1 floppy]# du
769    .
```

The picture file uses 769 kilobytes of the space on the diskette. The available options for the du command are shown in Table 9-18.

Table 9-18
Options for du

Option	Description
-a --all	Write counts for all files, not just directories.
--block-size=SIZE	Use SIZE-byte blocks.
-b --bytes	Print size in byte.
-c --total	Provide a grand total.
-D --dereference-args	De-reference PATHs when symbolic link.
-h --human-readable	Print sizes in human readable format, such as M for MB.
-H --si	Print sizes in human readable format but uses powers of 1000 instead of 1024, which the -h option uses.
-k --block-size=<size>	Used to assign the block size, normally 1024 but maybe assigned 512 or 256 and so on.
-l --count-links	Count sizes many times if hard linked.
-L --dereference	De-reference all symbolic links.
-m --megabytes	Sets block-size=1048576.
-S --separate-dirs	Do not include size of subdirectories.
-s --summarize	Display only a total for each argument.
-x --one-file-system	Skip directories on different file systems.
-X FILE --exclude-from=FILE	Exclude files that match any pattern in FILE.
--exclude=PAT	Exclude files that match PAT.
--max-depth=N	Print the total for a directory (or file, with --all) only if it is N or fewer levels below the command line argument.
--help	Provide help with the program.
--version	Provides version information about the program.

You can use the du command to estimate the free space used in the directory, as shown in the following.

```
[root@dhcppc1 /]# du /home/user
0    /home/user/tmp
0    /home/user/.kde/share/apps/RecentDocuments
0    /home/user/.kde/share/apps/konqiconview/kpartplugins
```

```
1     /home/user/.kde/share/apps/konqiconview
8     /home/user/.kde/share/apps/konqueror/dirtree/remote/
8     /home/user/.kde/share/apps/konqueror/dirtree/remote/
25    /home/user/.kde/share/apps/konqueror/dirtree/remote
46    /home/user/.kde/share/apps/konqueror/dirtree
62    /home/user/.kde/share/apps/konqueror
64    /home/user/.kde/share/apps
4     /home/user/.kde/share/fonts/override
5     /home/user/.kde/share/fonts
0     /home/user/.kde/share/icons/favicons
1     /home/user/.kde/share/icons
28    /home/user/.kde/share/config
99    /home/user/.kde/share
8     /home/user/.kde/Autostart
108   /home/user/.kde
16    /home/user/.netscape/cache
4     /home/user/.netscape/xover-cache/host-localhost
5     /home/user/.netscape/xover-cache
0     /home/user/.netscape/archive
467   /home/user/.netscape
0     /home/user/mydir
4     /home/user/Desktop/Trash
57    /home/user/Desktop
0     /home/user/nsmail
0     /home/user/.bluefish/projects
5     /home/user/.bluefish
3764  /home/user
```

Although the du command is capable of much more, it is ideal for determining the file usage in a single directory, such as how much space and which files are using what space in a user's home directory.

The df comand

The df command is similar to the du command but provides information about the amount of disk space available on the file system. The following is an example of the information provided by the df command:

```
[root@dhcppc1 /]# df -m
Filesystem  1M-blocks  Used  Available Use% Mounted on
/dev/hda1      248       77     171      31%  /
/dev/hda6      913      687     226      75%  /usr
/dev/hda7      453       59     394      13%  /var
```

The additional options available to the df command are shown in Table 9-19.

Table 9-19
Options for df

Option	Description
-a --all	Include file systems having 0 blocks.
--block-size=SIZE	Use SIZE-byte blocks.
-h --human-readable	Print sizes in human readable format, such as M for MB.
-H --si	Print sizes in human readable format but uses powers of 1000 instead of 1024, which the -h option uses.
-i	List inode information instead of block usage.
-k --block-size=<size>	Used to assign the block size, normally 1024 but maybe assigned 512 or 256 and so on.
-l --local	Used to limit listing to local file systems.
-m --megabytes	Sets block-size=1048576.
--no-sync	Do not invoke sync before getting usage info, the default.
-p --portability	Use the POSIX output format.
--sync	Invoke sync before getting usage info.
-t --type=TYPE	Limit the listing to file systems of type TYPE.
-T --print-type	Print the file system type.
-x --exclude-type=TYPE	Limit the listing to file systems not of type TYPE.
-v	Ignored.
--help	Provide help with the program.
--version	Provides version information about the program.

The ability to easily check usage of the created partitions with the df command is a valuable tool for anyone using the Linux system.

In the Real World   Most current systems have plenty of disk space, but you can use the df command to verify the current usage of that space displayed by percentage of used space.

Summary

This chapter explains many of the basics of administering a Linux system. This task is comprised of three areas:

✦ Users and Groups
  - Add, modify, and delete users
  - Add, modify, and delete groups

✦ Navigation and Management
  - Create, copy, move and delete files
  - Create and remove directories
  - Navigate the existing file system

✦ Controlling Access
  - Control user and group ownership of a file or directory
  - Change user and group ownership of a file
  - Change available file systems and devices

✦   ✦   ✦

STUDY GUIDE

The Study Guide section provides you with the opportunity to test your knowledge about the Linux+ exam objectives that are covered in this chapter. The Assessment Questions provide practice for the real exam, and the Scenarios provide practice with real situations. If you get any questions wrong, use the answers to determine the part of the chapter that you should review before continuing.

Assessment Questions

1. What command can you use to add the user name *john* for Johnny Jones?

   A. adduser john

   B. adduser John

   C. useradd john

   D. useradd John

2. Which command can you use to add the user name *contractor* that is disabled on the December 25, 2005?

   A. adduser contractor -d 2005-12-25

   B. adduser -e 2005-12-25 contractor

   C adduser contractor -e 2005-12-25

   D. adduser -d 2005-12-25 contractor

3. What command can you use to change user information for the finger command?

   A. chmod

   B. chgrp

   C. chfn

   D chsh

4. Which command will delete a user account, the user's home directory—including the user's files—and mail spool?

    A. `userdel -d <user name>`

    B. `userdel -h <user name>`

    C. `userdel -d /home/username <user name>`

    D. `userdel -r <user name>`

5. What files are modified when adding a group to a Linux system?

    A. `/sbin/group` and `/sbin/gshadow`

    B. `/etc/group` and `/etc/gshadow`

    C. `/var/group` and `/var/gshadow`

    D. `/proc/group` and `/proc/gshadow`

6. What command is used to delete a group from a Linux system?

    A. `groupdel`

    B. `groupmod`

    C. `delgroup`

    D. `grouprem`

7. What command will display the directory path that is currently in use?

    A. `dir`

    B. `shell`

    C. `path`

    D. `pwd`

8. Which command will move a user from his or her home directory to the /etc/X11 directory?

    A. `ls /etc/X11`

    B. `cd etc/X11`

    C. `cd /etc/X11`

    D. `ls -d /etc/X11`

9. Which command will list all the files and sub-directories in a directory and include the access rights?

    A. `ls -a`

    B. `ls -n`

    C. `ls -l`

    D. `ls -i`

10. Which command line will move the file named *myfile* from the home directory of user john to the /tmp directory?

    A. `[john@dhcppc1 /]$ cp myfile /tmp/`

    B. `[bob@dhcppc1 bob]$ cp /home/john/myfile /tmp/`

    C. `[john@dhcppc1 john]$ cp /home/john/myfile /tmp/`

    D. `[john@dhcppc1 john]$ cp /john/myfile /tmp/`

11. What is the correct format for the move command?

    A. `mv <file name> [options] [source] [destination]`

    B. `mv [options] [source] [destination]`

    C. `mv [options] [source] [destination] <file name>`

    D. `mv [source] [destination] <filename>`

12. What command may be used to remove a file interactively?

    A. `rm -d <file name>`

    B. `rm -i <file name>`

    C. `rm -f <file name>`

    D. `rm -a <file name>`

13. Which character allows the execute-only permission if the file is a directory when using the `chmod` command?

    A. r

    B. w

    C. x

    D. X

14. Which command will display confirmation of the change of ownership of a file from user to user2?

    A. `chown --verbose user2 /tmp/newfile`

    B. `chown --v user2 /tmp/newfile`

    C. `chgrp --verbose user2 /tmp/newfile`

    D. `chown -f user2 /tmp/newfile`

15. Which command is used to change only the group ownership of a file?

    A. `chmod`

    B. `chown`

    C. `chgrp`

    D. `grpch`

16. Which command *won't* mount the file system /mnt/win_c2?

    A. `mount /mnt/win_c2`

    B. `mount -f /mnt/win_c2`

    C. `mount -v /mnt/win_c2`

    D. `mount -w /mnt/win_c2`

17. Which file system is most likely to require the -t option to be mounted in Linux?

    A. vfat

    B. msdos

    C. iso9660

    D. smbfs

18. Which command would un-mount a diskette and provide verification of the dismount?

    A. `umount -l /mnt/floppy`

    B. `unmount -v /mnt/floppy`

    C. `umount -v /mnt/floppy`

    D. `umount -V /mnt/floppy`

19. Which command will display the total size of all files, without listing the files, in a user's home directory?

    A. du -c /home/user

    B. df -c /home/user

    C. du -c -s /home/user

    D. df -c -s /home/user

20. Which command will display the available space of each partition in megabytes (MB)?

    A. du -m

    B. du -M

    C. df -m

    D. df -M

Scenarios

1. The IT manager hires you to replace a neglectful administrator. The IT manager wants to have all the users who no longer work for the company completely removed from the system. How can you accomplish this?

2. The sales manager wants a new hard drive for his system. However, the IT manager won't approve the expenditure without proof. What tool can you use to resolve the situation?

Lab Exercises

Lab 9-1 File Management

The objective for this hands-on lab is to gain experience in navigating a Linux system and creating, copying, moving, and deleting files. You should be able to use any distribution of Linux for this installation exercise.

1. Log in to the Linux system.

2. Use the proper command(s) to determine the login directory.

3. Use the proper commands to move to every directory on the system and list the contents of those directories.

4. Return to the login directory and verify the directory.

5. Create a file in the home directory without opening an editor.

6. Copy that file to another directory on the system, try several and notice any that disallow access.

7. Create another file then move that file from directory to directory.

8. Remove all files that were created by navigating to the directory they are located in and listing them before removal.

Lab 9-2 Mounting and un-mounting drives

The objective for this hands-on lab is to gain experience in mounting and un-mounting. You should be able to use any distribution of Linux for this installation exercise.

1. Log in to the Linux system.

2. Use the proper commands to view the current mounted directories and devices.

3. Mount a diskette using a method that verifies that the mount was successful.

4. Un-mount the diskette.

5. Attempt to un-mount a system directory; take note of what can and can't be dismounted.

6. Repeat as often as possible trying several of the options available.

Answers to Chapter Questions

Chapter Pre-test

1. The creation of a user normally requires a user name, password, group assignment, user rights, and real world information, such as name, location, and contact numbers.

2. You need to know who is to be assigned to the group, what files and directories the group needs access to, and a name for the group.

3. The `adduser` command is the most often used command line method, and several GUI programs are available to create and manage users, such as kuser for KDE.

4. The `groupadd` command is the most often used command line method of adding groups to a Linux system. Several GUI programs are available for creating and managing groups,

5. The common directories in Linux are /, /bin, /boot, /dev, /etc, /home, /lib, /mnt, /opt, /proc, /root, /sbin, swap, /tmp, /usr, /usr/local and /var.

6. The common commands are ls, cd, cp, mv rm, touch, mkdir, and rmdir.

7. The common commands used to mount and manage file systems are `mount`, `umount`, `du`, `df`, `mkfs`, and `fsck`.

8. The use of chmod, chown, and chgrp are used to identify and manage file permissions

9. Normally, all commands used to manage the Linux system require root access.

10. Normally, users have no rights to manage users, groups, directories, file systems, or permissions.

Assessment Questions

1. A. The command `adduser john` should be used to add the user name *john* for Johnny Jones. The others won't create the proper account. For review, see the "Creating users" section.

2. B. The command `adduser -e 2005-12-25 contractor` is used to add the user name contractor that is disabled on December 25, 2005. The others will fail to create the user correctly. For review, see the "Creating users" section.

3. C. The `chfn` command is used to provide information for the finger command. The `chmod` and `chgrp` commands are used for access rights and the `chsh` command is used to change the login shell. For review, see the "Change user information" section.

4. D. The command `userdel -r <user name>` is used to remove a user and the user's home directory, including the user's files and mail spool. The -r option performs this task; the -d and -h options are not valid. For review, see the "Deleting users" section.

5. B. The files modified when performing any action on a group are `/etc/group` and `/etc/gshadow`. The others are not the typically files on a Linux system. For review, see the "Creating groups" section.

6. A. The `groupdel` command will delete a group from a Linux system. The `groupmod` will modify a group and the others are not typical programs used to perform group management. For review, see the "The `groupdel` command" section.

7. D. The command that displays the current directory is the print working directory or `pwd` command. The others won't display the current directory. For review, see the "The `pwd` and `cd` commands" section.

8. C. The command `cd /etc/X11` will move the user to the `/etc/X11` directory. The others fail due to the use of ls or a missing /. For review, see the "The `pwd` and `cd` commands" section.

9. C. The `ls -l` command will display a long listing format, including access rights. The -a option provides all entries, including all those normally not displayed; -n provides a list in long format but no access rights; and -i prints the i-node number for each file. For review, see the "The `ls` command" section.

10. C. The command `[john@dhcppc1 john]$ cp /home/john/myfile /tmp/` will move the file named *myfile* from the home directory of user john to the `/tmp` directory. The others won't perform the task. For review, see the "The `cp` command" section.

11. B. The correct format for the move command is `mv [options] [source] [destination]`. The use of <file name> is not used. For review, see the "The `mv` command" section.

12. B. The command used to remove a file interactively is `rm -i <file name>` due to the use of the -i option. The other options don't provide an interactive environment. For review, see the "The `rm` command" section.

13. C. The x option is used to allow execute only if the file is a directory. The r (read), w (write), and x (execute) don't perform this task. For review, see the "Setting File and Directory permissions" section.

14. A. The command `chown --verbose user2 /tmp/newfile` will display confirmation of the change of ownership of a file from user to user2. The -v and -f options don't provide confirmation and the chgrp command won't change ownership of the file for a user. For review, see the "The `chown` command" section.

15. C. The command `chgrp` is used to change only the group ownership of a file. The others provide a different service. For review, see the "The `chgrp` command" section.

16. B. The command `mount -f /mnt/win_c2` won't mount the file system /mnt/win_c2 due to the -f option. The other options won't fake the mount command. For review, see the "Mount" section.

17. D. The file system most likely to require the -t option is smbfs. The other file systems are normally mounted automatically by the mount command. For review, see the "Mount" section.

18. C. The command `umount -v /mnt/floppy` would un-mount a diskette and provide verification of the dismount. The other options don't provide verification. For review, see the "Umount" section.

19. C. The command `du -c -s /home/user` will display the total size of all files, without listing the files. The -c and -s options are required to provide the features needed. For review, see the "The `du` Command" section.

20. C. The command `df -m` will display the available space of each partition in MB. The -M is not used and the `du` command doesn't provide the correct information. For review, see the "The `df` Command" section.

Scenarios

1. You can move the users to a group called *remove* by using the `chgrp` command to remove any group affiliations, and then remove all their files by using the `userdel -r`.

2. The best way to justify the replacement or the denied replacement is to use the `df` command to verify the free space on the sales manager's current drive.

Linux Terminals and Shells

- ✦ 4.7 Perform administrative tasks while logged in as root, or by using the su command (e.g., understand commands that are dangerous to the system)

- ✦ 4.9 Describe and use the features of the multi-user environment (e.g., virtual terminals, multiple logins)

- ✦ 4.10 Use common shell commands and expressions

- ✦ 4.11 Use network commands to connect to and manage remote systems (e.g., telnet, ftp, ssh, netstat, transfer files, redirect Xwindow)

- ✦ 4.17 Manage and navigate the Graphical User Interface (e.g., menus, xterm)

- ✦ 4.18 Program basic shell scripts using common shell commands (e.g., grep, find, cut, if)

CHAPTER PRE-TEST

1. Is Linux a multi-user operating system?

2. Can multiple users simultaneously access a Linux system?

3. How does Linux provide multi-user access on the same terminal?

4. Can Linux provide Ethernet-based terminals?

5. Can Linux monitor remote connections?

6. What shells are commonly used in Linux?

7. What is the most common shell used in Linux?

8. What can you use to perform repetitive tasks in Linux?

9. What can you use to schedule tasks in Linux?

10. What is a "best practice" way to login as root?

✦ Answers to these questions can be found at the end of the chapter. ✦

One of the major advantages that Linux offers is a true multi-user environment. This environment includes virtual terminals, multiple logins, and remote logins — all on the same system at the same time. The remote access methods require the use of `rlogin`, `telnet`, or `ssh` to establish the connection. After the connection has been established, several common shell commands can help an administrator manage the Linux environment. These common shells can be used to create basic scripts to aid in the administration of a Linux system. Many of these administrative tasks are now included in the GUI interface tools that come with the most commonly used desktop environments, which are GNOME and KDE. To perform basic administration with these tools, you must have the ability to navigate the GUI environment. Also, you must have root access to perform many of the configurations on a Linux system. In fact, anyone administering a Linux system should be aware of the dangers of using root access, especially in a GUI environment.

Multi-User Environment

Objective

4.9 Describe and use the features of the multi-user environment (e.g., virtual terminals, multiple logins)

Linux is a true multi-user environment because it allows multiple users to simultaneously access a system locally or remotely. In fact, not only can several users access the system, they can also run several different applications on one computer at the same time. You can see this multitasking ability in action when using a console login, by pressing the key combination Alt+F2, which will switch to another login prompt terminal. This multiple console ability is enabled during the initialization of Linux, as several virtual consoles (or VCs) are created during startup. The number of consoles is controlled in the `/etc/inittab` file. You can switch back to the initial console by pressing Alt+F1. Most systems use four to six terminal sessions in order to provide local access to a system. Multiple virtual consoles can be used in environments where several users simultaneously access the same system, thus allowing each user to leave a session open while another user performs a task. Having several VCs is very useful, but VCs truly don't provide access for multiple users. However, they do demonstrate the ability to provide multiple logins.

Locally attached serial terminals can also provide access to the system, as this is another way to establish virtual consoles. Often called "dumb terminals," these serial devices are usually monochrome displays (color terminals do exist) and have a keyboard directly attached to provide input, and also a serial connection. A terminal server can host many serial connections — via serial hubs — that allow the daisy-chaining of clients. These clients log in to the server, which provides all the environmental and system resources, via terminals. The biggest advantage provided by a dumb terminal is the ability to provide clients with inexpensive devices that provide the computing power of a centrally located server. This central server can be easily upgraded to meet the future needs of the users.

The use of terminals has moved mostly to the Ethernet environment. All major vendors have some sort of terminal solution in place, which can be very useful and inexpensive.

The creation of Virtual Consoles

The administrator performs the creation of Virtual Consoles (VCs) for individual systems by using the /etc/inittab file. The following are the lines in the inittab file that control the virtual consoles:

```
# Run gettys in standard runlevels
1:2345:respawn:/sbin/mingetty tty1
2:2345:respawn:/sbin/mingetty tty2
3:2345:respawn:/sbin/mingetty tty3
4:2345:respawn:/sbin/mingetty tty4
5:2345:respawn:/sbin/mingetty tty5
6:2345:respawn:/sbin/mingetty tty6
```

For older versions of Linux, the lines may also look like this:

```
# Run gettys in standard runlevels
# Level 3 also getty on modem port.
1:2345:respawn:/sbin/getty tty1 VC linux
2:2345:respawn:/sbin/getty tty2 VC linux
3:2345:respawn:/sbin/getty tty3 VC linux
4:2345:respawn:/sbin/getty tty4 VC linux
S2:3:respawn:/sbin/uugetty ttyS2 M19200
```

Notice that the second configuration provides connection capabilities for modems to access the system. Because Linux supports the creation of up to 63 VCs on either local or remote connections, it can be used to create a small network using VCs.

The Linux Terminal Server Project

Linux uses the LTSP (Linux Terminal Server Project) to provide a simple way to utilize low cost workstations as either graphical or text-based terminals on a Linux server. A terminal is created from a diskless, or diskette-only system that boots from the network. To accomplish this, the terminal or workstation performs the following tasks:

✦ Obtains an IP address from a bootp or DHCP server by using a bootable BIOS or NIC

✦ Downloads the Linux kernel from a TFTP server

✦ Mounts the file systems needed and assigned on an NFS server

✦ Loads all system software, including the X Server, into memory and begins operation

✦ Contacts the XDM server and allows the user to log into the Linux system

These steps all require the use of a server to provide information for the terminals. The servers must be available to provide the following services:

✦ DHCP or bootp

✦ TFTP

✦ X Server

✦ NFS

These services allow the creation of graphical or text-based Linux terminals, which run over Ethernet. Graphical and text-based methods allow the creation of remote systems to augment the rlogin, TELNET, and ssh access methods.

Cross-Reference

See Chapter 7 for more information on rlogin, TELNET, and ssh.

These access methods require the basic user configuration on a Linux system and some additional configuration for the creation of terminal server clients.

Configurations for remote systems

Objective

4.9 Describe and use the features of the multi-user environment (e.g., virtual terminals, multiple logins)

4.11 Use network commands to connect to and manage remote systems (e.g., telnet, ftp, ssh, netstat, transfer files, redirect Xwindow)

The management of remote systems requires the creation of user accounts. After these user accounts have been created and the proper configurations have been made to the inittab file for virtual consoles, you need to configure additional services required by a terminal server.

To provide for the IP addressing of clients, you will need to enable the DHCP service or Bootp on your server.

After you have installed the automated method of assigning IP addresses, you need to install the lts_core package by using the command rpm -i lts_core-2.XX-XX.i386.rpm, where XX-XX is the release version. The installation of the Linux Terminal Server creates the /tftpboot/lts directory and the basic root hierarchy that will be mounted as the root filesystem of the workstation. The ltsp_initialize script is then run with the following commands:

```
cd /tftpboot/lts/templates
./ltsp_initialize
```

This installation script also modifies the following file:

```
/etc/exports
```

An entry is added in `exports` to allow machines in the 192.168.0.0 network to mount the `/tftpboot/lts/ltsroot` directory. Some other entries are created for other directories, but are commented out:

✦ /etc/bootptab: A partial entry is called `.ltsp`. An additional entry is created for workstation ws001, but is left commented out.

✦ /etc/X11/xdm/xdm-config: The "DisplayManager.requestPort" entry is commented out, thus allowing remote workstations to get an XDM Login screen.

✦ /etc/X11/xdm/Xaccess: The wildcard entry that starts with an asterisk (*) is un-commented, thus allowing remote workstations to get an XDM Login screen.

✦ /etc/hosts.allow: Entries are added by allowing `bootpd` to receive broadcast packets; `in.tftpd` and `portmap` are allowed to receive transfer requests from the 192.168.0.0 network.

✦ /etc/rc.d/init.d/syslog: This script is modified to allow remote clients to send `syslog` messages to the server.

✦ /etc/inetd.conf: This file is modified to turn on the `tftp` daemon.

✦ /etc/inittab: This file is modified to start the `xdm` process and the default run-level is set to 5.

✦ /etc/rc.d/rc5.d/S11portmap: This symbolic link allows the `portmapper` to be started when the system enters runlevel 5.

✦ /etc/rc.d/rc5.d/S60nfs: This symbolic link is created so that `nfs` will start when the system enters runlevel 5.

Because these file changes may introduce a security risk, you must restrict outside access by using a firewall. Then, install the kernels to be used for the remote stations by using some pre-configured kernels from the Linux Terminal Server Project or by creating a custom kernel. Either way, you must create the directory `/tftpboot/lts` that will contain the appropriate kernels. If you create a custom kernel, it must specify the following:

✦ Support for your specific network card

✦ RAM disk support

✦ IP kernel level auto-configuration

✦ BOOTP support

✦ `/proc` filesystem support

✦ NFS filesystem support

✦ Root filesystem on NFS

✦ Support for Parallel and/or serial ports for printer

After you create the kernel it must be set as a tagged image format with the `mknbi-linux` command. The `mknbi-linux` is included within the `Etherboot` package, which is available at `http://etherboot.sourceforge.net`, and uses the following command to convert the newly created kernel in the proper format:

```
mknbi-linux --output=/tmp/vmlinuz.ne2000      \
       --ipaddrs=rom               \
       --rootdir=/tftpboot/lts/ltsroot   \
       --append="ramdisk_size=1024"      \
       /usr/src/linux/arch/i386/boot/bzImage
```

After you create the kernel, you need to configure the X Server. These files are also available from the Linux Terminal Server Project and should be placed in the `/tftpboot/lts/ltsroot/ltsbin` directory. You must also verify several configuration files. The `tftpd` service must be started by `xinetd` or `inetd`. Newer distributions use the more secure `xinetd`, with `xinetd` requiring the command `xinetd`. Enabling `/etc/xinetd.d/tftp` and `inetd` requires the editing of the `inetd.conf` file. Include a command similar to the following example in the `inetd.conf` file:

```
#
tftp  dgram  udp   wait  root  /usr/sbin/tcpd in.tftpd
#bootps dgram  udp   wait  root  /usr/sbin/tcpd bootpd
#
```

Notice here that `tftp` is active — because it is not uncommented from the file — so no action is required. If you need to use bootp, you should uncomment it as well. Verify the configuration in the `inittab` file in order to confirm that `xdm` is running with the line; `id: 5:initdefault:` indicates that the server will boot into runlevel 5. Also, verify the configuration file for either `bootp` or DHCP. You can use `bootp` by configuring the following entries to the `/etc/bootptab` file:

```
# LTS-begins
.ltsp:\
 :ht=ethernet:\
 :ds=192.168.0.254:\
 :gw=192.168.0.254:\
 :lg=192.168.0.254:\
 :sm=255.255.255.0:\
 :hn:\
 :hd=/tftpboot/lts:\
 :rp=/tftpboot/lts/ltsroot:
```

```
#
# The following is an example of a line needed for a
# workstation
#
ws01:tc=.ltsp:ha=AABBCCDDEEFF:bf=vmlinuz.ne2000:ip=192.168.0.1:
# LTS-end
```

This `bootptab` file will set up the network on the 192.168.0.0 network; others may be used where appropriate. The line section ha=AABBCCDDEEFF is the MAC address of the Ethernet card in the system. `bootp` requires quite a bit of configuration, which is why DHCP is preferred. DHCP requires the configuration of the `/etc/dhcpd.conf` file. DHCP installs this configuration file, `/etc/dhcpd.conf.example`, but it will need editing to configure the system properly for your setup. The following is the default file:

```
default-lease-time 21600;
max-lease-time 21600;

option subnet-mask        255.255.255.0;
option broadcast-address    192.168.0.255;
option routers          192.168.0.254;
option domain-name-servers   192.168.0.254;
option domain-name        "ltsp.org";
option netbios-name-servers    192.168.0.254;

shared-network WORKSTATIONS {
    subnet 192.168.0.0 netmask 255.255.255.0 {
    }
}

group {
    use-host-decl-names        on;
    option log-servers        192.168.0.254;
    host ws001 {
        hardware ethernet     00:80:C8:D9:31:C1;
        fixed-address       192.168.0.1;
        filename         "/tftpboot/lts/vmlinuz.ne2000";
    }
    host ws002 {
        hardware ethernet     00:E0:18:E0:0C:09;
        fixed-address       192.168.0.2;
        filename         "/tftpboot/lts/vmlinuz.eepro100";
    }
}
```

This configuration allows the use of `bootp` or DHCP. Further configuration is needed for the workstation name and the IP resolution. This information must be entered in the `/etc/hosts` file or on a DNS server, because NFS needs to perform name to IP address resolutions to work properly. Another file `/etc/hosts.allow` will be created automatically and may need configuration if the following default is not used.

```
bootpd:  0.0.0.0
in.tftpd: 192.168.0.
portmap:  192.168.0.
```

Adjust the network address for the network in use. The creation of the /etc/
export file provides file systems. By default, the file resembles the following:

```
## LTS-begin ##

#
# The lines between the 'LTS-begin' and the 'LTS-end' were added
# on: Sun Aug 6 23:30:29 EDT 2000 by the ltsp installation script.
# For more information, visit the ltsp homepage
# at http://www.ltsp.org
#

/tftpboot/lts/ltsroot  192.168.0.0/255.255.255.0(ro,no_root_squash)

#
# The following entries need to be uncommented if you want
# Local App support in ltsp
#
#/usr        192.168.0.0/255.255.255.0(ro,no_root_squash)
#/bin        192.168.0.0/255.255.255.0(ro,no_root_squash)
#/sbin       192.168.0.0/255.255.255.0(ro,no_root_squash)
#/lib        192.168.0.0/255.255.255.0(ro,no_root_squash)
#/home       192.168.0.0/255.255.255.0(rw,no_root_squash)

## LTS-end ##
```

Notice that most of the file systems required to run local applications are remarked.
They may need to be un-remarked if you plan to use local applications. The LTSP
installation script modifies the /etc/rc.d/init.d/syslog startup script to
enable remote workstations to send their syslog messages to the server, in order to
verify that the line daemon syslogd -m 0 - is present. The configuration file for
the workstations is the /tftpboot/lts/ltsroot/etc/lts.conf file, and it contains most of the configurable parameters for the workstations. Use the following
example of a /tftpboot/lts/ltsroot/etc/lts.conf file if all workstations are
the same:

```
[Default]
    XSERVER        = XF86_SVGA
    SERVER         = 192.168.0.254
    X_MOUSE_PROTOCOL  = "PS/2"
    X_MOUSE_DEVICE  = "/dev/psaux"
    X_MOUSE_RESOLUTION = 400
    X_MOUSE_BUTTONS   = 3
    USE_XFS        = N
    UI_MODE        = GUI
```

```
[ws001]
    XSERVER       = XF86_SVGA
    X_MOUSE_PROTOCOL  = "Microsoft"
    X_MOUSE_DEVICE    = "/dev/ttyS1"
    X_MOUSE_RESOLUTION = 50
    X_MOUSE_BUTTONS   = 3
    X_MOUSE_BAUD     = 1200

[ws002]
    XSERVER       = XF86_Mach64

[ws003]
    XSERVER       = XF86_SVGA
    X_COLOR_DEPTH    = 24
    USE_XFS      = N

[ws004]
    UI_MODE      = CHAR
```

These parameters are used to create a basic configuration that allows the creation of terminals. These terminals may be GUI-based and can be configured to perform all the tasks required by the clients.

Monitoring remote connections

4.11 Use network commands to connect to and manage remote systems (e.g., telnet, ftp, ssh, netstat, transfer files, redirect Xwindow)

FTP, HTTP, TELNET, and ssh create remote connections to a system. They allow you to be able to login and use the remote machine as if you were sitting physically at the console.

Telnet

Telnet is a terminal emulation program for clients running on TCP/IP networks. It connects you to a terminal on another machine. This connection allows you to enter commands on that machine as if you were at the actual physical console. To connect to a host called server1, you would enter the command:

```
telnet server1
```

You should then receive a login prompt from where you can log into the system and start entering commands. To exit out of the telnet command, you simply have to logout, or use the quit command.

FTP

FTP (File Transfer Protocol) is a protocol that is part of the TCP/IP suite. It allows you to connect to a remote host and transfer files to or from the remote host. For example, to connect to a host called server1, you would enter the command:

```
ftp server1
```

This command will connect you to the FTP server process on server1, which will prompt you with a login. Once logged into the system, you can use the cd and ls commands to traverse and examine the directories on the system. Retrieving files from the remote host is accomplished by the get command. Uploading a file to the host is accomplished by using the put command.

SSH

SSH (secure shell) is similar to telnet, in that you use it to connect to a remote machine, but in this case, the communications and authentication are encrypted to prevent someone from listening in to the session.

X remote login

The X Windows system allows for remote X logins to other hosts, and also allows the ability of a client to run an X Windows session on another machine. For example, if you need to start an X login with server1, you would use the command:

```
X -query server1
```

You can also redirect your own display to a remote host, as long as the appropriate permissions are in place. For example, your client (client1) wants to open up an X Window on server that is from your client machine. First, the server has to give you permissions to do this:

```
xhost + client1
```

Now, you have to use the DISPLAY command to export your display:

```
DISPLAY=server1:0 xterm &
```

This command starts xterm in background mode (&), so you will not interfere with the main X session that is running on the server.

Netstat

The connections from these services, such as telnet, ssh, and ftp, may require detection by an administrator, so that any unauthorized attempts at logging in can be seen and logged. One of the most common tools used to perform this task is netstat. The netstat command provides information similar to the following:

```
[user@dhcppc1 user]$ netstat
Active Internet connections (w/o servers)
Proto Recv-Q Send-Q Local Address     Foreign Address      State
tcp    0    0 192.168.0.7:telnet  192.168.0.8:blackjack ESTABLISHED
tcp    0   20 192.168.0.7:ssh     192.168.0.6:1137    ESTABLISHED
Active UNIX domain sockets (w/o servers)
Proto RefCnt Flags    Type     State     I-Node Path
unix 8   [ ]     DGRAM        10679 /dev/log
```

```
unix 2   [ ]      DGRAM              16916
unix 3   [ ]      STREAM   CONNECTED   16330 /tmp/.X11-unix/X0
unix 3   [ ]      STREAM   CONNECTED   16329
unix 3   [ ]      STREAM   CONNECTED   16321 /tmp/.font-unix/fs-1
unix 3   [ ]      STREAM   CONNECTED   16320
unix 3   [ ]      STREAM   CONNECTED   16322 /tmp/.X11-unix/X0
unix 3   [ ]      STREAM   CONNECTED   16317
unix 2   [ ]      DGRAM              15166
unix 2   [ ]      DGRAM              14346
unix 2   [ ]      DGRAM              11463
unix 2   [ ]      DGRAM              10704
unix 2   [ ]      DGRAM              10691
unix 2   [ ]      STREAM   CONNECTED   10101
```

This output shows some of the current active UNIX domain sockets and remote hosts. In this example, the remote hosts use TELNET and ssh to connect to the system. Netstat is a powerful tool that uses the options shown in Table 10-1.

Table 10-1
Netstat Options

Option	Description
No Options	By default, netstat displays a list of open sockets.
-a --all	Shows both listening and non-listening sockets.
-A --protocol=family	Specifies the address families for which connections are to be shown.
-c --continuous	Causes netstat to print the selected information every second continuously.
-C	Prints the routing information from the route cache.
-e --extend	Displays additional information.
-F	Prints routing information from the FIB.
-g --groups	Displays multicast group membership information for IPv4 and IPv6.
-I --interface=iface	Displays a table of all network interfaces, or the specified iface.
-l --listening	Shows only listening sockets.
-M --masquerade	Displays a list of masqueraded connections.
-n --numeric	Shows numerical addresses instead of trying to determine symbolic host, port, or user names.
--numeric-hosts	Shows numerical host addresses but does not affect the resolution of port or user names.

Option	Description
--numeric-ports	Shows numerical port numbers but does not affect the resolution of host or user names.
--numeric-users	Shows numerical user IDs but does not affect the resolution of host or port names.
-o --timers	Includes information related to networking timers.
-p --program	Shows the PID and name of the program to which each socket belongs.
-r --route	Displays the kernel routing tables.
-s --statistics	Displays summary statistics for each protocol.
-v --verbose	Verbose mode that explains what is being done.

Netstat is a powerful tool that is used by experienced network administrators, but can also be used as a basic tool to see active connections to a system.

 Exam Tip   The use of any Linux command, such as netstat, requires the use of the proper syntax. Know the basic structure of the command and the switches.

Common Shell Commands

 Objective   4.10 Use common shell commands and expressions.

Basic tools are built into the shells, which are started as the environment when a user or administrator logs in to a Linux system. The most common shell for Linux is Bash or *Bourne Again SHell*. Other major shell programs used for Linux are Public Domain Korn Shell (PDKSH), the TCSH shell, and the Z-shell.

 Cross-Reference   See Chapter 8 for more information on shell programs.

Bash is an sh-compatible command language interpreter, which is intended to conform with the IEEE POSIX Shell and Tools specification. Bash also incorporates useful features from the Korn and C shells (ksh and csh). The following are the configuration files for Bash:

✦ /bin/bash: The bash executable

✦ /etc/profile: The system wide initialization file for login shells

✦ ~/.bash_profile: The personal initialization file for login shells

✦ ~/.bashrc: The individual per-interactive-shell startup file

✦ ~/.bash_logout: The login shell cleanup file that executed when the shell exits

✦ ~/.inputrc: Individual read line initialization file

Instructions for the Bash shell are very large and complex—in fact, the MAN page contains over 5000 lines of text, and thus covering this topic would require another book. Some of the most common and useful tools included in the shell are shown in Table 10-2.

Table 10-2
Bash Shell Commands and Tools Used

Option	Description
Arrow up and down	Scrolls through recent commands used.
|	Uses the format command1 | command2 and places the output of command1 and inputs into command2.
&&	Uses the format command1 && command2 and command2 is executed if, and only if, command1 returns an exit status of zero.
||	Uses the format command1 || command2 and command2 is executed if and only if command1 returns a non-zero exit status.
alias	Alias with no arguments or with the -p option prints the list of aliases in the form alias name=value on standard output.
bg [jobspec]	Resumes the suspended job jobspec in the background, as if it had been started with &. (background=bg)
break [n]	Exit from within a for, while, until, or select loop.
cd	Changes the current directory to dir.
continue [n]	Resumes the next iteration of the enclosing for, while, until, or select loop.
cut [options][FILE...]	Prints selected parts of lines from each FILE to standard output.
dirs	This displays the list of currently remembered directories.
echo	Outputs the args, separated by spaces, followed by a new line.
enable	Enables and disables built-in shell commands.

Option	Description
exit [n]	Causes the shell to exit with a status of n.
find [path...] [expression]	Searches the directory tree rooted at each given file name by evaluating the given expression from left to right, according to the rules of precedence until the outcome is known at which point find moves on to the next file name.
fg [jobspec]	Resumes jobspec in the foreground, and makes it the current job. (foreground=fg)
grep [options][FILE...]	Grep searches the named input FILE.
help [-s] [pattern]	Displays helpful information about built-in commands.
history	Displays the command history list with line numbers.
kill [-s sigspec	-n signum	-sigspec] [pid	jobspec]	Sends the signal named by sigspec or signum to the processes named by pid or jobspec.
logout	Exits a login shell.
pwd	Prints the absolute pathname of the current working directory.
read	One line is read from the standard input, and the first word is assigned to the first name, the second word to the second name, and so on, with leftover words and their intervening separators assigned to the last name.
umask [-p] [-S] [mode]	The user file-creation mask is set to mode.
unalias	Removes each name from the list of defined aliases.
wait [n]	Waits for the specified process and returns its termination status.

This is by no means the definitive list of tools for Bash. With experience, you will learn more of the included shell commands and the necessary commands for each environment. These common commands can help make Linux tools — especially the history tool — easier to use for everyone.

Basic shell scripts

Objective

4.18 Program basic shell scripts using common shell commands (e.g., grep, find, cut, if)

You can use the common shell commands to create some very simple scripts to perform routine tasks. You can chain together a number of basic commands to perform a specific task. Here is an example of a shell script:

```
#!/bin/sh
# This script changes to your home directory and does a
directory list
cd /home/user1
ls -al
```

In this simple script, all we are doing is changing to a user's home directory, and listing the contents of that directory.

The first line identifies this as a shell script that is passed to the BASH shell program at /bin/sh. This is important to ensure that the script is run under the BASH shell and not another one such as C shell.

The second line is a comment, telling the user what the script does. All comments are preceded with a "#" mark.

The next two commands are simply BASH shell commands to change to the user home directory, and list the contents.

Here is a list of common commands that can be very useful when programming shell scripts:

✦ grep — This command searches for a specific pattern of text in a file. This is useful for searching large amounts of text for a certain name or error message.

✦ find — This command is similar to grep, as it searches a directory for a pattern or file that you are looking for.

✦ cut — This command removes sections of text from lines of a file.

✦ if — If you need to perform some type of logical decision making within a script, you would use the if command. For example:

```
if [ "yes" = "yes" ]; then
    echo "The answer is yes"
```

These simple examples barely scratch the surface of the many large tasks you can perform using shell scripts.

Caution using root access

 4.7 Perform administrative tasks while logged in as root, or by using the su command (e.g., understand commands that are dangerous to the system)

Root access is required to perform most Linux administrative tasks. However, the powers of root access are unlimited and can permanently damage the system if performed incorrectly. Therefore, the common and "best practice" method for providing root access in Linux or UNIX is to log in as a user and then use the su (switch user) command to change to the root user, perform the required task, and then exit root privilege.

Exam Tip

You can use the su (switch user) command to move from any user login to another. If a user name is not given, the su command defaults to change to the root user. This command asks for the root password and provides all the necessary abilities. Notice that the prompt changes from a $ for users to # for the root user.

Even when performing routine tasks with root access, use due care to ensure that the system is backed up and user files are protected.

Navigating the GUI interface

 4.17 Manage and navigate the Graphical User Interface (e.g., menus, xterm)

Most Linux tasks can be performed in the X Window System, which requires you to be able to navigate the GUI interface. Today, most distributions use the GNOME or KDE desktop environment and provide many tools necessary for performing extensive management of the Linux system. Each distribution also provides its own tools to perform administrative tasks. The basic navigation of the system requires the use of a terminal session, which provides access to the command line in the GUI. Most instances of the GUI allow the right mouse button to provide a menu that allows you to select a terminal, or by using the standard GUI menus to select a terminal. This is typically called an "xterm", to denote a terminal within an X Windows session.

Exam Tip

The neutrality of the Linux+ exam limits the questions on navigating the GUI interface, so be prepared for only very general questions about GUI interfaces.

Summary

This chapter explains many of the basics of Linux system navigation, including the use of terminals, virtual consoles, shell navigation, and remote access. For the exam, keep these points in mind:

✦ Multi-user environments

  • Virtual Consoles (or VCs)

  • Serial Terminals

  • Ethernet Terminals and the Linux Terminal Server Project

✦ Shell, scripts, and scheduling

  • BASH

  • Creating scripts

  • Cron and crontab to schedule tasks

✦ Administration and navigation

  • Root access

  • GUI navigation

✦   ✦   ✦

STUDY GUIDE

The Study Guide section provides you with the opportunity to test your knowledge about the Linux+ exam objectives that are covered in this chapter. The Assessment Questions provide practice for the real exam, and the Scenarios provide practice with real situations. If you get any questions wrong, use the answers to determine the part of the chapter that you should review before continuing.

Assessment Questions

1. What keystroke is normally used to move from one virtual console to another virtual console?

   A. <Ctrl> <Tab>

   B. <Alt> <Fx>, where x is the console number

   C. <Alt> <Tab>

   D. <Ctrl> <Fx>, where x is the console number

2. How many virtual consoles does Linux normally support?

   A. 32

   B. 48

   C. 63

   D. 256

3. What can you use to provide a simple way to utilize low-cost workstations as either graphical- or text-based terminals in a Linux environment?

   A. Virtual Consoles

   B. Samba Server

   C. DHCP Server

   D. Terminal server

4. When creating terminals with a diskless or Ethernet client, how does the client receive the kernel from the server?

   A. tftp

   B. ftp

   C. DHCP

   D. bootp

5. Which file can be modified to allow Linux to provide more than the default number of virtual consoles?

   A. `/etc/rc.d/init.d/syslog`

   B. `/etc/inetd.conf`

   C. `/etc/inittab`

   D. `/tftpboot/lts/ltsroot/etc/lts.conf`

6. What services are used to provide IP addresses for clients on a terminal server system? (Choose all that apply.)

   A. `bootp`

   B. `DNS`

   C. `DHCP`

   D. `NFS`

7. What additional package may be used to help support the creation of terminals for the LTSP system?

   A. `lts_core`

   B. Etherboot

   C. XDM

   D. syslogd

8. What program may be used to monitor connections to a Linux system?

   A. `tracert`

   B. `nbstat`

   C. `ipconfig`

   D. `netstat`

9. BASH has incorporated useful features from what other shells? (Choose all that apply.)

   A. `ksh`

   B. `tcsh`

   C. `z-shell`

   D. `csh`

10. Where is the bash executable usually stored?

    A. `/.bashrc`

    B. `/.bash_profile`

    C. `/bin/bash`

    D. `/etc/bash`

11. What daemon is used to schedule automated tasks on a Linux system?

    A. `crontab`

    B. `cron`

    C. `cron.d`

    D. `crontab.d`

12. Which of the following indicates that the file is a shell script?

    A. #!/bin/sh

    B. #script

    C. !!/bin/bash

    D. * script *

13. What command may be used to move from one login to another without logging out?

    A. `vi`

    B. `su`

    C. `chmod`

    D. `chuser`

14. What provides access to other command line interfaces in a Linux system?

    A. <Alt> <Fx> where x is the number of the virtual console

    B. Command Prompt

    C. Only logging out to a command line

    D. Terminal

15. What is the Linux Terminal Server Project package name?

    A. `ltsp_initialize`

    B. `ltsp`

    C. `lts_core`

    D. `mknbi-linux`

16. What command is used to install the package `lts_core-2.XX-XX.i386.rpm`?

    A. `rpm -i lts_core-2.XX-XX.i386.rpm`

    B. `rpm -I lts_core-2.XX-XX.i386.rpm`

    C. `rpm -e lts_core-2.XX-XX.i386.rpm`

    D. `rpm -u lts_core-2.XX-XX.i386.rpm`

17. Which of the following lines in the `inittab` file will create a virtual terminal that may not be a local connection to the Linux system?

    A. `S2:3:respawn:/sbin/uugetty ttyS2 M19200`

    B. `2:2345:respawn:/sbin/getty tty2 VC linux`

    C. `# S2:3:respawn:/sbin/uugetty ttyS2 M19200`

    D. `# 2:2345:respawn:/sbin/getty tty2 VC linux`

18. Which file does the lts_core package create that may add in the starting of the `DHCP` service?

    A. `/etc/bootptab`

    B. `/etc/dhcpd.conf.example`

    C. `/etc/dhcpd.conf`

    D. `/etc/dhcp/dhcpd.leases`

19. What should be installed on any network using LTSP service to prevent vulnerability to unauthorized outside access?

    A. XDM

    B. firewall

    C. router

    D. portmapper

20. Which file contains most of the configurations for a workstation created for the Linux Terminal Server Project?

    A. `/etc/X11/xdm/xdm-config`

    B. `/tftpboot/lts`

    C. `/tftpboot/lts/ltsroot/ltsbin`

    D. `/tftpboot/lts/ltsroot/etc/lts.conf`

Scenarios

1. Your company must upgrade all the desktop systems because they are just too slow. The accounting department wants to know the best option available to reduce future cost. What solutions may be presented to reduce long-term cost?

2. The demands of a client site have escalated to require 24 hour/7day a week support. What features can be added to a Linux server to allow remote access to the system for preliminary testing before having to arrive on-site?

Lab Exercises

Lab 10-1 Configure virtual consoles

The objective for this hands-on lab is to gain experience in configuring virtual consoles. You should be able to use any distribution of Linux for this installation exercise.

1. Verify the number of virtual consoles available on a Linux system.

2. Double the number of virtual consoles by editing the `inittab` file.

3. Verify that the newly created virtual console works properly.

4. Change one of the virtual consoles to allow remote access to the Linux system.

5. Connect an external terminal and test the external virtual console.

6. Remove all configuration changes and repeat as needed.

Lab 10-2 Creating cron jobs

The objective for this hands-on lab is to gain experience in creating `cron` jobs. You should be able to use any distribution of Linux for this installation exercise.

1. Create several `crontab` compatible files to perform some routine tasks.
2. Use the `crontab` command to activate the `cron` jobs.
3. Verify that the jobs run correctly.
4. Repeat as often as needed.

Answers to Chapter Questions

Chapter Pre-test

1. Linux is a true multi-user environment that allows multiple users to access a system locally or remotely at the same time.
2. Linux includes the ability to use virtual terminals, multiple logins, and remote logins all on the same system at the same time.
3. Linux uses virtual consoles, serial terminals, and Ethernet workstations to allow multiple users access to the same system.
4. Linux can provide Ethernet terminals by using the tools available through the Linux Terminal Server Project.
5. Linux can use netstat to monitor remote connections.
6. The most common shells used in Linux today are BASH, PDKSH (often known as Korn Shell), TCSH, and Z-shell.
7. The BASH or Bourne Again SHell is the most common shell used in Linux.
8. A script can be created to perform repetitive tasks on a Linux system.
9. The use of the `cron` daemon and `crontab` command to convert shell commands into scheduled tasks is available on a Linux system.
10. The "best practice" way to login as the root user on a Linux system is to use a standard user account and then the `su` command to gain root access.

Assessment Questions

1. B. The keystrokes used to move from one virtual console to another is the <Alt> <Fx> combination. The other combinations don't normally produce the desired effect. For review, see the "Multi-User Environment" section.

2. C. Linux normally provides the ability to support 63 virtual consoles. The others are not correct for the standard Linux environment. For review, see the "The creation of Virtual Consoles" section.

3. D. A terminal server can provide the desired terminals. DHCP provides dynamic IP addresses, Samba provides services for Microsoft Windows clients, and Virtual Consoles are not normally considered the most inexpensive method of providing consoles. For review, see the "The Linux Terminal Server Project" section.

4. A. The download of the Linux kernel is performed via tftp when using the LTSP method of creating terminals. The abilities of ftp to transfer files are not used, and DHCP and bootp are used to provide IP addresses. For review, see the "The Linux Terminal Server Project" section.

5. C. The file /etc/inittab is used to adjust the number of virtual consoles. The other files are not used to adjust the number of virtual consoles. For review, see the "The creation of Virtual Consoles" section.

6. A and C. The bootp and DHCP services are used to provide IP addresses for the LTSP systems. For review, see the "Configurations for remote systems" section.

7. B. The Etherboot package may be used to create network bootable terminals for the Linux Terminal Server Project system. The lts_core package is the LTSP package, the XDM is a Linux system used to provide terminal logins, and syslogd controls the system messages. For review, see the "Configurations for remote systems" section.

8. D. The netstat command is used to monitor connections to a Linux system. The nbstat, tracert, and ipconfig programs are not normally used in the Linux environment. For review, see the "Monitoring remote connections" section.

9. A and D. The Bourne Again SHell uses features of the Korn and C shell. The others are available shells for Linux. For review, see the "Common Shell Commands" section.

10. C. The bash executable is normally located in /bin/bash. For review, see the "Common Shell Commands" section.

11. B. The daemon used to perform automatic tasks is the cron daemon. The crontab command is used with cron, cron.d is one of the support files systems, and crontab.d is normally not used in the Linux environment. For review, see the "Basic shell scripts" section.

12. A. The correct way to indicate a shell script is to use #!/bin/sh at the beginning of the file. For review, see the "Basic shell scripts" section.

13. B. The su command allows not only the ability to login as the root user but as any user on a system. The vi command is an editor, chmod is used to administer user accounts, and chuser is not a normal Linux command. For review, see the "Caution using root access" section.

14. D. The opening of a terminal in Linux can be used to provide a command line in the GUI. For review, see the "Navigating the GUI interface" section.

15. C. The package that is used to install the LTSP is `lts_core` and the others are not. For review, see the "Configurations for remote systems" section.

16. A. The command `rpm -i lts_core-2.XX-XX.i386.rpm` will install the Linux Terminal Server Project core packages. The others won't work because the options -I, -e and -u don't install packages. For review, see the "Configurations for remote systems" section.

17. A. The line `S2:3:respawn:/sbin/uugetty ttyS2 M19200` is the only line that will create a virtual console on a serial port to allow modem or external connections. For review, see the "Configurations for remote systems" section.

18. B. The file `/etc/dhcpd.conf.example` provides a starting point for the configuration file needed to start the `DHCP` service. The others are not provided to help start the `DHCP` service. For review, see the "Configurations for remote systems" section.

19. B. The need for a firewall is created to protect the LTSP server from outside access. A router can provide a firewall but does not always do so, `tftp` allows the download of the Linux kernel, and portmapper does not protect the system. For review, see the "Configurations for remote systems" section.

20. D. The file that provides most of the workstation information is `/tftpboot/lts/ltsroot/etc/lts.conf`. For review, see the "Configurations for remote systems" section.

Scenarios

1. The use of a system of Linux Terminal Servers will resolve most of the future cost needs. Because the servers provide the system resources such as processing and disk space, only the servers must be upgraded to provide most performance enhancements.

2. The creation of a virtual console on a serial port can allow remote access to a Linux system and provide some diagnostic abilities before traveling to the site.

Linux System Commands

EXAM OBJECTIVES

+ 4.12 Create, extract and edit file and tape archives using tar

+ 4.13 Manage runlevels using init and shutdown

+ 4.14 Stop, start, and restart services (daemons) as needed (e.g., init files)

+ 4.15 Manage print spools and queues

+ 4.16 Create, edit and save files using vi

CHAPTER PRE-TEST

1. What is the purpose of the `tar` command?

2. What does runlevel 0 indicate?

3. Why should the Linux system be shut down properly?

4. What process runs the print spooler?

5. Where are most startup scripts located?

6. What do "S" and "K" stand for when naming scripts?

7. How do you enter command mode in the vi editor?

8. What runlevel does the Graphical User Interface run at?

9. What command do you use to print from the command line?

10. How do you extract a tape archive file?

✦ Answers to these questions can be found at the end of the chapter. ✦

The Linux system administrator is responsible for the day-to-day operations of the Linux server. This chapter deals with some basic Linux system commands and services that administrators use in their daily tasks. One of the administrator's most important responsibilities is to stop, start, and restart services and daemons when needed. Configuring these services to automatically start at boot time involves an intricate knowledge of the different runlevels and startup scripts that Linux uses to maintain the system. This chapter also deals with setting up print spools and queues, which are very common tasks. `tar` and `vi` are also discussed in great detail.

Linux Runlevels

Objective

4.13 Manage runlevels using init and shutdown

Linux systems operate in different types of runlevels. A *runlevel* is a certain mode of operation for a system, which defines the services and processes that start for that particular runlevel.

As a Linux system boots, one process must be the first to start in order to be able to startup all other processes, daemons, and system-critical programs. This first process is called *init*.

init

init is the first process on a Linux system and is assigned a PID (Process Identification) of 1. The operating system kernel starts init and is responsible for starting all other services provided by the system. The services started by init are detailed in its configuration file, which is located in /etc/inittab.

The inittab file, located in /etc, is the primary configuration file for the init process. The inittab file controls how your system starts up and configures the different runlevels.

The following is a sample of an inittab file:

```
#
# inittab This file describes how the INIT process should set # up the system in
a certain run-level.
#
# Author:       Miquel van Smoorenburg,
#               Modified for RHS Linux by Marc Ewing and
#                     Donnie Barnes
#
# Default runlevel. The runlevels used by RHS are:
#   0 - halt (Do NOT set initdefault to this)
#   1 - Single user mode
```

```
#    2 - Multiuser, without NFS (The same as 3, if you do not #    have
networking)
#    3 - Full multiuser mode
#    4 - unused
#    5 - X11
#    6 - reboot (Do NOT set initdefault to this)
#
id:3:initdefault:

# System initialization.

si::sysinit:/etc/rc.d/rc.sysinit l0:0:wait:/etc/rc.d/rc 0
l1:1:wait:/etc/rc.d/rc 1
l2:2:wait:/etc/rc.d/rc 2
l3:3:wait:/etc/rc.d/rc 3
l4:4:wait:/etc/rc.d/rc 4
l5:5:wait:/etc/rc.d/rc 5
l6:6:wait:/etc/rc.d/rc 6

# Things to run in every runlevel.
ud::once:/sbin/update

# Trap CTRL-ALT-DELETE
ca::ctrlaltdel:/sbin/shutdown -t3 -r now

# When our UPS tells us power has failed, assume we have a # # few minutes of
power left.  Schedule a shutdown for 2
# minutes from now.
# This does, of course, assume you have powerd installed and # your UPS
connected and working correctly.
pf::powerfail:/sbin/shutdown -f -h +2 "Power Failure; System Shutting Down"

# If power was restored before the shutdown kicked in, cancel # it.
pr:12345:powerokwait:/sbin/shutdown -c "Power Restored; Shutdown Cancelled"

# Run gettys in standard runlevels
1:12345:respawn:/sbin/mingetty tty1
2:2345:respawn:/sbin/mingetty tty2
3:2345:respawn:/sbin/mingetty tty3
4:2345:respawn:/sbin/mingetty tty4
5:2345:respawn:/sbin/mingetty tty5
6:2345:respawn:/sbin/mingetty tty6

# Run xdm in runlevel 5
x:5:respawn:/usr/bin/X11/xdm -nodaemon
```

The most important line in this file is:

```
id:3:initdefault:
```

This line sets the default runlevel to 3. Therefore, when your Linux system starts, it will always boot into that runlevel.

Caution Never set your default runlevel as 0, which halts the system. If you do, your Linux system will automatically shut down when booted up!

You can set a number of other default runlevels, which are summarized in Table 11-1.

Table 11-1
Linux Runlevels

Runlevel	Description
0	Halt the system.
1	Single user mode. All file systems mounted, only small set of kernel processes running. Only root can login.
2	Multi-user mode, without remote file sharing.
3	Multi-user mode with remote file sharing, processes, and daemons.
4	User definable system state.
5	Used to start X-windows on boot.
6	Shutdown and reboot.

To initiate a runlevel from the command prompt, simply enter the following command:

```
init [runlevel]
```

To bring your system to a halt, use the following command:

```
init 0
```

Most systems have their default runlevel set to 3 because they usually don't need X windows to run. If you want your system to boot and start X windows, set the default runlevel to 5 by modifying the default runlevel entry to:

```
id:5:initdefault:
```

Exam Tip Know all of the characteristics of each runlevel, and when they should be used.

Login terminals

This section of the inittab file defines your terminal login sessions:

```
# Run gettys in standard runlevels
1:12345:respawn:/sbin/mingetty tty1
2:2345:respawn:/sbin/mingetty tty2
3:2345:respawn:/sbin/mingetty tty3
4:2345:respawn:/sbin/mingetty tty4
5:2345:respawn:/sbin/mingetty tty5
6:2345:respawn:/sbin/mingetty tty6
```

Startup scripts

This section of the inittab file defines the location for your startup scripts for each runlevel:

```
# System initialization.
si::sysinit:/etc/rc.d/rc.sysinit l0:0:wait:/etc/rc.d/rc 0
l1:1:wait:/etc/rc.d/rc 1
l2:2:wait:/etc/rc.d/rc 2
l3:3:wait:/etc/rc.d/rc 3
l4:4:wait:/etc/rc.d/rc 4
l5:5:wait:/etc/rc.d/rc 5
l6:6:wait:/etc/rc.d/rc 6
```

The /etc/rc.d directory contains several subdirectories named after the runlevel that they represent. Each subdirectory contains scripts that are run for that particular runlevel. These scripts start a number of services and also perform a number of configuration checks, including checking the disk file systems for errors, mounting the file systems, defining swap space, cleaning out temporary files, and starting up system daemons.

Each directory contains several scripts starting with the letter "S" or the letter "K." These letters represent start and kill scripts. Depending on your current runlevel and the runlevel that you want to switch to, the system must determine which processes need to be killed and which ones need to be started.

For example, the following are some of the scripts within the /etc/rc.d/rc 3 directory:

```
K20nfs
K34yppasswdd
S10network
S30syslog
S60lpd
S99linuxconf
```

As the system switches to runlevel 3, the K20nfs will kill the nfs process, and the S10network script will start the network services.

Shutting down Linux

As with most operating systems, you need to properly shut down your Linux system to avoid damaging the system and the user data on the file systems. If your file systems are not properly unmounted, the system runs a file system check the next time the system is booted.

Exam Tip Know how each of the shutdown commands work, and why to choose a certain command.

You may need to shut down a Linux system for several reasons, including the following:

✦ **General maintenance:** When you reboot a Linux system, it always performs some general maintenance tasks, such as deleting files from the temporary directories and performing checks on the machine's file systems. Restarting a system will also reset any dead or zombie processes that may be running.

✦ **System failure:** Often, your only recourse in the event of a system or process failure is to reboot the system. You may have to reboot for many reasons, including failure of system processes, locked devices, or runaway processes, which use up all the available CPU and RAM.

✦ **System upgrades:** Some system upgrades, such as a kernel update, only work if the system is rebooted.

The commands that you can use to safely shut down the system are shutdown, halt, and reboot. The shutdown command is the most commonly used command for shutting down a Linux system, and there are several options that can be used for it. For example:

```
shutdown -r now
```

The preceding option will shut down the Linux system immediately and initiate a reboot. If you don't want the system to reboot, and you'd rather have the system come to a halt, you can use the following command:

```
shutdown -h now
```

You should give your users warning *before* any type of scheduled shutdown in order to give them time to close their files and log out of the system. You can give the shutdown command a time parameter (in seconds) before it initiates shutdown:

```
shutdown -h 300
```

The halt command performs the same function as a shutdown -h now command, or init 0, and brings the system to a halt without rebooting. The reboot command performs the same function as a shutdown -r now command, or init 6. It brings the system down and reboots it. (Hitting the key combination, Ctrl-Alt-Delete can also start this function process).

In the Real World You should always warn your users before shutting down a system. It gives them a chance to close any open files and log out of the system. Shutdowns without warning can often damage files that are still open.

Managing Linux Services

Objective ➡ 4.14 Stop, start, and restart services (daemons) as needed (e.g., init files)

Managing Linux services is a job function that most Linux administrators will encounter on a daily basis. Most of the services that administrators must manage are applications, such as a Web or FTP servers. However, these services can also include system processes, such as DNS, DHCP, and other important services and daemons.

Most application and service scripts are located in /etc/rc.d/init.d, or /etc/init.d. For example, the following is the startup script for the Apache Web server httpd daemon:

```
#!/bin/sh
#
# Startup script for the Apache Web Server
#
# chkconfig: 345 85 15
# description: Apache is a World Wide Web server.  It is used to serve \
#        HTML files and CGI.
# processname: httpd
# pidfile: /var/run/httpd.pid
# config: /etc/httpd/conf/httpd.conf

# Source function library.
. /etc/rc.d/init.d/functions

# See how we were called.
case "$1" in
  start)
echo -n "Starting httpd: "
  daemon httpd
  echo
  touch /var/lock/subsys/httpd
  ;;
  stop)
  echo -n "Shutting down http: "
  killproc httpd
  echo
  rm -f /var/lock/subsys/httpd
  rm -f /var/run/httpd.pid
  ;;
  status)
```

```
    status httpd
    ;;
    restart)
    $0 stop
    $0 start
    ;;
    reload)
    echo -n "Reloading httpd: "
    killproc httpd -HUP
    echo
    ;;
    *)
    echo "Usage: $0{start|stop|restart|reload|status}"
    exit 1
eesac
exit 0
```

Most scripts utilize the arguments start, stop, restart, reload, and status.

✦ start: if it is not currently running, starts the process.

✦ stop: if it is currently running, stops the process.

✦ restart: stops, and then restarts the process.

✦ reload: restarts the process, reloading any configuration files.

✦ status: gives the current status of the process.

 Exam Tip   You don't have to memorize these startup scripts, but know where they are located and how to change the status of process.

As you can see from the example httpd daemon script above, each argument will run the corresponding part of the script that will change the status of the process as directed. You must be the root user to run these scripts.

For example, if you want to restart the httpd service, use the following command:

```
/etc/rc.d/init.d/httpd restart
```

You will have to restart a process or daemon after you have changed its configuration file. The process daemon won't reload any changes until you have stopped and started the service, or performed a reload or restart. Most configuration files are located in the /etc directory. For example, the configuration file for the httpd service is /etc/httpd/conf/httpd.conf.

You may also find that you may need to occasionally restart certain services if they become locked up. For example, you may find that your DHCP service is not providing IP addresses to clients, but if you restart the service, it will start operating normally.

Configuring Linux Printing

Objective   4.15 Manage print spools and queues

Printing is one of the most important user functions on a Linux system. Consequently, it is also one of the biggest contributors when it comes to day-to-day problems. Although each Linux distribution has its own method for setting up printers, they are usually based on the original Unix printing facility, which is the lpd daemon.

lpd daemon

Line Printer Daemon, or lpd, refers to the entire collection of programs that deal with print spooling. The lpd daemon is run when the Linux system first boots. The first operation that it performs is reading the configuration from the /etc/printcap file, which defines the printers that it will spool for. It then runs two programs, listen and accept, which wait for and accept user requests to print.

When the lpd daemon receives a request, the pages to be printed are copied to a different area on disk, which is the spool directory, usually located in /var/spool. This process frees up the current console shell after sending a print request.

The spool directory contains a file for every printer that is connected, either directly or remotely, to the system. When a print request is received for that printer, two files are created: A control file with the extension .cf, and a print file that is identified by a print ID number with a .df extension. The control file sends parameters to the printer, including information about the print job, such as the user's name and the name of the file. The data file contains the actual print job.

The lpd daemon then starts a process for that printer, which will begin queuing the file to the actual printer. After the job finishes, the files are deleted from the spool directory. When the print queue is empty, the daemon terminates.

/etc/printcap

The file /etc/printcap contains information about every printer (local or remote) that is connected to the Linux system. The lpd daemon and lpr command use this file to determine the type of characteristics for the printer. The following is a sample /etc/printcap file for an HP Laserjet printer:

```
# HP Laserjet
lp|hplj|hplaserjet|HP LaserJet4M:\
    :lp=/dev/lp0:\
    :sd=/var/spool/lp/lp0:\
    :lf=/var/spool/lp/errorlog:\
    :mx#0:\
    :of=/var/spool/lp0/hpjlp:\
```

Linux administrators are constantly changing the configuration files of their system services and applications to enable new services or to make them run more efficiently. All configuration files in Unix are simple text files, but in order to edit them, you need a text editor. A wide variety of editors are available for Linux and Unix. Some of the most popular editors include Emacs and Pico. Although each person has his or her own favorite editor, only the vi editor comes by default with every version of Unix.

The vi editor is certainly not the easiest and most user-friendly text editor, but because of its wide availability and existence on most Unix systems, it is extremely important that every Linux system administrator know how to use it.

In the Real World
vi exists on every Unix and Unix-like system; therefore, it is very important to know how to use vi.

vi operation modes

The vi editor operates in two basic modes: Command mode and insert mode. When vi is started, it is in command mode. This mode allows you to enter commands to edit files or navigate your text file. However, you can only add or insert text by using the insert mode. From command mode, you can enter into insert mode by typing the letter *i*. To return to command mode, use the Escape key.

Command mode

In command mode, you can enter commands to edit your files or navigate the file that you are working on. Table 11-2 summarizes some of the more common commands while using command mode.

<table>
<tr><td colspan="4" align="center">Table 11-2
vi commands</td></tr>
<tr><td>*Navigation*</td><td>*Text Insertion*</td><td>*Searching*</td><td>*File Commands*</td></tr>
<tr><td>l - Moves the cursor one position right</td><td>i - Insert before cursor</td><td>fx - Find x on current line</td><td><ESC> - Go to command mode</td></tr>
<tr><td>h - Move the cursor one position left</td><td>a - Insert after cursor</td><td>Fx - Find x on previous line</td><td>:q - Quit</td></tr>
<tr><td>k - Move up one line</td><td>I - Insert at start of line</td><td>; - Repeat last fx</td><td>:q! - Quit and don't save</td></tr>
<tr><td>j - Move down one line</td><td>A - Insert at end of line</td><td>' - Repeat last Fx</td><td>:w - Write file</td></tr>
</table>

Continued

Table 11-2 *(continued)*

Navigation	Text Insertion	Searching	File Commands
w – Move forward one word	x - Delete current character	/ - Search forward	:wq - Write and quit
b – Move backward one word	X - Delete to the left	? - Search backward	:r - Insert file at current position
[ctrl-f] - Move forward one page	o - Open after current line	n - Continue forward search	:n – Go to another file
[ctrl-b] - Move backward one page	O - Open before current line	N - Continue backward search	:! - Execute shell command
[ctrl-d] - Move down one half page	dd - Delete current line	" - Back to start of search	u - Undo last change
[ctrl-u] - Move up one half page	cc - Change current line		. - Redo last change
G - Move to end of file	r - Replace current character		U - Restore line
$ - Move to end of line			^| - Redraw the screen
0 - Move to beginning of line			
[n]G - Go to line number "n"			

Insert mode

In insert mode, you actually type text into the editor. You can type as many lines as you want; use Enter after you finish a line. You can correct mistakes by using the backspace key.

To perform any other command or function such as moving the cursor or saving the file, you need to hit the Escape key to bring you back into command mode.

Editing text files

To start the vi program, type the following at the command prompt:

```
vi [filename]
```

The filename can be a new or existing file. Remember that when you first start vi, you are initially in command mode. If you are working on a new file, you can immediately type the letter *i* to enter into insert mode and start adding text.

If you are working on an existing file, you can use the cursor keys, or the h, j, k, l keys to navigate to where you want to begin. You can use the [ctrl-f] or [ctrl-b] to move ahead or back a page.

To insert text at an exact point, you can type the letter *i* for insert and start adding your text. Other options include the letter *a*, which adds text next to the cursor location, and the letter *o*, which starts your text on the next line below the current one.

If you make a mistake while typing, you can use the backspace key to delete characters. If you want to delete characters in command mode, hit the Escape key, and then use the letter *x* to delete characters one at a time. If you want to delete an entire line, use the dd command. The command dw deletes only the entire word that your cursor is currently on.

To save your file, hit the Escape key to enter command mode, and then type :w. To save and exit out of the vi editor, use the :wq command. Or you can use an equivalent to the :wq command—type the letters *ZZ* in command mode to save and then exit.

If you want to exit without saving your file, use the :q command. This command asks you if you want to save the file before quitting. If you want to bypass the prompt, use the :q! command.

Using the `tar` Command

Objective   4.12 Create, extract and edit file and tape archives using tar

The tar command is short for for *tape archive*. Originally, it was used for combining a large number of files into a single file for archival to tape. Even if you don't plan to put files on tape, tar is a helpful archival tool that you can use to help manage your files.

Caution   The tar command does not compress files; it only combines them into one larger file. To compress files, you need to use the gzip or compress command.

The format of the tar command is:

```
tar [options] (file1) (file2) ...
```

You can use several options and arguments with the tar command:

✦ -c: Tells tar to create a new archive file

✦ -v: Prints each filename as it is archived

✦ -f: Specifies a filename for the archive

✦ -x: Tells tar to extract files from an archive

To back up the entire /home directory to a file called homebackup.tar, use the following command:

```
tar -cvf homebackup.tar /home
```

To extract the same file into the current directory, use the following command:

```
tar -xvf homebackup.tar
```

To back up three separate files, such as /etc/hosts, /etc/group, and /etc/passwd, to the archive etc.tar, use the following command:

```
cd /etc
tar -cvf  etc.tar hosts group passwd
```

Exam Tip   Know how to create and extract from a tar archive file.

Summary

This chapter details many system commands that are used routinely by the Linux system administrator. This chapter introduces the concepts of runlevels and how they interact with the `init` and `shutdown` commands, plus the location and purpose of startup scripts and how they can be used to stop and start services. This chapter discusses the management of print queues, including lpd daemon characteristics and print queue management commands. Finally, this chapter demonstrates the use of the tar command to create and extract archives, and explains some basic commands for the vi editor.

Here are some key points to remember from this chapter:

✦ Runlevels

- 0: Halt system
- 1: Single User Mode
- 2: Multiuser, no NFS
- 3: Multiuser mode, no X
- 4: Not used, user defined
- 5: Multiuser mode with X
- 6: Reboot

✦ Startup scripts for each runlevel—Located in /etc/rc.d/

✦ Service administration commands—Most scripts located in /etc/rc.d/init.d. Options include start, restart, reload, stop

✦ vi editor—Know the basic command to edit and save a text file

✦ tar command—Used for making tape archive files, combines several files into\ one archive

   `tar -xvf [file]` Used to extract files from archive

   `tar -cvf [file]` Used to create an archive

✦ Printing

   • `lpd`—Line Printer Daemon

   • `lpq`—Used to check queue status

✦   ✦   ✦

STUDY GUIDE

The Study Guide section provides you with the opportunity to test your knowledge about the objectives covered on the exam. The Assessment Questions provide an understanding of the basics of Linux, and the Scenarios provide practice with real situations. If you get any questions incorrect, use the answers to determine the part of the chapter that you should review before continuing.

Assessment Questions

1. A Linux system seems to start up fine, but as soon as it is almost loaded it shuts down again. What is the most likely cause of the problem?

    A. The Ctrl-Alt-Delete is stuck

    B. The default runlevel is set to 5

    C. The default runlevel is set to 0

    D. The kill command is corrupted

2. What command should be used to shut down the system and halt in 100 seconds?

    A. `shutdown -r now`

    B. `shutdown -h 100`

    C. `halt`

    D. `init 0 -100`

3. Your /etc/rc.d/rc3.d contains a script called *S10network*. What is the purpose of this script?

    A. To start the networking processes

    B. To kill the networking processes

    C. To reload the nfs daemon

    D. To start the login process

4. What runlevel does init 5 represent?

    A. Single User Mode

    B. Halt system

    C. Reboot

    D. Full multiuser mode with X-windows

5. What daemon controls the print spooling process?

 A. lprm

 B. lpd

 C. lpq

 D. lpstatus

6. What configuration file defines the default runlevel for the init process?

 A. /sbin/init

 B. /etc/rc.d/rc3.d

 C. /etc/inittab

 D. /etc/rc.d/init.d

7. What command should you use to save your file and quit the vi editor?

 A. `:wq`

 B. `:w`

 C. `:q!`

 D. `save`

8. What function can the `tar` comand *not* perform?

 A. Create an archive file

 B. Extract files from an archive

 C. Combine several files into one file

 D. Compress files

9. Which command can you use to shut down and halt a Linux System?

 A. `reboot`

 B. `halt`

 C. `init 1`

 D. `shutdown -r 300`

10. What init level should you set to bring the system to single-user mode?

 A. `init 1`

 B. `init 0`

 C. `init 3`

 D. `init 5`

11. What command do you use to check the status of a print queue?

   A. `lp`

   B. `lprm`

   C. `lpq`

   D. `lpstat`

12. A user wants to restart the Web server because they want to enable changes made in the configuration file. What command accomplishes this task?

   A. `/etc/rc.d/init.d/httpd start`

   B. `/etc/rc.d/init.d/httpd reload`

   C. `httpd reboot`

   D. `init 3`

13. What file contains information about specific printer configurations?

   A. /etc/printcap

   B. /etc/printers

   C. /etc/lpd

   D. /etc/printconf

14. What command can you use to reboot a Linux system?

   A. `init 5`

   B. `restart`

   C. `shutdown -h`

   D. `reboot`

15. What mode must you be in when using vi editor to input text into a file?

   A. super mode

   B. command mode

   C. text mode

   D. insert mode

16. Some users are complaining that the DHCP server is not running. After examining the running processes on the system, you notice that the process is not present. What command should you use to start the DHCP service?

    A. dhcp restart

    B. start dhcp

    C. /etc/rc.d/init.d/dhcpd start

    D. /etc/rc.d/init.d/dhcpd reload

17. What `tar` argument is used to extract files from an archive?

    A. -x

    B. -e

    C. -f

    D. -ext

18. What init runlevel should be set to shut down and reboot the system?

    A. init 6

    B. init 0

    C. init 3

    D. init 5

19. In what directory can you find the startup scripts for a system running in runlevel 5?

    A. /etc/rc.d

    B. /etc/rc.d/rc5.d

    C. /etc/init.d/rc5.d

    D. /etc/rc5.d

20. In the vi editor, what command should you use to quit without saving a file?

    A. `:wq!`

    B. `:wq`

    C. `:!`

    D. `:q!`

Scenarios

1. Your users are having problems being able to resolve names on the network. You suspect that the DNS server is not working, but when you check the running processes, it seems to be alive. What steps should you take to fix the problem?

2. You have just installed a new Linux system on your server. Unfortunately, it boots into X windows automatically, and you need the server to boot only to the command line interface. What steps should you take to fix the problem?

Lab Exercises

Lab 11-1 Runlevels and system shutdown

The objective for this hands-on lab is to gain experience in exploring different runlevels and how to properly shutdown a Linux system. You should be able to use any default Linux installation for this exercise.

1. Login as the root user on your system.

2. Enter the following command:

```
reboot
```

This should instantly reboot the system.

3. When the system comes back up, login as root again, and enter the following command:

```
shutdown -r now.
```

The system should perform the same function as in Step 2 and reboot.

4. When the system comes back up, login as root again, and enter the following command:

```
init 6.
```

The system should perform the same function as in Step 2 and reboot.

5. When the system comes back up, login as root again, and enter the key sequence: Crtl-Alt-Delete.The system should perform the same function as in Step 2 and reboot. Each of the last four commands (Steps 2-5) performed the exact same function.

6. When the system comes back up, login as root again, and enter the following command:

```
init 0
```

The system will shutdown and come to a halt without rebooting.

7. When the system comes back up, login as root again, and enter the following command:

```
halt
```

The system will shutdown and come to a halt without rebooting.

8. When the system comes back up, login as root again, and enter the following command:

```
shutdown -h now
```

The system will shutdown and come to a halt without rebooting. The last three commands (Steps 6-8) perform the same function.

Lab 11-2 Using the vi editor

The objective for this lab is to open and edit a simple text file using the vi editor.

1. Start the vi editor and edit a blank file called, text.txt. Use the following command:

```
vi text.txt
```

2. Enter the letter *i* to begin insert mode, and type the following sentence:

```
This is a test of the vi editor.
```

3. Hit Enter and then on the next line type the following sentence:

```
This is the second line of the test.
```

4. Hit Escape to enter command mode, and use the cursor keys to move the cursor on top of the first letter of the word *second*. Type the letters *dw* to delete the entire word.

5. Enter the letter *i* to begin insert mode again, and type the word *second*. After you finish, hit the Escape key to enter command mode.

6. Enter the letter *o* to begin inserting text on the next line.

7. Enter the following sentence:

```
This is the third line of the test.
```

8. Hit Escape and the :wq to save your file.

9. Enter the following command to see your edited file:

```
cat test.txt
```

Answers to Chapter Questions

Chapter Pre-test

1. The `tar` command, which stands for *tape archive*, archives several files into one single file for easier storage on disk or tape.

2. Runlevel 0 indicates a halted system that is shutdown.

3. If you don't shut down your Linux system properly with the shutdown or init commands, you risk causing damage to your hard drive data because the file systems aren't properly unmounted before shutdown.

4. The process that runs the print spooler is `lpd`.

5. Startup scripts are located in /etc/rc.d or /etc/init.d.

6. "S" stands for a start script, which will start a process, and "K" stands for kill script, which will kill a process.

7. To enter command mode in the vi editor, hit Escape.

8. The Graphical User Interface (GUI) will run in runlevel 5.

9. To print from the command line, use the `lpr` command.

10. With the tar command, use tar -xvf [filename].

Assessment Questions

1. C. In the /etc/inittab file, the default runlevel is probably set to 0, which tells it to shutdown right after the system has started. For review, see the "Linux Runlevels" section.

2. B. The correct command is `shutdown -h 100` to perform this action. For review, see the "Shutting down Linux" section.

3. A. This script is a startup script for the system's networking processes. For review, see the "Startup scripts" section.

4. D. Runlevel 5 is used to boot up a full multiuser system and to automatically start X-windows. For review, see the "Linux Runlevels" section.

5. B. The Line Printing Daemon (lpd) controls the print spooling process, and is started automatically at boot time. For review, see the "Printing management" section.

6. C. The correct location is the /etc/inittab file. For review, see the "Linux Runlevels" section.

7. A. The correct command is `:wq` used in command mode. For review, see the "Using the vi Editor" section.

8. D. The `tar` command doesn't compress data. To compress data, use the `gzip` or `compress` command. For review, see the "Using the `tar` command" section.

9. B. The `halt` command will shut down a Linux system without rebooting. For review, see the "Shutting down Linux" section.

10. A. `init 1` will bring the system to single-user mode. For review, see the "Linux Runlevels" section.

11. C. The correct command to check the printer queue status is `lpq`. For review, see the "Printing management" section.

12. B. The reload command will tell the system to stop the service, reload the configuration file, and restart the service. For review, see the "Managing Linux Services" section.

13. A. The file that contains specific printer configuration information is /etc/printcap. For review, see the "Printing management" section.

14. D. The command to reboot a Linux system is `reboot`. For review, see the "Shutting down Linux" section.

15. D. To insert text in the vi editor, you must be in insert mode. For review, see the "Using the vi Editor" section.

16. C. Because the service is currently not running, use the start command. For review, see the "Managing Linux Services" section.

17. A. To extract files from an archive, use the -x argument in the `tar` command. For review, see the "Using the `tar` command" section.

18. A. init runlevel 6 is used to shut down and reboot the system. For review, see the "Linux Runlevels" section.

19. B. The correct location for the startup scripts for runlevel 5 is /etc/rc.d/rc5.d. For review, see the "Linux Runlevels" section.

20. D. The correct command to quit without saving in the vi editor is `:q!` in the command mode. For review, see the "Using the vi Editor" section.

Scenarios

1. Because the DNS process (named) is already running, it may be in a locked state. Use the following commands to change into the startup script directory for the process, and then restart the service.

```
cd /etc/rc.d/init.d
./named restart
```

If you encounter no other problems, such as with the configuration file, the service should recover.

2. To change the default runlevel, edit the configuration file for init, which is /etc/inittab.

Use the vi editor to edit the file using the following command:

```
vi /etc/inittab
```

Use the cursor keys to jump down to the line that reads:

```
id:5:initdefault:
```

Position the cursor over the number 5, and hit the *x* key to delete the character. Press the letter *i* to enter insert mode, and type the number *3*.

The new entry should look like the following:

```
id:3:initdefault:
```

Now enter command mode by pressing Escape, and then use the following command to save the file:

```
:wq
```

Now reboot the system, and it should boot up into runlevel 3, without the X windows.

Maintaining the Linux System

System maintenance is another common task for the Linux administrator. Some of your specific duties that are necessary in maintaining a Linux system include creating and managing local storage devices and file systems, verifying user and root cron jobs, and identifying core dumps.

This part covers these topics, but also details how to run and interpret ifconfig; how to download and install patches and updates; how to identify, execute, and kill processes; and finally, how to monitor system log files. I also cover how to perform and verify backups and restores, along with how to perform and verify security best practices, how to set daemon and process permissions, and how to properly document work that is performed on a system. System maintenance is not only good to know in the real world but also for the Linux+ exam. Fourteen percent for the exam will focus of System Maintenance.

P A R T

V

◆ ◆ ◆ ◆

In This Part

Chapter 12
Linux Disk and
System Management

Chapter 13
Process Management

Chapter 14
Linux Security

Chapter 15
Backing Up Your
Linux System

◆ ◆ ◆ ◆

Linux Disk and System Management

CHAPTER PRE-TEST

1. What is the function of `cron`?

2. What kind of file has a tar.gz extension?

3. What kinds of information can the `ifconfig` command show you?

4. After creating a partition, what command do you use to make a file system?

5. Why should core dumps be analyzed?

6. What is the purpose of a program patch?

7. How does the `at` function differ from `cron`?

8. How can the `fsck` command help fix disk errors?

9. What is the best time to perform system updates and upgrades?

10. What is the purpose of the `fdisk` command?

✦ Answers to these questions can be found at the end of the chapter. ✦

The daily management activities of a Linux system administrator include many different tasks. From managing and configuring disk drives, to managing networks, to scheduling maintenance jobs, many parts of the system must be attended to on a routine basis.

For each of these system management activities, the administrator can use many tools and commands to ease the administration and configuration of various parts of the system.

This chapter deals with such system administration items as disk and file system management, by using the fdisk, mkfs, and fsck commands; system job scheduling, by using at and cron; network management, by using the ifconfig command; finding and analyzing core dumps; and finally, upgrading packages and installing patches.

Disk and File System Management

 5.1 Create and manage local storage devices and file systems (e.g., fsck, fdisk, mkfs)

The most common tool for managing your disks and file systems is the fdisk utility. This utility allows you to partition your drives and assign file systems to them.

To use fdisk on your hard drives, specify which hard drive you are using with the following conventions:

✦ The first ATA/IDE hard drive is called *hda*; the second is called *hdb*, etc.

✦ The first SCSI drive is called *sda*; the second is called *sdb*, etc.

With these hard drives, each partition is also numbered, so the first partition of the first IDE drive is hda1.

To start fdisk on the first ATA/IDE drive, use the following command:

```
fdisk /dev/hda
```

To view a list of commands that you can use from the fdisk prompt, type **?** (question mark). A display output similar to the following appears:

```
Command action
   a   toggle a bootable flag
   b   edit bsd disklabel
   c   toggle the dos compatiblity flag
   d   delete a partition
   l   list known partition types
   m   print this menu
   n   add a new partition
```

```
p    print the partition table
q    quit without saving changes
t    change a partition's system id
u    change display/entry units
v    verify the partition table
w    write table to disk and exit
x    extra functionality (experts only)
```

In addition, in expert mode (see the "x" command in the preceding example), you can use these advanced commands, but I recommend that you don't use these commands unless you know what you are doing. For most users, the following basic commands will suffice:

```
Command action
    b    move beginning of data in a partition
    c    change number of cylinders
    d    print the raw data in the partition table
    e    list extended partitions
    h    change number of heads
    m    print this menu
    p    print the partition table
    q    quit without saving changes
    r    return to main menu
    s    change number of sectors
    v    verify the partition table
    w    write table to disk and exit
```

I recommend that you begin with the "p" command to print a list of your current partition table. The following is a sample partition table from a Linux system:

```
Device   Boot   Start   End    Blocks    ID   System
/dev/hda1   *   1    949    1912152   83   Linux
/dev/hda2       950  1015   133056    5    Extended
/dev/hda5       950  1015   133024    82   Linux   Swap
```

In the preceding example, you can see that /dev/hda1 is the boot drive and that it contains the main Linux system. The system ID is the type of Linux file system, which, in this case, is the ext2 filesystem — the default for Linux.

The Linux swap file is ID 82, and is installed on the /dev/hda5 partition. The following is a list of other file system numbers:

```
0   Empty              9   AIX bootable      75   PC/IX          b7   BSDI fs
1   DOS 12-bit FAT     a   OS/2 Boot Manag   80   Old MINIX      b8   BSDI swap
2   XENIX root         40  Venix 80286       81   Linux/MINIX    c7   Syrinx
3   XENIX usr          51  Novell?           82   Linux swap     db   CP/M
4   DOS 16-bit <32M    52  Microport         83   Linux native   e1   DOS access
5   Extended           63  GNU HURD          93   Amoeba         e3   DOS R/O
6   DOS 16-bit >=32    64  Novell Netware    94   Amoeba BBT     f2   DOS Sec
7   OS/2 HPFS          65  Novell Netware    a5   BSD/386        ff   BBT
8   AIX
```

Exam Tip   The most important ID numbers to remember are the Linux specific designations, such as 82 for the Linux Swap file, and 83 for a typical Linux partition.

As the preceding examples demonstrate, you can see and format partitions for all types of systems. If you have a dual-boot system with Microsoft Windows, use the DOS fat file system.

You can use the fdisk tool to add and delete partitions. You must set the size of the partition by number of blocks. You must also set the file system with the file system ID number. After you finish, hit the "w" command to write the partition table to disk, and then exit the utility.

After you have set up your partitions, you won't be able to use them until you actually format the partitions with a valid file system. For Linux, the default file system is the ext2 system. If you have added another hard drive to your system, such as /dev/hdb, you will want to create another partition for Linux to use on that drive.

Using the fdisk tool, add a partition called /dev/hdb1. If you want, use all the available blocks to allocate the entire drive to one partition. After you finish using fdisk, format the partition with the ext2 file system.

For this, you need to use the mkfs command:

```
mkfs -t ext2 /dev/hdb2
```

This command tells the mkfs command to invoke the mke2fs utility to format the partition with the ext2 file system.

To mount the file system for use, use the mount command to mount your new partition:

```
mount /dev/hdb1 /home2
```

Exam Tip   The file system used by Linux is the ext2 file system.

Repairing Partitions

File systems can be very complex, and with a great amount of disk activity and read and writes, the occasional error is bound to happen. The utility that you use to repair these problems and inconsistencies is fsck, which is short for "File System Check." (This is similar in function to the Windows SCANDISK utility)

The fsck utility scans all disks and partitions, and if possible, repairs them when necessary. This utility runs automatically at boot time if the system has shut down abnormally. If your hard drives were unmounted improperly, they may contain errors and inconsistencies, which fsck will fix before remounting the file system.

This utility can never be run on a mounted file system. You must unmount any file system before checking it with fsck. This is important because fsck won't work properly if the file system is still in use, and the data it keeps on the drive is still changing.

To check your file system for errors, first unmount the drive:

```
umount /dev/hdb2
```

Then, you can run fsck manually on the partition:

```
fsck /dev/hdb2
```

The system asks you if you want fsck to fix any errors. Always let fsck fix the errors; otherwise, the file system will likely become more inconsistent through use.

You can use the -a option on fsck to have it automatically fix errors without manual intervention.

Using fsck on a large file system may take quite a long time to complete. If you are running fsck on a large file system manually, try to do it during off-hours so it won't affect your users.

 Tip   The fsck utility will run automatically if the system is shutdown abnormally. It will check the file systems for any errors caused by the abrupt shutdown.

System Automation and Scheduling

Objective ▶ 5.2 Verify user and root cron jobs and understand the function of cron

The daily tasks of running scripts, checking disk space, and performing CPU and memory utilization can take up most of an administrator's day. By utilizing program scheduling and automation tools, however, these tasks can be performed automatically, and the information and logs sent directly to the administrator's mailbox.

Two of the most heavily used commands for performing scheduling are at and cron.

at

Use the at command to set a specific command or batch file to run at a certain time. The atd daemon monitors the queue of at commands and executes the commands at their specified time.

To use the `at` command to set a scheduled job, you must first enter the `at` command with the time you want the job to begin:

```
at 8:00
```

This command tells the `at` command to start the job at 8:00 a.m. The format for the time and date can be fairly complex. If you are just setting the time, you can use the standard 24-hour clock to specify times. For example, 14:00 is 2:00 p.m. You can set a date by using the format dd.mm.yy., or mm/dd/yy. To set a job to start at 11:00 p.m. on February 22, 2002, use the following command:

```
at 23:00 22.02.01
```

After you have scheduled the time and date of the job, you can then enter as many commands at the at prompt that you want to schedule for execution. For example, to show the amount of disk space for all local drives to be performed at 11:00 p.m., use the following commands:

```
at 23:00
at> df -kl
<ctrl-d>
```

Use `<ctrl-d>` to end the list of commands after you are finished. When the job is run, it automatically mails output results to the user who issued the command. To monitor the current jobs in the queue, use the `at -l`, or `atq` command. User `at` jobs are saved in /var/spool/at/ with a directory for each user that stores all the user's `at` jobs.

You can remove jobs from the queue by using the `atrm` command. First, find the number of the job in the queue by issuing the `at -l`, then delete it with the `atrm` command:

```
atrm 2
```

The following list includes some of the options that you can use with the `at` command:

✦ V: Prints the version number to standard error.

✦ q: Uses the specified queue.

✦ m: Sends mail to the user when the job has completed — even if there was no output.

✦ f file: Reads the job from file rather than standard input.

✦ l: Shows completed but not yet deleted jobs in the queue; otherwise, shows the time the job will be executed.

✦ c: Cats the jobs listed on the command line to standard output.

cron

The disadvantage of the at command is that it can't schedule recurring jobs. So if you need to run a program every night at 11:00, you have to set it manually by using the at command each time. The cron command, however, can schedule recurring tasks.

The cron command is a powerful scheduling command and should be used by all Linux system administrators for automating tasks and scheduling programs. The system also uses this command to perform system cleanup jobs, such as rotating logs, updating the locate command database, and cleaning up temporary files.

Caution   Never delete the system cron files. They automate several important system tasks, including log rotation and temp file cleanup.

The crond daemon controls the cron command and constantly checks the queue for any jobs that need to be run. All cron jobs are stored in the /etc/crontab file. The default crontab file looks similar to the following:

```
SHELL=/bin/bash
PATH=/sbin:/bin:/usr/sbin:/usr/bin
MAILTO=root
HOME=/

# run-parts
01 * * * * root run-parts /etc/cron.hourly
02 4 * * * root run-parts /etc/cron.daily
22 4 * * 0 root run-parts /etc/cron.weekly
42 4 1 * * root run-parts /etc/cron.monthly
```

The first five columns in the preceding example show the specific times that the cron job will run (an asterisk means that any value will work):

✦ minute (0-59)

✦ hour (0-23)

✦ day of month (1-31)

✦ month of year (1-12)

✦ day of week (0-6 — Sunday to Saturday)

In the preceding example, the cron.monthly job will run at 4:42 in the morning on the first day of the month. The cron.hourly job runs at the first minute of every hour, every day. The /etc directory contains several cron subdirectories, which hold scripts that run as stated either hourly, daily, weekly, or monthly.

Exam Tip   Know the proper syntax for a cron job command.

To create an entry for `cron`, use the `crontab -e` command. This command brings you into the `vi` editor program, where you can write your `cron` entry in the format as listed in the preceding example. After you finish, save your file and exit `vi`.

User `crontabs` are saved in /var/spool/cron/ with a directory for each user that stores all the user's `cron` jobs.

To see your `cron` jobs, use the `crontab -l` command. To delete your `cron` jobs, use the `crontab -r` command.

Exam Tip Remember that the `at` command can only run a job at one particular time. `Cron` can schedule recurring tasks.

Core Dumps

Objective 5.3 Identify core dumps and remove or forward as appropriate

Inevitably, one of your system's applications or even a core system process will malfunction — causing a *core dump*. A core dump is a file that is created by an application or service that has crashed. The most serious type of system crash is a kernel crash, often called a kernel "panic." The information recorded in a core file is a snapshot of what was in memory at the time of the crash, and contains information important for debugging the application. A programmer can use this information to find out what caused the application to crash, and to modify the application to prevent future crashes. A program may crash for several reasons, such as lack of memory or disk space, invalid input, a hardware failure, or even a program bug.

This file, usually called the "core," is dumped into the current working directory. If you are not using this file at all to debug an application, you should delete it. Depending on the application, a core file may be extremely large, and can quickly use up valuable disk space. You can limit the size of a core file, or even turn off core dumping by using the `ulimit` command. I recommend against disabling core dumps because they contain very important debugging information that is needed to fix the application. The `ulimit` command sets various parameters for user environment settings. The core file size is specified in blocks. By default, the size is usually set to 1,000,000 blocks. You can turn off core dumps by issuing the following command:

```
ulimit -c 0
```

This command sets the core dump file size to zero, effectively disabling it. To see that the command worked, use the following command, which will show all of your user limit settings:

```
ulimit -a
```

Analyzing core dumps

Just by looking at the memory dump, the cause of the crash may not be immediately apparent. The information is very technical and confusing, showing actual memory addresses and program routines. Thankfully, many types of debugging tools are available that can help you analyze a core dump file and allow you to more accurately debug the problem. However, you may benefit more by forwarding the core dump to the programmer of the application, so that they can fix the bugs in their program.

GNU Debugger

By using the gdb (GNU Debugger) program, you can analyze your program's core dump files and also debug the application while it is actually running. You can invoke the program on a core file by issuing the following command:

```
gdb -c core
```

This command launches the gdb program on a core file called "core," and displays the name of the program that created the core file and the signal on which the program terminated.

The following is an example of the output of the gdb command on a core file from the Apache Web server:

```
Core was generated by `httpd'.
Program terminated with signal 11, Segmentation fault.
gdb> bt
#0   0x5c8b1674 in ?? ()
#1   0x4018df03 in zend_hash_add_or_update (ht=0x143280,
arKey=0x4018aa3d "stdclass", nKeyLength=9, pData=0x40253000,
nDataSize=128, pDest=0x0, flag=2) at zend_hash.c:284
#2   0x4018ab45 in register_standard_class () at zend.c:243
#3   0x4018ad06 in zend_startup (utility_functions=0xefbfd770, extensions=0x0,
start_builtin_functions=1) at zend.c:371
#4   0x401a548e in php_module_startup (sf=0xc8000) at main.c:807
#5   0x401a26dc in php_apache_startup (sapi_module=0xc8000) at mod_php4.c:270
#6   0x401a313c in php_init_handler (s=0xf6034, p=0xf600c) at mod_php4.c:694
#7   0x3d5d9 in ap_init_modules ()
#8   0x4b2b9 in main ()
```

The average user or system administrator may never need to use this information, but it is very valuable to programmers. The following is a list of commands that can be used in gdb.

✦ quit: Terminate gdb

✦ where: Show the call stack where execution has been halted

✦ p: Print the value of a variable or expression

✦ up: Refocus gdb up one function in the call stack

✦ down: Refocus gdb down one function in the call stack

✦ help: Get help for a command

✦ run: Start execution of a program

✦ b: Set a breakpoint at a line or function

✦ clear: Clear a breakpoint from a line or function

✦ commands: Set commands to be executed when a breakpoint is hit

✦ s: Execute one more line (possibly in a subroutine)

✦ n: Execute to next line of current function

✦ continue: Continue execution to next breakpoint

✦ watch: Watch for a change in an expression (this can be slow)

✦ list: List source lines of a function

Exam Tip
You don't need to know the gdb tool in detail, but you do need to know its function, and when to delete a core dump or forward it to a programmer.

Managing Networking Interfaces

Objective

5.4 Run and interpret ifconfig

Networking is one of the most basic and critical services run from the Linux system. The task of configuring, administering, and monitoring your network interfaces is not needed every single day, but is extremely important to know when troubleshooting network problems.

The central command for network interface management is the ifconfig command. Use this command to view information on all your network cards. You can also use this command to configure the network cards with a network address, subnet mask, gateway, and other network settings.

If you type the ifconfig from the command line, you will get the configuration of the first network interface in your machine. If you have multiple network cards, you should use the ifconfig, which is a command to list all network interfaces. You can also choose each interface by name. The first ethernet interface is called *eth0*; the next, *eth1*, and so on.

The following is a sample output of the ifconfig command:

```
> ifconfig eth0

eth0    Link encap: Ethernet    HWaddr 00:60:67:4A:02:0A
        inet addr:0.0.0.0  Bcast:0.0.0.0  Mask:255.255.255.255
```

```
UP BROADCAST RUNNING MULTICAST  MTU:1500  Metric:1
RX packets:466 errors:0 dropped:0 overruns:0 frame:0
TX packets:448 errors:0 dropped:0 overruns:0 carrier:0
collisions:85 txqueuelen:100
Interrupt:10 Base address:0xe400
```

This command shows a large amount of information on the card, including its type, its hardware MAC address, the IP address and subnet mask, and communications statistics, such as the number of network packets received and transmitted. This command also shows you how many network packets have been dropped. A high number of dropped packets indicate that you may be experiencing network problems, such as high traffic and network overload.

You should also have a local loopback address called interface "lo." This loopback interface is a special virtual interface that allows you to make network connections to your own system. This interface also allows you to test locally without sending any packets onto a network. The local loopback address is always assigned an IP address of 127.0.0.1.

To see the loopback interface, use the following command:

```
ifconfig lo
```

The output should look similar to the following:

```
lo      Link encap Local Loopback
        inet addr 127.0.0.1  Bcast [NONE SET]  Mask 255.0.0.0
        UP BROADCAST LOOPBACK RUNNING  MTU 2000  Metric 1
        RX packets 0 errors 0 dropped 0 overrun 0
        TX packets 0 errors 0 dropped 0 overrun 0
```

You can use the ifconfig to configure an interface. The following is the syntax of the ifconfig:

```
ifconfig interface options | address
```

To configure a network interface with a new IP address, use ifconfig, as in the following example, to enter all the information that you need to get the network connection live.

```
ifconfig eth0 192.168.1.1 netmask 255.255.255.0 broadcast 192.168.1.255
```

This command sets the first ethernet interface with the IP address of 192.168.1.1, a class C subnet mask of 255.255.255.0, and a broadcast address of 192.168.1.255.

You can also use the ifconfig to enable and disable an interface. For example, to disable the first ethernet interface, use the following command:

```
ifconfig eth0 down
```

To enable the interface, use the following command:

```
ifconfig eth0 up
```

The following list includes some of the options that you can set with the `ifconfig` command:

- ✦ interface: The name of the interface.
- ✦ up: This flag causes the interface to be activated.
- ✦ down: This flag causes the driver for this interface to be shut down.
- ✦ [-]arp: Enable or disable the use of the ARP protocol on this interface.
- ✦ [-]promisc: Enable or disable the promiscuous mode of the interface. If selected, all packets on the network will be received by the interface.
- ✦ [-]allmulti: Enable or disable all-multicast mode. If selected, all multicast packets on the network will be received by the interface.
- ✦ metric N: This parameter sets the interface metric.
- ✦ mtu N: This parameter sets the Maximum Transfer Unit (MTU) of an interface.
- ✦ netmask addr: Sets the IP network mask for this interface.
- ✦ [-]broadcast [addr]: If the address argument is given, set the protocol broadcast address for this interface.
- ✦ address: The IP address to be assigned to this interface.

Exam Tip   You don't need to use all the options of the `ifconfig` command, but know how to configure a basic ethernet or loopback interface.

Installing System Packages and Patches

Objective   5.5 Download and install patches and updates (e.g., packages, tgz)

Upgrading a system service or application is a common task for an administrator. You may need to upgrade a package or install a system or application patch for many reasons, including:

- ✦ Bug Fixes: Most upgrades fix a number of program bugs since the last release of the program. This ensures that you are using the most current stable version.
- ✦ Enhanced Functionality: Most new upgrades enhance the functionality of the program. This will help the user base by giving them additional tools with which to enhance their work.

✦ Increased Security: Many programs come with severe security flaws. These are usually patched up in later releases. It is extremely important to keep your programs up-to-date regarding security enhancements.

Any type of system upgrade or patch that you perform should take place during off-hours, so as not to affect the users. If users are logged into the system with files open, an upgrade or patch may cause data corruption — because you may need to stop or restart a program or service, or reboot the system. Remember to mention any upgrades or system maintenance in the "Message of the Day" file in /etc/motd. This reminds users to log off before they leave work, so no files will be open.

Software packages come in many different types. The most common method for packaging a group of files is using the `tar` and `gzip` utilities to create an archive file and compress it. These files are denoted by the extension tar.gz. Some distributions offer their own packaging format, such as RPM (Redhat Package Manager), or Slackware, which uses a modified `tar` and `gzip` package with the extension .tgz.

Compressed archive

Most programs and patches come in the form of a compressed archive. A program patch or upgrade contains several source code files, binaries, and program libraries. A compressed archive consists of all the files that are part of the update, tied together in a single file called a `tar` archive.

One problem with `tar` is that it doesn't actually compress the files in the archive; therefore, they can often be very large in size, which makes them more difficult to download over slow Internet connections, and impossible to fit on a floppy disk. To compress the archive, use the `gzip` utility. This utility compresses the data in a file into the smallest possible form. When used in conjunction with the `tar` utility, you can create a collection of files, and then compress them so that you only need one small file.

The resulting file has a .tar.gz extension, indicating that it is a `tar` file that has been compressed with `gzip`. To extract the file, use the gunzip command to unzip the file:

```
gunzip packagename.tar.gz
```

After the command completes, the file will be unzipped, and the remaining product is the `tar` archive file. Then, you can use the `tar` command to extract the files from the archive:

```
tar -xvf packagename.tar
```

The tar utility also comes with the capability of unzipping the archive while extracting files at the same time. To do this, use the -z switch:

```
tar -zxvf packagename.tar.gz
```

Performing the `gunzip` and `tar` extract commands together is a lot easier than using the two separate commands to extract and unzip the files.

After the file has been extracted, be sure to read the documentation before installing the upgrade or patch. Typically, a README file will give you installation instructions.

From the README file, you may have to compile the source code into a binary, and then execute the binary to start your upgrade or patch. Often, this process can be very tedious and time-consuming.

1. Run the `configure` command. This prepares the system for installation, and ensures that you have the proper compiler and any other dependencies for the operation.

2. Use the `make` command to compile the source code into binary format.

3. Use the `make install` command. This command installs your binary in the proper location.

After you finish, you can remove the original source files and the compressed file.

RPM

The RPM (Redhat Package Manager) format is another type of package installation. RPM is a utility that streamlines the method for installing applications, upgrades, and patches.

By installing an application through RPM, you only need to activate one command to uncompress and install your application package. You don't need to use tar, gzip, or tediously compile source code. The RPM manager does all this automatically. Although created by Redhat, the RPM format is used by many different distributions for package installation.

RPM packages come with the extension .rpm. To install it, simply use the install option:

```
rpm -i packagename.rpm
```

To see more information when installing, use the verbose and hash mark options, which allow you to see a better view of what is being installed.

```
rpm -ivh packagename.rpm
```

If you have an existing application that you want to upgrade, use the upgrade option. If the application doesn't already exist, it will install anyway.

```
rpm -Uvh packagename.rpm
```

To delete an application installed through RPM, use the erase function. This quickly and efficiently removes your application entirely:

```
rpm -e packagename.rpm
```

In the Real World Only update a package or install a patch if you are currently experiencing issues that are fixed by the update. Needlessly updating an application or applying a patch can often lead to system problems that you aren't prepared for.

Debian Package Installer

Packages for the Debian Linux distribution have the extension .deb. To install or manipulate these files, use the dpkg utility.

✦ To install a Debian package, use the following command:

```
dpkg -i packagename.deb
```

✦ To obtain a list of files that are contained in the package without installing them, use the following command:

```
dpkg -L packagename.deb
```

✦ To remove or uninstall a package, use the following command:

```
dpkg -r packagename.deb
```

Slackware Package Installation

Slackware's package management system utilizes .tgz files as its package format. Although the type of file is very similar to a standard tar.gz file, and can be unzipped and untarred as usual, the resulting package is only intended for installation on a Slackware system.

You can install Slackware packages by using a menu-driven tool called pkgtool. From the command line, you can use different utilities, depending on what you want to do with the package. For example, to install a package, use the following command:

```
installpkg packagename.tgz
```

The installpkg utility comes with an excellent installation option, which shows you what happens if you install a particular package. The "warn" option allows you to test a package before installing on a production system. To test install the package, use the following command:

```
installpkg -warn packagename.tgz
```

To remove a package from a system, use the removepkg command:

```
removepkg packagename
```

Summary

This chapter details many different system administration tasks. Disk and file system management, scheduling tasks, networking, analyzing core dumps, and installing new packages and patches are all routine tasks of the Linux system administrator. For the exam, keep the following points in mind:

✦ Disk and File Management

- `fdisk`: Formats disk partitions
- `mkfs`: Creates a file system on a partition
- `fsck`: File system check for fixing disk errors

✦ Job Scheduling

- `at`: Can only schedule a task for one time
- `cron`: Can schedule recurring tasks

✦ Core Dumps

- `core`: Typical name of the core file
- `gdb`: GNU debugger tool for debugging core files

✦ Networking

- `ifconfig -a`: Used to show information on all network interfaces
- `ifconfig eth0`: Configures the first ethernet interface
- `ifconfig lo`: Configures the loopback interface

✦ Package Upgrades and Patches

- `rpm -U`: Upgrades an RPM package
- `rpm -i`: Installs an RPM package
- `tar -xvf`: Extracts a tar archive, tar file has .tar extension
- `tar -zxvf`: Extracts and decompresses a tar archive compress with gzip
- `gunzip`: Unzips a compressed file with extension .gz
- `gzip`: Compresses a file
- `configure`, `make`, `make install` to compile and install source code binaries
- Upgrade after work hours to avoid affecting users

✦   ✦   ✦

STUDY GUIDE

The Study Guide section provides you with the opportunity to test your knowledge about the Linux+ exam objectives that are covered in this chapter. The Assessment Questions provide practice for the real exam, and the Scenarios provide practice with real situations. If you get any questions wrong, use the answers to determine the part of the chapter that you should review before continuing.

Assessment Questions

1. What command do you use to format a partition with a file system?

    A. `fdisk`

    B. `fsmake`

    C. `format`

    D. `mkfs`

2. On a Linux Web server, the Apache http server keeps crashing unexpectedly. What can the Linux administrator check to stop the crashes?

    A. process kill log

    B. core file

    C. /var/log/dmesg

    D. root cron file

3. An administrator wants to create the local loopback network interface on her Linux system. Which command will correctly perform the task?

    A. `ifconfig lo`

    B. `ifconfig -loopback`

    C. `ifconfig -a`

    D. `ifconfig 255.255.255.255`

4. Which of the following `cron` commands will create a `cron` job that will run at 5:00 a.m. every Sunday?

    A. `* 5 * * S /etc/cron.weekly`

    B. `/etc/cron.sunday`

    C. `* 5 * * 0 /etc/cron.weekly`

    D. `5 0 * * S /etc/cron.weekly`

5. What kind of file is stored with an extension of tar.gz?

   A. Backup files

   B. Temporary files

   C. A special compression executable

   D. A file that has been tar and gzipped

6. What command should be used to set a network interface to the IP address, 192.168.1.5, with a subnet mask of 255.255.255.0?

   A. `ifconfig eth0 192.168.1.5 netmask 255.255.255.0`

   B. `ifconfig lo 192.168.1.5 netmask 255.255.255.0`

   C. `ifconfig eth1 192.168.1.5 broadcast 255.255.255.0`

   D. `ifconfig -a 192.168.1.5 255.255.255.0`

7. Which option in `fdisk` will display the partition table?

   A. s (show partition table)

   B. p (print partition table)

   C. fdisk partition

   D. t (tables)

8. What command can you use to view and debug an application's core file?

   A. `cron`

   B. `debug`

   C. `vi`

   D. `gdb`

9. To create a recurring scheduled task, which Linux scheduling tool should you use to perform the task?

   A. `cron`

   B. `at`

   C. `timer`

   D. `gdb`

10. To upgrade an RPM package, which is the proper command to use?

    A. `rpm -upgrade`

    B. `rpm -i`

    C. `rpm -U`

    D. `rpm -upg`

11. What command can you use to enable an ethernet network interface that has already been configured?

    A. `ifconfig eth0 on`

    B. `ifconfig eth0 up`

    C. `ifconfig eth0 down`

    D. `ifconfig eth0 start`

12. What is the proper command to open and decompress a file with a tar.gz extension?

    A. `tar -zxvf filename`

    B. `gzip -txvf filename`

    C. `uncompress filename`

    D. `gunzip -txvf filename`

13. A core dump file contains this message, "Program terminated with signal 11, segmentation fault." What does this message indicate?

    A. The program is a kernel system process

    B. Signal 11 means the program is still running, but had an error

    C. The program halted because of a memory segment fault

    D. Nothing, this is informational only

14. What command runs fdisk on the first ATA/IDE hard drive?

    A. `fdisk /dev/hda`

    B. `fdisk /dev/sda1`

    C. `fdisk hda1`

    D. `fdisk /dev/hda2`

15. An application is creating several, very large core dump files. What should the administrator do if he has no intention of debugging these files?

    A. Copy them to gdb

    B. Delete the core files

    C. Move them to the root partition

    D. Change the name of the file, so that new core files can be created

16. What is the best reason to upgrade a package or application on your Linux system?

    A. Updated security

    B. Less program bugs

    C. More program functionality

    D. All of the above

17. When checking the partition information on your hard drive with fdisk, you notice that one of the partitions is formatted as "Linux Swap," and is approximately 128MB in size. What is the purpose of this partition?

    A. Special disk area for the Linux Swap file

    B. Overflow area in case the main partition runs out of space

    C. Virtual memory that is not used

    D. Holds temp files and deleted items

18. What sort of kernel error can cause a Linux system to crash and write a memory core dump?

    A. Cron daemon error

    B. Corrupt swap file

    C. Kernel panic

    D. Web server error

19. An administrator needs to create a second network interface with an IP address of 192.168.1.10, a subnet mask of 255.255.255.0, and a broadcast address of 192.168.1.254. What command will accomplish this task?

    A. `ifconfig eth1 192.168.1.10 netmask 255.255.255.0 broadcast 192.168.1.254`

    B. `ifconfig lo 192.168.1.10`

    C. `ipconfig eth0 192.168.1.10 netmask 255.255.255.0 bc=254`

    D. `ifconfig eth0 192.168.1.10 netmask 255.0.0.0 broadcast 192.168.1.254`

20. What command should you use to set up a job to run at 11:59 p.m. today?

    A. `cron 59 11 * * *`

    B. `at 23:59`

    C. `cron 11:59pm`

    D. `at 11:59am`

Scenarios

1. Management has instructed you to set up a schedule to perform automatic checks of disk space at least once a day. The company has had problems with running out of disk space on a routine basis, and they want to proactively monitor the situation to ensure that it won't happen again. How can you accomplish this task?

2. A company's Web server was recently upgraded with new Perl scripting code. Since the upgrade, the server crashes at least twice a day. What can the Linux administrator do to find and solve the problem?

Lab Exercises

Lab 12-1 Configuring Network Interfaces

The objective for this hands-on lab is to gain experience in setting up network interfaces by using the `ifconfig` command. This example assumes that you have one ethernet interface in the machine, and another machine on the network for testing purposes. You should be able to use any default Linux installation for this exercise.

1. See what your current interface configuration looks like by using `ifconfig`.

   `ifconfig -a`

2. In the output, there should be at least one ethernet interface, eth0, and possibly a loopback interface, lo. If there is no loopback interface, create it by using the following command:

   `ifconfig lo 127.0.0.1`

   Check to see if the loopback interface has been created by using the `ifconfig -a` command.

3. Now, set or change the IP address of the ethernet interface. The address is 192.168.1.1, and the subnet mask is 255.255.255.0.

   `ifconfig eth0 192.168.1.1 netmask 255.255.255.0`

   Check to see if the change worked by using the `ifconfig -a` command.

4. To check that the interface is working, use the `ping` command to test the address from another machine:

   `ping 192.168.1.1`

5. Use the `ifconfig` command to disable the interface:

   `ifconfig eth0 down`

   Try pinging it again from another computer; you should not get a response.

6. Use the `ifconfig` command to enable the interface again:

`ifconfig eth0 up`

You should be able to ping the address from another machine again.

Lab 12-2 Configuring Cron to Automate Tasks

The objective for this hands-on lab is to gain experience in using `cron` to automate tasks. You should be able to use any default Linux installation for this exercise.

1. Logged in as the root user, check your current crontab file:

`crontab-l`

2. Unless you have configured jobs before, it should be empty. Create a simple task that will run each day. Schedule a task for 5 minutes from the current time. So if your time is currently 1:00 p.m., set it to check the local disk space at 1:05 p.m.

`crontab -e`

Now use vi to enter the `cron` command:

`5 13 * * * df -kl`

3. Wait five minutes, and then check your root mail file by using the following command:

`mail`

You should have an e-mail with the output of the `df -kl` command.

4. Delete your crontab file so that it is empty again by using the following command:

`crontab -r`

Check to see that the job was removed by using the following command:

`crontab -l`

Answers to Chapter Questions

Chapter Pre-test

1. `Cron` is used to schedule recurring jobs. You can set it to run a program or script at any time you choose.

2. A file with a tar.gz extension is a file archive created by `tar`. Compress this file by using the `gzip` command.

3. The `ifconfig` command shows you information about the configuration of your network interfaces, including addresses, and packets transmitted and received.

4. The command to create a file system is `mkfs`. This command invokes another command specific for that file system, such as `mke2fs` for Linux file systems.

5. Analyze core dumps to find out why a program crashed. It may give you important information that can help you find what bug is causing the program to fail.

6. A program patch is an update to an application or service that was created to fix an existing bug, or to enhance security or functionality for a program.

7. The `at` command differs from `cron` in that it can only be used to schedule a job to run at one time. The `cron` command allows you to set up a job that will run at recurring times.

8. The `fsck` utility (File System Check) can scan your disk for errors, and actually fix them as it checks. This is helpful in recovering corrupted file systems that won't mount or boot.

9. Any system upgrades or patches should be performed in off-hours, so that it won't affect users currently logged into the system. If the system needs to be rebooted, you won't have any files still open by users, which may cause them to be corrupted.

10. The `fdisk` command is used to create partitions on a hard drive.

Assessment Questions

1. D. By invoking the `mkfs` command, you actually run a program specific to the file system that you are creating, such as mke2fs to format using the Linux ext2 file system. For review, see the "Disk and File System Management" section.

2. B. By analyzing the resulting core file from an application, the administrator may be able to debug the application and find out why the program is crashing. For review, see the "Core Dumps" section.

3. A. The administrator can select the loopback interface to configure by using the `ifconfig lo` command. The IP address for any loopback interface is 127.0.0.1. For review, see the "Managing Network Interfaces" section.

4. C. The proper format for `cron` entries is minute/hour/day/month/day of week (0-Sunday, 6-Saturday). For review, see the "System Automation and Scheduling" section.

5. D. To store and compress most file archives, a number of files are stored in a `tar` archive. To compress that archive, use the `gzip` command. For review, see the "Installing System Packages and Patches" section.

6. A. The correct command is `ifconfig eth0 192.168.1.5 netmask 255.255.255.0`. The eth0 option can be any Ethernet interface. The loopback interface must always use 127.0.0.1 for an IP address. For review, see the "Managing Network Interfaces" section.

7. B. Within the `fdisk` utility, the "p" command will print the partition table. This command does not "print" to a printer; the command displays the partition table on the terminal screen. For review, see the "Disk and File System Management" section.

8. D. The GNU debugger is the most popular tool for analyzing core dump files. You can use it to walk step-by-step through a program to identify bugs. For review, see the "Core Dumps" section.

9. A. The `cron` command allows you to create recurring tasks. The `at` command only allows you to execute a scheduled task at one particular time. For review, see the "System Automation and Scheduling" section.

10. C. The `rpm -U` command will update a currently existing package to the new version. If the program doesn't exist, `rpm` will install the package. For review, see the "Installing System Packages and Patches" section.

11. B. To enable an interface, use the `ifconfig eth0 up` command. If you need to disable the interface, use `ifconfig eth0 down`. For review, see the "Managing Network Interfaces" section.

12. A. The proper command is `tar -zxvf filename`. You can also complete the operation by using two separate commands, `tar` to extract the archive and `gunzip` to decompress the file. For review, see the "Installing System Packages and Patches" section.

13. C. The core file will tell you what exactly caused the program to crash. In this case, the program crashed because of a segmentation fault in memory. For review, see the "Core Dumps" section.

14. A. The first ATA/IDE hard drive is hda, so the correct command is `fdisk /dev/hda`. For review, see the "Disk and File System Management" section.

15. B. If you have no intention of keeping these files for debugging purposes, they should be deleted because they are wasting valuable disk space, and may cause your system to run out of space. For review, see the "Core Dumps" section.

16. D. Programs and applications should be kept up-to-date with the latest releases because the newest version will always have the latest security updates, bug fixes, and additional functionality. For review, see the "Installing System Packages and Patches" section.

17. A. The Linux swap file is used for virtual memory to store additional information that can't fit into current memory. This swap file allows information to be cached on disk, and can be retrieved very quickly. Heavy use of the swap file indicates a low memory condition. For review, see the "Disk and File System Management" section.

18. C. A kernel panic indicates that a kernel process has crashed. This is a very serious error that causes the entire Linux system to crash. These core dumps should be analyzed carefully to find the root cause of the problem. For review, see the "Core Dumps" section.

19. A. The second ethernet interface is called eth1, so the proper command is `ifconfig eth1 192.168.1.10 netmask 255.255.255.0 broadcast 192.168.1.254`. For review, see the "Managing Network Interfaces" section.

20. B. Because you are only running this job once at the specified time, you only need to use the `at` command. The `cron` command is more useful for setting up recurring jobs. The correct syntax is `at 23:59`. For review, see the "System Automation and Scheduling" section.

Scenarios

1. Because this must be a recurring task, the `at` command won't be an efficient method for performing the task in this situation. It is much easier to set up `cron` to run a script that will check the disk space daily at 1:00 p.m. The output will be e-mailed to the root account. You can compare the results from day to day to analyze disk space usage.

   Your `cron` file should look similar to the following:

   ```
   * 13 * * * df -kl
   ```

2. The crash of the Web server should create a core dump file in the Web server home directory. The administrator can save that file, and either debug it himself using the GNU debugger tool (gdb), or pass it along to the programmer who created the Perl code so that they can debug the program and remove the bugs that are causing the Web server to crash.

Process Management

CHAPTER PRE-TEST

1. What command is used to identify processes?

2. Which log file contains a list of user logins and logouts?

3. Why is maintenance documentation important?

4. What command is used to terminate a process?

5. What is the difference between a core process and a non-critical process?

6. What is the purpose of the `init` process?

7. What is a PID?

8. What command is used to send a running process into the background?

9. Which log contains system errors?

10. What command can be used to see real-time information on running processes and the resources that they are using?

✦ Answers to these questions can be found at the end of the chapter. ✦

Linux is a multi-user, multi-tasking operating system. Every time you run a program under Linux, you begin what is known as a *process*. A process is another name for a program that is run by a particular user. Depending on the processing and memory resources on your particular machine, a large number of processes can run simultaneously. Linux administrators must know what processes are running on their systems, and to what extent the processes are affecting system performance. This chapter deals with the subject of how to view, manage, stop, and start these processes.

The Linux administrator must also maintain system logs. The logs can provide excellent troubleshooting information by reporting system errors, user logins, and any unusual behavior that may affect the system. This chapter shows you where to find the different types of logs and how to interpret their data. Finally, this chapter also discusses the importance of documenting and maintaining the information on your Linux system and its performance.

Linux Processes

At any given time, your Linux system is constantly running several processes. These processes run concurrently and are simultaneously executed by the CPU. They also don't interfere with each other; for example, if one process crashes or ends abnormally, it won't affect any other process in the system. Some processes can spawn other processes, which are called *child processes*. If you stop a child process, the parent process will continue. However, if you stop the parent process, each child process is also stopped. A process uses several system resources when running, including the following:

✦ **CPU:** Runs the instructions for the process.

✦ **Memory:** Holds the process and any data that it is using.

✦ **File Systems:** Allows access to required physical files, and also allocates temporary storage for processing.

✦ **Physical Devices:** Allows processes to access physical devices, such as monitors, hard drives, and printers.

The system tracks each process for its usage of these resources, and allocates these resources as needed to the process that needs them the most. Some processes are given priority over others, while the other processes must "wait their turn" to use the CPU.

A process can be in one of the following states:

✦ **Running:** The process is currently assigned to a CPU and running.

✦ **Ready:** The process is waiting to be assigned to a CPU.

✦ **Waiting:** The process is waiting for a particular resource to become available.

✦ **Zombie:** The process has stopped but is still consuming resources; also often referred to as a "dead" process.

✦ **Stopped:** The process is in a stopped state.

The CPU uses a special identification number called a *PID*, or *Process ID*, which tracks each process. This number allows the administrator to more easily differentiate between processes while managing the system. The PID can also be used in conjunction with several commands to change the state of a process.

Core services versus non-critical services

Objective

5.6 Differentiate core services from non-critical services (e.g., ps, PID, PPID, init, timer)

Several core processes are integral to the Linux system because they run critical programs that the Linux kernel needs in order to function properly. These processes are run at boot time, and are usually referred to as "daemons."

Exam Tip

For the exam, be careful to differentiate the core services from regular application and user processes.

Init

The most important service in a Linux system is provided by init. Init starts when the system boots, and continues the boot process by performing various startup jobs, such as checking and mounting file systems, and starting services and daemons. When the system is shut down, the init process stops all other processes, unmounts the file systems, and halts the system.

All processes are spawned from init. Many Linux startup services and daemons are spawned from the init process. The command pstree gives you a list of all the processes in a "tree" format, so you can easily discern the parent and child processes. This is the sample output from the pstree command:

```
init-+-apmd
     |-atd
     |-crond
     |-gpm
     |-identd---identd---3*[identd]
     |-inetd
     |-kflushd
     |-klogd
     |-kpiod
     |-kswapd
     |-kupdate
     |-lockd---rpciod
     |-login---bash---pstree
     |-lpd
```

```
|-mdrecoveryd
|-5*[mingetty]
|-portmap
|-pump
|-rpc.statd
|-sendmail
|-syslogd
`-xfs
```

Getty

The getty process provides logins from terminals. The init program starts a separate instance of getty for each terminal on which logins are allowed. When the user types his or her name and password, the getty process begins the login program to authenticate the user.

Syslog

The syslog process allows the kernel and many other system programs to produce warnings, errors, and other messages. Syslog is configured to write these events to a file where the administrator can retrieve them at a later date.

Cron

The cron program schedules system tasks and other periodic maintenance programs. The cron program reads a configuration file, and then executes various programs and services at specified times.

Non-critical processes

Processes that are not part of the Linux system are considered non-critical, and are usually programs and applications, such as Web servers and FTP servers. Stopping and starting these processes won't affect the core functionality of the system.

When killing processes, be sure that you are not terminating a special core process, because you may cause your system to crash.

Process administration

The administrator can use several different commands to manage processes. The following sections detail these commands.

The ps command lists currently running processes. With the ps command, you can check the status of all running processes. You can also customize the way you view the list by using special arguments.

Using the ps command without any arguments only shows the running processes of the current user.

```
PID TTY TIME CMD
637 tty1 00:00:00 bash
913 tty1 00:00:00 ps
```

This example shows the user bash shell running, and the ps command that was just run. The PID shows the process identification number for that process. The TTY column defines which terminal the process was run from. The time lists how long the process has been active.

To see all running processes, use the ps -e command. If you are running as root, the ps command shows all running processes by default. The output looks something like this:

```
PID TTY TIME CMD
1     ? 00:00:07 init
2 ? 00:00:00 kflushd
3 ? 00:00:00 kupdate
4 ? 00:00:00 kpiod
5 ? 00:00:00 kswapd
6 ? 00:00:00 mdrecoveryd
287 ? 00:00:00 pump
301 ? 00:00:00 portmap
316 ? 00:00:00 lockd
317 ? 00:00:00 rpciod
326 ? 00:00:00 rpc.statd
340 ? 00:00:00 apmd
391 ? 00:00:00 syslogd
400 ? 00:00:00 klogd
414 ? 00:00:00 identd
416 ? 00:00:00 identd
418 ? 00:00:00 identd
420 ? 00:00:00 identd
421 ? 00:00:00 identd
432 ? 00:00:00 atd
446 ? 00:00:00 crond
464 ? 00:00:00 inetd
478 ? 00:00:00 lpd
522 ? 00:00:00 sendmail
537 ? 00:00:00 gpm
589 ? 00:00:00 xfs
628 tty2 00:00:00 mingetty
629 tty3 00:00:00 mingetty
630 tty4 00:00:00 mingetty
631 tty5 00:00:00 mingetty
632 tty6 00:00:00 mingetty
976 tty1 00:00:00 login
977 tty1 00:00:00 bash
1055 tty1 00:00:00 ps
```

This example shows all the processes that are currently running on the system. The notable processes include the core services, such as inetd, init, syslogd, and crond. The several mingetty processes refer to the number of terminal sessions

available for this instance of Linux. The current user is on tty1, which is why you
see the login, bash, and ps processes listed as originating from the terminal tty1.

ps a

This command is similar to ps -e, but this argument displays all processes that
originated from that particular TTY or terminal. For example:

```
PID TTY TIME CMD
976 tty1 00:00:00 login
977 tty1 00:00:00 bash
1055 tty1 00:00:00 ps
```

ps –u

This command displays all processes run by a particular user. For example, to see
all processes run by the user root, use this command: ps -u root.

ps –au

This command displays all processes listed by username.

ps -f

This command displays a more detailed listing of process information, including
the owner's ID, the start time of the process, and the parent process ID (PPID). For
example:

```
UID PID PPID C STIME TTY TIME CMD
user 636 628 0 06:31 tty1 00:00:00 -bash
user 667 636 0 06:42 tty1 00:00:00 ps -f
```

ps –ef

This is the most common command used to list processes. It displays all processes
by using the full listing format.

ps | more

The ps command can be piped through other commands to aid in displaying the
information. Sometimes, a process list can scroll by too quickly because of all the
entries, so you can pipe it through the more command to list it screen by screen.

ps > file.txt

You can use this command to send the output of the ps command to a text file to be
stored for later viewing, or to print it to a printer.

Exam Tip   Be sure to know and be able to use some of the more popular attributes of the
ps command.

Process control

Sometimes, a Linux system administrator may want to use certain commands in order to manually control processes. For example, the administrator may want to stop and restart a process, or shut down programs that are taking up too many resources.

Occasionally, a system administrator will have to manually control processes that have lapsed into a frozen state — meaning, they won't respond to conventional means of control. This tends to happen more often in a programming environment where a process may go out of control, and constantly use up resources until they have been depleted, which may cause the server to crash.

Foreground and background operation

A process can run either in the foreground or the background. When a process is running in the foreground, it is operating in your current shell, and any output or input is sent directly to that process. When a process is running in the background, it is still running, using resources, and completing its task, but it provides output or allows input from the current shell.

For example, to run a program from your shell, you simply type its name and hit Enter. At this point, you aren't able to get back to your current shell without stopping the process. To immediately put the process into the background at startup, append an ampersand (&) to the command. The difference between foreground and background processes is easily shown with this example:

```
/home/root# tail -f /var/log/messages
```

This command allows you to follow any additions to the /var/log/messages file, which is the main log file for your system. When the program is run, you won't be able to return to your shell until the program is stopped. This process is running in the foreground. To immediately put the program in the background, use the following command:

```
/home/root# tail -f /var/log/messages &
```

After using this command, the program will run in the background. Follow these steps to further manipulate the operation of the process:

1. After you press Enter, you are immediately returned to your shell prompt.

2. To return the application to the foreground, you can use [ctrl-z] to suspend the process, and then use the fg command to bring it back to the foreground.

3. If you have a process running in the foreground, and you need to return to your shell, you can use [ctrl-z] to suspend the process. Then, type **bg** to run the program in the background.

4. To end the process completely, use the [ctrl-c] command.

PIDs, PPID

Objective

5.7 Identify, execute and kill processes (ps, kill, killall)

Each process has its own unique PID that is assigned by the Linux system. This number represents the process when using various process control commands. The PPID, or *parent process identification*, is the identifier of the process that is the parent to the current process. Knowing the PPID is very beneficial because many parent processes have several child processes, and killing the parent process will stop all of the child processes in the chain.

In the Real World
It is very easy to mistake the PPID with the PID of a process in a ps command output listing. Killing the PPID of a process might kill a major parent process that will also terminate any child processes.

To see a list of all your processes — including PID numbers — you can use the ps -e command. Here is a sample output:

```
PID TTY TIME CMD
1 ? 00:00:07 init
2 ? 00:00:00 kflushd
3 ? 00:00:00 kupdate
4 ? 00:00:00 kpiod
5 ? 00:00:00 kswapd
6 ? 00:00:00 mdrecoveryd
287 ? 00:00:00 pump
301 ? 00:00:00 portmap
316 ? 00:00:00 lockd
317 ? 00:00:00 rpciod
326 ? 00:00:00 rpc.statd
340 ? 00:00:00 apmd
391 ? 00:00:00 syslogd
400 ? 00:00:00 klogd
414 ? 00:00:00 identd
416 ? 00:00:00 identd
418 ? 00:00:00 identd
420 ? 00:00:00 identd
421 ? 00:00:00 identd
432 ? 00:00:00 atd
446 ? 00:00:00 crond
464 ? 00:00:00 inetd
478 ? 00:00:00 lpd
522 ? 00:00:00 sendmail
537 ? 00:00:00 gpm
589 ? 00:00:00 xfs
628 tty2 00:00:00 mingetty
629 tty3 00:00:00 mingetty
630 tty4 00:00:00 mingetty
631 tty5 00:00:00 mingetty
632 tty6 00:00:00 mingetty
976 tty1 00:00:00 login
977 tty1 00:00:00 bash
1055 tty1 00:00:00 ps
```

To stop a certain process, use the kill command. To use this command, you need to know the PID number of the process that you want to terminate. For example, you can stop the sendmail process, which is PID 522, by issuing the following command:

```
kill 522
```

To ensure that the process has indeed ended, enter the ps -e command to examine the currently running processes, and to see if sendmail is still running.

Sometimes, a process won't stop even after receiving the kill command. If this happens, you will have to add an extra argument to force a kill signal to the process. To do this, use the following command:

```
kill -9 522
```

Signals are different types of commands that you can use with the kill command to change the state of a process. You can list the different types of signals that you can send by using the kill -1 command. The output is listed here:

```
1) SIGHUP 2) SIGINT 3) SIGQUIT 4) SIGILL
5) SIGTRAP 6) SIGIOT 7) SIGBUS 8) SIGFPE
9) SIGKILL 10) SIGUSR1 11) SIGSEGV 12) SIGUSR2
13) SIGPIPE 14) SIGALRM 15) SIGTERM 17) SIGCHLD
18) SIGCONT 19) SIGSTOP 20) SIGTSTP 21) SIGTTIN
22) SIGTTOU 23) SIGURG 24) SIGXCPU 25) SIGXFSZ
26) SIGVTALRM 27) SIGPROF 28) SIGWINCH 29) SIGIO
30) SIGPWR 31) SIGSYS
```

The most commonly used signals are 1 and 9, SIGHUP, and SIGKILL. Use the kill -9 command to force a kill to a process that won't stop after you've issued a conventional kill command. The signal HUP tells the process to restart. For example, if you need to restart your Sendmail program, which has a PID of 522, issue the following command:

```
kill -HUP 522
```

Use the killall command to kill multiple processes that use the same name. For example, an Apache Web server usually runs several httpd processes. In order to kill the process properly, you have to find which httpd process is the parent process. To make it easier, you can use the killall command to stop all of the httpd processes by using the following command:

```
killall httpd
```

The top command is another useful command for monitoring current processes. When you run this command, it shows all the current processes and their current resource usage in real time. The administrator can quickly see which program or process is taking up too much CPU time or memory space. Figure 13-1 shows the output of the top command.

```
  7:19am  up 17 min,   1 user,   load average: 0.01, 0.02, 0.04
37 processes: 36 sleeping, 1 running, 0 zombie, 0 stopped
CPU states:  0.1% user,  0.9% system,  0.0% nice, 98.8% idle
Mem:   127976K av,   81392K used,   46584K free,   12972K shrd,   48912K buff
Swap:  133016K av,       0K used,  133016K free                   21840K cached

  PID USER     PRI  NI  SIZE  RSS SHARE STAT  LIB %CPU %MEM   TIME COMMAND
  702 root      12   0   852  852   668 R       0  1.1  0.6   0:02 top
    1 root       0   0   476  476   404 S       0  0.0  0.3   0:07 init
    2 root       0   0     0    0     0 SW      0  0.0  0.0   0:00 kflushd
    3 root       0   0     0    0     0 SW      0  0.0  0.0   0:00 kupdate
    4 root       0   0     0    0     0 SW      0  0.0  0.0   0:00 kpiod
    5 root       0   0     0    0     0 SW      0  0.0  0.0   0:00 kswapd
    6 root     -20 -20     0    0     0 SW<     0  0.0  0.0   0:00 mdrecoveryd
  304 root       0   0   540  540   452 S       0  0.0  0.4   0:00 pump
  318 bin        0   0   420  420   332 S       0  0.0  0.3   0:00 portmap
  333 root       0   0     0    0     0 SW      0  0.0  0.0   0:00 lockd
  334 root       0   0     0    0     0 SW      0  0.0  0.0   0:00 rpciod
  343 root       0   0   560  560   472 S       0  0.0  0.4   0:00 rpc.statd
  357 root       0   0   480  480   412 S       0  0.0  0.3   0:00 apmd
  408 root       0   0   552  552   452 S       0  0.0  0.4   0:00 syslogd
  417 root       0   0   768  768   388 S       0  0.0  0.6   0:00 klogd
  431 nobody     0   0   628  628   520 S       0  0.0  0.4   0:00 identd
  439 nobody     0   0   628  628   520 S       0  0.0  0.4   0:00 identd
  440 nobody     0   0   628  628   520 S       0  0.0  0.4   0:00 identd
```

Figure 13-1: The output of the `top` command

Monitoring Log Files

Objective

5.8 Monitor system log files regularly for errors, logins, and unusual activity

Regularly monitoring log files is one of the most important tasks that a Linux system administrator can perform. Through this type of proactive maintenance, the administrator can take care of small problems before they become too serious. For example, a "low disk space" warning can give the administrator ample time to fix the problem before the file system becomes full. The administrator should check some logs on a daily basis, such as system and kernel logs. Other logs, such as boot messages or login information, can be examined with less frequency.

Linux log files are located in the /var/log directory. This directory contains several log files for both system functions and applications. The following list includes some of the more important logs that should be monitored on a regular basis.

✦ `/var/log/messages`: syslog is configured to write kernel and system errors in this log. This log should be checked daily for any warning messages.

✦ `/var/log/wtmp`: This log file keeps track of the time and date of user logins. This file can grow very quickly. The `last` command uses this log to show a list of users who have logged-in. This is helpful in tracking when certain users have logged in to the system at times that may indicate suspicious activity.

✦ `/var/log/dmesg`: This log file contains the results of your last system boot. It displays the various kernel messages that appeared on the monitor during the boot phase. This log file is helpful when debugging boot time problems.

Exam Tip   Know the different types of log files and what information they contain.

Because many of these log files can be very large, you may want to pipe it through the `more` command, or use `grep` to find only the keywords in the log file that you are looking for. For example, the following command searches the messages file for any reference to "mail:"

```
cat /var/log/messages | grep mail
```

Sometimes you may want to monitor a log file in real time in order to see the results of an application or process that you are testing. For this, you can use the `tail` command with the "follow" argument:

```
tail -f /var/log/messages
```

This command shows the messages file on the monitor screen. As entries are added to the log, they are immediately displayed.

Most log files are not set to roll over automatically, and you will find that these logs can grow very quickly, thus eating valuable disk space. Therefore, it's a good idea to use some sort of scheduling program, such as `cron`, to automate rolling over log files.

The easiest way to automate file rollover is to create a simple batch file that renames the current log file so that the system can start writing a new log file with the original name. Most administrators name the files by date, so they can easily track the files when looking for historical data.

Enter a log rotation into your `cron` schedule to run daily or weekly as required.

In the Real World   Unattended log files can quickly fill your disk file systems. Pay close attention to their sizes, or use the `cron` process to automate log retention.

Maintaining Documentation

Objective   5.9 Document work performed on a system

Linux system administrators often overlook the task of documenting their systems. This can be a major oversight, because without proper documentation, you won't have immediate access to the information that you need to restore a system in the event of a system crash or hardware failure.

You should keep accurate records of all the hardware and software on your system. Here are some of the more important items that you should be tracking:

✦ Hardware

- Vendor serial and model number

- Processor speed and type, and available multi-CPU slots

- Amount of RAM, including number of chips and empty slots

- Disk space and configuration, including any RAID or fault tolerance settings

- Network card type, configuration, and network address

- Peripheral cards, such as SCSI, and video

✦ Software

- Operating system version number, including kernel version and patches

- Versions of all other installed software

As part of your system documentation, you should also keep track of any hardware maintenance or software upgrades. You will greatly benefit from this information during troubleshooting, because you will always have an accurate record of what is currently running on the system, and what parts have been replaced or upgraded. This information is especially important when keeping track of kernel or software upgrades. By upgrading one component, you may create an incompatibility with another component. Only by keeping track of these changes can you go back to find which upgrade caused the problem.

You should routinely keep track of CPU, RAM, and disk usage so that you can proactively plan any resource upgrades that your system may need in the future. By plotting your usage trends, you can tell whether you need to order extra hard drives to correct any future disk space problems. Table 13-1 is an example of the type of information that you should be tracking.

Table 13-1 **Linux System Maintenance Log**		
Date	*Action Performed*	*Name*
May 13, 2001	Upgraded Apache Web Server to 1.3.2	J. Smith
June 22, 2001	Upgraded kernel to 2.4	T. Green
July 5, 2001	Upgraded Squid Proxy Server to 2.4	J. Smith
July 15, 2001	Replaced failed hard drive in RAID 5 array — bay 2	J. Smith

Summary

This chapter details many commands that you can use for process management. Commands like ps and kill have many different options that the Linux system administrator can utilize. The administrator should also regularly check the various system log files for errors, warnings, and information items that can help to proactively monitor the system. This chapter also emphasizes the importance of maintaining accurate hardware, software, and maintenance information. Here are some key points to remember from this chapter:

✦ ps: Lists current users' processes

✦ ps -e: Lists all processes

✦ ps -f: Uses full listing

✦ ps -u: Lists processes of a particular user

✦ kill: Terminates a process

✦ killall: Terminates several instances of the same process by name

✦ kill -9: Sends a kill signal if a conventional kill command does not work

✦ kill -HUP: Kills the process and restarts it

✦ top: Real-time list of all processes and resource usage

✦ System and kernel messages are written to /var/log/messages

✦   ✦   ✦

STUDY GUIDE

The Study Guide section provides you with the opportunity to test your knowledge about the Linux+ exam objectives that are covered in this chapter. The Assessment Questions provide practice for the real exam, and the Scenarios provide practice with real situations. If you get any questions wrong, use the answers to determine the part of the chapter that you should review before continuing.

Assessment Questions

1. An administrator wants to terminate the sendmail process on a Linux server. What is the best way to determine the PID of the sendmail process so it can be killed?

    A. pstree

    B. ps -ef | grep sendmail

    C. ps -u user1

    D. kill -9 sendmail

2. An administrator has tried to use the `kill` command to terminate a running process. Unfortunately, the command didn't work, and the administrator can still see the process when she uses the `ps` command to show running processes. What command should be used next to terminate the process?

    A. killall

    B. ps -k

    C. .top

    D. kill -9

3. When a Linux system boots, a kernel error message flashes across the screen, but it scrolls by before the user can determine the problem. What log file can be checked to examine boot time messages?

    A. /var/log/dmesg

    B. /var/log/messages

    C. /tmp/messages

    D. ./var/log/wtmp

4. What command can be used to send a running process to the background?

    A. `background`

    B. `fg`

    C. `bg`

    D. `#`

5. An administrator wants to kill all instances of the Web server process `httpd`. What command will most efficiently stop these processes?

    A. `killall httpd`

    B. `kill -9 httpd`

    C. `kill -SIGHUP httpd`

    D. `stop httpd`

6. What is the best command to use to show a full listing of all running processes?

    A. `top`

    B. `ps -ef`

    C. `ps -au user1`

    D. `ps -f`

7. A user has complained that his Web pages haven't displayed properly since the weekend. What should be checked first to troubleshoot the problem?

    A. Use `bg` to put the Web server process in the background

    B. Use `ps` to see if the Web server process is running

    C. Use the `top` program to examine the httpd process

    D. Check maintenance logs to see if the Web server was recently upgraded

8. An administrator needs to see what processes are being run by user jsmith. What is the correct command to use?

    A. `ps -ef`

    B. `kill jsmith`

    C. `ps -au jsmith`

    D. `top`

9. Which log file keeps track of all user logins and logouts?

    A. /var/log/dmesg

    B. /var/log/wtmp

    C. /var/log/last

    D. /var/messages

10. What is the first process that is run when a Linux system starts, and is responsible for starting all other system processes and services?

    A. cron

    B. syslogd

    C. getty

    D. init

11. A user wants to take her current process, which is running in the background, and move it to the foreground. What command will accomplish this task?

    A. fg

    B. [ctrl-z] bg

    C. [ctrl-c] bg

    D. kill

12. An administrator has accidentally killed a core process. What is the result of this action?

    A. The system could crash.

    B. Nothing, it won't harm the system.

    C. The parent of the process will terminate.

    D. The process will move into the background.

13. An administrator wants to monitor the /var/log/messages file in real-time to troubleshoot a problem. What is the best command to perform this function?

    A. fg /var/log/messages

    B. top /var/log/messages

    C. tail -f /var/log/messages

    D. head /var/log/messages

14. A Linux system that was running on a fault tolerant RAID array has crashed and needs to be rebuilt. How can the technician determine what level of RAID was being used on the hard drive system?

    A. By physically examining the hard drives

    B. Checking the /var/log/dmesg file

    C. Examining the RAID adapter card

    D. Checking the hardware documentation

15. When using the `ps` command to display processes, what number tells you the ID number of the parent process of a particular program?

    A. PID

    B. PPID

    C. TTY

    D. TIME

16. An administrator wants to terminate all instances of the sendmail process. What command would best perform this function?

    A. `killall sendmail`

    B. `kill sendmail`

    C. `kill -9 sendmail`

    D. `kill -9 522`

17. An administrator wants to kill a process and have it automatically restart. What kill signal should be sent to perform this function?

    A. SIGKILL

    B. SIGRESTART

    C. SIGHUP

    D. SIGTERM

18. While scanning the /var/log/messages file, an administrator notices an error stating an authentication failure for root. What could this mean?

    A. The administrator should not have access to the log file

    B. Someone has tampered with the log file

    C. Nothing, this is a common message

    D. Someone tried to break into the root account but failed

19. While using the `top` command, an administrator notices that an unidentified process is using up all CPU and memory. The administrator suspects that this is a programmer's process that has run away. What should be done to fix the problem?

    A. Nothing, the process will eventually terminate

    B. The process should be killed before the system crashes

    C. The user should be notified

    D. Add more memory to the server

20. What command can an administrator use to track real-time information on processes and the resources that they are using?

    A. `top`

    B. `ps -ef`

    C. `ps -aux | grep root`

    D. `fg`

Scenarios

1. A user has requested that the Apache Web server be restarted so that its configuration can be changed and enabled. What steps should be taken to ensure that all `httpd` services are restarted properly?

2. A programmer with username jsmith has told you that one of her processes seems to be locked up and can't be killed. The programmer is worried that a bug in the code may quickly use up all CPU and RAM resources on the server. What steps should be taken to track down the process and terminate it?

Lab Exercises

Lab 13-1 Process Management

The objective for this hands-on lab is to gain experience in using the `ps` and `kill` commands to manage processes. You should be able to use any default Linux installation for this exercise.

1. Logged in as a normal user, check your current running processes using just the `ps` command with no arguments.

2. Now, check all processes by using the `ps -e` command.

3. Get a full list of information, such as the PPID, by using the `ps -ef` command.

4. Switch to the root user by using the `su` command, and check your running processes by using the `ps` command. As you can see, the root user owns most of the processes.

5. Look for the entry for the `crond` process, and take note of its PID.

6. At your command prompt, type `kill -9 [PID of crond]`.

7. If you list all the processes again by using `ps -e`, you should see that crond is now no longer running.

8. To restart the crond process, at the command prompt, type `/etc/rc.d/init.d/crond start`.

9. To verify that it is running again, at the command prompt type `ps -ef | grep crond`.

Lab 13-2 Stopping and restarting jobs

The objective for this lab is to take a simple job process and practice stopping, starting, and sending the process between the foreground and background.

1. Logged in as a normal user, at the command prompt, type `yes`. This command runs the `yes` program, which simply displays the letter "y" repeatedly. This is useful for programs in which you want to answer "yes" to all questions that you are prompted for.

2. Press `[ctrl-c]` to stop the job.

3. Type `yes > /dev/null`.

   This runs the process, but points the output to a null device so that it won't appear on the monitor display.

4. At this point, you won't be able to get to your shell because the `yes` command is running in the foreground. Hit [ctrl-c] to stop the process.

5. Start the same program in the background by typing the command `yes > /dev/null &`.

6. After the program starts up again, it is running in the background so you can still use your shell prompt.

7. Return the program to the foreground by using the `fg` command.

8. Again, you have lost the shell, so return the program to the background by using `[ctrl-z]` to suspend the program, and then type `bg` to start the process again in the background.

Answers to Chapter Questions

Chapter Pre-test

1. The ps command is used to identify running processes. It can be used with many different arguments to modify the way the output is displayed.

2. The /var/log/wtmp file contains the user login information. It is used by the last command to show the last logged in users.

3. Keeping maintenance documentation allows you to keep track of any hardware and software changes on your system. This is helpful when you must troubleshoot a problem that may be related to recent upgrades.

4. The kill command is used to terminate a process.

5. A core process must always be running so that the Linux system can work properly. If these services are terminated, the entire system may crash. Non-critical processes are usually applications or services, such as a Web or FTP servers, that can be stopped or started without crashing the system.

6. The init process is the most important process in a Linux system. It is the parent of all other system processes; it runs at boot time to mount drives and starts critical system services.

7. A PID is a unique process identification number that is assigned to every process running in a Linux system.

8. The command used to send a process to the background is bg.

9. The main log that tracks kernel and system errors is /var/log/messages.

10. The command to see real-time information on running processes and their resources is the top command.

Assessment Questions

1. B. The ps -ef | grep sendmail command lists all processes with a full listing and pipes the results to grep, which only displays the sendmail process and its attributes. For review, see the "Process administration" section.

2. D. The kill -9 command sends the kill signal to the process to force it to terminate. For review, see the "Process Control" section.

3. A. The log file that contains kernel boot messages is /var/log/dmesg. For review, see the "Monitoring Log Files" section.

4. C. The bg command sends a running process to the background. This is helpful if you need to get back to your shell prompt. For review, see the "Process Control" section.

5. A. The correct command to kill all httpd processes is killall httpd. For review, see the "Process Control" section.

6. B. The best command to show a full listing of all running processes is `ps -ef`. For review, see the "Process administration" section.

7. D. Because the Web pages are working but not displaying properly, the maintenance logs should be checked to see if the server was upgraded over the weekend, thus causing the incompatibility. For review, see the "Maintaining Documentation" section.

8. C. The correct command is `ps -au jsmith`, which tells the `ps` command to display all processes owned by `jsmith`. For review, see the "Process administration" section.

9. B. The correct log file is /var/log/wtmp. You can output its data by using the `last` command. For review, see the "Monitoring Log Files" section.

10. D. The `init` process is the first process to be run. It is the parent process of all other Linux system processes, services, and daemons that are needed to run the system. For review, see the "Core services versus non-critical services" section.

11. A. The `fg` command immediately moves the program to the foreground. For review, see the "Process Control" section.

12. A. Killing a core process can potentially crash your system because many critical services rely on these core processes. For review, see the "Core services versus non-critical services" section.

13. C. The command `tail -f /var/log/messages` "follows" the log file and shows any new entries in real-time. For review, see the "Monitoring Log Files" section.

14. D. If the documentation has been kept up-to-date, it shows the RAID level that the hard drives were configured for. For review, see the "Maintaining Documentation" section.

15. B. PPID refers to the parent process identification number. For review, see the "PIDs, PPID" section.

16. A. The `killall sendmail` command terminates all instances of the sendmail process. For review, see the "Process Control" section.

17. C. The SIGHUP command is used to kill and restart a process. For review, see the "Process Control" section.

18. D. Any failed login attempts for root are logged into the /var/log/messages file. For review, see the "Monitoring Log Files" section.

19. B. The process should be immediately killed before it consumes so many resources that the server can't run properly, and therefore crash. For review, see the "Process Control" section.

20. A. The `top` command is used to monitor processes and resources in real-time. For review, see the "Process Control" section.

Scenarios

1. Your first step is to first determine what PID the parent `httpd` process is using. Because the Web server normally starts several `httpd` processes, you must use the `ps` command to determine which one is the parent:

```
ps -ef | grep httpd
```

The output is similar to the following:

```
root 853 1 8 10:58 ? 00:00:00 httpd
nobody 856 853 0 10:58 ? 00:00:00 httpd
nobody 857 853 0 10:58 ? 00:00:00 httpd
nobody 858 853 0 10:58 ? 00:00:00 httpd
nobody 859 853 0 10:58 ? 00:00:00 httpd
nobody 860 853 0 10:58 ? 00:00:00 httpd
nobody 861 853 0 10:58 ? 00:00:00 httpd
nobody 862 853 0 10:58 ? 00:00:00 httpd
nobody 863 853 0 10:58 ? 00:00:00 httpd
```

As you can see by the output, the first `httpd` process is the parent, as all other processes have a PPID of 853, which is the PID of parent process.

Next, you must kill the parent `httpd` process, and send it the SIGHUP signal so that it will reload its configuration file and restart the `httpd` services:

```
kill -HUP 853
```

If you enter another `ps -ef | grep httpd` command, you can verify that the services have been restarted because the start time will now reflect your current time.

2. You need to identify which process must be stopped. To narrow down the search, you can you use the `ps` command and search by user:

```
ps -au jsmith
```

After you have a list of his processes, you can then run the `top` program to compare the processes running, and verify which one is using the most resources.

After you have identified the problem process, you can use the `kill` command to terminate it. Because the user was unable to stop the process, you should probably force a kill signal to make sure that the process stops:

```
kill -9 [PID of process]
```

Now, to verify that it has stopped, run the `ps` command again on the user:

```
ps -au jsmith
```

Linux Security

EXAM OBJECTIVES

- ◆ 5.11 Perform and verify security best practices (e.g., passwords, physical environments)
- ◆ 5.12 Assess security risks (e.g., location, sensitive data, file system permissions, remove/disable unused accounts, audit system services/programs)
- ◆ 5.13 Set daemon and process permissions (e.g., SUID - SGID - Owner/groups)

CHAPTER PRE-TEST

1. Why should passwords be changed on a regular basis?
2. What is the purpose of setting an expiration date on a user account?
3. What security setting can let a user run a program as a root user?
4. What is an advantage of having system and user files on separate partitions?
5. Who should know the root passwords of a Linux system?
6. What is the purpose of file security audits?
7. What do the terms *SUID* and *GUID* mean?
8. What can protect a networked server from access by external networks?
9. Why must you be careful in choosing which user can run an application service or daemon?
10. Why are remote access programs, such as FTP and telnet, insecure?

✦ Answers to these questions can be found at the end of the chapter. ✦

Your company's data is under your protection. Security threats can come from almost anywhere—a disgruntled employee, a hacker, or a rival company. Network and system security is one of the greatest concerns facing the Linux system administrator.

Security threats arrive in many forms, such as physical theft of a system, a stolen password, or an attack from a remote network user in another country. These security threats can cost your company great amounts of money and time spent on recovering data or fixing a hacked system.

Implementing a proper security policy for your company—and having it backed by management—is integral to protecting your company's systems and data. This chapter deals with implementing these security policies within the physical environment, and with the users, the system administrators, and the company's data.

Securing the Environment

Objective

5.11 Perform and verify security best practices (e.g., passwords, physical environments)

5.12 Assess security risks (e.g., location, sensitive data, file system permissions, remove/disable unused accounts, audit system services/programs)

The physical security of your Linux system is one of the most overlooked areas in the creation of a secure environment. When planning the physical environment for your Linux system, you need to address some key issues in order to support your security policies.

Location

You don't want your system sitting out in the open, where it may be damaged, vandalized, stolen, or tampered with. The best place to store your server is in a proper server room or a closet that can be locked. In large environments, many servers are individually locked in cages or server racks, along with the keyboard, mouse, and monitor, to prevent unauthorized people from attempting to access the system.

The server room area should be consistently monitored, and the log files containing information about who has entered and exited the room should be periodically examined for any strange behavior.

The locking device for this cage or closet can be any type, but the traditional method of using keys can be a drawback. For example, if an employee with access to the room leaves the company, the locks must be re-keyed—just in case that employee has made copies of the originals before turning them in. Keys are also easily lost, and therefore, must be replaced often. A better method for securing your cage or closet is to use special keycode doors with a combination lock in place. This method, however, also suffers from some of the disadvantages of regular keys because the combination must be changed whenever an employee leaves the company. The most useful method for securing the cage or closet is magnetic swipe cards. With this method, each employee that needs access to the room has his or her own card. If an employee is terminated, that card is simply denied access to the area.

In smaller environments, you may not have room for a server room — or even a wiring closet. In order to ensure security in this case, make sure that the terminal is locked with a password so that no user passing by can access the system.

Environment

Your computer system is very susceptible to natural environmental issues, such as heat, fire, and flood. Your server location should be safe from any and all of these natural disasters. It should also be equipped with a proper air conditioning system, dehumidifier, and adequate ventilation to prevent overheating.

System Security

After you have secured your physical environment, you must take steps to secure your virtual environment. Although physical security is extremely important, unauthorized users can still access your system over the network or through a remote terminal. The following sections detail some general tips on keeping your internal system secure.

System/user files

You must ensure that your core system and application files are kept separate from your general user files and home directories. Most standard Linux installations already perform this partitioning scheme by setting up /home and the root / partition separately. Allowing only the system partitions to be accessed by the root user is an effective tool for security, and it is helpful in the event that the user directories run out of disk space because it won't affect the system partition.

Permissions

Even within the user directories, you must take care to set up appropriate access permissions for user and group directories. Consider the example of a payroll or human resources directory, which contains sensitive personal and salary information. Even though it is within the same /home directory, such as /home/HR, its file and directory permissions can be set up so that only certain users can read and modify its contents.

Each user should have his or her own separate directory within /home. Users should only have read and write permissions for their own individual directory. Also, if the user is part of any group, they should also have access to that directory. You can accomplish this by employing group permissions. For example, users jsmith and bjones are part of the Engineering group. You can create a separate group called *Engineering*, and give it read and write access to the /home/engineering directory. With this setup, each user has only the necessary access to reach his or her files. Users can't read or modify data for a directory or file that they don't have permission to access.

Log auditing

On a periodic basis, the Linux administrator should examine log files for any strange behavior or invalid login attempts. Multiple failed attempts, especially for the root user, should raise a warning flag that someone is trying to break into a user account.

Failed login attempts are logged in the file /var/log/secure. It is especially important that you check the file for failed attempts to reach the root user. The general system log file, /var/log/messages, also logs attempts (both successful and non-successful) for accessing the root account.

Backups

The security of your backup media is also a serious concern. The standard security method is to back up your media, and then remove it to an offsite storage facility to prevent damage from natural disasters, such as fire, flood, and theft.

Linux Security Best Practices

You can run a wide variety of applications and services from your Linux server. Each additional application or service that you install and run, however, creates a potential security hole. During the initial installation of your Linux system, install only the minimum amount of applications and services that you need, and add more as you need them. Some default Linux installations install many unnecessary services that create more security risks for your system.

The following sections highlight some "best practices" to use when running a Linux system, including specific configurations for applications and services that can potentially create a security risk.

Network security

After physical security, the most important aspect of Linux security is protecting the network. Although your system may be physically secure, a networked computer is open to unauthorized access at all times. This is because a user can access the system from any terminal or computer on the same network. If the system is connected to the Internet, it is instantly exposed to millions of people all over the world.

Firewall

The most popular method for protecting a networked computer from other networks is the use of a firewall. A firewall can be a stand-alone device or a special server configuration that stands between your system and the outside world. Using rule-based filtering, the firewall lets only authorized network traffic in and out of the system and network. A firewall enables you to set up your system so that only local users have access — effectively rendering the machine invisible to the outside world.

If your system is running as an FTP or Web server, you can set up the firewall to allow only those services and protocols to the server and to deny all others.

Linux has network packet filtering built right into the kernel. The utility to create firewall filter rules is called ipchains, but in newer versions of the kernel it has been renamed iptables.

System security

There are a variety of ways to increase security on your Linux system. They range from simple things such as user passwords and legal banners, to more advanced techniques such as encryption and system service management. Only by taking the time to go through your entire system and remove all the possible locations that an unauthorized user can use to gain access to your system will you be able to fully secure your system.

Package installations

Linux distributions typically come with hundreds of different application packages. One of the most common mistakes made by a new Linux system administrator is to install all distribution packages by default.

If you make this choice, you will have every application and service that you will ever need, but you are creating security holes by running so many different applications and services that you don't use. There are known security hole exploits for a large number of these programs, such as Apache web server and early versions of Secure Shell, and the more programs you install, the more you make yourself vulnerable to attack. Needlessly installing a default FTP or Web server package will immediately render your system insecure. Install only those packages that you will be using for your system. If you need more in the future, you can always install them from the CD-ROM.

In the Real World   Most Linux distributions are insecure if installed straight out of the box. You must take the time to properly secure the system after the initial installation by updating all software to the most current version, and by disabling any unused services.

Package updates

After you have installed only the packages that you need, the next task for increasing security is to update these programs to the latest version. The version that came with your distribution is already several months out of date. In that interim, many security holes have been exploited and patched. By obtaining the latest release, you are ensuring that you have all the most recent security patches for your application. The latest versions of your packages can be found either from your particular Linux distribution web page, or the home page of the program itself.

Legal banners

Every system should have some form of legal policy that displays when a user logs in to the system. This policy will give you some legal protection in the event that an unauthorized user breaks into the system. The message should briefly explain that any unauthorized access or usage is prohibited. If you want this message to display *before* a user logs in, you can enter the text into /etc/issue or /etc/issue.net. If you want the message to display *after* the user logs in, you can put it in /etc/motd, which stands for "Message of the Day."

Caution It's not a good idea to mention your company name in the login banner. This way, if an unauthorized user does get access to the system, they won't know whose system it is.

Root password

The most important password on your Linux system is the root password. Because the root user is the most powerful user on the system, you must take extreme care to ensure that only a very few people in your organization know the password. At the very most, only the system administrator, their designated backup, and a member of management should know the password.

Your root password should not be any common word, and should contain at least six to eight characters. The password should have both lower and uppercase letters and one or two numbers. This way, the password can't be easily guessed, and a brute force attack, which allows an unauthorized user to try password combinations rapidly in succession, won't be able to break the password.

You should always memorize the password. You should *never* write it down somewhere where someone else can find it. Never store your password on your hard drive or in e-mail. If your password is stored electronically, someone can easily find it by hacking your machine or e-mail.

The best solution for storing root and other administrative passwords is to write them down, seal them in an envelope, and keep them in a safe that can only be accessed by the system administrator or one or two key members of management. In the event that the passwords are forgotten, or if the administrator is fired, management or the new administrator can retrieve the passwords.

Password encryption

The password file for Linux is located in /etc/passwd. It contains a list of users, their passwords, which are shown in encrypted form, and various items of information that users can access. Unfortunately, the basic encryption is somewhat weak and a directed effort can reveal passwords — especially if common words are used. To compound this fact, the file is actually readable by all and is easy prey for unauthorized users. By enabling "shadow" passwords, the passwords are encrypted and stored in /etc/shadow, which is only accessible by the root user.

By enabling the more advanced MD5 encryption, you can encrypt passwords beyond the basic default Linux encryption, and you can use up to 256 characters.

Enabling both shadow and MD5 passwords is vital to the system's security. This option is usually selected by default at installation time, but can be changed whenever needed.

User account and password management

Enabling the user account and password are the first steps in the creation of a secure system. In fact, these two steps are considered the simplest form of protecting system resources and data from unauthorized users. Although securing your system with passwords is an effective security measure, without a proper user account and password policy, this system may quickly break down and offer an unauthorized user many access points to the system.

Many users tend to use very simple passwords — and most of the time — would rather not use any passwords at all. Users will create simple passwords, such as their names, birth dates, names of family and pets, and even their phone numbers. These types of passwords are easy to remember, but are also much easier for an unauthorized user to break into.

Setting a policy for your user's passwords will force them to use more complicated passwords that are not so easy to guess or to decipher through brute force. You can set several options in a password policy:

✦ **Minimum Length:** Your minimum password length should be set to at least six to eight characters long. Many hackers use a method of brute force, in which a password-hacking program attempts many combinations of passwords until the right one works. If the password is only three letters long, it won't take very long for a hacker to go through every combination. The longer the password, the harder it is to be cracked.

✦ **Password Types:** Many versions of Linux will warn a user if they choose a password that is too easy to guess, such as a dictionary word. Because Linux is case-sensitive, using a combination of uppercase and lowercase characters and numbers will greatly decrease the possibility of the password being guessed or cracked.

✦ **Password Attempts:** An administrator can set a specific number of times or chances that a user has to enter his or her user name and password incorrectly before the account disables. This device prevents brute force type of attacks, in which an unauthorized user attempts many combinations of passwords to find the one that works. Setting the number of attempts to between three and five is an acceptable range.

✦ **Password Rotation:** The longer a password remains the same, the more easily it can be guessed or cracked by an unauthorized user through brute force. By requiring your users to change their passwords after a certain time period, you can greatly increase security. Some high-security institutions require their users to change their passwords every week or month. Setting your rotation to three months is acceptable for general use.

✦ **Account Expiration:** Set expiration dates on accounts for employees that are temporary or contract. When their term of employment ends, their account is automatically expired, and they won't be able to log in to the system. This way, the administrator won't forget to disable the account when the person leaves, and outdated accounts won't clutter the system. When a full time employee leaves the company, you must disable his or her account immediately, including any type of remote access.

✦ **Account Auditing:** Periodically, you should audit your user accounts to ensure that you have no old and outdated accounts from past employees. Old and outdated accounts create a security risk, because even though former employees no longer work for the company, they still have access to the system.

Exam Tip   Know the different types of password and account policies that you can enable to enhance security.

Remote logins

Use `telnet` to remotely log in to a system. It is the most common form of remote login, but is very insecure because it uses plain text passwords, which can easily be logged and captured by a network packet sniffer. Other remote access programs include rsh, rlogin, and rexec, which allow you to log in remotely to a system and execute programs on that host. These other access programs are also security risks, which you should disable from a default installation by removing their respective configuration lines from `inetd.conf`.

An excellent replacement for `telnet` and other remote access programs is SSH or *secure shell*. It allows you to log in remotely to a system while encrypting the entire session. This encryption prevents any transmissions or passwords from being passed along the network as clear text.

inetd services

`inetd` is the main process daemon that controls many network services on your Linux system. `inetd` handles communications for a number of services by listening on their specific TCP/IP port numbers, and enabling the service when a request comes in.

Many Linux distributions install the services by default. They are configured through the `inetd` configuration file, which is `/etc/inetd.conf`. Typical entries in the inetd.conf file look like the following:

```
ftp stream tcp nowait root /usr/sbin/tcpd in.ftpd -l-a
telnet stream tcp nowait root /usr/sbin/tcpd in.telnetd
#
# Shell, login, exec, comsat and talk are BSD protocols.
#
shell stream tcp nowait root /usr/sbin/tcpd in.rshd
login stream tcp nowait root /usr/sbin/tcpd in.rlogind
#exec stream tcp nowait root /usr/sbin/tcpd in.rexecd
talk dgram udp wait nobody.tty /usr/sbin/tcpd in.talkd
ntalk dgram udp wait nobody.tty /usr/sbin/tcpd in.ntalkd
#dtalk stream tcp wait nobody.tty /usr/sbin/tcpd in.dtalkd
#
# Pop and imap mail services et al
#
#pop-2  stream tcp   nowait root  /usr/sbin/tcpd ipop2d
#pop-3  stream tcp   nowait root  /usr/sbin/tcpd ipop3d
#imap   stream tcp   nowait root  /usr/sbin/tcpd imapd
```

To disable a certain service, simply comment the specific line relating to that service out of the file by preceding the line with a # character. Disable any services that you aren't using because if you don't, you will leave many open ports on your system that may be exploited.

The following sections list several services that you should consider disabling if you are not using them.

Exam Tip   Know where and how to identify and disable unused services and daemons.

POP/IMAP/sendmail

If you aren't using your server for any type of mail service, you should disable these daemons and services. Remote servers use the POP and IMAP protocols to retrieve mail from a system, and the sendmail daemon acts as a mail relay agent. POP and IMAP send their passwords in clear text format, and can pose a security risk. You can disable these protocols by commenting their specific configuration lines in the `inetd.conf` file.

Outside users often abuse the sendmail service by relaying their mail through your server to somewhere else on the Internet. This abuse often takes the form of so-called "spam" mail, which sends unsolicited advertisements to hundreds of thousands of e-mail addresses. By using your server as a mail relay, the offending mail appears to come from your company. If you aren't using the mail service on your server, you should remove it. If this is a mail server, you can turn off the relay function so that it only relays mail from your authorized hosts. Information on how to stop sendmail from relaying unauthorized mail can be found at `www.sendmail.org/tips/relaying.html`.

`finger`

This command is used to find out information about a particular user or host. You should disable the `finger` service because it allows an outside user to gain valuable information about your system. Disable the service in the `inetd.conf` file, specifically the daemons `fingerd` and `cfingerd`.

`nmap`

`nmap` is a special utility that you can use to see what open ports you have on your system. Commonly called a *port scanner*, you can use it to determine what services you are currently enabling for the outside world. This tool is very useful because it lets you know exactly what services you are providing from your system. You can then decide which ones you want to keep, and then disable the others that aren't being used, which pose a security risk.

Securing a Web server

The most widely used Web server for Linux is the Apache Web server. It currently runs on approximately 60 percent of all Web servers on the Internet. Web server attacks have become increasingly common in the last few years, and hacking or disabling a Web site has become an everyday occurrence. To prevent this from happening, there are number of precautions that you can take to protect your web server.

Apache versions

You must ensure that you are using the most recent version of Apache. The most recent version, as of July 2001, is 1.3.20. You can always obtain the latest release of Apache from `www.apache.org`.

Modifying httpd.conf

The configuration file for Apache is usually located in `/usr/local/apache/conf/httpd.conf`, or in `/etc/httpd/conf/httpd.conf`. You can modify a number of settings to make your server more secure than the default installation.

User/Group

The httpd.conf configuration file contains a user and group directive, which tells the Apache Web server which server to use when running its service daemon. By default, these directives are set to nobody, which is a special user with only limited rights. You can set the user to anyone, but this poses a security risk. If you run the Web server as user root, malicious users may be able to gain root access to your machine via the Web server. If you need to switch it from the default, ensure that the user has only read and execute permissions for only your Web directories.

DocumentRoot

This directive sets the initial root directory for your Web pages. Ensure that this value is not a different directory. For example, if it is set to /etc, any user connecting to the Web server is able to see all the system configuration files.

Indexes

By removing the indexes directive, you can prevent users from seeing an index of a directory if they access a URL that doesn't point to a specific document.

CGI scripts

Some default installations of Apache come with a set of example CGI scripts. Delete these because some of these scripts contain known security holes.

Modules

Apache comes with a system of loadable modules for extra functionality, which you can add and remove as needed. Ensure that only the modules that you need are loaded, and remove all others. Having extra modules increases the complexity of your system, and thereby increases the number of possible security holes.

Securing an FTP server

Along with Web servers, FTP servers are one of the most popular applications that can be easily run from Linux. Unfortunately, many FTP server software configurations contain a number of security holes that can be easily compromised. There are a number of ways in which you can increase security for your FTP server — especially by utilizing the FTP configuration files to reduce the risk of being compromised.

FTP program version

Ensure that you are using the most recent version of your FTP server. The most recent release will always have updated security patches that have fixed previous holes in the system. Check the website of your particular Linux distribution, or the web page of the FTP program you are using for the most recent updates.

FTP configuration files

The FTP daemon uses several configuration files to control access to the FTP server. Adding and removing certain users from these files will greatly enhance the security on your system because you can ensure that only a select group of user accounts can get access. These files are located in the /etc directory.

ftpusers

This file contains a list of user names that are not allowed to log in to the FTP server (this file is usually blank by default). Copy all special accounts (such as root, bin, daemon, adm, lp, sync, shutdown, halt, mail, news, uucp, operator, games, gopher, ftp, nobody, lists, and xfs) so they can't access FTP services.

ftphosts

This file allows access to the FTP server from a selected set of hosts. They can be identified either by IP addresses or hostnames. The default file is blank, which allows any host to access the system. For example, if you want to give access to only machines from your own domain, add the following line to the ftphosts file:

```
allow * *.mycompany.com
```

You can also deny specific hosts by using the deny command within the configuration file:

```
deny * *.hackers.org
```

Anonymous users

Depending on your FTP server setup, you may not want anonymous users to have access, especially if the FTP files are for your company use only. Disable the anonymous account, which is usually the `ftp` user.

In the Real World The most vulnerable applications are any type of Internet application, such as Web and FTP servers. They are the most commonly hacked services, and therefore, you must give special attention to the security of these systems.

Process security

Objective 5.13 Set daemon and process permissions (e.g., SUID - SGID - Owner/groups)

Every process and daemon that is running on your system employs a user ID to create its permission base. Many important system services need to use the root user ID to perform their functions, which may involve killing and starting other processes. Other less important daemons employ user IDs with limited rights, such as nobody or daemon.

Any service or daemon running as a root user poses a security risk to your system. If that service can be interrupted or be directed to perform other activities not related to its function, it will do so as the root user. Effectively, this gives the unauthorized person control of the daemon root access to your machine.

Ensure that all services and daemons are using the most appropriate user ID for their function, and that they have the least amount of permission rights possible.

Set-user-ID permission (SUID) is a special permission that can be set on executable files. It allows any user that is executing the file to run that file as if they were the file's owner. The *Set-Group-ID permission* (GUID) performs the same function, but for groups.

The SUID and GUID permissions must be used carefully, because they are usually set on root-owned programs. Effectively, this means that the user is actually running as the root user when they run that executable. Most hacking attempts involve some attempt at overriding a SUID set executable by feeding it bogus scripts with out-of-range variables. Sometimes, this causes the process to stop, but allows you to exploit the root access. This is called a "buffer overflow" type of bug, and is one of the most common security holes in a system. Check any executable programs, applications, and services that may have this value set if it isn't necessary.

Summary

This chapter explains many of the basics of Linux system security, and discusses the best security practices. System security is directed at three main areas:

✦ Physical Environment Security

- Ensure that your system is stored in a locked, temperature-controlled room.

- Only those authorized to administer the server should be allowed into the area.

✦ Network Security

- Keep your network separated from the outside world by using a firewall.

- Filter the incoming network traffic to prevent unauthorized users and services from accessing local resources.

✦ System Security

- Create and maintain a proper user account and password policy.

- Keep system files and user files separated on different partitions.

- Enable file and directory permissions to give access to only the files that each user needs.

- Ensure that processes and daemons are using the least privileged accounts necessary for operation.

- Shutdown unnecessary services.

✦   ✦   ✦

STUDY GUIDE

The Study Guide section provides you with the opportunity to test your knowledge about Linux. The Assessment Questions will help you to understand the basics of Linux, and the Scenarios provide practice with real situations. If you get any questions incorrect, use the answers to determine the part of the chapter that you should review before continuing.

Assessment Questions

1. After the initial installation of a Linux system, what is the first action that you should take to enhance security on your system?

   A. Change the root password to be blank

   B. Update your kernel and packages

   C. Immediately back up the system

   D. Turn off the Web and FTP services

2. Which of the following is the *least* secure way to administer a Linux system remotely?

   A. telnet

   B. ssh

   C. root

   D. bash shell

3. A contract employee recently had her contract renewed with the company for another six months. What should the Linux administrator do to enhance security on the employee's account?

   A. Set a minimum password length of eight characters

   B. Disable the account

   C. Set the expiration date to six months from now

   D. Set permissions for the /home directory

4. Which of the following services should be disabled on a server that is acting as both a Web and FTP server?

    A. inetd

    B. http

    C. ftp

    D. finger

5. Where should backup tapes be stored to increase security and safety of the data?

    A. Administrator's briefcase

    B. Locked server room

    C. Offsite storage

    D. Locked file cabinet

6. Which of the following is a misconfiguration on an FTP server, thus creating a security risk?

    A. Username and password required

    B. FTP root directory set to /

    C. Anonymous logins disabled

    D. FTP server behind a firewall

7. A user is trying to set a new password for their account. They want to use the name of the company "ABC" as their password. Why won't the system allow this password?

    A. Minimum length is set to six characters

    B. Characters can't be in alphabetical order

    C. Can't use capital letters in a password

    D. Password is already in use by another user

8. An administrator wants to set the Web server so that it won't show a directory listing if a user requests a page that is a directory. Which modification should be set in httpd.conf?

    A. User

    B. ServerName

    C. Remove `indexes` from configuration file

    D. Document Root

9. What settings can you enable to ensure that the password file is encrypted and hidden?

   A. hide_passwd

   B. tar and zip

   C. Encrypted ssh

   D. shadow passwords

10. Which of the following services should be disabled on a machine that does not use or send e-mail?

    A. POP

    B. IMAP

    C. Sendmail

    D. All of the above

11. A Linux system has just been installed. The kernel and packages have been upgraded to the latest versions, and any unnecessary services and daemons have been turned off. What else should you do to enhance security on the system?

    A. Change the root password

    B. Set up a telnet session

    C. Audit your log files

    D. Turn off network card

12. While auditing user accounts, an administrator notices that one of the users has a blank password. What should he do to the account?

    A. Set an expiration date on the account

    B. Ask the user to change it at their convenience

    C. Disable the account, and set a temporary password for the user

    D. Set up shadow passwords

13. What is the most important security aspect of a server room?

    A. Fire extinguishers

    B. Proper humidity should be maintained

    C. It should have a good air conditioning system

    D. It should be secure and locked

14. A company has two system administrators, and one of them has just been terminated from their position. What is the first thing that the current administrator should do to enhance security?

    A. Change the employee's account password

    B. Set an expiration date on the employee's account

    C. Disable the employee's account

    D. Change the root password

15. A system administrator is setting up an FTP server. Only company employees are allowed to use the FTP services. What should be configured on the FTP server to enhance security?

    A. Disable anonymous logins

    B. Set DocumentRoot in httpd.conf

    C. Allow only encrypted sessions

    D. Create a legal banner that is shown when users log in

16. What permission setting allows a user to run an executable with the permissions of the owner of that file?

    A. Read

    B. SUID

    C. Write

    D. SSH

17. A company is concerned about the length of time that employees use their current passwords. What can the system administrator do to help enforce a new password policy?

    A. Expiration dates on accounts

    B. Maximum password length

    C. Set password rotation

    D. Set number of allowed login attempts

18. Which of the following is the *most* secure way of remotely connecting to a system?

    A. telnet

    B. ssh

    C. rlogin

    D. ftp

19. What password setting can allow encrypted passwords of up to 256 characters in length?

    A. md5

    B. ssh

    C. shadow

    D. rotation

20. What device or services can you use to protect a networked Linux system from other outside networks?

    A. inetd daemon

    B. Router

    C. Proxy server

    D. Firewall

Scenarios

1. A company wants to implement a proper password security policy for the users. In the past, the company has had problems with users using easily guessed passwords or even no password at all. Employees have left or have been terminated, yet are still able to use their accounts to access the system. What sort of policy should be set regarding the best security practices for user accounts and passwords?

2. A company's internal Web server was recently hacked into. The company has no network protection, and the Web server was improperly configured to allow access to the root file system. What changes can you make to ensure the security of this system?

Lab Exercises

Lab 14-1 Removing Unused Inetd Services

The objective for this hands-on lab is to gain experience in altering the inetd.conf file to turn the services that you require on and off. Turning off unused services is a good security practice. You should be able to use any default Linux installation for this exercise.

1. Try to telnet and FTP to the local machine:

```
ftp localhost
telnet localhost
```

You should be able to get a prompt for these services. Afterwards, turn these services off.

2. Logged in as root, switch to the /etc directory, and use any text editor — vi, for example — to edit the file inetd.conf

```
vi inetd.conf
```

3. The file contains listings of popular services. Turn off the FTP and telnet services because the server is not going to be an FTP server, and you should always use SSH to remotely administer the machine.

Look for these lines in the file:

```
ftp stream tcp nowait root /usr/sbin/tcpd in.ftpd -l-a
telnet stream tcp nowait root /usr/sbin/tcpd in.telnetd
```

4. To disable the services, simply comment them out of the file. Using the vi editor, add a "#" sign in front of these two statements so they look like the following:

```
#ftp stream tcp nowait root /usr/sbin/tcpd in.ftpd -l-a
#telnet stream tcp nowait root  /usr/sbin/tcpd in.telnetd
```

5. Restart the inetd daemon and reload the configuration file to enable the new settings:

```
killall -HUP inetd
```

6. Try to telnet and FTP to the system; it should tell you that the connection was refused because you have turned off the services.

```
ftp localhost
telnet localhost
```

Answers to Chapter Questions

Chapter Pre-test

1. The longer a password remains on an account, the easier it can be cracked or guessed through brute force methods.

2. If users are on a data-specific contract, you should set the expiration date for their last day to ensure they can't access the system when they are no longer employees.

3. You can set the SUID (Set-User-ID) permission to allow a user to run an application with the privileges of the owner of that file.

4. Creating separate partitions enhances security by keeping system files separate from user operations, where they won't be able to affect them.

5. Only the system administrators and one or two key members of management should know the root password.

6. By periodically auditing your filesystems, you can keep track of any odd behavior, such as repeated attempts at failed logins or file access. This should be a warning flag that an unauthorized user is attempting to access the system.

7. SUID and GUID stand for Set-User-ID and Set-Group-ID, respectively, which are permissions that can be set on executable files to allow users to run that file as if they were the file's owner.

8. A firewall can filter incoming network traffic so that only authorized network traffic can reach the local network.

9. If that application or daemon is using a root account, the service can be exploited, and an attacker may be able to gain root access through a vulnerability with that service.

10. Telnet and FTP use unencrypted clear text within their sessions, which can easily be picked up by unauthorized users using network analyzing devices.

Assessment Questions

1. B. By updating your kernel and package versions, you can ensure that you are using the latest versions that contain the most recent security updates. For review, see the "System Security" section.

2. A. Telnet is a very insecure method of remotely logging in to a Linux system, because the session is sent across the network with unencrypted text, and someone can easily use a network tool to find out the password. For review, see the "Remote logins" section.

3. C. Because the contract will run out in six months, the administrator should set the expiration date for their account at that time, so that if the employee leaves or does not have their contract renewed, the account will be automatically disabled. For review, see the "User account and password management" section.

4. D. The finger service should be disabled because a remote user can get important information about the system by using that command. The other services are essential for this system to function. For review, see the "inetd services" section.

5. C. The tapes should be sent to an offsite storage facility. This prevents the tapes from being destroyed during a natural disaster at the server site. It also prevents the tapes from being stolen. For review, see the "System Security" section.

6. B. When a user logs in to the server, they are immediately put into the root directory of the system, which gives the person a full view of the entire server. The FTP root directory should be in its own directory, away from any system critical files. For review, see the "Securing an FTP server" section.

7. A. To enhance password security, the minimum length should be set for at least six to eight characters. No rules exist for having ordered or capital letters; multiple users can duplicate a password. For review, see the "User account and password management" section.

8. C. By removing the "Options Indexes" directive from the configuration file, the server won't show directory listings if requested by a user. This is a security measure so that remote users can't scan the directory tree of the server looking for security holes. For review, see the "Securing a Web server" section.

9. D. By enabling shadow password, the /etc/passwd file is "shadowed" to /etc/shadow, where only the root user can access the file, and the file is encrypted. For review, see the "Password encryption" section.

10. D. All of these services should be disabled if the server is not being used for mail purposes. Leaving them running can increase the chance of a security vulnerability being exploited, and unauthorized use of sendmail relay. For review, see the "inetd services" section.

11. A. Your root password should be immediately changed from your initial installation to a more secure password. For review, see the "System Security" section.

12. C. To prevent further use of the account, which is an immediate security risk, disable it and set a temporary password for the user for the next time they login. For review, see the "User account and password management" section.

13. D. Environmental security is helpful, but the most important security aspect of a server room is its ability to be secured and locked from unauthorized users. For review, see the "Securing the Environment" section.

14. D. Because the system administrator knows the root password for the system, it should be changed immediately to prevent them from tampering with the system. For review, see the "System Security" section.

15. A. The anonymous FTP account should be disabled, so that only users with a username and password can access the system. For review, see the "Securing an FTP server" section.

16. B. The Set-User-ID is a special permission that can be set on executable files so that anyone running that application can do so with the equivalent permissions of the owner of that file. This is a dangerous permission because it can create security vulnerabilities when the file owner is a root login. For review, see the "Process security" section.

17. C. By enabling password rotation, the administrator can set up a time period for which the users must change their password; for example, every 90 days. For review, see the "User account and password management" section.

18. B. SSH (secure shell) is the most secure method of remotely connecting to a system because it encrypts the entire session. Traditional access methods such as telnet or FTP use clear text during their sessions, which can be easily intercepted by unauthorized users. For review, see the "Remote logins" section.

19. A. Encryption using md5 algorithms allows encrypted passwords of up to 256 characters in length. For review, see the "Password encryption" section.

20. D. A firewall is used to filter packets coming into a local network in order to protect internal systems from external networks, such as the Internet. For review, see the "Network security" section.

Scenarios

1. You can configure many different settings to enhance account and password security.

   - The minimum password length should be set to six to eight characters.

   - Password rotation should be set up so that users are required to change their passwords periodically. A good setting is between 90-180 days.

   - Expiration dates should be set on accounts for contract or temporary employees.

   - An account should be locked after a certain amount of failed login attempts. A good setting is three to five attempts.

2. Because the company's network has no network protection, the first item to set up is a firewall. This will filter incoming network packets, and only allow certain protocols and networks to access the system. It should be set up so that only users on the local network can access the machine.

   The original Web server was set up with the DocumentRoot setting set to the root filesystem. The Web documents should be in their own directory or partition, away from critical system files. Create a new directory called /home/httpd/docs, and set the DocumentRoot to this new location.

Backing Up Your Linux System

EXAM OBJECTIVES

+ 5.10 Perform and verify backups and restores

CHAPTER PRE-TEST

1. What do you use the `dump` command for?

2. Why should Linux system files be backed up?

3. What is the purpose of the `cpio` command?

4. Why should restores not be sent to the original location?

5. What is the importance of offsite storage?

6. How often should you back up critical user data?

7. What is the purpose of the `tar` command?

8. What backup method backs up all files that have been modified since the last full backup?

9. What is the purpose of the `restore` command?

10. What backup method backs up only files that have been modified since the last backup?

One of the Linux system administrator's most critical responsibilities is the backup and recovery of system and user data. Companies spend hundreds of thousands of dollars on their network infrastructure, yet they never take into account the amount of money that may be wasted due to lost data and downtime because of a deficient backup plan. The importance of having a proper backup system that is routinely monitored and tested can't be understated.

It's not enough just to back up your user data; critical Linux system files must also be backed up on a regular basis. In the event of system file corruption or disk failure, you will be able to quickly restore your system to its original state if you have regularly backed up system files.

You should also regularly test your restore procedures. Many companies only test their backup procedures and never test their restores. This is a big mistake because the only way you can verify that a backup system is working properly is to test the restore procedure.

This chapter deals with planning, executing, and routinely testing a backup and restore system.

Disaster Recovery Planning

In planning a system for backup and recovery, the Linux system administrator must analyze several factors:

✦ Types of backup data: What different types of data must be backed up, and what is their importance?

✦ Frequency and scheduling: When and how to backup data?

✦ Storage and media type: What types of storage units and media are available?

✦ Recovery options: Is this regular user data, or special proprietary database information?

✦ Media Storage: Should backup media be stored onsite or offsite? What extra safety precautions or facilities will be needed?

Types of data

Basically, two types of data must be backed up — user files and system files.

User files

Your Linux user files are typically stored in the /home partition or directory. Keep all user data in its own partition, so it won't affect critical system partitions. For example, your user directories will quickly use up disk space because they continuously add files, programs, data, and personal software. If the /home partition runs out of space, it won't affect any of the system drives. If your system runs out of disk space, it may create a condition in which the server can crash.

Keeping all user files in the /home partition also aids your backup strategy by having all your user files backed up in one location. This means you won't have to search all over your file systems for user files that need to be backed up, thus saving the administrator the task of creating lengthy backup scripts to accommodate all locations.

Some user data, however, may not be located in the /home partition; for example, special databases that all users can access. You must ensure that these are also backed up properly. Many databases store their information in a proprietary format that may involve special software or procedures to properly back up the data. For transactional databases, for example, you must back up both the database data and the transaction logs in order to recover from a disaster.

System files

Linux system files are critical programs and the data that they contain are necessary in order for the system to run properly. These critical programs include the core operating system, configuration files, and user-installed programs.

In the event of a severe system crash, you can install the base operating system by using the installation disks or CD-ROM. You can also reinstall patches and programs. However, some files can't be reinstalled in this manner, such as special configuration files, user mail, and log files. Back up these files because they can't be reinstalled by default.

Some of the major Linux system partitions and directories include:

- ✦ /etc: Configurations for your services, programs, and daemons reside here. This partition is critical when restoring a system to its previous state.

- ✦ /usr/local or /opt: Most user-installed files are kept in these partitions and directories.

- ✦ /var/spool/mail: User mail that has not been downloaded resides here.

- ✦ /var/log: This directory contains all your log files. It is a good idea to backup up your system log files on a frequent basis, as they contain information that can help you troubleshoot your system.

Frequency and Scheduling

After you know exactly what to back up, you must create a schedule to determine the frequency for performing backups. Certain data, such as Linux system files, change rarely and can be safely backed up once a week, or whenever an important configuration change takes place. User files that change very frequently should be backed up daily — at the very least. Some heavily used transactional database environments back up their data several times a day because of the large number of changes that happen within a short period of time.

Backup types

You can perform four main types of backups:

Full

In this type of backup, all files are backed up every night. This is the most simple and effective type of backup, but can be limited by the amount of data that you have. A full backup may be impractical if your file systems are very large, containing hundreds of gigabytes. Depending on the size and speed of your backup device, a full backup may involve many sets of backup media, and the process may take a very long time to complete. The advantage of a full backup is that you always have the most recent files backed up properly, which makes restores very easy and convenient to perform.

 Exam Tip Full backups should be performed prior to adding new applications or hardware, and prior to a change in server configuration.

Incremental

In this type of backup, all files that have changed since the previous backup are backed up. For example, a certain file is only updated on Wednesday mornings. Therefore, the next backup, which happens at 11:00 p.m., will backup that file. The following day, the file will not be modified, so it won't be saved during that night's backups. The advantages of using an incremental backup system is that you don't use as much tape because you aren't performing a full backup each night. Incremental backups also cut down the amount of time required to perform a nightly backup. One major disadvantage of an incremental backup system is lengthy restore times. If you need to restore a full set of files, you will need the last full backup and every incremental backup to restore them in order. Another disadvantage is that your backups will be spread across multiple media, making the restore process more complicated.

Differential

In the differential backup scheme, all files that have changed since the last full backup are backed up. For example, a certain file is only updated on Wednesdays. The backup that takes place at 11:00 p.m. will back up that file. On the Thursday night backup, the file is still backed up because it changed since the last full backup — even though the file did not change that day. The advantage of a differential backup is that to restore a full system, you only need the last full backup and the last differential backup. The downside of the differential scheme is that it uses much more disk media than an incremental backup.

Archive

In an archive backup, data from your file systems are backed up to a storage device, but the original files are then removed from the server. Use archive backups to permanently remove data that has not been used in a long time to a storage media, such as CD-ROM or tape. This frees up space on your file systems, and keeps your data directories clear of outdated files.

Backup rotation methods

After you have chosen backup types, you also need to organize your media to deal with these backups and to keep them for a certain period of time. Depending on the type of data, you may only want to keep it for one month, one year, or indefinitely.

You can choose from several existing backup media rotation methods, and you can always customize your own schedule, depending on the type and sensitivity of your data. Choose from the following:

Son

With this method, you perform a full backup, and then use the same tape for each subsequent backup. In other words, whatever has been backed up to tape is written over by the next backup operation. This format is not suitable for most environments, and does not offer much retention time for your files. It also causes the media to wear out much faster, which can cause corruption.

Father/Son

This method uses a full set of tapes, which are rotated every week. For example, suppose that you have five tapes representing Monday through Friday, and a sixth tape for Saturday. For the daily tapes, you perform an incremental or differential backup. For the Saturday tape, you perform a full backup. With this format, you can go back at least once a week to restore a file. In the event that you have to restore a full system, you only need the full backup, and up to five of the daily tapes. Although this scheme is better than the Son method, it still doesn't offer enough retention time for most environments.

Grandfather/Father/Son

This is the most popular method of backup operations. Similar to the Father/Son method, this method's cycle is an entire month, and allows for daily, incremental, or differential backups, with four weekly backups and one monthly backup. This method gives you a very large retention window for data because your weekly tapes are kept for up to a month, and your monthly tapes are kept for up to a year. You can also extend this time with a yearly tape at the end of the year. Although this method uses the greatest amount of backup media, it's a worthwhile expenditure because you receive excellent data protection and retention.

Storage and media types

When you think of backups, the most typical type of storage media that probably comes to mind is the tape drive. Although the tape drive is still the backbone of most backup strategies, you can use other devices for backup purposes. Your choice for storage device and media will ultimately depend on the number of servers and size of your data backup requirements:

✦ **Floppy Disk:** Good for making copies of your configuration files, such as /etc directory, because the size is very small and the disk can only hold 1.44MB. Not suitable for regular backups of your data.

✦ **Magnetic Cartridge:** This type of magnetic media can hold from 100MB to 2GB of information on one cartridge. This is a good size media for use with small partitions, but not very useful in a larger environment.

✦ **CD-ROM:** Can hold up to 600MB of information. Most often, CDs are used to archive data because of their durability and portability. For regular backups, however, CD-ROMs aren't recommended.

✦ **Disk:** This type simply copies your data to a different location (preferably another machine). Usually, the files are combined and compressed into an archive for easy retrieval. Disk backups, however, are susceptible to disk failures — just like regular data. Therefore, they are usually used in conjunction with tape backups. Disk backups can also take an enormous amount of space.

✦ **Tape:** The most popular type of backup system. Tape drives come in a variety of sizes and media capacities. Magnetic tapes are reliable, can store a large amount of information, and can easily be transported to another location for protection in offsite storage. However, the drives must be constantly maintained through regular cleanings to remove buildup on the tape heads and to prevent tapes from being damaged.

Exam Tip   Know the different types of backup methods, rotation schemes, and devices that can be used for backing up different types of files and systems.

Recovering data

Administrators commonly restore files from backup because users regularly delete files, and because files become corrupt or accidentally overridden. The most difficult task in restoring files is finding the media that holds the correct files. If the file was deleted, the administrator simply returns to the last backup before the deletion took place. If the file is corrupted, the administrator may have to search for a version of the file that doesn't appear to be corrupted. When restoring files from your backup media to your system, keep in mind some general rules:

✦ **Never overwrite the original.** If it still exists, never overwrite the original file with the restored file. If the owner has already added some work to that file, you may be deleting data that can't be recovered. Always create a separate directory called "restore," and restore the files to that directory. This way, users can compare the files and replace their data as needed.

✦ **Restore incremental and differential backups after a full backup.** In the event that you are restoring a full file system, always restore your last full backup first, and then restore any necessary incremental or differential back-ups after that. If you restore your full backup after the incremental or differential backups, it may overwrite any newer versions of the files that you just restored.

✦ **Always test your restore procedure.** Companies spend much time and money formalizing a backup process without ever properly testing restores. Testing a backup is pointless unless you also test a restore from that backup. Problems with the backup device or media may render the backup useless, even if it appears that the backup process worked.

Offsite storage

Offsite storage involves transporting your most current backup media to a safe, off-site location. A reputable records management company can perform this service for you; many of these companies specialize in the storage of magnetic backup media. Offsite storage of your backup media will protect your valuable data in the event of a physical disaster at your current site. Only the system administrator and key management personnel who might need access to the data should have security access to retrieve and send tapes offsite.

Realistically, you should send your most recent full backup of all systems and any archived data to your offsite location. Make two copies of your full backups — one to keep onsite for availability of restores, and one to keep offsite for protection from disaster.

Don't send your only copy of a full backup offsite. If the tapes are lost in transit or at the offsite storage facility, you have nothing to fall back on. This is rare, but it can happen, so protect yourself by making duplicate copies.

Linux Backup Tools and Commands

5.10 Perform and verify backups and restores

To back up your system, you can utilize several tools and commands to perform the necessary tasks.

Third party tools

The best way to properly back up your system is to use third-party software to schedule backups and perform restores. These types of specialized software make the process of scheduling and performing backups much simpler than using basic command line tools. They also ease tape administration by allowing you to assign tape and volume labels, and support bar-coded labels as well.

A simple point-and-click interface simplifies the process of file restoration because you can search down your directory trees and tape histories to find the exact file that you need. Third party backup programs also offer extensive reporting and management features that let you easily customize reports from backup logs in order to focus on the information that you need the most.

If you are performing simple file system dumps, you probably don't need extensive backup software. If you are in an enterprise environment, however, you may need to back up several different systems, such as Linux, Unix, NT, and Netware, and third party tools give you a central, common interface to do so. The disadvantage of using third party tools is that they usually back up files by using a proprietary database. If you try to restore files by using a different program or command line tool, it may not work.

 If you change the program that you use to back up files, you should retain the older version for at least one year — just in case a restore is needed of a file that was backed up by using the older system.

Most third party solutions also come with modules for specialized backup needs, such as databases or mail servers, which need different backup configurations than regular user files. Modules are also available to take care of open files during a backup. For example, if some users have left their computers on with files still open, the backup system can't back them up. These specialized modules allow the files to be backed up, even if they are open.

The following are some of the most popular programs available for backing up Linux systems:

✦ Arcserve for Linux: `www.ca.com/arcserve/arcserve_linux.htm`

✦ Legato NetWorker for Linux: `www.legato.com/products/protection/networker`

✦ Veritas NetBackup for Linux: `www.veritas.com/us/products/netbackup`

✦ Merlin PerfectBackUP+: `www.merlinsoftech.com/products/backup.htm`

Tape devices

In order to back up data, you need a device to send the data to, which can be another disk, a floppy, or a tape drive. Copying to another disk is a simple matter because you only need to refer to it by its pathname, such as /mnt/backup.

For other devices, such as tape and floppy, all devices in Linux are defined in the /dev directory. For example, the first SCSI tape drive is referred to as /dev/st0. The device name /dev/nst0 means that the tape is non-rewinding, so for each backup, it won't overwrite the previous session. Table 15-1 shows an example of the device names that may be used for tape backup.

	Table 15-1	
Linux Backup Devices		
Device	**Device Name**	
First SCSI Tape Drive	/dev/st0	
First "No-Rewind" SCSI Tape Drive	/dev/nst0	
Second SCSI Tape Drive	/dev/st1	
First ATAPI Tape Drive	/dev/ht0	
First "No-Rewind" ATAPI Tape Drive	/dev/nht0	
Second ATAPI Tape Drive	/dev/ht1	
Floppy Drive	/dev/fd0	

Commands

The following command examples utilize a default device of /dev/tape to avoid confusion.

Tape device commands

The tape device must be mounted before it can be used by any other backup command or tool. Technically, you are not mounting the tape drive as a file system; rather, you are using the mount command to direct the tape drive to fast-forward or rewind the tape to the proper position. The following commands work on the first tape device, but if you need to specify the device, use the -f option (for example, `mt -f /dev/tape status`).

- ✦ `mt status`: Tells status of tape drive
- ✦ `mt fsf 2`: Fast-forwards the specified number of files on the tape
- ✦ `mt asf 2`: Fast-forwards to the specified file number
- ✦ `mt rewind`: Rewinds the tape to the beginning

tar

The `tar` command, short for *tape archive*, is one of the oldest Unix commands for creating archive files for storage on magnetic tape. The `tar` command isn't limited for use on tape devices; it is commonly used to create any type of file archive and to save it to any type of device.

Caution   The `tar` command does not compress data; it only creates file archives. For backup use, you should use the hardware compression that's built into your storage unit. If you want to compress files with `tar`, you can use it in conjunction with the `compress` or `gzip` commands.

The format of the `tar` command is:

```
tar [options] (file1) (file2) ...
```

You can use several options and arguments with the `tar` command:

- ✦ c: Tells tar to create a new archive file
- ✦ v: Verbose mode; this will print each filename as it is archived
- ✦ f: Lets you specify a filename for the archive
- ✦ x: Tells tar to extract files from an archive
- ✦ p: Tells tar to keep permissions on files when extracted from an archive

To back up the entire /home directory to a tape device, use the following command:

```
tar -cvf /dev/tape /home
```

To extract the same file into the current directory, use the following command:

```
tar -xvfp /dev/tape
```

To see the contents of a tar archive on tape, use the following command:

```
tar -tvf /dev/tape
```

To restore a single file from tape, use the following command:

```
tar -xvfp /dev/tape /home/file
```

Exam Tip   Know how to create and extract from a `tar` archive file on tape.

cpio

The `cpio` command, which means "copy in, copy out," is similar to the `tar` command in that it is used for copying files in and out of archives, including `tar` and its own binary format. The `cpio` command has three operating modes:

- ✦ **Copy-in mode:** `cpio` copies files out of an archive or lists the archive contents. Only files in the archive whose names match one or more of those patterns are copied from the archive. If no patterns are given, all files are extracted.

- ✦ **Copy-out mode:** `cpio` copies files into an archive. It reads a list of filenames, one per line, on the standard input and writes the archive onto the standard output. Typically, use the `find` command to generate the list of filenames.

- ✦ **Copy-pass mode:** `cpio` copies files from one directory tree to another, combining the copy-out and copy-in steps without actually using an archive. It reads the list of files to copy from the standard input. The directory into which it will copy them is given as a non-option argument.

These are some command options that are often used when using the `cpio` command:

- ✦ i: Copy-in mode, extract
- ✦ o: Copy-out mode, create
- ✦ t: Lists the contents of the input
- ✦ p: Copy-pass mode
- ✦ d: Create directories as required

To use the `cpio` command to list the contents of the archive, use the following command:

```
cpio -it < [archivefile]
```

To extract files from an archive, such as an entire /home directory, use the following command:

```
cpio -id "/home" < [archivefile]
```

Most often, the `cpio` command is used in conjunction with the `find` command to more precisely find the files that are needed in an archive:

```
find /home -print | cpio -p /dev/tape
```

dump and restore

Use the `dump` command to dump entire Linux file systems to the output device of your choice, which can be a disk file or a tape device.

Here are some of the command options that can be used with the `dump` command:

- ✦ [0-9]: This option sets the dump level for the current operation. A dump level of 0 indicates a full backup. Any level higher than 0 indicates an incremental backup, so `dump` copies all new or modified files since the last dump of the same or lower level.
- ✦ f: This option indicates the file or device that the command is writing to.

To dump the entire /home partition to a tape device, use the following command:

```
dump -f /dev/tape -0 /home
```

Use the `restore` command to restore files that were backed up by using the `dump` command. The `dump` command saves the directory structure of the files that were backed up, so when you invoke the `restore` command, you can navigate up and down the directory tree to choose the files to restore.

You must properly mount the tape, and fast-forward or rewind it to the archive that contains the file that you want to restore.

When you type the `restore` command, you receive a prompt similar to the following:

```
restore>
```

Type ? for a list of commands; the most used commands are `add` and `extract`. You can also use `cd` and `ls` to find the files that you want. Then use the following command:

```
restore> add filename
```

Continue to `add` all the files that you want to restore, and then use the following command:

```
restore> extract
```

This command will then restore the files into your current directory, so before invoking the `restore` command, you should navigate to the directory where you want to place the recovered files.

Exam Tip   Be aware of all the command line tools that can be used for backup and file restoration.

Summary

This chapter details the topic of backing up your Linux system. I also discuss several backup methods, along with their advantages and disadvantages. This chapter explains specific commands that are used to backup and restore files from a command prompt, supported by examples, while an overview of third-party backup applications gave you a look at what high-end programs can accomplish for your backup strategy.

For the exam, remember these key points from this chapter:

✦ Backup Types:

• Full: Full backup of all data

• Incremental: Backs up all files that have changed since last backup

• Differential: Backs up all files that have changed since last full backup

• Archive: Backs up files and removes them from the filesystem

✦ Backup Methods: Grandfather/Father/Son method is the most popular and most useful tape rotation scheme, utilizing daily, weekly, and monthly tapes to achieve a thorough backup strategy with excellent data retention.

✦ Command Line tools:

- tar
- cpio
- dump
- restore

✦   ✦   ✦

STUDY GUIDE

The Study Guide section provides you with the opportunity to test your knowledge about the Linux+ exam objectives that are covered in this chapter. The Assessment Questions provide practice for the real exam, and the Scenarios provide practice with real situations. If you get any questions wrong, use the answers to determine the part of the chapter that you should review before continuing.

Assessment Questions

1. During a recent basement flood, several archive tapes of the system were damaged and ruined. What can be done with these tapes in the future to prevent physical damage?

    A. Offsite storage

    B. Keeping the tapes in a safe

    C. Storing tapes at the administrator's home

    D. Grandfather/Father/Son rotation

2. A Linux FTP server was hacked into over the weekend. Due to the amount of damage, the entire server needs to be restored. How should the administrator restore the original kernel system files?

    A. Restore from floppy disk

    B. Restore from tape

    C. Reinstall the OS

    D. Restore from offsite archive

3. What type of backup strategy only backs up files that have changed since the last full backup?

    A. Incremental

    B. Full

    C. Offsite

    D. Differential

4. Approximately how many tapes will be needed to implement the Grandfather/ Father/Son method, when the administrator wants to use five daily tapes a week, four weekly tapes a month, a monthly tape, and a yearly backup?

   A. 64

   B. 22

   C. 8

   D. 120

5. What type of tape media solution should be used to fully back up a 20GB database every night?

   A. Disk

   B. Floppy Disk

   C. Tape

   D. CD-ROM

6. What command should be used to rewind a tape from the command line?

   A. `mt back 0`

   B. `mt status`

   C. `mt asf`

   D. `mt rewind`

7. What is the best backup media solution for an administrator who only wants to backup the /etc directory to save the system configuration files?

   A. Floppy Disk

   B. Tape

   C. Offsite storage

   D. `tar` archive

8. An administrator needs a backup solution that will offer extensive reporting and management features. Which backup solution would be the most useful?

   A. `dump` and `restore`

   B. third party backup software

   C. `tar` archive

   D. offsite storage

9. What command can you use to make a tape archive file of a /home directory, and send it to the /dev/tape device?

   A. `archive /home /dev/tape`

   B. `tar -xvf /dev/tape /home`

C. `archive /home`

D. `tar -cvf /dev/tape /home`

10. Which backup strategy backs up all files that have changed since the last backup?

    A. Archive

    B. Differential

    C. Incremental

    D Full

11. What command should be used to make a `tar` archive to a disk file system located in /mnt/backup?

    A. `tar -cvf /mnt/backup`

    B. `dump /mnt/backup`

    C. `restore -cvf /mnt/backup`

    D. `cpio - /mnt/backup`

12. An administrator must restore files from a backup that was performed three months ago using an older third party solution. The administrator is currently using a different type of program for backups. Will the restore work?

    A. No, because the administrator should have used `tar`

    B. Yes, the restore will work fine

    C. Yes, but the administrator will have to use `dump` and `restore`

    D. No, the original program will be needed

13. A file is unable to be restored from tape due to several device and media errors. What is most likely the cause?

    A. The tape is damaged

    B. The tape is not properly mounted by the system

    C. The tape needs to be rewound

    D. The file is not a `tar` archive

14. To save disk space, an administrator wants to backup files, and then remove them from the server permanently. What kind of backup operation is this?

    A. Full

    B. Differential

    C. Incremental

    D. Archive

15. What command can you use to back up an entire file system most efficiently?

    A. `archive`

    B. `dump`

    C. `tar`

    D. `cpio`

16. What is the location of important Linux system configuration files that should be backed up on a regular basis?

    A. /usr/local

    B. /var/log

    C. /etc

    D. /home

17. What type of backup strategy can you use to fully back up a system every night?

    A. Incremental

    B. Differential

    C. Full

    D. Archive

18. What command can you use to scan an archive for a particular file (file.txt), and print the output to the screen?

    A. `grep /dev/tape "file.txt"`

    B. `find file.txt -print | cpio -p /dev/tape`

    C. `dump /dev/tape > file.txt`

    D. `restore -p /dev/tape file.txt`

19. What command is the opposite of the `dump` command and used for file restores?

    A. `extract`

    B. `cpio`

    C. `archive`

    D. `restore`

20. What is the device name of the first SCSI tape drive?

    A. /dev/nst1

    B. /dev/st1

    C. /dev/st0

    D. /dev/ht0

Scenarios

1. A company wants to implement a new backup plan for their enterprise network. They have several large database servers that need to be backed up nightly, and they need to receive extensive reports on the backup logs and messages. The data needs to be retained for at least two years. What backup system would you recommend for this company?

2. A user's home directory, /home/jsmith needs to be restored from tape. The files were backed up using the dump command, which backs up the entire /home directory every night. It is always the first file archive on the tape, and the tape can be accessed using the device /dev/tape. What commands would you use to restore the file?

Lab Exercises

Lab 15-1 Dump and Restore files

The objective for this hands-on lab is to gain experience in using the dump and restore commands to back up and extract files. You should be able to use any default Linux installation for this exercise.

1. Logged in as root, change to your home directory of /home/root, and create a test file by using this command:

```
ls -al > file.txt
```

This will take a directory listing, and print the output to a file called file.txt.

2. Logged in as root, use the dump command to dump the entire /home directory to tape. Use the zero level argument to indicate a full backup.

```
dump -f /dev/tape -0 /home
```

3. Delete the file you just created after the backup is complete.

```
rm file.txt
```

4. Rewind the tape to the beginning, and mount it to the first file archive dump that you just created:

```
mt rewind
mt -f /dev/tape asf 0
```

5. After the command finishes, you can invoke the restore command to begin the restore process.

```
restore
```

6. Use the cd command to go down to the location of your file in /home/root:

```
restore> cd /home/root
```

7. Add the file to your list of files to extract from the archive:

```
restore> add file.txt
```

8. Begin the restore process by using the extract command from the restore prompt:

```
restore> extract
```

9. After the operation completes, exit the restore process, and check to see if your file has been restored:

```
ls /home/root
```

Answers to Chapter Questions

Chapter Pre-test

1. The dump command is used to back up entire file systems and directories.

2. In case the system has crashed and needs to be restored, you will have copies of your original configuration files.

3. The cpio command is used to copy files in and out of an archive file.

4. You may overwrite the original file that has new data in it.

5. Offsite storage will protect your tape data in the event your location suffers a natural disaster, such as a fire or flood.

6. Critical user data should be backed up at least once a day. If the data is from a high-volume transactional database system, it should be backed up several times a day.

7. The tar command can create a tape archive file, which can combine several files and directories into one archive file.

8. The differential backup method backs up all files since the last full backup.

9. The restore command is used to restore files that were backed up using the dump command.

10. The incremental backup method backs up files that have changed since the last backup, which may have been a full, differential, or incremental backup.

Assessment Questions

1. A. By sending the tapes offsite, you protect them from physical damage that may occur if a natural disaster strikes the office building. For review, see the "Offsite storage" section.

2. C. The entire operating system can't be restored from tape. It is best to reinstall the core operating system, and then restore system configuration files and user data from tape. For review, see the "System files" section.

3. D. A differential backup will backup files that have changed since the last full backup. In an incremental scheme, files will be backed up that have changed since the last incremental backup. For review, see the "Backup types" section.

4. B. The administrator will need five tapes for the daily backups, four tapes for the weekly backups, twelve tapes for each of the monthly backups, and one tape for the end-of-the-year backup. For review, see the "Backup rotation methods" section.

5. C. A tape drive has the capacity for these requirements. Backing up to disk will use up too much space, and a CD-ROM and floppy are not nearly big enough to hold that amount of data. For review, see the "Storage and media types" section.

6. D. The command to rewind a tape from the command line is `mt rewind`. For review, see the "Tape devices" section.

7. A. Because the /etc is fairly small, it can easily fit on a floppy disk. For review, see the "System files" section.

8. B. Third party backup software offers these types of advanced features for users who need excellent reporting and management capabilities. For review, see the "Linux Backup Tools and Commands" section.

9. D. The correct command is `tar -cvf /dev/tape /home`. The -xvf option is used to extract files from an archive. For review, see the "Commands " section.

10. C. An incremental backup will only back up files that have changed since the last backup. A differential backup will back up all files that have changed since the last full backup. For review, see the "Backup types" section.

11. A. The correct command is `tar -cvf /mnt/backup`. The /mnt/backup directory should be on another machine to be fully effective as a backup strategy. For review, see the "Commands" section.

12. D. Because third party backup programs use proprietary formats for backups, you need the same program to perform a restore. For review, see the "Third party tools" section.

13. A. Media errors usually indicate that the tape media is damaged, or that the tape drive heads need cleaning. For review, see the "Storage and media types" section.

14. D. An archive operation will take the files, back them up to a device, and then remove the files from the original server. This helps save disk space that's taken up by outdated files that can be moved offsite. For review, see the "Backup types" section.

15. B. The easiest command to use to back up an entire file system is the `dump` command. Files can be restored from a `dump` operation by using the `restore` command. For review, see the "Commands" section.

16. C. The /etc directory contains most of the Linux system configuration files. Just using a floppy drive can easily back it up, but you can use any backup media. For review, see the "System files" section.

17. C. A full backup strategy will always perform a full backup of all files. This takes much more time and space than other methods, but is it the most

complete method and allows for easy file restoration. For review, see the "Backup Types" section.

18. B. The `find file.txt -print | cpio -p /dev/tape` command will find the file file.txt within the tape archive, and print the output to the screen. For review, see the "Commands" section.

19. D. The `restore` command will restore files that have been backed up using the `dump` command. For review, see the "Commands" section.

20. C. The device name of the first SCSI tape drive is /dev/st0. The drives are numbered starting from zero. The drive type /dev/nst1 means that the tape drive is the second SCSI drive, and it is non-rewinding. For review, see the "Tape devices" section.

Scenarios

1. Because these databases consume a large amount of space, you will definitely use a tape backup method, which can handle large size backups quickly and efficiently.

   Since the data needs to be retained for a long period of time, the best backup method to use is the Grandfather/Father/Son method, which implements both weekly and monthly backups. A yearly backup can also be enabled at the end of the year.

   For backup software, you need a third party solution to offer the reporting and management tools that they need. Using command line backup tools, such as `tar` and `dump`, don't give the functionality to create extensive reports on backup logs.

2. Because the dump command was used to back up the files, you must use the restore command to extract them. Find the right file on tape before invoking the command. Since it is the first file, you can mount the tape, and forward it to the first archive:

   ```
   mt -f /dev/tape asf 0
   ```

   This command chooses the first file on the tape because they are numbered beginning with zero. Then, invoke the restore command:

   ```
   restore
   ```

   At the restore prompt, you can simply use the `cd` command to change directory to the /home/ directory:

   ```
   restore> cd /home
   ```

   Now you can `add` the jsmith directory to the list that you want to extract, and then invoke the `extract` command.

   ```
   restore> add jsmith
   restore> extract
   ```

Troubleshooting and Maintaining System Hardware

As an administrator, one of your main responsibilities on the job will be troubleshooting. The chapters in this part provide you with an overall troubleshooting procedure that you can apply to most situations. The first step in this process is to determine what the specific problem is.

Many tools and utilities are available to help you solve the problem — after you know what it is — and you will need to know how to use them. I explain how to use troubleshooting resources, such as existing documentation and vendor resources, to examine configuration files based on symptoms of a problem to help resolve the issue. This part also explores how to recognize common errors (for example, package dependencies, library errors, version conflicts), and how to identify backup and restore errors. You will also learn how to take appropriate action on boot errors and use network utilities to identify network and connectivity problems.

This part also explores basic knowledge and skills of core and peripheral hardware installation, configuration, and trouble-shooting in a Linux environment, focusing on both generic hardware issues and Linux-specific hardware issues.

The end of this part will teach you how to identify basic terms, concepts, and functions of system components, including how each component should work during normal operation and during the boot process; configuring IRQs, BIOS, DMA, SCSI settings and cabling; and removing and replacing hardware accessories. You will also learn to identify basic networking concepts, procedures for diagnosing and trouble-shooting ATA, SCSI, peripheral devices, and supported hardware. Finally, you will learn to troubleshoot core system hardware, and to identify and maintain mobile system hardware, such as PCMCIA and APM.

Linux Troubleshooting Basics

EXAM OBJECTIVES

+ 6.1 Identify and locate the problem by determining whether the problem is hardware, operating system, application software, configuration, or the user

+ 6.2 Describe troubleshooting best practices (i.e., methodology)

+ 6.3 Examine and edit configuration files based on symptoms of a problem using system utilities

+ 6.4 Examine, start, and stop processes based on the signs and symptoms of a problem

+ 6.7 Inspect and determine cause of errors from system log files

+ 6.14 Identify and use trouble shooting commands (e.g., locate, find, grep, ?, <, >, >>, cat, tail)

+ 6.15 Locate troubleshooting resources and update as allowable (e.g., Web, man pages, howtos, infopages, LUGs)

CHAPTER PRE-TEST

1. Where can you find the manual pages for commands on your system?

2. What is the purpose of the `locate` utility?

3. Why is it useful to `tail` the system log file?

4. Where are most hardware problems first detected in the boot process?

5. What is the name and location of the main system log file?

6. Where are the system configuration files located?

7. What is your first step in identifying a problem?

8. What is the purpose of using the | during a command?

9. Where can you find the most valuable collection of Linux documentation?

10. What command can you use to view current running processes?

✦ Answers to these questions can be found at the end of the chapter. ✦

Linux administrators really earn their pay when troubleshooting the Linux system. If a system process or application halts, and the user is unable to perform his or her job, the problem must be fixed as soon as possible. Even minor problems can quickly fill up an administrator's time if they aren't dealt with efficiently and correctly.

Troubleshooting is an art, but if you use the proper methodology and best practices, your troubleshooting attempts can be accurate and efficient, too. For example, you don't do yourself any favors by replacing several hardware parts if the actual problem is software-related. Using a proper step-by-step methodology will help you avoid wasting your time on such procedures.

This chapter deals with the basics of troubleshooting and focuses on step-by-step methodical methods that you can use to efficiently solve a problem. This chapter emphasizes the importance of log files as a troubleshooting resource, along with the techniques of stopping and starting processes, and modifying their configuration to aid in the troubleshooting process. You can use a wide variety of command line tools for help when you need to carefully examine your processes and log files.

Finally, this chapter includes a section devoted to troubleshooting resources that you can refer to for help when fixing a problem.

Identifying the Problem

`Objective` ▶ 6.1 Identify and locate the problem by determining whether the problem is hardware, operating system, application software, configuration, or the user

When troubleshooting, stick to a step-by-step method to determine a solution to your problem. This way, you avoid making common mistakes, such as ignoring the obvious or following a path of examination that directs you away from the cause of the problem.

Methodology and Best Practices

`Objective` ▶ 6.2 Describe troubleshooting best practices (i.e., methodology)

This section provides a sample step-by-step process for you to follow when troubleshooting a problem. This is a good general overview of how you should examine a problem. Sometimes, however, extended downtime for a close examination is not an option. With some luck and quick thinking, though, you can achieve a solution as fast as going through step by step.

In the Real World It is much too easy to overlook the most obvious things when troubleshooting. Always start with the simplest things first. (Is the machine plugged in?)

1. **Examine the symptoms:** Take the time to get all the facts when the first signs of the problem are reported. Explore the following questions: Is this happening to one user or is it happening to everyone? Does the problem only happen on one particular system? Does it happen in an application, or is this a system process problem? By gathering as many facts as possible, you can get started in the right direction.

2. **Examine the obvious:** The seemingly most difficult problems often have a simple source. Don't overlook the obvious! Even simple things, such as loose power cords, network cables, malfunctioning fans, or a caps lock key can all cause larger problems than you may think. On the software side, make sure that the user knows how to use a particular program. Does the system have enough disk space? Is this a simple permissions problem? By checking the obvious problems first, you can quickly move to more in-depth examinations of the systems that you are checking.

3. **Work your way from the simple to the complex:** Always start troubleshooting from the simplest systems to the more complex systems. For example, if the problem is reported at a user's system, start troubleshooting from the user's system, and then work your way up the chain from the network to the server. By using this methodical practice, you can eliminate the most simple and obvious systems first.

4. **Hardware or software:** You should also quickly narrow down whether the problem is hardware- or software-related. You will waste a great deal of time and money by swapping and replacing hardware parts if the source of the problem is actually software-related (and vice-versa). Make sure that all of the hardware is operating normally, and that no warning lights, strange sounds, or smells are emanating from any mechanical or electrical components. On the software side, take the time to recreate the problem with the same system. Try the same thing on another person's workstation to attempt to recreate the problem, and then narrow it down to the server or a workstation.

5. **OS or application:** After you have determined that the problem is software-related, you must again narrow the issue down to either an operating system or application issue. If it is an operating system issue, something within the system itself is causing the problem, such as incompatible versions or conflicting programming libraries. You can easily test application problems by trying to recreate the problem on another machine with the same application.

6. **Examine log files:** Check all log files for the operating system and applications. Examine the system log file for any warnings or error messages, and check the application logs for malfunctions.

7. **Examine configuration:** If you have narrowed down the problem to a specific process or application, examine the configuration file to ensure that it has been set up properly. Compare them to configuration files on other servers, and ensure that they don't contain any errors. If you make a change to a

configuration file, remember to restart the particular process or application that you are working on.

8. **Use as many resources as possible:** When you are stumped, don't be afraid to use as many outside resources as possible. If you have a maintenance contract with your software or hardware vendor, call them immediately. Utilize resources on the Internet, such as technical and vendor Web sites with searchable troubleshooting databases.

9. **Document your solution:** After you have solved your problem, document the solution in detail. You may need this information again in the future if the same problem appears, and you can avoid the additional troubleshooting time by referring to your own notes.

Troubleshooting Resources

Objective ➡

6.15 Locate troubleshooting resources and update as allowable (e.g., Web, man pages, howtos, infopages, LUGs)

A wide variety of resources are available for the Linux user and system administrator when troubleshooting problems. From the inception of Linux (and due to its Open Source model), most companies have never provided any official software support for Linux. Linux users and experts support the system by communicating with each other the tips and tricks that make Linux run smoothly. Any problem that you may have with a Linux system, you can bet that someone, somewhere, has already encountered the same problem and has created and documented a solution. The documentation support for Linux is massive, and several resources are available to you when troubleshooting a problem.

 Exam Tip   Know what is the best troubleshooting resource for the situation.

Documentation resources

A vast amount of documentation for Linux is available for administrators, developers, and users, who have all shared information on Linux configuration, troubleshooting, and general operating issues. This section details the different types of documentation that you can access when troubleshooting your Linux system.

MAN pages

MAN pages, or manual pages, are the original Unix way to look up information on specific commands and processes on your system by consulting an online manual. By using a command's MAN page, you can find out exactly what the command does, how to execute it, and all of the options that you can use with the command. The MAN page is split into different sections, each giving the command name and its function, a synopsis of the syntax for the command, and a description, which lists all of the available options for that command.

When troubleshooting, you often need to quickly check the options that you can use with a particular command—using the MAN page command is the fastest way to do so. To use the man command, simply type the name of the command that you want to look up:

```
man lilo
```

For example, here is a listing of the MAN page for the lilo command:

```
Name
        lilo - install boot loader
Synopsis
Main function:
    /sbin/lilo - install boot loader

Auxiliary uses:
 /sbin/lilo -q - query map
        /sbin/lilo -R - set default command line for next reboot
        /sbin/lilo -I - inquire path name of current kernel
        /sbin/lilo {-u|-U} - uninstall lilo
Description
        lilo  installs  a  boot loader that will be activated next
        time you boot.  It has lots of options.
-v      Increase verbosity. Giving one or more  -v  options
            will make lilo more verbose.

-q      List  the currently mapped files.  lilo maintains a
            file, by default /boot/map, containing the name and
            location  of  the  kernel(s)  to boot.  This option
            will list the names therein.

-m map-file
            Use specified map file instead of the default.

-C config-file
            lilo reads its instructions about what files to map
            from  its  config  file, by default /etc/lilo.conf.
            This option can be used to  specify  a  non-default
            config file.

-d delay
            If  you  have  specified several kernels, and press
            Shift at boot-time, the boot  loader  will  present
            you  with a choice of which system to boot. After a
            timeout period the first  kernel  in  the  list  is
            booted.  This option specifies the timeout delay in
            deciseconds.

-D label
            Use the kernel with the given label, instead of the
            first  one  in  the  list, as the default kernel to
            boot.
```

```
-r root-directory
          Before doing anything else,  do  a  chroot  to  the
          indicated  directory.  Used  for  repairing a setup
          from a boot floppy.

-t    Test only. Do not really write a new boot sector or
          map  file.  Use  together with -v to find out what
          lilo is about to do.

-c    Enable  map  compaction. This  will   merge   read
          requests from adjacent sectors. Speeds up the
          booting (especially from floppy).

-f disk-tab
          Specify disk geometry parameter file. (The  default
          is /etc/disktab.)

-i boot-sector
          Specify  a  file to be used as the new boot sector.
          (The default is /boot/boot.b.)

-l Generate linear sector addresses  instead  of  sec-
          tor/head/cylinder addresses.

-P {fix|ignore}
          Fix  (or  ignore) 'corrupt' partition tables, i.e.,
          partition tables with linear and sector/head/
          cylinder addresses that do not correspond.

-s save-file
          When  lilo overwrites the boot sector, it preserves
          the  old   contents   in   a   file,   by  default
          /boot/boot.NNNN  where  NNNN depends on the device.
          This option specifies an alternate  save  file  for
          the  boot sector. (Or, together with the -u option,
          specifies from where to restore the boot sector.)

-S save-file
          Normally, lilo will not overwrite an existing  save
          file.  This   options  says  that  overwriting  is
          allowed.

-u device-name
          Uninstall lilo, by copying the  saved  boot  sector
          back. A time-stamp is checked.

-U device-name
          Idem, but do not check the time-stamp.

-R command line
          This  option  sets the default command for the boot
          loader the next time it executes. The  boot  loader
          will then erase this line: this is a once-only
```

```
                    command. It is typically used in reboot scripts,  just
                    before calling 'shutdown -r'.

  -I label

                    The label of the running kernel can be found in the
                    environment variable BOOT_IMAGE after startup. This
                    command  will  print the corresponding path name on
                    stdout.

  -V       Print version number.

The above command line options correspond to the key words
in the config file indicated below.

   -b bootdev       boot=bootdev
                    -c             compact
                    -d dsec        delay=dsec
                    -D label       default=label
                    -i bootsector  install=bootsector
                    -f file        disktab=file
                    -l             linear
                    -m mapfile     map=mapfile
                    -P fix         fix-table
                    -P ignore      ignore-table
                    -s file        backup=file
                    -S file        force-backup=file
                    -v             verbose=level

See Also
        lilo.conf(5).
        The lilo distribution comes with very extensive documenta-
        tion.
Author
        Werner Almesberger (almesber@bernina.ethz.ch).
```

Linux Documentation Project

The Linux Documentation Project was created to store all available Linux-related documentation, and to offer a central source for all types of documentation that is easy to navigate and search. It is a repository for all types of documentation, such as HOWTOs, guides, MAN pages, and information for new Linux users. For more information, see the home page of the Linux Documentation Project, which is located at www.linuxdoc.org.

The following sections list the types of documents that can be found through the Linux Documentation Project.

HOWTO

The Linux HOWTOs are detailed "how to" documents for specific subjects. A large number of HOWTO documents detail how to configure everything from PPP, to firewalls, to writing CDs. They come in a variety of formats, such as plain text, HTML, PDF, Postscript, and SGML.

The HOWTO documents are very efficient, concise manuals on how to perform certain tasks. For example, if you need to learn how to set up your Linux system as a DNS server, consult the DNS-HOWTO document, which takes you step-by-step through the process of configuring DNS.

Linux Guides

Linux Guides generally have a broader scope than the smaller HOWTO documents because they deal with subjects such as networking, security, and programming. These guides provide an excellent way to quickly research a topic for your Linux system, and are a good free source of information, so you don't have to spend money on a large, expensive textbook on the same subject.

MAN Pages

The Linux Documentation project also contains a searchable database of the MAN pages that are located on your system.

Internet resources

Due to its collaborative nature, Linux support on the Internet offers a wide variety of ways to locate troubleshooting solutions and advice. Because most Linux users continuously communicate new technologies, solutions to problems, and compatibility issues, you should always be able to find someone out there who knows the answer to your question.

World Wide Web

A large number of Linux Web sites are available that cater to everyone from the new Linux user to the advanced system administrator. Some of them are:

✦ `www.linux.org`: Good starting point for new Linux users.

✦ `www.linuxdoc.org`: The Linux Documentation Project, which contains a vast amount of material, such as HOWTOs, READMEs, MAN pages, and FAQs.

✦ `www.linux.com`: General Linux information site.

✦ `www.linuxhq.com`: Good information on kernel versions.

The following sites offer online Linux magazines:

✦ `www.linuxgazette.com`

✦ `www.linuxtoday.com`

✦ `www.linuxworld.com`

✦ `www.linux-mag.com`

Depending on your Linux distribution, you may find that the distribution's home page offers many troubleshooting resources that are dedicated to that version of Linux. You may need these resources because some distributions package their own special software, which may not be used by another Linux distribution.

Newsgroups

Usenet is a form of distributed discussion forums that offer special newsgroups about every conceivable topic, which can be read and posted to. It should be no surprise, then, that a number of Linux newsgroups are helpful for asking questions and getting solutions for system problems.

Here is a list of popular Linux newsgroups that you can consult for troubleshooting purposes:

✦ comp.os.linux.answers: Posts READMEs, FAQs, HOWTOs, and other documents that answer questions about Linux.

✦ comp.os.linux.hardware: Consult for questions and answers that are specific to hardware and how it works with Linux.

✦ comp.os.linux.networking: Consult for questions, answers, and discussions relating to networking topics.

✦ comp.os.linux.x: Consult for questions and answers on the X Windows System.

✦ comp.os.linux.setup: Consult for questions and answers on Linux installation, configuration, and administration.

✦ comp.os.linux.misc: Consult for postings on anything else related to Linux that is not covered by other newsgroups.

 In the Real World   A good answer to your problem can often take many days to arrive from a newsgroup, so be sure the problem is not critical!

Linux User Groups

The Open Source nature of Linux is based on a sharing of knowledge — and your local Linux User Group is just another extension of this philosophy. A Linux User Group is a regionally based group of users who regularly meet to discuss Linux issues and problems, and to exchange ideas on everything that comprises Linux. Most groups also have their own mailing lists, where general information and questions and answers can be posted. You can find a local Linux User Group in your area by consulting the GLUE (Groups of Linux Users Everywhere) database at `www.linuxjournal.com/glue`. You can also check the Linux User Groups Worldwide page for a list of groups all over the world, located at `http://lugww.counter.li.org/`.

Friends and co-workers

Finally, one of the greatest resources for Linux information (and one of the most underrated) is your friends and co-workers who use Linux. The Open Source concept of Linux combined with its emphasis on sharing knowledge forms the basis of this openness between users; you will constantly be sharing knowledge with your fellow Linux users and administrators. Communication with your friends and co-workers through e-mail and instant messaging programs offer another great resource for you to use when troubleshooting a problem.

System Log Files

Objective

6.7 Inspect and determine cause of errors from system log files

Most system processes and applications keep a running log file. When examining a Linux problem, check these log files first to define the actual problem. Log file entries can be very verbose, but can instantly point you in the right direction when you're trying to narrow down the source of a problem.

The type of problem that you are having can guide you to which log file you should check first. For example, if you are having general system problems or if you are having issues with main system services, such as DNS or NFS, you should check the main system log file, which is located in `/var/log/messages`.

Exam Tip   `/var/log/messages` is the most important log file in your system. Check it frequently for error and other informative messages.

You may also find that odd server problems may be the result of something very simple, such as low disk space, which are indicated in `/var/log/messages` with an entry similar to the following:

```
Mar 22 14:41:16 system kernel: /home is out of disk space
```

Log files for an application may also be found in the `/var/log` directory, but they can often be located with the main program files themselves, such as `/usr/local/apache`.

Other important logs include:

✦ `/var/log/dmesg`: A log file that tracks kernel boot messages

✦ `/var/log/boot.log`: A log file that contains service and device status at boot time

✦ `/var/log/lastlog`: A log file that shows the last person who logged into the system

✦ `var/log/maillog`: A log file of sendmail activity

✦ `/var/log/cron`: A log file of activity performed by the `cron` daemon

Tools for Log Files

Objective 6.14 Identify and use trouble shooting commands (e.g., locate, find, grep, ?, <, >, >>, cat, tail)

Examining large amounts of log files can be very time-consuming. When you need information quickly, skimming through a large log file by using a text editor (such as vi), can be a daunting task.

You have many command line tools at your disposal, which will aid you in getting through your log files much easier.

✦ cat: To view log files, use the cat command. cat is short for *concatenate*, which prints your file to a standard output. cat is usually used in conjunction with other commands to make viewing the log file an easier process. Using cat by itself prints the output of the specified file to the screen, but if the output comprises more than one page, it will quickly scroll to the end of the file, without giving you a chance to read it.

✦ cat /var/log/messages: This command will print the entire file to the screen. If the file is very large, it will scroll by very quickly, and you may have to pause or cancel the output to read a particular section.

✦ cat /var/log/messages | more: The pipe, "|", takes the output of cat and sends it through the more command. The more command displays a text file one screen at a time, so that after you finish reading the first screen, you can press the spacebar to move to the next screen. This gives you a chance to review every line in the file.

✦ head / tail: Sometimes, you may only want to view the first or last few lines of a log file because these include the first and most recent log entries. If you are using the cat or more command, you must wait until you reach the end of the file before you can see the last few log entries. The commands head and tail show you the first and last ten lines of the log file, respectively. For example, to see the first ten lines of your /var/log/dmesg file, use the following command:

```
head /var/log/dmesg
```

You can also input the number of lines that you want to see in the command output by adding an option with the number. For example, if you want to see the last fifty lines of dmesg log file, use the following command:

```
tail -50 /var/log/dmesg
```

You can also use the tail command to watch a log file as entries are being logged. This is useful if you are testing a command, process, or application in real-time, and you want to see the immediate result in the log file. For this situation, use the tail command with the "follow" option. For example:

```
tail -f /var/log/messages
```

This command opens up the /var/log/messages file, and outputs log entries as they are added to the file.

✦ **grep:** Because some of these log files can be very large, use other tools to narrow down the search so you can find an answer much more efficiently. One of the best tools to use is the grep command. Grep searches through a particular output file, and returns the results of a substring that you have specified. For example, you may want to scan your entire /var/log/messages file for any error messages by using the following command:

```
cat /var/log/messages | grep error
```

This sequence of commands tells the system to view the /var/log/messages file by using the command cat, which then sends the output to the grep command. The grep command searches the output for any lines in the log file that contain the word "error" and outputs them to the screen.

You can also use grep on its own to search a text file. The following example uses grep to search for the string "error" within the file /var/log/messages:

```
grep error /var/log/messages
```

✦ **special "operators":** operators, such as the question mark (?), will help you find expressions within a file. The question mark signifies that the preceding character is optional, and matched once at most. For example:

```
grep err?or /var/log/messages
```

This command will find the words, "error", "eror", but not "errror".

Output to another file

You can also send the output of a file to another file by using the > and >> options. For example, suppose that you want to save the result of the preceding grep command to a separate file. The > option sends the output to a file of your choice:

```
cat /var/log/messages | grep error > error.log
```

The > option creates or overwrites the file that you specified. The >> option creates a new file if none exists, or adds the data to an existing file.

Locating files

If you are having difficulty finding a particular log or configuration file, you can use one of two commands for help. The locate command finds the location of any file that you are looking for. Simply enter a search string, and the locate command queries an internal database that stores the location of all the commands.

For example, if you need to find the location of your `resolv.conf` file, simply enter the following command:

```
locate resolv.conf
```

The following is the output of the command:

```
/etc/resolv.conf
```

If you don't know the name of the file, you can type a certain amount of characters, and `locate` it will match all files with that string of characters. Using this functionality, however, may bring up a large number of matches that you will have to search through.

The database of files is updated routinely by a system `cron` job. You can also update the database manually by using the command `updatedb`.

Another command that you can utilize for file searching is `find`. The `find` command searches the specified directory for the file that you are looking for. This command is helpful if you already know the general directory. For example, you may be looking for a configuration file that you know resides in the /etc directory, but you aren't sure of the subdirectory. You can use the following command:

```
find /etc -name "httpd.conf"
```

This command provides the following output:

```
/etc/httpd/conf/httpd.conf
```

Exam Tip   Know how to use the various command line tools to help you navigate your log and configuration files more efficiently.

Process Configuration and Management

Objective   6.4 Examine, start, and stop processes based on the signs and symptoms of a problem

Often, you will find that a system process ends or becomes unresponsive. Usually, the users notice this situation right away — especially if the process is very important, such as a Web or Samba server. Knowing how to stop, start, and restart these services is a very important troubleshooting skill. Sometimes, you can quickly fix a problem by stopping and restarting a service, or by changing a process configuration file and restarting the service with new values.

The basic command that you can use to identify current running services is the `ps` command. This command shows all running processes on the system by using the `ps -ef` command.

By using the `grep` command, you can narrow the list down to the process that you are currently examining. For example, if you want to see whether the httpd Web server daemon is running, you can issue the following command:

```
ps -ef | grep httpd
```

If users are complaining that the Web server is not running, you can use this command to see if the process even exists. If it does exist, it may be a stuck process, but if it isn't present, it may have stopped abnormally.

In either case, examine the applications log file to see if any error messages are present to indicate why the process may have become frozen or stopped. You should also check the general system log file `/var/log/messages` for any system-wide problems, such as lack of disk space. If you can't find any immediate reason, the best thing to do is to start or restart the process.

Stopping, Starting, and Restarting Processes

Most services and daemons have their process script stored in `/etc/rc.d/init.d`. Each script contains detailed commands to execute, stop, start, or restart the process as required. You can run this script with the particular option that you need to perform. For example, if you want to stop the running `httpd` process, change directories to `/etc/rc.d/init.d/` and issue the following command:

```
./httpd stop
```

In the Real World
If the process is frozen, stopping the process with its own script doesn't always work. In this event, you may need to use the "kill" command to end the process.

This command runs the script with the "stop" parameter and the process should halt. You can check the results by performing the `ps -ef` command again to see if it is still running.

If you want to start the process again, you can issue the following command:

```
./httpd start
```

Use the `ps -ef` command again to ensure that the process is running properly.

To restart a running process — which you may need to do if the process is frozen — or if you need to read new values from the application's configuration file, use the following command:

```
./httpd restart
```

Exam Tip Always restart a process after changing the configuration file. If you don't, the changes won't take effect.

Configuration Files

Objective 6.3 Examine and edit configuration files based on symptoms of a problem using system utilities

You may find that a process is not working properly because an error has occurred in its configuration file. Even a simple typing mistake can cause an application or process to run abnormally, so you must take great care when editing these configuration files.

The config files for most system processes and applications are stored in the /etc directory with files ending in the .conf extension. These configuration files are mere text files, and can be manipulated with any good text editor.

This example employs the `httpd.conf` file for the Web server. Consider this problem: You have set your document root directory to a wrong location. Users that are trying to access the Web server find that they can't access any documents, or (even worse) the document root location is set to a directory with sensitive files.

In this case, the administrator must edit the `httpd.conf` file and set the DocumentRoot directive to its correct location. Change it back to the default directory of `/home/httpd/html` and then save the `httpd.conf` file.

At this point, if your users try to immediately access the Web page, you will still have the original problem. This is because the process is still running with the original configuration file. To have the program read the new configuration file, you must tell the process to stop and start, or perform a restart.

Summary

This chapter details some basic steps of troubleshooting a problem. This chapter describes many tools and resources to aid in finding a solution to your issue as efficiently as possible. For the exam, keep in mind the following key points:

✦ Methodology and Best Practices

- Never overlook the obvious
- Work your way from the simple to the complex
- Document your solution

✦ Resources

  • Linux User Groups, Linux Documentation Project

  • News groups, mailing lists

  • MAN pages, HOWTOs

✦ System Log Files

  • `/var/log/messages`: Main system kernel log file — examine it frequently

  • `/var/log/mesg`: Kernel boot messages

✦ Command Line Tools

  • `cat`: Print a file to the screen

  • `grep`: Find a pattern of text in a file

  • `head` / `tail`: Examine the top or bottom of a text file

  • `more`: Read files a screen at a time

  • `|` and `>`, `>>`: Used to redirect output to another program or output file

  • `locate`, `find`: Used to find the location of files

✦ Process management

  • Scripts located in `/etc/rc.d/init.d`

  • Commands include start, stop, restart

  • Use `ps -ef` to find running processes

✦ Configuration files: Most are located in `/etc`, end in .conf extension

✦   ✦   ✦

STUDY GUIDE

The Study Guide section provides you with the opportunity to test your knowledge about the Linux+ exam objectives that are covered in this chapter. The Assessment Questions provide practice for the real exam, and the Scenarios provide practice with real situations. If you get any questions wrong, use the answers to determine the part of the chapter that you should review before continuing.

Assessment Questions

1. Users are complaining that Samba services are not working properly. The administrator checks that the service is running. What can the administrator do to fix the problem?

    A. Reboot the system

    B. Reload the samba configuration file

    C. Kill the samba service

    D. Restart the samba service

2. A Linux system has been rebooted. When it starts up, no display appears on the screen and the system is beeping. What may this indicate?

    A. The monitor is not connected

    B. BIOS is indicating a system board problem

    C. One of the hard drives is out of space

    D. The Linux kernel is corrupted

3. A Linux system has crashed. The server is restarted, but a message appears, indicating that the operating system can't be found. What is the most likely cause of the problem?

    A. The hard drive has failed

    B. The kernel needs to be upgraded

    C. The motherboard has failed

    D. The network card has failed

4. A Linux administrator is having a difficult time locating the configuration file httpd.conf for the Web server. What command line tool can aid in finding the file?

    A. `tail`

    B. `cat`

    C. `grep`

    D. `locate`

5. A Linux administrator is noticing odd system behavior. Which log file can be examined to find general system log messages?

    A. `/var/cron/messages`

    B. `/var/log/maillog`

    C. `/var/log/messages`

    D. `/etc/httpd/log`

6. A Linux administrator is having trouble with the options for a particular command. What is the best resource to use for information on the command?

    A. MAN pages

    B. Linux Documentation Project

    C. Linux distribution home page

    D. Usenet newsgroups

7. An administrator is reading through a lengthy log file in order to find out why a certain application keeps crashing. What command can be used to simplify the log search using a search string?

    A. `find`

    B. `cat`

    C. `grep`

    D. `locate`

8. A programmer is constantly making changes to his application's configuration file, and then running the application to see if anything comes up in the error log. Which command lets the user see the log file in real-time, as entries are being added?

    A. `tail logfile`

    B. `tail -f logfile`

    C. `head -50 logfile`

    D. `more logfile`

9. In order to fix a bug in a process, an administrator has made changes to the daemon's configuration file. When she checks the process, it is still exhibiting the same behavior. What is the most likely cause of the problem?

    A. The file was saved with a different name

    B. The process has to be restarted to enable the new configuration

    C. The process needs to be reinstalled

    D. The system needs to be rebooted

10. An administrator is having problem with a specific Linux distribution's installation program. What is the best resource to use to troubleshoot the problem?

    A. HOWTO networking guide

    B. Linux Documentation Project home page

    C. Local Linux users group

    D. The distribution's Web page

11. What is the best source of information for local Linux concerns within a Linux administrator's geographic region?

    A. Linux Users Group

    B. Mailing List

    C. Usenet group

    D. MAN pages

12. A Linux administrator is trying to read through a large log file using the `cat` command. Because it is so large, the `cat` command scrolls the file right to the end without allowing the start of the file to be read. What command can be used to more easily read the file?

    A. Use `head` to read the first ten lines of the log

    B. Pipe the `cat` command to the `head` command

    C. Copy the output to another file

    D. Pipe the `cat` command to the `more` command

13. A user is complaining that he can't connect to the company's Web server. You have checked that the Web service is running and no one else is having problems connecting to the server. What is the most likely cause of the problem?

    A. The server needs to be restarted

    B. The httpd daemon needs to be stopped then started

    C. The user is not using their program correctly

    D. The Web server configuration is flawed

14. When troubleshooting a problem, what should be an initial step in narrowing down the issue?

    A. Examine if the problem is hardware or software related

    B. Determine if the problem persists when the server is rebooted

    C. Determine the time of day the issue occurred

    D. Determine if other servers exhibit the same behavior

15. A user is complaining that the printing service is not working. What is the quickest way to check whether the service is indeed running or not?

    A. Restart the server

    B. Check the running processes with the `ps` command

    C. Have the user log out then in again

    D. `grep` the main log file for printer errors

16. What command should be used to show the first 100 lines of a file?

    A. `grep -100 filename`

    B. `head -100 filename`

    C. `tail -100 filename`

    D. `tail -f filename`

17. A Linux administrator is currently examining a problem involving a user who is unable to login. After checking the appropriate services and examining the user's account properties, a problem can't be found. What is the most likely cause of the issue?

    A. The user's password is expired

    B. The login process is not available

    C. The user is locked out of their account

    D. The user's caps lock key is on

18. A Linux administrator is trying to set up networking on a new system, but is running into problems. What is the best source of troubleshooting information in this case?

    A. Networking HOWTO

    B. MAN pages

    C. Mailing List

    D. Linux Users Group

19. A user is unable to save her file in the home directory. The administrator checks the system log file for any type of errors that may help solve the issue. Which of the following entries would most likely indicate the source of the problem?

    A. sendmail starting daemon

    B. http shutdown succeeded

    C. /home is out of space

    D. Xwindow unable to open

20. Which log should be checked for errors that may have happened during the boot process?

    A. `/etc/httpd/log/httpd.log`

    B. `/var/log/maillog`

    C. `/etc/init.d`

    D. `/var/log/dmesg`

Scenarios

1. A user is having problems getting access to a file located on a Linux server. What steps should you take to solve the problem?

2. You are experiencing odd behavior with your current Web server configuration, which was modified the day before. What steps should you take to solve the problem?

Lab Exercises

Lab 16-1 Using log files and process management

The objective for this hands-on lab is to gain experience in examining log files and checking running processes. You should be able to use any default Linux installation for this exercise.

1. Check to see if the `crond` process is running by using the following command:

   ```
   ps -ef | grep crond
   ```

2. Stop the `crond` process by using the script files in `/etc/rc.d/init.d`:

   ```
   ./crond stop
   ```

3. Take a look at the last few lines of the `/var/log/messages` file using the `tail` command:

   ```
   tail /var/log/messages
   ```

   You should see a message indicating that `crond` was stopped. Check the running processes to ensure this by using the following command:

   ```
   ps -ef | grep crond
   ```

4. Open another console window, and watch the `/var/log/message` file in real time:

   ```
   tail -f /var/log/messages
   ```

5. Now, start the crond process by using its startup script in /etc/rc.d/init.d:

   ```
   ./crond start
   ```

   You should see a message show up in the `/var/log/messages` file that `crond` was started.

6. Check to see if crond is running by using the following command:

   ```
   ps -ef | grep crond
   ```

Answers to Chapter Questions

Chapter Pre-test

1. You can find the MAN pages directly on your system by simply typing the word *man* and the command that you want to look up.

2. The `locate` utility is used to find the location of a specified program.

3. By using the `tail` command, you can watch the log file in real-time, and see entries as they happen.

4. Most hardware problems are detected at boot time by the BIOS.

5. The main system kernel log file is `/var/log/messages`.

6. Most system configuration files are located in `/etc`.

7. You must first examine the symptoms of the problem to understand where to begin looking for a solution.

8. The pipe "|" option is used to send the output of one command to another one.

9. The best place to look for Linux documentation is the Linux Documentation Project.

10. You can examine current running processes by using the ps `-ef` command.

Assessment Questions

1. D. The service, even though it is currently running, may be in a frozen state, and will need to be restarted. For review, see the "Process Configuration and Management" section.

2. B. Because the system has a problem even before the operating system is loaded, the problem is hardware-based, and is most likely caused by a problem with the system board. For review, see the "Methodology and Best Practices" section.

3. A. Because the area on the disk that stores the operating system can't be found, the problem must lie with the hard disk. This can also indicate a problem with the master boot record of the drive. For review, see the "Methodology and Best Practices" section.

4. D. The `locate` command is able to find the location of the file very quickly. It is most helpful if you know the full name of the file that you are looking for. For review, see the "Tools for Log Files" section.

5. C. The general log file for the Linux system is `/var/log/messages`. For review, see the "System Log Files" section.

6. A. The quickest way to find out information on a system command is to use the internal MAN pages, which give you a full description of the command, and information on how to use all of its options. For review, see the "Troubleshooting Resources" section.

7. C. By outputting the log file through the `grep` command, a user can specify a certain keyword to look for, which then displays all instances of that word in the log file. This greatly reduces the time required for searching through a log file for relevant information. For review, see the "Tools for Log Files" section.

8. B. To see a file being updated in real time, you can use the `tail -f` command, which stands for "follow." This way, you don't have to keep opening and closing the file to see any changes. For review, see the "Tools for Log Files" section.

9. B. In order for the process to see the new configuration, it has to be restarted. For review, see the "Process Configuration and Management" section.

10. D. Because the installation program is specific to that distribution, it is best to visit that distribution's home page for information on the installation. The other options may only give you general Linux support. For review, see the "Troubleshooting Resources" section.

11. A. Joining a local Linux Users Group allows you to interact with people within your city or region on any number of Linux issues. User groups are a great place to exchange information, and to get questions and answers on your system. For review, see the "Troubleshooting Resources" section.

12. D. By sending the output of the `cat` command to the `more` command, you can read the log file screen-by-screen. Thus, you can see the entire file from start to finish while using the spacebar to move ahead in the file. For review, see the "Tools for Log Files" section.

13. C. Because the service seems to be working properly and no one else is having any problems, it is most likely that the user is not using her application correctly. For review, see the "Methodology and Best Practices" section.

14. A. To quickly narrow down your problem, you should initially determine whether the problem is hardware- or software-related. This puts you in the right direction from the beginning. For review, see the "Methodology and Best Practices" section.

15. B. By checking the running processes, you can quickly ascertain whether the suspected service is running or not. Even though the service may be running, it may be in a frozen state, so you should next test the service for functionality. For review, see the "Process Configuration and Management" section.

16. B. The command to show the first 100 lines of a file is `head -100 filename`. The `tail` command shows the last line of a filename, while `grep` searches for a specified search string within a file. For review, see the "Tools for Log Files" section.

17. D. The most overlooked item is often the item that can cause a problem. In this case, the user's caps lock key was on, thus causing them to input their password incorrectly (Linux is case-sensitive). For review, see the "Methodology and Best Practices" section.

18. A. In this case (a broad topic like setting up networking), the best resource is a HOWTO document on the topic of networking. For review, see the "Troubleshooting Resources" section.

19. C. In this case, the most likely cause of the problem is that the /home partition is out of space, which is where the user is most likely trying to save his file. For review, see the "System Log Files" section.

20. D. Bootup kernel messages can be viewed in the `/var/log/dmesg` file. For review, see the "System Log Files" section.

Scenarios

1. You must begin with the obvious and most simple scenarios first, such as going to the user's desk and trying to recreate the problem. Can the user access other files? Is the user logged in as themselves? Should the user even have rights to that file?

   If this doesn't work, you must move up the chain of systems from the most simple to the complex. Examine the user's networking settings to make sure that they are correct. Try to access the same files from another point on the network.

   Then, check your server for the problem. Most likely, the user doesn't have permission to the file in question.

2. Because the Web server was recently upgraded, it may be easy to assume that something is wrong with the software configuration. However, always start with the simplest and most obvious things first.

Check the log file of the Web server, and note any warning or error messages. This should give you a quick clue as to the location of the problem.

Judging by the log file, you can then narrow down the exact configuration issue that is affecting the server. You find that a typographical error has occurred in the configuration.

Using a text editor, you fix the problem. However, it won't go into affect until you stop and restart the Web server process.

First, set up a console to actively view your application log file by using the following command:

```
tail -f /var/log/httpd/httpd.log
```

Then, stop and restart the Web server process, by paying close attention to any error messages that may appear in the log file.

Troubleshooting the Boot Process

- ✦ 6.5 Use system status tools to examine system resources and statuses (e.g., fsck, setserial)

- ✦ 6.6 Use systems boot disk(s) and root disk on workstation and server to diagnose and rescue file system

- ✦ 6.8 Use disk utilities to solve file system problems (e.g., mount, umount)

- ✦ 6.11 Take appropriate action on boot errors (e.g., LILO, bootstrap)

CHAPTER PRE-TEST

1. Why should you always create a system rescue boot disk?

2. What is the purpose of the `fsck` utility?

3. What command can you use to examine current system resources usage?

4. What sort of utilities should be saved on a boot disk?

5. Why would you want to connect to your server using a terminal connection?

6. What command can you use to check current running processes?

7. What is the purpose of LILO?

8. What command can you use to format the master boot record?

9. What log can you check to analyze boot time errors?

10. What is the purpose of the `setserial` command?

✦ Answers to these questions can be found at the end of the chapter. ✦

A problem with booting your Linux system is probably one of the most serious malfunctions that can happen. If the system can't load, its hard drives and file systems won't mount and its services won't start. Essentially, the machine is rendered useless.

A system will fail to boot for many reasons. The most serious problem is a hardware malfunction, such as a hard drive or disk controller failure. Another problem that can prevent your machine from starting is corrupt files. A file system can be corrupted if it is not shut down properly; for example, if an administrator accidentally turns a server off without properly unmounting the file systems, they can easily become corrupted. Files can also become corrupt in the event of a power failure because the system has no time to close opened files and shut down properly. Another problem that can hinder your system boot is misconfigured software and hardware. For example, you may have made a mistake in the name of a file system in one of your boot configuration files, and the file system will not load.

A wide variety of tools and utilities are available to help you troubleshoot and fix a boot problem. This chapter deals with several of these tools, including system rescue boot disks, hard drive utilities, and system hardware and software status commands.

Examining the Startup Process

Between the time you turn the machine on and the time you get to login, the boot process goes through many different steps and stages to get to that point. Each step along the way can break down because of a hardware or software problem, which will prevent the system from booting at all. A good theoretical knowledge of the Linux boot process is essential when troubleshooting boot problems.

Boot process steps

The following is a list of events that transpire from the moment you start to boot the Linux system.

1. **BIOS:** The system's BIOS (Basic Input Output System) initializes and performs internal checks on the hardware components of the system, including the CPU, memory, hard drives, and video system. If an error occurs with a component, the system will emit audible beeps and halt the process during initialization.

2. **MBR:** The system checks the MBR (Master Boot Record) of the boot hard drive, which loads into memory the boot manager for the system. In this case, the boot manager is LILO.

3. **LILO:** LILO stands for LInux LOader. LILO is a Linux boot manager, which is responsible for loading the Linux kernel and system into memory. LILO can also boot the computer into different operating systems if they are running

on separate partitions from the Linux system, such as a dual boot system. For example, you may have Linux and Windows 98 operating on the same system. LILO tells the system the location of the kernel image and begins to load it.

4. **Boot prompt:** After LILO has finished loading, you are given the following prompt:

```
boot:
```

Press the tab key to see a list of operating systems that have been configured with LILO. Choose Linux (it may be the default) to enable the boot loader to start loading the kernel image file specified in the `/etc/lilo.conf` file.

5. **Kernel initializes:** At this point, the kernel is uncompressed and loaded into memory. The kernel then initializes the processor, memory, and console and console settings. From there, the kernel starts the disk bus subsystems, networking is initialized, and hardware device drivers are loaded.

6. `init` **process:** After hardware and device initialization has been completed, the kernel spawns the first Linux process, which is `init`. The `init` process is the "father" of all processes in a Linux system. It reads your startup configuration file in `/etc/inittab`, and brings the system up to the appropriate runlevel.

7. **Startup scripts execute:** As part of the init process initialization, the appropriate scripts for the designated runlevel are run. These scripts start the necessary processes and services for the runlevel, mount your file systems, and initiate the console sessions.

8. **Login:** At this point, your system is completely loaded. To begin working on the system, enter your username and password to gain access.

Exam Tip For the exam, know the general boot-up process and what happens at each step.

Analyzing Boot Process Errors

Objective 6.11 Take appropriate action on boot errors (e.g., LILO, bootstrap)

In order to fully understand problems with the boot process, you must be able to analyze the existing data up to the point where the boot process halted. By carefully analyzing error messages and log files of your boot process, you can quickly narrow down the point of failure. Interpreting boot errors, warnings, and informational messages is an extremely important aspect of troubleshooting, that allows you to reduce the time it takes to solve a problem.

Common Boot Problems

After you know the steps in the boot-up process, you should examine some of the common problems that are related to each step.

Hardware

Any sort of hardware problem will most likely occur during the BIOS initialization process because the BIOS must examine these systems before loading the operating system. This is called the POST (Power-On Self Test). The POST routing examines all internal and external hardware for faults and proper configuration. The following is a list of common components that may fail, along with the error messages or warnings that you may encounter.

✦ **Motherboard:** Typically, if you boot up your system and get no response at all except for a number of beeps from the systemboard, then you have a hardware problem with the systemboard circuitry. The beeps from the systemboard are in a sequence, which you can look up in the manual to determine which component — including the video subsystem, cache, memory, or CPU — may be faulty.

✦ **Memory:** The POST routine performs checksum tests on the memory, and if any part of the memory addresses fail, it may halt the boot process altogether.

✦ **Peripherals:** The system checks for the presence of a keyboard, mouse, and any other input devices. These devices aren't needed for full operation — especially if you can use the network to connect to the machine or serial port — but sometimes a faulty keyboard or mouse can lock up a system.

✦ **Hard Drive subsystems:** The system examines the hard drives and disk drive controllers, which may be SCSI or IDE. The system checks that they are using proper addresses that don't conflict with each other.

✦ **Other Cards and Peripherals:** At this time, any other cards and peripherals you have may be tested, such as SCSI cards, or network cards. Any type of IRQ or IO address conflict may render the device inoperable, and these can be detected in the POST process

Software

Software processes take over from the hardware checking routines after the BIOS has examined the master boot record (MBR) of the machine for a boot loader. The following sections explore some of the most common problems that can occur at boot time.

MBR

The BIOS loads the master boot record of the first boot hard drive. If it can't find a hard drive, an "Operating system not present error" results. If there is a drive that contains Linux, BIOS loads LILO (the Linux Loader boot manager). If your MBR has become corrupt — as is often the case if you happen to get a virus from a diskette or Windows partition — you can reset it by booting from a DOS disk and using the fdisk/mbr to wipe the master boot record. Then, you must reinstall LILO by booting into your system with a boot disk, mounting your root partition, and running LILO again.

LILO

At this point, LILO takes over the boot process and presents you with options regarding which operating systems are present and can be loaded. The system prints the word *LILO* on the screen as it initializes. Each letter that appears indicates that a certain process has been started. The first letter "L" indicates that it has moved itself into a proper area of memory. As this process finishes, the letter "I" displays and the second stage begins the secondary boot loader code. The second letter "L" displays when special descriptors are initiated to load the kernel. After the process has completed, the final letter "O" displays. You can troubleshoot boot problems with LILO by noting the number of letters that were displayed before the process halted. Table 17-1 shows a list of possible LILO error codes and their causes.

Table 17-1
LILO Error Codes

LILO Prompt	Error Description
L (n)	Indicates a disk error code
LI	Second stage boot loader loaded, but not run. Kernel cannot be found.
LIL	Descriptor table unable to be read
LIL?	Second stage boot loader loaded at incorrect address
LIL-	Corrupt descriptor table
LILO	The LILO process ran successfully

The most common error message usually occurs when LILO prints only the first two letters "LI" and then freezes. This usually means that LILO can't run the second stage of the boot loader because it can't find the kernel image specified in the LILO configuration file, which is /etc/lilo.conf.

The lilo.conf file is used to configure LILO with the operating systems that can be loaded and their location. A typical Linux /etc/lilo.conf looks similar to the following example:

```
boot=/dev/hda
map=/boot/map
install=/boot/boot.b
prompt
timeout=50
message=/boot/message
lba32
default=linux

image=/boot/vmlinuz-2.4.0-0.43.6
    label=linux
```

```
initrd=/boot/initrd-2.4.0-0.43.6.img
read-only
root=/dev/hda5
```

The kernel image is located in `/boot/vmlinuz-2.4.0-0.43.6` on partition `/dev/hda5`. If it can't find this image, the LILO boot loader will fail when it tries to load the Linux system. Therefore, if you need to change the location of the kernel image, you will have to use a boot disk to mount the partition, fix the `/etc/lilo.conf` file, run LILO to activate the changes, and reboot.

A dual-boot system with Windows contains an extra section to identify where the Windows partition is located:

```
other=/dev/hda1
    label=windows
    table=/dev/hda
```

This section of the `lilo.conf` file tells the system that the Windows partition can be found on `/dev/hda1`.

When installing a dual-boot system with Windows, always install Windows first, and Linux second. If you install in reverse order, Windows will overwrite LILO and the MBR.

Kernel initialization and `init` process

The last steps of the boot process are kernel initialization and the beginning of the `init` process. The kernel loads into memory and initializes. Then the `init` process (which is the "father" of all processes in a syste) begins by loading the various services and mounting the hard drives.

The main problem that you will run into at this stage is a system inability to mount one or more of the file systems on your Linux partitions. This problem will occur either because of a corrupted file system — in which you will have to run the `fsck` (File System Check) utility to fix any errors and inconsistencies — or because your location of the file systems is incorrect in your `/etc/fstab` file.

The `/etc/fstab` file is consulted whenever the mount command is started. The table lists the different file systems that are located on each partition, and gives options on how they are loaded. A typical `/etc/fstab` looks something like this:

```
/dev/hda1 /dos     msdos   defaults    0 3
/dev/hda5 /boot    ext2    defaults    1 2
/dev/hda6 /        ext2  defaults    1 1
/dev/hda7 swap     swap  defaults    0 0
/dev/fd0 /mnt/floppy ext2  user,noauto 0 0
/dev/hdc /cdrom     iso9660 user,ro,noauto 0 0
none     /proc     proc  defaults    0 0
none     /dev/pts  devpts gid=5,mode=620 0 0
```

If the file contains an invalid entry, it won't mount the file system properly. In this case, you will need to edit the /etc/fstab file to fix the error. If this happens with the root partition, you will have to mount it manually, and then make your change to the file.

Any error messages that occur during the boot process are logged to the file /var/log/dmesg.

Using System Status Tools

6.5 Use system status tools to examine system resources and statuses (e.g., fsck, setserial)

You have a number of tools at your disposal for help in troubleshooting your Linux system. These tools allow you to check the status of your hardware and software, and can greatly shorten the troubleshooting process by narrowing down the source of the problem.

File System Check

6.8 Use disk utilities to solve file system problems (e.g., mount, umount)

Depending on the type of boot process problem that you are troubleshooting, you may have to use special utilities to rescue your disk from a corrupted state. Disk data can be easily damaged by file systems that are not unmounted properly—a situation that can result from a power failure or improper shutdown. You can use these special utilities to quickly analyze and fix any inconsistencies in your file systems, thus restoring them to a normal state.

> **Tip**
> The most important utility you will need for repairing your Linux system is the fsck utility. This program will check your file system for errors and inconsistencies, and can repair them while it is running.

During a normal shutdown procedure, the file systems are properly closed and unmounted before the machine shuts down. If Linux is improperly shut down because of a power failure or because someone uses the on/off switch, the file systems and disk tables may become corrupt. If your file systems are not unmounted properly, fsck will run automatically at the next boot-up to attempt to fix the errors.

> **Tip**
> fsck is actually a front-end for more specific utilities. For example, Linux uses the ext2 file system, so when fsck is invoked to check this system, it will run the e2fsck utility.

The following is the syntax for using the `fsck` command:

```
fsck [option] device
```

For example, if you need to run a file system check on `/dev/hda1`, use this command:

```
fsck /dev/hda1
```

The file system must be unmounted in order to run properly. If the file system was mounted and in use, the contents would be constantly changing and `fsck` would not be able to examine it properly.

If you need to check the root file system, you must either boot into the system by using a boot floppy disk or run the check in single-user mode.

Options for `fsck`

You can use a number of options with `fsck`, which is shown in Table 17-2.

Table 17-2 `fsck` **Options**	
s	Serialize `fsck` operations. Use this option if you want to check multiple file systems in order.
-t	Specifies the type of file system to be checked (for example, ext2).
-A	Walk through the `/etc/fstab` file and try to check all file systems in one run.
-C	Display completion/progress bars.
-N	Don't execute, just show what would be done if the file system check was run.
-T	Don't show the title on startup.
-V	Produce verbose output, including all file system-specific commands that are executed.
-a	Automatically repair the file system without any questions.
-r	Interactively repair the file system (ask for confirmations).

You may receive a message stating that you must manually run `fsck` on a file system. If you receive this message, `fsck` was unable to fix the problem normally. Therefore, you must use a more specific utility. You may also receive an error message stating that the superblock is damaged and could not be read. The superblock is a special area that contains pointers to where the file systems are located on the disk. In this case, you have to specifically use the `e2fsck` and pass the superblock parameter manually.

```
e2fsck -b 8193 /dev/hda
```

Exam Tip   Know how to properly use the `fsck` command to check file systems.

System Resource Commands

The following are some commands that can help you examine your current resources and where they are being used. This is helpful when troubleshooting your system for resource conflicts, or over use. For example, if one of your processes uses too much memory, it may cause other programs or even your whole system to crash.

Top

You can use the `top` command to check current resource usage. This utility lets you see on one screen how much memory and CPU resources you are currently using. This screen also displays the resource usage by each program and process. Figure 17-1 shows a screenshot from the output of the `top` command.

```
  7:19am  up 17 min,  1 user,  load average: 0.01, 0.02, 0.04
37 processes: 36 sleeping, 1 running, 0 zombie, 0 stopped
CPU states:  0.1% user,  0.9% system,  0.0% nice, 98.8% idle
Mem:   127976K av,   81392K used,   46584K free,      12972K shrd,     48912K buff
Swap:  133016K av,       0K used,  133016K free,                      21840K cached

  PID USER     PRI  NI  SIZE  RSS SHARE STAT  LIB %CPU %MEM   TIME COMMAND
  702 root      12   0   852  852   668 R       0  1.1  0.6  0:02 top
    1 root       0   0   476  476   404 S       0  0.0  0.3  0:07 init
    2 root       0   0     0    0     0 SW      0  0.0  0.0  0:00 kflushd
    3 root       0   0     0    0     0 SW      0  0.0  0.0  0:00 kupdate
    4 root       0   0     0    0     0 SW      0  0.0  0.0  0:00 kpiod
    5 root       0   0     0    0     0 SW      0  0.0  0.0  0:00 kswapd
    6 root     -20 -20     0    0     0 SW<     0  0.0  0.0  0:00 mdrecoveryd
  304 root       0   0   540  540   452 S       0  0.0  0.4  0:00 pump
  318 bin        0   0   420  420   332 S       0  0.0  0.3  0:00 portmap
  333 root       0   0     0    0     0 SW      0  0.0  0.0  0:00 lockd
  334 root       0   0     0    0     0 SW      0  0.0  0.0  0:00 rpciod
  343 root       0   0   560  560   472 S       0  0.0  0.4  0:00 rpc.statd
  357 root       0   0   480  480   412 S       0  0.0  0.3  0:00 apmd
  408 root       0   0   552  552   452 S       0  0.0  0.4  0:00 syslogd
  417 root       0   0   768  768   388 S       0  0.0  0.6  0:00 klogd
  431 nobody     0   0   628  628   520 S       0  0.0  0.4  0:00 identd
  439 nobody     0   0   628  628   520 S       0  0.0  0.4  0:00 identd
  440 nobody     0   0   628  628   520 S       0  0.0  0.4  0:00 identd
```

Figure 17-1: Output of `top` command

If one of your processes is not working properly, it may be using up all of your available CPU and memory resources. If this is the case, kill the process and restart it.

Setserial

You can use the `setserial` utility to obtain information about your serial port resource usage, such as IRQ and IO addresses. A device uses an IRQ (Interrupt Request) to signal the CPU that it has a request that needs processing. The IO address is a special address reserved in memory for a particular device. If any of these addresses conflict with another device, it may disable them or cause erratic behavior. You can use `setserial` to examine your serial ports and ensure that no conflicts exist.

By default, the Linux system loads serial ports COM1-4 with the default and IRQ values. You can change these settings if you need to set up a device with a non-standard IRQ or IO address.

For example, the following is the default configuration of the first serial port, COM1:

```
setserial /dev/ttyS0
```

The output should look something like this:

```
ttyS0, UART: 16550A, Port: 0x03f8, IRQ: 4
```

The four default com ports are listed in Table 17-3.

Table 17-3 Linux Serial Port Settings			
PORT	**Device**	**IRQ**	**IO Address**
COM1	ttyS0	4	0x03f8
COM2	ttyS1	3	0x02f8
COM3	ttyS2	4	0x03e8
COM4	ttyS3	3	0x02e8

If you need to set a serial port with different settings to be compatible with a certain device, you can use the `setserial` command to change them. Just remember that the device needs to have the settings or it won't work.

For example, if you need to set COM4 to a different IRQ, you can use the following command:

```
setserial /dev/ttyS3 irq 10
```

This command sets the COM4 serial port to use IRQ 10.

Using the System Boot Disk

6.6 Use systems boot disk(s) and root disk on workstation and server to diagnose and rescue file system

If your system fails and won't restart, you can rescue your system instead of installing it from scratch and recovering your data from backup tape. The use of a system boot rescue disk can quickly get your system operational again by booting directly to your hard drive and allowing you to make changes so that the boot process can continue properly.

A boot/rescue disk is one of your most important troubleshooting tools. Always have one on hand, and update it when you update your system.

Types of boot disks

You can make several different types of boot disks, and many can be combined onto one disk to give you the most options and utilities for rescuing a system.

✦ **Boot Disk:** A bootable diskette that contains the Linux kernel. This can point to a root file system located on another disk, such as your hard drive.

✦ **Root/Rescue Disk:** A disk containing a root file system that can run the Linux system from the floppy disk. This disk doesn't necessarily have to be a boot disk.

✦ **Utility Disk:** A disk containing all the system utilities that you need to rescue a file system. This should include utilities such as mount, fsck, and the vi editor.

Be aware that a basic boot disk doesn't contain a root file system; it merely points to the location of the root partition on the original drive.

Creating a boot disk

To create a boot disk, you need to copy a version of the kernel and the boot loader LILO to the boot disk. Use the following general steps to create a boot disk:

1. Insert a floppy disk into the drive and mount it. If you have not formatted it yet, use the following command to create a Linux file system on the floppy:

   ```
   mke2fs /dev/fd0
   ```

2. Mount it:

   ```
   mount -t ext2 /dev/fd0 /mnt
   ```

3. Copy the contents of your /boot partition to the floppy disk:

   ```
   cp -dp /boot/* /mnt
   ```

4. Create a new lilo.conf on the floppy by adding these commands (hda1 assumes that your system is on the first partition of the first hard drive):

```
boot = /dev/fd0
root = /dev/hda1
```

5. Install lilo on floppy with:

```
/sbin/lilo -C /mnt/lilo.conf
```

This disk enables you to boot from the floppy, and to mount a root file system from your hard drive. Use this disk if you are having problems with LILO and the master boot record. With this disk, you will be able to boot into your system and make the appropriate changes to fix the system. These changes usually involve running `/sbin/lilo` to install it back into the master boot record.

Most Linux distributions also come with a bootable installation CD-ROM, which can perform the same functions as the boot floppy diskette.

Creating a rescue/utility disk

The drawback of having only a boot disk is that you won't be able to boot into the root file system on your main Linux machine if you are having problems it. You would benefit more by having a minimal root file system and some disk utilities on your boot floppy to help troubleshoot severe boot problems.

This process can vary quite a bit, depending on the Linux distribution that you are using. Most distributions come with their own bootable installation CD-ROM, which contains an excellent rescue environment for recovering systems.

Keep these points in mind when creating a rescue/utility disk:

✦ **Kernel:** Try to use a compressed version of your kernel if at all possible. Some distributions already have a compressed version of the kernel, usually called *vmlinuz*, which fits much better on a floppy disk.

✦ **Basic File System:** Copy as many directories that you need to your floppy disk to be able to boot into a functional system. For example, at the very least you need `/dev`, `/proc`, `/bin`, `/etc`, `/lib`, `/usr`, and `/tmp`.

✦ **Utilities:** You need several basic utilities to be able to rescue your system, including programs, such as `fsck`, `mount`, and the `vi` editor, and even basic commands, such as `ls`, `cp`, `mv`, and shells.

✦ **Config files:** You need many of your config files from `/etc`, such as `fstab`, `lilo.conf`, and rc/init scripts.

Summary

This chapter details the processes and possible problems that you may encounter during the Linux boot process. For the exam, keep these points in mind:

✦ **Boot Process Steps:** BIOS, MBR, LILO, kernel initialization, `init`, and process startup

✦ **Boot Problems**

- BIOS can detect many hardware errors during the POST routine

- `fdisk /mbr` to format master boot record

- Reinstall LILO into the MBR by running `/sbin/lilo`

- Make sure entries in `/etc/fstab` are correct

✦ **Disk and Resource Utilities**

- `fsck` — Repairs file systems, the file systems must be not mounted

- `setserial` — Identifies and configures serial port properties

- `top` — Shows current resource usage

✦ **Boot and Rescue Disks**

- Boot Disk — Will be able to boot into the root partition on your hard drive

- Root/Rescue Disk — The floppy contains its own condensed root file system

- Utility Disk — Contains important disk utilities and command line tools to help repair a system

✦ ✦ ✦

STUDY GUIDE

The Study Guide section provides you with the opportunity to test your knowledge about the Linux+ exam objectives that are covered in this chapter. The Assessment Questions provide practice for the real exam, and the Scenarios provide practice with real situations. If you get any questions wrong, use the answers to determine the part of the chapter that you should review before continuing.

Assessment Questions

1. A Linux system was recently turned into a dual boot system after the installation of Microsoft Windows. When the system was rebooted, however, no LILO prompt appeared, and the system booted directly into Windows. What is the most likely cause of the problem?

   A. The Windows installation removed LILO.

   B. Linux is incompatible with Windows.

   C. The Linux partition was erased.

   D. Two hard drives are needed for dual boot.

2. What is the purpose of the POST routine?

   A. To load Linux into the BIOS

   B. To initialize LILO

   C. To examine and test the system's hardware at boot time

   D. To load the Linux kernel

3. After a one-minute power outage, your system starts up from a powered off state. You receive a warning error stating that the machine was not shut down properly, and `fsck` will be run. What is the cause of this message?

   A. `fsck` will run randomly after any shutdown.

   B. The `fsck` utility will run if there is no UPS on the system.

   C. `fsck` will always run after a power outage.

   D. The `fsck` utility will run automatically when file systems are not unmounted properly.

4. When you try to boot a Linux system, you receive a message stating that it can't mount the /home partition because of errors. What can you do to fix the problem?

   A. Run LILO

   B. Run an fdisk /mbr to clear the problem

   C. Format the partition and restore from backup

   D. Run the `fsck` utility on that partition to attempt recovery

5. During the bootup of a Linux system, there is no output on the monitor, the machine beeps, and then halts the boot-up process. What is the most likely cause of the problem?

   A. Systemboard failure

   B. Linux kernel is corrupted

   C. The master boot record is corrupt

   D. LILO has not been properly run

6. During the startup of a Linux system, the machine halts with the error that it can't mount the root file system. What is the best way to fix the problem?

   A. Force a mount using the `mount -f` command

   B. Try to run LILO to replace the root partition

   C. Use a boot disk, and then run `fsck` on the root partition

   D. Reinstall Linux

7. As the LILO prompt appears on a booted machine, it halts with only the letters "LI" showing. What is the cause of this problem?

   A. LILO is waiting for a user prompt.

   B. LILO is not finished running yet.

   C. The boot loader could not run.

   D. Windows has been installed on the same hard drive.

8. What is the most important utility that should be on your Linux boot rescue disk?

   A. `vi`

   B. `fsck`

   C. `init`

   D. setserial

9. During a system's POST routine, the system halts halfway through the memory check. What is the most likely cause of the problem?

    A. One of the memory chips has failed

    B. Not enough memory exists to run Linux

    C. The system cache is corrupt

    D. The systemboard is faulty

10. What must you do before performing `fsck` on a file system?

    A. `setserial` must be run first

    B. `fsck` must be run from a boot disk

    C. The file system must be mounted

    D. The file system must be unmounted

11. What is the purpose of the `setserial` command?

    A. To configure modems for dialing

    B. It allows you to examine and set properties for serial ports

    C. Run by `fsck` during drive checking

    D. A boot loader

12. Where is LILO normally stored by default?

    A. Floppy disk

    B. On a DOS partition

    C. First boot device

    D. Master Boot Record

13. What command can be used to remove LILO from the system?

    A. `LILO -remove`

    B. Boot with a DOS disk and use `fdisk /mbr`

    C. `format /dev/hda1`

    D. `ULILO`

14. A Linux administrator wants to review the messages that scrolled up the screen during a system boot. How can this be accomplished?

    A. View the log `/var/log/dmesg`

    B. `show bootlog`

    C. Reboot the system and pause the screen

    D. `vi bootlog`

15. Instead of properly shutting down a Linux system, an administrator mistakenly just turned the machine off with the on/off switch. What will happen when the system restarts?

   A. `fsck` will automatically check the disks

   B. Nothing, the system will boot up normally

   C. The kernel will fail to load

   D. LILO won't be able to run

16. As a Linux system is booting up, the LILO prompt halts when the letter *L* and some numbers are displayed. What is the cause of this error?

   A. LILO is waiting for a user prompt

   B. LILO is corrupted

   C. It indicates a disk error

   D. The Linux kernel can't be loaded

17. After installing Linux on a system, the administrator reboots the machine. After the POST routine is completed, a message stating "No Operating System Found" error appears. What is the most likely cause of the error?

   A. The hard drive is corrupt

   B. The Linux installation did not finish formatting the drive

   C. The system does not support Linux

   D. LILO did not install properly

18. During a Linux startup, one of the partitions — /dev/sda7 — did not mount properly because of errors. What command can you use to repair the problem?

   A. fsck /dev/sda7

   B. fdisk /dev/sda

   C. fdisk /mbr

   D. fsck /dev/hda7

19. During a Linux system startup, the LILO program loaded, and the word *LILO* appeared on the screen. What does this message mean?

   A. You have a physical hard drive error

   B. The kernel can't be found

   C. You have a problem with the boot loader

   D. LILO loaded successfully

20. After installing Linux on a system that also dual boots into Windows, you aren't given the option to boot into the Windows partition at the LILO prompt. How can Linux be configured so that it will give the option to boot into Windows?

    A. Reinstall Windows

    B. Add a Windows section to the `/etc/lilo.conf` file

    C. Run fdisk to set the Windows partition

    D. Run LILO -w to install a Windows prompt

Scenarios

1. A power outage happened overnight and brought down a server that didn't have a UPS attached. When you come in to work in the morning, the system has rebooted, but it won't mount the root file system. What can you do to fix the problem?

2. A user has installed Windows onto a machine that already has Linux installed. The Windows installation has overwritten the MBR, and you aren't given the option to boot into Linux. What can you do to fix the system so that it will dual boot into both Linux and Windows?

Lab Exercises

Lab 17-1 Using the `fsck` utility

The objective for this hands-on lab is to gain experience in using the `fsck` utility to check file systems. You should be able to use any default Linux installation for this exercise.

1. Logged in as root, you want to unmount the root partition so that you can run a filesystem check on it:

```
umount /
```

You should get a warning message that the device is busy and can't be unmounted. Because this is the root partition, you can only safely use the `fsck` utility when booting from a floppy, or when booting Linux into single user mode.

2. Change to single user mode by issuing the command:

```
init s
```

3. Run the `fsck` utility with the -C and -V and -r options. This enables you to see as much information as possible, and interactively choose to repair errors.

   `fsck -C -V -r /`

   (Notice how the `fsck` utility actually invokes the `e2fsck` program to check an ext2 file system.)

4. The program will warn you about running fsck on a mounted file system, but since because you are in single user mode, this is okay, so confirm the prompt. Watch the process run, and watch it detect for errors. Say yes to any prompt that asks if you want to fix errors.

5. When the process is finished, you can safely return to normal running by either rebooting the machine, or by going back to your default runlevel.

Answers to Chapter Questions

Chapter Pre-test

1. By using a boot disk, you will be able to boot your system, and mount a basic file system so that you can fix the errors that are preventing your system from starting.

2. The `fsck` utility, short for *file system check*, checks your file systems for inconsistencies and errors, and fixes them automatically.

3. The `top` command will show you all your running processes, including the CPU time and amount of memory that they are using.

4. Your boot disk should contain utilities that can be used to safely rescue your system, such as disk utilities, a text editor, and hardware and communication utilities.

5. By connecting to a serial port on your Linux system, you can access the console directly. This is useful if networking services are not working, and if you can't log into the system remotely.

6. The command to check current processes is the `ps` command.

7. LILO stands for *LInux LOader*, which is a special boot loader that loads the operating system into memory and starts it.

8. To format the master boot record on a system, you can use the `fdisk /mbr` command.

9. The `/var/log/dmesg` file contains the kernel messages from your last boot.

10. The `setserial` command is used to configure the serial ports on your system.

Assessment Questions

1. A. If Windows is loaded after an installation of Linux, it will write over the master boot record with its own boot loader. To retrieve LILO, you will have to use a boot CD to boot onto your Linux partition and run LILO. For review, see the "Analyzing Boot Process Errors" section.

2. C. The POST (Power On Self Test) goes through a number of internal checks of all hardware and systemboard components, such as CPU, memory, and hard drives. It has nothing to do with Linux itself. For review, see the "Examining the Startup Process" section.

3. D. If your hard drive file systems are not unmounted properly, the fsck utility will automatically run the next time the system is started to fix any inconsistencies before they are mounted again. If they are not fixed, the file system can quickly become corrupt. For review, see the "Using System Status Tools" section.

4. D. The system can't mount that particular partition because of data errors. Running the fsck utility should enable you to recover from the errors. Because the other file systems were not affected, it is most likely not a physical problem with the hard drive. For review, see the "Analyzing Boot Process Errors" section.

5. A. If the system won't even get to the POST stage, the problem is most likely with the systemboard itself. You can compare the number of beeps to the BIOS manual in order to determine which specific component failed. For review, see the "Examining the Startup Process" section.

6. C. Because you can't load any utilities that are on the root partition, you must use a boot disk and run the fsck utility on the damaged file system. For review, see the "Using the System Boot Disk" section.

7. C. When the LILO prompt gets this far and halts, this means that the boot loader has been loaded, but can't run. For review, see the "Analyzing Boot Process Errors" section.

8. B. The most important and useful utility to have is fsck. If you run into the problem of a corrupted file system, and you can't mount any drives, you will need access to the fsck utility, which can repair them. For review, see the "Using System Status Tools" section.

9. A. If the system fails the memory test during a POST routine, one of the memory chips is probably faulty. For review, see the "Examining the Startup Process" section.

10. D. The fsck utility can only run on a file system that is unmounted. If it were active, this utility wouldn't be able to properly repair the drive, and may cause further corruption. For review, see the "Using System Status Tools" section.

11. B. The `setserial` command is used to configure settings for your serial ports. This is helpful if you need to communicate with the terminal on one of these ports. For review, see the "Using System Status Tools" section.

12. D. By default, LILO is installed on the master boot record of your hard drive. The master boot record is a special area that is loaded by the BIOS. You can then use LILO to choose which operating system you will enter. For review, see the "Analyzing Boot Process Errors" section.

13. B. To remove LILO, it is easiest to boot from a DOS diskette and run `fdisk/mbr` which will format the master boot record. For review, see the "Analyzing Boot Process Errors" section.

14. A. The boot kernel messages are saved to the log file `/var/log/dmesg`. For review, see the "Analyzing Boot Process Errors" section.

15. A. When the system shuts down abnormally and the file systems are not properly mounted, the `fsck` utility will automatically check the disks for errors and inconsistencies in order to repair them. For review, see the "Using System Status Tools" section.

16. C. If a disk error is encountered during the LILO initialization, it will print the first "L" and a special numeric error code that maps to a specific disk error. For review, see the "Analyzing Boot Process Errors" section.

17. D. The Linux boot loader LILO did not install properly. After the BIOS initializes, it loads code from the master boot record, where LILO should reside. If it isn't there, no operating system will load. For review, see the "Analyzing Boot Process Errors" section.

18. A. To repair the damaged partition, you can use the `fsck` command to fix any errors and inconsistencies. For review, see the "Using System Status Tools" section.

19. D. This is normal operating procedure for LILO. After it has finished loading, and the word *LILO* appears on your screen, you can now choose which operating system you want to load, or you can let Linux load by default. For review, see the "Analyzing Boot Process Errors" section.

20. B. In order for LILO to be able to boot into the Windows partition, you must configure it within the `/etc/lilo.conf` file. You must re-run LILO when you are finished in order to reload the new configuration. For review, see the "Analyzing Boot Process Errors" section.

Scenarios

1. You will need to use a boot rescue disk that contains a boot image of the kernel, and a basic root file system. This disk may be a self-made floppy disk, or you can use the installation CD-ROM for the Linux distribution.

   a. Boot from the rescue disk.

   b. You must run a filesystem check on all your drives. You can use the following command if your root file system is on the first partition of the first drive:

   ```
   fsck /dev/hda1
   ```

   c. Repeat for any other damaged file systems. Tell the program to repair any errors or inconsistencies it finds.

   d. After you are finished, remove the boot disk and reboot your system. It should start up normally—unless severe damage was caused to the file system.

2. The Windows installation has overwritten LILO, which was installed in the MBR.

   a. To recover LILO, you must use a boot disk to gain access to the Linux partition.

   b. After you have booted with the boot disk, you need to mount the root file system somewhere so you can work on it (assuming the root is on /dev/hda5):

   ```
   mount -t ext2 /dev/hda5 /mnt
   ```

   c. The preceding command mounts the root file system into the directory /mnt. Now you need to reload LILO by running /sbin/lilo:

   ```
   cd /mnt/sbin
   lilo
   ```

   d. LILO should now be reinstalled back into the master boot record.

   e. Before you reboot, however, you should add the Windows partition to the lilo.conf file. Using a text editor, such as vi, edit the /etc/lilo.conf and add these entries (assuming Window is on /dev/hda1):

   ```
   other=dev/hda1
   label=win
   table=/dev/hda
   ```

   f. Run LILO again, so that the configuration is saved.

   g. Now reboot, and when the LILO prompt appears, you can choose between booting Linux or Windows.

Troubleshooting Software and Networking

+ 6.9 Resolve problems based on user feedback (e.g., rights, unable to login to the system, unable to print, unable to receive or transmit mail)

+ 6.10 Recognize common errors (e.g., package dependencies, library errors, version conflicts)

+ 6.12 Identify backup and restore errors

+ 6.13 Identify application failure on server (e.g., Web page, telnet, ftp, pop3, snmp)

+ 6.16 Use network utilities to identify network and connectivity problems (e.g., ping, route, traceroute, netstat, lsof)

CHAPTER PRE-TEST

1. What sort of hardware problems can cause a tape backup to fail?

2. How does the `ping` command help you diagnose network connectivity problems?

3. Why do some software programs suffer from version and library conflicts?

4. What command can you use to send a job to a printer?

5. What happens when you send an e-mail to a misspelled e-mail address?

6. What is the purpose of the `traceroute` command?

7. What command can you use to check your current running processes?

8. Why should a user be locked out of his or her account after a certain number of unsuccessful logins?

9. What should you examine after the failure of an application?

10. What is the purpose of issuing a `telnet localhost` command on the system console?

Troubleshooting common user problems is a daily task for the Linux system administrator. The applications, software packages, services, and server processes that allow the end user to login, print, and send mail offer many different points of failure that the administrator must sort out. This chapter details many of the common user problems that need to be fixed on a daily basis.

Connecting all these services and devices is the network, and any problem with the network will interfere with all applications and services. This chapter also looks at a number of utilities that you can use to troubleshoot networking problems in a quick and efficient manner.

Other frequent problems that the administrator faces include backup and restore errors, and software package version conflicts and dependencies. This chapter helps you to resolve errors with these services and applications.

Common User Problems

Objective

6.9 Resolve problems based on user feedback (e.g., rights, unable to login to the system, unable to print, unable to receive or transmit mail)

A wide variety of common user problems happen daily, and they are usually centered on the basic functions that are used each day. Problems with logins, mail, permissions to files and directories, and printing are the most common. Most of these problems can be fixed very quickly with the right knowledge of troubleshooting basics.

Login problems

A user may not be able to login for several reasons:

✦ **Username/Password:** The user may be simply using the wrong name or password. Ensure that his or her password is being typed properly — especially if the password is case-sensitive. If the user has forgotten his or her password, change it to something else, and have the user change it when he or she logs in again. If the user is still unable to login, you may have to check the networking settings, or check the server login services.

✦ **Networking:** Make sure that the client can `ping` the login server, and that the client has full network connectivity, including DNS resolution. You may have more serious networking or server problems if the server can't be contacted.

✦ **Server Login Services:** Examine the server logs and processes to ensure that login services are available, running, and accepting connections. Try logging in from another workstation to see if the problem is on the client side. If no one in the organization can log in, then you have a serious server problem.

✦ **Account problems:** A number of account restrictions may be enabled, thus causing the login problems. Some administrators configure time or machine restrictions so that a user can only logon at certain times or from a certain host. The account may have expired if an expiration date was enabled. The account may also be locked if the user entered an incorrect password more than the maximum times allowed, thus causing the account to be locked out.

In the Real World   Many user password problems in Linux stem from the fact that they are case-sensitive. Make sure that the user's caps lock key is not depressed.

File and directory permissions

Sometimes a user will try to access a file or directory that they don't have permission to access. They will be denied access unless they are given rights to the files in question. This is a good security practice — users should never be able to access more than they are authorized for.

Most permission problems involve shared or group directories rather than a user's home directory. In this case, you must list the contents of the file and directories to which they are seeking access, and then examine the permissions by using the command `ls -al` to see who is allowed to access those files. In most cases, you only need to add that user to the authorized group to allow them access.

If the user is currently not assigned to a particular group with access to that directory, don't add the user until you receive permission from his or her management. The user may be trying to access files that he or she has been denied (for good reason).

Printing problems

Printing is a very common function performed by the end user, and is prone to many different types of errors. Sometimes the problems have simple causes that are easily overlooked, such as the printer being turned off or out of paper. Sometimes, however, printer problems can be complex — dealing with printer server and queue issues. The best practice of any troubleshooting operation is to start with the simplest causes before moving on to more complex issues.

Printer hardware

Check some of the simple causes first to ensure that the printing problem is not a server issue. Some of the most obvious problems are easily overlooked:

✦ **Printer turned off:** Users rarely check to see if the printer is turned on. A person may have unplugged the printer to use the power outlet, or a janitor may have moved the printer and unplugged it the night before. After the printer is turned on, it should start printing from print queue again.

✦ **Printer out of paper:** A very simple problem, but you can't know for certain until you actually look at the message on the printer.

✦ **Printer Offline:** Another easily overlooked problem, which you won't know about until you actually examine the printer to see if it is online or offline.

✦ **Printer networking problems:** Most printers connect directly to the network via a built-in network port, while some are attached directly to a print server machine or device. If the printer can't connect to the network, it won't service requests, which will build up in a queue on a print server. If your printer is set with an IP address, you can `ping` it to see if it's alive. You can also try to print a configuration from the printer, and examine the statistics for the built-in network card to check for any activity.

Client printer setup

Examine the settings on the client machine that is having difficulty printing because the settings may be misconfigured.

If users are printing from an X application, try printing from a different application to see if that works. If not, try printing from the command line. Use the `lpr` command to print a test file to the same printer, and if that doesn't work, try sending it to a different printer. This way, you will know if the problem is only affecting the ability to print to one particular printer, or all printing functions.

Check for other problems, such as lack of disk space, system resources, and proper network connectivity.

Make sure that clients have the proper print driver for the printer they are using. For example, if users are printing a Postscript file, they should be using a Postscript driver of their printer.

In the Real World Users often think that they are printing to a specific printer, when they are actually using a different printer somewhere else in the organization.

Print server problems

If you can't find any problems with the client computer printing setup, and if all files are being properly spooled to the print queue, your next step is to check the print server to see what is happening with the queue.

Use the `lpq` command to obtain information about the jobs in your print queue for a specific printer:

```
lpq -P[printername]
```

If you find that a job is stuck or perhaps corrupted and holding up the queue, you can remove it by using the `lprm` command:

```
lprm -P[printername] [job id]
```

The line printer daemon may not be functioning, and is not processing requests for printing. Ensure that the `lpd` daemon is running by using the following command:

```
ps -ef | grep lpd
```

If the service is not running, or is running but not responding to requests, you should stop and start the service as required.

Exam Tip   Know how to properly troubleshoot a printing problem, especially by using the available command line tools.

Mail problems

A common user complaint is the inability to send or receive mail. When trouble-shooting mail problems, it is generally best to start from the client end and then check connectivity up to the mail server. Most likely, you have a problem with the client, whether it's misconfiguration or a networking problem. If no one in your organization can send or receive mail, then you know that something is wrong with the central mail services on your mail server.

When examining the client for mail problems, check the following general items before moving on to the possibility of a server problem:

✦ **Username/Password:** Is the user using their proper username and password to login to mail?

✦ **E-mail addressing:** Is the user typing an invalid or misspelled e-mail address? Generally, the server will send back a message stating that the e-mail was undeliverable if this is the case, but other problems may prevent this message from arriving.

✦ **Configuration:** Are the incoming and outgoing mail servers set to the correct servers? Is the client using the proper protocol on the right port, such as `pop3` (port 110) and `imap` (port 143)? The outgoing server should be using the `smtp` (port 25) protocol.

✦ **Networking:** Is the client having any networking problems, such as slow or no network activity? Try to `ping` the mail server to make sure that you have connectivity. Is DNS resolving names properly? You can test DNS by using the IP address of a mail server instead of using its full domain name.

If everything on the client side seems in order, you must then move up to the server level to ensure that the mail processes are running properly. If other users are having the same problem, then you probably have a server problem. For more information of server mail problems, see the "Application Failures" section in this chapter.

Software Package Problems

Objective

6.10 Recognize common errors (e.g., package dependencies, library errors, version conflicts)

Sometimes, when trying to install a software package, you will find that the package requires extra programs to run properly, or that the package conflicts with a version of another application that you are running.

Software package problems are very common, but fairly easy to solve after you know what you're looking for.

In the Real World Some advanced package managers will install dependent programs for you. Sometimes, this can cause more problems than it solves because the dependent program may conflict with another existing application.

Package dependencies

Software package managers, such as RPM (Redhat Package Manager) and DPKG (the Debian package manager), will tell you immediately if you are lacking any dependencies that the current package requires. Applications can have all types of dependent programs, such as programming run-time libraries or modules. Package managers contain special control files, which keep track of the dependencies for the package. If you don't have the required dependent software, the new package won't install and you will receive an error message telling you what you're missing.

Using this information from the error message, you can obtain the correct dependent software, install it, and then try to install your original package again.

Package managers also keep track of dependencies when you are removing a package, so you won't accidentally delete a file or library that another program depends on.

Software and version conflicts

When a new software program is installed, it may have components that conflict with other programs already installed. For example, if you installed a new package that contains newer versions of run-time libraries that another program requires, you may cause the already existing program to stop working. This happens because the existing program was dependent on the older version of the run-time library that you replaced. If you need both programs, you may have to track down a library that is compatible with both programs.

When installing a new package, read over the installation README file to ensure that what you are installing won't conflict with existing software.

Exam Tip   Be able to recognize the symptoms of a software dependency or conflict.

Backup and Restore Errors

Objective ➤   6.12 Identify backup and restore errors

Backup failures are common, but are serious problems that you must deal with immediately. I can't stress enough the importance of backing up your data. When you experience continual failures of the backup system, you put your organization's valuable data on the line every day the problem persists.

Backup failures can originate from a variety of causes, including hardware, software, and misconfiguration of the programs and their restore procedures.

Backup hardware

Tape backup systems are mechanical in nature and are very prone to failure, especially due to lack of periodic maintenance and cleaning.

Most backup errors are caused by media write errors, meaning that the backup application was unable to write to the tape during the operation. The tape may be faulty, or the tape mechanism may be dirty or in need of maintenance.

Cleaning the magnetic heads of your tape drive on a regular basis with a cleaning tape will reduce the number of errors.

Tape robots, sometimes called a *jukebox*, have special mechanical components that automatically load and eject tapes into a drive. These robots are easily prone to mechanical failure, and should be periodically serviced to maintain optimum operation.

The tapes themselves may also be faulty. A tape may be faulty, despite being used numerous times, or may be faulty straight out of the package. Whenever a backup fails due to a media tape error, remove the tape from your rotation scheme and throw it out. If you use the tape again, more than likely it will repeat the failure.

You should always set a maximum time, or specific number of backups, that a tape can be used. Tapes should be used for about one year and then removed from rotation, especially if they are reused frequently. The constant writing and rewriting of the magnetic media will slowly deteriorate it, making it more likely to fail.

 In the Real World   Most media errors are caused by neglecting to periodically clean the tape drive heads.

Backup software

Misconfiguration and software errors may also cause your backups to fail. When you have a backup failure, your first task should be to examine your backup logs.

These logs will give you specific error messages, and help you narrow down the problem fairly quickly.

Other failures can be caused by misconfiguration of your backup scheme. If you have your software set to put all of your backups on one tape, you increase the possibility that the tape will become full before the operation is complete — causing the backup to fail.

Retention settings may also be misconfigured. *Retention* is a setting that lets the application know how long data on a tape should be retained before it is written over. If you try to backup to a tape that is still retaining data, the system won't overwrite the data, and therefore, cause the backup to fail.

Another cause of backup failures is open files. If you're trying to back up your Linux server during working hours, your users may have many open files, which won't be backed up. Schedule your backups for off-hours when those files will be closed.

If you aren't using a special backup application, you may be simply dumping file systems to tape, scheduled by the `cron` daemon. Examine your cron logs to make sure that the system is being backed up properly. If cron is not running or not executing the schedule, your system is not being backed up.

File restore errors

When restoring files from tape, you may run into problems other than mechanical or media problems.

For example, the backup application must have the proper permissions to restore a file to a particular directory. You must also be careful about restoring a file with the same name as the original. Restore the file to a different directory than the original file so it won't be overwritten. This way, the user can compare the files if they need to copy any changes or retain information entered in the new file.

When restoring large files and directories, take note of how much disk space the restored files will consume. If you don't have enough disk space, the restore operation will fail, and as a result, may cause other problems to occur on the server.

Application Failures

Objective

6.13 Identify application failure on server (e.g., Web page, telnet, ftp, pop3, snmp)

On a stable Linux system, you will rarely encounter a problem on the operating system. This process reliability is different for actual application programs and process daemons, which can cause problems due to misconfiguration, errors from bad input, and general process failure. Most of the time, the users will see the symptoms of the problem before the administrator because they are the ones constantly using the applications throughout the day. These problems can range from simple, non-critical services to critical application processes and programs, such as mail, Web, and file-sharing services.

You can discover and remedy application and process errors in a number of ways by using the process logs and startup script tools of the Linux system.

Exam Tip   Know how to properly test and troubleshoot systems for various application errors, including Web, FTP, and telnet.

Log files

When you first discover an application failure, check the log file for that application, or check the main system log file if the application is a system process.

By examining the error messages, you may be able to quickly ascertain the exact problem. The problem may have been a misconfiguration error that occurred after changes were made to an application configuration file, or the problem may have occurred for other general reasons, such as low disk space or system resources.

Most application and process log files are stored in the /var/log directory. The main system log file is located in /var/log/messages. In this log file, you will find the informational and error messages from any system processes or applications, including kernel system messages.

You can find other more application-specific log files in the /var/log directory as well. Some applications, however, store their log information in the same directory where the application is located.

Process and daemon errors

You and your users will notice most process errors when a certain service won't perform its function. Process errors can range from the non-critical services, such as cron or snmp, to system-critical functions, such as a live Web server, logins, or file sharing.

You can examine most of these problems through the system and application log files. Most process errors stop due to an error, or have lapsed into a frozen state because of some system error.

You can stop, start, or restart services by using their respective scripts in the /etc/rc.d/init.d directories. For example, to stop, start, or restart the cron daemon, use the following commands:

```
crond stop
crond start
crond restart
```

Web server errors

If your Web server is not serving pages, check for the existence of the Web server daemon, `httpd`, by using the following command:

```
ps -ef | grep httpd
```

If your Web server is running but not working, or if the process does not seem to be running, then it is either in a frozen state or stopped.

You can stop, start, and restart the service using the script in `/etc/rc.d/init.d/httpd`. For example, if the process is not running, use the following command:

```
httpd start
```

If the Web server is running but not working properly, use the following commands:

```
httpd stop
httpd start
```

Check to see if the Web server is running by first checking the process with `ps`, then try connecting to a Web page.

Telnet

You can easily check telnet services for a host by attempting to connect from the same machine to its local port. For example, to test that your `telnet` daemon is properly listening for connections, use the following command:

```
telnet localhost
```

If the `telnet` command does not respond with a login prompt, then your `telnet` service may be turned off or the network services daemon `inetd` is not running.

Examine the `/etc/inetd.conf` file for the `telnet` section. Many people turn off the `telnet` services as a security measure. You can disable the `telnet` service by commenting the appropriate line out from `inetd.conf`. If you want to re-enable the service, uncomment it from the file, and restart the `inetd` daemon.

FTP

FTP services are also run from the `inetd` daemon, which is similar to the `telnet` service. Examine the `/etc/inetd.conf` file to see if `ftp` services are disabled, and enable them if necessary.

You can always test the service by using the following command:

```
ftp localhost
```

Or, try using FTP from a different machine to verify that the service is running.

Mail services

The failure of mail services — whether it's incoming mail services, such as `pop3`, or `imap`, or sending services, such as `smtp` — is among the most frustrating problems. You can check most of these services by using the ps -ef command to find the running processes.

You can also test to see if these protocols are accepting connections for their particular port. For example, pop3 uses port 110 to listen for requests. By using the telnet command, you can telnet to that port to see if you get a reply:

```
telnet hostname 110
```

You can do the same for imap (port 143) and smtp (port 25).

If neither of these tests succeeds, then you must check your /etc/inetd.conf file to ensure that these services are enabled. If they are commented out, then that service is disabled. You must uncomment the line and restart the inetd process.

Basic Networking Troubleshooting

6.16 Use network utilities to identify network and connectivity problems (e.g., ping, route, traceroute, netstat, lsof)

Networks are very complex systems. Several devices, hosts, and software comprise a network, and problems with any one of these can have consequences ranging from smaller problems, such as the inability of a host to connect to the network, to an enterprise-wide network of problems.

You should always check network problems starting from the client side and moving up. Check the client's networking settings and check the cables, and then move up the chain to the local wiring closet, and to the servers, central hubs, switches, and routers of your network.

By starting with the most obvious areas first and moving up, you can methodically trace a network problem to its root.

Networking connectivity

You can benefit from several Linux commands and utilities when troubleshooting network connectivity.

Ping

You can use the `ping` command to test connectivity from one machine or device to another. Ping stands for *Packet Internet Groper*, and basically sends out a network packet to a specified machine. That machine, in turn, will send a packet back to the signal, stating that it is alive and on the network.

Ping uses the ICMP (Internet Control Message Protocol) to perform its functions. ICMP is an extension of the IP protocol, and allows error, control, and informational packets to be sent and received.

Suppose that you have just installed a Linux server on your network, and you want to test the connection from a client machine to see if the server is on the network. You can `ping` the server from your machine. If you don't receive a reply, your server network is not set up properly. Similarly, you can test connectivity from the new server by trying to `ping` another host on the network—or, more commonly—the default gateway for the network.

The following is an example of the `ping` command:

```
ping www.hungryminds.com
PING hungryminds.com (168.215.86.100) from 10.1.1.5: 56(84) bytes of data.
64 bytes from websrv.hungryminds.com (168.215.86.100): icmp_seq=0 ttl=49
time=26.549 msec
64 bytes from websrv.hungryminds.com (168.215.86.100): icmp_seq=1 ttl=113
time=19.972 msec
64 bytes from websrv.hungryminds.com (168.215.86.100): icmp_seq=2 ttl=113
time=29.972 msec
```

In the preceding example, you try to `ping` a Web site to check for connectivity. `Ping` will show you how long it takes for the specified host to `ping` back a reply. Very long `ping` response times result in a "Request Timed Out" error. This error can occur during times of high network activity, if the host is not available.

Attempting to `ping` an address on the Internet is quite common, but if you are trying to `ping` a local host on your own private network, this may indicate network and routing problems. If you receive repeated request errors with no `ping` replies, then that host is experiencing networking problems, or it isn't connected at all.

In the Real World

Some Internet and corporate sites use a firewall to block `ping` requests from outside hosts. Allowing ping requests can be a security risk, because a hacker can have a machine send repeated `ping` requests to a server to prevent it from processing any other network requests. This action is often called the "ping of death" type of attack.

Traceroute

Use the `traceroute` utility to trace a network packet from one host to another so you can see how many "hops" or Internet routers it passes through before reaching its destination. `Traceroute` is used most often to troubleshoot routing and latency issues between hosts in a WAN or Internet environment. As with the `ping` utility, `traceroute` also uses the ICMP protocol for its functions, specifically the TTL (Time to Live) data for each packet. When you initiate the `traceroute` command, network packets are sent to the destination host. The TTL setting for each packet is a measurement of how long that packet can remain alive in between hops until it is returned. If the TTL is too short, it is eventually returned without reaching its target. After each hop or router in a traceroute operation, the packets are sent with longer TTL settings until the final destination is reached.

The following example shows how to trace the amount of hops between a local machine and a Web site:

```
traceroute www.hungryminds.com
traceroute to hungryminds.com (168.215.86.100),30 hops max, 38 byte packets
 1 gateway (10.1.1.1) 4.863 ms 1.264 ms 2.130 ms
 2 Router (10.1.2.254) 3.907 ms 5.014 ms 2.315 ms
 3 216.191.195.169 (216.191.195.169) 4.221 ms 4.088 ms 4.421 ms
 4 atm7-0-71.core1-tor.bb.attcanada.ca (216.191.67.65) 8.745 ms 8.053
ms 12.336 ms
 5 srp2-0.gwy1-tor.bb.attcanada.ca (216.191.65.243) 8.676 ms 8.692 ms
14.571 ms
 6 12.125.142.5 (12.125.142.5) 23.113 ms 23.146 ms 22.749 ms
 7 gbr6-p80.cgcil.ip.att.net (12.123.5.222) 19.464 ms 19.108 ms 19.437
ms
 8 12.122.9.133 (12.122.9.133) 25.734 ms 73.168 ms 42.280 ms
 9 12.122.11.57 (12.122.11.57) 43.276 ms 20.764 ms 21.492 ms
10 12.122.11.50 (12.122.11.50) 19.267 ms 19.324 ms 19.239 ms
11 gr1-p340.cgcil.ip.att.net (12.123.4.249) 26.212 ms 19.618 ms 19.271
ms
12 pa2-atm0-1-aads-igr01.chi.twtelecom.net (206.220.243.116) 29.284 ms
24.657 ms 45.476 ms
13 jr-01-at-0-1-0-1.chcg.twtelecom.net (207.67.50.85) 23.328 ms 23.336
ms 31.708 ms
14 jr-04-so-2-0-0-155m.chcg.twtelecom.net (168.215.53.37) 23.143 ms
27.103 ms 22.529 ms
15 jr-01-so 2 0 0 622m.iplt.twtelecom.net (168.215.53.18) 31.682 ms
31.464 ms 31.775 ms
16 cr-01-pos-5-0-0-155m.iplt.twtelecom.net (207.67.94.194) 32.500 ms
31.575 ms 32.648 ms
17 168-215-52-186.twtelecom.net (207.67.94.186) 40.461 ms 30.792 ms
29.252 ms
18 websrv.hungryminds.com (168.215.86.100) 30.077 ms 30.092 ms 30.376 ms
```

You can see the number of routers or "hops" that your network packets have to hit before reaching their final destination. If the request times out at some point, you will see a group of asterisks (*) in the destination, and it won't go any further. These asterisks will let you know the exact point at which your network has lost communication. The `traceroute` command is particularly useful in internal local or wide area networks — especially if you are experiencing communication problems with a particular router or site in your network.

Route

Use the `route` command to show and manipulate your local machine's IP routing table. The routing table configures your system to route packets to certain addresses through another gateway or router. The routing table also allows you to choose which network interface you need to use for routing, because you have more than one network card in a system.

Note   The entire topic of routing is beyond the scope of this chapter, but when troubleshooting network problems, you may have to make adjustments to your routing table in order for networking to function properly.

By simply issuing the following command, you can display your current routing table, which shows the destination address, gateway, and interface for each routing entry:

```
route
```

The following is a sample output from the `route` command:

```
Kernel IP routing table
Destination Gateway     Genmask      Flags Metric Ref  Use Iface
10.1.0.0    *           255.255.0.0   U    0      0     0 eth0
127.0.0.0   *           255.0.0.0     U    0      0     0 lo
default     10.1.0.254  0.0.0.0       UG   0      0     0 eth0
```

This example shows the default gateway, 10.1.0.254, which is a central router for that particular network. The interface shows which network card is using that route; in this case, the network card is an ethernet card, "eth0", and the local loopback interface "lo" is a virtual networking adapter used for internal loopback tests.

If you can't reach a host because it is located on another network or subnet, you can add a static route to the proper destination gateway that will forward your request. The general syntax for adding routes is similar to the following:

```
route add -net 192.168.1.0 netmask 255.255.255.0 gw 192.168.1.254
```

This syntax tells the system to add the network 192.168.1.0 to the routing table, and to go through the gateway address of 192.168.1.254, which can be a router, or routing interface on a device or host.

Similarly, you can delete static routes by using the `route del` command.

Netstat

Netstat is a very powerful command that can provide a wide variety of information about your network interface cards and network connections. Use the `netstat` command to show which network connections are currently being used on your system. This command also provides you with information about which daemons are listening on certain ports. This information is helpful in determining which ports are currently active, and waiting for network requests. If you are worried about security and want to see which connections you are using or listening to, use the following command:

```
netstat -l
```

This command shows information on all listening ports, while the netstat command on its own can be used to show active network connections. The following is a sample output from the netstat command showing connections, such as telnet, ssh, and ftp:

```
Active Internet connections (w/o servers)
Proto Recv-Q Send-Q Local Address   Foreign Address      State
tcp    0    124 host:telnet 10.1.0.188:4339 ESTABLISHED
tcp    0     0 host:ssh 10.1.0.189:4014 ESTABLISHED
tcp    0     0 host:ssh 10.1.0.189:3560 ESTABLISHED
tcp    0     0 host:ftp 10.1.0.190:21 ESTABLISHED
Active UNIX domain sockets (w/o servers)
Proto RefCnt Flags    Type     State     I-Node Path
unix 7   [ ]    DGRAM          338 /dev/log
unix 0   [ ]    DGRAM          1037545
unix 0   [ ]    DGRAM          181851
unix 0   [ ]    DGRAM          723
unix 0   [ ]    DGRAM          520
unix 0   [ ]    DGRAM          425
unix 0   [ ]    DGRAM          361
unix 0   [ ]    DGRAM          348
```

The netstat command has many other powerful options:

✦ netstat -r: Shows the Routing table

✦ netstat -I: Shows statistics for network interfaces

```
Kernel Interface table
Iface MTU Met RX-OK RX-ERR RX-DRP RX-OVR TX-OK TX-ERR TX-DRP TX-OVR Flags
lo   0   0  4256    0    0    0 3185    0    0    0 BLRU
eth0 1500  0 873009   19   23  156 647383  123    0    0 BRU
```

These interface statistics show you the number of packets transmitted and received, including any errors that were encountered. A high number of errors indicate very high network traffic or a faulty interface card.

Lsof

Lsof (List open files) lists information about any files that are open by processes, and whether those files are currently running on any system. An open file may be a regular file, a directory, a library, a stream, or a network file, such as a network socket. Lsof is a great security tool for a Linux system administrator because it can show you open network sockets and files on your system.

Lsof doesn't always come by default on some Linux distributions, but it is a handy tool to have. The latest release of Lsof is always available via anonymous FTP from `ftp://vic.cc.purdue.edu/pub/tools/unix/lsof`.

Exam Tip Know when and how to properly use networking utilities to troubleshoot a networking problem.

Network hardware problems

When troubleshooting networking problems, don't forget to check your hardware systems — they are just as important as the computer networking software. Networking can be interrupted at many points, ranging from a faulty router port to a bad ethernet cable. Knowing how to examine and test your hardware for network connectivity problems is an important skill — and is just as important as your networking software knowledge.

Cabling

One of the most common sources of network connectivity problems is the network cabling. Defective cables, crossed wires, broken jacks, and cut cabling all contribute from minor to major effects on the network.

Basic, twisted-pair Ethernet cabling, which simply consists of four pairs of twisted wires, is very susceptible to damage and improper installation. If the administrator is making his or her own cables, it can be very easy to mismatch wires or not crimp the end connectors properly. The easiest way to avoid mistakes is to use commercially purchased cables. However, remember that these cables may also have defects.

Coaxial network cabling is more impervious to damage, and is typically used in industrial environments where the cables are in greater danger of being damaged. However, improper terminations or split or cut cabling can quickly bring down this type of network because it's using a bus technology for network communications, and any break in one part of the cabling will bring down the entire network.

When troubleshooting networking problems, ensure that the problem is not simply the cabling. You can easily test the cabling by exchanging the cable with a known good one. This very short test can save you a lot of time if your problem is simply a faulty cable.

Switches and routers

The source of network problems can often be traced back to a main switch or hub. A faulty port can often project thousands of network packets onto the network, thus causing large scale, general network congestion.

In most cases, a faulty port won't work at all, and if you trace your problems back to the port, you can simply plug it into another port to establish connectivity. Other, more serious problems with the main networking equipment include overall equipment malfunction, misconfiguration, or even just loss of power.

Summary

This chapter deals with a number of troubleshooting procedures, tips, and utilities for several different Linux applications, networking, and user problems. For the exam, keep the following points in mind:

✦ User problems

- Examine account information, including expiration dates and locked status

- Make sure that usernames and passwords are entered properly, especially if the password is case-sensitive

- Printing: `lpr` to send print job, `lpq` to check printer status

- Mail: Check that the address is correct, right servers and mail ports are configured

✦ Application Problems

- Check application logs for detailed error messages

- Stop, start, and restart services with the scripts in `/etc/rc.d/init.d`

- Telnet to application ports for testing (pop3-110, imap-143, smtp-25, ftp-21)

✦ Networking Utilities

- `ping`: Test network connectivity

- `traceroute`: Trace communications and see routers between local and remote host

- `netstat`: Used to show routing tables, port status, interface card statistics

✦   ✦   ✦

STUDY GUIDE

The Study Guide section provides you with the opportunity to test your knowledge about the Linux+ exam objectives that are covered in this chapter. The Assessment Questions provide practice for the real exam, and the Scenarios provide practice with real situations. If you get any questions wrong, use the answers to determine the part of the chapter that you should review before continuing.

Assessment Questions

1. During the tape backups from the last two evenings, several media write errors have occurred. Different tapes were used for each night's backup. What is the most likely cause of the problem?

   A. The wrong type of tape is being used

   B. Tape drive heads need cleaning

   C. There is a backup configuration error

   D. Tape retention is not set properly

2. A user is trying to login to the network from their Linux machine. After several attempts at logging in, a message displays that the account has been locked. What is the most likely cause of the problem?

   A. The machine is experiencing network problems

   B. The username was entered incorrectly

   C. The account is expired

   D. The user entered the wrong password too many times

3. A user is having problems accessing a file in a directory reserved for accounting users. What is the most likely cause of the problem?

   A. The user is not part of the accounting department

   B. The user does not have permissions for that directory

   C. The filename does not exist

   D. The user is not logged in to the system

4. What command can an administrator use to see the status of a print queue?

    A. `lpq`

    B. `lpr`

    C. `lp`

    D. `pq -l`

5. A Linux administrator is trying to troubleshoot a networking problem with a company's WAN. All offices except one can be contacted. What is the best command to use to find out where the problem occurred along the network connection?

    A. `netstat -r`

    B. `route`

    C. `traceroute`

    D. `lp`

6. During a software package installation, an error occurs warning that a certain library is missing, and the installation aborts. What is the most likely cause of the problem?

    A. The package does not contain the programming library

    B. The software package is corrupted

    C. The software package is dependent on another program

    D. The program is not compatible with that version of Linux

7. A contract user has just had their contract renewed. The following week, the user logs in to the system and finds that her account is locked. What is the most likely cause of the problem?

    A. The username has changed

    B. The password is incorrect

    C. The password has been changed

    D. The user's account had expired

8. An application process has just failed on a Linux system. What should you examine first to find out the root of the problem?

    A. Application logs

    B. Process statistics

    C. Cron log

    D. Application configuration file

9. A user has sent a print job to the printer, but it has not printed. The administrator checks the print queue, and finds that this job and previous jobs are still in the queue. What is the most likely cause of the problem?

   A. The user did not use the `lpr` program

   B. The print queue is full

   C. The printer is turned off

   D. The user is using the wrong printer driver

10. A user is trying to check his mail by using the `pop3` protocol and port 143. The mail program can't connect to the mail server to retrieve mail. What is the most likely cause of the problem?

    A. The mail server is down

    B. The `pop3` protocol uses port 110

    C. The mail server `smtp` process is not running

    D. You have a network problem

11. A Linux administrator is trying to connect to a remote server by using `telnet`, but the connection won't work. The remote server is on the network because the administrator can `ping` it. What is the most likely cause of the problem?

    A. The administrator should be using `ftp`

    B. The administrator should be using `traceroute` to trace the connection

    C. You can't `telnet` to a remote server

    D. The `telnet` service has been disabled

12. A user has decided to come into work overnight to get some work done. Unfortunately, she isn't able to login, even though she is using her proper name and password. What is the most likely cause of the problem?

    A. Time restrictions exist on the user's account

    B. The account has expired

    C. The server is not available overnight for backup purposes

    D. The password is incorrect

13. A Linux administrator can't connect to a remote server. What command can he use to test if the remote server is on the network?

    A. `telnet`

    B. `netstat`

    C. `ping`

    D. `route`

14. What command can you use to send a file to a printer?

    A. `lpq`

    B. `lpr`

    C. `lprm`

    D. `print`

15. A user in the engineering department wants to be able to use her department's shared directory to share files with her co-workers. What should the administrator do to give her access?

    A. Mail the user the shared directory password

    B. Add the user to the engineering group

    C. Delete the current account, and make a new account with access

    D. Temporarily give them root access

16. A user is trying to login to the system. After he enters his username, the machine hangs and won't prompt for a password. What is the most likely cause of the problem?

    A. There is a networking problem and the machine can't contact the server

    B. The username is invalid

    C. The account is expired

    D. The account is locked

17. A user has sent an e-mail, but within minutes the e-mail is returned stating that the address could not be found. What is the most likely cause of the error?

    A. The user was not using `imap`

    B. The user was using the wrong mail port

    C. The mail server is down

    D. The e-mail address is incorrect

18. A user's print job has been successfully queued, and according to the queue status is printing, but nothing is coming out of the printer. What is the most likely cause of the problem?

    A. The request was sent to a different printer

    B. The printer server is not running

    C. The printer is out of paper

    D. The printer specified was invalid

19. During a tape backup job, a recycled tape that should have been empty was full and the backup was aborted. What is the most likely cause of the problem?

   A. The tape drive needs to be cleaned

   B. The retention settings of the tape are incorrect and set too long

   C. The software is backing up the wrong servers

   D. There was too much data to back up to one tape

20. The Web server on a Linux system keeps crashing five minutes after it starts. What is the first step in trying to troubleshoot the problem?

   A. Reboot the system

   B. Check the `httpd.conf` file for errors

   C. Examine the Web server application logs

   D. Stop and restart the `httpd` daemon

Scenarios

   1. A Linux administrator is having trouble connecting to a server at a remote office. The IP address of the server is 10.1.2.100. What utilities can she use to try and troubleshoot the network connectivity problem?

   2. A user is trying to send a print job to a printer with no success. What are the steps that he should take to troubleshoot the problem?

Lab Exercises

Lab 18-1 Application and process management

The objective for this hands-on lab is to gain experience in checking system applications and processes and being able to stop and start them. You should be able to use any default Linux installation for this exercise.

   1. Logged in as root, test the `telnet` services. Examine the `/etc/inetd.conf` file, and look for the line that configures `telnet`.

   ```
   cat /etc/inetd.conf | grep telnet
   ```

   If the section is commented out with a pound (#) sign before the section, then telnet is disabled. If it isn't commented out, then edit the file and add the pound sign to the beginning of the telnet line.

   2. Restart the inetd daemon to make sure that your changes are enabled:

   ```
   killall -HUP inetd
   ```

3. Try to telnet to the local host.

```
telnet localhost
```

If the local host doesn't respond, `telnet` service is disabled.

4. Edit the `/etc/inetd.conf` file to uncomment the `telnet` line by removing the pound sign.

After you finish, restart the `inetd` process:

```
killall -HUP inetd
```

5. Use telnet again to connect to your own machine:

```
telnet localhost
```

You should now get a connection.

Answers to Chapter Questions

Chapter Pre-test

1. The most common hardware problems that cause a tape backup to fail include bad tapes, neglecting to periodically clean tape heads, and failed drive mechanisms.

2. The `ping` command sends a network packet to a host. If the host replies with an acknowledgment, then you know that it has received the request. If a reply is not received, a problem has occurred between the two hosts.

3. Many programs use the same libraries, or two different versions of the same library. If the library is updated, it may cause the other program to stop functioning.

4. The `lpr` command can be used to send a job to the printer.

5. The destination e-mail server should respond with a reply, sometimes called a "bounced" message letting you know that the e-mail did not reach its destination.

6. The `traceroute` command is used to identify the number of router hops from one host to another host. It is helpful in identifying the source of network communication problems.

7. The command to show your current running processes is `ps`.

8. If an unauthorized person is trying to break into someone's account, the system will lock out login attempts after a certain number of failures. This decreases the chance of an intruder breaking into an account by attempting multiple passwords.

9. The logs of the application should be examined to narrow down the source of the failure.

10. You can try using `telnet` on your own host to ensure that the `telnet` services are working.

Assessment Questions

1. B. Because the same errors occurred using different tapes, the error probably originated from the drive, and most likely the tape heads need cleaning. For review, see the "Backup and Restore Errors" section.

2. D. The user's account is set to lock after too many failed logins. This helps stop an unauthorized user from breaking into an account. For review, see the "Login problems" section.

3. B. The user does not have permissions for the directory. If the user should not be seeing the data, then this error is normal because they are trying to access files that they are unauthorized to see. For review, see the "File and directory permissions" section.

4. A. The `lpq` command can be used to see the status of a print queue. For review, see the "Printing problems" section.

5. C. To trace the network connection to locate where the break in communications exists, use the `traceroute` command. For review, see the "Networking connectivity" section.

6. C. Many software packages are dependent on other programs to function properly. If these dependencies do not exist, you must install them before installing your software package. For review, see the "Software Package Problems" section.

7. D. Set expiration dates for employees who may only be contracted for a certain amount of time. When their contracts expire, their account will automatically be locked. For review, see the "Login problems" section.

8. A. When an application fails, the first thing that you should do to help troubleshoot the problem is to examine the application logs for the particular error that caused the application to fail. For review, see the "Application Failures" section.

9. C. Because the print jobs have made it to the queue, the most likely problem is that the printer is turned off, or is offline. For review, see the "Printing problems" section.

10. B. If the user is trying to connect using the `pop3` protocol, the proper port to use is 110 because port 143 is for the `imap` protocol. For review, see the "Application Failures" section.

11. D. If the `telnet` service is commented out from the `/etc/inetd.conf` file, it will disable connections on that protocol. For review, see the "Application Failures" section.

12. A. Some organizations choose to implement time restrictions on accounts, so in high security environments, no one is able to log in during certain time periods. For review, see the "Login problems" section.

13. C. The best command to use for testing network communications is the `ping` command. The `ping` command sends a network packet to the remote server, and if it is on the network, will send a reply back. For review, see the "Networking connectivity" section.

14. B. The `lpr` command is used to send a file to a printer. `lpq` and `lprm` are commands used for examining and manipulating the print queue. For review, see the "Printing problems" section.

15. B. Typically, shared directory permissions are issued by using groups rather than by assigning them on an individual basis. For review, see the "File and directory permissions" section.

16. A. If a problem occurs with the login process, and no responses are received from the server, most likely you have a networking problem or a problem with the server. For review, see the "Login problems" section.

17. D. If the e-mail was returned, all mail services are working properly, but the destination e-mail address was wrong. For review, see the "Application Failures" section.

18. C. If the print job makes it to the destination print queue, you most likely have a problem with the printer, as this is the last destination for the print job. For review, see the "Printing problems" section.

19. B. The retention setting on your backup tapes tells your system how long to keep data on a tape before allowing it to be overwritten and recycled. If the time is set for too long, it won't write over the older data, causing the tape to quickly fill up. For review, see the "Backup and Restore Errors" section.

20. C. You should always check the logs of a failed application because they will give you more detailed error messages to help you troubleshoot the problem. For review, see the "Application Failures" section.

Scenarios

1. To initially test network communications, use the `ping` command, which will immediately tell you if the server is alive on the network or not:

```
ping 10.1.2.100
```

If your `ping` request times out, and you haven't received a reply, move on to using the traceroute command to find where the network communication breakdown is occurring:

```
traceroute 10.1.2.100
```

The `traceroute` command sends out network packets to find out at which point on the chain of routers the communication stops.

2. To troubleshoot a problem like this, start with the most obvious things:

- Is the printer on?

- Is the printer online?

- Is the printer out of paper?

After you have gone through the basic questions, examine how the client is trying to print the file:

- Is the user printing from an X application?

- Can the user print from another X application?

- Can the user print from the command line?

If you find that the user can successfully print from other applications or the command line, then the problem may be the printing configuration of that particular program.

If this does not solve your problem, check the server print queues to see if any problems occurred there:

```
lpq -P[printername]
```

The administrator can use this command to check the status of any print queue. From this point, you can tell whether the user's print job actually made it to the queue, and is awaiting to be printed.

You may need to ensure that the lpd daemon is running so that it can service jobs in the print queue and send it to the appropriate printer:

```
ps -ef | grep lpd
```

If the daemon is not running, you need to start it again.

Installing and Maintaining System Hardware

Continued

✦ 7.7 Remove and replace hardware and accessories (e.g., cables and components) based on symptoms of a problem by identifying common symptoms and problems associated with each component and how to troubleshoot and isolate problems

✦ 7.9 Identify proper procedures for diagnosing and troubleshooting ATA devices

✦ 7.10 Identify proper procedures for diagnosing and troubleshooting SCSI devices

✦ 7.11 Identify proper procedures for diagnosing and troubleshooting peripheral devices

✦ 7.12 Identify proper procedures for diagnosing and troubleshooting core system hardware

✦ 7.13 Identify and maintain mobile system hardware (e.g., PCMCIA, APM)

CHAPTER PRE-TEST

1. What is an IRQ?

2. What should be the SCSI ID of the host adapter?

3. What is APM?

4. When does a kernel need SMP support?

5. What do you use to configure an IDE hard drive as a master or slave?

6. What type of memory can perform error checking and correcting?

7. What is the function of the BIOS?

8. What support does the kernel require in order to run laptop devices?

9. Why does a SCSI bus need to be terminated?

10. What is USB?

✦ Answers to these questions can be found at the end of the chapter. ✦

You need to make several considerations when installing or configuring new or existing hardware on your Linux system. For example, the most overlooked aspect of installation and configuration is hardware compatibility—every piece of hardware needs corresponding kernel or driver support.

You may have a difficult time finding drivers for newer devices or older, more obscure devices. Linux developers need time to understand how a new device reacts in a Linux system, and then to create a proper driver for it.

This chapter focuses on the installation and maintenance of your system hardware, and relates considerations and tips for all types of devices—from SCSI and IDE disk drives to multi-processor support—and makes special considerations for laptops.

 Exam Tip   Most of the questions on the exam concerning hardware are not Linux-specific, and are more general hardware questions—much like the A+ exam.

Mainboard Components

 Objective   7.1 Identify basic terms, concepts, and functions of system components, including how each component should work during normal operation and during the boot process

7.12 Identify proper procedures for diagnosing and troubleshooting core system hardware

Your system mainboard, or *motherboard*, is the heart of your computer. It contains all the essential devices that make your system run, including the BIOS, CPU, RAM, and caching. The following section gives you a quick overview of these components, and many special considerations for Linux installations.

BIOS

BIOS (Basic Input Output System) is built-in software on the system mainboard that contains all the code required to control most of the basic devices and operations, and provides the interface to the underlying hardware of your server for the operating system.

Modern systems contain flash BIOS, and you can access three possible sources for a BIOS update: Your system vendor (for major brand systems), your motherboard vendor, or your BIOS vendor (if you've already purchased a replacement BIOS chip). Contact the system or motherboard vendor for the flash BIOS file that you must download. Most major system vendors have a database of models and the matching BIOS files.

Note   You must ensure that your BIOS can support Linux on your system prior to installation.

After you find the correct BIOS version, you can download it as a single compressed file that contains the BIOS image file. Most upgrades involve saving the BIOS upgrade image to a bootable floppy diskette. To update the flash BIOS, simply boot your server with the image floppy and follow the instructions.

Caution It is extremely important to not power down or reboot the server during a BIOS upgrade. If you do, you may render the BIOS inoperable.

CPU

The CPU (central processing unit) is the main component of any computer system. It is the brain that controls all aspects of a system's operations, processes program instructions, and programs data. The following sections detail some of the basic characteristics and processes that comprise the CPU.

Clock frequency

The clock frequency of a CPU refers to how often its internal clock "ticks." Each tick represents the execution of an instruction in the CPU. The faster the ticking, the faster each instruction is being processed. The clock frequency is measured in Megahertz (MHz).

Cache

To prevent bottlenecks in communications between the CPU and RAM, a special memory area, called the *cache*, holds information that is mostly used by the CPU, without having to go to RAM. Caches are available in two types — the type just described is a Level 1 cache. A Level 2 cache is a second cache layer outside of the CPU that is larger and slower than the Level 1 cache, but is included in the system to allow a second buffer between the CPU and system RAM.

Multiprocessing

The term *multiprocessing* describes a system that is using more than one processor to service requests. In order for this service to work, multiprocessing must be supported by both your hardware and your software. If your operating system does not recognize other processors, it won't use the additional CPU's.

In Linux, you must specify multiprocessor support directly into the kernel. You need a special kernel version that includes SMP (Symmetric Multi-Processing) support. SMP is the operating system's ability to assign tasks to any one of the processors in the system. The other type of processing is called *asymmetrical processing*, in which certain processors are designated for certain tasks only. Most modern systems use SMP due to its higher performance and efficiency.

System memory

RAM (Random Access Memory) is the system memory in which the server stores running applications and data. Memory is crucial to system performance because no amount of CPU power will help a machine without enough memory to store its operations. Many different types of memory are available, so it's very easy to make a mistake when choosing the right RAM for your particular system. The memory type, size, packaging, and supported chip sets are all items that you should keep in mind when upgrading server memory.

Basic types of server memory

There are two basic types of server memory: ROM and RAM. Each is very different in the way they store information and the ways they are put to use within the computer system.

ROM

Read Only Memory (ROM) is a type of memory that can't be written to; its information is static. When your system is turned off and on, the information stored in ROM will remain. ROM is most commonly used in the system BIOS because they store basic information about your computer, which rarely changes.

RAM

Random Access Memory (RAM) can be both read and written to. This type of memory is one of the most important contributors to the performance of your system. If you don't have enough RAM, your server won't be able to run as many applications, and large applications won't run very well. RAM is volatile, and when the server is switched off, anything that was in memory will be lost. There are two main types of RAM: SRAM and DRAM.

✦ **SRAM** (Static RAM) continues to hold on to its data without a refresh, as opposed to DRAM (Dynamic RAM), which must be refreshed constantly to retain its information. SRAM is much faster, but more expensive than DRAM, and is typically used for cache memory.

✦ **DRAM** (Dynamic RAM) is refreshed every few milliseconds, hence its dynamic nature. It is used for main system memory because it's much less expensive than SRAM, and the memory modules are smaller and can fit into a smaller area. There are several different types of DRAM:

- **FPM:** Fast Page Mode RAM was the traditional RAM used in computers for many years. It came in modules of 2MB to 32MB. It is considered too slow for fast, modern system memory buses.

- **EDO:** Extended Data Out DRAM is slightly faster than FPM RAM. It is similar to FPM RAM, but the timing mechanisms have been changed so that no access to the memory can begin before the last access has finished. It is therefore slightly faster than FPM memory, but still too slow for modern high-speed memory bus requirements.

- **ECC:** Error-Correcting Code memory is a type of memory that includes special parity operations for testing the accuracy of data as it passes in and out of memory. ECC RAM is used mostly in servers that require high availability. ECC RAM can prevent server crashes due to memory errors.

- **SDRAM:** Synchronous DRAM is different from earlier types of RAM in that it doesn't run asynchronously with the system clock. SDRAM is specifically designed to be synchronized with the system clock speed of your computer. SDRAM is the most common form of RAM in modern servers, due to its ability to scale to the faster bus speeds of newer motherboards. Another technique that sets SDRAM apart from other memory types is *memory interleaving*. Interleaving is used by high-end motherboards to increase performance. Memory interleaving allows simultaneous access to more than one area of memory. This improves performance because it can access more data in the same amount of time. This type of memory is helpful with large, enterprise databases and application servers.

- **RAMBUS (RDRAM):** Rambus Direct RAM is a revolutionary new RAM type created by Rambus, a company partnered with Intel. It contains an intelligent micro-channel memory bus, which can run at a very high clock speed. Although the memory module is only 16-bits wide, compared to the traditional 64-bit SDRAM module, this allows a much higher clock frequency. Adding more memory channels increases the throughput to even greater levels.

Memory packaging types

Memory comes in all sorts of types, shapes, and sizes. You must be careful in choosing the right type of memory for your particular system. The following are the most common types of memory packaging.

SIMM

Single Inline Memory Modules (SIMM) are the older standard of memory modules. They are available in two types — an older 8-bit 30-pin version, and a newer 32-bit 72-pin version. They are connected into sockets on the motherboard, which contain clips to keep them in place.

DIMM

The Dual Inline Memory Module (DIMM) are 64-bit modules and have 168 pins, and are used in most modern computer systems. They won't work in older motherboard SIMM sockets because of the difference in size. They are the most common form of packaging for SDRAM types of memory.

There are three DIMM types: Buffered, registered, and unbuffered. Most memory modules are unbuffered.

- ✦ Buffered modules contain a buffer to isolate the memory from the controller in order to minimize the load that it sees. Buffered modules are typically used in high-load server environments.

- ✦ Unbuffered modules do not contain any intermediary buffer, thereby making the system faster for certain types of applications.

✦ Registered modules, which are used in newer Fast RAM modules, contain a register that delays all information transferred to the module by one clock cycle, allowing the information to be buffered before going to the controller.

Serial Presence Detect (SPD) is a small EEPROM that resides on newer fast RAM DIMMS. When a computer system boots up, it detects the configuration of the memory modules in order to run properly.

RIMM

RDRAM memory modules are called *Rambus Inline Memory Modules* (RIMM) and contain 184 pins. Because RDRAM works in channels, any empty sockets have to be filled with a blank memory module called a *Continuity Rambus Inline Memory Module*.

Linux memory considerations

All types of memory — EDO, DRAM, and SDRAM — can be used with Linux. The only problem that you may run into is that older Linux kernels may not recognize an amount of RAM of 64MB. If you run into this problem, you need to pass parameters to the kernel from the LILO (Linux Loader) configuration file in /etc/lilo.conf:

```
append="mem=<amount of RAM>M"
```

If you have 128MB or RAM, enter the following:

```
append="mem=128M"
```

Caution Don't state an amount of memory that you don't have, or your system may crash.

System Resources

Objective 7.5 Assure that system hardware is configured correctly prior to installation (e.g, IRQs, BIOS, DMA, SCSI, cabling) settings by identifying available IRQs, DMAs, and I/O addresses and procedures for device installation and configuration

To function properly, devices and peripherals must be able to communicate directly with the system resources, such as the CPU, memory, and disk drives. To facilitate this process, and to ensure that a device can talk to these resources when needed, the computer assigns certain lines and channels for that particular device to operate on. This allows the computer's resources to be allocated and shared among all the devices. These resources are Interrupt Request Lines (IRQ), Input/Output addresses, and Direct Memory Access (DMA) channels.

Exam Tip Pay close attention to some of the system resources that are used for popular devices, such as floppy drives or sound cards.

IRQ

Interrupt Request Lines (IRQs) allow a device to communicate directly with the CPU. The process of getting the computer's attention is referred to as "using an *interrupt*." The name accurately describes its use because the device will actually interrupt the CPU to allocate a resource to it. IRQs are assigned by numbers from 0 to 15. Each device is assigned its own IRQ to use. No more than one device can use the same interrupt or a conflict will occur, causing the device to not function properly. Some devices actually share IRQs, including serial COM ports. Table 19-1 summarizes a list of common IRQs and the devices that use them.

Table 19-1
Standard Interrupts and Device Assignments

IRQ	Device Assignment	Typical Uses
0	System Timer	-
1	Keyboard	-
2	Cascade for IRQ's 8-15, redirected to IRQ 9	Modems, COM 3, COM 4 serial ports
3	Serial Port (COM 2)	COM 4 Serial Port, Modems, Sound Card, Network Card
4	Serial Port (COM 1)	COM 3 Serial Port, Modems Sound Card, Network Card
5	Parallel Port (LPT 2)	Sound card, Network Card
6	Floppy Controller	-
7	Parallel Port (LPT 1)	Sound Card, Network Card, other peripherals
8	Real-time Clock	-
9	Unassigned (Redirected from IRQ 2)	Sound Card, Network Card, SCSI Adapter, other peripherals
10	Unassigned	Sound Card, Network Card, SCSI Adapter, other peripherals
11	Unassigned	Video Card, Sound Card, Network Card, SCSI Adapter, other peripherals
12	Mouse	Video Card, Sound Card, Network Card, SCSI Adapter, other peripherals
13	Math Co-processor	-
14	Hard Disk Controller (Primary IDE)	SCSI Adapter
15	Hard Disk Controller (Secondary IDE)	SCSI Adapter, Network Card

I/O addresses

Input/Output (I/O) addresses represent special locations in system memory that are reserved for a particular device. As information is passed back and forth between the peripheral device and the CPU, the I/O address is a common place for this information to reside. I/O address ranges can vary in size, depending on the type of device. As with IRQs, I/O addresses must be unique for each device. Table 19-2 is a list of the most frequently used I/O addresses and the devices that use them.

Table 19-2 Summary of Common I/O Addresses and Devices	
I/O Address Range	*Device*
1F0-1F8	Hard Drive Controller
200-20F	Game Controller
201	Game I/O
278-27F	Parallel Port (LPT 2)
2F8-2FF	Serial Port (COM 2)
320-32F	Hard Drive Controller
378-37F	Parallel Port (LPT 1)
3B0-3BF	Graphics Adapter (Mono)
3D0-3DF	Graphics Adapter (Color)
3F0-3F7	Floppy Controller
3F8-3FF	Serial Port (COM 1)

Direct memory access

Direct Memory Access (DMA) channels are used to facilitate the transfer of data from a peripheral device directly to system memory. Information transfer is faster and more efficient because it doesn't have to go through the CPU to get to system memory. DMA channels are used most often by sound cards, but they are a scarce resource — only seven of them exist.

Laptop Considerations

 7.13 Identify and maintain mobile system hardware (e.g., PCMCIA, APM)

Running Linux on a laptop can often be more difficult than running Linux on a regular system because laptop hardware is much different. Also, the drivers to properly control laptop devices have not yet been created under Linux.

Most hardware driver problems occur with the video system, PCMCIA support, infrared ports, sound cards, and modems. When you want to buy a laptop for use with Linux, do a careful investigation of hardware compatibility, and see if you can get appropriate Linux drivers and support for the laptop's devices.

Beyond basic peripherals, such as video and sound, you need two specific items for use on a laptop: PCMCIA and APM support.

PCMCIA

PCMCIA (Personal Computer Memory Card International Association) is a standard set by hardware companies for interface and device cards that can fit into a small laptop slot.

For installation under Linux, you need to install PCMCIA support as part of your kernel. The kernel must also be able to support loadable modules for devices.

APM

APM (Advanced Power Management) is an excellent feature for laptops because it allows the laptop to suspend operations for a period of time for actions including turning off the monitor and powering off the hard drive, to reduce battery usage.

APM must be supported by your laptop BIOS because this is where hardware control initiates. You also need to have APM support enabled in your Linux kernel.

Linux Peripheral Configuration

7.4 Assure that system hardware is configured correctly prior to installation (e.g., IRQs, BIOS, DMA, SCSI settings, cabling) by identifying proper procedures for installing and configuring peripheral devices

7.11 Identify proper procedures for diagnosing and troubleshooting peripheral devices

You can install many different peripheral devices on your Linux system. You must also check many different characteristics and settings before performing installation, compatibility, system resource settings, and expansion slot availability.

With most devices, you must ensure that you are using free IRQ, DMA, and I/O resources that don't conflict with another device. If you do have conflicts, certain peripherals may not work, or may conflict with critical devices, such as disk controllers and network cards. Here are some points to consider when installing certain devices under Linux:

✦ **Video Cards:** Linux works with all video cards in simple text mode. Unless you need X-windows capability, you have no need to install an X server on your Linux system — especially if you are running it as a server. X-windows uses a lot of RAM, and you must also carefully check that you have drivers available for your video card to work in X-windows.

✦ **Sound Cards:** Generally, you have no need for a sound card on a server system, but if you need it on a desktop multimedia system, keep a few things in mind. Be careful when choosing which I/O port, IRQ, and DMA resources that the sound card will use. Network and SCSI cards are often configured with the same resources. This will cause a resource conflict, and it may disable your SCSI hard drive bus, resulting in a system that won't boot. In the case of a network card conflict, the server won't be able to communicate with the network.

Installing and Configuring SCSI Devices

Objective ➡

7.3 Assure that system hardware is configured correctly prior to installation (e.g., IRQs, BIOS, DMA, SCSI settings, cabling) by identifying proper procedures for installing and configuring SCSI and IEEE 1394 devices

7.6 Remove and replace hardware and accessories (e.g., cables and components) based on symptoms of a problem by identifying basic procedures for adding and removing field replaceable components

7.7 Remove and replace hardware and accessories (e.g., cables and components) based on symptoms of a problem by identifying common symptoms and problems associated with each component and how to troubleshoot and isolate problems

7.10 Identify proper procedures for diagnosing and troubleshooting SCSI devices

SCSI (Small Computer Systems Interface) is an advanced system bus built for high performance disks and peripheral communications. Although much more expensive than IDE/ATA, SCSI is preferred in server installations for its robust performance and flexible expansion options. Many devices can be chained together on a SCSI bus, which is required for large disk space installations and fault-tolerant RAID systems.

SCSI definitions

Before describing some of the wide variety of SCSI technologies, I need to define several key characteristics of SCSI devices in order to compare the different technologies:

✦ Clock Speed: The clock speed of the SCSI bus, measured in MHz.

✦ Bus Speed: The speed of the SCSI bus, measured in MB/s.

✦ Bus Width: The width of the SCSI bus. Narrow SCSI is 8-bit, Wide SCSI is 16-bit.

✦ Signaling: The type of voltage signaling used to trigger events. The three types are Single Ended (SE), Low-Voltage Differential (LVD), and High Voltage Differential (HVD).

✦ Termination: Describes the various types of terminators needed on the SCSI bus. Termination of a SCSI bus is critical to block signal reflection noise.

✦ Cable Type and Length: Different SCSI technologies require certain cable types and lengths.

✦ Devices Supported: The number of devices allowed at one time on the SCSI bus chain.

SCSI technologies

There have been a wide variety of SCSI standards — each building upon the other in terms of newer technologies that increase the speed and the bandwidth of SCSI communications. The following lists each of the SCSI types that you may encounter and their technical characteristics.

✦ SCSI: The original SCSI 1 standard introduced an 8-bit parallel bus that can perform transfers of up to 5 MB/sec.

✦ WIDE SCSI: Also part of the SCSI 2 standard, it increased the width of the bus from 8 bits to 16 bits. This allows double the amount of information transfer, and also increases the maximum number of devices on the SCSI chain to 16 — the normal SCSI can only have a maximum of 8.

✦ FAST SCSI: Part of the SCSI 2 standard that raised speeds to 10 MB/sec. It also introduced a different type of bus called a *differential bus*, as opposed to the single-ended bus of SCSI 1. The differential type of bus offered better protection from interference, and increased the bus length to 25 meters from 6 meters.

✦ ULTRA SCSI: Another implementation in the SCSI 2 standard, Ultra SCSI technology doubles the transfer information using the same clock rate speed. This doubles the speed of the bus to 20 MB/sec.

✦ ULTRA WIDE SCSI: This technology refers to using the same doubled transfer capability over a wide SCSI bus. Because the ULTRA SCSI bus is running over 16 bits instead of 8, the effective transfer rate is 40 MB/sec.

✦ ULTRA 2 WIDE SCSI: Utilizing a Low Voltage Differential signaling method, this allows the ULTRA 2 WIDE SCSI bus to double its clock speed, offering an effective transfer rate of 80 MB/sec. This LVD bus can also run in single-ended mode to be compatible with older UTLRA technology. If you do run an Ultra SCSI device on an Ultra2 bus, the bus will always run at the speed of the slowest component.

✦ ULTRA 160 SCSI: This technology improves on the transfer rate again, and offers a transfer rate of 160 MB/sec over a 16-bit bus.

✦ ULTRA 320 SCSI: A new type of SCSI bus that uses a 16-bit wide LVD bus with a doubled clock speed to offer transfer rates up to 320 MB/sec. It is also backwards-compatible with older devices.

Table 19-3 shows a comparison of different SCSI technologies:

Table 19-3
Comparison of different SCSI technologies

SCSI Type	Bus Clocking Speed (MHz)	Bus Width (Bits)	Transfer Speed (MB/s)	Signaling Method
SCSI	5	8	5	SE/HVD
Wide SCSI	5	16	10	SE/HVD
Fast SCSI	10	8	10	SE/HVD
Ultra SCSI	20	8	20	SE/HVD
Ultra Wide SCSI	20	16	40	SE/HVD
Ultra 2 Wide SCSI	40	16	80	LVD/SE
Ultra 160 SCSI	80	16	160	LVD/SE
Ultra 320 SCSI	160	16	320	LVD/SE

SCSI cabling and termination

Because SCSI comes in a wide of variety of bus speeds, clock rates, and signaling methods, it also offers a wide variety of cable and termination requirements for the different SCSI types:

✦ **SCSI 1 50-Pin Connectors (Narrow):** SCSI 1 devices use either a 50-pin "D" connector, or a 50-pin Centronics type of connector. The "D" connector is named for the shape of the shell that surrounds the pins. It is also called a DB-50, and resembles a DB25 or DB9 type serial and parallel connector. The Centronics connector (which is named after the type of printer that used this type of connector for a parallel interface) does not actually have pins, but 50 flat contacts. Internally, SCSI 1 devices use a rectangular connector of 50 pins, split into two 25-pin rows.

✦ **SCSI 2 High density 50 and 68-Pin (Wide) Connectors:** Similar to the "D" shaped connectors used by SCSI 1 devices, but they are much smaller, with the pins closer together. The 68-pin versions are also referred to as *Wide connectors*. For internal cabling, SCSI-2 devices use high-density 50-pin or 68-pin wide connectors.

✦ **SCSI-3 68-Pin Centronics Connector (VHDCI):** The Very High Density Cable Interconnect resembles the large 50-Pin Centronics connector. These connectors use 68 contacts, which sit very close to each other. Its size makes it much easier to plug two cables into the back of a host adapter.

✦ **SCA Adapters:** For RAID or multi-disk systems with many SCSI hard drives, the connectors used are Single Connector Attachment adapters. Their special connections allow all signaling and power to be fed through one connector (that the hard drive plugs right into) without any cabling. This technology is most important for hot swapping drives: The ability to remove and replace drives without having to power off the system. The SCA connector utilizes 80 pins in a Centronics type of setting. The server will usually consist of a SCSI backplane with several of the connectors where the hard drives can be plugged into.

Cable lengths

Depending on the type of signaling technology that is employed, maximum cabling lengths can vary. For older single-ended signaling, the degradation rate for the signal increases dramatically as the cable length increases. For a fast bus speed on a single-ended system, the maximum cable lengths are fairly short. For LVD-type signaling, the signal degradation is much less, resulting in longer maximum cable lengths for the SCSI bus. Refer to Table 19-4 for a summary of SCSI cable lengths.

<table>
<tr><td colspan="3" align="center">Table 19-4
Summary of SCSI cable lengths</td></tr>
<tr><td>*SCSI Type*</td><td>*Contacts/Pins*</td><td>*Cabling Length(meters)*</td></tr>
<tr><td>SCSI</td><td>50</td><td>6 SE/25 HVD</td></tr>
<tr><td>Wide SCSI</td><td>68</td><td>6 SE/25 HVD</td></tr>
<tr><td>Fast SCSI</td><td>50</td><td>3 SE/25 HVD</td></tr>
<tr><td>Fast Wide SCSI</td><td>68</td><td>3 SE/25 HVD</td></tr>
<tr><td>Ultra SCSI</td><td>50</td><td>3 SE/25 HVD</td></tr>
<tr><td>Wide Ultra SCSI</td><td>68</td><td>3 SE/25 HVD</td></tr>
<tr><td>Ultra 2 SCSI</td><td>50</td><td>12 LVD/25 HVD</td></tr>
<tr><td>Wide Ultra 2 SCSI</td><td>68</td><td>12 LVD/25 HVD</td></tr>
<tr><td>Ultra 3 SCSI</td><td>68</td><td>25 LVD</td></tr>
</table>

Termination

Termination of the SCSI bus is necessary to provide a way of stopping cable signals from reflecting from the end of the bus back onto the wire and causing data corruption. The terminator must be connected to the end of the SCSI bus at the end of the chain of devices. Some SCSI devices are self-terminating, but if yours isn't, you will need a separate terminator. Older SCSI-1 devices used simple passive termination, which uses resistors to stop the signal from reflecting back onto the bus. Faster speed single-ended devices also use active termination, which adds voltage regulators to the resistors to more efficiently terminate signals.

SCSI-2 and SCSI-3 devices need terminators based on the type of signaling being used. LVD (Low voltage differential), HVD (High voltage differential), and Single-ended devices need a terminator for each specific type.

SCSI device configuration

When configuring a SCSI bus, you must be aware of several rules and limitations. These include host adapter settings, SCSI ID setting, and mixing different SCSI types.

Exam Tip   Know how to configure a SCSI bus with a host adapter and devices; pay careful attention to IDs, cable lengths, and termination.

Host adapters

The SCSI host adapter facilitates communications between the system bus and the devices on the SCSI chain. The host adapter must be compatible with the SCSI devices that you are using. Most host adapters are backwards-compatible, so older devices can still be used with your system. The host adapter must also be electrically compatible with your devices. You can't mix HVD types of devices on the same bus with single-ended or LVD type devices. Single-ended and LVD devices are electrically compatible, but your devices must support multimode operations. The only limitation is that the bus will only run as fast as your slowest device. Newer host adapters don't have this speed limitation, because they use special segments on the same SCSI channel to separate the devices, or sometimes run a separate SCSI channel for devices running on a different mode.

Devices configuration

The SCSI system is configured as a bus topology because devices are chained together from one end to the other and terminated at each end. Original 8-bit SCSI devices can have up to 8 devices on the bus. The wide 16-bit versions can have up to 16 devices.

Device IDs

Each device on a SCSI bus must have its own separate identification number. This is how the system allocates control of the bus to a specific device. The numbers also give a priority level for the devices; higher device IDs have greater priority than lower numbers. This is why the SCSI host adapter is usually designated as device 7.

To set the device ID, older SCSI devices use jumpers on the card to configure the ID. Newer devices use a small button that, when pressed, can cycle through the choices of ID numbers. SCSI IDs can also be regulated through software.

Device mixing

The best way to mix different SCSI types, such as wide and narrow, is to use a host adapter that supports segmentation. In this configuration, each segment has its own cabling and termination that won't conflict with the other. Using different SCSI types on the same bus channel is possible, but you should keep in mind some important configuration items. You will need to use cable adapters that will facilitate connections between 50-pin devices and 68-pin wide devices. Ensure that these special cables support termination so a wide-to-narrow adapter will terminate the extra wide connections.

Linux SCSI devices

You can find the device names of SCSI devices within the /dev directory. For SCSI disk drives, the /dev directory contains IDs for each of the drives. For example, the first drive on the first SCSI bus is called /dev/sda, and the second drive is /dev/sdb. Each disk is divided into partitions, such as /dev/sda1, or /dev/sdb2.

SCSI CD-ROM devices have traditionally used /dev/sr as an identifier, but more recent distributions use /dev/scd, so the first CD-ROM is /dev/scd0.

SCSI tape devices are slightly different — as the device name indicates — if the tape will or won't use rewind. For example, the first tape drive is /dev/st0, but the first tape with no rewind uses /dev/nst0.

Most other SCSI devices, such as scanners, use the device names of /dev/sg0, /dev/sg1, and so on.

ATA/IDE Devices

7.2 Assure that system hardware is configured correctly prior to installation (e.g., IRQs, BIOS, DMA, SCSI settings, cabling) by identifying proper procedures for installing and configuring ATA devices

7.6 Remove and replace hardware and accessories (e.g., cables and components) based on symptoms of a problem by identifying basic procedures for adding and removing field replaceable components

7.7 Remove and replace hardware and accessories (e.g., cables and components) based on symptoms of a problem by identifying common symptoms and problems associated with each component and how to troubleshoot and isolate problems

7.9 Identify proper procedures for diagnosing and troubleshooting ATA devices

ATA/IDE is the most often-used disk type on desktop systems. IDE (Integrated Drive Electronics) places the bulk of the IO "intelligence" on the disk controller card. Early drives had a separate controller and disk drive.

Most new ATA drives are available in the following types:

✦ Ultra ATA/33: Includes UDMA (which is an advanced DMA technique that essentially doubles the speed of data transfer clocking) allowing a throughput of 33 MB/s. ATA/33 also introduced a new 80-conductor IDE cable to support reliability with the faster speeds. It also uses CRC (Cyclical Redundancy Checking) to provide error checking.

✦ Ultra ATA/66: This type of drive features faster UDMA modes that allow up to 66 MB/s data transfer. The special 80-conductor IDE cable, which was optional with ATA-33, is mandatory for ATA-66.

✦ Ultra ATA/100: The latest standard that brings data transfer speeds to 100 MB/s, and also improves LBA support for extremely large hard drives.

IDE drive configuration

One IDE channel can support up to two devices. To differentiate between the devices, one drive is configured as the master drive and the other as the slave. No performance difference exists because these are just identifiers for the drives. It is often easier to think of master and slave alternately as Drive 0 and Drive 1.

You must follow certain rules when configuring the master and slave designations for IDE hard drives. With two devices present, one must be configured to be the master, and the other the slave. You can't have two masters or two slaves; this will typically result in a boot failure because the system won't be able to properly identify the boot disk drive.

Some systems also have a third option, called *cable select*, in which the master and slave are configured using a special cable with specific connectors for each drive.

Jumpers

IDE drives use jumpers to set their configuration. A *jumper* is a small connector that fits over two pins on the hard drive. The jumper will make a connection between those two pins to signal the configuration for the hard drive. Even though manufacturers have their own sets of pins on the hard drive for these configurations (typically six to ten pins), most pin configurations are generally the same.

Typically, the proper settings for the jumpers are printed on the hard drive, but you may have to consult the manufacturer's documentation or Web site for the information.

Master/Slave settings

To set the drive as the Master: Use a jumper to join the two pins that are labeled as Master or "MA." Most hard drives ship from the manufacturer configured as the master, so you may have to adjust the jumper if you need to use the hard drive as a slave.

To set the drive as the Slave: Use a jumper to join the two pins that are labeled as Slave, or "SA."

Cabling

IDE cables are 40- or 80-pin ribbon cables. They can only go on one way on the hard drive or mainboard connector, with the designated pin 1 of the cable going to pin 1 of the connector. Most ribbon cables have a red stripe along the wire that designates it as pin 1.

Linux ATA/IDE Drive configuration

In Linux, the first IDE hard drive is given the device name of /dev/hda. The second drive is /dev/hdb. When partitioning the drives, the first partition of the first IDE drive is designated /dev/hda1, and so on.

Exam Tip   Know how to install and configure ATA/IDE hard drives, including master/slave settings, jumpers, and cabling.

Linux Support for Other Devices

7.11 Identify proper procedures for diagnosing and troubleshooting peripheral devices

Support for newer technologies, such as IEEE 1394 and USB, can only come as fast as Linux developers and related project work can come up with drivers for these devices.

IEEE 1394 (Firewire)

This communications technology standard, sometimes called "Firewire" as trade-marked by Apple and "iLink" as trademarked by Sony, is a serial bus that can run at up to 400 Megabits/sec. It is similar to a USB bus, but allows a SCSI command set to be sent over a standard IEEE 1394 bus. It is most often used for high speed periph-erals, such as digital video cameras, CD writers, DVDs, optical drives, and scanners.

Linux has limited support for IEEE 1394 devices, and you must download special drivers to use them.

USB

The Universal Serial Bus (USB) is an advanced serial bus that can perform at speeds up to 12 MB/sec. Up to 127 devices can be connected using a series of USB hubs, which can connect up to 7 devices. USB is a hot pluggable and plug-and-play compatible technology, so you can attach or remove peripherals without having to power off the system. Many different types of devices use USB, such as printers, scanners, mouses, and keyboards. USB allows faster data transfer rates than typical methods, such as a serial or parallel interface.

Only the latest kernel versions contain code for USB support at this time. Be sure to check hardware compatibility lists for a list of supported hardware.

Summary

This chapter gives you an overview of hardware components and how they work under Linux. In most cases, they work the same as in any other operating system, but for some devices, you must make some special considerations, including kernel support and availability of drivers. For the exam, remember the following key points:

✦ Pay close attention to hardware compatibility and kernel support for Linux devices

✦ Many devices need special drivers of kernel modules to work

✦ Know the typical IRQ and I/O ports of popular devices

✦ Know how to install and configure SCSI and ATA/IDE drives

✦   ✦   ✦

STUDY GUIDE

The Study Guide section provides you with the opportunity to test your knowledge about the Linux+ exam objectives that are covered in this chapter. The Assessment Questions provide practice for the real exam, and the Scenarios provide practice with real situations. If you get any questions wrong, use the answers to determine the part of the chapter that you should review before continuing.

Assessment Questions

1. What is the default IRQ for a floppy drive?

   A. 6

   B. 5

   C. 4

   D. 7

2. A SCSI host adapter came factory-installed with a SCSI ID of 1. What SCSI ID should the technician set the host adapter to?

   A. 1

   B. 0

   C. 7

   D. 2

3. Parallel port LPT 1 uses what I/O address?

   A. 1FO – 1F8

   B. 278 – 27F

   C. 2F8 – 2FF

   D 378 – 37F

4. You have just installed 2 IDE drives on one IDE channel of your system. How will each one be configured?

   A. Master, Servant

   B. First, Second

   C. Primary, Secondary

   D. Master, Slave

5. How many devices can be added to a typical IDE or EIDE controller?

    A. 7

    B. 2

    C. 4

    D. 1

6. What type of slot is usually found on a laptop computer that can be used to install modem and network cards?

    A. PCMCIA

    B. PCI

    C. AGP

    D. SCSI

7. How many USB peripherals can you connect at once?

    A. 127

    B. 7

    C. 27

    D. 1

8. The red stripe on the edge of an IDE/ATA cable identifies what feature?

    A. The cable supports cable select

    B. The cable is UDMA cable

    C. The wire that should be connected to Pin 1 on the hard drive

    D. The cable is self-terminating

9. Which drive under Linux is indicated by /dev/sda?

    A. Raid controller

    B. Second SCSI drive

    C. First IDE drive

    D. First SCSI drive

10. What support needs to be added to the Linux kernel for multiprocessing?

    A. APM support

    B. SMP support

    C. PCMCIA support

    D. API support

11. What application in Linux must properly support your video card to use GUI features?

    A. X-windows

    B. AGP

    C. Screensaver

    D. APM

12. What support is needed by your BIOS and Linux kernel to run power management on your laptop?

    A. API

    B. APG

    C. PCMCIA

    D. APM

13. Which IRQ does the serial port COM 1 use?

    A. 3

    B. 1

    C. 4

    D. 5

14. A second hard drive is being installed in a SCSI bus system. What should you do to the bus after the installation is complete?

    A. The system should be rebooted

    B. The bus should be reset

    C. The bus should be terminated

    D. The host adapter should be rebooted

15. What two serial com ports share IRQ 3?

    A. COM 1 and COM 5

    B. COM 2 and COM 3

    C. COM 1 and COM 3

    D. COM 2 and COM 4

16. A Linux administrator has installed a second CPU on a dual CPU system. When tests are run afterwards, there is still no performance. What is the most likely cause of the problem?

    A. The kernel must be able to support SMP

    B. The system needs to be rebooted twice

    C. There is not enough memory

    D. No applications are currently running

17. What should you check before installing a hardware device on a Linux system?

    A. Video support

    B. Hardware compatibility

    C. Bug reports

    D. Memory usage

18. What type of RAM supports error checking?

    A. SIMM

    B. EDO

    C. ECC

    D. ROM

19. What is the device name of the first rewinding SCSI tape device in a Linux system?

    A. /dev/nst1

    B. /dev/st0

    C. /dev/st1

    D. /dev/nst0

20. A system is installed with 128MB of memory, but when the system boots up, it only recognizes 64MB. What is mostly likely the cause of the problem?

    A. The RAM does not support error checking

    B. The RAM is bad

    C. The amount of memory needs to be set in LILO

    D. The RAM is not compatible with the kernel

Scenarios

1. An administrator is installing two ATA/IDE hard drives, and an IDE CD-ROM drive into a Linux machine. The system contains two IDE controllers. What is the best configuration for these devices?

Answers to Chapter Questions

Chapter Pre-test

1. An IRQ is an interrupt request line — a resource used to tell the CPU that a device has data that needs to be processed.

2. The SCSI host adapter should be ID 7 to give it the highest priority on the SCSI bus.

3. APM stands for *advanced power management*, which can help with saving battery power on laptops by shutting down devices when not in use.

4. The kernel will need SMP support for multiprocessing capabilities.

5. To configure an IDE hard drive as a master or slave, you need to set its jumpers to a particular setting.

6. ECC memory can perform error checking and correcting.

7. The BIOS (Basic Input Output System) contains code to control all basic devices and operations of the computer, and provides an interface between the operating system and hardware.

8. The kernel needs to support PCMCIA, which is used for laptop card and devices.

9. A SCSI bus needs to be terminated to prevent electronic signals from reflecting back onto the bus.

10. USB stands for *Universal Serial Bus*, an advanced form of serial bus that is very fast, and can connect several devices together at once.

Assessment Questions

1. A. The default IRQ for a floppy drive is IRQ 6. IRQ 4 is for COM1, IRQ 5 is for LPT2, and IRQ 7 is for LPT 1. For review, see the "System Resources" section.

2. C. The host adapter should be set to ID 7 to give it the highest priority on the bus. For review, see the "SCSI device configuration" section.

3. D. The parallel port uses I/O address 378-37F. The I/O address 1F0 – 1F8 is used for the Hard drive controller, I/O address 278 – 27F is used for LPT 2, and 2F8 – 2FF is used for COM2. For review, see the "System Resources" section.

4. D. For two IDE drives, one should be configured as the master, and one should be configured as the slave. If you had another channel, you could take the slave drive and install it as a master on that channel. For review, see the "IDE drive configuration" section.

5. B. A single IDE controller can handle up to two devices. For review, see the "IDE drive configuration" section.

6. A. A laptop card slot uses the PCMCIA standard. For review, see the "Laptop Considerations" section.

7. A. Utilizing USB hubs, you can theoretically use up to 127 devices. For review, see the "Linux Support for Other Devices" section.

8. C. The red stripe on the edge of an IDE cable signifies that it should go to pin 1 on the drive and mainboard connectors. If it is reversed, it may damage the components. For review, see the "IDE drive configuration" section.

9. D. The drive /dev/sda is the first SCSI drive on the system. IDE drives are indicated by /dev/hda, hdb, etc. For review, see the "Linux SCSI Devices" section.

10. B. To support multiprocessing, your kernel needs to have SMP (Symmetrical Multiprocessing) support. For review, see the "CPU" section.

11. A. In order for your video card to be supported under Linux, it needs to be supported by your X-windows application. For review, see the "Linux Peripheral Configuration" section.

12. D. To utilize power management on laptops running Linux, the BIOS and the Linux kernel need to support APM (Advanced Power Management). For review, see the "Laptop Considerations" section.

13. C. The serial port COM 1 uses IRQ4. It also shares this with COM 3. For review, see the "System Resources" section.

14. C. The bus should always be properly terminated at the ends of the chain. For review, see the "SCSI Device Configuration" section.

15. D. Serial ports COM2 and COM4 share IRQ 3. For review, see the "System Resources" section.

16. A. In order to run multiprocessing, the kernel must support SMP. This must be compiled into the kernel if it does not already support it. For review, see the "CPU" section.

17. B. Before installing any device, you should check to see if it's compatible with the Linux kernel, and if you have a proper driver for the device. For review, see the "Linux Peripheral Configuration" section.

18. C. ECC memory performs error checking and correction. For review, see the "System memory" section.

19. B. The first rewinding SCSI tape drive is set to /dev/st0. The no-rewind tape would be set at /dev/nst0. For review, see the "Linux SCSI devices" section.

20. C. Some older kernels won't recognize memory over 64MB. To enable the extra RAM, it has to be specified in the LILO configuration file. For review, see the "System memory" section.

Scenarios

1. It is easiest to assign the two hard drives to one controller, and the CD-ROM to the other controller. If you have the CD-ROM and a hard drive on the same controller, it may cause performance issues because the CD-ROM is much slower than the hard drive.

   Configure the first hard drive as the master, and the second hard drive as a slave on the first controller.

   The CD-ROM can then be installed as a master on the second controller.

What's on the CD-ROM

This appendix provides you with information on the contents of the CD-ROM that accompanies this book.

The following programs are included on this CD:

+ Linux+ Bible Certification Test Engine
+ FrazierWall Linux
+ System Manager In a Box
+ Big brother system and network monitor
+ Nettest
+ Sysmon
+ RPM
+ Yafc
+ Encompass
+ Squid Web Proxy Cache
+ AbiWord The Open Source, Cross-Platform Word Processor
+ Phat Linux
+ Apache
+ Apache 2.0 White Papers

Also included is an electronic, searchable version of the book that you can view with Adobe Acrobat Reader.

System Requirements

Make sure that your computer meets the minimum system requirements listed in this section. If your computer doesn't match up to most of these requirements, you may have a problem using the contents of the CD.

For Microsoft Windows 9*x*/ME or Windows NT/2000:

+ PC with a Pentium processor running at 120 MHz or faster
+ At least 32 MB of RAM
+ At least 100 MB of free hard drive space
+ Ethernet network interface card (NIC) or modem with a speed of at least 28,800 bps
+ A CD-ROM drive — double-speed (2x) or faster

For the Linux-only programs, the minimum requirements are:

+ PC with a Pentium processor running at 120 MHz
+ 32 MB of RAM (64 MB recommended)
+ 500 MB of available hard drive space
+ Ethernet network interface card (NIC)
+ A CD-ROM drive — double-speed (2x) or faster

Using the CD with Microsoft Windows

To install the items from the CD to your hard drive, follow these steps:

1. Insert the CD into your computer's CD-ROM drive.
2. Click Start ➪ Run.
3. When the Run dialog box appears, choose Browse, locate your CD-ROM drive, and double-click your CD-ROM drive to view the contents of the CD-ROM.
4. Double-click the folder of the software that you want to install and then choose the Install.exe or Setup.exe program.
5. Click OK.
6. In the Run dialog box, you should see the path of the software that you want to install. Click the OK button.

Using the CD with Linux

To install items from the CD to your Linux system, follow these steps:

1. Insert the CD into your computer's CD-ROM drive.

2. From the command prompt, type `mount /dev/cdrom /mnt/cdrom`.

3. To change to the CD-ROM directory, type `cd /mnt/cdrom`.

4. To change to a directory that contains the application that you want to install, type `cd/mnt/cdrom/[directory name]`.

5. To install the application, follow these guidelines:

   - For RPM, type rpm -i [filename]

   - For Debian (files ending in .deb), type dpkg -i [filename]

   - For Slackware, type (.tgz) installpkg [filename]

   - For binaries that are tarred and zipped (files ending in tar.gz), type tar -zxvf [filename]

   - If your version of tar doesn't support gunzip options, use these two separate commands: To unzip the file type `gunzip [filename]` or to extract the file from the tar archive type the command: `tar -xvf [filename]`

For further installation instructions, please consult the README file for the program.

The CD-ROM contains some great applications that I think you will enjoy. Also included on the CD-ROM are the Linux+ Bible Certification Test Engine and the electronic version of the book in Adobe PDF format. The next section is a summary of the contents of the CD-ROM.

Microsoft Windows applications

Every program on the CD-ROM is located in the folder name associated with the name of the software. The following applications that install under Microsoft Windows are on the CD-ROM.

Electronic version of the Linux+ Certification Bible

The complete (and searchable) text of this book is on the CD-ROM in Adobe's Portable Document Format (PDF), readable with the Adobe Acrobat Reader (also included). For more information on Adobe Acrobat Reader, go to `www.adobe.com`.

Linux+ Bible Certification test engine

The Linux+ Bible Certification test engine will help you test your knowledge of all the objectives covered in this book. The test engine has over 250 sample test questions that mimic the real Linux+ exam. Also included are detailed explanations of the correct answers.

Linux links

This is a standard text document that provides you with Web address links that you can use to progress your studies. No need to search the Internet for the most popular Linux URLs — this file has them all.

Phat Linux

Phat Linux is a full running version of Linux, but it can run on your current Windows partition. You don't need to partition drives for this installation of Linux. Phat Linux is a user-friendly Linux distribution that is easy to install and can co-exist with Microsoft Windows. Phat Linux allows Windows users to run Linux while preserving their Windows partition.

Linux applications

Every program on the CD-ROM is located in the folder name associated with the name of the software. The following applications that install under Linux are on the CD-ROM.

FrazierWall Linux

FrazierWall Linux was originally created to be a customized firewall. It was based on the Linux Router Project and Coyote Linux 1.03 (`www.frazierwall.com`). Frazier Wall continued to modify and develop, as a separate distribution of Linux.

System Manager In a Box

Linux is difficult to configure and to maintain; in fact, computer professionals should really do this job. System Manager in a Box performs basic Linux administration tasks, including:

✦ Reports configuration problems with common Linux packages

✦ Gives tuning tips for common Linux packages

✦ Gives an overview of activity and job control on a computer

✦ Performs daily administration tasks

✦ Runs your own regular administration scripts

You can run System Manager in a Box directly in a terminal window, call it from other programs, or install it as a Web server CGI plug-in.

Big Brother system and network monitor

Big Brother is designed to enable any user to check the status of his or her network in near real-time, from any Web browser, and at any location.

Nettest

Nettest is a Perl script that tests the integrity of a net connection. If the connection is down, Nettest will beep the speaker, send e-mail, write in the system logs, or all of the above.

Sysmon

Sysmon is a network-monitoring tool designed to provide high performance and accurate network monitoring. Currently supported protocols include SMTP, IMAP, HTTP, TCP, UDP, NNTP, and PING tests.

RPM

RPM is a powerful package manager, which can be used to build, install, query, verify, update, and uninstall individual software packages. A *package* consists of an archive of files and package information, including name, version, and description.

Yafc

Yafc stands for "yet another ftp client." It was developed under Linux and supports features, such as:

- ✦ Directory cache
- ✦ Tab completion (including remote filename completion)
- ✦ Aliases
- ✦ Autologin and bookmarks
- ✦ Redirection to local command or file
- ✦ Proxy support
- ✦ Kerberos authentication
- ✦ SSH2 support (sftp)

Encompass

Encompass is a Web browser for the Gnome Desktop Environment. It uses the GtkHTML rendering engine and the Bonobo component architecture.

Squid Web Proxy Cache

Squid Web proxy cache is a full-featured Web proxy cache designed to run on Linux/Unix systems. Squid supports:

+ Proxying and caching of HTTP, FTP, and other URL's
+ Proxying for SSL
+ Cache hierarchies
+ ICP, HTCP, CARP, Cache Digests
+ Transparent caching
+ WCCP (Squid v2.3 and above)
+ Extensive access controls
+ HTTP server acceleration
+ SNMP
+ Caching of DNS lookups

AbiWord

AbiSource is developing seamless cross-platform, Open Source desktop applications. The first is the AbiWord word processor, currently available for free on Windows, Unix, GNOME, BeOS, and QNX.

SSH Secure Shell

SSH Secure Shell for Servers is intended for server computers (Web servers, file servers, database servers, mail servers, and so on) that need to provide secure remote access to multiple users. This version of the software runs on all major versions of the Unix or Linux operating systems.

Apache

Since April 1996, Apache has been the most popular Web server on the Internet. The February 2001 Netcraft Web Server Survey found that 60 percent of the Web sites on the Internet are using Apache (around 62 percent if Apache derivatives are included). Thus, it is more widely used than all other Web servers combined.

Apache 2.0 white papers

The Apache 2.0 white papers are the technical documentation associated with the Apache Web server. These are the different kinds of software distribution terms:

Shareware

Shareware programs are fully functional, free trial versions of copyrighted programs. If you like particular programs, register with their authors for a nominal fee and receive licenses, enhanced versions, and technical support.

Freeware

Freeware programs are free copyrighted games, applications, and utilities. You can copy them to as many PCs as you like, but they have no technical support.

GNU

GNU software is governed by its own license, which is included inside the folder of the GNU software. There are no restrictions on distribution of this software. See the GNU license for more details.

Trial, demo, evaluation, and unregistered versions

Trial, demo, evaluation, or unregistered versions are usually limited either by time or functionality (for example, they are unable to save projects), or you may need to purchase a registration code to unlock the full version of the software.

Troubleshooting

If you have difficulty installing or using the CD-ROM programs, try the following solutions:

✦ **Turn off any anti-virus software that you may have running.** Installers sometimes mimic virus activity and can make your computer incorrectly believe that it is being infected by a virus. (Be sure to turn the anti-virus software back on later.)

✦ **Close all running programs.** The more programs you're running, the less memory is available to other programs. Installers also typically update files and programs; if you keep other programs running, installation may not work properly.

If you still have trouble with the CD, please call the Hungry Minds Customer Service phone number at (800) 762-2974. Outside the United States, call (317) 572-3994 or e-mail at techsupdum@hungryminds.com. Hungry Minds will provide technical support only for installation and other general quality control items; for technical support on the applications themselves, consult the program's vendor or author.

✦   ✦   ✦

Objective Mapping Table

This appendix provides a table listing the exam objectives for the Linux+ Certification Exam. The table is an exhaustive cross-reference chart that links every exam objective to the corresponding materials (text and labs) in this book, and includes where the subject matter is covered.

Table B-1 Exam XK0-001 — Linux+ Certification	
Exam Objective	*Chapter*
Domain 1.0 Planning the Implementation	
1.1 Identify purpose of Linux machine based on predetermined customer requirements (e.g., appliance, desktop system, database, mail server)	4
1.2 Identify all system hardware required and validate that it is supported by Linux (e.g., CPUs, RAM, graphics cards, storage devices, network interface cards, modem)	3
1.3 Determine what software and services should be installed (e.g., client applications for workstation, server services for desired task), check requirements and validate that it is supported by Linux	3 and 4
1.4 Determine how storage space will be allocated to file systems. (e.g., partition schemes)	4
1.5 Compare and contrast how major Linux licensing schemes work (e.g., GNU/GPL, freeware, shareware, open source, closed source, artistic license)	1
1.6 Identify the function of different Linux services (e.g., Apache, Squid, SAMBA, Sendmail, ipchains, BIND)	3
1.7 Identify strengths and weaknesses of different distributions and their packaging solutions (e.g, tar ball vs. RPM/DEB)	2 and 4

Continued

Table B-1 *(continued)*

Exam Objective	Chapter
Domain 1.0 Planning the Implementation	
1.8 Describe the functions, features, and benefits of a Linux solutions as compared with other operating systems (e.g., Linux players, distributions, available software)	3 and 4
1.9 Identify how the Linux kernel version numbering works	2 and 4
1.10 Identify where to obtain software and resources	2 and 3
1.11 Determine customer resources for a solution (e.g., staffing, budget, training)	3

Exam Objective	Chapter
Domain 2.0 Installation	
2.1 Determine appropriate method of installation based on the environment (e.g., boot disk, CD-ROM, Network (HTTP, FTP, NFS, SMB))	4 and 5
2.2 Describe the different types of Linux installation interaction and determine which to use for a given situation (e.g., GUI, text, network)	4 and 5
2.3 Select appropriate parameters for Linux installation (e.g., language, time zones, keyboard, mouse)	4
2.4 Select packages based on the machine's "role" (e.g., Workstation, Server, Custom)	4
2.5 Select appropriate options for partitions based on pre-installation choices (e.g., FDISK, third party partitioning software)	4 and 5
2.6 Partition according to your pre-installation plan using fdisk (e.g., /boot, / , /usr, /var/home, SWAP)	4 and 5
2.7 Configure file systems (e.g., (ext2) or (ext3) or REISER)	4 and 5
2.8 Select appropriate networking configuration and protocols (e.g., modems, Ethernet, Token-Ring)	4 and 5
2.9 Select appropriate security settings (e.g., Shadow password, root password, umask value, password limitations and password rules)	4
2.10 Create users and passwords during installation	4
2.11 Install and configure Xfree86 server	4
2.12 Select Video card support (e.g., chipset, memory, support resolution(s))	4
2.13 Select appropriate monitor manufacturer and settings (e.g., custom, vertical, horizontal, refresh)	4

Exam Objective	Chapter
Domain 2.0 Installation	
2.14 Select the appropriate window managers or desktop environment (e.g., KDE, GNOME)	4
2.15 Explain when and why the kernel will need to be recompiled	5
2.16 Install boot loader (e.g., LILO, MBR vs. first sector of boot partition)	4 and 5
2.17 Install and uninstall applications after installing the operating system (e.g., RPM, tar, gzip)	5
2.18 Read the Logfiles created during installation to verify the success of the installation	5
2.19 Validate that an installed application is performing correctly in both a test and a production environment	5

Exam Objective	Chapter
Domain 3.0 Configuration	
3.1 Reconfigure the Xwindow with automated utilities (e.g., Xconfigurator, XF86Setup)	6
3.2 Configure the client's workstation for remote access (e.g., ppp, ISDN)	7
3.3 Set environment variables (e.g, PATH, DISPLAY, TERM0)	8
3.4 Configure basic network services and settings (e.g., netconfig, linuxconf; settings for TCP/IP, DNS, DHCP)	7
3.5 Configure basic server services (e.g., X, SMB, NIS, NFS)	7
3.6 Configure basic Internet services (e.g., HTPP, POP, SMTP, SNMP, FTP)	7
3.7 Identify when swap space needs to be increased	8
3.8 Add and configure printers	8
3.9 Install and configure add-in hardware (e.g., monitors, modems, network interfaces, scanners)	8
3.10 Reconfigure boot loader (e.g., LILO)	8
3.11 Identify the purpose and characteristics of configuration files (e.g., BASH, inittab, fstab, /etc/*)	8
3.12 Edit basic configuration files (e.g., BASH files, inittab, fstab)	8
3.13 Load, remove, and edit list modules (e.g., insmod, rmmod, lsmod, modprobe)	7

Continued

Table B-1 *(continued)*

Exam Objective	Chapter
Domain 3.0 Configuration	
3.14 Document the installation of the operating system, including configuration	6, 7, and 8
3.15 Configure access rights (e.g., rlogin NIS, FTP, TFTP, SSH, Telnet)	7

Exam Objective	Chapter
Domain 4.0 Administration	
4.1 Create and delete users	9
4.2 Modify existing users (e.g., password, groups, personal information)	9
4.3 Create, modify and delete groups	9
4.4 Identify and change file permissions, modes and types by using chmod, chown and chgrp	9
4.5 Manage and navigate the Linux hierarchy (e.g., /etc, /usr, /bin, /var)	9
4.6 Manage and navigate the standard Linux file system (e.g., mv, mkdir, ls, rm)	9
4.7 Perform administrative tasks while logged in as root, or by using the su command (e.g., understand commands that are dangerous to the system)	10
4.8 Mount and manage filesystems and devices (e.g., /mnt, /dev, du, df, mount, umount)	9
4.9 Describe and use the features of the multi-user environment (e.g., virtual terminals, multiple logins)	10
4.10 Use common shell commands and expressions	10
4.11 Use network commands to connect to and manage remote systems (e.g., telnet, ftp, ssh, netstat, transfer files, redirect Xwindow)	10
4.12 Create, extract and edit file and tape archives using tar	11
4.13 Manage runlevels using init and shutdown	11
4.14 Stop, start, and restart services (daemons) as needed (e.g., init files)	11
4.15 Manage print spools and queues	11
4.16 Create, edit and save files using vi	11
4.17 Manage and navigate the Graphical User Interface (e.g., menus, xterm)	10
4.18 Program basic shell scripts using common shell commands (e.g., grep, find, cut, if)	10

Exam Objective	Chapter
Domain 5.0 System Maintenance	
5.1 Create and manage local storage devices and file systems (e.g., fsck, fdisk, mkfs)	12
5.2 Verify user and root cron jobs and understand the function of cron	12
5.3 Identify core dumps and remove or forward as appropriate	12
5.4 Run and interpret ifconfig	12
5.5 Download and install patches and updates (e.g., packages, tgz)	12
5.6 Differentiate core services from non-critical services (e.g., ps, PID, PPID, init, timer)	13
5.7 Identify, execute and kill processes (ps, kill, killall)	13
5.8 Monitor system log files regularly for errors, logins, and unusual activity	13
5.9 Document work performed on a system	13
5.10 Perform and verify backups and restores	15
5.11 Perform and verify security best practices (e.g., passwords, physical environments)	14
5.12 Assess security risks (e.g., location, sensitive data, file system permissions, remove/disable unused accounts, audit system services/programs)	14
5.13 Set daemon and process permissions (e.g., SUID – SGID – Owner/groups)	14

Exam Objective	Chapter
Domain 6.0 Troubleshooting	
6.1 Identify and locate the problem by determining whether the problem is hardware, operating system, application software, configuration or the user	16
6.2 Describe troubleshooting best practices (i.e., methodology)	16
6.3 Examine and edit configuration files based on symptoms of a problem using system utilities	16
6.4 Examine, start, and stop processes based on the signs and symptoms of a problem	16
6.5 Use system status tools to examine system resources and statuses (e.g., fsck, setserial)	17
6.6 Use systems boot disk(s) and root disk on workstation and server to diagnose and rescue file system	17

Continued

Table B-1 *(continued)*

Exam Objective	Chapter
Domain 6.0 Troubleshooting	
6.7 Inspect and determine cause of errors from system log files	16
6.8 Use disk utilities to solve file system problems (e.g., mount, umount)	17
6.9 Resolve problems based on user feedback (e g , rights, unable to login to the system, unable to print, unable to receive or transmit mail)	18
6.10 Recognize common errors (e.g., package dependencies, library errors, version conflicts)	18
6.11 Take appropriate action on boot errors (e.g., LILO, bootstrap)	17
6.12 Identify backup and restore errors	18
6.13 Identify application failure on server (e.g., Web page, telnet, ftp, pop3, snmp)	18
6.14 Identify and use trouble shooting commands (e.g., locate, find, grep, ? , <, >, >>, cat, tail)	16
6.15 Locate troubleshooting resources and update as allowable (e.g., Web, man pages, howtos, infopages, LUGs)	16
6.16 Use network utilities to identify network and connectivity problems (e.g., ping, route, traceroute, netstat, lsof)	18

Exam Objective	Chapter
Domain 7.0 Identify, Install, and Maintain System Hardware	
7.1 Identify basic terms, concepts, and functions of system components, including how each component should work during normal operation and during the boot process	19
7.2 Assure that system hardware is configured correctly prior to installation (e.g., IRQs, BIOS, DMA, SCSI settings, cabling) by identifying proper procedures for installing and configuring ATA devices	19
7.3 Assure that system hardware is configured correctly prior to installation (e.g., IRQs, BIOS, DMA, SCSI settings, cabling) by identifying proper procedures for installing and configuring SCSI and IEEE 1394 devices	19
7.4 Assure that system hardware is configured correctly prior to installation (e.g., IRQs, BIOS, DMA, SCSI, cabling) settings by identifying proper procedures for installing and configuring peripheral devices	19

Exam Objective	Chapter
Domain 7.0 Identify, Install, and Maintain System Hardware	
7.5 Assure that system hardware is configured correctly prior to installation (e.g, IRQs, BIOS, DMA, SCSI, cabling) settings by identifying available IRQs, DMAs, and I/O addresses and procedures for device installation and configuration	19
7.6 Remove and replace hardware and accessories (e.g., cables and components) based on symptoms of a problem by identifying basic procedures for adding and removing field replaceable components	19
7.7 Remove and replace hardware and accessories (e.g., cables and components) based on symptoms of a problem by identifying common symptoms and problems associated with each component and how to troubleshoot and isolate the problems	19
7.8 Identify basic networking concepts, including how a network works	7
7.9 Identify proper procedures for diagnosing and troubleshooting ATA devices	19
7.10 Identify proper procedures for diagnosing and troubleshooting SCSI devices	19
7.11 Identify proper procedures for diagnosing and troubleshooting peripheral devices	19
7.12 Identify proper procedures for diagnosing and troubleshooting core system hardware	19
7.13 Identify and maintain mobile system hardware (e.g., PCMCIA, APM)	19

✦   ✦   ✦

Sample Exam

This eighty-question Linux+ sample exam tests your knowledge on all the Linux+ text objectives, which are fully covered in this book. By using this exam — it is similar to the real one — you can prepare by identifying any weak areas that you need to review. At the end of the sample exam, you will find the correct answers, along with explanations and the chapter where the topic is covered.

Exam Questions

1. A technician is downloading files for an application for his Red Hat Linux system. What is the proper term for identifying these sets of files?

   A. Package

   B. Open Source software

   C. Linux distribution

   D. Freeware

2. What file extension is associated with the Red Hat Package manager?

   A. .zip

   B. .tar

   C. .rpm

   D. .deb

3. A technician is implementing a new e-mail server for a customer. Which of the following is the most commonly used protocol for an e-mail server?

   A. SNMP

   B. SMTP

   C. IPX

   D. TCP

4. A customer has asked a technician to install a new network card into the workstation that is running Linux. Before installing the new network card, the technician wants to see if the network card is compatible with the operating system. Where can the technician find this information?

   A. MAN pages

   B. The operating system's HCL list

   C. Documentation provided by the network card vendor

   D. The network card vendor's Web site

5. A customer is having a new Linux workstation built. The customer has told the technician that she wants to install a word processor for her new Linux system that offers a similar version for her Microsoft Windows system. Which of the following is a word processor that offers versions for both Linux and Microsoft Windows?

   A. Microsoft Office

   B. Star Office

   C. Corel Word Perfect

   D. Netscape

6. Which Web browser is not compatible with Linux?

   A. Netscape

   B. Opera

   C. Internet Explorer

   D. Konqueror

7. An administrator wants to see what processes are running, so she uses the `ps` command. When the current running processes are shown, the administrator notices a process that she terminated 5 minutes ago by using the `kill` conmmand is still running. What command should the administrator use next to terminate this process?

   A. `Kill-All`

   B. `Kill-9`

   C. `Kill -1`

   D. `Kill -a`

8. During the boot process, a technician quickly notices a kernel error message on the screen. Unfortunately, the error message didn't display long enough for the technician to read it all. What log file can the technician use to examine boot-time messages?

    A. /var/log/dmesg

    B. /etc/logs

    C. /dev/dmesg

    D. /var/dmesg/log

9. A technician wants to view a list of all running processes on the server. Which of the following is the best command to use to show a list of all running processes?

    A. ps-t

    B. ps-ef

    C. ps-r

    D. ps-z

10. In what directory is the Inittab file located?

    A. /dev

    B. /etc

    C. /sbin

    D. /boot

11. A technician is editing the Inittab file so that the system will boot X on startup. What runlevel will the technician assign for the system to boot X on startup?

    A. 3

    B. 2

    C. 5

    D. 0

12. A technician wants to bring a Linux server to a halt. What command will the technician use?

    A. init 2

    B. init 4

    C. init 1

    D. init 0

13. What command will shut down a Linux system?

    A. Shutdown

    B. Logout

    C. Unmount

    D. Exit

14. A technician has to perform a scheduled shutdown. The technician has informed the users that the shutdown will occur in 15 minutes. What command will the technician use to shut down the server in 15 minutes?

    A. shutdown -h 200

    B. shutdown 300

    C. shutdown - 15

    D. shutdown - h 900

15. What command will halt the system?

    A. halt

    B. shutdown -halt

    C. halt now

    D. stop -h

16. A technician wants to restart the httpd service. What command will the technician use to restart httpd?

    A. /etc/rc.d/init.d/httpd restart

    B. /etc/rc.d/httpd restart

    C. /etc/init.d/httpd restart

    D. /etc/rc.d/init.d/restart

17. What file contains information about every printer connected to the Linux system?

    A. Pine.conf

    B. Printcap

    C. Printinto

    D. Print.config

18. What line printer control command is used to control the operation of the line printer system?

    A. flp

    B. ccp

    C. clp

    D. lpc

19. What print command terminates an active spooling daemon on the local host immediately and then disables printing for the specified printers?

    A. lpc abort

    B. lpc end

    C. lpc down

    D. lpc quit

20. What print command stops a spooling daemon after the current job completes and disables printing?

    A. lpc disable

    B. lpc abort

    C. lpc stop

    D. lpc topg

21. What command allows you to directly see what jobs are currently in a printer queue?

    A. lpq

    B. lrq

    C. lpc

    D. flp

22. What line printer command lets you remove print jobs from the printer queue?

    A. ipc

    B. ipq

    C. lprm

    D. lrmp

23. What text editor comes included with every version of Linux by default?

    A. Emacs

    B. vi

    C. Pico

    D. Ledit

24. What command is used for combining a large number of files into one single file for archival to tape?

    A. deb

    B. zip

    C. tba

    D. tar

25. A technician starts up a Linux system, but after the system has booted up, the system shuts down. What is the most likely cause of this?

    A. In the /etc/inittab, file the runlevel is set to 3

    B. In the /etc/inittab, file the runlevel is set to 5

    C. In the /etc/inittab, file the runlevel is set to 0

    D. In the /etc/inittab, file the runlevel is set to 6

26. Where do all your configurations for your services, programs, and daemons reside by default?

    A. /dev

    B. /etc

    C. /root

    D. /bin

27. What type of backup tape will only back up files that have changed since the previous backup and clear the archive bit?

    A. Full

    B. Differential

    C. Incremental

    D. Daily

28. Which of the following is NOT a recognized backup rotation method?

    A. Son

    B. Grandfather/Father/Son

    C. Son/Father

    D. Father/Son

29. What option of the `tar` command will tell `tar` to create a new archive file?

    A. -p

    B. -c

    C. -f

    D. -x

30. What option of the `tar` command will tell `tar` to extract files from an archive?

    A. -p

    B. -c

    C. -f

    D. -x

31. What type of installations do most modern Linux installations default to?

    A. Text

    B. GUI

    C. Network

    D. NFS32

32. A technician is installing a new version of Linux on a workstation. The workstation doesn't have the proper video requirements to perform a GUI type installation. What other choice does the technician have besides a GUI installation that will be sufficient to install the new version of Linux?

    A. Network

    B. NFS

    C. Text

    D. GUI –t

33. When performing a Linux installation, what partitioning program is available in most modern Linux distributions?

    A. Fdisk

    B. Disk Partition

    C. Disk Druid

    D. Scan Disk

34. What is the purpose of a boot loader?

    A. A boot loader is used to load the necessary files for a GUI installation.

    B. A boot loader is used to boot the operating system into the intended operating system.

    C. A boot loader is used to load packages after the installation is complete.

    D. A boot loader is a file in the /root directory that saves all information about the current Linux hardware configuration.

35. What is the first thing a technician should do to a current Linux system before planning to install a second OS for dual-boot configuration?

    A. Check the HCL for the new OS to verify that all hardware is supported.

    B. Flash the BIOS to recognize the new OS.

    C. Back up the current system before installing the second OS.

    D. Recompile the Kernel.

36. What is another name for a root user?

    A. Administrator

    B. Super User

    C. Manager

    D. Account user

37. What account is usually created first in most modern Linux installations?

    A. Manager

    B. Account User

    C. Guest

    D. Root

38. What program is most often used to configure a GUI installation?

    A. XFree86

    B. fdisk

    C. Disk Druid

    D. linuxconf

39. A technician is going to install Linux on a workstation. The technician wants to customize the installation. What type of installation will the technician use to customize the installation?

    A. Server

    B. Custom

    C. Manual

    D. Workstation

40. During a Linux installation, the technician is asked where he would like to install LILO. The technician is installing Linux on a Microsoft Windows 2000 system that already has an NTFS partition. With this configuration, where is the proper place to install LILO for a dual-boot system?

    A. First sector of the boot partition

    B. Master boot region

    C. First sector of the NTFS partition

    D. Last sector of the boot partition

41. What command can be used to activate a created swap partition during a text-based installation?

    A. mount

    B. chmod

    C. swapon

    D. remadmin

42. A technician is trying to decide a proper location for his new Linux server. Which of the following choices would NOT be a proper location to place the new Linux Server? Choose *all* that apply.

    A. In a locked ventilated room

    B. In an unlocked ventilated room

    C. In a locked air conditioned closet

    D. On a table beside the technician's desk for quick access

43. Which password on a Linux system is the most important password?

    A. User password

    B. Network password

    C. Root password

    D. Mail password

44. Where is the password file for Linux located?

    A. /etc/passwd

    B. /bin/passwd

    C. /dev/passwd

    D. /usr/passwd

45. Which of the following programs can be used to remotely log into a Linux system?

    A. Netstat

    B. Telnet

    C. Ping

    D. ifconfig

46. What file contains a list of user names (set by a Linux administrator) that is not allowed to log in to the FTP server?

    A. ftpadmin

    B. ftppasswd

    C. ftpusers

    D. ftproot

47. Which of the following commands can be used to schedule recurring tasks?

    A. Cron

    B. Schedule

    C. AT

    D. Time

48. In which directory would you find crontab files for particular users?

    A. /var/log/cron/

    B. /var/log/cron

    C. /var/tmp/cron

    D. /var/spool/cron/

49. What program can you use to analyze your program's core dump files and to debug the application while it is actually running?

    A. xconf

    B. gdb

    C. ulimit

    D. cpio

50. What at command option will send mail to the user when the job has completed — even if there was no output?

    A. at -m

    B. at -v

    C. at -f

    D. at -c

51. A technician wants to adjust the X Windows system configuration. What file will the technician manually edit to adjust the X Windows system configuration?

    A. /etc/XF86Config

    B. /usr/X11R6/bin/XF86Config

    C. /etc/X11/XF86Config

    D. /bin/XF86Config

52. A technician wants to set up his Linux system to access the Internet. What protocol will the technician install on the Linux system so the system can access the Internet after configuration?

    A. IPX/SPX

    B. NetBEUI

    C. TCP/IP

    D. IPX

53. A technician is verifying the network configuration of a Linux server. Which of the following commands should be used to accomplish this?

    A. Config

    B. ifconfig

    C. ipconfig

    D. netstat

54. What type of server will a technician set up to be able to automatically assign IP addresses to all the systems that will connect to the server?

    A. DHCP server

    B. Wins server

    C. DNS server

    D. Database server

55. A Linux administrator wants to add a new user to the current domain. What command will the administrator use to accomplish this?

    A. `newuser [username]`

    B. `adduser [username]`

    C. `username [adduser]`

    D. `useradd [username]`

56. What command should you use to activate a swap partition?

    A. `<partition> mkswap/dev/`

    B. `mkswap /dev/<partition>`

    C. `/dev/hda5 swap <partition>`

    D. `mkswap/<partition>`

57. What option of the `mkfs` command should you use to check the device for bad blocks before building the file system?

    A. -c

    B. -V

    C. -t

    D. -I

58. A technician has just finished installing a new hard drive on a Linux System. What command will the technician use to create a new file system on the new hard drive?

    A. `linuxconf`

    B. `cfdisk`

    C. `fdisk`

    D. `mkfs`

59. A technician wants to verify the current active shell. Which command will the technician use?

    A. `bash`

    B. `env`

    C. `shell`

    D. `ver`

60. What command can you use on a Linux system to help you search for a specific file?

    A. `cat`

    B. `tar`

    C. `locate`

    D. `mkdir`

61. What is the first thing that a technician should do at the first sign of a problem?

    A. Examine the symptoms

    B. Reboot the server

    C. Check the link lights on the severs NIC card

    D. Type `halt` at the command prompt

62. What is one source that a technician can quickly refer to for help for a specific command?

    A. The previous technician's documentation

    B. The Linux distribution's Web site

    C. The installation media

    D. The MAN pages

63. A technician is having problems with main system services, such as DNS or NFS. Where should the technician look first to help determine the problem?

    A. MAN Pages

    B. Log files

    C. Previous technician's documentation

    D. Vendor's Web site

64. What option should you use to send the output of a file to another file?

    A. >

    B. ^

    C. $

    D. #

65. What is the purpose of the Linux Loader?

    A. Responsible for loading the Linux kernel and system into memory

    B. Responsible for loading device drivers at boot time

    C. Responsible for loading the video drivers at boot time

    D. Responsible for trapping errors at boot time

66. During the boot process, an error of LI is displayed on the screen and the system stops loading. What is the cause of the problem?

    A. Descriptor table unable to be read

    B. Can't find kernel

    C. Indicates a disk error code

    D. The LILO process ran successfully

67. What utility is your best choice for repairing your Linux system?

    A. fdisk

    B. ifconfig

    C. cat

    D. fsck

68. What is the -t option with fsck command used for?

    A. Interactively repair the filesystem

    B. Display completion/progress bars for those filesystem's checkers

    C. Specifies the type of filesystem to be checked

    D. Don't show the title on startup

69. What command should you use to display CPU processes?

    A. top

    B. show

    C. grep

    D. setserial

70. What command can you use to obtain information about your serial port resource usage, such as IRQ and IO addresses?

    A. top

    B. Mem

    C. setconfig

    D. setserial

71. What command can a Linux administrator use to add a new user?

    A. adduser

    B. addprofile

    C. addroot

    D. addaccess

72. Using the usermod command, what option can a Linux administrator use with this command to unlock a user's password?

    A. -L

    B. -U

    C. -l

    D. -h

73. What command can a Linux administrator use to delete a user from the system?

    A. userdel -o

    B. deluser

    C. adduser -d

    D. userdel

74. What command can you use to change from one directory to another?

    A. ls

    B. cd

    C. dir

    D. dir -c

75. A Linux administrator wants to copy a file from the /bin directory to the /root directory. Which command would the administrator use?

    A. copy

    B. ls

    C. cp

    D. mv

76. What command can you use to mount a CD-ROM drive?

    A. install

    B. attach

    C. mount

    D. connect

77. A technician wants to monitor connections to a Linux server. Which of the following programs would the technician use?

    A. netstat

    B. ifconfig

    C. ping

    D. tracert

78. Which of the following commands can you use to exit a login shell?

    A. Shutdown

    B. Halt

    C. Logout

    D. Stop

79. A Linux administrator is having problems connecting to a mail server. What command can he use to test if the mail server is on the network?

    A. ping

    B. FTP

    C. telnet

    D. netstat

80. A Linux administrator wants to send a file to the printer. Which of the following commands can the Linux administrator use?

    A. `print`

    B. `lpq`

    C. `lpr`

    D. `lprm`

Exam Answers

1. A. A *package* is the proper term used to identify sets of files. For review, see Chapter 2.

2. C. .rpm is the proper extension associated with the Red Hat Package manager. For review, see Chapter 2.

3. B. SMTP stands for *Simple Mail Transfer Protocol*. This protocol is the most commonly used protocol for an e-mail server. This protocol can be used for Linux e-mail servers and many others, such as UNIX or Microsoft Windows. For review, see Chapter 3.

4. B. To verify that specific hardware is compatible with the operating system, it is best to check the operating system's HCL (hardware compatibility list). The operating system's HCL list contains the most up-to-date information about supported hardware. For review, see Chapter 3.

5. C. Some versions of Corel Word Perfect can run on Linux systems and Microsoft Windows systems. Star Office is only specific to Linux. Netscape is a Web browser and Microsoft Office is only compatible for Microsoft Windows systems. For review, see Chapter 3.

6. C. The Microsoft Internet Explorer Web browser is only specific to Microsoft Windows and not compatible with Linux. Netscape, Opera, and Konqueror are available for Linux systems. For review, see Chapter 3.

7. B. Using the -9 argument with the `kill` command will send a kill signal to the process. This will stop the specific process immediately. For review, see Chapter 13.

8. B. The /etc/logs file contains the boot time messages that a technician can use to examine error messages. For review, see Chapter 13.

9. B. The `ps-ef` command can be used to show a list of all running processes. The `ps-t` command will only show processes on the specific terminal on which the command is run. The `ps-r` command will show only running processes, and the `ps-z` is not a recognized command. For review, see Chapter 13.

10. B. By default, the Inittab file is located in the /etc directory. The Inittab file describes which processes are started at boot up and during normal operations. For review, see Chapter 11.

11. C. The level 5 runlevel is assigned in the Inittab file so that the system will boot X on start-up. Level 3 is for multi-user mode with remote file sharing, processes, and daemons, level 2 is for multi-user mode, without remote file sharing, and level 0 is for halting the system. For review, see Chapter 11.

12. D. The command `init 0` brings the Linux server to a halt. For review, see Chapter 11.

13. A. The `Shutdown` command shuts down a Linux system. `Logout` will log the current users out of the system, but won't shut down the system. `Unmount` is a command used to disconnect devices, and `Exit` is the same as `Logout`. For review, see Chapter 13.

14. D. The only correct answer `is shutdown -h 900`. All the other answers will shut down the system before or after 15 minutes. For review, see Chapter 11.

15. A. `halt` is the only correct command to halt the system. For review, see Chapter 11.

16. A. `/etc/rc.d/init.d/httpd restart` is the only correct command out of the list that will restart httpd. For review, see Chapter 11.

17. B. The Printcap file contains information about every printer connected to the Linux system. For review, see Chapter 11

18. D. Lpc is used by the system administrator to control the operations of the line printer system. For each line printer configured in /ect.printcap, lpc may be used to disable or enable a printer, disable or enable a printer's spooling queue, rearrange the order of jobs in a spooling queue, or find the status of printers and their associated spooling queues and printer daemons. For review, see Chapter 11.

19. A. `lpc abort` terminates an active spooling daemon on the local host immediately and then disables printing for the specified printers. For review, see Chapter 11.

20. C. The `lpc stop` command stops a spooling daemon after the current job completes and disables printing. For review, see Chapter 11.

21. A. The `lpc` command allows you to directly see what jobs are currently in a printer queue. For review, see Chapter 11.

22. C. The `lprm` command will let you remove print jobs from the printer queue. For review, see Chapter 11.

23. B. vi is a text editor that can be used to edit any ASCII text. It is especially useful for editing programs. For review, see Chapter 11.

24. D. The `tar` command is used for taking a large number of files and combining them into one single file for archival to tape. For review, see Chapter 11.

25. C. If the /etc/inittab file runlevel is set to 0, the system will shut down right after it has booted. This is because the 0 runlevel is used for halting the system. For review, see Chapter 11.

26. B. By default, all configurations for your services, programs, and daemons reside in the /etc directory. For review, see Chapter 15.

27. C. An Incremental backup will backup only files that have changed since the previous backup and clear the archive bit. For review, see Chapter 15.

28. C. The Son/Father rotation method is the only answer that is not a true recognized backup rotation method. Son, Grandfather/Father/Son and Father/Son are all true recognized backup rotation methods. For review, see Chapter 15.

29. B. The –c option of the tar command will tell tar to create a new archive file. The –p option will tell tar to keep permissions on files when extracted from an archive. The –f option will let you specify a filename for the archive, and the –x option tells tar to extract files from an archive. For review, see Chapter 15.

30. D. The –x option tells tar to extract files from an archive. The –c option tells tar to create a new archive file. The –p option tells tar to keep permissions of files when extracted from an archive. The –f option well let you specify a filename for the archive. For review, see Chapter 15.

31. B. Most modern Linux installations will default to a GUI installation after you press enter from the main installation screen. If you would like a text-based installation all you need to do is type **Text,** then hit enter and the installation will continue in a text-based install. For review, see Chapter 4.

32. C. A text-based installation would be necessary if you did not have the proper video requirements to perform a GUI installation. For review, see Chapter 4.

33. A. Fdisk is the most common partitioning program that is available in most modern Linux Distributions. For review, see Chapter 4.

34. B. The boot loader is used to boot the operating system into the intended operating system. For review, see Chapter 4.

35. C. Before any upgrading or installation of another operating system, it is imperative to back up the current system before installing the second operating system. This way, your data is backed up in case of major problems with the new OS installation of your data. For review, see Chapter 4.

36. B. The most common term used for the root user is a *super user*. The super user has more powerful rights on the network then any normal user. For review, see Chapter 4.

37. D. The root user is the first account that is created by default during most modern Linux installations. After the root user has been set up, the administrator can then create regular users. For review, see Chapter 4.

38. A. XFree86 is the underlying software that is located between the hardware and graphical user interface. For review, see Chapter 4.

39. B. Only a custom installation can be used to customize what is installed during an installation. A custom installation will allow you to choose what packages you want to install and what packages you don't want to install. For review, see Chapter 4.

40. A. The proper place for the technician to install LILO is in the first sector of the boot partition. For review, see Chapter 4.

41. C. The swapon command during a text-based installation can be used to activate a created swap partition. For review, see Chapter 5.

42. B, D. Placing your new server in an unlocked room or beside the technician's desk is not a good place because these environments are not secure and the server can be tampered with when the technician is not present. Always place your server in a room with a locked door that has proper ventilation. For review, see Chapter 5.

43. C. The Root password or the super user password is the administrator's password. The administrator account has all the privileges necessary to control the network properly, unlike the limited regular user accounts. For review, see Chapter 14.

44. A. The password file for Linux is located by default in the /etc/passwd location. For review, see Chapter 14.

45. B. Telnet is the only program in the list that can be used to remotely log into a Linux server. Netstat, Ping, and ifconfig do not have remote capabilities. For review, see Chapter 14.

46. C. The ftpusrs file contains a list of usernames that a Linux administrator has previously set to not allow specific users to login to the FTP server. For review, see Chapter 14.

47. A. Unlike the at command, the Cron command can be used to set scheduled recurring tasks. For review, see Chapter 12.

48. D. The /var/spool/cron is the directory where user's crontabs are saved with a directory for each user in which all user's cron jobs are stored. For review, see Chapter 12.

49. B. The gdb program is the only program in the list that can be used to analyze your program's core dump files and also debug the application while it is actually running. For review, see Chapter 12.

50. A. The at -m command option will send mail to the users when the job has completed even if there was no output. at- v shows completed but not yet deleted jobs in the queue, at -f reads the job from the file rather than standard input and at -c displays the jobs listed on the command line to standard output. For review, see Chapter 12.

51. D. The default location of the configuration file for the X Window System is /etc/X11/XF86Config. For review, see Chapter 6.

52. C. The TCP/IP protocol suite is used extensively in the Linux environment, and most other operating systems, because it is the protocol used on the Internet. For review, see Chapter 7.

53. B. `ifconfig` is the proper command to examine network information on a Linux server or workstation. `Ifconfig` is used to configure the kernel-resident network interfaces. It is used at boot-time to set up interfaces as necessary. For review, see Chapter 12.

54. A. A DHCP server runs the Dynamic Host Configuration Protocol, which assigns the network IP address to clients on the network at start-up. With this configuration, each client workstation does not need to be set up with a static IP address. When the client computer starts, it sends a request to the DHCP server, which assigns the client and IP address. For review, see Chapter 7.

55. D. The command `useradd` followed by the username will create a new user or update default new user information. After the new user has been added, Linux will prompt you to specify a password for the new user. For review, see Chapter 9.

56. B. To activate the swap partition, use the command `mkswap /dev/ <partition>`. For review, see chapter 8.

57. A. The –c option when used with the mkfs command will check the device for bad blocks before building the file system. For review, see Chapter 8.

58. D. The `mkfs` command is used to create the file system. `linuxconf` is used to configure the Linux system, and `format` is not a standard Linux command. `cfdisk` and `fdisk` are used to create partitions. For review, see Chapter 8.

59. B. The technician should use the `env` command to verify the current active shell. The other commands listed won't perform this function. For review, see Chapter 8.

60. C. The `locate` command will search and quickly find the location of a file. The `cat` command will concatenate files and print on the standard output. The `tar` command is an archiving utility and the `mkdir` command is used to make directories. For review, see Chapter 16.

61. A. The first thing that a technician should do at the first sign of a problem is to examine the symptoms. The technician should take the time to get all the facts by asking the following questions: Is this happening to one user? Is it happening to everyone? Does the problem only happen on one particular system? Does it happen in an application, or is this a system process problem? By gathering as many facts as you can, this will help get you started in the right direction. For review, see Chapter 16.

62. D. Manual Pages, or MAN pages, is the original Unix way to look up information on specific commands and processes on your system by consulting an online manual. By using a command's manual page, you can determine exactly what that command does, how to execute it, and all of the options that you can use with that command. For review, see Chapter 16.

63. B. Most system processes and applications keep a running log file. When examining a Linux problem, it is a good idea to check these log files first to try to define the actual problem. For review, see Chapter 16.

64. A. The > option is used to send the output of a file to another file. The ">" option will send the output to a file of your choice: cat /var/log/messages | grep error > error.log for example. For review, see Chapter 16.

65. A. The Linux Loader, or LILO, is responsible for loading the Linux kernel and system into memory. LILO can also boot the computer into different operating systems if they are running on separate partitions from the Linux system, such as in the case of a dual boot system. For review, see Chapter 17.

66. B. If only LI is present on the screen and the system does not continue to boot usually means that it cannot run the second stage of the boot loader. This happens because it cannot find the kernel image specified in the LILO configuration file, /etc/lilo.conf. For review, see Chapter 17.

67. D. The fsck utility checks your filesystem for errors and inconsistencies, and can repair them while they are running. Your filesystems can become damaged for any number of reasons. The number one reason is improper shutdown of the Linux system. For review, see Chapter 17.

68. C. The –t option used with fsck is used to specify the type of filesystem to be checked. Option –r is used to interactively repair the filesystem, -C is the option used to display completion/progress bars for those filesystem checkers, and –T is used to depress the title on startup. For review, see Chapter 17.

69. A. Use the top command to check current resource usage. This utility lets you see all on one screen how much memory and CPU usage that you are currently using, and also the resource usage by each program and process. For review, see Chapter 17.

70. D. setserial is a utility that you can use to obtain information about your serial port resource usage, such as IRQ and IO addresses. An IRQ (Interrupt Request) is used by a device to send a signal to the CPU that the device has a request that needs processing. For review, see Chapter 17.

71. A. The adduser command is used to add a new user to the network. For example: adduser <username>. To use the adduser command the Linux administrator must be logged in as root. For review, see Chapter 9.

72. B. The –U option used in conjunction with the usermod command is used to unlock a user's password. The –U option is the opposite of the –L option, which is used to lock a user's password. For review, see Chapter 9.

73. D. The userdel command is used to delete a user from the system. The administrator must be logged in as root to use this command. For review, see Chapter 9.

74. B. The cd command stands for Change Directory. To navigate the Linux hierarchical file system structure, use the cd command to change from one directory to another. For review, see Chapter 9.

75. C. To move a file from one directory to another in Linux use the `cp` command. To move a file to another directory, use the `mv` command. For review, see Chapter 9.

76. C. The `mount` command is a powerful tool used to `mount` directories and devices on a Linux system. For review, see Chapter 9.

77. A. The `netstat` command is used to monitor connections to a Linux system. `Netstat` is a perfect way to see and monitor connections (both inbound and outbound). This program can also be used to view packet statistics so you can see how many packets have been sent and received. For review, see Chapter 10.

78. C. The `logout` command will exit you from a login shell. After you have logged out, the system will automatically prompt you for a login username followed by the password for that account. For review, see Chapter 10.

79. A. The `ping` command is the most basic TCP/IP utility. To ping a server with an ip address of 192.123.12.2, the syntax would be: `ping 192.123.12.2`. The most common reason for using the ping utility is to find out if you can reach a host or to find out if a host is responding. For review, see Chapter 18.

80. C. The `lpr` command is used to send a file to a printer. `lpq` and `lprm` are commands used for examining and manipulating the print queue. For review, see Chapter 18.

✦   ✦   ✦

Exam-Taking Tips

The CompTIA exams are not easy—they require a great deal of preparation. The exam questions measure real-world skills. Your ability to answer these questions correctly will be enhanced by hands-on experience with the product.

Taking a CompTIA Exam

This section contains information about registering for and taking an exam, including what to expect when you arrive at the testing center to take the exam.

How to register for an exam

CompTIA testing and certification is administered by the worldwide networks of Prometric and VUE. You can find a testing center in your area by following the links from the CompTIA Web site. Which testing center that you use is up to you.

If you visit the Web sites of Prometric and VUE, you will find the necessary information on how to register for an exam, and what to expect when you get there. In fact, both Web sites, www.prometric.com and www.vue.com offer electronic registration for the CompTIA exams to help speed up the testing process.

What to expect at the testing center

As you prepare for your certification exam, it may be helpful to know what to expect when you arrive at the testing center on the day of your exam. The following information gives you a preview of the general procedure that you'll go through at the testing center:

+ You will be asked to sign the log book upon arrival and departure.

+ You will be required to show two forms of identification, including one photo ID (such as a driver's license or company security ID), before you may take the exam.

✦ The test administrator will give you a Testing Center Regulations form that explains the rules that you will be expected to comply with during the test. You will be asked to sign the form, indicating that you understand and will comply with the regulations.

✦ The test administrator will show you to your test computer and will handle any preparations necessary to start the testing tool and display the exam on the computer.

✦ You will be provided a set amount of scratch paper for use during the exam. All scratch paper will be collected from you at the end of the exam.

✦ The exams are all closed book. You may *not* use a laptop computer or have any notes or printed material with you during the exam session.

✦ Some exams may include additional materials or exhibits. If any exhibits are required for your exam, the test administrator will provide you with them before you begin the exam and collect them from you at the end of the exam.

✦ Before you begin the exam, the test administrator will tell you what to do when you complete the exam. If the test administrator doesn't explain this to you, or if you are unclear about what you should do, ask the administrator *before* beginning the exam.

Because you'll be given a specific amount of time to complete the exam, if you have any questions or concerns, ask the test administrator *before* the exam begins.

As an exam candidate, you are entitled to the best support and environment possible for your exam. In particular, you are entitled to the following:

✦ A quiet, uncluttered test environment

✦ Scratch paper

✦ The tutorial for using the online testing tool, and time to take the tutorial (which is time used that is not part of your 90 minute exam time limit)

✦ A knowledgeable and professional test administrator

✦ The opportunity to submit comments about the testing center and staff, or the test itself

Your exam results

As soon as you finish the test, you receive the final score. You will see the results immediately on the computer screen. In addition, you are provided a hard copy of the score report at the testing center.

The score report shows whether or not you passed the certification. You can also see how you did on each section of the test and on each type of technology. Retain this score report because it contains your unique ID number, which is also your certification number. It can be used to verify your certification until your certificate arrives.

If you pass the examination, a certificate will be mailed to you within a few weeks. If you don't receive your certificate and information packet within five weeks of passing your exam, contact CompTIA by e-mail at fulfillment@comptia.org or by calling 630-268-1818 (ask for the fulfillment department).

Certification indicates that you have completed the steps and have the knowledge required to perform at a specified level. It shows your employer and clients that your expertise has been attested by a recognized industry organization. Today, virtually every technology professional can benefit from pursuing a well-chosen certification. Becoming certified can increase your salary, enhance your skill set, and make your job more satisfying.

If you don't receive a passing score

If you don't pass a certification exam, you may call the testing center to schedule a time to retake the exam. Before retaking the exam, you should review this book and focus additional study on the topic areas where you can improve your exam results. Please note that you must pay again for each exam retake. For the best up-to-date information about CompTIA's retake policy, visit www.comptia.org

One way to determine areas where additional study may be helpful is to review your individual section scores carefully. The section titles in your score report generally correlate to specific groups of exam objectives.

Here are some specific ways that you can prepare to retake an exam:

✦ Go over the section-by-section scores on your exam results, noting objective areas where you can improve your score.

✦ Review the objectives for the exam, with a special focus on the tasks and objective areas that correspond to the exam sections where you can improve your score.

✦ Increase your real-world, hands-on experience and practice performing the listed job tasks with the relevant products and technologies.

About the Linux + Exam

An important aspect of passing the CompTIA Linux+ exam is to understand the "big picture." This includes understanding how the exams are developed and scored.

Every job function requires different levels of cognitive skills, from memorization of facts and definitions to the comprehensive ability to analyze scenarios, design solutions, and evaluate options. To make the exams relevant in the real world, CompTIA exams test the specific cognitive skills that are necessary for the job functions being tested. These exams go beyond testing rote knowledge — you need to apply your knowledge, analyze technical solutions, solve problems, and make decisions, just as you would on the job.

The CompTIA Linux+ exam is based on a "how to" approach. Thus, it is recommended that you have some hands-on experience before actually taking the test. The CompTIA Linux+ exam tests the skills for an individual who has at least six months of practical experience.

The CompTIA Linux+ Certification exam consists of 80 questions. You must have a passing score of 75 percent, and you have 90 minutes to complete the exam. The certification test is administered on a computer in an easy-to-use format; you will take the test at a Prometric or VUE authorized testing center. The format of the test is very similar to other multiple-choice examinations. The difference is that you take this examination on a desktop computer that is connected to a testing network, where all the data is stored centrally and securely. Directions for using the testing software are displayed on the screen. You are also provided a tutorial, and you can seek assistance from a nearby proctor. Onscreen "help" is also available, including information at the bottom of the screen that lets you know how to enter your answer, move forward in the test, mark a question for answering later, or review a previous question. Of course, the software tells you *how* to enter the answer, not *what* answer to enter.

Usually, each question has only one correct response. However, some questions do have multiple correct responses. When multiple correct answers are possible, a message at the bottom of the screen prompts you to "choose all that apply." Be sure to read the messages at the bottom of the screen.

For the most updated information concerning the CompTIA Linux+ exam, please consult the CompTIA Web site, located at `www.comptia.org`.

Preparing for the Linux+ Exam

The best way to prepare for the CompTIA Linux+ exam is to study, learn, and master the job function on which you'll be tested. For the CompTIA Linux+ exam — or any certification exam, for that matter — you should follow these important preparation steps:

1. Identify the objectives on which you'll be tested.

2. Assess your current mastery of those objectives.

3. Practice tasks and study the areas that you haven't mastered.

If you visit the CompTIA Web site at `www.comptia.org`, you will find relevant information about the Linux+ certification exam, including test centers in your area and any fees that are involved. They also have links to help you find study resources, and hands-on training centers in your area.

The CompTIA Web site also has the exam objective blueprint in an Adobe Acrobat format. This blueprint will help you to determine what areas you need to cover to pass the exam.

For More Information

VUE has teamed with Self Test software (a world leader in certification practice tests) to help you to prepare for the actual test. Visit their Web site for more information at www.vue.com. VUE also lists several resources on how to pass the CompTIA exams.

The Prometric Web site located at www.prometric.com also contains information about how to pass the CompTIA exams

✦   ✦   ✦

Glossary

Application Server Any server that acts as a middle-tier in a multi-tiered application that uses transactional database data and processes client requests to use that data.

Artistic License Artistic license requires that any modifications to a software package remain in some control of the copyright holder.

BIOS (Basic Input Output System) A set of detailed instructions for system startup; usually stored in ROM on the system board.

Boot Manager A boot loader is used to boot the existing operating system into the intended operating system. The boot loader accomplishes this by loading a bootstrap onto the HDD. This bootstrap then tells the computer system where to find the next part of the operating system to be loaded.

Browser A computer program that uses the Hypertext Transfer Protocol (HTTP), which is used to access hosts on the Web.

Cable A physical transmission medium that has a central conductor of wire or fiber, surrounded by a plastic jacket.

Closed Source The creators of Closed Source software are the only ones who are supposed to see the software code, and they are the only ones who are authorized to refine it, add to it, and fix bugs in the software.

CPU (Central Processing Unit) The main chip on the motherboard where instructions are executed.

Cron A utility that helps the system administrator automate repetitive tasks.

DAT A type of backup tape. Digital Audio Tape is a type of magnetic tape that uses a scheme called *helical scan* to record data. This is the same type of recording that is used in common videotape recorders and is somewhat slower than the linear type.

Database Server A server that stores structured data in a filing system that can be retrieved by multiple users simultaneously.

DHCP Server A DHCP server runs the Dynamic Host Configuration Protocol, which assigns network IP addresses to a client as the startup on the network. With this configuration, each client workstation does not need to be set up with a static IP address. When the client computer starts, it sends a request to the DHCP server to be assigned an IP address.

Differential Backup Backs up data that has changed since the last full backup.

Disk Druid A utility that can partition your hard drive.

DLT (Digital Linear Tape) A hardware solution for tape backup and storage that enables multiple tapes to be loaded into the system — provides unattended back-ups and easy access for keeping data in online storage.

DNS Server (Domain Name Service) A server that keeps a database of tables that translate fully qualified Internet domain names to their respective IP addresses.

Ethernet A networking technology defined by the Institute for Electrical and Electronic Engineers (IEEE) as the IEEE standard 802.3.

Father-Son The father-son backup media rotation method uses a combination of full and differential (or incremental) backups for a two-week schedule.

Fdisk A utility that can partition your hard drive.

File and Print Server A server that provides file storage and printing services to clients. Client files are stored on the server, then they are centralized in a common place that can be more easily backed up. Print services enable clients to send a request to a printer. The print requests are queued by the print server for delivery to the final destination printer.

Firewall Software that prevents unauthorized traffic between two networks by examining the IP packets that travel on both networks.

Freeware Freeware programs are free of charge, and consist of copyrighted games, applications, and utilities. You can copy them to as many PCs as you like but they have no technical support.

FTP File Transfer Protocol is used to download files from an FTP server to a client computer.

FTP Server FTP is an Internet-based protocol for file transfers. Its function is to facilitate these transfers with proper integrity, efficiency, and security. A client computer will connect to an FTP server (which supplies log on credentials) and then is granted access to retrieve files on the server.

Full backup A full backup occurs when all the files on all the selected devices are backed up.

Gnome A windows-based desktop environment for users.

GNU GNU software is governed by its own license, which is included inside the folder of the GNU software. No restrictions exist on the distribution of this software.

Grandfather A type of backup method that typically uses 19 tapes.

Grandfather-Father-Son A type of backup method. The Son consists of daily backups, the Father consists of the last full backup of the week, and the Grandfather consists of the last full backup of the month.

GZIP A compression utility used to compress files into an archive.

Hardware Compatibility List (HCL) A list of supported devices that will work on a particular operating system.

Hub A central device that connects several computers together or several networks together.

Ifconfig Used to assign an address to a network interface and/or to configure network interface parameters.

Incremental Backup Backs up data that has changed since the last full or incremental backup.

Init The process that is the ultimate parent of all user processes on a Linux system. Init is started by the operating system kernel and is responsible for starting all other services provided by the system.

Inittab The primary configuration file for the init process; controls how your system starts up and configures the different run levels.

Internet A global network that consists of a large number of individual networks interconnected through the use of public telephone lines, cable lines, and satellites.

KDE A windows-based desktop environment for Linux users.

Kernel The core of the operating system; enables other software to access hardware.

Konqueror A Linux Web browser provided with the KDE desktop environment.

LAN A Local Area Network is created when two or more computers in a limited geographic area are linked by high-performance cables. With a LAN, users can exchange information, share peripheral devices, or access a common server.

Link Light A small Light-Emitting Diode (LED) that is found on both the NIC and the Hub. It is usually green to indicate a successful connection; yellow indicates no connection.

Linux An Open Source implementation of UNIX that was created by Linus Torvalds, which runs on many different hardware platforms, including Intel, Sparc, PowerPC, and Alpha Processors.

Log File A file that keeps a running list of all errors and notices, the time and date that they occurred, and any other pertinent information.

lpd daemon (line printer daemon) Refers to the entire collection of programs that deal with print spooling. The lpd daemon is run when the Linux system first boots.

Mail Server A type of server that stores e-mail. Clients connect to the mail server by supplying their mail account information, with which they can send and receive e-mail.

Man Pages (Abbreviation for Manual Pages) Refers to the online documentation for a particular function call, program, or command.

Microsoft Internet Explorer A Web browser developed by Microsoft that is not available for Linux systems.

Minix A free UNIX clone that is available with all the source code. Minix is well suited to people who want to run a UNIX-like system on their personal computers and learn about the inner workings of such systems.

Netscape A Web browser that is available for Linux and Microsoft Windows.

Network Interface Card (NIC) A physical device that connects computers and other network equipment to the transmission media.

Network Media The physical cables that link computers in a network; also known as *physical media*.

Network Operating System (NOS) The software that runs on a network server and offers file, print, application, and other services to clients.

Offsite Storage A method for storing backup media in an off-site location. Protects the company's data in the event of a disaster, such as a fire or flood in the main building. Also ensures the integrity of the data and improves the company's ability to quickly resume operations.

Open Source The creators of an Open Source program distribute the code along with the program so that other developers can view it and add to it.

Opera A Web browser available for Linux, Microsoft Windows, Macintosh, OS/2, and many others.

Operating System (OS) A set of computer instruction codes; its purpose is to define input and output device connections, and to provide instructions for the computer's central processor to retrieve and display data.

Packages A collection of files necessary for combining a program or application into one installable file.

Partition A hard drive that is sectioned into separate virtual drives from one logical drive.

Plug-and-Play An Intel standard that allows components to be automatically configured when added to a PC. The standard requires support from the BIOS, the expansion card, and the operating system.

Proxy Server Forwards network requests on behalf of another client or server. A proxy server is typically configured to facilitate Web server requests between a client and a Web server.

RAM (Random Access Memory) The computer's main workspace. Data stored in RAM can be accessed directly; it is not necessary to read information stored before or after the desired data.

ReadME file A text file that comes with most software and gives additional information that may not appear in the manual.

Root The main administration account on a Linux system; sometimes referred to as the *Super user*.

SCSI (Small Computer System Interface) A hardware interface that allows the connection of up to seven devices.

Shareware Shareware programs are fully functional, free trial versions of copyrighted programs. If you like particular programs, you can register with their authors for a nominal fee and receive licenses, enhanced versions, and technical support.

Son A backup method that performs a full backup every day.

Super User Another term for the Root user. The main administration account on a Linux system.

Tape Drives A device that holds magnetic tape; enables the computer to read and write to it.

Tarball Archiving with Tar places several files or the contents of a directory (or directories) in one file, commonly called a *Tarball*.

TCP/IP A protocol suite that runs the Transmission Control Protocol (TCP) on top of the Internet Protocol (IP). These protocols were developed by DARPA to enable communication between different types of computers and computer networks. The Internet Protocol is a connectionless protocol that provides packet routing. TCP is connection-oriented and provides reliable communication and multiplexing.

Third Party Refers to manufacturers other than the manufacturers of the specific application or hardware.

Topology The configuration of a network, or the pattern in which the computers are interconnected. Common network topologies are the Star, Bus, and Token-ring.

UNIX A 32-bit, multitasking operating system developed in the 1960s for use on mainframes and minicomputers.

Vi A text editor that is included with most popular distributions of Linux.

Web server A server that delivers Web pages to client computers. The client runs a Web browser, which requests an HTML Web page from the server. The server receives that request and sends the desired page, which is displayed in the\ client's Web browser.

X Also known as *X11* or the *X Windows system*; X is a protocol for exchanging information that is used to present a graphical user interface.

Index

Continued

Continued

Hungry Minds, Inc.
End-User License Agreement

READ THIS. You should carefully read these terms and conditions before opening the software packet(s) included with this book ("Book"). This is a license agreement ("Agreement") between you and Hungry Minds, Inc. ("HMI"). By opening the accompanying software packet(s), you acknowledge that you have read and accept the following terms and conditions. If you do not agree and do not want to be bound by such terms and conditions, promptly return the Book and the unopened software packet(s) to the place you obtained them for a full refund.

1. **License Grant.** HMI grants to you (either an individual or entity) a nonexclusive license to use one copy of the enclosed software program(s) (collectively, the "Software") solely for your own personal or business purposes on a single computer (whether a standard computer or a workstation component of a multi-user network). The Software is in use on a computer when it is loaded into temporary memory (RAM) or installed into permanent memory (hard disk, CD-ROM, or other storage device). HMI reserves all rights not expressly granted herein.

2. **Ownership.** HMI is the owner of all right, title, and interest, including copyright, in and to the compilation of the Software recorded on the disk(s) or CD-ROM ("Software Media"). Copyright to the individual programs recorded on the Software Media is owned by the author or other authorized copyright owner of each program. Ownership of the Software and all proprietary rights relating thereto remain with HMI and its licensers.

3. **Restrictions On Use and Transfer.**

   (a) You may only (i) make one copy of the Software for backup or archival purposes, or (ii) transfer the Software to a single hard disk, provided that you keep the original for backup or archival purposes. You may not (i) rent or lease the Software, (ii) copy or reproduce the Software through a LAN or other network system or through any computer subscriber system or bulletin-board system, or (iii) modify, adapt, or create derivative works based on the Software.

   (b) You may not reverse engineer, decompile, or disassemble the Software. You may transfer the Software and user documentation on a permanent basis, provided that the transferee agrees to accept the terms and conditions of this Agreement and you retain no copies. If the Software is an update or has been updated, any transfer must include the most recent update and all prior versions.

4. Restrictions on Use of Individual Programs. You must follow the individual requirements and restrictions detailed for each individual program in Appendix A of this Book. These limitations are also contained in the individual license agreements recorded on the Software Media. These limitations may include a requirement that after using the program for a specified period of time, the user must pay a registration fee or discontinue use. By opening the Software packet(s), you will be agreeing to abide by the licenses and restrictions for these individual programs that are detailed in Appendix A and on the Software Media. None of the material on this Software Media or listed in this Book may ever be redistributed, in original or modified form, for commercial purposes.

5. Limited Warranty.

(a) HMI warrants that the Software and Software Media are free from defects in materials and workmanship under normal use for a period of sixty (60) days from the date of purchase of this Book. If HMI receives notification within the warranty period of defects in materials or workmanship, HMI will replace the defective Software Media.

(b) **HMI AND THE AUTHOR OF THE BOOK DISCLAIM ALL OTHER WARRANTIES, EXPRESS OR IMPLIED, INCLUDING WITHOUT LIMITATION IMPLIED WARRANTIES OF MERCHANTABILITY AND FITNESS FOR A PARTICULAR PURPOSE, WITH RESPECT TO THE SOFTWARE, THE PROGRAMS, THE SOURCE CODE CONTAINED THEREIN, AND/OR THE TECHNIQUES DESCRIBED IN THIS BOOK. HMI DOES NOT WARRANT THAT THE FUNCTIONS CONTAINED IN THE SOFTWARE WILL MEET YOUR REQUIREMENTS OR THAT THE OPERATION OF THE SOFTWARE WILL BE ERROR FREE.**

(c) This limited warranty gives you specific legal rights, and you may have other rights that vary from jurisdiction to jurisdiction.

6. Remedies.

(a) HMI's entire liability and your exclusive remedy for defects in materials and workmanship shall be limited to replacement of the Software Media, which may be returned to HMI with a copy of your receipt at the following address: Software Media Fulfillment Department, Attn.: *Linux + Certification Bible*, Hungry Minds, Inc., 10475 Crosspoint Blvd., Indianapolis, IN 46256, or call 1-800-762-2974. Please allow four to six weeks for delivery. This Limited Warranty is void if failure of the Software Media has resulted from accident, abuse, or misapplication. Any replacement Software Media will be warranted for the remainder of the original warranty period or thirty (30) days, whichever is longer.

(b) In no event shall HMI or the author be liable for any damages whatsoever (including without limitation damages for loss of business profits, business interruption, loss of business information, or any other pecuniary loss) arising from the use of or inability to use the Book or the Software, even if HMI has been advised of the possibility of such damages.

(c) Because some jurisdictions do not allow the exclusion or limitation of liability for consequential or incidental damages, the above limitation or exclusion may not apply to you.

7. **U.S. Government Restricted Rights.** Use, duplication, or disclosure of the Software for or on behalf of the United States of America, its agencies and/or instrumentalities (the "U.S. Government") is subject to restrictions as stated in paragraph (c)(1)(ii) of the Rights in Technical Data and Computer Software clause of DFARS 252.227-7013, or subparagraphs (c) (1) and (2) of the Commercial Computer Software - Restricted Rights clause at FAR 52.227-19, and in similar clauses in the NASA FAR supplement, as applicable.

8. **General.** This Agreement constitutes the entire understanding of the parties and revokes and supersedes all prior agreements, oral or written, between them and may not be modified or amended except in a writing signed by both parties hereto that specifically refers to this Agreement. This Agreement shall take precedence over any other documents that may be in conflict herewith. If any one or more provisions contained in this Agreement are held by any court or tribunal to be invalid, illegal, or otherwise unenforceable, each and every other provision shall remain in full force and effect.

Preamble

The licenses for most software are designed to take away your freedom to share and change it. By contrast, the GNU General Public License is intended to guarantee your freedom to share and change free software — to make sure the software is free for all its users. This General Public License applies to most of the Free Software Foundation's software and to any other program whose authors commit to using it. (Some other Free Software Foundation software is covered by the GNU Library General Public License instead.) You can apply it to your programs, too.

When we speak of free software, we are referring to freedom, not price. Our General Public Licenses are designed to make sure that you have the freedom to distribute copies of free software (and charge for this service if you wish), that you receive source code or can get it if you want it, that you can change the software or use pieces of it in new free programs; and that you know you can do these things.

To protect your rights, we need to make restrictions that forbid anyone to deny you these rights or to ask you to surrender the rights. These restrictions translate to certain responsibilities for you if you distribute copies of the software, or if you modify it.

For example, if you distribute copies of such a program, whether gratis or for a fee, you must give the recipients all the rights that you have. You must make sure that they, too, receive or can get the source code. And you must show them these terms so they know their rights.

We protect your rights with two steps: (1) copyright the software, and (2) offer you this license which gives you legal permission to copy, distribute and/or modify the software.

Also, for each author's protection and ours, we want to make certain that everyone understands that there is no warranty for this free software. If the software is modified by someone else and passed on, we want its recipients to know that what they have is not the original, so that any problems introduced by others will not reflect on the original authors' reputations.

Finally, any free program is threatened constantly by software patents. We wish to avoid the danger that redistributors of a free program will individually obtain patent licenses, in effect making the program proprietary. To prevent this, we have made it clear that any patent must be licensed for everyone's free use or not licensed at all.

The precise terms and conditions for copying, distribution and modification follow.

Terms and Conditions for Copying, Distribution, and Modification

0. This License applies to any program or other work which contains a notice placed by the copyright holder saying it may be distributed under the terms of this General Public License. The "Program", below, refers to any such program or work, and a "work based on the Program" means either the Program or any derivative work under copyright law: that is to say, a work containing the Program or a portion of it, either verbatim or with modifications and/or translated into another language. (Hereinafter, translation is included without limitation in the term "modification".) Each licensee is addressed as "you".

   Activities other than copying, distribution and modification are not covered by this License; they are outside its scope. The act of running the Program is not restricted, and the output from the Program is covered only if its contents constitute a work based on the Program (independent of having been made by running the Program). Whether that is true depends on what the Program does.

1. You may copy and distribute verbatim copies of the Program's source code as you receive it, in any medium, provided that you conspicuously and appropriately publish on each copy an appropriate copyright notice and disclaimer of warranty; keep intact all the notices that refer to this License and to the absence of any warranty; and give any other recipients of the Program a copy of this License along with the Program.

   You may charge a fee for the physical act of transferring a copy, and you may at your option offer warranty protection in exchange for a fee.

2. You may modify your copy or copies of the Program or any portion of it, thus forming a work based on the Program, and copy and distribute such modifications or work under the terms of Section 1 above, provided that you also meet all of these conditions:

   a) You must cause the modified files to carry prominent notices stating that you changed the files and the date of any change.

   b) You must cause any work that you distribute or publish, that in whole or in part contains or is derived from the Program or any part thereof, to be licensed as a whole at no charge to all third parties under the terms of this License.

   c) If the modified program normally reads commands interactively when run, you must cause it, when started running for such interactive use in the most ordinary way, to print or display an announcement including an appropriate copyright notice and a notice that there is no warranty (or else, saying that you provide a warranty) and that users may redistribute the program under these conditions, and telling the user how to view a copy of this License. (Exception: if the Program itself is interactive but does not normally print such an announcement, your work based on the Program is not required to print an announcement.)

These requirements apply to the modified work as a whole. If identifiable sections of that work are not derived from the Program, and can be reasonably considered independent and separate works in themselves, then this License, and its terms, do not apply to those sections when you distribute them as separate works. But when you distribute the same sections as part of a whole which is a work based on the Program, the distribution of the whole must be on the terms of this License, whose permissions for other licensees extend to the entire whole, and thus to each and every part regardless of who wrote it.

Thus, it is not the intent of this section to claim rights or contest your rights to work written entirely by you; rather, the intent is to exercise the right to control the distribution of derivative or collective works based on the Program.

In addition, mere aggregation of another work not based on the Program with the Program (or with a work based on the Program) on a volume of a storage or distribution medium does not bring the other work under the scope of this License.

3. You may copy and distribute the Program (or a work based on it, under Section 2) in object code or executable form under the terms of Sections 1 and 2 above provided that you also do one of the following:

   a) Accompany it with the complete corresponding machine-readable source code, which must be distributed under the terms of Sections 1 and 2 above on a medium customarily used for software interchange; or,

   b) Accompany it with a written offer, valid for at least three years, to give any third party, for a charge no more than your cost of physically performing source distribution, a complete machine-readable copy of the corresponding source code, to be distributed under the terms of Sections 1 and 2 above on a medium customarily used for software interchange; or,

   c) Accompany it with the information you received as to the offer to distribute corresponding source code. (This alternative is allowed only for noncommercial distribution and only if you received the program in object code or executable form with such an offer, in accord with Subsection b above.)

The source code for a work means the preferred form of the work for making modifications to it. For an executable work, complete source code means all the source code for all modules it contains, plus any associated interface definition files, plus the scripts used to control compilation and installation of the executable. However, as a special exception, the source code distributed need not include anything that is normally distributed (in either source or binary form) with the major components (compiler, kernel, and so on) of the operating system on which the executable runs, unless that component itself accompanies the executable.

If distribution of executable or object code is made by offering access to copy from a designated place, then offering equivalent access to copy the source code from the same place counts as distribution of the source code, even though third parties are not compelled to copy the source along with the object code.

4. You may not copy, modify, sublicense, or distribute the Program except as expressly provided under this License. Any attempt otherwise to copy, modify, sublicense or distribute the Program is void, and will automatically terminate your rights under this License. However, parties who have received copies, or rights, from you under this License will not have their licenses terminated so long as such parties remain in full compliance.

5. You are not required to accept this License, since you have not signed it. However, nothing else grants you permission to modify or distribute the Program or its derivative works. These actions are prohibited by law if you do not accept this License. Therefore, by modifying or distributing the Program (or any work based on the Program), you indicate your acceptance of this License to do so, and all its terms and conditions for copying, distributing or modifying the Program or works based on it.

6. Each time you redistribute the Program (or any work based on the Program), the recipient automatically receives a license from the original licensor to copy, distribute or modify the Program subject to these terms and conditions. You may not impose any further restrictions on the recipients' exercise of the rights granted herein. You are not responsible for enforcing compliance by third parties to this License.

7. If, as a consequence of a court judgment or allegation of patent infringement or for any other reason (not limited to patent issues), conditions are imposed on you (whether by court order, agreement or otherwise) that contradict the conditions of this License, they do not excuse you from the conditions of this License. If you cannot distribute so as to satisfy simultaneously your obligations under this License and any other pertinent obligations, then as a consequence you may not distribute the Program at all. For example, if a patent license would not permit royalty-free redistribution of the Program by all those who receive copies directly or indirectly through you, then the only way you could satisfy both it and this License would be to refrain entirely from distribution of the Program.

If any portion of this section is held invalid or unenforceable under any particular circumstance, the balance of the section is intended to apply and the section as a whole is intended to apply in other circumstances.

It is not the purpose of this section to induce you to infringe any patents or other property right claims or to contest validity of any such claims; this section has the sole purpose of protecting the integrity of the free software distribution system, which is implemented by public license practices. Many people have made generous contributions to the wide range of software distributed through that system in reliance on consistent application of that system; it is up to the author/donor to decide if he or she is willing to distribute software through any other system and a licensee cannot impose that choice.

This section is intended to make thoroughly clear what is believed to be a consequence of the rest of this License.

8. If the distribution and/or use of the Program is restricted in certain countries either by patents or by copyrighted interfaces, the original copyright holder who places the Program under this License may add an explicit geographical distribution limitation excluding those countries, so that distribution is permitted only in or among countries not thus excluded. In such case, this License incorporates the limitation as if written in the body of this License.

9. The Free Software Foundation may publish revised and/or new versions of the General Public License from time to time. Such new versions will be similar in spirit to the present version, but may differ in detail to address new problems or concerns.

Each version is given a distinguishing version number. If the Program specifies a version number of this License which applies to it and "any later version", you have the option of following the terms and conditions either of that version or of any later version published by the Free Software Foundation. If the Program does not specify a version number of this License, you may choose any version ever published by the Free Software Foundation.

10. If you wish to incorporate parts of the Program into other free programs whose distribution conditions are different, write to the author to ask for permission. For software which is copyrighted by the Free Software Foundation, write to the Free Software Foundation; we sometimes make exceptions for this. Our decision will be guided by the two goals of preserving the free status of all derivatives of our free software and of promoting the sharing and reuse of software generally.

No Warranty

11. BECAUSE THE PROGRAM IS LICENSED FREE OF CHARGE, THERE IS NO WARRANTY FOR THE PROGRAM, TO THE EXTENT PERMITTED BY APPLICABLE LAW. EXCEPT WHEN OTHERWISE STATED IN WRITING THE COPYRIGHT HOLDERS AND/OR OTHER PARTIES PROVIDE THE PROGRAM "AS IS" WITHOUT WARRANTY OF ANY KIND, EITHER EXPRESSED OR IMPLIED, INCLUDING, BUT NOT LIMITED TO, THE IMPLIED WARRANTIES OF MERCHANTABILITY AND FITNESS FOR A PARTICULAR PURPOSE. THE ENTIRE RISK AS TO THE QUALITY AND PERFORMANCE OF THE PROGRAM IS WITH YOU. SHOULD THE PROGRAM PROVE DEFECTIVE, YOU ASSUME THE COST OF ALL NECESSARY SERVICING, REPAIR OR CORRECTION.

12. IN NO EVENT UNLESS REQUIRED BY APPLICABLE LAW OR AGREED TO IN WRITING WILL ANY COPYRIGHT HOLDER, OR ANY OTHER PARTY WHO MAY MODIFY AND/OR REDISTRIBUTE THE PROGRAM AS PERMITTED ABOVE, BE LIABLE TO YOU FOR DAMAGES, INCLUDING ANY GENERAL, SPECIAL, INCIDENTAL OR CONSEQUENTIAL DAMAGES ARISING OUT OF THE USE OR INABILITY TO USE THE PROGRAM (INCLUDING BUT NOT LIMITED TO LOSS OF DATA OR DATA BEING RENDERED INACCURATE OR LOSSES SUSTAINED BY YOU OR THIRD PARTIES OR A FAILURE OF THE PROGRAM TO OPERATE WITH ANY OTHER PROGRAMS), EVEN IF SUCH HOLDER OR OTHER PARTY HAS BEEN ADVISED OF THE POSSIBILITY OF SUCH DAMAGES.